S0-AAC-259

American Universities in a Global Market

A National Bureau
of Economic Research
Conference Report

American Universities in a Global Market

Edited by **Charles T. Clotfelter**

The University of Chicago Press

Chicago and London

CHARLES T. CLOTFELTER is the Z. Smith Reynolds Professor of Public Policy, professor of economics and law, and director of the Center for the Study of Philanthropy and Voluntarism at Duke University. He is a research associate of the National Bureau of Economic Research.

The University of Chicago Press, Chicago 60637
The University of Chicago Press, Ltd., London

Printed in the United States of America

19 18 17 16 15 14 13 12 11 10   1 2 3 4 5
ISBN-13: 978-0-226-11044-8 (cloth)
ISBN-10: 0-226-11044-3 (cloth)

Library of Congress Cataloging-in-Publication Data

American universities in a global market / edited by Charles T. Clotfelter.
p. cm.— (National Bureau of Economic Research conference report)
Includes bibliographical references and index.
ISBN-13: 978-0-226-11044-8 (alk. paper)
ISBN-10: 0-226-11044-3 (alk. paper)
1. Education, Higher—United States. 2. Education and globalization. 3. Universities and colleges—United States. 4. Competition, International. I. Clotfelter, Charles T. II. Series: National Bureau of Economic Research conference report.
LA227.4.A517 2010
338.73—dc22

2009043758

♾ The paper used in this publication meets the minimum requirements of the American National Standard for Information Sciences—Permanence of Paper for Printed Library Materials, ANSI Z39.48-1992.

Relation of the Directors to the Work and Publications of the National Bureau of Economic Research

1. The object of the NBER is to ascertain and present to the economics profession, and to the public more generally, important economic facts and their interpretation in a scientific manner without policy recommendations. The Board of Directors is charged with the responsibility of ensuring that the work of the NBER is carried on in strict conformity with this object.

2. The President shall establish an internal review process to ensure that book manuscripts proposed for publication DO NOT contain policy recommendations. This shall apply both to the proceedings of conferences and to manuscripts by a single author or by one or more co-authors but shall not apply to authors of comments at NBER conferences who are not NBER affiliates.

3. No book manuscript reporting research shall be published by the NBER until the President has sent to each member of the Board a notice that a manuscript is recommended for publication and that in the President's opinion it is suitable for publication in accordance with the above principles of the NBER. Such notification will include a table of contents and an abstract or summary of the manuscript's content, a list of contributors if applicable, and a response form for use by Directors who desire a copy of the manuscript for review. Each manuscript shall contain a summary drawing attention to the nature and treatment of the problem studied and the main conclusions reached.

4. No volume shall be published until forty-five days have elapsed from the above notification of intention to publish it. During this period a copy shall be sent to any Director requesting it, and if any Director objects to publication on the grounds that the manuscript contains policy recommendations, the objection will be presented to the author(s) or editor(s). In case of dispute, all members of the Board shall be notified, and the President shall appoint an ad hoc committee of the Board to decide the matter; thirty days additional shall be granted for this purpose.

5. The President shall present annually to the Board a report describing the internal manuscript review process, any objections made by Directors before publication or by anyone after publication, any disputes about such matters, and how they were handled.

6. Publications of the NBER issued for informational purposes concerning the work of the Bureau, or issued to inform the public of the activities at the Bureau, including but not limited to the NBER Digest and Reporter, shall be consistent with the object stated in paragraph 1. They shall contain a specific disclaimer noting that they have not passed through the review procedures required in this resolution. The Executive Committee of the Board is charged with the review of all such publications from time to time.

7. NBER working papers and manuscripts distributed on the Bureau's web site are not deemed to be publications for the purpose of this resolution, but they shall be consistent with the object stated in paragraph 1. Working papers shall contain a specific disclaimer noting that they have not passed through the review procedures required in this resolution. The NBER's web site shall contain a similar disclaimer. The President shall establish an internal review process to ensure that the working papers and the web site do not contain policy recommendations, and shall report annually to the Board on this process and any concerns raised in connection with it.

8. Unless otherwise determined by the Board or exempted by the terms of paragraphs 6 and 7, a copy of this resolution shall be printed in each NBER publication as described in paragraph 2 above.

Contents

Preface and Acknowledgments

Charles T. Clotfelter

It was the best of times, it seemed, for American universities, especially those at the highest echelons of world rankings. Through at least the last several decades of the twentieth century and into the first years of the twenty-first, the top US research universities enjoyed a collective international reputation unmatched by universities in any other country or region. Paradoxically, these American institutions held their exalted position at the same time the country's elementary and secondary schools were receiving considerably less praise. The nation's K–12 schools, buffeted at home by criticisms and exposed abroad to unflattering comparisons in international tests of science and mathematics, were increasingly viewed as America's educational Achilles' heel. American universities, at any rate, appeared to have no rivals and few worries.

But in the new century that brought with it a horrendous demonstration of terrorism and threats to American geopolitical ascendency, there arose as well a newly articulated anxiety about the country's ability to compete in the global economy; in particular, its ability to produce the innovations and educated workforce necessary to remain economically competitive. Not since the Soviet *Sputnik* touched off a paroxysm of self-doubt in the 1950s had alarm over the inadequacy of American research and training in science and technology reached such a crescendo. In his 2005 book, *The World is Flat,* Thomas Friedman argued that the consequence of a shrinking American advantage in education could very well be the loss of American world lead-

Charles T. Clotfelter is the Z. Smith Reynolds Professor of Public Policy, professor of economics and law, director of the Center for the Study of Philanthropy and Voluntarism at Duke University, and a research associate of the National Bureau of Economic Research.

ership in high-tech industries.[1] Then in 2007 a prestigious committee of the National Academy of Sciences weighed in with its own call to arms, *Rising Above the Gathering Storm,* which emphatically echoed the alarm raised by Friedman.[2] It argued that, through decades of neglect, the United States had fallen behind in science and engineering, leaving the country in a weakened position to compete in knowledge-intensive industries. It issued an urgent call for boosting the number of college students who major in science and engineering. At the same time, some observers saw the continued dominance of American research universities as vulnerable, as the dramatic advances occurring in communication such as the Internet were diminishing the importance of physical proximity and thus lessening the advantage of established institutions.

I found these issues to be compelling in part because of my own interest and research in the economics of higher education. Another reason was an opportunity I had in 2002 to get a firsthand look at higher education in China, when I took part in a conference jointly sponsored by the National Bureau of Economic Research (NBER) and the China Center for Economic Research in Beijing. These things led me to consider organizing a conference to examine US research universities through a global lens, one that would ask how the changing market for research and advanced training in the world would affect American universities and their continued prominence. I proposed the idea to Martin Feldstein, then president of the NBER, in 2005. Over the next two years, I discussed the project with dozens of experts in an effort to identify important questions and knowledgeable scholars who could undertake new research to address them. From the first, and at many points along the way, I turned to two long-standing members of the NBER higher education study group, Ronald Ehrenberg and Paula Stephan, for advice. Their counsel and support has been invaluable to me. Others from whom I received helpful suggestions include William Bowen, Michael Bradley, Richard Brodhead, Kanchan Chandra, Mihir Desai, Craufurd Goodwin, Roger Gordon, Diana Hicks, Caroline Hoxby, Andrea Ichino, Charlotte Kuh, Peter Lange, Michael Rothschild, John Siegfried, and Shang-Jin Wei.

After securing financial support from the Kauffman Foundation, we held a preconference at the Bureau's Cambridge offices on September 28, 2007. This session, plus ensuing communication among the authors, allowed for active collaboration and communication among participants that, I believe, is a major reason why the resulting volume has cohered to become a single, integrated whole. Reaffirming the irreplaceable value of face-to-face com-

1. Thomas L. Friedman, *The World Is Flat: A Brief History of the Twenty-First Century* (New York: Farrar, Straus and Giroux, 2005).

2. US National Academy of Sciences, Committee on Science, Engineering, and Public Policy, *Rising Above the Gathering Storm: Energizing and Employing America for a Brighter Economic Future* (Washington, DC: National Academy Press, 2007).

munication, however, the authors met together again, this time in Woodstock, Vermont, from October 2 to 4, 2008, to present and discuss their finished papers. This meeting included a dozen scholars who had agreed to be discussants. These participants brought with them research knowledge of education, innovation, and labor markets; extensive experience in university administration, or both. The group included three former deans (Peter Doeringer, Michael Rothschild, and Debra Stewart), one former vice president and current university trustee (Ronald Ehrenberg), two former provosts (Paul Courant and Charles Phelps), and two former university presidents (Harold Shapiro and Hugo Sunnenschein). The remaining discussants (Elizabeth Cascio, Caroline Hoxby, Arvind Panagariya, Bruce Sacerdote, and Michael Teitelbaum), like the former administrators, have both worked inside universities and also figured prominently in research and public policy that touch upon the issues addressed in this volume. The dialogue these discussants engendered at the conference was lively, provocative, and constructive, and the resulting published chapters in this volume benefited greatly from their active participation.

A final and emphatic word of thanks is due to Martin Feldstein. As a distinguished economist who has spent most of his career working for the same university, he became an astute observer of universities as firms.[3] But his impact on American higher education has been arguably greater in his role as president of the NBER, a position he held for some three decades. In that role, he left an indelible imprint on both the character of the economics profession and the nature of "competition" among universities in this discipline. Under his leadership the number of economists affiliated with the National Bureau grew tremendously at the same time that the organization retained its strong culture of free exchange of ideas. Together, these two features fostered enhanced scholarly communication and collaboration among active researchers in the profession, while paying little heed to institutional or national affiliation. For his early and sustained support of this project and its editor, I am happy to dedicate this volume to him.

3. See, for example, his written comment in Charles T. Clotfelter and Michael Rothschild (eds.), *Studies of Supply and Demand in Higher Education* (Chicago: University of Chicago Press, 1993), 37–42.

Introduction

Charles T. Clotfelter

Since World War II, American universities have occupied an unchallenged position of preeminence in the world. Owing to high rates of educational attainment, vigorous governmental support of scientific research, and a massive influx of scholars from Europe seeking refuge, America during the twentieth century supplanted Europe as the home of most of the world's leading universities. Today, American institutions dominate the highest rungs of the various world rankings of great universities. When universities around the world seek to improve themselves, they commonly look to universities in the United States as their model. As a result of America's comparative advantage in this industry, higher education has become one of our major exports.

But there are signs that this position of preeminence could be in jeopardy. The flow of foreign graduate students and scholars into American universities, while still massive, has shown signs of slowing, in the wake of heightened security concerns and competition from foreign universities. Not only are European universities girding themselves for more vigorous international competition, but those in Australia, China, and other parts of Asia have signaled their intention to become major players in the global higher education market. Meanwhile, America's own production of uni-

Charles T. Clotfelter is the Z. Smith Reynolds Professor of Public Policy, professor of economics and law, and director of the Center for the Study of Philanthropy and Voluntarism at Duke University. He is a research associate of the National Bureau of Economic Research.

This introduction was shaped and informed not only by the chapters contained in this volume, but also by the formal comments delivered by the papers' assigned discussants and the lively discussion among all the participants at the NBER conference held October 2–4, 2008. I am also especially grateful for the helpful comments I received on an earlier draft from Peter Doeringer, Lex Borghans, Frank Cörvers, Ronald Ehrenberg, Richard Freeman, Caroline Hoxby, Han Kim, Charles Phelps, and Debra Stewart.

versity graduates has slowed relative to that of other developed nations, a trend that was highlighted with alarm in the National Academy of Sciences' 2007 call to arms, *Rising above the Gathering Storm.* Adding to the sense of crisis were the unmistakable signs that America's position of leadership in the world—financial, military, intellectual, and moral—is increasingly being challenged.

The purpose of this volume is to examine aspects of American higher education today that will affect its future global standing. Will American universities retain their leading role? Surely the advantages of scope and scale that they currently enjoy will continue to redound to their advantage. But the ultimate outcome is far from clear. A warning issued by Roger Noll posed a decade ago seems all the more relevant today: "American research universities have enjoyed a wonderful century, rising from a distinctly inferior status to world domination. But in the waning years of this golden age of American science and engineering, the future of these institutions is in doubt."[1]

This volume contains eleven chapters addressing key issues surrounding the position of American universities in the global higher education market. This introduction provides an overview of those issues. It begins by considering the evidence of US preeminence among the world's universities as well as indications that this position might be in jeopardy. Next, I discuss aspects of American higher education that distinguish it as an industry and highlight the ways it has responded to global pressures. The third section addresses the nature of the foreign competition that the United States faces in the global higher education market. I then conclude by considering what is at stake for the United States in its standing in the world in this industry.

A Golden Age for American Universities

Roger Noll's evocative phrase aptly describes for American higher education the current period of unrivaled ascendancy, a period that began sometime during the first half of the twentieth century and continues to this day. To introduce the analyses that follow, I offer some evidence in support of this claim, list some of the advantages enjoyed by American universities, and take note of storm clouds on the horizon.

Documenting American Preeminence

The modern university took shape in Europe, and Europe retained unquestioned world leadership in scientific research through the nineteenth century.[2] In the United States, some of the colleges that had been founded

1. Noll (1998, 1).

2. For a comparison of the development of universities in the United States and Europe, see Windolf (1997). For analyses of the comparative standing of American and European universities in the nineteenth and twentieth centuries, see, for example, Noll (1998, 2–3) or Weinberg (2008).

for the purpose of training teachers and ministers in the nineteenth and early twentieth century, including some public institutions operated by state governments, began to take on some of the characteristics of the renowned German universities, including a serious devotion to research and graduate training. These fledgling universities continued to expand opportunities for undergraduate education, they grew larger, increasingly incorporated professional training, and adopted the structures and attitudes to enable them to conduct research at levels that would allow the best of them to compete with European universities.[3]

Today there can be little doubt that most of the world's leading universities are in the United States. One ready indication of this high standing can be found in the various rankings of top universities that have appeared in recent years. The oldest and most prominent of these is a ranking that is published by Shanghai Jiao Tong University. A research-oriented, global version of the familiar *US News and World Report* ranking of US colleges, this ranking employs a collection of quantitative measures of research output and scholarly awards, heavily weighted on science, to produce an ordered list based on an arbitrary weighting of these measures.[4] In its most recent ranking, for 2008, seventeen out of its twenty top-ranked universities were American. The other frequently cited ranking, by the *Times* of London, produces a list featuring fewer American universities and more from Britain and Commonwealth countries.[5] Of the thirteen universities that made both of these top-twenty lists for 2008, one was Japanese (Tokyo University), two were British (Oxford and Cambridge), and ten were American (Harvard, Stanford, MIT, California Institute of Technology, Columbia, Princeton, University of Chicago, Yale, Cornell, and University of Pennsylvania). Interestingly, a total of seven public universities in the United States appeared on one of these two lists for 2008, but none appeared in both.[6] If one expands the list of top universities (for example, to the top fifty), the dominance of American universities remains apparent. As shown in

3. For a discussion of the development of American universities in the period 1890 to 1940, see Goldin and Katz (1999).

4. As explained on its website, the Shanghai Jiao Tong University Academic Ranking of World Universities employed "several indicators of academic or research performance, including alumni and staff winning Nobel Prizes and Fields Medals, highly cited researchers, articles published in Nature and Science, articles indexed in major citation indices, and the per capita academic performance of an institution." (see http://www.arwu.org/rank2008/ARWU2008_A(EN).htm). As noted by Aghion et al. (2009, 2), this ranking scheme places heavy weight on research in science.

5. Times World University Rankings 2008. Available at: http://www.timeshighereducation.co.uk/hybrid.asp?typeCode=243&pubCode=1&navcode=137.

6. Two other rankings available on the web include those produced by Webometrics (http://www.webometrics.info/top4000.asp) and *Newsweek* (http://talk.collegeconfidential.com/graduate-school/226863-newsweek-ranks-world-s-top-100-global-universities.html). In these two rankings, American universities occupied twenty and fifteen, respectively, of the top twenty spots in the worldwide ranking.

table I.1, thirty-six of the Shanghai Jiao Tong top fifty universities for 2008 are in the United States.[7]

It is instructive to see how the American hegemony suggested by such rankings manifests itself in a single discipline. Drèze and Estevan (2007) spell this out for the discipline of economics, showing how American economists have dominated international recognition and American economics departments have led in training top economists. Coming from a country with a population just three-fourths the size of Europe's, American economists accounted for more honors and more research output than their European counterparts. As an illustration, the United States-to-Europe ratio in Nobel laureates was 2.9; in Econometric Society Fellows, 3.2; in entries in *Who's Who in Economics,* 4.8; and in various measures of publications, 1.9 to 8.3.[8] American leadership is also revealed by the tendency for top economists to obtain their PhDs in the United States, even if they subsequently return to their home countries. Among 585 economists listed in *Who's Who in Economics* who received their PhDs at American universities, 26 percent came from abroad (that is, having received their first degrees outside of the United States). By contrast, fewer than 20 percent of the 112 of economists so listed who received their PhDs outside of the United States were Americans (Drèze and Estevan 2007, table 3a, 273–74). In advanced training in economics, therefore, the United States is a net exporter.

Indeed, one of the primary by-products of America's leadership in higher education is the huge number of foreign students who come to the United States to study, especially at the most advanced graduate levels. In 2006 the United States enrolled a fifth of the world's international students (OECD 2008, chart C3.3, 354). Except for the years immediately after the 9/11 attacks, international enrollments in all US programs have grown rapidly, increasing at an average rate of 4.8 percent a year between 1997 and 2001 and a rate of 5.0 percent a year between 2005 and 2007.[9] In 2007 this amounted to some 623,000 foreigners studying in the United States. Of these international students, about 44 percent were enrolled in graduate programs.[10] Although foreign students account for larger shares of bachelor's-level

7. It is worth noting that the United States is markedly less dominant in global rankings of business schools. For example, the *Financial Times* ranking for 2009 listed just twenty-four American business schools among its top fifty (see http://rankings.ft.com/businessschoolrankings/global-mba-rankings). Note that business schools require less physical capital than is required in science and engineering and that business education is one of the most active areas for overseas operations of US universities.

8. Drèze and Estevan (2007, table 1, 273). For Europe, the authors used the EU fifteen plus Norway, whose population in 2000 was 382,283, compared to the United States' 282,339 (see www.demographia.com/db-eu-pop.htm). *Statistical Abstract of the United States* 2006, table 1314.

9. Beth McMurtrie, "Foreign Students Pour Back into the US," *Chronicle of Higher Education,* November 21, 2008.

10. Between 2005 to 2006 and 2007 to 2008, the number of international students in graduate programs in the United States increased from 259,704 to 276,842, for a growth rate of 3.2 percent a year. (Elizabeth Redden, "Record Year" for Foreign Student Enrollment," *Inside Higher Ed,* November 17, 2008.)

Table I.1 **World ranking of universities, Shanghai Jiao Tong University, 2008**

World rank	Institution	Country
1	Harvard University	US
2	Stanford University	US
3	University of California-Berkeley	US
4	University of Cambridge	UK
5	Massachusetts Institute of Technology (MIT)	US
6	California Institute of Technology	US
7	Columbia University	US
8	Princeton University	US
9	University of Chicago	US
10	University of Oxford	UK
11	Yale University	US
12	Cornell University	US
13	University of California-Los Angeles	US
14	University of California-San Diego	US
15	University of Pennsylvania	US
16	University of Washington-Seattle	US
17	University of Wisconsin-Madison	US
18	University of California-San Francisco	US
19	Tokyo University	Japan
20	Johns Hopkins University	US
21	University of Michigan-Ann Arbor	US
22	University College London	UK
23	Kyoto University	Japan
24	Swiss Federal Institute of Technology-Zurich	Switzerland
24	University of Toronto	Canada
26	University of Illinois-Urbana Champaign	US
27	Imperial College London	UK
28	University of Minnesota-Twin Cities	US
29	Washington University-St. Louis	US
30	Northwestern University	US
31	New York University	US
32	Duke University	US
33	Rockefeller University	US
34	University of Colorado-Boulder	US
35	University of British Columbia	Canada
36	University of California-Santa Barbara	US
37	University of Maryland-College Park	US
38	University of North Carolina-Chapel Hill	US
39	University of Texas-Austin	US
40	University of Manchester	UK
41	University of Texas Southwestern Medical Center	US
42	Pennsylvania State University-University Park	US
42	University of Paris 06	France
42	Vanderbilt University	US
45	University of Copenhagen	Denmark
46	University of California-Irvine	US
47	University of Utrecht	Netherlands
48	University of California-Davis	US
49	University of Paris 11	France
50	University of Southern California	US

Source: Shanghai Jiao Tong World Rankings, http://www.arwu.org/rank2008/ARWU2008_A(EN).htm.

college and university enrollments in many other countries than in the United States, the foreign share in US advanced research programs is one of the highest in the world and has risen over time (OECD 2008, table C3.3). As a consequence, the percentage of graduate students in American universities who are foreign has risen steadily over time. For example, the percentage of science and engineering doctoral degrees received by foreign nationals increased from 26 percent in 1985 to 40 percent in 2005 (National Science Board 2008, figure 2-23). There is no more emblematic sign of the growing number of foreign graduate students than the fact noted by Richard Freeman in chapter 11 that two Chinese universities—Tsinghua and Peking—have pushed aside the likes of Berkeley, Cornell, and Michigan to become the two most common sources of bachelor's degrees among those obtaining PhDs in American universities.[11]

Explaining America's Dominance

Numerous explanations have been offered for the rise and prominence of American higher education in the twentieth century. There are four that I believe deserve particular emphasis: generous government support, the industry's decentralized structure, openness to people and ideas, and the so-called first-mover advantage.

Beginning with the first of these, American universities have benefited from government support, both direct and indirect, and at both the state and the federal levels, and this support, in turn, was made possible by America's buoyant economy and relative affluence. Unlike the public support typical of European universities, which has mostly been in the form of direct funding from central governments, the most common form of direct public support in the United States first came from state governments. Inspired both by the desire to see the benefits of education spread widely across the population and an appreciation of the value of imparting practical knowledge, the state universities, especially those in the newer states of the Midwest and West, grew in scale. Federal support was important as well. Before 1900 it came by way of the Morrill Acts of 1862 and 1890. In the twentieth century it took other forms, including military-related research during World War II, the subsequent GI Bill (1944), which provided generous financial support for veterans to attend college, the National Defense Education Act (1957), which supported graduate students intending to become college and university professors, and numerous other programs to give financial aid to students.

Of particular significance was federal support of nondefense spending through agencies such as the National Science Foundation (NSF) (1950)

11. In 2006, the top six bachelor's degree-granting institutions represented among recipients of American PhDs were, in order, Tsinghua, Peking, University of California Berkeley, Seoul National, Cornell, and Michigan. See Mervis (2008, 185).

and the National Institutes of Health (NIH).[12] Not only did these agencies provide funding for university research, they helped to foster collaboration among researchers, and not only those in universities. According to Owen-Smith et al. (2002, 40) the NIH. played a critical role in integrating regional collaborative clusters in US biomedical research. The federal government's contribution to American leadership in this research did not arise, therefore, principally from the dollar value of federal support that universities received. In contrast to that conducted in European universities, biomedical research in American universities relied on a greater variety of funding sources, including a significant share from industry. In 2006 federal support for academic R&D amounted to about $30 billion, which was just 63 percent of the $48 billion total from all sources. The chief federal funding agencies were the Department of Health and Human Services, the National Science Foundation, and the Department of Defense. Taking into account all sources of support, funding for academic R&D grew in real terms for over three decades. In 2006 it represented 0.4 percent of gross domestic product (GDP) (National Science Board 2008, chapter 5 and table 5.2).

Indirect government aid may have been equally important for American success, however, especially for private nonprofit universities. Not only did the federal income tax exempt all nonprofit organizations from income taxation, most donations to universities were deductible in calculating the personal income tax, the corporate income tax, and the estate tax. Private foundations, a noteworthy beneficiary of the tax laws, also provided support to universities. At the local level, universities both public and private were exempted from paying most property taxes. In sum, these various forms of government support, both direct and indirect, made more potent by America's affluence, were instrumental in creating research universities that, unlike the specialized research institutions in Europe, simultaneously served several major aims: broad-based undergraduate education, practically-oriented professional training, basic research in arts and sciences, and applied research and outreach to industry and farm.[13]

A second reason that has been offered for the success of American higher education is its decentralized market structure. In 2005 there were over 4,000 colleges and universities in the United States, of which about 200 were research universities.[14] Small in number but relatively large in size (they

12. The Public Health Service Act (1944), which launched a period of tremendous growth in spending on public health after World War II, was a significant step toward the creation of the National Institutes of Health (see http://history.nih.gov/exhibits/history/docs/page_06.html). Morris (1965, 419, 464); National Science Foundation (see http://www.nsf.gov/about/history/).

13. For discussions of the multiplicity of functions in American research universities, see Goldin and Katz (1999, 45) and Ash (2006, 251).

14. For 2005, the Carnegie Foundation for the Advancement of Teaching listed a total of 4,391 institutions, of which 199 were research universities (see http://www.carnegiefoundation.org/classifications/index.asp?key=805).

accounted for 23 percent of total college and university enrollment), these research universities count among their number both private and public institutions. It is precisely their large number, the diversity of their funding, and their autonomy one from another that create the conditions that have allowed them to develop a tradition of vigorous but friendly competition that has proven to be conducive to the pursuit of their core research mission. This friendly competition embodies two seemingly contradictory components. On the one hand, these research universities compete for resources and prominence. They bid against each other to attract prominent and promising faculty. The top, most desired faculty members are highly mobile and are responsive to both financial incentives and attractive working conditions. This responsiveness and mobility is summed up in the apocryphal comment of one dean: "I don't control what they make, only where they work." Owen-Smith et al. (2002, 25, 41) note, for example, the higher levels of mobility among young scientists in the United States as compared to Europe. Significantly, such responsiveness operates, albeit for a more limited number of faculty, at the international level as well.[15] In a parallel contest, research universities also actively compete for top students—from applicants for doctoral programs to the high school seniors applying for undergraduate spots. These universities (and their faculty) also compete against one another to attract donations and grant funding. In some instances, the availability of public funding provides public universities with a natural edge. In other instances, the freedom from outside interference plus access to pots of private money give the private universities the upper hand.[16]

Competition also occurs within universities, and its widespread use and acceptance as a mechanism for resources allocation in the United States contrasts with the resistance it has run into in many European universities (Liefner, Schätzl, and Schröder 2004, 35–36). In support of the value of this competition at various levels, Aghion et al. 2009 present evidence that university research output is positively correlated with institutional autonomy and market-like competition.

As fierce as the competition may be between universities, it is joined by a cooperative way of doing business that is as deeply embedded in scholarly custom as it is alien to commercial competition. This cooperation, arising from the openness and collaborative attitudes that are core values in the long tradition of scientific scholarship, means that—contrary to what happens in other industries—employees of different institutions have no compunction about forming partnerships with each other to do research. And this willingness to partner extends beyond universities, to government research shops and industry as well. Although there is nothing uniquely American about

15. See, for example, Drèze and Estevan (2007, 287).

16. Charles Phelps particularly emphasized the value of having private institutions, with their relative freedom to act, as competitors in the American higher education market.

this second component, its combination with the distinctly decentralized structure of the US higher education industry has produced an environment quite conducive to independent research, powered by strong incentives to be first and be the best. To be sure, a system so rooted in social Darwinism will be one in which some institutions rise at the expense of others. In fact, during most of the three decades preceding the economic shocks of 2008, the entire public sector appears to have languished relative to the wealthiest of the private institutions, as large endowments ballooned while state funding lagged. This public-private divide is a theme touched on by several of the chapters in this volume.

One historical factor sometimes cited as a reason for the twentieth-century American leadership in higher education is the influx of European scholars that took place in the wake of Nazi ascendancy and rule. This episode serves as a vivid illustration of a third, more general characteristic to explain the success of American universities: their openness to people and ideas. Many of the émigrés who fled European universities in the early 1930s, including such luminaries as Albert Einstein and Edward Teller, ended up in the United States. Not only did this immigration and the terror that motivated it cause leading scholars to move to American universities, it dealt a double blow to German universities, by also revealing their subservience to the Third Reich (Ash 2006, 252–53). Historians do not agree on the ultimate importance of the migration of European scientists. One side argues that it was an essential ingredient for American ascendency in higher education, while the other maintains that it was helpful but not necessary.[17] In either case, the boon from this historical event surely may be viewed as one illustration of a larger advantage that American universities have enjoyed by virtue of being American, that of a general spirit of openness to both people and ideas. Despite some glaring exceptions to the contrary, it is no mere expression of chauvinism to distinguish American policies toward immigration and free expression from those of many other countries in the world. This openness turns out to be powerfully complementary with creativity and the vitality of the research university as an enterprise. When taboos are few on the questions that can be asked and the restrictions are few on who can participate in inquiry, scholarly investigation has its best climate in which to thrive.

Fourth among the reasons why America emerged as world leader in higher education is also an argument for why it may remain so for a while. It is a set of factors that can be lumped together under the heading of "first-mover

17. For example, Weinberg (2008, 1) quotes Robert Fogel making the former argument. Ash (2006, 253) takes the latter view, saying that, while it may have influenced content in some disciplines, the migration "had no transformative impact on the structure or philosophy of American higher education." Likewise, Weinberg (2008, 19) assigns to the migration "a modest role" in America's twentieth-century scientific leadership. See Siegmund-Schultze (2009) for an analysis of how the Nazi ascendency affected the field of mathematics.

advantage." By establishing a position of leadership, the United States has in effect erected barriers to entry into the top rungs of higher education. That is, being at the top makes it easier to stay there and harder for others to get there.[18] One aspect of this advantage is the collection of favorable local externalities created by faculty, other researchers, and trained resource and support personnel within universities. Despite the marvelous advances in communication of the late twentieth century, many of the production relationships in higher education stubbornly retain a reliance on face-to-face communication. These spillover effects on research productivity seem especially strong when it comes to having others in one's own field and in lab settings that require hands-on work. In the terms of textbook economics, universities enjoy economies of scope, and these economics of scope require a certain degree of scale before they become operational. So when a scholar chooses between two universities, one an established university with a full complement of active scholars in his or her discipline, and another just starting to undertake a research program, the established university will have an obvious appeal. Where the prominent universities are, therefore, is also where academic jobs will carry automatic advantages. A similar, but more general, advantage that American universities share with those in other English-speaking countries is the use of English itself, the language that became in the twentieth century the dominant language in science, engineering, and other technical fields. As Drèze and Estevan (2007, 278) noted, with admirable irony, "English is the undisputed *lingua franca* of economics!"

Trouble Ahead?

Despite the abundant evidence that American universities are in fact kings of the global hill, troubling pieces of evidence have appeared that cast some doubt on the permanence of the present state of affairs. To be sure, it may be that a certain degree of equalization across countries is simply to be expected, as incomes elsewhere rise relative to those in the United States, causing demand for higher education to rise abroad. From this perspective, if America loses its dominant position in terms of numbers of students and institutions, this should not be a major concern. Such a sanguine point of view is evident in part of Richard Freeman's chapter of the volume. But evidence of a loss of leadership at the top rungs of institutions, a weakening of the ability to attract the top graduate students and scholars, or an absolute decline in scholarly output would be cause for genuine concern, at least from the standpoint of the United States.

One source of concern lies in the diminishing numbers of American college students who undertake advanced study in science, technology, engineering, and math (STEM) fields, a trend that is aided by high rates of attrition among college students who start out majoring in a STEM field, only to

18. For an application to biomedical research, see Owen-Smith et al. (2002, 40).

switch majors (US National Academy of Sciences 2007, 327). These falling STEM enrollments among American college students may be connected to two other troubling indicators: the stagnation of US college completion rates and the lackluster performance of American students on international tests. In the last two-and-a-half decades, the expansion of college degree attainment in the United States has been eclipsed by advances in other developed countries. In 1980 the US rate of college completion was 22 percent, exactly twice that of the median of thirteen other Organization for Economic Cooperation and Development (OECD) countries. By 2004, this rate had risen in the United States to 39 percent, but the median in the thirteen comparison countries had caught up with and soared ahead of the United States, to 46 percent.[19] In international comparisons of math and science, American youngsters turn in middling performances. In the Programme for International Student Assessment (PISA) international test of science performance in 2006, for example, the percentage of American fifteen-year-olds who scored in the top two levels (7.5 percent), was near the median of thirty OECD countries.[20] In the 2007 Trends in International Mathematics and Science Study (TIMSS) math tests, American fourth and eighth graders scored above some advanced countries and below others, consistently being beaten by Japan and England.[21] To be sure, some observers believe that such international tests paint an unfairly negative portrait of American education. Gary Becker has argued, for example, that what American students lack in rigor at the high school level they make up for with creative thinking and more diligence in college.[22]

In chapter 2 of this volume, Eric Bettinger examines the decline in the propensity of American college students to obtain PhDs in math, science, and engineering. Between 1970 and 2005, the numbers of US citizens who obtained doctoral degrees in these STEM disciplines declined in absolute terms.[23] The decline was 23 percent in engineering, 44 percent in physical sciences, and 50 percent in mathematics (see chapter 2). He endeavors to explain these troubling declines by looking closely at the pipeline that produces Americans with PhDs in STEM fields. One likely culprit is insufficient

19. Cascio, Clark, and Gordon (2008, table 2). The thirteen OECD countries in this comparison group were: Australia, New Zealand, Britain, Austria, France, Germany, Italy, the Netherlands, Spain, Switzerland, Denmark, Finland, and Sweden.

20. PISA stands for Programme for International Student Assessment, a test administered by the OECD. The fourteen countries whose fifteen-year-olds surpassed the United States were Australia, Austria, Belgium, Canada, the Czech Republic, Finland, German, Ireland, Japan, Korea, the Netherlands, New Zealand, Switzerland, and the United Kingdom (OECD 2008, table A5.2, 116).

21. US National Center for Education Statistics, *Trends in International Mathematics and Science Study (TIMSS)* (see http://nces.ed.gov/timss/table07_1.asp).

22. Gary Becker, "Test Scores and Economic Performance," *The Becker-Posner Blog*, September 10, 2006 (http://www.becker-posner-blog.com/archives/2006/09/).

23. Bettinger focuses on these fields: computer science, math, engineering, and natural sciences.

preparation at the K through 12 level, illustrated by the humble standing of US students in international tests such as those previously noted. But Bettinger finds that the pipeline leaks in several places. Among students who start college in a STEM major, even for those with high test scores, there are high rates of attrition. Instead of science and engineering, American undergraduates tend to gravitate toward business, education, and the social sciences. Some of these defections can be attributed to the lure of more lucrative earnings possibilities, but certainly not all. At the end of the day the question remains just how serious a problem such leaks in the pipeline are when market signals appear to make at least some of it quite rational.[24]

Another sign that American universities might be losing ground is revealed in a marked deceleration in science and engineering research publications. Between 1995 and 2005 the number of science and engineering articles authored by Americans grew at an average rate of 0.6 percent a year, a rate that was outpaced by authors in Europe (1.8 percent) and Asia (6.6 percent) (National Science Board 2008, table 5-19). The result of these disparate growth rates is that the US share of global science and engineering articles has fallen. As table 2 shows, the US share of world article production fell from 34.2 to 28.9 percent over this ten-year period. Europe's share also fell slightly, while that of ten Asian countries jumped from 13.5 percent to 20.4 percent. Declines also mark the US share in most-cited articles (62.3 to 54.6 percent) and in citations (49.6 to 40.8 percent).

In his chapter, James Adams examines evidence of both American preeminence and America's weakening position. Its undeniable dominance after World War II, he argues, can be attributed not only to the previously noted emigration to the United States of European scientists and other scholars, but also to the growth in US federal funding for research and development during the after the war, the burgeoning access in America to college and university training, and the growth of technology-intensive industries. By the 1980s, however, the growth of research output in Europe and Asia had begun to outpace that of American universities. As an illustration, the American share of world citations declined from 52 percent in 1992 to 42 percent in 2003. To explain this slippage, Adams examines factors associated with scholarly output in American research universities, using data compiled by field, university, and year. He documents, and then seeks to explain, a marked slowdown in research output beginning in the mid-1990s, especially in public universities and in lower-ranked disciplines within universities. Over the same period, private universities strengthened their ability to bid for top faculty.

24. The plentiful supply of foreign graduate students and post docs is one probable cause for unattractive prospects in STEM fields. One conference participant, Michael Teitelbaum, has argued that the avoidance of STEM careers by Americans should not be a cause of concern, in light of the uncertainties and relatively low wages that characterize many careers in STEM disciplines (Teitelbaum 2007).

Table I.2 **Share of world science and engineering articles, citations, and most cited articles, United States, European Union, and ten Asian countries, 1995 and 2005**

Category	US	EU	Ten Asian countries
S&E articles			
1995	34.2	34.7	13.5
2005	28.3	33.1	20.4
Top 1% of cited S&E articles			
1995	49.6	30.6	8.2
2005	40.8	33.7	12.9
Citations of S&E articles			
1995	62.3	24.7	4.9
2005	54.6	29.0	7.5

Source: National Science Board, *Science and Engineering Indicators 2008,* table 5-19, Appendix table 5-19, and table 5-28.

Note: The ten Asian countries include China (including Hong Kong), India, Indonesia, Japan, Malaysia, Philippines, Singapore, South Korea, Taiwan, and Thailand.

Universities as Firms in Global Competition

Before one can analyze the effects of global forces on American universities and their international standing, it is necessary to look closely at the research university as an organization, as a firm. How are the large numbers of foreign students flowing into the United States utilized in the production that research universities undertake? How do universities respond to growing demand for training and research abroad? In the vocabulary of economics, questions such as these go to the heart of two aspects of these firms: their production functions and their objective functions. Thus, it is vital to begin by trying to answer these basic questions concerning universities as firms. Doing so leads directly to a consideration of two issues directly related to the link between American universities and the global higher education market: the role of foreign students and post docs in the production of research and decisions by universities to set up overseas programs.

A Peculiar Kind of Firm

As a "firm," the modern research university differs from the modern corporation in at least three important respects. As explained by sociologist James Coleman in a 1973 essay, the university as an organizational form retains one of the essential characteristics of its medieval forebear: it is more a community than it is a hierarchy. Top-down decision making is rare; today's successful university presidents are those who can persuade or coax various groups of stakeholders to do what needs to be done. Two other features follow from this community structure. The first is that the university has no overarching aim, except "to be the best." Second, those who carry out its main functions are not employees in the traditional sense, but rather "semi-independent professionals" (Coleman 1973, 369). These characteristics produce a "firm" whose production process resembles a neighborhood of busy bee hives or independent shops more than it does an assembly line tended by workers performing specialized tasks. Not only must the CEO and his lieutenants—president, provost, and deans—suffer the indignity of their employees occasionally refusing their requests, these corporate officers must also accustom themselves to seeing these employees routinely join with those working for rival universities in projects of joint production, sharing ideas and expertise in the process.[25] This is not to suggest that presidents and provosts are without the power to nudge their institutions in one direction or the other, especially when this can be accomplished by creating new entities under the university's umbrella. It is simply to say that top-down, disciplined, hierarchical control, a pillar of the modern corporation, has no real parallel in the modern research university.

Production in these firms yields research (of many highly differentiated varieties, to be sure), training, and a variety of activities loosely described as "service." Some of this training is highly complementary with the research function, illustrated by the graduate student who acts as lab assistant in a research project while she learns advanced skills and collects data as part of her doctoral training. In such labs and other collaborative research projects in the university, the utility of face-to-face contact and common access to research facilities makes it infeasible for universities to set up branch plants. Another feature that discourages branches may be fear of possible damage to the university "brand" that could result from subpar or disreputable research. Whether or not these are in fact the reasons for it, one distinctive feature of research universities is the remarkable rarity of branches and franchises as they are defined in the corporate world.[26] These peculiarities in production have particular relevance for the likely effects of foreign graduate students and for decisions regarding overseas programs.

The Role of Foreign Students in Production

The high percentage of foreign graduate students in American graduate programs has a double significance. On the one hand, it is a sure sign of quality, a natural by-product of the high standing enjoyed by American universities. The best universities in the world attract the best graduate students in the world. On the other hand, it is at the same time a sign of vulnerability, of the fragility of American hegemony. Should the high quality graduate

25. Feldstein (1992, 38–39) argues that university administrators not only lack power, they lack the incentive to bring about any changes that would make too many waves, or enemies.

26. To be sure, many state universities have branches, but these are typically branches in name only. A state's branch campuses are more aptly described as a loose confederation linked by a common source of funding and a single regulatory body. They seldom constitute branches of a single research university in the sense of an auto manufacturer's plants or an accounting firm's regional offices.

students whom we have become accustomed to welcoming and putting to work in our universities decide instead to stay at home or go elsewhere for graduate training, American universities could be in for a painful adjustment.

John Bound and Sarah Turner document the flows of international students into American universities, noting that the sources and effects of flows of graduate students are quite distinct from those of undergraduates. At the doctoral level, where complementarities with research are the highest, the flows of graduate students have been massive, leading to the marked increases in the shares of foreign graduate students noted before. Tracking doctoral students by the beginning dates of their programs, they show an increase of 20 percentage points in the share of PhD candidates from abroad, that share having risen from 29 percent for the cohort beginning study in 1980 to 49 percent in the 1996 cohort. This growing share of foreigners has been especially noteworthy in science, social science, and engineering. In some fields it was the result of absolute declines in Americans as well as increases among the foreign born. The absolute number of foreign doctoral students has exceeded that of Americans since the late 1970s in engineering, since the late 1980s in economics, and since the mid-1990s in physical sciences. In the life sciences, enrollments by US citizens have continued to grow, but at a slower rate than foreign enrollments.

It is not enough simply to count the number of students, however. A full accounting requires attention to differences in quality as well. Bound and Turner show that the growth in numbers of foreign students in US universities has generally occurred outside the top programs. They find little evidence to suggest that foreign students are "crowding out" American students in these graduate programs. One implication of their analysis is that American universities have less to fear from any future declines in the number of foreign doctoral students, as long as they are limited to second-tier US programs. Bound and Turner are also attentive to geographical patterns, showing that the top three source countries for doctoral students in science and engineering are China, India, and Korea.

What do these waves of foreign graduate students mean for the productivity of research universities? It has become a truism that doctoral training is complementary with the production of research, but can that complementarity be documented? How dependent have American universities become on the ready availability of foreigners to work in their labs and collaborate on research projects? These are the questions that motivate chapter 4, by Grant Black and Paula Stephan. To assess the role of foreigners in the research of American universities, Black and Stephan get under the hood of university research by concentrating on the central role of collaborative work in the sciences, most of which occurs within labs. While most previous research has focused on the importance of faculty who are foreign nationals, Black and Stephan take a new approach that allows them to ferret out the role of graduate students and post docs in research projects. They document the role of these participants in university research by analyzing authorship patterns for articles published in the journal *Science.* Analyzing articles whose last authors were affiliated with a US university and that had fewer than ten authors, they determine the position and ethnicity of all authors as a way of characterizing the role of foreign graduate students and post docs in the research projects associated with these articles. They document that graduate students and post docs are quite important, serving as authors in over 85 percent of all articles and as first authors in three-quarters of the cases. Using ethnic identification of names to suggest country of origin, they find that over half of the articles had a foreign student or post doc as a coauthor. They conclude that foreign graduate students and post docs are not simply important in staffing the labs of American universities; they actually play leading roles in university research projects.

Overseas Programs

International figures on post-secondary enrollments make clear that the market for higher education, like those for a multitude of other goods and services, is growing at much faster rates abroad than at home. This burgeoning of foreign demand has led American corporations of all stripes to boost exports and establish beachheads of production and distribution abroad. A similar instinct is evident among American universities, although it is restrained by the strong reluctance, noted before, to establish branches away from the main campus.

In spite of this reluctance, instances of American universities setting up overseas programs have occurred with surprising regularity in recent years. In addition to programs offering distance learning, this export instinct has manifested itself primarily in professional education. For example, Cornell Medical College's branch in Qatar, opened in 2002, graduated its first class in 2008. It was the first time an American medical school had awarded degrees overseas. Other universities, including Duke, Johns Hopkins, Indiana, and Ohio State, have gone partway toward setting up full-fledged branches by forming partnerships with foreign medical schools.[27] A different sort of partnership, one that is designed to create a new research university out of whole cloth, is the partnership between three prominent American universities with the new King Abdullah University of Science and Technology (KAUST) in Saudi Arabia. The University of Texas, Berkeley, and Stanford will each receive at least $25 million in return for assistance in establishing programs in computer science and engineering.[28] In yet another model of outreach, Duke University proposed to establish partnerships and branch

27. Katherine Mangan, "Cornell Graduates Its Inaugural Class at Its Medical College in Qatar," *Chronicle of Higher Education,* May 7, 2008.

28. Tamar Lewin, "US Universities Join Saudis in Partnerships," *New York Times,* March 6, 2008.

campuses in five different locations—Dubai, London, New Delhi, Shanghai, and St. Petersburg—where it plans to offer an MBA plus other professional degrees in what they are calling the "first global business school."[29]

Not only are they of obvious relevance to the future global position of American universities, programs such as these raise the question of just what objectives universities are pursuing. Given the view put forth by Coleman, that universities have no clearly defined purpose, this becomes a doubly interesting category of programs to study. This is the backdrop to chapter 5, by E. Han Kim and Min Zhu. They view universities as firms, to be sure, but firms that are different in some important ways from conventional for-profit corporations. For one thing, one of their principal outputs, research, is a public good that often has no immediate payoff. The other principal output, teaching, is a largely private good whose payoff is both tangible and rapidly realized. They argue that, in their consideration of overseas commitments, universities act like multinational firms. The authors argue that universities appear to maximize the present value of their net revenues, and that this orientation is most evident in their practice of price discrimination.

Not all universities are the same, of course. Kim and Zhu divide universities into two groups. One is composed of research-oriented institutions with high intellectual capital, whose fortunes are heavily dependent on their reputations. These universities are reluctant to put their reputations on the line by starting programs or forming alliances that might produce substandard research. The other group, universities with modest research reputations, depend mainly on teaching for revenue, can afford to be less picky about their partners, and are consequently more likely to offer overseas programs. Asia and the Middle East have become popular destinations for such programs. The authors note two waves of foreign programs. The first, beginning in the 1980s and reaching a peak in 1995 before declining, was marked by the failure of almost all of the programs started in Japan. The second wave, after 2000, has involved some high profile universities, such as the ones noted previously. Kim and Zhu conclude that the actions of American universities in the global market for advanced training reveal that economics, not altruism, guides their decisions.

External Forces on American Universities

The future position of American higher education in the world is not, of course, entirely in its own hands. As the previous discussion makes clear, that position depends in part on a large and continuing flow of talented graduate students from abroad to help fill a university's graduate rosters and staff its labs. More generally, the fortunes of American universities will be directly

29. Elizabeth Redden, "An Ambitious Approach to Overseas Expansion," *Inside Higher Ed*, September 16, 2008 (http://www.insidehighered.com/news/2008/09/16/duke).

influenced through two main channels by a host of forces and developments, ranging from economic growth and geopolitical alignments to government policies directly affecting higher education. One of these channels is obviously the flow of students from abroad to American universities. Although undergraduates are a part of this flow, the critical component is the graduate student portion. The number of such students, their quality (and thus their suitability as researchers), and their desire to remain in the United States after they finish their degrees are all aspects that are both important to American universities and influenced by conditions in the students' home countries. The chapters in this volume that cover three Asian countries well illustrate how these kinds of influences make themselves felt. The other primary channel through which conditions and institutions abroad directly affect American universities is in the international academic labor market. Next to ideas and graduate students, probably the most mobile of factors important to higher education is research faculty. To the extent that foreign universities are able to attract and keep top scholars, the competitive position of American universities is clearly going to be challenged. Indeed, this is the ultimate threat to the continued preeminence of American universities.

The Competition for Graduate Students and Faculty

The number of foreigners willing and able to enroll in American graduate programs depends on the number who obtain appropriate undergraduate training and the availability and quality of graduate programs outside the United States, both in their own countries and in third countries. Growth in the first of these—undergraduate education—has been strong worldwide and breathtaking in a few countries. According to United Nations Educational, Scientific, and Cultural Organization (UNESCO) figures, the number of students worldwide enrolled in all postsecondary ("third level") programs grew at an annual rate of 5.0 percent between 1990 and 2004. (This compares to growth of only 1.6 percent a year in the United States) But enrollment growth was spectacular in the world's two largest countries: it was 6.2 percent a year in India and 12.3 percent a year in China. As of 2004 China had 21.3 million students enrolled in these postsecondary programs, more than the United States' 17.3 million. India had another 11.8 million in such programs (US Department of Education 2007, table 385).

While these figures clearly overstate the number of students who are prepared to enter doctoral programs, let alone top-ranked ones, they surely suggest the kind of growth that has taken place in potential graduate enrollments. All of which lends significance for the United States of the inability of China and India to provide sufficient high-quality graduate programs to accommodate the burgeoning demand for graduate training by their own citizens. Given the vast disparity between the growing numbers of potential graduate students and suitable places for them in their home countries, it is little wonder that American universities—as well as those in Britain, Europe, Australia, and elsewhere—have enjoyed a flood of applications from Chinese and Indian students. Nor is it surprising that China and India account for the two largest groups of foreign students in the United States, followed by South Korea.

Besides these wellsprings of enrollment growth, the other element in determining America's success in attracting the best graduate students is the ability of competing universities to attract these students. The stronger the competition, the more successful foreign universities will be in attracting top faculty as well as strong applicants for advanced study. Thus, the prospects for continued American preeminence in higher education depend in large part on the rate of improvement of universities abroad, particularly in the two giant countries producing so many of the world's aspiring scholars and researchers. And, indeed, a number of countries around the world have set out explicitly to bring about just such improvement.

One prominent effort at reforming higher education is Europe's so-called Bologna Process, a series of concerted efforts begun in 1999 to rationalize and standardize degree requirements throughout much of Europe. As Ofer Malamud describes in chapter 6 of this volume, these reforms will make European programs more closely resemble those of American universities. More significantly, it will cause them to resemble each other, and this uniformity will make it easier for students to transfer between institutions in Europe. Interestingly, similar changes have recently occurred in Australia, where six universities have revised their academic programs in an attempt to put them more in line with the American model.[30]

Particularly important for the issues stressed in the current volume are reforms that seek to beef up universities' capacity to do research and, as a by-product, undertake high-level doctoral training. The most audacious among these policies are the efforts by China to build world-class universities, discussed by Haizheng Li in chapter 8. To provide incentives for high-quality research, countries have adopted policies with explicit incentives. For example, Britain adopted rating procedures for departments in its universities, wherein funding is directed to those departments rated highly by review boards using criteria based on publication records. Similarly, Germany allocated funds to universities largely on the basis of quality of research, and faculty salaries in Chinese and Australian universities were made dependent in part on the basis of numerical scores based on publications and citations.[31] And India announced in 2008 plans to set up a quasi-independent National Science and Engineering Research Board, patterned after the American

30. Martha Ann Overland, "Australian Universities Revamp Degree Programs to Become More Like Those in the US." *Chronicle of Higher Education,* September 30, 2008.

31. Aisha Labi, "Obsession with Rankings Goes Global," *Chronicle of Higher Education,* October 17, 2008; Hicks (2007, 236).

National Science Foundation, and to double such government funding for science and technology.[32]

Reforming European Higher Education

After the United States, Europe is the world's leading region for higher education. It awards more PhD-equivalent degrees than the United States, and its universities are among the most storied and prestigious in the world. According to the Shanghai Jiao Tong ranking for 2008, Europe contained over a third of the world's top 100 universities. Through the Bologna Process, Europe is setting about to reform its system of higher education by homogenizing various countries' degree programs and creating a system of course credits, making it easier to transfer between institutions and generally making European courses of study be more comparable to those in American colleges and universities. Ofer Malamud's chapter in this volume examines the scope and likely effects of these reforms. By shortening the time required for a bachelor's degree and making many course credits transferable between different institutions, the cost of false starts will be reduced, possibly allowing students to obtain degrees that better fit their own skills and predilections, and degree completion should be speedier. These changes should also, he argues, make European universities more attractive to foreign students and therefore more successful in competition against American universities.

An entirely different aspect of reform in Europe is addressed by Lex Borghans and Frank Cörvers in chapter 7. They focus on research and graduate training, using the discipline of economics in Dutch universities as a case in point. They observe a broad shift in perspective from national to international among faculty in European research universities in the last two decades, a shift that is heavily influenced by American standards and practices. The internationalization of research has brought with it a set of changes that have tended to break down national boundaries and deemphasize purely national concerns. English has become the language of internationally-focused professional writing, a change that is evident not only in professional journals but in dissertations as well. English is becoming the language of teaching at the doctoral level. Research faculty increasingly strive to publish in foreign (especially American) journals, and international travel to professional meetings has become almost commonplace. Structurally, faculties and graduate programs in European universities have come to look more and more like American ones. As Borghans and Cörvers explain, although faculty must incur costs in making some of these changes, the professional benefits are palpable. But these benefits differ by field (they

32. Shailaja Neelakantan, "India to Double Spending on Scientific Research," *Chronicle of Higher Education,* December 4, 2008.

are greater in the sciences, where research interests differ little across countries) and by language area (they are greater in smaller language areas, in such countries as Sweden or the Netherlands). Accordingly, the switch to English tended to start earlier in these fields and countries. Like the reforms embodied in the Bologna Process, these changes have the effect of making European universities more competitive with American ones for the best trained international students.

Developments in Asia

As the aforementioned enrollment figures attest, there is no area of the world to rival the large countries of Asia when it comes to potential for future development in university research and training. With the exception of Japan, however, Asia has so far failed to develop universities on a par with the scholarly accomplishments of its native sons and daughters. It remains a huge and alluring question just when the region will produce world-class universities. Thus, Asia bears attention on two planes: the contribution of its natives to research universities abroad and its development of domestic research universities. Separate chapters analyze, in turn, China, India, and South Korea.

No country boasts a longer or richer history of cultural and scientific achievement than China. Yet, owing to the cataclysm of the Cultural Revolution, modern higher education in China had a very late start, as Li spells out in his chapter. Following a ten-year hiatus, China resumed administering its national college entrance exam in 1978. Thereafter, enrollments grew with breathtaking speed. In recent years the Chinese government has announced an objective of launching as many as 800 colleges in the next fifteen years.[33] Over the last three decades, the flow of talented students from China to the United States has made Chinese education an important complement, or input, in the work of American universities. An alternative role that the Chinese education system could play vis-à-vis American universities is that of a competitor. In an effort to enhance its competitiveness, China has embarked on a bold effort to create world-class institutions by pouring resources into China's most established institutions and adopting policies to enhance their quality. One strategy described by Li is to recruit scholars from abroad, focusing particularly on the thousands of native Chinese who have built academic careers in the United States and elsewhere. To bolster this effort, Chinese universities are offering markedly higher salaries, as Li documents, using data for the discipline of economics. Whether such efforts, added on top of preexisting trends and the undeniable realities of

33. Mooney, Paul, "The Wild, Wild East; Foreign Universities Flock to China, But Are There Riches to Be Made, or Just Fool's Gold?" *Chronicle of Higher Education,* February 17, 2006.

scale, will someday thrust Chinese universities into the top rungs of global ranking seems clear. The only question is, how soon.

India presents a starkly different situation. In contrast to the ambitious plans laid out by the Chinese, Devesh Kapur describes in chapter 9, on Indian higher education, a state-supported structure of universities and training institutes weighed down by a brittle bureaucracy and patronage politics. The few flashes of brilliance on the Indian higher education scene seem to occur as much in spite of government policy as because of it. Traditional, state-supported universities in India, Kapur writes, are plagued by insufficient funding, debilitating centralized regulation, rent-seeking, a weak culture of research, and massive faculty shortages. Public institutions have also become subject to an extensive system of ethnic quotas designed to increase the enrollment rates of students from lower castes. The weaknesses of the established universities have led to wholesale flight by elite students to doctoral programs overseas, chiefly to those in America. As for professional training, the market has responded to the state-supported system's shortcomings by sprouting homegrown private substitutes—new private institutions and corporate-sponsored training programs. The private sector's growth has produced a doubling since 1980 in the shares of engineering and medical degrees awarded in the private sector. Even if recently announced plans to launch new institutes in technology and management come to pass, however, India's institutions of higher education appear likely to continue to keep lagging behind the educational achievements of its best students.

The case of South Korea, as described in chapter 10 by Sunwoong Kim, is a vivid demonstration of the interplay between home-country conditions and American opportunities in guiding the career decisions of foreigners who obtain doctoral training in American universities. This case also illustrates the bonds of influence that are created and sustained when foreigners receive their training in American universities, although the case of Korea is distinctive, since relations with the United States have been close for over a century. Having achieved more economic prosperity sooner than either China or India, South Korea could more effectively beckon to its scholar-expatriates abroad with the prospect of university or other professional employment back home. The strength of this pull to return has varied over time, depending on economic conditions and education policy in Korea, alternately fostering brain-drain of scholars to the United States, and later encouraging them to return home. An underlying but powerful theme of this history is the legacy created by the massive number of Koreans who obtained their doctoral training in America. One lasting result is that Korean higher education has a heavy American flavor; half of the faculty with PhDs at Seoul National University got them from American universities. Not only have Korean students and scholars contributed on a large scale to the American higher education enterprise, the resulting ties, both professional and personal, illustrate the dimensions of interrelationships evident in the global position of American universities.

Looking Ahead and Taking Stock

After at least a half century as undisputed global leaders, American research universities face a future that in many ways looks as promising as the recent past. Yet unbridled confidence seems quite unwarranted. Chief among the items that give pause is a global financial crisis whose first calamitous shocks were unfolding just as this conference was taking place, in early October of 2008. The events that shook the world's financial system in the fall of 2008 made a dramatic dent on the endowments of private American universities, and the accompanying recession seems destined to put a crimp on both state revenues and household income, posing an equal or greater threat to the well-being of public universities. In considering future prospects for American universities, and for the country itself, it is important to look beyond the likely effects of the recession to the longer-run trends analyzed in the studies contained in this volume.

To assess how American universities will fare in the next decade or two, a natural starting place is to consider the favorable characteristics and circumstances that have made possible their current high standing. The four traits noted in the first section of this introduction were: government support, decentralized competition, openness, and first-mover advantage. The prospects for continued American advantage arising from the first two traits—government support and decentralized competition—rest to some degree on the shape and severity of the current economic recession and on the federal government's response to it. As American dominance in higher education has in part been a function of its strong economy, economic vulnerability will surely raise questions about the continuation of public, as well as philanthropic, support. If federal spending for research and development in the United States fails to grow at least as fast as such spending in European universities, that would surely not auger well for future world standing. Even before the financial crisis of 2008, however, a distinguished science panel was calling for the federal government to construct a new giant particle accelerator so that the United States would not be left behind in physics.[34] Early indications from the Obama administration, building on a promise to double federal funding of basic research over a decade, appeared to bode well for federal support.[35] But in the wake of the 2008 global financial collapse, neither government support nor private resources can be taken for

34. Dennis Overbye, "Science Panel Report Says Physics in US Faces Crisis," *New York Times,* April 30, 2006.

35. Kelly Field, "Cautiously, Scientists Put Faith in Obama Promise," *Chronicle of Higher Education,* January 30, 2009.

granted; this goes for American universities and their foreign competitors alike. Stay tuned.

Equally difficult to predict is the effect of recession and other forces yet unseen on the vigorous competition among universities for faculty and other resources, dependent as it is on those universities having the financial wherewithal to compete. In light of the daunting economic conditions of the current moment, any jaunty confidence remaining from the heady decades of the recent past must surely be tempered with caution. For some time observers have expressed concerns about the ability of the top public research universities to remain competitive with elite private universities, given evidence of divergences in faculty salaries and other spending useful in attracting top scholars. It seems likely that a severe recession will do nothing but further weaken the economic position of public universities, but large question marks will hover over future private donations as well as the performance of endowments, both of which have been critical to the achievements of private universities in recent decades. In a backhanded way, the advantages of institutional autonomy and market competition may work against the continued dominance by American universities, if this structure is emulated elsewhere. In a recent statement, French President Nicolas Sarkozy signaled his support for greater institutional autonomy: "there is not a single example in the world of great universities that are not autonomous."[36]

As for the third advantage—openness—the prospects for continued openness would appear fairly good. There remain, for example, few restrictions on permissible topics and methods of research, although federal restrictions on embryonic stem cell research are a conspicuous exception to this general rule. A greater threat to openness lies in manifestations of post-9/11 national security concerns, such as delayed visa approvals, restrictive visa policies, and an unwelcoming attitude toward foreign visitors, which discourage foreigners from visiting or studying in the United States.[37]

What of that last item, the first-mover advantage? Although it has not gone away, the efforts of scholars and universities abroad to adopt American modes of operation—ranging from the structure of degree programs to the use of English—will surely serve to lessen its power. As Malamud argues in his chapter, the Bologna reforms promise to make European universities as

36. "French President Attacks 'Infantilizing System' of 'Weak Universities,'" *Chronicle of Higher Education,* January 28, 2009. If Western Europe is now partially emulating American higher education, it would reflect the similar, limited Americanization of European economic institutions in the decades after World War II. See Djelic (1998).

37. The National Academy (US National Academy of Sciences 2007, 34) stated, "Immigration procedures implemented since 9/11 have discouraged students from applying to US programs, prevented international research leaders from organizing conferences here, and dampened international collaboration. As a result, we are damaging the image of our country in the eyes of much of the world. Although there are recent signs of improvement, the matter remains a concern." Regarding restrictive visa policies, see also p. 36 of the previously quoted report. For a report reflecting these various influences, see Eugene McCormack, "US Visa Data Suggest a Coming Rise in Foreign Enrollments," *Chronicle of Higher Education,* July 21, 2008.

a whole a more homogeneous product and its component programs more comparable and therefore interchangeable. Not only will this increase the attractiveness of European universities within Europe, it could also make them more attractive for those outside Europe to the extent that the European degree structure, particularly its three-year bachelor degree, becomes widely accepted. Indeed, European authorities are actively working to build on the standardization achieved through the Bologna reforms to establish linkages to universities in Canada, Australia, and Latin America.[38]

In research, the first-mover advantage remains a potent force to the extent that universities depend on face-to-face contact, but it is diminished to the extent that new modes of communication and data retrieval lessen the need for geographical propinquity and physical access. Change there has been. Whether they constitute the revolutionary democratizing agent that many believe they have become (Friedman 2005), digital innovations such as JSTOR (short for "journal storage") and Google, not to mention the Internet itself, have dramatically reduced the advantage of having an office within walking distance of the reference desk of a world-class university library or, for that matter, the office of a coauthor. To borrow the words of Black and Stephan, advances such as these have surely transformed "the technology of discovery." Kim, Morse, and Zingales (2009) argue that such innovations have already begun to nullify the advantages arising from physical proximity. Using research output data of economics faculty from the 1970s to the 1990s, they document the decline and disappearance of the benefit of being affiliated with a top twenty-five university, although average productivity of top departments remains high, owing to the effect of past agglomeration patterns. Thus, as cell phones have allowed late-developing countries to dispense with the need to lay landlines, the Internet will render superfluous many of the reference volumes that were considered indispensible in 1980. Countries and universities attentive to new technologies and intent on improvement, then, may benefit from a second-mover advantage.[39]

In short, American universities will continue to benefit from a having arrived there first, but the potency of this advantage seems destined to diminish over time. This advantage could be further reduced if American higher education as a whole rests on its laurels, a possibility that is more than a little bit credible. Consider, for example, the changes in work processes and productivity being wrought by technological innovations.

Any close examination of such changes in higher education compared to those in other service industries will reveal that the changes in higher educa-

38. The European University Association on its website describes its efforts, including "forging institutional alliances and partnerships which, as European universities respond to global challenges and increasingly seek to position themselves internationally, become more and more important" (http://www.eua.be/international-relations/).

39. The concept is not unlike the advantages of backwardness once put forth by Gerschenkron (1962).

tion have been relatively modest. While many processes in other industries have been "re-engineered," universities continue to do many things in much the same way they were done in the nineteenth century: lecturers employ blackboards, journals are printed and bound, and bachelor's programs take four years. At the undergraduate level, colleges and universities have resisted calls for greater accountability and assessment, at the same time that worrisome trends continue, including a long-term secular decline in the amount of time undergraduates spend on academic work and the aforementioned drop in STEM enrollments.[40] To the extent that dominance breeds self-satisfaction, American universities could be vulnerable. One need look no farther than the case of automobiles to see how an American industry, once the envy of the world, can quickly fall from grace.[41]

In chapter 11, Richard Freeman takes a broad look at the implications for the United States of the changes in the global market for higher education and America's position in it. To a great extent, he reminds us, the catching-up in enrollments abroad, and the concomitant fall in America's share of global enrollment, are natural outcomes of rising propensities for higher education in both advanced countries and very populous developing ones. Thus, the US share of all higher education enrollments worldwide fell from 29 percent in 1970 to 12 percent in 2006.[42] Our share of science and engineering PhDs is higher than these, but is also falling over time. At the same time, international students are accounting for a larger share of students in American doctoral programs. This trend is fueled by the very elastic supply of foreign graduate students. Freeman points out that these trends hold benefits for our universities, by giving them access to the world's most promising graduate students and, by the way, raising the quality of applicants to those American universities beyond the most elite group, all of which should result in yet higher rates of research output for American universities as a whole. The resulting research output will contribute to the growth of knowledge, and thus to growth and rising incomes worldwide, and to the supply of highly trained graduates who can be hired by American corporations both domestic and multinational. In addition, the heavily international flavor of graduate enrollment in American universities means that many leadership roles abroad, both in universities and outside of them, will be held in the future, as is now the case, by individuals who once studied in the United States. Freeman's chief caveat to this largely sanguine view is that these benefits will accrue only to the extent that American universities hold onto their sizable competitive advantage over universities in Europe and elsewhere. Inevitably, however, this advantage is likely to diminish.

40. See the American Association of University Professors' reaction to recommendations of the Spellings Commission (AAUP 2006) and Babcock and Marks (2008).

41. For a narrative of the auto industry's fall, see Halbersham (1986).

42. For an analysis of broad trends in enrollments around the world, see Schofer and Meyer (2005).

In the near term, therefore, the rising share of foreign graduate students in our universities is cause for celebration rather than concern. Those students represent high-quality inputs into what remains a vibrant American industry. The benefits accrue to the United States and to the world at large. These benefits come in the form not only of scientific knowledge itself, but also in the model provided by American universities and funding agencies of how to undertake academic research. In the words of Diana Hicks:

> The institutions of modern science have in many ways been a gift from the United States to the rest of the world. The US has demonstrated that the best-quality scientific research is fostered when funding is awarded competitively, when plentiful, rigorously trained PhD students and post-docs are available cheaply, when substantial amounts of money are spent, when modern equipment is used, and when transfer of research to technological application is encouraged. (Hicks 2007, 242)

Thus, neither the shrinking US share of global enrollments nor the rising share of foreign students in American universities should themselves be a cause for special concern. One is a largely natural consequence of catching-up and relative population size, and the other holds important benefits for our universities as well as the American economy and nation. Not the least of these broader benefits is the extensive yet intangible advantage that accrues from that fact that so many leaders around the world have lived in the United States for at least the years of their graduate training. The bonds of affection and appreciation that so often accompany such experience constitute an important source of what has been deemed "soft power," an element of foreign policy that can only become more vital to US national security in the coming decades.[43]

It seems likely, indeed, that global leadership in higher education is tethered in a real sense to leadership defined more broadly. In assessing the position of American universities in the world, it may be useful to look beyond the campus walls and consider economic, political, and ideological leadership. Such a broader view may be necessary in order to reach a full understanding of why American universities were able to push aside British and European ones in the twentieth century to achieve preeminence. Although America's position of leadership in the world remains fairly secure in the first decade of the twenty-first century, it is difficult to ignore the existence of widespread negative attitudes toward the United States, especially with regard to its foreign policy and especially after its invasion of Iraq in 2003 (Katzenstein and Keohane 2007, 15). One perhaps small but telling sign of waning American influence is the decline among supreme courts in other countries in the frequency with which they cite decisions issued by our

43. For an explanation of this concept, see Nye (2004). See also US National Academy of Sciences [2007, 36] for an application to foreign students in US universities.

own US Supreme Court.[44] The actual importance for higher education of leadership in these disparate domains is unknown, of course. What seems more certain is that the future standing of American universities will depend largely upon their continued ability to take advantage of those features of higher education in this country that have served it well over the past half century. One need only consider the demise of the US automobile industry to realize that even a position of global preeminence can be a vulnerable one.[45]

References

Aghion, P., M. Dewatripont, C. Hoxby, A. Mas-Colell, and A. Sapir. 2009. The governance and performance of research universities: Evidence from Europe and the US. NBER Working Paper no. 14851. Cambridge, MA: National Bureau of Economic Research, April.

American Association of University Professors. 2006. Statement of the Committee on Government Relations regarding the report *A test of leadership: Charting the future of US higher education,* September 26. Available at: http://www.aaup.org/AAUP/GR/federal/FutureofHigherEd/spellrep.htm.

Ash, M. G. 2006. Bachelor of what, master of whom? The Humboldt myth and historical transformations of higher education in German-speaking Europe and the US. *European Journal of Education* 41 (2): 245–67.

Babcock, P., and M. Marks. 2008. The falling time cost of college: Evidence from half a century of time use data. University of California. Unpublished Manuscript, June.

Cascio, E., D. Clark, and N. Gordon. 2008. Education and the age profile of literacy into adulthood. NBER Working Paper no. 14073. Cambridge, MA: National Bureau of Economic Research, June.

Coleman, J. S. 1973. The university and society's new demands upon it. In *Content and context,* ed. C. Kaysen, 359–99. New York: McGraw-Hill.

Djelic, M.-L. 1998. *Exporting the American model: The postwar transformation of European business.* Oxford: Oxford University Press.

Drèze, J. H., and F. Estevan. 2007. Research and higher education in economics: Can we deliver the Lisbon objectives? *Journal of the European Economic Association* 5 (April/May): 271–304.

Feldstein, M. 1993. Comment. In *Studies of Supply and Demand in Higher Education,* ed. C. T. Clotfelter and M. Rothschild, 37–42. Chicago: University of Chicago Press.

Friedman, T. 2005. *The world is flat: A brief history of the twenty-first century.* New York: Farrar, Straus, and Giroux.

Gerschenkron, A. 1962. *Economic backwardness in historical perspective.* Cambridge, MA: Harvard University Press.

Goldin, C., and L. Katz. 1999. The shaping of higher education: The formative years

44. Adam Liptak, "US Court is Now Guiding Fewer Nations," *New York Times,* September 18, 2008.

45. For a short history, see Halbersham (1986).

in the United States, 1890–1940. *Journal of Economic Perspectives* 13 (Winter): 37–62.

Halbersham, D. 1986. *The reckoning.* New York: William Morrow and Co.

Hicks, D. M. 2007. Global research competition affects measured US academic output. In *Science and the university,* ed. P. E. Stephan and R. G. Ehrenberg, 223–42. Madison: The University of Wisconsin Press.

Katzenstein, P. J., and R. O. Keohane, eds. 2007. *Anti-Americanisms in world politics.* Ithaca, NY: Cornell University Press.

Kim, E. H., A. Morse, and L. Zingales. 2009. Are elite universities losing their competitive edge? *Journal of Financial Economics* 93 (3): 353–81.

Liefner, I., L. Schätzl, and T. Schröder. 2004. Reforms in German higher education: Implementing and adapting Anglo-American organizational management structures at German universities. *Higher Education Policy* 17 (1): 23–38.

Mervis, J. 2008. Top PhD feeder schools are now Chinese. *Science* 321 (July): 185.

Morris, R. B., ed. 1965. *Encyclopedia of American history.* New York: Harper and Row.

National Science Board, National Science Foundation. 2008. *Science and engineering indicators 2008.* Arlington, VA: National Science Board, January. Available at: http://www.nsf.gov/statistics/seind08/.

Noll, R. G., ed. 1998. *Challenges to research universities.* Washington, DC: Brookings Institution Press.

Nye, J. 2004. *Soft power: The means to success in world politics.* New York: Public Affairs.

Organization for Economic Cooperation and Development (OECD). 2008. *Education at a glance 2008.* Available at: http://www.oecd.org/dataoecd/23/46/41284038.pdf.

Owen-Smith, J., M. Riccaboni, F. Pammolli, and W. W. Powell. 2002. A comparison of US and European university-industry relations in the life sciences. *Management Science* 48 (January): 24–43.

Schofer, E., and J. W. Meyer. 2005. The worldwide expansion of higher education in the twentieth century. *American Sociological Review* 70 (December): 898–920.

Siegmund-Schultze, R. 2009. *Mathematicians fleeing from Nazi Germany: Individual fates and global impact.* Princeton, NJ: Princeton University Press.

Teitelbaum, M. S. 2007. Testimony before the Subcommittee on Technology and Innovation, Committee on Science and Technology, US House of Representatives, November 6. Washington, DC.

US Department of Education, National Center for Education Statistics. 2007. *Digest of education statistics.* Available at: http://nces.ed.gov/programs/digest/d07/tables/dt07_385.asp?referrer=list.

US National Academy of Sciences, Committee on Science, Engineering, and Public Policy. 2007. *Rising above the gathering storm: Energizing and employing America for a brighter economic future.* Washington, DC: National Academy Press.

Weinberg, B. A. 2008. Scientific leadership. Ohio State University. Unpublished Manuscript, August.

Windolf, P. 1997. *Expansion and structural change: Higher education in Germany, the United States, and Japan, 1870–1990.* Boulder, CO: Westview Press.

I

Storm Clouds for American Higher Education?

1

Is the United States Losing Its Preeminence in Higher Education?

James D. Adams

1.1 Introduction

For more than fifty years, US universities have led the world in research and graduate education, building on firm foundations laid down in the nineteenth century, and rising to new heights during the twentieth century. But in recent years doubts have begun to arise concerning the future of US higher education, considered as a producer of graduate and professional students as well as scientific discoveries. The two are complementary: faculty that are not at the research frontier are less likely to produce top PhDs and MDs, and conversely, faculty who lack top students are less likely to do cutting-edge research. It follows that this chapter's emphasis on research extends to advanced students.[1] Furthermore, a strong research enterprise improves the quality of undergraduate education in the long run and contributes to the ability to undertake advanced training. As far as higher education is concerned, none of this is new.

The United States is losing share in scientific research, and perhaps in papers accepted in top journals (Hicks 2007), in part because the number of countries that devote significant resources to scientific research has

James D. Adams is professor of economics at Rensselaer Polytechnic Institute and a research associate of the National Bureau of Economic Research.

The Andrew W. Mellon and Alfred P. Sloan Foundations supported data collection underlying this project. I thank Charles Clotfelter, Charles Phelps, two readers, and conference participants for comments. The staff of Folsom Library, Rensselaer Polytechnic Institute, provided valuable assistance in locating the historical data discussed in this paper. Of course, I am responsible for any remaining errors. This paper was presented at the NBER Conference on American Universities in a Global Market held in Woodstock, Vermont, October 2–4, 2008.

1. In confirmation of this point, the National Research Council rankings of graduate programs reveal a strong positive correlation between research and the quality of graduate programs. See National Research Council (1995).

increased. This implies intensified competition for scientific and engineering talent and also greater competitiveness of foreign high technology firms (Freeman 2006). But in addition to growth overseas, a slowdown has taken place within the United States. The growth rate of financial resources of US public universities has declined and this has reduced the growth rate in their publications.[2] This development is important, because public universities account for a large share of US science.

It may come as a surprise to hear that US universities could be in danger of losing their preeminence, since top US private and public universities invariably rank near the pinnacle of world institutions (Shanghai Jiao Tong University 2005). But university growth overseas implies that this dominance may not last forever. Moreover, public universities in the United States have struggled in recent years.

To understand how top private universities in the United States have reached unparalleled heights at the same time that top public universities have fallen behind, it is necessary to explain the organization of US higher education. It is a mixed public-private system. Top US private universities rely on federal grants, endowments, gifts, and tuition to hire the best faculty, select the best students, and sustain their competitive advantage. In this they are not constrained by state interests. The situation is otherwise with US public universities, whose charter, beginning with the Morrill Act of 1862, enjoins them to support state industries by providing affordable and practical higher education. If state budgets contract, or if competition for state funds strengthens, then funding diminishes and the competitive advantage of US public universities declines. A pillar of public support for higher education, its accountability to state interests erodes and becomes a constraint on university growth. In recent years this appears to have taken place.

The chapter's focal point is a panel of universities and fields observed over time. Main findings from an analysis of these data are as follows. Starting with growth facts, I find that research output grows at about the same rate in the late twentieth century in private schools as in public, until the 1990s, when public university growth slows down. This is despite the fact that stocks of Research and Development (R&D), which are mostly federally funded, rise appreciably faster in public universities. A slowdown in papers and in papers per dollar of R&D is evident in the late 1990s, again in public universities. Given the challenges of measuring R&D, I provide faculty counts as a supplementary measure. It turns out that faculty grow at a slower rate than papers, so research productivity indeed rises. Once again, though, it rises more slowly in public universities, especially during the late 1990s. In addition, the evidence reveals that current funds rise more rapidly in private universities, suggesting that in public universities, faster growth of (mostly federal) R&D stocks is cancelled by slower growth in tuition and state appropriations. Hence, faster growth of current funds in private

2. See Ehrenberg (2006) and Adams and Clemmons (2009).

schools contributes to faster growth of wages and research output in these universities.

Continuing with regression findings, I show that public and private universities obtain similar percentage increases in scientific papers and citation-weighted papers from equal (percentage) increases in R&D, graduate students, and current funds, so that differences in growth of research output between the two sets of institutions are the result of differences in growth of resources. Here private universities have recently held the advantage. Departments ranked in the top 20 percent of their disciplines obtain a larger increase in papers for the same increase in R&D and students than departments of lower rank. Graduate students contribute more to papers in top 20 percent departments than elsewhere, suggesting the high degree of complementarity of faculty and graduate students at the top of the quality distribution.

Compensation in private universities rises faster than it does in public universities by almost 1 percent per year. Compared to public universities, where the wage structure is relatively flat, compensation in private schools is higher at all ranks and rises more markedly for full professors. This suggests incentives for researchers, especially senior researchers, to migrate from public to private universities. Combined with slower growth in current funds in public universities, this helps to produce slower growth in their research output than in that of private universities.

The rest of the chapter proceeds as follows. Sections 1.2 and 1.3 provide an historical perspective on US universities. Section 1.2 recounts the expansion of research in US universities before, during, and after World War II. This is the period in which US universities progress relative to the rest of the world. Section 1.3 considers the US contribution to world scientific output since the 1980s. The share of the United States declines sharply during this period. While this is inevitable in the face of post-war recovery and world economic development, the section also points to a slowdown in research output during the 1990s in the United States, due largely to a deceleration in the growth rate of resources in US public universities.

Section 1.4 introduces panel data covering 110 top US universities and twelve main science fields during 1981 to 1999. Section 1.5 presents growth facts concerning university research. Section 1.6 begins with regressions in which research output is the dependent variable and concludes with wage regressions. Section 1.7 discusses the evidence and draws conclusions for the future of US higher education.

1.2 US Universities Since World War II

1.2.1 Pre-War Setting

Prior to World War II and unlike the present day, federal R&D was located inside the US military (Mowery and Rosenberg 1989, 92 ff.). Agricultural research is the exception. It was conducted in land-grant colleges founded by the Morrill Act of 1862 and the Land-Grant Act of 1890, extending the 1862 Act to state agricultural and mechanical colleges for blacks. In addition, the Hatch Act of 1887 established experiment stations close to the land-grant colleges. Huffman and Evenson (1993, ch. 1) provide a summary of these developments.[3]

The first statistical evidence on university R&D in the United States derives from balance sheet data in 1935 and 1936. The data are contained in *Research—A National Resource, Volume I* (National Resources Committee 1938, section 6).[4] A survey of sixty universities yielded total research expenditures of $50 million. Of this amount, $16 million was earmarked for experiment stations, much of this funded by the Department of Agriculture.[5] Of the remaining $34 million, seventeen derived from endowment, eight from foundations, four from gifts, two from contract research, and two from state government. Therefore, the federal government's main role in university research was its support for agriculture.

Bush (1945, 86) contains estimates of research expenditure by sector from the 1930s through World War II. The data are limited to natural science.[6] Using as a basis the figure of $50 million reported in National Resources Committee (1938), this yields $25 million for natural science research in 1936. Using survey data on research faculty, this figure is then extrapolated backward to 1930 and forward to 1942 to arrive at natural science R&D for universities. This is the relatively crude university series shown in figure 1.1.[7]

The aforementioned summarizes the pre-war setting. Events surrounding World War II led to a vast expansion of university R&D. First, before the war, immigration of scientists from Europe significantly increased the science and engineering workforce. Second, during the war, a sharp rise in defense research increased the demand for scientists and engineers, which the Cold War institutionalized.[8] Third, after the war, the GI Bill helped

3. The democratic and equal-opportunity conditions set by the early US patent system (Khan 2005) may have complemented the later establishment of universities focused on the agricultural and mechanical arts—the very type envisaged by the Morrill Act.

4. Individual evidence on university R&D exists before 1935 to 1936. The University of Chicago conducted an internal survey of research costs in 1929 and 1930 and the University of California undertook a similar survey in 1928 and 1929. But these data lack the comparative breadth of the National Resources Committee survey.

5. In 1940 federal R&D expenditures were $74 million, of which $29 million or 39 percent, consisted of Department of Agriculture R&D (Mowery and Rosenberg 1998, 27). Clearly, agricultural research assumed a much larger role in the federal government and universities than it does today.

6. In these early data, natural science includes biological, mathematical, and physical science, plus engineering.

7. Industrial R&D statistics are obtained by multiplying industrial researchers by R&D per worker of $4,000. See *Research—A National Resource, Volume II* (National Resources Committee 1941, section IV).

8. By an increase in demand I mean throughout a shift to the right of the demand curve for scientists and engineers.

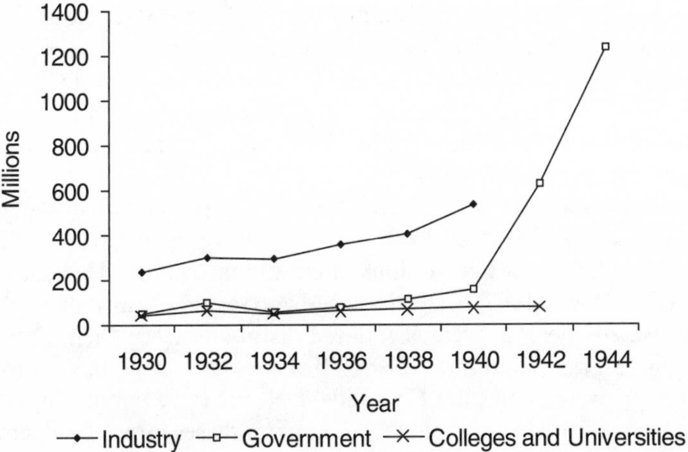

Fig. 1.1 R&D in the United States, 1930–1944 (millions of 1958 dollars)
Sources: R&D dollars, Bush (1945, 86); implicit GDP deflator, US Department of Commerce, Bureau of the Census (1975, part 1, series E13).

finance college education for returning soldiers, which subsequently produced a spike in enrollments and increased post-war demand for faculty. I discuss each of these factors in turn.

1.2.2 The Intellectual Migration from Europe, 1933–1944

The supply of highly skilled scientists to the United States increased due to the flight from Hitler's Europe, but by how much, and in what proportion? The main statistical source is Davie (1947), who directed data collection for the Committee for the Study of Recent Immigration from Europe.[9] Using the criterion of "refugee, arrival from Europe as place of last residence," statistics of immigration and naturalization yielded 22,842 refugees in the professions during 1933 to 1944. The refugees were assigned to detailed occupations: 507 were chemists, 2,471 engineers, 3,415 professors and teachers, and 1,907 were "scientists or literary persons," yielding a total of 8,300 refugees in science, engineering, and related professions. In 1938 the National Resources Committee, using *American Men of Science*, 6th edition (1938), estimated that 28,000 US men and women were researchers in the natural sciences, and that 22,000 more were in the humanities and social sciences (National Resources Committee 1938, 171) for a total of 50,000 across all sectors of the economy.[10] Thus, while the intellectual migration from Europe during the 1930s was small by modern standards, it was large

9. Fermi (1971) recounts individual biographies of this wave of immigrants by detailed occupation, including scientists and engineers by their separate specialties. Her time period, 1930 to 1941, is earlier than that of Davie (1947), whose perspective I adopt here.

10. The committee judged that of the existing stock of 50,000 researchers, 5,000 or (10 percent) were in the first rank.

for the time. Put another way, if half of the roughly 8,000 refugees in science and engineering and related fields were engaged in research—not excessive, given their occupations—then this constitutes an increase of 4,000 persons on a base of 50,000, or 8 percent. And since they specialized in natural science and engineering, then the increase could be almost 4,000 on a base of 28,000, or 14 percent.[11]

There is reason to think that even this understates growth at the highest levels of research. Table 1.1 illustrates.[12] Twelve refugees had won a Nobel Prize by 1947, the most prestigious international award.[13] Using a sample collected by Davie (1947) of 707 refugees who served on university faculties in Europe, 203 persons were accounted distinguished in their disciplines, of which 181 were in natural science. To assess the meaning of this, turn to table 1.2, which compiles US-resident Nobel Prize winners by decade. The number of foreign-born is shown in parentheses for each subject area, except for the sum across areas, where the foreign-born appear as column (2).[14] Noting that twenty-three prizes had been won by US residents by 1940, with none foreign-born except for one award, I conclude that the intellectual migration from Europe increased resident Nobel Prize winners by 50 percent.[15]

Table 1.2 also shows that major improvements in US universities were under way by the 1930s. Across areas, the number of native-born prizes rises from one to seventeen per decade during 1901 to 1940. Excluding economics prizes—since these did not exist until 1969—the total of seventeen prizes for the 1930s is half the native-born total, per decade, during 1971 to 2007.

1.2.3 Increase in Federal R&D During World War II

Besides the increase in the pre-war supply of highly skilled scientists and engineers, the increase in military R&D during and after the war produced a sustained rise in demand for scientists and engineers. Figures 1.1 and 1.2 illustrate.[16]

Figure 1.1 shows R&D expressed in millions of 1958 dollars in industry, government, and colleges and universities during 1930 to 1944. The data are

11. Following the usage of Bush (1945) and Davie (1947), in this section natural science refers to biology, medicine, mathematics and statistics, and engineering, in addition to chemistry and physics.

12. The data are compiled from appendix C of Davie (1947).

13. The Fields Medal in mathematics dates from 1936 and competes with the Abel and Wolf prizes. Other awards of distinction, such as the National Medal of Science in the United States, are national in scope.

14. In this table, Nobel Prizes in science include chemistry, physics, and physiology or medicine.

15. The foreign-born award belongs to Albert A. Michelson, for the Michelson-Morley experiment on the invariance of the speed of light.

16. The data on federal R&D are of higher quality during this period than the data on academic and industrial R&D, because they derive from annual cost accounts. All these data are crude by standards of the present day.

Table 1.1 **Statistics of the intellectual migration from Europe to the United States, 1933–1944**

Field	Nobel Prize winners[a]	Distinguished refugees[b]	Sample of refugee professors[c]
Biology; physiology or medicine	2	72	91
Chemistry	1	28	63
Physics or astronomy	6	40	77
Mathematics	n.a.	41	53
Literature	3	15	65
Economics	n.a.	7	60
Total	12	203	409

Note: n.a. = not applicable.

[a]These are Nobel Prize winners by the time of Davie (1947).

[b]Distinguished Refugees are compiled by Davie (1947, 432–40), from *Who's Who in America* (1944–1945) and *American Men of Science* (1944).

[c]Sample consists of 707 refugees in Davie (1947) who were formerly on university faculties in Europe, of which 409 were in the disciplines shown.

Table 1.2 **Nobel Prizes won by US residents, 1901–2007**

Period	Total laureates	Total (foreign-born)	Science[a] (foreign-born)	Literature (foreign-born)	Peace (foreign-born)	Economics[b] (foreign-born)
1901–1910	2	1	1 (1)	0	1	n.a.
1911–1920	3	0	1	0	2	n.a.
1921–1930	5	0	2	1	2	n.a.
1931–1940	13	0	9	2	2	n.a.
1941–1950	22	5	15 (5)	2	5	n.a.
1951–1960	29	7	27 (7)	1	1	n.a.
1961–1970	32	10	27 (10)	1	3	1
1971–1980	52	14	40 (7)	3 (3)	1 (1)	8 (3)
1981–1990	48	15	37 (11)	1 (1)	1 (1)	9 (2)
1991–2000	52	12	39 (9)	1	1	11 (3)
2001–2007	46	9	31 (6)	0	2	13 (3)
All years	304	73	229 (56)	12 (4)	21 (2)	42 (11)

Note: n.a. = not applicable.

[a]Science Nobel Prizes include separate awards in physics, chemistry, and in physiology or medicine.

[b]The Nobel Prize in economics began in 1969. Thus, economics prizes for the 1961 to 1970 decade are limited to 1969 and 1970. Data compiled from Nobel Archives at www.nobel.org.

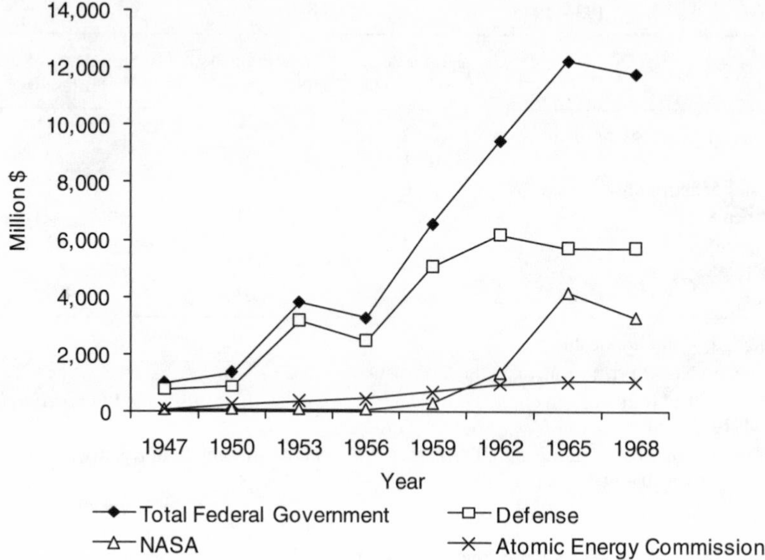

Fig. 1.2 Federal R&D, 1947–1968 (millions of 1958 dollars)

Sources: R&D dollars, US Department of Commerce, Bureau of the Census (1975, part 2, series W126, W129, W137, and W138); implicit GDP deflator, US Department of Commerce, Bureau of the Census (1975, part 1, series E13).

reported every two years.[17] They show that federal R&D rises from less than 200 million in 1940 to over 1.2 billion by 1944.

To the benefit of US universities the Cold War produced a sustained rise in the demand for scientists and engineers. Figure 1.2 shows Federal R&D in 1958 dollars for the years 1947 to 1968.[18] Total federal R&D amounted to $1 billion in 1947, rising to $12 billion by 1968. Nearly all R&D expenditures were on defense, the Atomic Energy Commission, or NASA.

1.2.4 Post-War Demand for Higher Education

Mobilization produced a wartime decline in male college enrollment and degrees. But under the GI Bill this decline was succeeded by a large spike around 1950. Figure 1.3 shows BA and BS degrees from 1932 to 1960.[19] Baccalaureate degrees earned by men rise during the 1930s, then decline from a peak of 100,000 in 1940 to a trough of 50,000 in 1946, and finally spike to 350,000 in 1950. By comparison, the decline and recovery of degrees

17. To convert current into constant dollars I have used the implicit GDP deflator with 1958 set to 1.0. This chart, as I have noted, derives from Bush (1945, 86).

18. The source of the R&D data is US Department of Commerce, Bureau of the Census (1975, Part 2, series W 126, 129, 137, and 138). These are deflated by the implicit GDP deflator for government purchases of goods and services (indexed to 1958) that appears in US Department of Commerce, Bureau of the Census (1975, Part 1, series E 13).

19. The data on BA and BS degrees derive from US Department of Commerce, Bureau of the Census (1975, Part 1, series H 752–754).

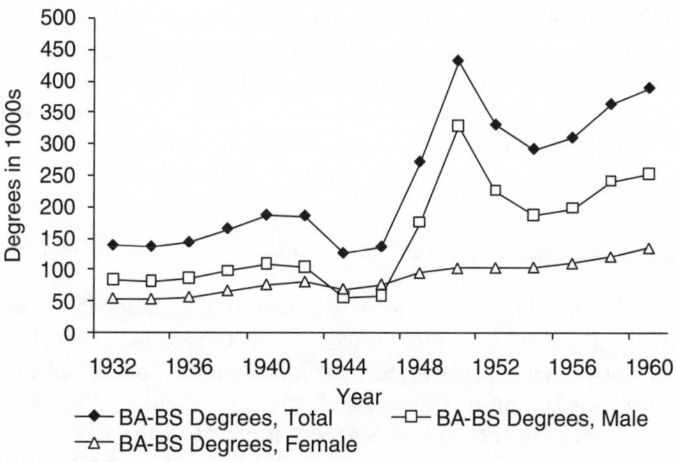

Fig. 1.3 Baccalaureate degrees in the United States, 1932–1960
Source: US Department of Commerce, Bureau of the Census (1975, part 1, series H752–H754).

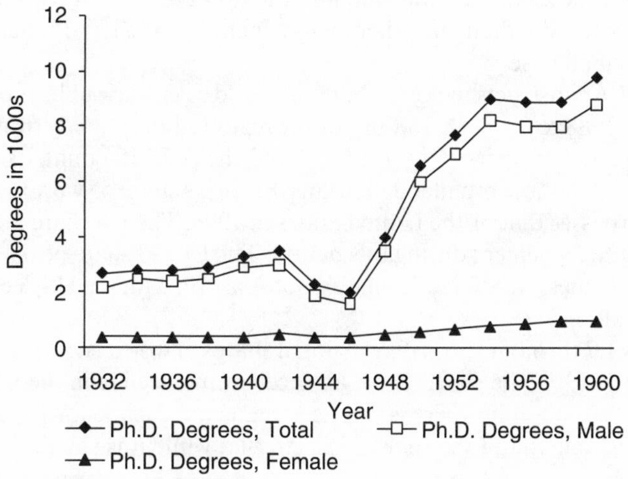

Fig. 1.4 PhD degrees in the United States, 1932–1960
Source: US Department of Commerce, Bureau of the Census (1975, part 1, series H761–H763).

earned by women are slight. As the stock of excess demand for education diminished during the 1950s, baccalaureate degrees fell and did not regain their 1950 peak until the mid-1960s.

Figure 1.4 shows PhD degrees from 1932 to 1960.[20] These increase from 2,000 to almost 4,000 during the 1930s, decline to 2,000 by 1946, and increase

20. The data on PhD degrees derive from US Department of Commerce, Bureau of the Census (1975, Part 1, series H 761–763).

to 10,000 in 1960. Unlike baccalaureate degrees, the flow of PhDs rises smoothly, reflecting the strength of long-run prospects for advanced skills.

World War II and the Cold War led to sustained growth in US academic science. Throughout the subsequent period, growing demand for undergraduate and graduate education fueled continued expansion of US universities.

1.3 World Scientific Output Since the 1980s

Having discussed forces that led to expansion of research in US universities from the 1930s to the 1980s, I now examine the recent role of the United States in world scientific research. I shall use scientific papers as a measure of the public or "commons" aspects of science.[21] Figure 1.5 shows relative growth of papers in the United States compared to the EU-15 group of European countries, East Asia, and rest of the world.[22] Clearly, US papers grow slowly compared to most regions, and growth equals zero from 1997 to 2002. The EU-15 countries surpass the United States in total publications by 1997 and they maintain this lead into the twenty-first century. East Asia grows more rapidly than any other region, including the EU-15, but it does so from a small base.

Figure 1.6 constructs regional shares in world scientific publications over the period 1988 to 2005. Definitions of the regions differ slightly from figure 1.5.[23] The EU-23 supersedes the EU-15 and the Asia-10 countries replace East Asia.[24] On these broader definitions, Europe's share of world scientific papers surpasses that of the United States in 1996. The US share falls from 38 percent to 29 percent during this period. The EU-23 share peaks in 1998 but then declines. All shares decline except Asia-10, with the US decline the fastest of all.

Figures 1.7 through 1.9 display regional shares in world citations in 1992, 1997, and 2003.[25] The charts show an accelerating decline in the US share of citations, though nowhere is this as great as the decline for papers. The EU-15 gain share; and the share of East Asia, while it is small, grows the

21. Alternative measures of commercial licenses and patents are beyond the scope of this chapter.

22. The EU-15 consists of Austria, Belgium, Denmark, Finland, France, Germany, Greece, Ireland, Italy, Luxembourg, Netherlands, Portugal, Spain, Sweden, and the United Kingdom. These are the EU countries before the addition of countries of Eastern Europe. East Asia consists of Japan, China, South Korea, Singapore, and Taiwan. The source of figure 1.5 is appendix table 41, chapter 5, National Science Board (2006).

23. The source of these data is appendix table 41, chapter 5, National Science Board (2006) and appendix table 34, chapter 5, National Science Board (2008).

24. The EU-23 countries are the EU-15 plus new member countries Bulgaria, Czech Republic, Estonia, Latvia, Lithuania, Poland, Romania, and Slovenia. The Asia-10 countries consist of East Asia (Japan, China, South Korea, Singapore, and Taiwan) plus India, Indonesia, Malaysia, Philippines, and Thailand.

25. The data source is appendix table 61, chapter 5, National Science Board (2008).

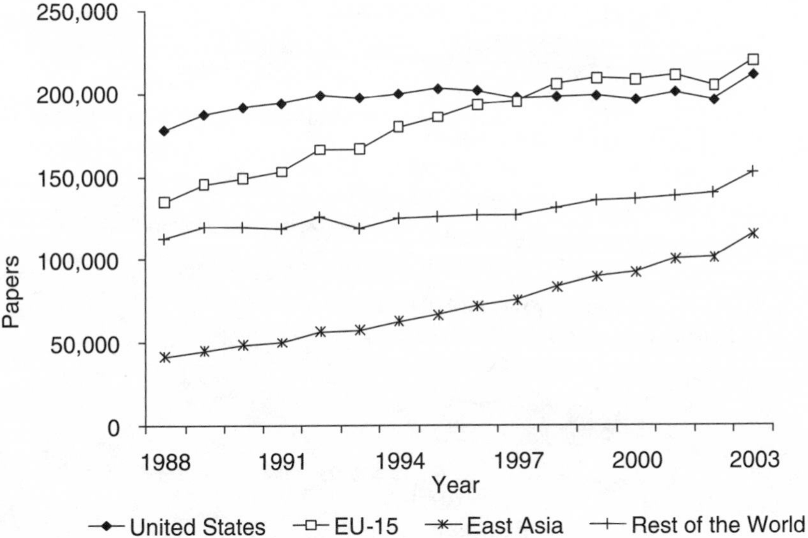

Fig. 1.5 Scientific papers by region, 1988–2003
Source: National Science Board (2006, chapter 5, appendix table 41).

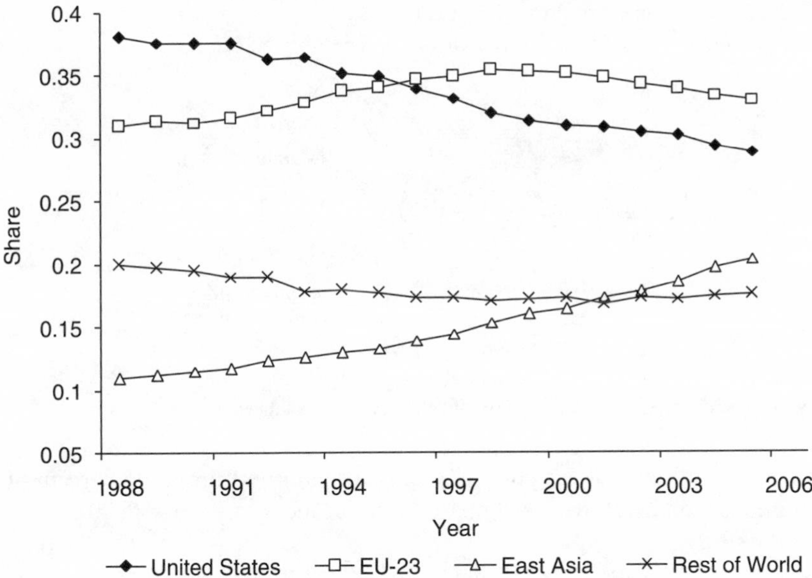

Fig. 1.6 Shares in world scientific papers, 1988–2005
Sources: National Science Board (2006, chapter 5, appendix table 41); National Science Board (2008, chapter 5, appendix table 34).

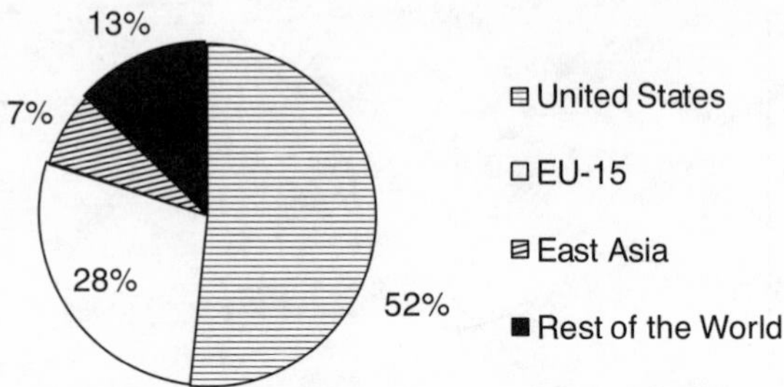

Fig. 1.7 Citation shares by region, 1992
Source: National Science Board (2008, chapter 5, appendix table 61).

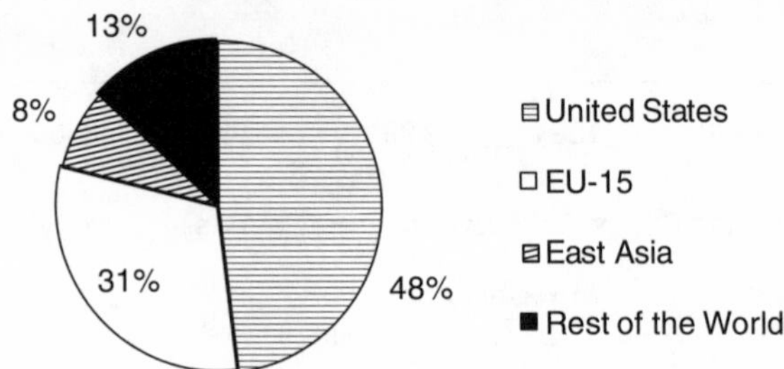

Fig. 1.8 Citation shares by region, 1997
Source: National Science Board (2008, chapter 5, appendix table 61).

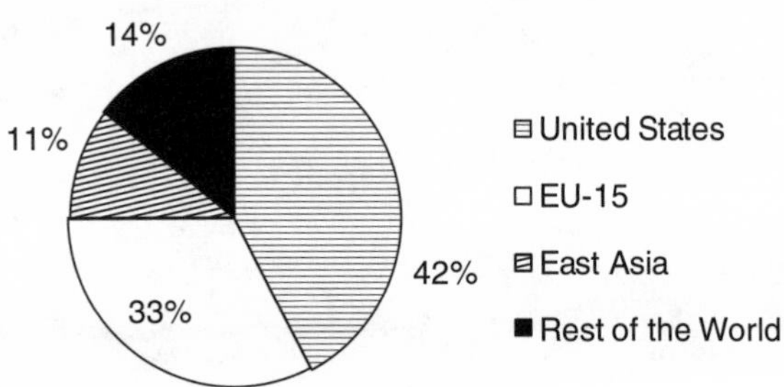

Fig. 1.9 Citation shares by region, 2003
Source: National Science Board (2008, chapter 5, appendix table 61).

fastest. At the end of the period, because of gains in Europe, 75 percent of citations are still received by America and Europe compared with 70 percent at the start.

Figure 1.10 depicts the US share in the top 1 percent, top 5 percent, and top 10 percent most cited papers from 1992 to 2005.[26] The share erodes at every level, and though it is hard to see, the percentage decline is less for top 1 percent papers than top 5 percent papers. The top 1 percent share declines

26. The data source is appendix table 63, chapter 5, National Science Board (2008).

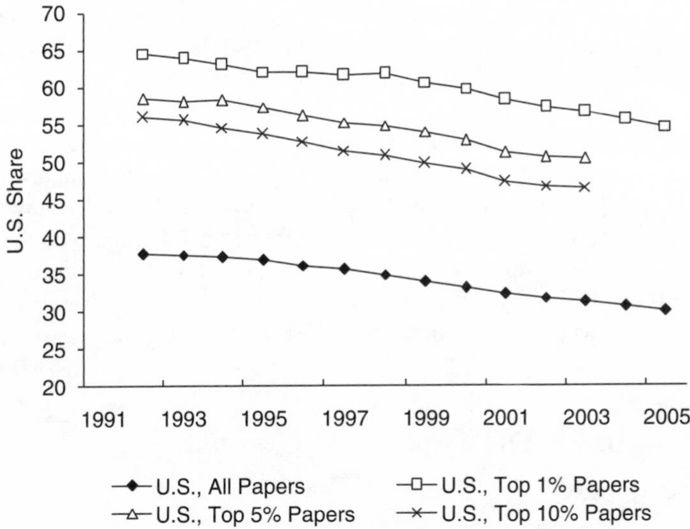

Fig. 1.10 US share in world output of highly cited papers, 1992–2005
Source: National Science Board (2008, chapter 5, appendix table 63).

from 65 percent of the world total in 1992 to 55 percent in 2005. This is a decline of 15 percentage points (10/65). The top 5 percent share declines from 38 percent to 30 percent, a decline of 21 percentage points. So erosion in share is less at higher levels of citation impact, though some may see this as cold comfort.

But what does all this mean? Share data tell us little about welfare. Output adjusted for quality, and output relative to input, are what matter for growth and technical efficiency of an industry, and universities are no exception to this rule. All we can say is that the growth rate of US scientific publications has fallen and that growth is slow relative to other regions, but we have not addressed the factors that drive this slowdown.

Foreign competition for science and engineering students is unlikely to be responsible.[27] If that were the reason, then the skill of foreign science and engineering graduate students entering US universities would have undergone serious decline in recent years. But this seems implausible given the attractiveness of US education and employment. Alternatively, the slow-

27. In the long run, arguments concerning the diffusion of science and R&D vary in their implications for welfare of advanced countries like the United States. If technology converges in science and in industrial research then the share of innovative products produced in advanced countries will decline. Standard models build on the theory of trade with differentiated products (Helpman and Krugman 1986). North-South models of innovation, imitation, and trade based on this approach (Krugman 1979; Grossman and Helpman 1991) assume that all innovation occurs in the North, while the South merely imitates. But if advanced human resources arise in the South as well, then innovation is distributed across both North and South, as Freeman (2006) points out. In that case the profits from new products are also distributed across both

down could represent crowding out of US authors in top journals (Hicks 2007), or diversion to commercial activities (Toole and Czarnitski 2007), or earmarking to less efficient institutions (De Figueiredo and Silverman 2006).

The recent slowdown could derive from other domestic causes and this is the approach that I am about to pursue. I show in section 1.5 that growth of scientific publication in US private universities did not slow down much in the 1990s compared with the 1980s. In contrast, a pronounced deceleration did occur in public universities. In explaining the difference, a deceleration in resource growth during the 1990s seems to be the most likely explanation for the slowdown in public universities. I explore this hypothesis in sections 1.5 and 1.6.

1.4 Panel Data on US Universities

1.4.1 Data Construction

With the goal of explaining the slowdown in US academic research, I turn to empirical work using a panel of 110 top US universities. I begin by describing the data. In their raw form they consist of 2.4 million scientific papers, published during 1981 to 1999, that have at least one author from a top 110 US university. These universities account for more than 80 percent of US academic research during this period.[28]

Papers consist of articles, reviews, notes, and proceedings. The data source is Thomson-Reuters Scientific.[29] Papers follow the field that Thomson assigns to the journal in which they appear.[30] "Field," in this case, is one of eighty-eight subfields. To link the data to the National Science Foundation's

regions and the North can lose some industries with supra-normal profits. Applying this line of reasoning to universities as an industry suggests that the United States could lose the lead in some sciences, which in turn might contribute to less effective industrial research in the United States. But countervailing forces also apply if product varieties grow with the world economy. First, knowledge flows to industries in advanced countries will increase, including universities, so that scientific discoveries and inventions of new products could increase. Second, the larger world economy that results from the South's entry into advanced nation status would create markets for the North, including in scientific research. So it is not clear whether the North gains or loses as a result of the South's development.

28. According to National Science Board (2002), appendix table 5-4, in 1999 the top 100 US universities account for $22.10 billion of R&D out of $27.49 billion of R&D for all US universities. This equals 80.4 percent. National Science Board (2008), appendix table 5-11 indicates that in 2006 the top 100 account for $38.09 billion out of $47.76 billion for all US universities. This equals 79.8 percent. Since the sample consists of the top 110 and not the top 100, its share in R&D expenditures exceeds 80 percent. Publication data reflect R&D spending, so the publication share also exceeds 80 percent.

29. The journal set consists of approximately 5,500 journals that were active in 1999, as well as 1,600 inactive (renamed or out of print) journals that were cited by active journals.

30. This assignment is reasonable for specialized journals because of the breadth of fields that I use. But the method produces serious errors for the 1 percent of journals (about 70) that fall into Thomson-Reuters's Multidisciplinary category. Thomson treats this category as part

(NSF) Computer-Aided Science Policy Analysis and Research (CASPAR) database, I assign each of the eighty-eight to one of NSF's twelve main fields.[31]

The data record publication year, journal field, institutional affiliation, address information on city, state, and country, and author names, as well as number of authors.[32] Address information is used to identify university affiliations of those who collaborate on a paper and to compute fractional papers. By fractional, I mean that if a paper is written by researchers in two universities, then each university is assigned half the paper. If three collaborate, then each receives a third, and so on.[33] I add up fractional papers by university, field, and year to form "effective" papers produced in a university-field. By treating the data in this way I avoid multiple counting of papers of US universities taken as a whole. Likewise I compute (forward) citations received by a paper in its first five years, including year of publication, and I calculate fractional five-year citations in the same manner as for papers, but excluding citations from the same institution. I accumulate fractional citations by university, field, and year to form an estimate of "effective" citation-weighted papers in a university-field.[34]

These steps yield research "output" in a university, field, and year. Following along these lines I form a panel of universities, fields, and years. The panel combines papers and citations with university-field level R&D, university-field PhD students and post-doctoral students, and characteristics of doctoral programs; as well as financial characteristics of parent universities. The measure used for R&D is a calculated depreciated stock based on past R&D expenditures. The NSF-CASPAR database of universities, a compendium of NSF surveys, is the source for university R&D and for graduate and post-graduate students. The HEGIS (Higher Education General Information Surveys) surveys of the US Department of Education provide financial data at the university level on tuition revenues, state appro-

of biology because biology accounts for the largest number of its papers. Multidisciplinary journals include *Nature, Science, Proceedings of the National Academy of Sciences USA,* and *Philosophical Transactions of the Royal Society.* Wholesale assignment to biology here is clearly wrong. But to correct the problem would require article (not journal) assignments to fields. Also, some Multidisciplinary journals are primarily focused on biology. Therefore, the problem applies to less than 1 percent of the journals.

31. The twelve fields are: agriculture, astronomy, biology, chemistry, computer science, earth sciences, economics and business, engineering, mathematics and statistics, medicine, physics, and psychology.

32. There is no limit on the number of authors. The maximum number in the sample is 210, while the mean is 2.36.

33. The cumulative distribution of universities listed on papers is: one university, 79.6 percent; two universities or less, 96.8 percent; three universities or less, 98.3 percent; and four universities or less, 99.5 percent. It follows that the fractions assigned are almost always 1, 1/2, 1/3, or 1/4.

34. It is tempting to think of university-fields as departments, but this is misleading. The same field can be practiced by more than one department and (rarely) multiple fields can be practiced within one department.

priations (for public universities), endowments, auxiliary revenues from fees, and total revenues. The National Research Council (NRC) 1993 Survey of Doctoral Programs (NRC 1995) includes rankings of PhD programs, and I use these to stratify departments by relative standing.[35]

In the basic panel of universities I consider only leading university-fields ("departments") from the top 110. Their number depends on size of field: I include the top twenty-five universities in astronomy, the top fifty in agriculture, chemistry, computer science, economics and business, earth sciences, mathematics and statistics, physics, and psychology, and the top seventy-five in biology, medicine, and engineering. Summing across fields, and accounting for the fact that forty-eight formal schools of agriculture exist, the panel consists of 648 top university-fields. My purpose in breaking out few individual schools in small fields and more in large fields is to avoid empty cells for universities where fields are small or nonexistent.[36] The result is a panel that contains papers and citation-weighted papers for 648 university-fields in twelve main sciences during 1981 to 1999. This implies a total of 12,312 observations before exclusions due to missing values. In some cases I stratify the data into top 20 percent, middle 40 percent, and bottom 40 percent university-fields. A field that contains fifty university-fields has ten in the top 20 percent, twenty in the middle percent, and twenty in the bottom 40 percent, and so on. The university-field dimension allows for greater variability of R&D stock, graduate students, and other variables within a university. It increases the robustness of the findings when university dummies are included. The price of this detail is that lagged faculty counts must be replaced by lagged R&D stocks and a moving average of graduate students. These are the primary indicators of resources that are available at the university, field, and year level.

1.4.2 Descriptive Statistics

Table 1.3 contains descriptive statistics for major variables. The table reports means, standard deviations, minima, and maxima. Groups consist of "all," "private," and "public" universities. The last two are the groups used in the rest of the empirical work.

I begin with research output. Mean (fractional) papers in all universities are 177 per university-field and year. They are slightly larger in private schools. The data indicate considerable variation, especially among private schools. The field with the most papers is in a private university. The mean of five-year (fractional) citations received (citation-weighted papers) is 520

35. The NRC ranks are not available for agriculture and medicine. For these fields I sort universities by their 1998 R&D and assign a rank of 1 to the university with the largest R&D and so on in descending order.

36. The size of the remainder of the top 110 equals an average university-field in the individual top twenty-five, fifty, or seventy-five schools. This reflects the positive skew of academic R&D. For more on this point see Adams and Griliches (1998).

Table 1.3 **Descriptive statistics, panel of universities, fields, and years**

Variable	Analytical level	Mean	Standard deviation	Min	Max
Papers[a]					
All universities	University-field	176.8	210.9	0.5	2,559.1
Private		183.1	256.2	1.3	2,559.1
Public		173.6	183.2	0.5	1,317.6
Five-year citations received[a]					
All universities	University-field	520.1	1,078.9	0	21,954.2
Private		693.8	1,518.7	0.9	21,954.2
Public		430.8	743.4	0	7,710.8
Number of faculty[b]					
All universities	University	1,236.3	614.6	42	3,083
Private		802.1	371.6	179	2,461
Public		1,459.9	595.0	42	3,083
Stock of R&D (millions of 1992 US$)[c]					
All universities	University-field	83.3	112.7	0.0	1,441.1
Private		83.4	116.6	0.0	828.9
Public		83.3	110.6	0.2	1,441.1
Tuition revenues (millions of 1992 US$)[d]					
All universities	University	120.4	83.9	0.7	547.4
Private		158.1	94.7	13.0	547.4
Public		101.0	70.2	0.7	413.0
State appropriations (millions of 1992 US$)[d]					
All universities	University	155.9	132.0	0	489.7
Private		11.1	30.6	0	160.8
Public		230.5	97.8	23.9	489.7
Endowment (millions of 1992 US$)[d]					
All universities	University	553.9	890.7	0.013	6,553.7
Private		1,118.9	1,029.4	55.3	6,553.7
Public		258.7	632.7	0.013	5,089.6
Graduate students[e]					
All universities	University-field	258.7	343.1	0.0	4,904.0
Private		198.3	363.1	0.0	4,904.0
Public		289.8	328.1	0.0	2,705.0
Auxiliary/total revenues[d]					
All universities	University	0.096	0.045	0.006	0.302
Private		0.077	0.040	0.006	0.245
Public		0.105	0.045	0.007	0.302
Enrollment/faculty[f]					
All universities	University	21.5	6.4	4.8	40.1
Private		16.4	4.9	6.5	28.9
Public		24.1	5.4	4.8	40.1

Notes: Period is 1982 to 1999. Sources of the data are described in the text and include: Thomson-Reuters Scientific, the CASPAR database of the National Science Foundation, and the HEGIS database of the National Center for Education Statistics.

[a]Papers and citations received are fractionally assigned to universities in the manner described in the text.

[b]The number of faculty is the number of tenure-track plus nontenure-track faculty. These data derive from HEGIS.

[c]The stock of R&D is defined at the university-field level. It derives from the NSF-CASPAR database of universities.

[d]All the financial variables derive from HEGIS.

[e]The number of lagged graduate students is for a university-field. It is an average over the previous three years. These data derive from the NSF-CASPAR database of universities.

[f]The enrollment data derive from HEGIS.

per university, field, and year. This is 33 percent higher in private schools and 17 percent lower in public schools. Again the maximum occurs in a private university.

For comparison I report faculty counts. Since these exist only at the university level they indicate total research labor.[37] The average school employs slightly more than 1,200 faculty, private schools employ 800, and public schools employ 1,500. A smaller faculty in private schools produces the same papers per university-field, but appreciably more citation-weighted papers, than do faculty in public schools. Note that I compare total faculty in universities with papers and citations at the university-field level. But this comparison is also valid at the university level (Adams and Clemmons 2009).

Research & Development stock signifies lagged resources that enter into research. It is the depreciated sum of total R&D from federal and other sources in a university-field over the previous eight years.[38] The depreciation rate is 15 percent; underlying R&D flows are expressed in millions of 1992 dollars using the Bureau of Economic Analysis (BEA) university R&D deflator (Robbins and Moylan 2007). The R&D stock in field i, university j, at time t, is

$$\text{(1)} \qquad \text{R\&D Stock}_{ijt} = \sum_{\tau=1}^{8} (0.85)^{\tau} r_{ij,t-\tau}.$$

Mean R&D stock is about \$80 million. Research output varies more than R&D, and private universities produce more research than expected, given their R&D stocks, suggesting that other, less readily observed resources are greater in these universities.

Financial statistics of tuition, state appropriations, and endowment derive from HEGIS. These are expressed in millions of 1992 dollars using the implicit gross domestic product (GDP) deflator. The data are at the university level.[39] Financial resources could be used to support more and better faculty. For example, tuition in private universities is used to cover start-up packages for assistant professors in science and engineering (Ehrenberg, Rizzo, and Jakubson 2007). Not surprisingly, and despite smaller enrollments, private schools have larger tuition revenues and larger (nontax) endowments. State appropriations capture the "tax endowment" of public universities. I construct the following measure of current revenue in university j:

37. The data include untenured as well as tenure track faculty. In the top 110 about 90 percent are tenure track according to HEGIS. Note that data on faculty by university and field have not been collected since 1985.

38. I chose an eight-year lagged stock because the NSF CASPAR R&D data begin in 1973 and papers begin in 1981. It is therefore the maximum length of stock that is available given the data.

39. One difficulty with the financial variables is that they are not available for the late 1990s. This causes an appreciable loss of data as we shall see.

(2) $\text{Revenue}_{j,t} = \text{Tuition}_{j,t-1} + \text{Public} * \text{State Appropriations}_{j,t-1}$.

In equation (2) "public" is a dummy indicator equal to one in public universities and zero otherwise so that in private universities revenue is tuition, since "public" equals zero. But in public universities it is tuition plus state appropriations on the assumption that appropriations substitute for tuition in public universities. I lack a history of revenue, but I lag equation (2) by one year in the research output equations to approximate lagged resources. I treat endowment separately from revenue, since it is a stock, and since it may be earmarked for different uses. Note that I use the endowment stock because endowment income is poorly measured in HEGIS.

The moving average of the stock of graduate students over the previous three years captures numbers of research assistants:

(3) $$\text{Graduate Students}_{ij,t} = 0.333 * \sum_{\tau=1}^{3} \text{Students}_{ij,t-\tau}.$$

Table 1.3 shows that public universities employ more graduate students. But numbers of undergraduates are also larger, requiring more of the graduate students to serve as teaching assistants. Besides this, large public university programs in engineering include masters as well as PhD students. For these reasons, equation (3) is likely to be a noisy indicator of research assistance, and yet it is the best measure that I have.

I use the ratio of auxiliary/total revenues (from HEGIS) to indicate financial duress. Auxiliary revenues are fee-for-service charges for residence halls, food services, athletics, student unions, stores, and movie theaters.[40] I divide auxiliary by total revenues to abstract from size of university. The mean of this ratio is 0.10, although it ranges from zero to 0.30.

To motivate the use of auxiliary/total revenues, suppose that tuition is price-controlled in a public university. This could occur in states that guarantee tuition to families of students, since the states must then cover tuition if the price cap were to be lifted (Rizzo 2006). If fees were increased in small amounts, then they might substitute for tuition in this setting. Likewise, private universities with small endowments and gifts could use fees to finance their operations. Fees in this interpretation resemble hidden prices for university attendance.

Table 1.4 reports correlations among auxiliary/total revenue, enrollment/faculty, tuition plus state appropriations per student, and endowment per student. The enrollment/faculty ratio, or the student-teacher ratio, is positively correlated with auxiliary/total revenue. Since an increase in the student-teacher ratio spreads limited resources over more students, it also may indicate financial duress.[41] Tuition plus state appropriations per student

40. Hospital revenues are separate from auxiliary revenues.

41. An alternative view is that a higher student-teacher ratio automatically increases the share of auxiliary fees. It is by no means perfect as an indicator of financial duress.

Table 1.4 **Correlations among financial indicators**

	Auxiliary/ total revenue	Enrollment/ faculty	Tuition + state appropriations/ student	Endowment/ student
Auxiliary/total revenue	1.00			
Enrollment/faculty	0.17	1.00		
	(< 0.0001)			
Tuition + state appropriations/student	–0.41	–0.50	1.00	
	(< 0.0001)	(< 0.0001)		
Endowment/student	–0.25	–0.35	0.21	1.00
	(< 0.0001)	(< 0.0001)	(< 0.0001)	

Notes: See text and table 1.3 for data sources and definitions of the financial indicators. (Significance levels in parentheses).

and endowment per student capture more abundant resources per student. They are the opposite of financial duress (Ehrenberg 2002). They should be, and are, negatively correlated with the financial duress indicators, which in this study are auxiliary/total revenue and enrollment/faculty.

1.5 Growth of University Research

I now use the university panel data described in section 1.4 to provide an overview of the growth of university research. Understanding these facts is helpful in interpreting the regression analysis of university research in section 1.6. To this end, I have composed three summary tables that are designed to facilitate discussion of trends in university research productivity and the US slowdown in publication rates during the 1990s.

Table 1.5 presents totals of papers, citation-weighted papers, PhD degrees awarded, and R&D stock in private and public universities. The data consist of 620 university-fields (out of 648 possible), observed over 1982 to 1999, for which there are no missing values. To aid in the interpretation, I report values relative to 1982 in square brackets. In brief, the data tell us that the output of papers grows by slightly more (slightly less) than 50 percent in private (public) universities; that citations grow by 125 percent in both groups (from 1982 to 1995); and that PhDs grow by a third in both. Since citations rise with the growing ease of citation and with the number of researchers who cite, citation growth is best regarded as an upper bound on the growth of research output. But since papers have genuinely become more influential, growth of papers is a lower bound. Therefore, growth of research output lies between 50 and 125 percent.

This provides a broad range of growth in research output, but what about input? I start by examining the behavior of R&D stock deflated by the implicit GDP deflator. This grows by 105 percent (130 percent) in private

Table 1.5 **Scientific papers, PhDs, and R&D stock by university type, selected years**

University type, variable	1982	1986	1990	1995	1999
A Private schools					
Papers	27,591	30,776	33,342	40,022	41,952
	[1.00]	[1.12]	[1.21]	[1.45]	[1.52]
5-year citations	83,641	110,371	140,938	187,763	—
	[1.00]	[1.32]	[1.69]	[2.24]	
PhD degrees[a]	48,374	48,512	55,178	60,278	63,840
	[1.00]	[1.00]	[1.14]	[1.25]	[1.32]
R&D stock (mill. of 1992 US$)[b]					
Using GDP implicit price deflator	10,296	11,709	14,641	17,775	21,099
	[1.00]	[1.14]	[1.42]	[1.73]	[2.05]
Using BEA university R&D input deflator	11,927	13,109	15,435	17,873	20,478
	[1.00]	[1.10]	[1.29]	[1.50]	[1.72]
B Public schools					
Papers	49,851	56,312	63,566	73,985	74,158
	[1.00]	[1.13]	[1.28]	[1.48]	[1.49]
5-year citations	101,746	125,394	173,066	229,657	—
	[1.00]	[1.23]	[1.70]	[2.26]	
PhD degrees[a]	116,709	117,402	126,311	153,026	155,505
	[1.00]	[1.01]	[1.08]	[1.31]	[1.33]
R&D stock (mill. of 1992 US$)[b]					
Using GDP implicit price deflator	18,400	21,771	27,963	36,385	42,257
	[1.00]	[1.18]	[1.52]	[1.98]	[2.30]
Using BEA university R&D input deflator	21,312	24,366	29,468	36,567	41,030
	[1.00]	[1.14]	[1.38]	[1.72]	[1.93]

Notes: Value relative to 1982 in brackets. See the text and table 1.3 for data sources and definitions of the variables. Data are a balanced panel of university-fields, defined as a matched sample that includes the same observations in all years. The sample includes all the data. Papers and five-year citations received are fractional and are adjusted for collaboration among universities. Dashed cells indicate that data are not available for the data set.

[a]PhD degrees are specific to university-fields and belong to twelve main fields of science and engineering: agriculture, astronomy, biology, chemistry, computer science, earth science, economics and business, engineering, mathematics and statistics, medicine, physics, and psychology.

[b]R&D stock is deflated by the GDP implicit price deflator in the first row, and by the BEA University R&D input deflator (Robbins and Moylan 2007) in the second row. Both price indexes are normalized to 1992.

(public) schools. The R&D growth exceeds publication and PhD growth: surely, one supposes, this is a recipe for a slowdown in research productivity. But R&D growth is overstated, because the GDP deflator understates cost increases in universities and overstates growth of real R&D. The evidence in table 1.12, on rising real compensation of faculty, helps to make this clear.

For this reason I prefer the BEA price index for university R&D (Robbins and Moylan 2007), because it takes university wage costs into account, and I use the BEA index to deflate R&D stock in all the regressions to follow. When I use the BEA index instead of the implicit GDP deflator to calculate real R&D, I find that R&D in private universities grows by 72 percent, not

105 percent. Likewise I find that growth in public schools is 93 percent, not 130 percent. Using the improved deflator, real R&D grows by 70 (90) percent in private (public) universities, while research output grows by 50/125 percent in both. In this way the gap narrows between growth of articles and growth of real R&D.

Even so, growth of real R&D is likely to be overstated despite the use of the BEA deflator. First, interuniversity grants probably grow in importance during this time because of large projects in biology and other fields. Since grants are not apportioned among schools in the statistics until well after 1999, R&D is increasingly overcounted because of this. Second, an increasing amount of funding could be targeted for training of graduate students rather than faculty research. To assess research productivity with more accuracy it would be useful to separate funds for research from funds for pure training. A related point might be important, if universities move from institutional to grant support of graduate students. To that extent, grants replace internal funds and they are not additional funds for research. I mention these problems not because I have solutions to them but in the interest of producing better statistics on university R&D in the future.

Table 1.5 shows that publications in private universities grow more slowly than R&D stock. The same point applies even more strongly to public universities. While growth of papers slows down during 1995 to 1999 in private universities, it virtually stops in public universities. However, the growth rate of papers recovers somewhat during 2000 to 2005 (see figure 1.5) so this slowdown is to some extent temporary.[42]

Table 1.6 constructs ratios of papers, citations, and PhD students to R&D stocks using the GDP and BEA deflators, and it examines their growth. Using the BEA deflator, papers per million dollars decline over time in private schools by –11 percent, but the decline is –23 percent in public universities. Citations per million also grow significantly faster in private universities. In comparing research productivity, it is useful to remember that faculty compensation rises by almost 1 percent faster a year in private universities. Almost paradoxically, this may explain why papers (citations) per million dollars of R&D fall *less* (rise *more*). It is because labor quality grows at a faster rate in private universities due to faster wage growth in these universities. Finally, PhD students per million dollars decline by 50 percent in both types of university.

Table 1.7 takes a different look at university resources. It records enrollment, tenure track and non-tenure track faculty, and tuition (in public universities, tuition plus state appropriations). All variables are at the university level. Values relative to 1982 are again placed in square brackets. These

42. For all academic institutions, total scientific papers published fell from 139,168 in 1995 to 138,472 in 1999. But by 2005 this total had increased to 159,972. Numbers of scientific papers reflect year of entry into the database rather than year of publication. See National Science Board (2008, chapter 5, appendix table 5-36).

Table 1.6 Research output/R&D stock by university type, selected years

University type, variable	1982	1986	1990	1995	1999
A Private schools					
Papers/R&D stock					
Using GDP implicit price deflator	2.68	2.63	2.28	2.25	1.99
Using BEA university R&D input deflator	2.31	2.35	2.16	2.24	2.05
5-year citations/R&D stock					
Using GDP implicit price deflator	8.12	9.43	9.63	10.56	—
Using BEA university R&D input deflator	7.01	8.42	9.13	10.51	—
PhD degrees/R&D stock					
Using GDP implicit price deflator	4.70	4.14	3.77	3.39	3.03
Using BEA university R&D input deflator	4.06	3.70	3.57	3.37	3.12
B Public schools					
Papers/R&D stock					
Using GDP implicit price deflator	2.71	2.59	2.27	2.03	1.75
Using BEA university R&D input deflator	2.34	2.31	2.16	2.02	1.81
5-year citations/R&D stock					
Using GDP implicit price deflator	5.53	5.76	6.19	6.31	—
Using BEA university R&D input deflator	4.77	5.15	5.87	6.28	—
PhD degrees/R&D stock					
Using GDP implicit price deflator	6.34	5.39	4.52	4.21	3.68
Using BEA university R&D input deflator	5.48	4.82	4.29	4.18	3.79

Notes: See the text and table 1.3 for data sources and definitions of the variables. Data are a balanced panel of university-fields, defined as a matched sample that includes the same observations in all years. Papers and 5-year citations received are fractional and adjusted for collaboration among universities. R&D stock is deflated by the GDP implicit price deflator in the first row for each of the variables, and by the BEA University R&D input deflator (Robbins and Moylan 2007) in the second row. Both price indexes are normalized to 1992. Dashed cells indicate that data are not available for the data set.

measures track teaching loads as well as human and financial resources over time.

Growth in enrollments in both private and public institutions is about 10 percent by 1997. Since PhD degrees increase by one-third, enrollment shifts toward (more costly) graduate education. Numbers of faculty grow by 25 percent in private universities, but by 8 percent in public universities. Most of the growth in private universities occurs at the end, during a period of rapid growth in stock market and endowment values. Its effects will be felt in the twenty-first century. Tuition revenue grows by 124 percent in private universities but tuition plus state appropriations in public universities grow by just 46 percent. The divergence in resources becomes obvious during the 1990s. It helps to account for differences in private-public productivity, since we shall show that current revenues support research.

Endowments grow at the same rate in all institutions, though the difference in endowment per faculty remains large. It is 1.39 million in private universities versus 0.15 million in public universities. Endowment is simply too small in most public institutions to affect faculty resources very much.

Table 1.7 **Enrollment, faculty, and financial resources by university type, selected years**

University type, variable	1982	1986	1990	1997
	A Private schools			
Enrollment	403,875	413,824	428,522	446,495
	[1.00]	[1.02]	[1.06]	[1.11]
Faculty	21,527	22,352	23,246	26,960
	[1.00]	[1.04]	[1.08]	[1.25]
Tuition (mill. of 1992 US$)[a]	2,975	4,034	5,026	6,668
	[1.00]	[1.36]	[1.69]	[2.24]
Endowment (mill. of 1992 US$)[b]	13,768	19,531	27,645	37,361
	[1.00]	[1.42]	[2.01]	[2.71]
	B Public schools			
Enrollment	1,895,564	1,908,438	1,999,802	2,053,056
	[1.00]	[1.01]	[1.06]	[1.08]
Faculty	80,112	80,458	84,448	86,158
	[1.00]	[1.00]	[1.05]	[1.08]
Tuition + state appropriations (mill.	14,554	17,400	19,706	21,242
of 1992 US$)[a]	[1.00]	[1.20]	[1.35]	[1.46]
Endowment (mill. of 1992 US$)[b]	4,524	6,879	8,309	12,619
	[1.00]	[1.52]	[1.84]	[2.79]

Notes: Value relative to 1982 in brackets. See the text and table 1.3 for data sources and definitions of the variables. Data are a balanced panel, defined as a matched sample that includes the same observations in all years. Enrollment consists of all students, both graduate and undergraduate, in the fall of each year. Faculty include both tenure-track and non-tenure-track personnel.

[a]Tuition and state appropriations end in 1997 owing to suspension of data collection in the HEGIS surveys beginning in 1998.

[b]Endowment data end in 1996 instead of 1997 owing to suspension of data collection in the HEGIS surveys beginning in 1997. The endowment data are missing for about 20 percent of universities so the matched sample is smaller than for other variables. Deflator for revenue and endowment is the implicit GDP deflator indexed to 1992.

Together, tables 1.5 and 1.7 provide a new perspective on university research productivity. Table 1.5 shows that papers increase by 50 percent during this period, while citation-weighted papers increase by 125 percent. Table 1.7 shows that faculty increase by 10 to 25 percent. Papers per faculty increase by either measure, and this draws attention to the point made earlier, that growth of university R&D is overstated. At the same time, research productivity in public universities has clearly fallen behind that of the privates.

1.6 Regression Findings

1.6.1 Equation Setup

To better understand the determinants of research productivity, I turn to a regression analysis of the university, field, and year panel. Tables 1.8 and

1.9 present pooled ordinary least squares (OLS) regressions for private and public universities. By pooled, I specifically mean regressions that combine fields in a given university. As I have shown, the university-field dimension of the data allows for variability within universities that helps to identify effects of R&D stock and other variables.

The regressions follow three basic formats that we describe next. Let y_{ijt} be the logarithm of research output (papers or citations) in field i, university j, at time t; let the vector $\mathbf{x_{ijt}}$ consist of logarithms of R&D stock, graduate students, and current revenue defined by equations (1), (3), and (2); and let the vector $\mathbf{z_{jt}}$ stand for financial variables at the university level (endowment in logarithms; auxiliary/total revenue, and enrollment/faculty). Also, $\mathbf{D_i}$ is a vector of field dummies.[43] Then the "total" equation that omits university dummies is:

$$y_{ijt} = \alpha + \beta_0 t + \boldsymbol{\beta}'_{\mathbf{x}}\mathbf{x_{ijt}} + \boldsymbol{\delta}'_{\mathbf{i}}\mathbf{D_i} + e_j + u_{ijt}. \tag{4}$$

Financial variables z_{jt} are omitted from equation (4), but they are included in (4′):

$$y_{ijt} = \alpha + \beta_0 t + \boldsymbol{\beta}'_{\mathbf{x}}\mathbf{x_{ijt}} + \boldsymbol{\gamma}'_{\mathbf{z}}\mathbf{z_{jt}} + \boldsymbol{\delta}'_{\mathbf{i}}\mathbf{D_i} + e_j + u_{ijt}. \tag{4′}$$

In equations (4) and (4′), e_j is a university error component that may be correlated with the right-hand variables, while u_{ijt} is a transitory component that is uncorrelated over time both with itself and with the contemporaneous right-hand variables.

The "within" equation adds university dummies to equation (4′):

$$y_{ijt} = \alpha + \beta_0 t + \boldsymbol{\beta}'_{\mathbf{x}}\mathbf{x_{ijt}} + \boldsymbol{\gamma}'_{\mathbf{z}}\mathbf{z_{jt}} + \boldsymbol{\delta}'_{\mathbf{i}}\mathbf{D_i} + \boldsymbol{\delta}'_{\mathbf{j}}\mathbf{D_j} + u_{ijt}. \tag{5}$$

In equation (5), the vector of university dummies D_j absorbs the university error component, so that $e_j = \boldsymbol{\delta}'_{\mathbf{j}}\mathbf{D_j}$.[44]

I also include time trend in equations (4), (4′), and (5) to indicate residual growth. If trend increases when university effects are included, then this may indicate that research output shifts toward universities where output grows more slowly (Adams and Clemmons 2009).

1.6.2 Pooled Regressions: Private Universities

Table 1.8 reports estimates for private universities. Following (4), column (8.1) includes trend, R&D stock, and the stock of graduate students. All are highly significant, and together they explain most of the variation in papers.[45] The elasticity of R&D stock is 0.41, while that of graduate stu-

43. In other regressions I include shares of full and associate professors to capture aging effects. The shares are insignificant. Unlike individual productivity of scientists (Stephan and Levin 1991, 1992) where age is significantly negative, at the university and field level rank is insignificant. One explanation for the difference is that selective pressures favor more productive researchers. Promotion in the aggregate counteracts individual aging.

44. See Hsiao (2003, chapters 2 and 3) for derivations of estimators of the slope coefficients in total and within regressions.

45. See Adams and Griliches (1998) for a related analysis.

Table 1.8 **Ordinary least squares research regressions: Private universities**

Variable or statistic	Log (papers)			Log (5-year citations)		
	8.1	8.2	8.3	8.4	8.5	8.6
Field dummies included	Yes	Yes	Yes	Yes	Yes	Yes
University dummies included	No	No	Yes	No	No	Yes
Regression structure	Total	Total	Within	Total	Total	Within
Time trend	0.0102**	–0.0018	–0.0035	0.0333**	0.0097	–0.0112
	(0.0025)	(0.0050)	(0.0087)	(0.0042)	(0.0070)	(0.0121)
Log (R&D stock in mill. of 1992 US$)	0.413**	0.369**	0.294**	0.563**	0.474**	0.377**
	(0.045)	(0.039)	(0.036)	(0.059)	(0.052)	(0.043)
Log (graduate students)	0.157**	0.127**	0.132*	0.092	0.083	0.088
	(0.049)	(0.047)	(0.055)	(0.054)	(0.057)	(0.066)
Log (tuition rev. in mill. of 1992 US$)		0.137	0.270*		0.186	0.624**
		(0.086)	(0.129)		(0.130)	(0.214)
Log (endowment in mill. of 1992 US$)		0.102*	0.055		0.205**	0.196**
		(0.050)	(0.071)		(0.070)	(0.076)
Auxiliary/total rev.		–1.912	–1.832*		–1.517	–1.233
		(0.985)	(0.796)		(1.438)	(1.001)
Enrollment/faculty		–0.015	–0.009*		–0.029*	–0.004
		(0.008)	(0.004)		(0.012)	(0.005)
Number of observations	3,255	2,636	2,636	2,523	2,454	2,454
R^2	0.84	0.86	0.88	0.85	0.87	0.90
Root MSE	0.471	0.448	0.407	0.641	0.597	0.536

Notes: Robust, clustered standard error in parentheses. See the text and table 1.3 for data sources and definitions of the variables. MSE = mean squared error.

***Significant at the 1 percent level.

**Significant at the 5 percent level.

*Significant at the 10 percent level.

dents is 0.16. It follows that an expansion of R&D and graduate students of 10 percent results in 5.7 percent more papers in private universities, indicating diminishing returns to research resources. Following equation (4′), column (8.2) adds financial variables. Lagged tuition is linked to an increase in papers, but this is not statistically significant. The coefficient of endowment is positive and marginally significant. Auxiliary/total revenue and enrollment/faculty (financial duress) reduce research output, but again are not statistically significant. As in equation (5), column (8.3) adds university dummies. Tuition revenue now enters significantly as do the indicators of financial duress. In columns (8.2) and (8.3), trend becomes insignificant so that growth of research output is fully explained. R&D stock and graduate students decline slightly, but remain significant.

Columns (8.4) through (8.6) explain five-year citations received. While the elasticity of R&D stock increases compared to the earlier regressions for papers, that of graduate students declines and becomes insignificant. Endowment is linked to an increase in citations, suggesting that private universities use endowment to buy release time and hire star faculty. As with papers, trend is not significant once the financial indicators are included.

In all these production functions and those in succeeding tables, the sum of the output elasticities across R&D stock, graduate students, tuition revenue, and endowment is less than 1.0. This suggests decreasing returns to scale in university research and limits to university size, consistent with Adams and Clemmons (2009). The relevance of this point is that, allowing for fixed costs of research and after the efficient scale is reached, research may be better shifted to universities in which it was previously missing. We shall return to this point in the summary and conclusion in section 1.7.

1.6.3 Pooled Regressions: Public Universities

Table 1.9 reports results for public universities. In general, output elasticities of R&D stock are less than in table 1.8 for private schools. One difference, though, is the larger elasticity of the stock of graduate students,

Table 1.9 Ordinary least squares research regressions: Public universities

Variable or statistic	Log (papers)			Log (5-year citations)		
	9.1	9.2	9.3	9.4	9.5	9.6
Field dummies included	Yes	Yes	Yes	Yes	Yes	Yes
University dummies included	No	No	Yes	No	No	Yes
Regression structure	Total	Total	Within	Total	Total	Within
Time trend	0.0115**	0.0023	0.0144**	0.0415**	0.0236**	0.0448**
	(0.0017)	(0.0026)	(0.0018)	(0.0031)	(0.0049)	(0.0028)
Log (R&D stock in mill. of 1992 US$)	0.341**	0.338**	0.335**	0.416**	0.406**	0.397**
	(0.034)	(0.034)	(0.035)	(0.042)	(0.041)	(0.042)
Log (graduate students)	0.288**	0.215**	0.173**	0.232**	0.156**	0.127**
	(0.042)	(0.038)	(0.041)	(0.053)	(0.046)	(0.046)
Log (tuition + state appropriations in mill. of 1992 US$)		0.267**	0.142**		0.224*	0.163
		(0.063)	(0.048)		(0.092)	(0.084)
Log (endowment in mill. of 1992 US$)		0.019	–0.018		0.050**	–0.044**
		(0.011)	(0.010)		(0.018)	(0.018)
Auxiliary/total rev.		–1.384**	0.124		–2.389**	0.459
		(0.401)	(0.157)		(0.634)	(0.349)
Enrollment/faculty		–0.009*	–0.004*		–0.008	–0.002
		(0.004)	(0.002)		(0.006)	(0.005)
Number of observations	6,552	4,678	4,678	5,088	4,378	4,378
R^2	0.84	0.86	0.90	0.83	0.85	0.89
Root MSE	0.429	0.400	0.342	0.634	0.595	0.506

Notes: Robust, clustered standard error in parentheses. See the text and table 1.3 for data sources and definitions of the variables. MSE = mean squared error.

***Significant at the 1 percent level.

**Significant at the 5 percent level.

*Significant at the 10 percent level.

about 0.1 higher and significant throughout. This may indicate that graduate student assistants are funded in public universities, to a larger extent, by means other than R&D, such as teaching assistantships. Research output rises, usually significantly, with tuition plus state appropriations. Endowment does not contribute to research output in public universities, because amounts per faculty member are too small to matter. Auxiliary/total revenues and enrollment/faculty enter with the expected negative signs, but are insignificant once university effects are taken into account.

The trend coefficient is also greater in the public university regressions. The coefficient of trend is even higher in the "within" regressions (columns [9.3] and [9.6]) than in total. Again, this may reflect a shift of research toward schools where output growth is slower (Adams and Clemmons 2009). Some of trend growth could also be due to knowledge flows from private universities, since knowledge flows are more likely to take place from higher to lower ranked departments (Adams, Clemmons, and Stephan 2006) and since top departments are more often found in private universities.

1.6.4 Regressions Stratified by Rank of University-Field

Let us now consider university-fields stratified into groups according to top 20, middle 40, and bottom 40 percent rankings. Table 1.10 contains frequency distributions of the top 20, middle 40, and bottom 40 by private and public ownership. The top 20 and middle 40 percent account for most of the private school observations. In contrast, public school observations cluster in the middle and bottom 40 percent. Even so, public universities contain almost half of the top 20 percent university-fields. The stratified regressions take this into account by analyzing differences in quality wherever they occur.

Table 1.11 reports estimates of equations (4′) and (5). It shows results for the top 20, middle 40, and bottom 40 percent in panels A, B, and C, respectively. Because I separate university-fields into groups by rank, the

Table 1.10 **Relationship of rank of university-fields to private and public schools**

	Rank of university-field			
University type	Top 20%	Middle 40%	Bottom 40%	All
Private	72 (33.6%)	90 (42.1%)	52 (24.3%)	214 (100%)
Public	56 (13.8%)	160 (39.4%)	190 (46.8%)	406 (100%)

Notes: Row percents in parentheses. See the text for data sources and a description of the underlying panel data. Data consist of 620 private and public university-fields from 103 universities after exclusion of missing values. Top ten universities include eight private and two public schools.

Table 1.11 **Stratified OLS research regressions: Top 20, middle 40, and bottom 40 percent university-fields**

Variable or statistic	Log (papers)		Log (5-year citations)	
	Total regression	Within regression	Total regression	Within regression
A Top 20 percent university-fields				
Equation no.	11.1	11.2	11.3	11.4
Time trend	0.0089*	0.0119**	0.0249**	0.0158*
	(0.0035)	(0.0044)	(0.0050)	(0.0079)
Log (R&D stock in mill. of 1992 US$)	0.310**	0.284**	0.278**	0.270**
	(0.057)	(0.076)	(0.058)	(0.077)
Log (graduate students)	0.157**	0.196**	0.139**	0.193**
	(0.049)	(0.062)	(0.052)	(0.075)
Number of observations	1,501	1,501	1,407	1,407
R^2	0.89	0.91	0.91	0.92
Root MSE	0.365	0.328	0.447	0.413
B Middle 40 percent university-fields				
Equation no.	11.5	11.6	11.7	11.8
Time trend	0.0063*	0.0178**	0.0337**	0.0475**
	(0.0030)	(0.0034)	(0.0046)	(0.0057)
Log (R&D stock in mill. of 1992 US$)	0.297**	0.266**	0.301**	0.304**
	(0.034)	(0.037)	(0.042)	(0.048)
Log (graduate students)	0.151**	0.135**	0.075	0.043
	(0.041)	(0.053)	(0.047)	(0.062)
Number of observations	3,077	3,077	2,877	2,877
R^2	0.89	0.93	0.89	0.92
Root MSE	0.349	0.283	0.492	0.420
C Bottom 40 percent university-fields				
Equation no.	11.9	11.10	11.11	11.12
Time trend	0.0114*	0.0231**	0.0414**	0.0539**
	(0.0041)	(0.0030)	(0.0054)	(0.0064)
Log (R&D stock in mill. of 1992 US$)	0.222**	0.203**	0.264**	0.252**
	(0.044)	(0.038)	(0.049)	(0.051)
Log (graduate students)	0.083	0.100	–0.006	0.089
	(0.051)	(0.057)	(0.055)	(0.069)
Number of observations	2,736	2,736	2,548	2,548
R^2	0.81	0.87	0.84	0.89
Root MSE	0.447	0.374	0.624	0.541

Notes: Robust, clustered standard error in parentheses. See the text and table 1.3 for data sources and definitions of the variables. Top 20, middle 40, and bottom 40 percent groups are ranked according to field using 1993 NRC rankings, except for agriculture and medicine, where, because of missing data, university-fields are ranked by size of R&D expenditure. All regressions include field dummies. Total regressions exclude university dummies while within-regressions include them. Also included are Log (tuition + public * state appropriations), Log (endowment), auxiliary/total revenue, and enrollment/faculty. MSE = mean squared error.

***Significant at the 1 percent level.

**Significant at the 5 percent level.

*Significant at the 10 percent level.

regressions are stratified, though they are pooled across fields.[46] I focus on key variables consisting of trend, R&D, and graduate students, not reporting results for the financial variables, although these are included in the regressions.

Top 20 percent university-fields obtain more research output from R&D and graduate students than the middle or bottom 40 percent.[47] Indeed, graduate students in the bottom 40 percent fail to make any significant contribution to research. This implies that their primary duties are to teach and work on thesis research. This and the faculty time needed for dissertation work, reduce the net student contribution to zero in bottom 40 percent university-fields.

Below the top 20 percent the pattern in the trend coefficients suggests that research output grows more rapidly in the within regressions, which include university effects, than in the total regressions that exclude these effects. As before, this pattern could be due to a shift in output toward universities in which growth is less (Adams and Clemmons 2009).

1.6.5 Faculty Compensation and Wage Structure

The empirical work concludes with a regression analysis of faculty compensation by professorial rank—or in other words, the academic wage structure. Studying this structure could help us to further understand the financial condition of universities. The dependent variable is the logarithm of wages plus fringe benefits in 1992 dollars at the full and assistant professor ranks.[48] These are university-wide averages, since HEGIS, which is their source, does not collect wage data by university-field. Since compensation is an average I cannot estimate a typical wage equation where wages are a function of education, experience, and tenure. But faculty quality is reflected in the logarithm of the university-wide R&D stock per faculty, the logarithm of tuition revenue per faculty (private schools) or tuition plus state appropriations per faculty (public schools), the logarithm of endowment per faculty, and the financial duress indicators, auxiliary/total revenue and

46. Following section 1.4, top 20 percent regressions include the top five in astronomy; the top 15 in biology, medicine, and engineering; and the top 10 in all other fields. Middle 40 percent regressions include the next 10 in astronomy; the next 30 in biology, medicine, and engineering; and the next 20 in all other fields. Bottom 40 percent regressions include the bottom 10 in astronomy; the bottom 30 in biology, medicine, and engineering; and the bottom 20 in all other fields.

47. These results are similar to findings for top ten universities not reported here. The top ten are selected on the basis of top ten citation impact per paper in a set of twenty-one fields during 1981 to 1993. Schools ranked as top ten most frequently among these fields are considered a top ten university. They include eight private schools (Harvard, Yale, Chicago, MIT, Stanford, Princeton, Cornell, and California Institute of Technology) as well as two public schools (Berkeley and the University of Washington). It should come as no surprise that top 20 percent university-fields predominate in top ten universities.

48. All monetary variables besides R&D are deflated by the GDP implicit price deflator indexed to 1992.

enrollment/faculty. In constructing per capita variables on the right-hand side of the wage equations, I lag the number of faculty to limit division error bias. Besides the aforementioned, I include trend to capture general wage growth, and a cost of living indicator for whether a university is located in a large city (in the United States, a Consolidated Metropolitan Statistical Area). The specification is:

$$\text{(6)} \qquad \text{Log}(\text{Wage}_{jt}) = \alpha + \beta_0 t + \beta_L \text{Large City} + \boldsymbol{\beta}'\mathbf{x}_{jt} + u_{jt}.$$

These are "total" wage regressions that omit university effects because wage variation is insufficient in the within-university dimension to permit a "within" specification.

Table 1.12 contains the results. The dependent variable in columns (12.1) and (12.4) is the logarithm of full professor compensation; in columns (12.2)

Table 1.12 **Faculty compensation equations**

	Private universities			Public universities		
Variable or statistic	Full 12.1	Asst. 12.2	Full-asst. 12.3	Full 12.4	Asst. 12.5	Full-asst. 12.6
Year	0.0174**	0.0257**	–0.0083**	0.0139**	0.0155**	–0.0014
	(0.0031)	(0.0031)	(0.0021)	(0.0016)	(0.0015)	(0.0010)
Large city (1 if yes, 0 if no)	0.098**	0.052*	0.046**	0.032	0.017	0.016
	(0.025)	(0.024)	(0.014)	(0.029)	(0.020)	(0.024)
Log (R&D stock/faculty)	0.039**	0.054**	–0.015	0.017	0.019	–0.003
	(0.015)	(0.017)	(0.010)	(0.021)	(0.018)	(0.011)
Log [(tuition + public * state appropriations)/faculty][a]	0.080	–0.035	0.116**	0.137	0.121*	–0.002
	(0.057)	(0.053)	(0.042)	(0.073)	(0.056)	(0.037)
Log (endowment/faculty)	0.040	–0.014	0.054**	0.011	–0.003	0.013
	(0.021)	(0.023)	(0.012)	(0.008)	(0.008)	(0.007)
Auxiliary/total revenue	–0.068	–0.260	0.192	–0.095	–0.329	0.206
	(0.287)	(0.245)	(0.148)	(0.271)	(0.182)	(0.170)
Enrollment/faculty	–0.006	–0.001	–0.005*	–0.004	–0.002	–0.002*
	(0.003)	(0.004)	(0.002)	(0.003)	(0.002)	(0.001)
No. of observations	485	485	485	879	879	879
R^2	0.77	0.68	0.44	0.47	0.55	0.12
Root MSE	0.078	0.088	0.053	0.108	0.093	0.068

Notes: Robust, clustered standard error in parentheses. See the text and table 1.3 for data sources and definitions of the variables. Dependent variable is Log (wage + fringe benefits) in equations labeled "Full" for full professors, and "Asst." for assistant professors; it is the difference in the logarithm of wage + fringe benefits for full and assistant professors in equations marked "Full-Asst."

[a]The variable "Public" equals 1 if a university is public, and 0 otherwise, so the variable equals the logarithm of tuition for private universities and the logarithm of tuition + state appropriations in public universities.

***Significant at the 1 percent level.

**Significant at the 5 percent level.

*Significant at the 10 percent level.

and (12.5) it is the logarithm of assistant professor compensation; and in columns (12.3) and (12.6) it is the difference of the two.

Starting with the results for full and assistant professors, the trend coefficients show that real compensation grows at about 1.5 percent a year, all else equal, but faster in private universities, especially at the assistant professor level, where it grows at 2.5 percent.[49] Location in a large city raises private school wages by 5 to 10 percent, although it has no significant effect on wages in public schools, probably because state institutions are mostly located outside large cities. For full professors in private universities, R&D stock and endowment increase compensation. Besides trend, the only significant determinant of compensation in public universities is current revenue consisting of tuition plus state appropriations.

Columns (12.3) and (12.6) display the results for the difference in compensation for full and assistant professors. In the private university column (12.3), we see that location in a large city, tuition, and endowment increase the wage premium for senior faculty, but trend and enrollment/faculty decrease it. In the public university column (12.6), the wage structure is flat across ranks. Together the findings suggest that successful researchers have an incentive to move to private universities that increases with the rank of full professor.

1.7 Discussion, Synthesis, and Conclusion

Is the United States losing its preeminence in higher education? The evidence presented in this chapter suggests that in a relative sense it is. Sections 1.2 and 1.3 tell a story of rapid post-war expansion of US universities, followed by a tapering off after 1980. A series of natural experiments took place in the 1930s and 1940s that contributed to this growth. Because of their exogeneity, these early events may in time capture the imagination of researchers studying higher education.

In the early years, growth of US universities was aided by refugee scientists, with foreign graduate students playing a larger role after 1980. Additional early factors that contributed to expansion of US universities include a broadening of access to universities, increased military research during World War II and the Cold War, and the expansion of high technology industries during the post-war period. Since the 1980s we observe more rapid growth of academic research in Europe, and especially East Asia, that implies convergence in world science and engineering and a decline in the US share.

49. The compensation gap between private and public universities rises at the rate of 0.8 percent a year. In simple regressions that include trend and intercept, I find that, relative to the GDP deflator, both full and assistant professor compensation grows at 2.3 percent per year in private universities and at 1.5 percent per year in public universities. Top ten university compensation grows at 2.2 percent per year. R^2s for these regressions range from 0.3 to 0.5.

But this is not the entire story. Most recently, in the 1990s, we observe a slowdown of publication output in the United States. This becomes the central puzzle of the chapter, and sections 1.4 through 1.6 address it using panel data on universities, fields, and years. In section 1.4 we describe the panel, and in section 1.5 we present growth facts concerning US university research. These reveal that much of the slowdown in publication is located in public universities. While R&D stocks grow more rapidly in public than private schools, current revenues grow more slowly. This suggests that public universities fall behind because of slower growth in their financial resources.

The regression findings in section 1.6 indicate a fairly similar if not perfectly identical production process in public and private universities. On average, both obtain similar increases in scientific papers from similar combined increases in R&D, graduate students, tuition revenues, and endowment. This is true even though graduate students play a larger role in public universities, perhaps because research is cross-subsidized by teaching assistantships more of the time. In view of this broad similarity, a divergence in research output over time, in which public universities fall behind, can only be accounted for by a lower rate of increase in public university resources, as section 1.5 reveals.

In support of this hypothesis, compensation in private universities rises almost 1 percent a year faster than in public universities. And besides, wages are flat across professorial rank in public universities, whereas they rise noticeably with rank in private universities. All this suggests reasons for top scientists to migrate from public to private universities. Therefore, in several ways slower growth in current revenues in public universities produces slower growth of research as well.

At the same time, (mostly federal) research funding expands at a faster rate in public schools (Adams and Clemmons 2009). Together this tells an interesting story of state and federal policy interactions. Even as (mostly federal) R&D is expanding, the states are subjected to a portion of rising health care costs under Medicaid. In addition, some are subject to mandated equalization of K through 12 education expenditures that raise the cost of elementary and secondary education (Murray, Evans, and Schwab 1998). Toward the end of the period some states commit themselves to prepaid tuition plans that are inadequately funded (Rizzo 2006). So growth of mostly federal research dollars is cancelled out by the slower growth of state dollars in public universities.

An obvious question that arises is whether this situation will persist. If it is temporary, then the downward fluctuations of finances of public universities during the 1990s would be compensated by upward fluctuations at a later time, leaving public institutions on the same unaltered trend line with little to be concerned about in the long run. But if the situation is permanent and state funding remains below trend and perhaps increasingly so, then top public universities would have to seek alternative sources of funding to begin to catch up to top private universities. They might, for example, seek to obtain freely floating tuition from parents of students anywhere in the world. But this solution seems unlikely given the charters of state universities and ownership of their real assets by the states. More likely is a gradual removal of tuition price controls to in-state families amidst a frank recognition that price caps deny public universities the resources that are essential to a good education. Still another solution revolves around increased commercialization of university inventions as well as increased sales of merchandise and entertainment, though the latter are hardly consistent with the academic missions of these institutions. All these adjustments to the new realities seem destined to occur slowly, so that relative shortfalls of public universities are likely to persist for years to come.

On a worldwide scale, the relatively faster growth of universities in newly industrializing countries will continue. This is because this growth is part of a convergence process in the developing world, in which steady-state incomes and growth rates increase as a function of increases in education and stocks of knowledge. Even if funding problems of US public universities could be resolved through improved mechanisms of finance, the decline in the US share of world science will likely persist.

Yet another possibility arises. All that we have seen in this chapter, which covers more than 80 percent of academic research in the United States, consists of a fixed set of top 110 institutions. Tables 1.8, 1.9, and 1.11 show that these universities are subject to decreasing returns to scale in research, since the sum of the output elasticities of R&D stock, graduate students, and financial resources is less than one. Since this is the definition of decreasing returns, one might suppose that beyond the efficient scale, more growth could be obtained at less cost by spreading research funds over a wider range of universities. Of course, organizational assets in smaller research institutions are not necessarily the equal of those in top 110 schools. It follows that if sustained growth of research output is the objective, then the challenge is not only that of spreading resources across more schools, but also that of replicating the assets of top universities. At present, growth appears to be more rapid in universities where this kind of replication remains an open question.

References

Adams, J. D., and J. R. Clemmons. 2009. The growing allocative inefficiency of the US higher education sector. In *Science and engineering careers in the United States,* ed. R. B. Freeman and D. Goroff, 349–82. Chicago: University of Chicago Press.

Adams, J. D., J. R. Clemmons, and P. E. Stephan. 2006. Standing on academic shoulders: Measuring scientific influence in universities. *Annales D'Economie et de Statistique* 79/80:1–30.

Adams, J. D., and Z. Griliches. 1998. Research productivity in a system of universities. *Annales D'Economie et de Statistique* 49/50:127–62.

Bush, V. 1945. *Science: The endless frontier.* Washington, DC: US Government Printing Office.

Davie, M. R. 1947. *Refugees in America: A report of the committee for the study of recent immigration from Europe.* New York: Harper and Brothers.

De Figueiredo, J. M., and B. S. Silverman. 2006. Academic earmarks and the returns to lobbying. *Journal of Law and Economics* 49 (October): 597–625.

Ehrenberg, R. G. 2002. *Tuition rising: Why college costs so much.* Cambridge, MA: Harvard University Press.

———. ed. 2006. *What's happening to public higher education?* Westport, CT: Praeger.

Ehrenberg, R. G., M. J. Rizzo, and G. H. Jakubson. 2007. Who bears the growing cost of science at universities? In *Science and the university,* ed. R. G. Ehrenberg and P. E. Stephan, 19–35. Madison: University of Wisconsin Press.

Fermi, L. 1971. *Illustrious immigrants: The intellectual migration from Europe, 1930–1941.* Chicago: University of Chicago Press.

Freeman, R. B. 2006. Does globalization of the scientific/engineering workforce threaten US economic leadership? *Innovation Policy and the Economy* 6:123–58.

Helpman, E., and P. R. Krugman. 1986. *Market structure and foreign trade: Increasing returns, imperfect competition, and the international economy.* Cambridge, MA: MIT Press.

Hicks, D. M. 2007. Global research competition affects measured US academic output. In *Science and the university,* ed. P. E. Stephan and R. G. Ehrenberg, 223–42. Madison: University of Wisconsin Press.

Hsiao, C. 2003. *Analysis of panel data,* 2nd ed. New York: Cambridge University Press.

Huffman, W. E., and R. E. Evenson. 1993. *Science for Agriculture,* 1st ed. Ames, IA: Iowa State University Press.

Khan, Z. 2005. *The democratization of invention: Patents and copyrights in American economic development, 1790–1920.* New York: Cambridge University Press.

Krugman, P. R. 1979. A model of innovation, technology transfer, and the world distribution of income. *Journal of Political Economy* 87 (April): 253–66.

Mowery, D.C., and N. Rosenberg. 1989. *Technology and the pursuit of economic growth.* New York: Cambridge University Press.

———. 1998. *Paths of innovation: Technological change in 20th-century America.* New York: Cambridge University Press.

Murray, S. E., W. N. Evans, and R. M. Schwab. 1998. Education-finance reform and the distribution of education resources. *American Economic Review* 88 (September): 789–812.

National Research Council. 1995. *Research-doctorate programs in the United States: Continuity and change.* Washington, DC: National Academy Press.

National Resources Committee. 1938. *Research—A national resource, volume I.—Relation of the Federal Government to research.* Washington, DC: US Government Printing Office.

———. 1941. *Research—a national resource, volume II.—Industrial research.* Washington, DC: US Government Printing Office.

National Science Board. 2002. *Science and engineering indicators 2002* (in two volumes). Arlington, VA: National Science Foundation.

———. 2006. *Science and engineering indicators 2006* (in two volumes). Arlington, VA: National Science Foundation.

———. 2008. *Science and engineering indicators 2008* (in two volumes). Arlington, VA: National Science Foundation.

Nobel Laureates Facts. Available at: http://nobelprize.org/nobel_prizes/nobelprize_facts.html.

Rizzo, M. J. 2006. State preferences for higher education spending: A panel data analysis, 1977–2001. In *What's happening to public higher education?,* ed. R. G. Ehrenberg, 3–36. Westport, CT: Praeger.

Robbins, C. A., and C. E. Moylan. 2007. Research and development satellite account update: Estimates for 1959–2004, new estimates for industry, regional, and international accounts. *Survey of Current Business* 87 (October): 49–92.

Shanghai Jiao Tong University, Institute of Higher Education. 2005. Academic ranking of world universities. Available at: http://ed.sjtu.edu.cn/ranking.htm.

Stephan, P. E., and S. G. Levin. 1991. Research productivity over the life cycle: Evidence for academic scientists. *American Economic Review* 81 (March): 114–32.

———. 1992. *Striking the mother lode in science: The importance of age, place, and time.* New York: Oxford University Press.

Toole, A. A., and D. Czarnitzki. 2007. Life scientist mobility from academe to industry: Does academic entrepreneurship induce a costly "brain drain" on the not-for-profit research sector? Discussion Paper no. 07-072, Center for European Economic Research, Mannheim, Germany.

US Department of Commerce, Bureau of the Census. 1975. *Historical statistics of the United States: Colonial times to 1970,* parts 1 and 2. Washington, DC: US Government Printing Office.

2

To Be or Not to Be
Major Choices in Budding Scientists

Eric Bettinger

2.1 Introduction

Over the last forty years, the supply of US-born scientists and engineers has dropped dramatically. In 1970, 3,547 US citizens received doctoral degrees in the physical sciences. By 2005, this number had fallen to 1,986. Over the same period, the number of Americans earnings doctorates in math fell from 1,088 to 541, and the number in engineering fell from 2,957 to 2,284.[1] From 1966 to 2000 the proportion of US-trained doctorates born in the United States declined from 77 percent to 61 (Freeman, Jin, and Shen 2004).

These trends in science and math, coupled with the increase in foreign-born, US-trained doctorates in science, technology, engineering, and math (STEM) fields have led to great consternation among policymakers and industry analysts. The National Academy of Science (2007, 3), for example, stated,

> "Having reviewed trends in the United States and abroad, the committee is deeply concerned that the scientific and technological building blocks critical to our economic leadership are eroding at a time when many other nations are gathering strength. . . . [W]e are worried about the future prosperity of the United States. Although many people assume that the United States will always be a world leader in science and technology, this may not continue to be the case inasmuch as great minds and ideas exist throughout the world. We fear the abruptness with which a lead in science and

Eric Bettinger is associate professor of education at Stanford University School of Education and a faculty research fellow of the National Bureau of Economic Research.

1. Figures 2.1 and 2.2 show the relative change in the number of math, physical science, and engineering doctorates awarded each year relative to 1970 for US citizens and permanent residents.

technology can be lost—and the difficulty of recovering a lead once lost, if indeed it can be regained at all."

Similar pronouncements have come from the American Council on Competitiveness, the American Association of Universities, and other government agencies. Many of the statements bring up the concern that the increased reliance on foreign-born scientists may have ramifications for national security. For example, the Hart-Rudman Commission on National Security (2001, ix) claimed that the "U.S. government has seriously underfunded basic scientific research in recent years" and that the "inadequacies of our systems of research and education pose a greater threat to U.S. national security over the next quarter century than any potential conventional war that we might imagine."

There are several possible reasons for the decrease in US-born students pursuing advanced studies in STEM[2] fields. One possibility is that US schools have become worse in either fostering interest in the sciences or in actually teaching the material. For example, over the last forty years, a period in which the overall number of students attending college increased by 84 percent, the number of US-born students intending to major in a science or engineering field has either been constant (through 1995) or falling (since 2001) (ACT 2006). Additionally, indicators of students' aptitude in science and math in primary and secondary school provide similar hints that the United States is lagging behind other countries. In the 2003 math scores on the Trends in International Mathematics and Science Study (TIMSS), fourth graders scored twelfth out of twenty-four countries and sixth among the ten participating Organization for Economic Cooperation and Development (OECD) countries. Eighth graders performed similarly, ranking nineteenth of the forty-four participating countries and tenth of the twelve participating OECD countries.[3]

Another potential explanation for the decline in US-born students pursuing advanced studies in STEM fields is that students have become more attuned to labor market outcomes and the rewards for pursuing STEM careers. Indeed, the annual survey of college freshmen conducted since 1966 by the Higher Education Research Institute at UCLA suggests a high and growing attention to pecuniary rewards as a life goal. In 1966, 54 percent of freshmen claimed that it was important to them to be "very well-off financially" and by 2006 this figure had climbed to 73 percent (Pryor, et al. 2007).

2. The definition of STEM is somewhat amorphous. Many early studies on the shortage of STEM workers focused on "scientists and engineers." Modern definitions focus on science, technology, engineering, and mathematics although the range of included fields can also include economics. For the purpose of this chapter, our definition of STEM includes computer science, mathematics, engineering, engineering technologies, and the physical and biological sciences. When we refer to "scientists and engineers," we include all workers included in our definition of STEM workers.

3. The TIMSS results are accessible at http://nces.ed.gov/timss/.

Over that same period, salaries in many non-STEM fields have increased more rapidly than salaries in STEM fields.

Some have argued that, despite the falling numbers, there is no "shortage" of US-born scientists. Addressing Sputnik-era concerns over STEM pipelines, articles by Alchian, Arrow, and Capron (1958), Arrow and Capron (1959), and Blank and Stigler (1957) argued that a key distinction of the labor market for scientists and engineers was the high degree of inelasticity in the short run supply of engineers. The training of new engineers and scientists can take years as students progress through four to five years of undergraduate training, eight to ten years of graduate training, and then postdoctoral work. As a result, the supply of scientists may take years to respond to shifts in demand, and the labor market conditions may change between the time that students enter the labor market and the time that they finish their training (Freeman 1976).

Because supply may take years to respond, the labor market can go through periods of surplus and shortage—called "cobwebs" in the labor market literature. Indeed, the market for scientists and engineers has fluctuated between shortage and surplus throughout the last half century. While many academics and policymakers have argued that there is a shortage of scientists and engineers (e.g., NSF 1989; Atkinson 1990), others (e.g., Teitelbaum 2007; Ryoo and Rosen 2004) have suggested that the STEM labor market continues to function as one might expect.

This chapter focuses on an earlier point in the pipeline of scientists and engineers—specifically, the development of scientists and engineers in undergraduate studies. As the labor market models underscore, the decision to become a scientist or engineer largely starts when students enter their undergraduate study and choose their major. For many students, this may even start in high school as they develop skills and interest in science and engineering and start to choose a major. As students progress through college, they have the opportunity to stay in their major or change. Once they graduate, the probability that students will pursue careers in science and engineering is quite small if they do not major in a relevant field during their undergraduate careers.

This chapter seeks to do four things. First, we review what is meant by the "STEM pipeline," specifically focusing on how students' major choice plays a role in the development of scientists and engineers. Second, we present a number of frameworks that may shed light on students' major choices and the perceived shortage of STEM professionals. We focus extensively on how relative earnings have changed in different professions. Third, we present new data showing that many of the brightest undergraduate students who are arguably the most prepared to pursue graduate studies in STEM fields are systematically moving away from the hard sciences into fields where earnings might be 5 to 15 percent higher (e.g., finance and accounting). While we make few statements about the state of science and math instruction in primary and secondary education, we show that there is a significant pipeline of students who are prepared to enter careers in the sciences. Finally, we examine how women and minorities choose STEM fields. Over the last forty years, the number of women and minorities majoring in STEM fields has dramatically increased (see figures 2.3 and 2.4). The trends for women and minorities seem to be opposite that of the overall profession. Yet among the top performing students in our sample, we find that African Americans are more likely than other top performers to persist in STEM majors while top performing women are less likely to do so.

2.2 The STEM Pipeline

Our focus is on a particular part of the STEM pipeline—students' major choices. To help motivate why major choices are central to the STEM pipeline, we first review what we mean by the STEM pipeline and the role that major choice plays in that pipeline. Then to help shed light on why students choose STEM majors, we discuss the three key phases of career selection. We discuss when and how students make initial indications as to what major they want to pursue, how major choices evolve in college, and how career choices change after college.

2.2.1 STEM Major Choices and the STEM Pipeline

The STEM pipeline is the phrase used to describe STEM education throughout schooling levels and eventually culminating in the labor force. The development of a new scientist begins quite early and can only be effectuated through a series of steps. It starts with primary and secondary school, where students have to acquire both the skills and the interest in STEM fields to be successful in postsecondary studies. It continues grade by grade as students continue to acquire the skills and interests that might shape their decision as to whether or not to study STEM fields after secondary school.[4]

At any level, students must acquire the skills and the interest in STEM fields which will enable them to continue progressing in the field and help qualify them for the next level. Once students enter a postsecondary school, students in the STEM pipeline may continue to prepare for graduate school admission in a STEM postgraduate program. Similarly, a student's performance in their graduate program helps them attain productive employment related to their STEM training. As the STEM pipeline has been popularized, the failure at any level of schooling to spawn interest or to prepare students academically leads to decreased supply of STEM workers.

4. The STEM pipeline as it has been popularized is similar to a model of sequential production in economics (e.g., Kremer 1993). In a model of sequential production, each step in production depends on the previous. The final product can only be produced if the sequential steps leading to have been completed successfully.

Alarm over the state of the pipeline largely focuses on the fact that the supply of US-born scientists and engineers with doctoral degrees is extremely low relative to the levels from the early 1970s, as shown in figures 2.1 and 2.2. In the various STEM fields, there was a systematic and constant decline in the number of doctorates throughout the 1970s. In the physical sciences, the downward trends begin to level off in the late 1970s. Since 1980, the trend has been relatively constant, reflecting a 50 percent decline from the 1970 peak.

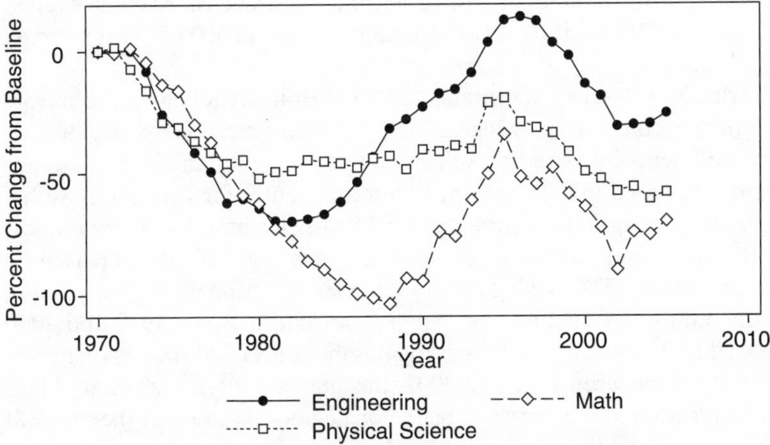

Fig. 2.1 Growth of total doctorates among US citizens and permanent residents relative to 1970
Source: Data from NSF Survey of Earned Doctorates.

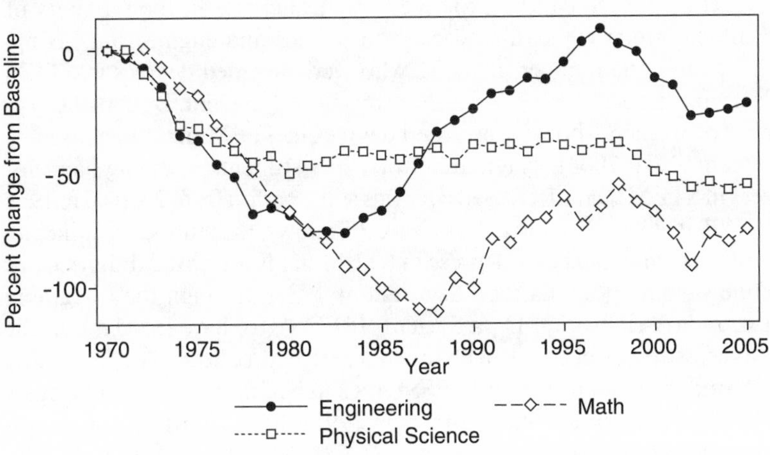

Fig. 2.2 Growth of total doctorates among US citizens relative to 1970
Source: Data from NSF Survey of Earned Doctorates.

In engineering, the downward trend in the number of earned doctorates continued through the early 1980s. In the early 1980s, the trend started to reverse itself and more and more students began entering doctoral studies in engineering. This upward trend continued through the mid-1990s, where it actually surpassed the level from 1970. Thereafter, the number of students earning doctorates declined again.

In math, the drop in the number of earned doctorates continued throughout the 1970s and most of the 1980s. In its lowest years, the decline in math doctorates among US citizens had gone from 1,030 awarded in 1970 to 342 in 1988. While the number of math doctorates awarded each year has failed to reach its 1970 level it has also increased to around 500 per year from its low in 1988.

The decline in earned doctorates contrasts dramatically with the college enrollment patterns from 1970 to 2005. Over that time, undergraduate full-time enrollments increased by 86 percent, and the total number of college students increased by 104 percent (National Center for Education Statistics [NCES] 2008). Yet enrollments in STEM fields have had more modest growth. The number of undergraduate engineering students increased by 14 percent from 1979 to 2002 (National Science Foundation [NSF] 2004), and the number of engineering degrees awarded between 1979 and 2000 increased by 11 percent. Although the number of STEM majors increased by 31 percent between 1977 and 2002, this increase masks substantial heterogeneity: while the number of bachelor degrees awarded in the physical sciences and in math decreased over this period, the number of students majoring in computer science increased by 482 percent (NSF 2004).

The proportion of students stating that they wanted to major in science and engineering increased from the mid-1970s to the mid-1990s; however, most of this growth can be explained by an increase in the numbers of women who are now pursuing careers in science and engineering. As figure 2.3 shows, the number of males who were awarded degrees in STEM fields decreased between 1977 and 2000 by about 1 percent. By contrast, the number of women who were awarded degrees in STEM fields increased by 91 percent (NSF 2004). The number of white students receiving bachelor degrees in STEM fields decreased over this same period from 292,800 in 1979 to 270,420 in 2000. By contrast, as figure 2.4 shows, the number of minority students receiving bachelor degrees in STEM fields increased dramatically.

While we have good data on degree completion through the Integrated Postsecondary Education Data System (IPEDS), we have less data on the dynamics of major choice when students arrive at college. The Beginning Postsecondary Student Survey (BPSS) tracked beginning freshmen over six years. At the start of students' careers in 1995, about 20 percent of all students indicated a desire to major in a STEM field. Among students who indicated a major, 28 percent indicated a desire to major in a STEM field. By 2001, only about 48 percent of those who had started out in the biologi-

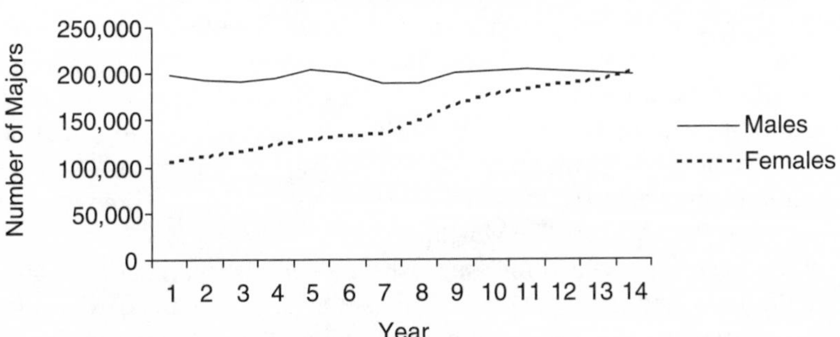

Fig. 2.3 STEM majors by gender, 1977 to 2000
Source: NSF (2004).

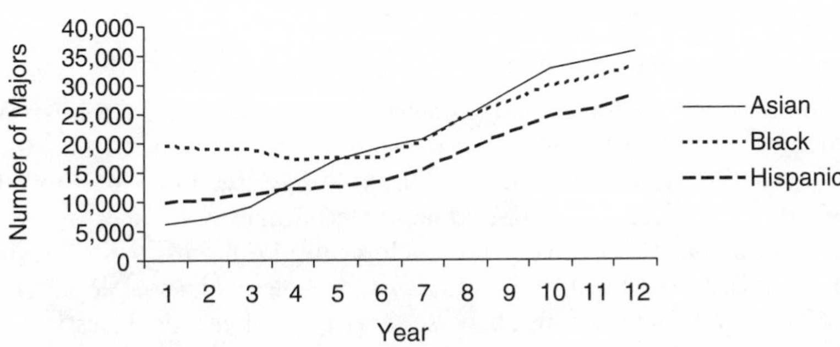

Fig. 2.4 STEM majors by race, 1977 to 2000
Source: NSF (2004).

cal sciences had persisted in the major and only 71 percent of students in physical sciences, engineering, and math had stayed in the major.

Additionally, upon entering college, students lack significant coursework in math and science (ACT 2006). The ACT estimates that only 26 percent of students met the necessary benchmarks in terms of the science curriculum that they took in high school in preparation for college. Only 41 percent of students took the ACT's recommended classes in math. Given that these percentages of students focus only on students who actually took the ACT exam, they likely overestimate the preparedness of students in math and science in the overall population.

Worries about the STEM pipeline have been the motivation for policy decisions affecting education at all levels—primary, secondary, undergraduate, and postgraduate. For example, according to the Academic Competitive Council (ACC 2007), the federal government invested $574 million across twenty-four programs focused on elementary and secondary school students. The federal government allocated $2.4 billion across seventy undergraduate, graduate, and postgraduate programs. The federal government funded an additional eleven informal projects with an overall budget around $137 million. Additionally, the United States introduced the National Science and Mathematics Access to Retain Talent (SMART) Grant in the 2006 and 2007 school year. This grant augments a Pell Grant by up to $4,000 per year if students are US citizens, have a grade point average (GPA) over 3.0, and are enrolled in a key STEM field.[5]

While these statistics certainly suggest a level of unpreparedness for many students, they shed little light on the choices and decisions made by the most prepared students. In section 2.4 of the chapter, we present some data on students who are seemingly prepared to enter STEM fields upon entry into college. Before moving on to those results, we first outline how students choose careers and theories of how students aim to choose majors.

2.2.3 Major and Career Choice

Frameworks for Major Choices

We focus on two conceptual frameworks that researchers have used to characterize students' choice of majors and careers. The first framework is attributed to Holland (1966, 1973) and is widely used by colleges to help students choose between majors. The second framework comes from the economic model of human capital development. We discuss these in turn.

Holland's model has its foundations in psychology and sociology.[6] Holland's theory is that there are six personality types (Realistic, Investigative, Artistic, Social, Enterprising, and Conventional). People with each personality type have competencies and values that draw them to specific activities and give them a certain self-perception. When a student is trying to decide on a major, college career centers usually offer a battery of questions aimed at deriving competencies, activities, self-perceptions, and values that interest or characterize a specific student. These competencies, activities, self-perceptions, and values are then mapped into specific careers.[7] Specific environmental characteristics are similarly linked to specific "environment types" using the same six personality descriptors. Batteries and surveys that attempt to help students choose majors and occupations try to identify specific majors and specific occupations/settings that bring together both students' internal personality and an appropriate environment.

5. As of June 2009, Congress was strongly considering eliminating this program.

6. Holland's theories are reviewed extensively by Smart, Feldman, and Ethington (2000) and Pascarella and Terenzini (2005). Holland's early work is among the most cited papers in psychology on occupational choice.

7. There are a number of resources that map job titles to college majors including Rosen, Holmberg, and Holland (1989) and Gottfredson and Holland (1996).

According to the theory, students persist or initially adopt majors if their personality characteristics and their environment are compatible. For example, an investigative student in an investigative environment will be able to pursue a major compatible with their interests (e.g., engineering). By contrast, a student who is not in a "compatible" environment will likely switch majors multiple times and is at risk of not succeeding. Much of the application of Holland's theory to choice of major has focused on the degree to which an institution creates an environment that fosters students' personality development (e.g., Feldman, Smart, and Ethington 2004).

Because Holland's theory focuses heavily on the institution and its compatibility, it has led policymakers and scholars in psychology and sociology to focus extensively on institutional characteristics in the retention of students in specific majors and their development within majors. Research in both education and economics has shown that institutional characteristics matter for major choice. For example, Bettinger and Long (2009) find that college remediation affects students' major choice. Feldman, Smart, and Ethington (2004) shows that institutions can affect competencies, values, and self-perceptions, which in turn can alter students' dominant personality traits. Other research in economics finds that peer effects influence students' study habits and perceptions (e.g., Sacerdote 2001; Kremer and Levy 2003).

Another theory of major choice comes from models of human capital formation (e.g., Manski 1993). The standard idea is that students will choose a specific major (or course/degree in education) if the expected, present-value of lifetime utility for choosing that major is higher than the expected value of any other. Equation (1) demonstrates this relationship in more mathematical terms:

$$(1) \qquad E\left[\sum_{t=K_j}^{T} R^{t-1}(y_{jt}) - \sum_{t=1}^{K_j} R^{t-1}(c_{jt})\right] > E\left[\sum_{t=K_i}^{T} R^{t-1}(y_{it}) - \sum_{t=1}^{K_i} R^{t-1}(c_{it})\right],$$

where R is the discount rate, T represents the working lifetime of an adult, K_i is the length of training in the field of study i, $E[.]$ is the expectation operator, and y_i and c_i refer to the earnings and cost of training in the field of study i. The equation shows that a student will choose field j so long as the expected earnings in that field net of the cost of training exceed that of another field i. The length of training, the earnings, and costs can differ by field.

Supporting the relevance of the human capital model to decision making of students is the fact that American students have become more focused on vocational offerings. Many have noted that the students' shifts away from STEM majors have often gone toward more "market-based utilitarianism" (Smart, Feldman, and Ethington 2006). Several authors have noted that over the last two decades students are increasingly pursuing more vocational course offerings (e.g., Adelman 1995; Brint 2002; Grubb and Lazerson

2005). Students are moving toward majors related to specific professions, a trend that is consistent with the rise, noted previously, in the percentage of American college freshmen who highly value being "very well off financially" in their future and the decline in the percentage who count as an important goal to "develop a meaningful philosophy of life" (Pryor et al. 2007, ?).

Similarly, work by Montmarquette, Cannings, and Mahseredjian (2002) find that expected earnings is the major determinant of students' college choices. Del Rossi and Hersch (2008) find that double majors that include business are even more lucrative to students than double majors not involving business. This may also explain why business accounts for half of students who eventually move away from STEM majors.

In the human capital model, students' discount rates play a vital role in helping balance the trade-offs between current costs and future rewards. The more impatient that students are, the more they will eschew long periods of training before entering the labor force. Additionally, the years of training and the earnings profile within careers can also discourage investment in specific careers. In science and engineering, especially in the case of students pursuing doctoral careers, the median completion time for students to complete their doctorate following their bachelor degree work is high, ranging from 8.5 in engineering, 8.0 years in mathematics, and 8.1 years in the biological sciences, to 9.5 years in computer science (NSF 2004).

A student's choice of careers can be costly. It takes time to search through several possible fields of study, and the costliness of the search may encourage students to reduce the amount of search that they do (e.g., Oi 1974) or to trust other students. In the standard model, students incur search costs as they try to identify the optimal career. They may be content to take a "lesser" career rather than to continue searching. Alternatively, they may overvalue information from their peers and allow peer effects (or "herd" behavior) to influence their choices of careers.

A variation of the search cost model is one of limited information. Students may not have full access to information about careers when they make their decisions to study. A student who pursues business and commits early on may not explore other fields in which the student may have experienced similar success. Students, especially those who wish to study in high credit degree areas like in the sciences, must commit to their field of study early in order to complete the degree requirements and to graduate in a timely fashion. The rigidity of the degree requirements in science and engineering fields often discourages exploration of other disciplines.

Holland's model and the human capital model are not mutually exclusive. For example, suppose that students compute the expected value of a profession given their current information about their skills. As students acquire new information about their abilities or as institutions improve students' capabilities in a specific dimension, students will have new information about their skills and potential returns in a given field. If students are

Bayesian updaters, then they will reevaluate equation (1) continuously. If the expected value of an alternative major (given students' current beliefs about their abilities) exceeds that of their current major, students will change majors.

Both of these frameworks provide conceptualization about both the process of initially choosing a major and about persistence within that major. We now turn our attention to the timing of initial major choices and subsequent persistence in the major.

Timing of Major Choice

Students initially decide on a major at the end of high school or the beginning of college. College admissions tests and application forms ask students to indicate a potential field of study when they enter college. When UCLA began surveying incoming students in 1966, only 2 percent of students were undecided as to what major they wanted to pursue when they entered college. Over time, this has increased to over 8 percent of students entering without majors chosen (Astin et al. 1997).

Although an overwhelming majority of students have indicated a potential major, there is much less certainty about whether they will persist in the major. According to UCLA's survey of first-year students, 49 percent of students entered college saying that there was "some chance" or "a very good chance" that they would change their major at some point in college (Saenz and Barrera 2007). Similarly, 55 percent of students thought that they would change their choice of careers. The large number of students who think that they may change fields suggests that students are consciously and actively considering multiple major and career options as they enter college.

Students' movements across majors begin in their first semesters. Within the first year of college, 30 percent of students change their major (Saenz and Barrera 2007). What has changed in that first year? According to the UCLA student survey, there have been increases in students' reported computer skills, public speaking ability, and writing. Students also report higher levels of cooperation and "self-understanding." By contrast, students report less mathematical ability, less "drive to achieve," and less academic ability than they thought they had when they first arrived. Holland's model would predict that these changes should push students toward majors requiring less mathematical ability and where the competitive environment is less intense.

Once students formally choose a major (typically by the start of the second year), they still frequently switch majors. One institution, for example, found that 51 percent of students changed their majors at least once after formally indicating a major, and 19 percent of students changed their major two or more times after formally declaring a major (Sethi and Shi 2008). Given that the formal declaration of a major need not be the same major as indicated on a student's application or college entrance exam, it is clear that there is substantial mobility across majors once students arrive at school.

Even if a student enters a specific STEM major, there is no guarantee that their eventual career will be in a STEM field. To illustrate, about 50 percent of engineering majors aim to pursue an advanced degree in business or law. Similarly, 50 percent of students in biology and physics pursue advanced degrees in fields other than biology or physics. Medical degrees are the most common training among these students, although many also pursue advanced degrees in business or law. Depending on the field of study, only 30 to 40 percent of engineering, physical or computer science, or math students go on to study these same fields in graduate school.

2.3 The Role of Relative Wages

The heart of the human capital model is the idea that individuals make educational decisions by comparing their lifetime utilities in alternative prospective careers. This calculation applies to major choice as well. Generally speaking, economists have largely used earnings as the measure of the overall lifetime utility of careers, and so economics typically examines major choice by comparing the returns to earnings across many disciplines. Identifying the economic returns to a particular major is difficult since students' choices of majors may be correlated with students' underlying abilities. Perhaps the best measures of returns to various disciplines come from Donald and Hammermesh (2004). Using data from a single, large university, they tracked earnings profiles across majors. They control for students' ability to separate the financial rewards from a specific major and those from students' abilities. Their estimates appear in table 2.1. The estimates represent the percent differences in wages across majors relative to majoring in education.

The highest earning field was "hard" business. This category included the more quantitative fields in business, including accounting, finance, and

Table 2.1 Returns to major by discipline

Major choice	Percent difference in wages relative to education
Humanities	.097
Social science	.314
Communications	.366
Natural sciences	.293
Business—soft	.413
Business—hard	.522
Engineering	.372
Architecture	.165
Education	.000
Social work	.212

Notes: Estimates come from Donald and Hamermesh (2004 table 5, column 2).

business engineering. Hard business majors earned about 52 percent more than students in education. Students in the "soft" business majors, which include management and marketing, made 41 percent more than students in education. Social science majors earned 31 percent more than education. The STEM fields fared far better than education, with engineers making 37 percent more and natural science majors making 29 percent more, but in both cases students make less money than they do in the business fields.

Similarly, older data from the Bureau of Labor Statistics seem to support Donald and Hamermesh's evidence. Hecker (1995) reports that there was very little difference between the earnings of business majors and STEM majors. In fact, women in business and accounting earned more money than women whose degrees were in chemistry, biology, or mathematics. They earned less than those with degrees in architecture or engineering. Women in economics earned more than women in any of the STEM fields. Men in accounting and business had similar earnings to those in the highest-paid STEM fields—engineering, math, physics, and computer science—and they had higher earnings than men who had majored in biology and chemistry. Business majors had similar earnings to those in biology and chemistry. For both males and females, majors in business and economics had higher earnings than majors in the other social sciences, humanities, and education.

Not only are the absolute wages of non-STEM fields often higher than those in STEM fields, the wage growth has also been higher. From 1991 to 2001, business wages increased by 27 percent, compared to only 19 percent for engineering and 21 percent for math and computer science. These divergent wage increases are not only indicative of demand shocks, but they may also provide one key input to students' decision making. They help students project future earnings in a given profession, making business even more attractive relative to STEM fields. As we show following, at least half of students who started as STEM majors and eventually moved to other majors ended up pursuing business as a major.

There are still other job-related differences that could contribute to the attractiveness of non-STEM majors over STEM majors. For example, one factor that influences major decision and labor market participation is the duration of the training needed to enter a career. Each additional year that a student needs to pursue training means another year of foregone earnings. Since the returns to majors may be dynamic, students have to project into the future their potential earnings in a given career. Arrow and Capron (1959) were among the first to explore how labor supply responded given the fact that training took time. They published their paper shortly after Sputnik had been launched and at a time when the United States was heavily encouraging the development of more US-born scientists. They claimed that a model of "dynamic shortage" could explain the labor market for scientists. As noted before, the type of labor market adjustments described by Arrow and Capron is an example of a cobweb model.

In Arrow and Capron's model, an increase in labor demand leads to a shortage of engineers and an increase in real wages. This wage increase makes a career as a scientist or engineer more attractive to potential students. As students' expected earnings in STEM fields increase relative to other majors, college students should respond accordingly by switching their majors. As more workers respond to the higher wages by changing careers, the labor supply curve shifts out leading real wages to decline. As each person finishes their training, they lead the supply curve to shift out, but there is no guarantee that the supply curve will not shift "too far" out.

The duration of training in STEM fields is longer than that of other fields. For example, the eight to ten years that students typically spend earning a doctorate in a STEM field is quite a bit longer than the two years needed for a business degree or the three years needed for a law degree. Not only do students forego more years in the labor market, but the labor market conditions may have changed dramatically from when they entered their training to the end of their training, and while workers are getting their training. If the labor supply curve shifts too far, it could actually lead to declining real wages among scientists and engineers. It could also lead to periods of surplus and shortage in the market for scientists and engineers—cobwebs left over from the previous shift in supply. The key factor in the adjustment is the elasticity of the supply of scientists and engineers.

The cobweb model has been tested over and over again. Freeman (1971, 1975, 1976) and Breneman and Freeman (1974) provided early tests examining the market for engineers. It has also been applied to the market for lawyers (Freeman 1975, Pashigian 1977). More recent work by Ryoo and Rosen (2004) extends these models with advances made in economic theory. As in the earlier studies, Ryoo and Rosen (2004) find that the cobweb model of supply and demand accurately characterizes the market for engineers. They note that there have been several periods of surplus in the market over the last four decades. They also pay special attention to identifying the lifetime earnings that an engineer can reasonably expect at the time that they commit to a specific area of study. They find that the supply of engineers closely corresponds with variations in the lifetime earning cycle of engineers at the time that engineers commit to their career. Periods of shortage and surplus correspond to unexpected demand shocks in the labor market for engineers. One important consequence of the resulting gyrations in wages has been to make engineering a riskier, and thus less attractive, career option for American students.

2.4 Major Choices and Transitions

To shed some light on the STEM pipeline during college, we present some evidence based on students' transcripts in college. We do not present any new evidence on the STEM pipeline leading to college. Instead, we focus on how college students make decisions about major choice once enrolled in college.

The data that we use come from the Ohio Board of Regents and represent students who entered college for the first time during the 1998 and 1999 school year. Beginning in the 1998 and 1999 school year, the Ohio Board of Regents began tracking students' transcripts at all of Ohio's fifty-two public colleges and universities. Additionally, the Ohio Board of Regents collaborates with the College Board to match students' collegiate records to the students' ACT exam scores and survey. Hence, for each student, we observe the students' ACT exam scores and self-reported high school transcript data from the ACT survey. During the ACT survey, students indicate which majors they intend to pursue while in college. With the transcript data from the Ohio Board of Regents, we observe all of the classes that they take in college, and ultimately we observe their major choices.

Our sample consists of students who first enrolled in the 1998 and 1999 school year at one of Ohio's four-year campuses. We further restrict our sample to those students who took the ACT exam when they entered college and who designated a major at that time.[8] We need this last restriction to identify students who have interests in STEM fields.

The Ohio data are advantageous in that we can track students across schools within the Ohio public higher education system (four-year and two-year institutions). If a student transfers and changes majors, we can observe the outcome. We cannot track students who leave the state, although previous work has suggested that any bias from this is small (Bettinger 2004).

Table 2.2 shows the pre-college major choices for students in our data. We show this for a variety of samples. For example, only about 2 percent of the sample claims that they want to major in the humanities at the start of college. The social sciences attract 13.3 percent while the sciences attract 8.0 percent of students. Business and education are the most attractive pre-college majors, with 23.4 and 17.5 percent of students choosing these topics, respectively. Engineering also attracts a significant number of students, with nearly 11.7 percent of students choosing this major before college.

The other columns of table 2.2 refine the sample somewhat. The second column focuses on students scoring 25 or over on their ACT exams. This represents the top 28 percent of all students taking the ACT exam. This is likely a subsample that is more likely to pursue the sciences or engineering in college. Similarly, the other columns of table 2.2 include, respectively, students with science ACT exam scores 25 and over, with math ACT exam scores 25 and over, and with high school GPAs 3.5 and over in math.

Of these subsamples, each of them is more likely to major in science and engineering than the overall sample. For example, of the students scoring

8. The ACT survey allows students to declare a specific discipline (e.g., economics) or a more general distinction (e.g., social studies).

Table 2.2 Major intentions of incoming first-year college students, Ohio public colleges and universities, fall 1998

	Sample				
Intended major	All students	Students with overall ACT > 24	Students with science ACT > 24	Students with math ACT > 24	Students with HS math GPA ≥ 3.5
Humanities	2.1	3.2	2.7	2.2	1.6
Foreign language	0.5	0.8	0.6	0.8	0.8
Social science	13.3	14.6	13.3	11.6	12.3
Communications	8.1	8.0	6.7	5.9	6.4
Science (biological or physical)	8.0	11.7	12.6	10.7	10.5
Math	0.6	1.0	1.1	1.3	1.3
Business	23.4	19.1	18.4	22.4	22.9
Computers	4.7	6.3	6.9	6.4	5.2
Engineering	11.7	18.0	19.9	20.9	17.5
Engineering technology	2.4	2.5	3.0	2.8	2.5
Architecture	3.8	3.0	3.5	3.8	3.7
Education	17.5	10.2	9.7	9.6	13.3
Social work	4.0	1.5	1.7	1.6	2.1
N	17,969	5,031	4,702	5,676	6,265

Notes: Data are from the Ohio Board of Regents and include traditional-aged (age eighteen to twenty) students who entered a four-year Ohio public college in the fall 1998. The sample is further restricted to students who declared a major on their ACT survey.

over 24 on the ACT science exam, 12.6 percent hope to major in science and 19.9 percent hope to major in engineering. As a whole, science and engineering are more attractive than education and business combined. In thinking about the STEM pipeline, these subsamples of students are likely the ones who may eventually pursue careers in science and engineering and go on for study in those fields.

Table 2.3 shows some descriptive statistics for these samples. We have restricted our sample to full-time, traditional age (i.e., eighteen to twenty), first-time students, so students' age at the start of college is around eighteen. About 86 percent of students are white. This is slightly higher than the Ohio's overall system, but given that we are focused on students who took the ACT exam, this is not surprising.

About 7 percent of students are African American and 52 percent of students are female. The average ACT score is 22 and this is true for the math and science tests as well. About 78 percent of the sample currently or last attended a four-year college. Twenty-two percent of this sample took math remediation during their college careers.

The subsamples of students, generally speaking, have fewer minority students, fewer women, higher ACT scores, higher likelihoods of attending four-year colleges, and lower likelihoods of attending math remediation

Table 2.3 Student characteristics, Ohio public colleges and universities, fall 1998

	Sample				
Student characteristic	All students	Students with overall ACT > 24	Students with science ACT > 24	Students with math ACT > 24	Students with HS math GPA ≥ 3.5
Age	18.4	18.3	18.4	18.4	18.4
	(0.5)	(0.5)	(0.5)	(0.5)	(0.5)
White	0.86	0.92	0.93	0.92	0.90
Black	0.07	0.02	0.01	0.02	0.04
Female	0.52	0.47	0.40	0.40	0.52
Overall ACT	22.0	27.4	26.9	26.2	24.4
	(4.3)	(2.2)	(2.8)	(3.1)	(4.0)
Math ACT	21.9	27.1	26.6	27.7	25.0
	(4.8)	(3.4)	(3.8)	(2.4)	(4.5)
Science ACT	22.0	26.7	27.5	25.6	24.0
	(4.3)	(3.2)	(2.6)	(3.7)	(4.2)
Attending 4-year college	0.78	0.92	0.90	0.92	0.87
Attended math remediation	0.22	0.02	0.04	0.01	0.06
N	17,969	5,031	4,702	5,676	6,265

Notes: Data are from the Ohio Board of Regents and include traditional-aged (age eighteen to twenty) students who entered a four-year Ohio public college in the fall 1998. The sample is further restricted to students who declared a major on their ACT survey. The STEM includes computer science, mathematics, engineering, engineering technologies, and the physical and biological sciences.

than the overall sample. The one point that table 2.3 accentuates is that women and minorities continue to be underrepresented among students who enter college highly prepared to study in science and technology. Similar to national patterns, at least at this point in the pipeline, these groups are continuing to be underrepresented.

Our focus is to see what majors students eventually choose. To do that, we focus simply on whether students intended to major in a STEM field or not.[9] In table 2.4, we compare students' pre-college choices of major to their college decisions. For students originally desiring to major in STEM fields, only about 43 percent of them actually go on to major in STEM fields. The rest transfer to non-STEM majors. For students who originally desired to major in non-STEM fields, most (95 percent) stay in non-STEM fields. Only 5 percent of them ever transfer into STEM fields.

As we focus on a more science- and/or math-oriented population, there is some improvement, but STEM majors have a poorer retention rate than non-STEM majors. The STEM majors retain only between 50 and 54 percent of students interested in STEM fields. The retention rate is highest

9. We include math, sciences, computer science, engineering, and engineering technology as the key STEM fields.

Table 2.4 **STEM major choices by pre-college STEM decisions**

	Pre-college STEM major		Pre-college non-STEM major	
Sample	STEM major	Non-STEM major	STEM major	Non-STEM major
All students	42.9	57.1	5.5	94.6
ACT > 24	52.2	47.8	7.7	92.3
ACT science > 24	51.6	48.4	8.7	91.3
ACT math > 24	54.2	45.8	8.5	91.5
HS math GPA ≥ 3.5	50.4	49.6	7.0	93.0

Notes: Data are from the Ohio Board of Regents and include traditional-aged (age eighteen to twenty) students who entered a four-year Ohio public college in the fall 1998. The sample is further restricted to students who declared a major on their ACT survey. The STEM includes computer science, mathematics, engineering, engineering technologies, and the physical and biological sciences.

among the sample of students with high math scores. The STEM majors attract away 7 to 9 percent of students who originally wanted to major in non-STEM fields.

One way to examine major choice and STEM retention is to look at the timing of students' defections from STEM majors. When we observe students at the end of high school, we know their major intentions. The nature of our data allows us to then track their course schedules as they start college. We focus on the first semester schedules, as these are likely the most exogenous to institutional efforts to increase STEM participation. Students commit to these schedules when they arrive at college, and we focus on the classes that they attempt rather than those that they complete successfully.

In figure 2.5, we plot the proportion of STEM courses that students take during the first semester. Students who are interested in STEM fields clearly take more STEM classes than students who expressed interest in another major. The STEM majors take, on average, 52 percent of their first semester courses in STEM fields, compared to 28 percent for non-STEM majors.

Figure 2.6 repeats the previous exercise, but it divides the pre-college students who were interested in STEM into two categories: those who eventually majored in STEM and those who did not. Students who would stay in STEM majors took about 63 percent of their credit hours in STEM fields in their first semester, whereas those who would eventually abandon STEM majors averaged only 42 percent. Figure 2.7 plots the difference between STEM "stayers" and "defectors."

This difference in the content of students' first semester schedules can be seen not just in the overall sample, but also within subsamples of high-achieving students. For example, if we restrict our sample to students with the highest ACT scores, the highest ACT math scores, the highest ACT science scores, or high school math GPAs greater than 3.5, we find similar differences between eventual STEM majors and those who abandon STEM

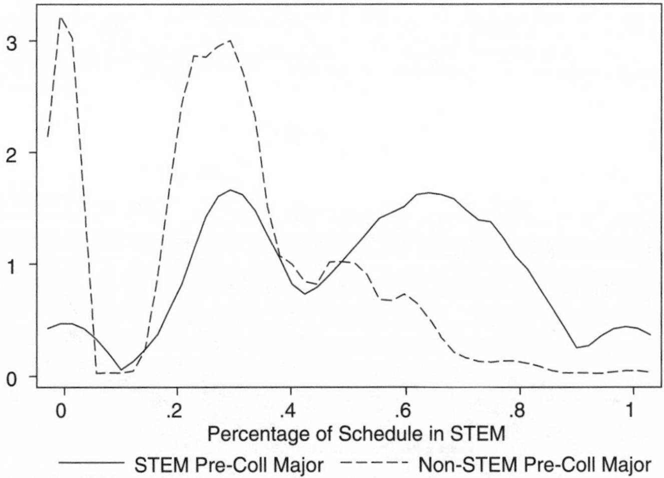

Fig. 2.5 Proportion of first-semester courses in STEM fields for pre-college majors in STEM and non-STEM fields

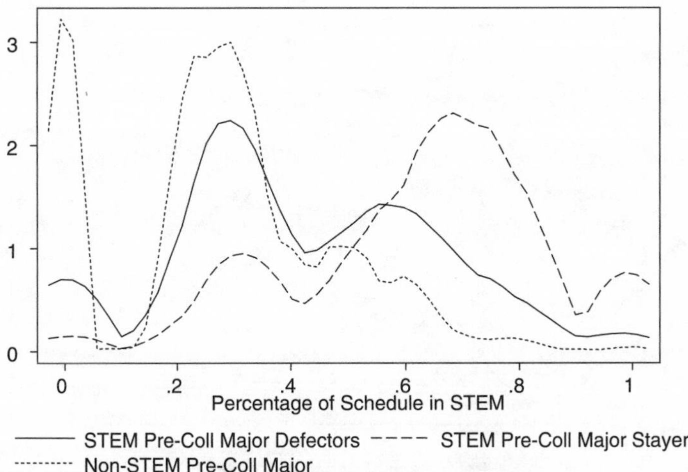

Fig. 2.6 Proportion of first-semester courses in STEM fields for pre-college majors in STEM and non-STEM fields, by students' eventual major

fields (figures 2.8 through 2.11). Even from the first semester, differences emerge in the types of schedules that students take.

It is not clear which way the causality runs in these cases. On the one hand, students who take fewer STEM courses may be identifying themselves as students who want to defect. On the other hand, taking more courses may generate more interest and consequently more commitment to the STEM major. Regardless, we see that students who more fully immerse themselves in STEM classes at the start are more likely to persist in the major. Although

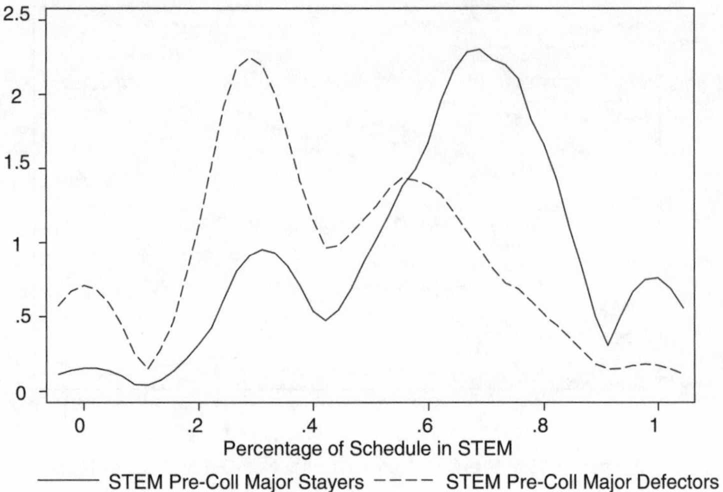

Fig. 2.7 Proportion of first-semester courses in STEM fields for pre-college majors in STEM fields, by eventual major

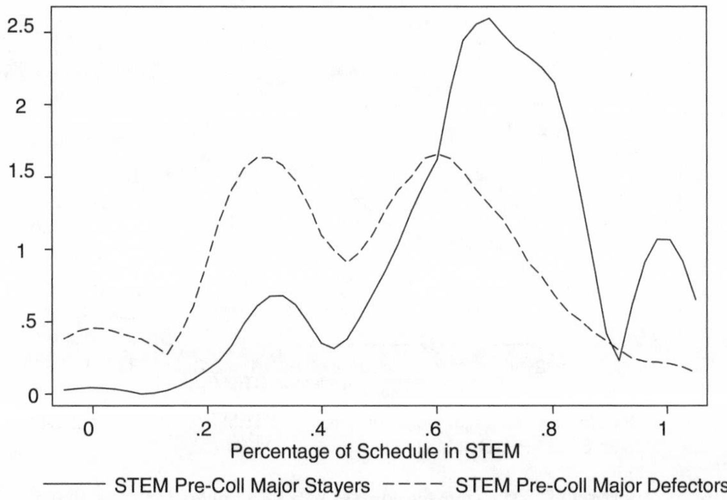

Fig. 2.8 Proportion of first-semester courses in STEM fields for pre-college majors in STEM fields, by eventual major for students with ACT scores over 24

we do not present the figures here, the differences between those who stay in STEM majors and those who defect increases with each successive semester, as one might expect.

What about the other students who switch to STEM fields from other fields? At least in the first semester, they look quite similar to the students who originally declared a STEM major and then left. We plot their distribu-

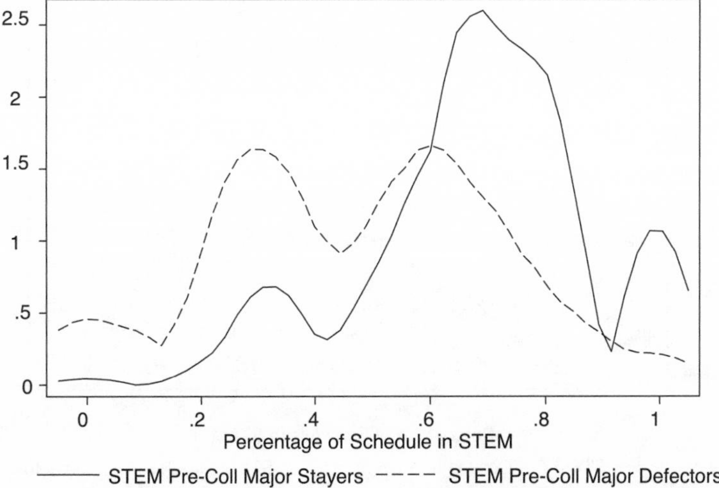

Fig. 2.9 Proportion of first-semester courses in STEM fields for pre-college majors in STEM fields, by eventual major for students with ACT science scores over 24

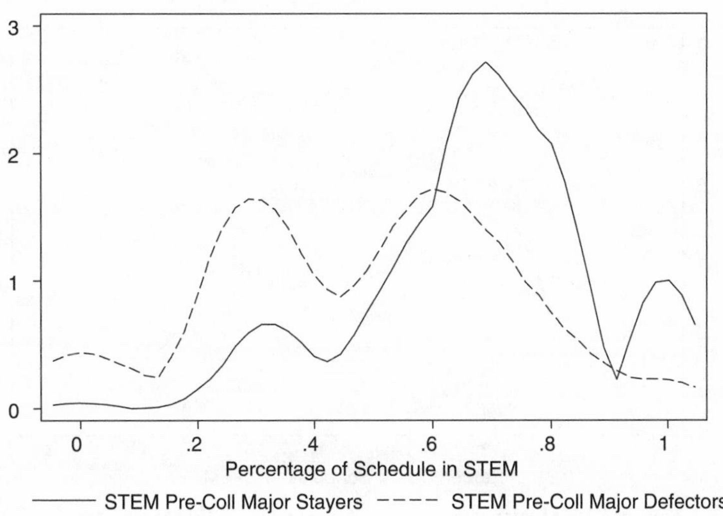

Fig. 2.10 Proportion of first-semester courses in STEM fields for pre-college majors in STEM fields, by eventual major for students with ACT math scores over 24

tions in figure 2.12. The distributions also look similar when we focus on students with higher ACT scores.

Another way to view the same results is to figure out the probability that students eventually major in STEM according to the proportion of the courses they took in STEM fields during their first semester and according to whether they indicated before college a desire to major in STEM fields. This

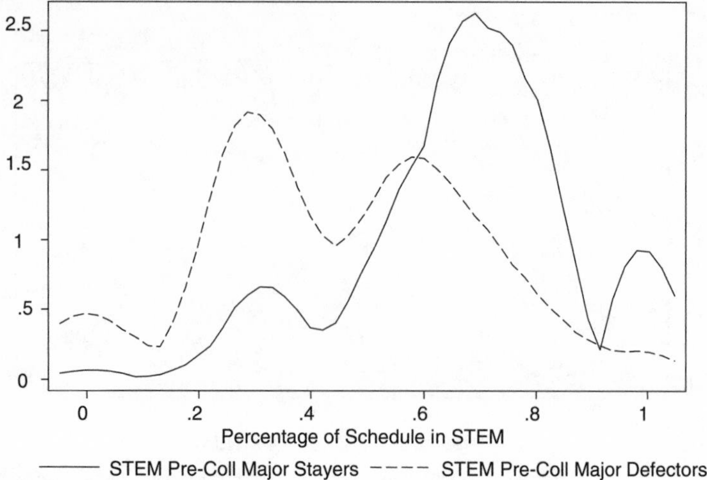

Fig. 2.11 Proportion of first-semester courses in STEM fields for pre-college majors in STEM fields, by eventual major for students with high school math GPA's 3.5 and over

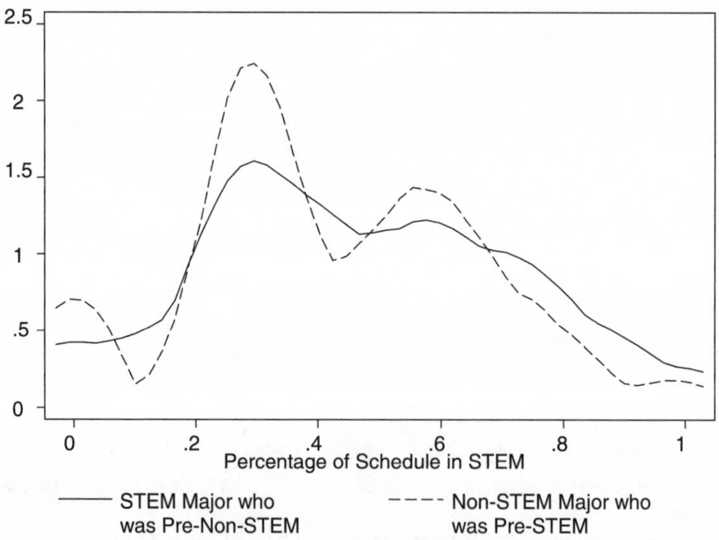

Fig. 2.12 Proportion of first-semester courses in STEM fields for students who later switch to STEM fields and those who switch out

is plotted in figure 2.13. Declaring a major in STEM fields before college automatically increases the probability that a student eventually majors in STEM fields. There is also a positive association of the proportion of STEM courses in the first semester and eventual major choice for both groups.

So what do we make of these results, and why do STEM fields have such

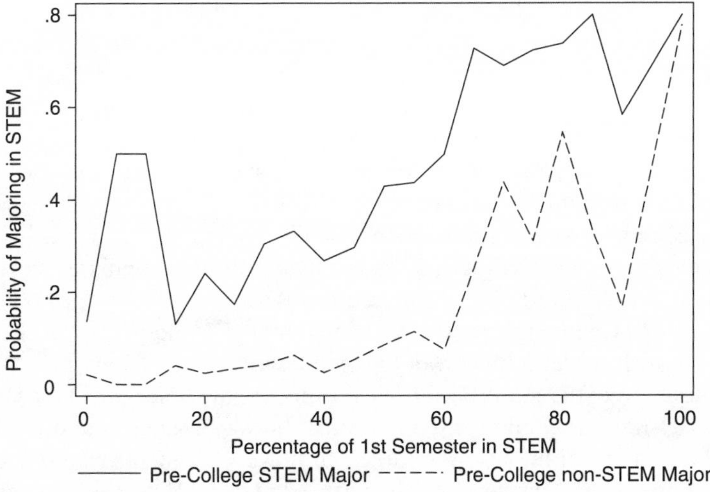

Fig. 2.13 Probability of majoring in STEM field by the percentage of first-semester courses in STEM fields, by pre-college major

lower retention rates? One possible explanation is that students formulate their interest prior to college and only deviate slightly thereafter. For example, many studies (e.g., NAC 2007) report that students in STEM majors decided to pursue this major prior to college. These findings are supported in figures 2.5 through 2.13 in that the differences between individuals' commitment to STEM already appears in students' first semesters. Students who originally declared that they wanted to be a STEM major take a more STEM-filled schedule in their first semester than other students. Students who are moving either away from STEM fields or toward them seem to take a lighter STEM load, but one that is still significantly larger than students who have never expressed interest in STEM and eventually major in non-STEM fields.

Another possible explanation is based on the rigidity of STEM majors. The STEM majors typically have high credit requirements. For example, engineering fields at the Ohio State University, the largest campus in our sample, require between 150 and 165 quarter hours for the core major requirements and technical electives.[10] Students have an additional requirement to complete roughly forty hours of general education requirements. A majority of students' first couple of years at the university are spent taking prerequisites for upper-division classes, so a student majoring in one of these fields would have little space to explore other majors in their early careers.

By contrast, a student majoring in economics or political science at Ohio

10. Electrical engineering is an exception only requiring ninety-two hours.

State has substantial flexibility. They must take forty-five to fifty quarter credits within their major. Students in these majors must complete an additional forty to forty-five credit hours in general education as well. Given that the university requires 180 credit hours for graduation, students have almost two quarters of "free time" to explore other majors.

In the first year, a student in the sciences takes only required classes. If after that first year the student chooses to pursue a program outside the sciences, he or she can still graduate in a timely fashion. On the other hand, a student who begins by exploring a major in one of these popular social studies majors will not complete the prerequisites necessary to change majors to the sciences. Changing to a STEM-related major would necessarily extend the time such students must wait for their degree.

If hours were the sole criterion for shifting major choices, then the largest shifts of students would likely be toward the social sciences and humanities, but that is not the case. As Table 2.5 shows, of students who started as STEM majors and then eventually switched majors, 21 percent changed to the social sciences and 8 percent to the humanities. In comparison, 60 percent of defectors chose either business or education, majors that are much more demanding in terms of hours than the social sciences. For example, an accounting major at Ohio State must complete eighty-eight hours within the major and ninety-five general education hours, and an education major needs at least 101 hours within the major and ninety-five general education hours. While the general education hours may provide more flexibility (and interchangeability with other majors), the hours in the major are almost twice that required in most social science or humanities majors.

The same pattern appears when we look at high performing students who

Table 2.5 **Major choices among STEM defectors**

	Sample				
Major	All students	ACT > 24	ACT science > 24	ACT math > 24	HS math GPA ≥ 3.5
Humanities	8.2	10.7	8.4	7.9	6.4
Foreign language	1.0	1.5	1.4	1.3	0.9
Social science	21.2	24.3	23.9	21.3	20.5
Communications	6.5	5.4	5.9	4.8	5.6
Business	48.7	46.2	47.8	53.2	53.9
Architecture	2.2	1.5	1.3	2.0	2.1
Education	11.1	9.6	10.6	9.3	9.8
Social work	2.0	1.0	0.6	0.3	0.8

Notes: Data are from the Ohio Board of Regents and include traditional-aged (age eighteen to twenty) students who entered a four-year Ohio public college in the fall 1998. The sample is further restricted to students who declared a major on their ACT survey. The STEM includes computer science, mathematics, engineering, engineering technologies, and the physical and biological sciences.

decided to change their major from a STEM field to another. Half of these students choose business, while 20 to 24 percent of them choose social studies. As before, most of the transitions are going to hour-intensive majors.

Part of the criticism of the hour-intensity of STEM majors is that students have little chance to explore other majors. While there may be some validity to this, we find that many students who did not indicate interest in STEM prior to college are in fact able to switch to STEM majors. Students who switch out of STEM are not forced to do so because they took too many non-STEM classes in their first semester. Another fact that undercuts the rigidity argument is that a number of students who are switching into STEM fields take similar schedules and are able to complete the hours needed for a STEM major. However, there are two facts that might still suggest some rigidity. First, when we look at figure 2.13, we see that the probability of majoring in STEM fields is quite low for students who did not indicate interest in STEM prior to college and who take less than about 60 percent of their first semester schedule in non-STEM fields. Second, we have only examined students' first semester schedules. It could be that students have very little flexibility after the first semester.

What are the implications of these patterns in major choice on the STEM pipeline? On the one hand, the defection of many top students suggests that the STEM pipeline is leaky. Only about half of students in the top of the ability distribution who wanted to major in sciences before college continue in those majors through the end of college.

On the other hand, many talented students who are prepared for and in a position to major in STEM fields make seemingly rational decisions to do otherwise. Significant numbers have taken the early courses in STEM majors and switch majors to fields that are almost or perhaps even more lucrative both contemporaneously and in the long run.

2.5 Changing Patterns for Women and Minorities

As we have already shown, much of the growth in STEM majors over the last thirty years has taken place among women and minorities. Over that period, the number of women majoring in STEM fields increased by 91 percent. The number of African Americans and hispanics majoring in STEM fields increased dramatically as well.

To examine how gender and race predict the likelihood that students major in STEM fields, we run linear probability models comparing the likelihood of switching out of a STEM major to the covariates in table 2.3. Our purpose is not to obtain causal estimates of any individual factor but to determine what correlates with the likelihood that students persist in a STEM major. Our sample focuses solely on students who indicated that they intended to major in STEM fields prior to college. The results appear in table 2.6.

Table 2.6 Predictors of persisting in STEM majors

	All		ACT > 24	ACT math > 24	ACT science > 24	HS GPA ≥ 3.5
Age	–.027	–.029	–.019	–.000	–.011	–.010
	(.013)	(.019)	(.022)	(.020)	(.021)	(.019)
White	–.014	–.016	.033	.004	.037	–.006
	(.027)	(.027)	(.044)	(.039)	(.043)	(.040)
Black	.087	.063	.056	.080	.186	.161
	(.037)	(.037)	(.094)	(.081)	(.096)	(.064)
Female	–.141	–.101	–.114	–.140	–.090	–.129
	(.015)	(.016)	(.027)	(.026)	(.028)	(.024)
Overall ACT	–.013	–.011	.006	–.003	–.006	–.004
	(.005)	(.004)	(.008)	(.007)	(.007)	(.007)
Math ACT	.029	.027	.027	.028	.027	.027
	(.003)	(.003)	(.004)	(.005)	(.004)	(.004)
Science ACT	.009	.009	.002	.005	.013	.007
	(.003)	(.003)	(.005)	(.005)	(.006)	(.005)
Attending 4-year college	.021	.016	.032	.062	–.056	.045
	(.019)	(.019)	(.043)	(.039)	(.040)	(.034)
Attended math remediation	.000	.001	–.139	–.053	–.081	.005
	(.023)	(.023)	(.076)	(.088)	(.069)	(.056)
Attended English remediation	.036	.035	.178	.085	.097	.076
	(.024)	(.024)	(.117)	(.069)	(.083)	(.051)
Pre-college major FE	No	Yes	Yes	Yes	Yes	Yes
N	4,914	4,914	1,988	2,387	2,040	2,321

Notes: Sample = students indicating STEM major before college. Dependent variable = Probability of persisting in STEM major. FE = fixed effects. Data are from the Ohio Board of Regents and include traditional-aged (age eighteen to twenty) students who entered a four-year Ohio public college in the fall 1998. The sample is further restricted to students who declared a major on their ACT survey. The STEM includes computer science, mathematics, engineering, engineering technologies, and the physical and biological sciences.

In the first column, we report results for the full sample. In the full sample, females and older students are less likely to stay in STEM majors. African Americans are more likely to persist in STEM majors than other students. Students' overall ACT scores are negatively correlated with the likelihood of staying in a STEM major after controlling for students ACT math and science scores. These other scores are strongly and positively correlated with persistence in STEM fields. In column (2) we add fixed effects for the specific major that students indicated prior to college. The results are very similar to those in column (1).

In the third column, we focus only on students whose ACT scores are high. Within that group, women are about 11 percentage points less likely to stay in STEM majors, a result that is statistically significant. This is similar to the finding by Dickson (2010) that women are less likely to major in STEM fields even after controlling for SAT scores and high school rank.

The coefficient on being African American is positive but not statistically significant. The ACT math scores remain the strongest indicator among the achievement variables. Remediation also seems to matter. Math remediation is marginally significant, suggesting that it decreases the likelihood that students persist in STEM fields. English remediation seems to have the reverse relationship but is not significant. It is hard to decipher the causal relationship of these remediation estimates, although work by Bettinger and Long (2009) shows that math remediation causes a decrease in the probability that students major in math fields.

The results in the other columns of table 2.6 are similar. In every case, females, even among the top students who previously indicated an interest in STEM fields, are less likely to major in STEM fields. The ACT math scores seem to predict greater likelihoods of persistence in STEM fields. The coefficient on African Americans is always positive, suggesting that, among high achievers, African Americans are more likely to persist in STEM majors, but it is not always statistically significant.

The only results that are robust across all of the specifications are those for gender and ACT math scores. Those for ACT math scores seem fairly obvious: STEM fields require higher math skills and students' retention in these fields is tied to their abilities. On the other hand, the gender result is less obvious. The fact that women are underrepresented has long been discussed in academic literature. What is different here is that we have focused on the highest ability students; among them, women who have previously expressed interest in STEM fields are 9 to 14 percentage points less likely to stay in STEM majors than men.

2.6 Conclusion

This chapter presents new descriptive evidence on the STEM pipeline. Using data from Ohio's four-year colleges, the chapter shows that STEM fields retain only about half of their students, and this retention rate does not improve significantly when we restrict the analysis to top performing students. Even among top performing students, almost half of the students who indicated interest in STEM majors did not persist in STEM majors. Almost half of them switched and became business majors. Detection from STEM fields is particularly acute among high performing women.

We also show how students' experimentation of STEM fields varies in the first semester with their early and ultimate interest in STEM fields. During students' first semester in college, the proportion of courses that they take in STEM fields is directly correlated with their eventual major. It is not clear which direction causality runs: students with less commitment to a STEM major may take fewer courses, or taking fewer courses may lead to less commitment.

Nonetheless, students who eventually major in STEM fields take, on average, over 60 percent of their first semester courses in STEM topics. To be sure, there are some students who take less than 60 percent of their schedule in STEM fields who still may major in STEM fields; however, students' chances of successfully completing STEM majors decline significantly if they take less than 60 percent of the first semester courses in STEM fields.

What are the implications for the STEM pipeline? The first observation is that some strongly prepared students who are interested in STEM fields nevertheless depart from STEM majors. Often they move to other fields that are more lucrative; as we showed in the previous section, wages in business can often be 5 to 15 percent higher than in STEM fields. These defections appear to be rational decisions. Evidence from other economists suggests that periods of surplus and shortage are endemic to the STEM market because of the prolonged training required. Given the responsiveness of students to wages, it may be that, as Ryoo and Rosen (2004, S110) observe, public policies that "build technical talent ahead of demand are misplaced unless public policy makers have better information on future market conditions than the market participants do."

The second observation is that students who depart STEM majors tend to do so early in their careers. As early as students' first semesters, there is already a separation between the STEM course-taking intensity of eventual majors compared to the STEM intensity of students who previously expressed interest in STEM fields but eventually depart. If indeed the decision to depart from STEM fields occurs early in students' careers, public policy or institutional efforts aimed at improving retention in STEM majors must happen early in students' careers, or in enough time so that students can incorporate their expectations of the effects of such efforts in their career decision making.

Third, women even at the top of the ability distribution are not pursuing STEM majors. In part because many are switching to more lucrative majors, they remain underrepresented in STEM fields. Other research by Bettinger and Long (2005) suggests that women's early experiences in STEM subjects in college affects their likelihood of persisting in these subjects.

Finally, as other chapters in this volume have highlighted, the United States remains a net importer of scientific talent. While fewer US citizens are pursuing doctoral degrees in STEM fields, the US continues to lead the world in the production of doctorates and a significant proportion of these students stay in the United States (NSF 2004). These facts, coupled with the choices that students make in choosing college majors, support the claims of Teitelbaum (2007) and others that the shortage of scientists and engineers is overstated.

References

Academic Competitive Council (ACC). 2007. *Report of the Academic Competitive Council.* Washington, DC: US Department of Education.

ACT. 2006. ACT National high school profile report. Data available at: http://www.act.org/news/data.html.

Adelman, C. 1995. *The new college course map and transcript files: Changes in course-taking and achievement, 1972–1993* (NCES PE 95-800). Washington, DC: US Department of Education, National Center for Education Statistics.

Alchian, A. A., K. J. Arrow, and W. M. Capron. 1958. *An economic analysis of the market for scientists and engineers.* Santa Monica, CA: The RAND Corporation.

Arrow, K. J., and W. M. Capron. 1959. Dynamic shortages and price rises: The engineer-scientist case. *Quarterly Journal of Economics* 73 (May): 292–308.

Astin, A. W., S. A. Parrott, W. S. Korn, and L. J. Sax. 1997. *The American freshman: Thirty-year trends.* Los Angeles: Higher Education Research Institute, UCLA.

Atkinson, R. 1990. Supply and demand for scientists and engineers: A national crisis in the making. *Science* 248 (4954): 425–32.

Bettinger, E. 2004. Is the finish line in sight? Financial Aid's impact on retention and graduation. In *College choices: The economics of where to go, when to go, and how to pay for it,* ed. C. M. Hoxby, 207–83. Chicago: University of Chicago Press.

Bettinger, E., and B. Long. 2009. Addressing the needs of under-prepared students in higher education: Does college remediation work? *Journal of Human Resources* 44 (3): 736–71.

———. 2005. Female role models for female college students. *American Economic Review Papers and Proceedings* 95 (2): 152–57.

Blank, D. M., and G. J. Stigler. 1957. *The demand and supply of scientific personnel.* New York: National Bureau of Economic Research.

Breneman, D., and R. Freeman. 1974. Forecasting the PhD labor market: Pitfalls for policy. Technical Report no. 2. Washington, DC: National Board of Graduate Education.

Brint, S. 2002. The rise of the "Practical Arts." In *The future of the city of intellect,* ed. S. Brint, 231–59. Stanford: Stanford University Press.

Del Rossi, A. F., and J. Hersch. 2008. Double your major, double your return? *Economics of Education Review* 27 (4): 375–86.

Dickson, L. 2010. Race and gender differences in college major choice. *Annals of the American Academy of Political and Social Science* 627:108–24.

Donald, S., and D. Hamermesh. 2004. The effect of college curriculum on earnings: Accounting for non-ignorable non-Response Bias. NBER Working Paper no. 10809. Cambridge, MA: National Bureau of Economic Research, October.

Feldman, K., J. Smart, and C. Ethington. 2004. What do college students have to lose? Exploring the outcomes of differences in person-environment fits. *The Journal of Higher Education* 75 (5): 528–55.

Freeman, R. 1971. *The labor market for college-trained manpower.* Cambridge, MA: Harvard University Press.

———. 1975. Legal "cobwebs": A recursive model of the market for new lawyers. *The Review of Economics and Statistics* 57 (2): 171–79.

———. 1976. A cobweb model of the supply and starting salary of new engineers. *Industrial and Labor Relations Review* 29 (2): 236–48.

Freeman, R., E. Jin, and C.-Y. Shen. 2004. Where do US trained science engineering PhDs come from? NBER Working Paper no. 10554. Cambridge, MA: National Bureau of Economic Research, June.

Gottfredson, G. D., and J. L. Holland. 1996. *Dictionary of Holland occupational codes,* 3rd ed. Odessa, FL: Psychological Assessment Resources.

Grubb, W. N., and M. Lazerson. 2005. Vocationalism in higher education: The triumph of the education gospel. *The Journal of Higher Education* 76 (1): 1–25.

Hart-Rudman Commission on National Security. 2001. Road map for national security: Imperative for change. Available at: http://govinfo.library.unt.edu/nssg/PhaseIIIFR.pdf.

Hecker, D. 1995. Earnings of college graduates, 1993. *Monthly Labor Review* 118 (2): 3–17.

Holland, J. L. 1966. *The psychology of vocational choice.* Waltham, MA: Blaisdell.

———. 1973. *Making vocational choices.* Englewood Cliffs, NJ: Prentice-Hall.

Kremer, M. 1993. The O-ring theory of economic development. *The Quarterly Journal of Economics* 108 (3): 551–75.

Kremer, M., and D. Levy. 2003. Peer effects and alcohol use among college students. NBER Working Paper no. 9876. Cambridge, MA: National Bureau of Economic Research, July.

Manski, C. 1993. Identification of social effects: The reflection problem. *Review of Economic Studies* 60 (3): 531–42.

Montmarquette, C., K. Cannings, and S. Mahseredjian. 2002. How do young people choose college majors? *Economics of Education Review* 21 (6): 543–56.

National Academy of Science (NAC). 2007. Rising above the gathering storm: Energizing and employing America for a brighter economic future. Washington, DC: National Academy Press.

National Center for Education Statistics. 2008. *Digest of education statistics, 2007.* US Department of Education (NCES 2008-022).

National Science Foundation. 1989. *Science and engineering indicators.*

———. 2004. *Science and engineering indicators.* NSB 04-01.

Oi, W. 1974. Scientific manpower forecasts from the viewpoint of a dismal scientist. Princeton University Industrial Relations Section Working Paper 47.

Pascarella, E. T., and P. T. Terenzini. 2005. *How college affects students: A third decade of research.* San Francisco: Jossey-Bass.

Pashigian, B. 1977. The market for lawyers: The determinants of the demand for and supply of lawyers. *Journal of Law and Economics* 20 (1): 53–85.

Pryor, J. H., S. Hurtado, V. B. Saenz, J. L. Santos, and W. S. Korn. 2007. The American freshman: Forty-year trends, 1966–2006. University of California, Los Angeles. Higher Education Research Institute. Available at: http://www.gseis.ucla.edu/heri/40yrtrends.php.

Rosen, D., K. Holmberg, and J. L. Holland. 1989. *The college majors finder.* Odessa, FL: Psychological Assessment Resources.

Ryoo, J., and S. Rosen. 2004. The engineering labor market. *Journal of Political Economy* 112 (1): S110–40.

Sacerdote, B. 2001. Peer effects with random assignment: Results for Dartmouth roommates. *The Quarterly Journal of Economics* 116 (2): 681–704.

Saenz, V. B., and D. S. Barrera. 2007. *Findings from the 2005 College Student Survey (CSS): National aggregates.* Los Angeles: Higher Education Research Institute.

Sethi, S. J., and S. Shi. 2008. Major migration by college at UTPA. Available at: http://www.texis-air.org/conference/2008/presentations/C3_Major_Migration-Feb_2008-Tair.ppt#256.

Smart, J. C., K. A. Feldman, and C. A. Ethington. 2000. *Academic disciplines: Holland's theory and the study of college students and faculty.* Nashville, TN: Vanderbilt University Press.

Teitelbaum, M. 2007. Testimony before the Subcommittee on Technology and Innovation, Committee on Science and Technology, US House of Representatives. Washington, DC. Available at: http://democrats.science.house.gov/Media/File/Commdocs/hearings/2007/tech/06nov/Teitelbaum_testimony.pdf

II

Universities as Firms in a Global Market

3

Coming to America

Where Do International Doctorate Students Study and How Do US Universities Respond?

John Bound and Sarah Turner

Globalization and *internationalization* are two of the most widely used (and overused) terms in contemporary higher education discourse. There is no question that doctorate education at US universities has drawn an increasing number of students from around the world in recent decades. The growth of foreign students in US doctorate education may produce a wide range of benefits and costs for universities. Foreign graduate students may enhance output in science and engineering—including research innovations—and contribute to teaching in undergraduate and professional education. As foreign students increase the supply of workers with advanced degrees, the flow into doctorate education may also change the wage structure for those with advanced degrees in science and engineering fields (Bound and Turner 2006).

One point is clear: the expansion of foreign student participation in US colleges and universities is far from uniform. The flow of foreign students has been particularly marked outside the most highly ranked programs and at public sector universities.

In this chapter, we begin by describing the trends in doctorate attainment among foreign students at US universities. We distinguish significant trends by country of origin and type of US doctorate program. Our analysis demonstrates substantial shifts in country of origin over the last three

John Bound is professor of economics at the University of Michigan, and a research associate of the National Bureau of Economic Research. Sarah Turner is university professor of economics and education at the University of Virginia, and a research associate of the National Bureau of Economic Research.

We would like to thank Casey Cox and Xiaohuan Lan for exemplary research assistance. We are grateful to Michael Teitelbaum and Charles Clotfelter for excellent comments.

decades among doctorate students, with the growth in foreign students coming largely from Asian countries, including China and India. In the main, the growth in foreign PhD students has led to expansion in program size, with this growth concentrated at programs at public institutions and those programs outside the most highly ranked.

The expansion of foreign participation in doctorate education is notably distinguished from expansion of foreign participation in other margins of US higher education, such as undergraduate education and professional training. Not only does country of student origin differ markedly, but so does institutional destination and source of funding. Highlighting the comparison between the internationalization of doctorate education and undergraduate education serves to sharpen understanding of the impact of foreign doctoral students in the production of university research and undergraduate education. In section 3.2, we present evidence relevant to these points.

Rising numbers of foreign students and the associated expansion of doctorate education may impact undergraduate education through complementarities in the university production function. We consider the link between the number of undergraduates, their distribution by field, and the scale of doctorate training. Increased foreign flows of graduate students may serve to lower the cost of undergraduate degree production resulting in expansion in undergraduate majors; alternatively, the flow of foreign students may have substantial complementarity with university research outputs. It follows that those institutions with the highest benefits from extra products in research and teaching generated by additional graduate students will have been most likely to recruit from the expanding pool of foreign doctorate students. Data on changes in undergraduate concentrations and sources of funding for graduate students provide some evidence: in the main, effects of foreign flows on undergraduate degree production are small in magnitude, while there is corresponding evidence that expansions in foreign PhDs in recent years have come with expansion in research funding. Doctorate student flows in the sciences are concurrently outputs of university education and inputs to the production of research and, to a much more modest extent, teaching.

3.1 Setting the Stage: The Flows of Foreign PhDs over Time by Country of Origin and University Destination

3.1.1 Basic Trends

While foreign students have been drawn to US universities since the first part of the twentieth century, there has been an unambiguous rise in PhDs awarded to students from abroad from the late 1950s to the mid-1990s, with considerable acceleration in growth concentrated in science and engineering fields beginning in the late 1970s.[1] The *Survey of Earned Doctorates* provides a census of doctorates awarded by US universities by country of origin from the late 1950s to the present, and we use these data to show the broad trends by field in figure 3.1.[2] In economics and engineering, degrees awarded to students from abroad have outnumbered those awarded to US students for a number of years; in all but the life sciences, the foreign-born share has equaled or exceeded the share of US-born PhD recipients.

Focusing on explaining the rise in the participation of students from abroad in US doctorate programs, Bound, Turner, and Walsh (2009) emphasize that expanding undergraduate attainment in countries like South Korea and India produced increased demand for US doctorate education. In addition, sharp changes in political circumstances in countries like China opened a new port of entry to US graduate education that had been largely closed in the 1960s and 1970s. A further explanatory factor on the supply side of US graduate education is that substantial increases in public support for science and engineering research (and, in turn, graduate education) generate a response that may be particularly strong among students from abroad.[3]

A point of emphasis in prior descriptions of the doctorate education market is that the pattern of international flows differs quite markedly by country of origin, program characteristics, and university control and resources (see Black and Stephan [2007]) and Bound, Turner, and Walsh [2009] for further discussion). Understanding these patterns requires consideration of the nature of demand among foreign students and, significantly, the supply-side response of US universities in the context of differential funding structures for graduate education and university research across institutions.

1. Note that even in the first part of the twentieth century, universities in the United States attracted a substantial number of students from abroad, particularly in the sciences. In the period from 1936 to 1956, nearly 20 percent of PhDs in engineering and about 12 percent of PhDs in the life sciences were awarded to students who had completed undergraduate studies abroad. Bound, Turner, and Walsh (2009), and Blanchard, Bound, and Turner (2008) provide additional discussion of long-term trends in doctorate receipt by country of origin; this introductory section draws substantially on these earlier papers.

2. The *Survey of Earned Doctorates* is an individual-level census of recipients of doctorates at US institutions. Because survey participation is often coupled with the formal process of degree receipt, response rates have been quite high. Note that we focus our analysis on trends in doctorate degree recipients, though it would be conceptually preferable to examine all enrolled students; data on the latter group are much more limited in time horizon and do not allow for the examination of country of origin (see *Survey of Graduate Students and Postdoctorates in Science and Engineering,* conducted by the National Science Foundation [NSF] and National Institutes of Health [NIH]).

3. When funding in the United States for science (and, in turn, graduate education in the sciences) increases, the pool of students from abroad with preparation in scientific fields who are well-positioned to shift into US PhD programs may be relatively larger than the similar pool of recent BA degree recipients from US universities in the sciences. As such, the elasticity of demand among foreign students may be somewhat larger than among US students if foreign students are simply choosing where to attend graduate school rather than weighing the choice between a graduate program and an alternate profession. In turn, short term enrollment expansion in response to funding expansion may come disproportionately from foreign students.

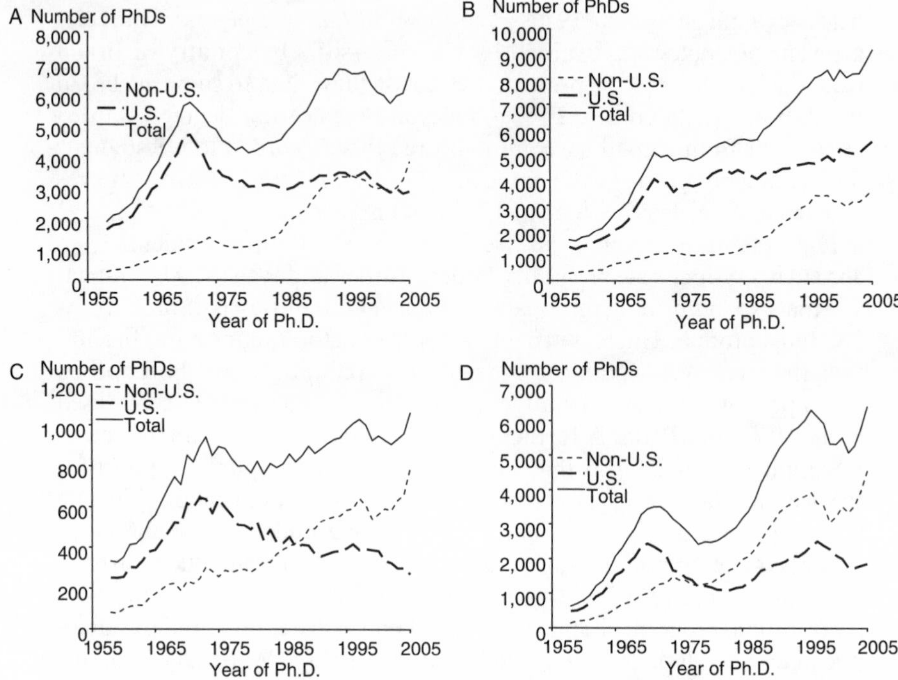

Fig. 3.1 Degrees awarded by US universities and national origin, 1958–2005: *A*, Physical Sciences; *B*, Life Sciences; *C*, Economics; *D*, Engineering

Source: NSF, *Survey of Earned Doctorates* microdata. National origin is defined by the country in which an individual went to high school. Fields defined using NSF classification, from SED annual reports.

3.1.2 Changes by Country of Origin

There is considerable variation in the source of doctoral students from abroad by country of origin, and the patterns of attendance by country have changed markedly over time in distribution and scale. Table 3.1 shows the distribution of PhDs from US institutions in science and engineering fields by country of origin for the decade from 1966 to 1975 and the more recent decade from 1996 to 2005. Much of the growth has come from new demand for advanced study in science and engineering from countries rapidly climbing a development trajectory; particularly South Korea, India, Taiwan, and, more recently, China. Black and Stephan (2007) note the relatively recent concentration of doctorate students from these four Asian countries, which account for about 60 percent of doctorate recipients among non-US residents in the most recent year.

Why students from some countries are particularly likely to pursue doctorate education in the United States surely depends on opportunity costs. In general, demand for doctorate education will be lower for those students

Table 3.1 **Doctorates awarded by US universities by student country of origin, science, and engineering fields**

	1966–1975	Rank 1966–1975	1996–2005	Rank 1996–2005
China	945	5	25,334	1
India	5,255	1	9,520	2
Korea	1,252	4	7,905	3
Taiwan	4,389	2	6,820	4
USSR	8		2,958	5
Turkey	481		2,403	6
Canada	2,274	3	2,356	7
Mexico	311		1,635	8
Germany	528		1,614	9
Brazil	401		1,420	10
Japan	816	7	1,126	
Iran	684	8	996	
Greece	532	10	931	
United Kingdom	916	6	892	
Israel	636	9	342	
United States	98,679		105,955	
Total	131,946		213,113	

Source: NSF, *Survey of Earned Doctorates* microdata.
Notes: National origin is defined by the country in which an individual went to high school. Fields defined using NSF classification, from SED annual report.

with more abundant home country opportunities and, in turn, students from countries with relatively substantial university systems will be unlikely to study in the United States unless they can attend top tier doctorate programs.[4] What matters for students potentially pursuing study in the United States is the expected return to a US PhD program relative to the best alternative in the home country. Students in each country face a choice based on the expected benefit to doctorate study in the United States, and an expected return to persistence in the home country, which may include attending graduate school in the home country or pursuing some other vocation. Home

4. The decision by students from different countries to pursue doctorate education in the United States is in many respects similar to the occupational choice selection problem set forth in the Roy model (1951). Because options for post-baccalaureate study vary appreciably across countries, it follows that the opportunity cost of pursuing a doctorate degree at a US university varies among countries of origin. The result is that there are differences across countries in the total share of a nation's PhD recipients trained in the United States and variation in the representation of students by the quality of graduate programs in the United States. The predictions we outline follow from the case where expected success as a PhD in the home country and the United States are positively correlated, and the variance in returns is greater in the United States than the home country (e.g., the rewards to a top mathematician—relative to a median mathematician—will be greater in the United States than in home country). To this end, US programs tend to be dominant in the top tail of the international distribution of program quality.

country university systems differ and, as a result, the opportunity cost of pursuing a doctorate degree at a US university varies among countries of origin. What is more, receipt of a doctorate from a US university may well provide increased opportunities for employment in the United States.[5]

In the cross section, both the level of undergraduate degree attainment in foreign countries and the extent to which there are established doctorate-level programs in these countries have a substantial effect on the flow of PhD students to US institutions. Countries without large university systems but with recent expansion in undergraduate attainment will have the greatest representation of doctorate students at US institutions; students from these countries will also be represented in other well-developed university systems such as the United Kingdom, Canada, and Australia. To this end, it is not surprising that the ratio of PhDs awarded by US institutions to home country institutions is high for countries like China (0.5), South Korea (.3), and India (.75); relative to European countries like France (0.013) or the United Kingdom (0.003) (Bound, Turner, and Walsh 2009, table 1).

3.1.3 Foreign PhD Flow By Program Rank

For countries in which forgone opportunities are close to those in the United States—for example, countries with large and well-established university sectors—only a select few individuals will pursue graduate studies in the United States. These individuals will be among those with relatively high ability and receive admission offers from some of the best programs in the United States.[6] In contrast, individuals from countries with much more limited higher education systems will have fewer opportunities for graduate study in their home countries and will be much more likely to choose to pursue graduate study at a US university. In turn, these individuals may choose to come to the United States to pursue studies at programs outside the most highly ranked departments. To illustrate, the proportion of a country's PhD recipients receiving degrees from top five programs differs markedly across countries (and, to some degree, over time). For a num-

5. Most foreign students hold F-status (student) visas while in school and; to work in the United States requires adjusting the student visa to the H1B status for high-skilled visa employment with the assistance of a institutional sponsor. As such, limited provision of visas and the restrictions related to HIB employment often leave foreign doctorate recipients with a more limited set of employment options than permanent visa holders and US residents. Using an exogenous change in visa status associated with the Chinese Student Protection Act of 1992, Lan (2008) shows that permanent visa holders are about 24 percent less likely to take post-doctoral positions than temporary visa holders.

6. A related implication is that the average quality or achievement of students and the associated graduate programs selected of PhDs receiving PhDs in the United States from a particular country is inversely related to the share of a country's potential doctorate students completing advanced study in the United States. Less formally, students from a country like France receiving PhDs in the United States will likely be among the best in their home country cohorts, and attend the very top tier doctorate institutions like MIT and Stanford, while students from a country like Turkey will be spread among a broader range of US institutions as their home country options are more limited.

ber of Asian countries—notably Taiwan, South Korea, and China—PhD recipients in science are underrepresented in the top five departments and are much less likely to receive their degrees from these programs than PhD recipients from the United States in these fields. For example, while students from China are about 15.5 percent of all chemistry PhDs, they are only 5.3 percent of degree recipients from top five programs. At the other extreme, students from Canada and European countries tend to be represented in the top programs in shares in excess of their overall representation among PhD recipients from US universities.

Over time, much of the growth in doctorate education has come outside the most highly ranked programs and, in turn, expansion in foreign doctorate receipt at US institutions has been most concentrated outside the most elite—or highly ranked—programs. Figure 3.2 presents trends in doctorate awards to PhDs in selected fields distinguishing programs in the top fifteen, ranks sixteen to thirty, ranks thirty-one to fifty, outside the top fifty, and unranked. What is unambiguously clear is that in chemistry, physics, and biochemistry, foreign degree expansion is concentrated outside the top fifty and starts a dramatic upward trend in the 1980s. In engineering, the growth

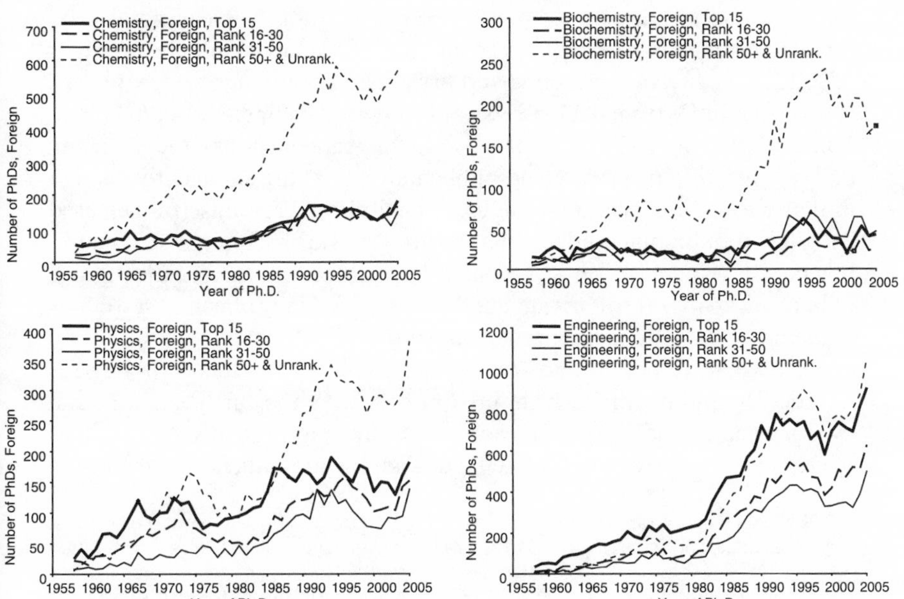

Fig. 3.2 Degrees awarded by US universities to non-US citizens by program rank, 1958–2005

Source: NSF, *Survey of Earned Doctorates* microdata. National origin is defined by the country in which an individual went to high school. Fields defined using NSF classification, from SED annual reports.

in degrees awarded occurs more broadly across program ranks, though as we will subsequently discuss, large public universities have greater representation in the top tier of engineering than in other scientific fields.

3.1.4 Expansion of Doctorate Education by Type of University

The US market for doctorate education is differentiated and highly stratified. Of the more than 3,000 four-year institutions of higher education, 413 universities in the United States awarded doctorates in 2002, with the mean number of degrees per institution ninety-seven, and the median number thirty-eight degrees. Overall, production is relatively concentrated, with twenty institutions awarding 27 percent of the 2002 total of 39,955 degrees.[7]

Both private and public universities award PhDs, with public universities dominant in the number of institutions awarding degrees and the scale of doctorate programs. In 2005, public universities awarded over 15,000 degrees in science and engineering fields, compared to about 6,500 degrees awarded by private universities. This margin has grown appreciably since 1960, when the comparative totals were 2,989 and 2,011 doctorate degrees awarded by public and private universities, respectively. At the same time, a small number of elite private universities often occupy the top program rankings, though there is unquestioned competition between public and private universities for faculty, students, and resources. While the products of graduate education at public and private universities are widely seen as substitutes (PhDs from the University of Michigan compete with PhDs from Yale and the University of Pennsylvania for academic jobs), the financing and organization of private and public universities are sufficiently distinct in that we might expect quite different institutional response to increased demand from foreign students. Substantial subsidies from the state, combined with a much larger scale of undergraduate education, distinguish public universities from private universities, potentially affecting responses to increased demand from foreign students.

Figure 3.3 presents broad trends in the number of doctorate degrees awarded by public and private institutions, with the further distinction by Carnegie classification.[8] In each graph, there are broadly two regimes of expansion—a peak in the late 1960s, and a subsequent upturn in the

7. While this concentration is considerable, it is appreciably less than at the start of the century or the middle of the twentieth century. The interval of expansion in US higher education between 1950 and the early 1970s brought many new entrants to the higher education market. Focusing on the interval between 1958 and 1972, Bowen and Rudenstine (1992) document the extraordinary growth in the number of institutions and departments operating PhD programs. In economics, the number of PhD granting institutions increased nearly 90 percent from 57 to 108, while in mathematics the number of programs increased more than 130 percent, from 60 to 139.

8. We employ the Carnegie codes (as classified in 1994) to distinguish broad types of institutions. The primary categories are as follows.

Research Universities 1: Award fifty or more doctoral degrees1 each year. In addition, annually more than $40 million in federal support.

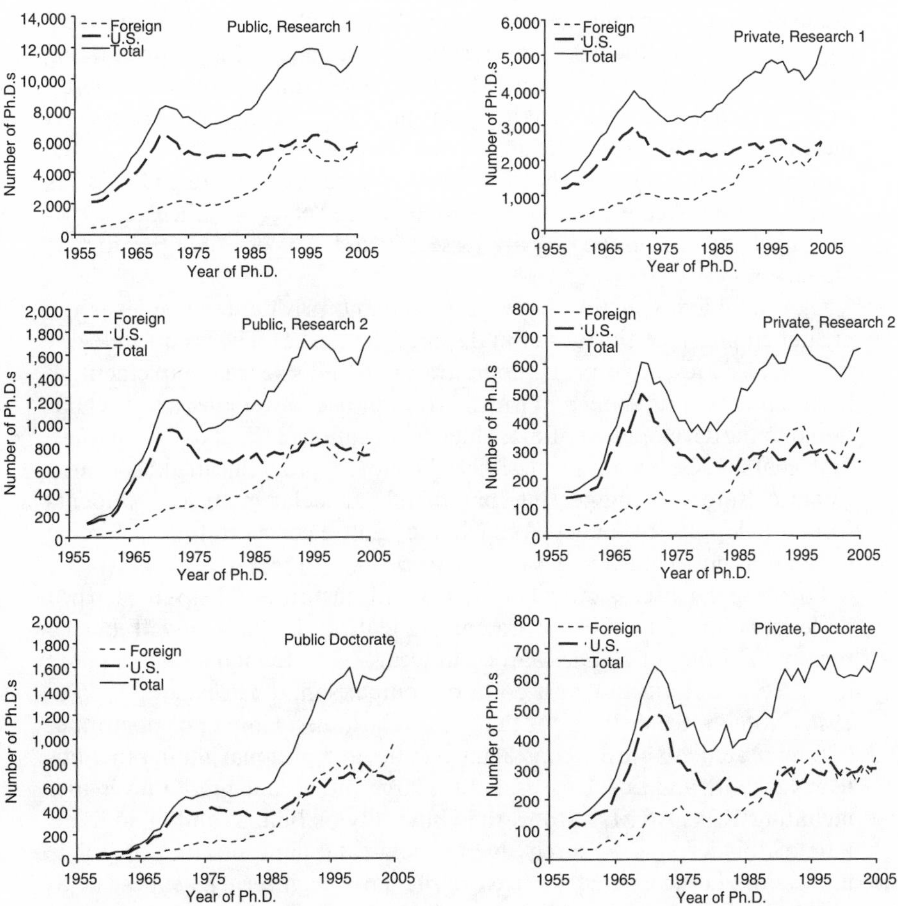

Fig. 3.3 Degrees awarded by US universities to US and foreign students by institutional control and Carnegie Classification, 1958–2005

Source: NSF, *Survey of Earned Doctorates* microdata. National origin is defined by the country in which an individual went to high school. Fields defined using NSF classification, from SED annual reports.

1980s—with the relative magnitude of fluctuations over time differing by type of institution. Private Research 1 and public Research 1 Universities have experienced more muted changes than the other institution types in the number of doctorates awarded. A clear point from the graphs is that while the early expansion was fueled by a substantial rise (and then contraction) in domestic PhDs, much of the growth in the later period comes through

Research Universities 2: Award fifty or more doctoral degrees1 each year. In addition, they receive annually between $15.5 million and $40 million in federal support.

Doctoral Universities 1 & 2: Award annually at least ten doctoral degrees—in three or more disciplines—or twenty or more doctoral degrees in one or more disciplines.

the expansion in the number of foreign PhD students in the science and engineering fields. Indeed, at all but the institutions in the doctorate category, the number of PhDs awarded to US residents only increased modestly from 1980 to the present. Strikingly, the number of foreign PhD recipients increased by a factor of 3.25 in the public sector overall, and 5.15 in the public doctorate sector. In the private sector, expansion in foreign PhDs has also been a significant force, with increases of 230 percent in the Research 1 sector, 390 percent in the Research 2 sector, and 270 percent in the doctorate sector.

One notable distinction between public and private universities is the greater emphasis of the former in the applied sciences. The unique integration of basic research, professional training, and science complementing local industry is fundamental to American public universities and foundational to the development of mass higher education at the start of the twentieth century (Goldin and Katz 1999). Doctorate programs in areas related to agriculture and engineering may be of particular interest to students from developing economies. As such, the relative concentration of foreign students at public universities is not surprising.

Focusing the discussion to consider specific institutions helps to sharpen understanding of the flow of foreign students at the PhD level. Table 3.2 presents a listing of PhDs awarded in total and to foreign students in the most recent decade and, as a point of comparison, the decade of 1966 to 1975. Notably, the institutions that award the largest number of doctorates to foreign students are not coastal universities in traditional immigrant hubs like New York and Los Angeles, but the large, public land grant universities including Texas A&M, Purdue, the University of Illinois, and Ohio State. Part of this response is surely due to the greater concentration of public universities in the applied sciences, particularly engineering, as these fields may have close ties to local industries, while also being of greatest demand among foreign students from developing countries.

3.1.5 The Question of "Crowd Out": Evidence and Supply Elasticity In Doctorate Education

While there is no question that foreign participation in US doctorate education has increased, it is less clear whether this expansion represents net new doctorate awards or some displacement of potential US doctorate students. The growth of foreign students among overall PhD recipients and PhD recipients from US institutions affects the flow of potential US doctorate students through two potential channels. First, US students may face increased competition for slots (admission) to graduate programs. At the most competitive graduate programs, where there is typically considerable excess demand for enrollment, the admission of additional foreign students is likely to be accompanied by reductions in admissions of domestic students. Second, beyond potential crowd out effects in higher education, the overall growth in the number of foreign doctorates (both those who obtained

Table 3.2 **Doctorate degrees conferred in science and engineering by top producing public and private universities**

	1966–1975		1996–2005	
	Foreign	Total	Foreign	Total
Public universities				
Stanford University	744	3,004	1,639	4,069
MIT	958	3,528	1,530	4,297
Cornell University	941	2,881	1,485	3,149
University of Southern California	256	960	1,298	1,910
Columbia University	522	1,769	1,175	2,075
Johns Hopkins University	301	1,280	911	2,702
Harvard University	409	2,102	854	2,796
University of Pennsylvania	542	1,767	849	2,041
Princeton University	364	1,363	824	1,610
Northwestern University	364	1,614	798	1,997
Public universities				
Texas A&M University	338	1,548	2,018	3,455
Ohio State University	561	2,505	1,945	3,364
Purdue University	718	3,294	1,944	3,410
University of Illinois	1,136	4,037	1,933	4,068
University of Texas (Austin)	377	1,994	1,786	3,519
University of Michigan (Ann Arbor)	629	2,854	1,720	4,042
University of Wisconsin (Madison)	1,064	3,924	1,709	4,087
University of Minnesota (Twin Cities)	814	2,479	1,690	3,614
University of California (Berkeley)	1,452	4,500	1,608	4,783
Pennsylvania State University	381	1,838	1,590	3,237

Source: NSF, *Survey of Earned Doctorates* microdata.
Notes: National origin is defined by the country in which an individual went to high school. Fields defined using NSF classification, from SED annual report.

their degrees in the United States and those who migrated after receiving their degrees) is likely to have had a substantial effect on the labor market returns to PhD awards in science (Bound and Turner 2006).

Measuring the degree of direct crowd out in graduate education is not straightforward empirically: changes in the rate at which US students complete PhD programs may reflect both increased demand among foreign students, and other factors such as funding shocks, which would lead to increases in scale of graduate programs. While a number of studies have attempted to estimate the magnitude of potential crowd out effects, there is little conclusive evidence to support substantial crowd out effects.[9]

9. Using data from the *Survey of Graduate Students and Postdocs* and variation within academic departments, Regets (2001) finds a largely positive association between enrollment of US students and foreign students. Borjas (2004) uses within institution variation in graduate student enrollment measured in the IPEDS surveys and finds a negative effect of foreign enrollment on the level of enrollment of white men, though little effect on domestic enrollment in aggregate. Finally, Zhang (2004) used the *Survey of Earned Doctorates* and reports essentially

The case of the sharp increase in demand among Chinese graduate students beginning in the early 1980s presents a relatively clear opportunity to assess the adjustment of the US market to a sharp demand shock. Focusing on the field of physics as an illustration, consider the change in doctorate completion by year of program entry for Chinese students, other foreign students, and US residents (Bound, Turner, and Walsh 2009). At top ranked programs, the number of additional students from China is small and there is little discernable change in the overall number of PhDs awarded. Outside the most highly ranked programs, the number of Chinese students receiving PhDs from universities outside the top fifty increased from 7 to 202 between the 1980 year of graduate entry and the 1985 year of graduate school entry. Notably, this large "shock" produced no notable decline in PhDs awarded to US students at these institutions, with this number actually rising slightly from 164 to 199, while the number of students from other countries receiving PhDs also rose over this interval of graduate school entry. Data for other fields show similar patterns. Remarkably, this large cohort of Chinese students had no discernable impact on the number of US, or for that matter, other foreign students receiving PhDs in the sciences. The example produced by the particularly large and rapid influx of Chinese students in the early 1980s may be hard to reproduce in other periods, both given its scale and its arrival during a period in which funding for the sciences in general—and the physical sciences in particular—was expanding rapidly. Nevertheless, this evidence does suggest that it is plausible that realized expansions in the representation of foreign doctorate students need not crowd out domestic doctorate attainment by US students.

Our conclusion is that outside the most highly ranked programs, many doctorate programs are relatively elastic in scale.[10] "Supply elasticity" at the PhD level is much greater outside the top tier universities, particularly outside the top fifty; these are institutions with programs often below the minimum efficient scale, many of which experienced sharp declines in domestic student interest in the mid-1970s. In turn, at the universities and programs where the expansion of foreign doctorate recipients has been the largest, our interpretation is that crowd out is minimal in the sense that additional doctorate recipients from abroad do not substitute for domestic PhD production at the institutional level.

no evidence of crowd-out of native students associated with additional PhDs awarded to native students. A limitation of this broad line of inquiry is that expansion in the representation of foreign students in US graduate programs may well be endogenously related to other factors such as the availability of funding which simultaneously affect the demand for graduate students.

10. Indeed, for the programs that are unranked or ranked very modestly, the period of growth in the 1960s and early 1970s represented both expansion in scale and the entry of new programs; the entry of new programs in this category was extraordinary, with a threefold increase in the primary science fields. As the market contracted in the 1970s, and then expanded in the 1980s, the adjustment came in terms of the scale of programs, with apparently few programs either exiting or entering the market.

Proceeding from this assessment, we offer the marked comparison between doctorate students and undergraduate students from abroad in the next section, as differences in country of origin, sources of funding, and institutional destination are substantial. In section 3.3, we consider the expansion in doctorate education generated by foreign students in the context of the university production function, focusing on the link with university research support and undergraduate education.

3.2 The Differentiation of Doctorate Education and Undergraduate Education for Foreign Students

To understand the distinct context of the participation of foreign students in doctorate education, it is instructive to examine broad comparisons with the flow of international students to US undergraduate programs. Overall, one might be tempted to regard the flow of undergraduate students and graduate students from abroad as closely coupled trends. Figure 3.4 shows total enrollment of graduate and undergraduate students from abroad at US colleges and universities from 1955 to 2005; the trends are largely overlapping, and the levels for 1965 and 2000 are close to identical. However, this broad correlation hides substantial differences in country of origin, source of support, and institutional destination. Moreover, foreign students are a much larger share of doctorate recipients from US institutions than under-

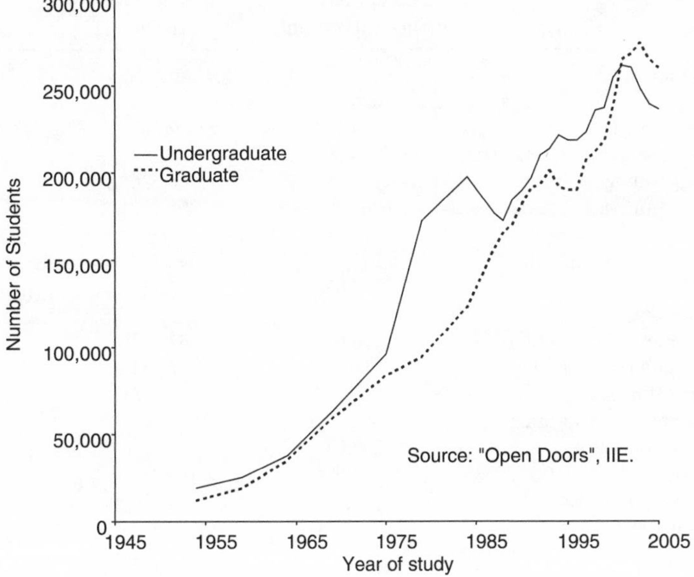

Fig. 3.4 Comparing growth of foreign undergraduate and doctorate enrollment
Source: Enrollment data are from *Open Doors* surveys (IIE, various years).

graduate degree recipients and, as such, shifts in the pattern of matriculation among foreign doctorate students would likely have substantial equilibrium effects and implications for university research.

3.2.1 College and University Choices in the United States

Graduate students are much more likely to be concentrated at public universities, while undergraduates are more likely to gravitate to private institutions. An obvious—if tautological—explanation is that many private institutions, such as liberal arts colleges, do not have substantial graduate programs in the sciences or do not have graduate programs at all. However, the distribution of noncitizens enrolled at the undergraduate level at US institutions is appreciably different than domestic students, as shown in table 3.3. While noncitizens are about 2.1 percent of aggregate undergraduate enrollment, these students comprise about 3.2 percent of the undergraduate body at private institutions, where they are even more likely (4.4 percent) to be represented among the institutions awarding PhD degrees.

A number of institutions in the United States, such as Boston University, Northeastern University in Massachusetts, and Babson College in the northeast, actively recruit foreign students. At Babson College, about one-quarter of the students are from abroad, while at Boston University, inter-

Table 3.3 Citizenship of undergraduate enrollment, 2005

	US citizens & permanent residents	Temporary residents	Percent temporary residents
Public institutions			
Doctorate-granting institutions	3,020,268	70,864	2.3
First professional institutions	89,408	2,163	2.4
Master's-granting institutions	1,849,660	40,251	2.1
Bachelor's-granting institutions	277,580	6,536	2.3
Two-year institutions	5,967,200	91,920	1.5
Other/unknown degree level	90,515	397	0.4
Two-year institutions and other	6,057,715	92,317	1.5
Total, public	11,294,631	212,131	1.8
Private institutions			
Doctorate-granting institutions	716,683	33,083	4.4
First professional institutions	117,761	2,953	2.4
Master's-granting institutions	1,003,922	36,978	3.6
Bachelor's-granting institutions	698,870	15,808	2.2
Two-year institutions	267,049	3,555	1.3
Other/unknown degree level	38,086	275	0.7
Two-year institutions and other	305,135	3,830	1.2
Total, private	2,842,371	92,652	3.2
All institutions	14,137,002	304,783	2.1

Sources: Authors' tabulations from Webcaspar. IPEDS Fall Enrollment Survey, 2005.

national students are typically about 7 percent of the freshman class (Jan 2008; Schworm 2008). Some in the field of college recruiting have posited that favorable exchange rates increase the attractiveness of US institutions, while concurrently, US universities have been more aggressively recruiting from abroad.[11] While a select few institutions are able to offer full financial aid to international students, much of the impetus for overseas recruiting is tied to the capacity of students to pay substantial tuition expenses either directly, or through home country fellowship support.

3.2.2 Country of Origin

The countries that send a high fraction of students to study in the United States at the undergraduate level are very different from those with large flows of students to US doctorate education (or graduate school, more generally). While the overall ratio of foreign undergraduate to foreign graduate students was about 0.9 in 2007, there are many countries well above and well below this ratio, as shown in table 3.4. The countries with disproportionately high representation of undergraduates enrolled in the United States relative to graduate students tend to be those with substantial income inequality. Oil-rich countries are well-represented in this list. At the other extreme, countries with relatively high representations of graduate students include countries like China and India that are on rapid development trajectories, with modest existing university infrastructure. In addition, European countries like Italy and France—with well-developed state higher education systems—appear much lower on the list; as few undergraduate from these countries pay to study in the United States, while very top tier students may pursue graduate study in the United States.

The data certainly suggest a model in which capacity to finance undergraduate education is a determinant of undergraduate enrollment. Indeed, there is some evidence that commodity price shocks—particularly oil—are an important determinant of undergraduate enrollment flows from a number of Middle Eastern countries. Figure 3.5 provides an illustration of the fluctuation in enrollment from oil-rich countries in association with oil prices. In these countries, it may well be that American undergraduate education is a luxury good, with changes in income leading to increased enrollment rates. But, a college education is certainly more than a consumption good; and it seems likely that access to capital afforded by positive oil shocks generates financing for higher education for students from these countries, as there are certainly many more well-qualified students from other countries

11. A July 2008 article, written when the dollar to pound exchange rate was about two, quotes a number of students as benefiting from the weak dollar, with the price of a US education declining relative to substitutes in the UK (Schworm 2008). For example, Martin Prochazka, a student from the Czech Republic, notes, "It wasn't the only reason but it was pretty important. I checked into London but it was twice the price."

Table 3.4 Undergraduate and graduate enrollment by country of origin, 2007

Place of origin	Undergraduate	Graduate	Total	Ratio: UG/grad
High undergraduate/graduate				
Qatar	201	27	228	7.444
Haiti	962	137	1,099	7.022
El Salvador	772	160	932	4.825
Hong Kong, China	5,148	1,594	6,742	3.230
Japan	22,247	7,008	29,255	3.175
Saudi Arabia	3,394	1,270	4,664	2.672
United Arab Emirates	523	202	725	2.589
Kuwait	1,050	421	1,471	2.494
Venezuela	2,691	1,187	3,878	2.267
Low undergraduate/graduate				
Germany	3,218	3,702	6,920	0.869
Russia	1,884	2,308	4,192	0.816
France	2,201	2,848	5,049	0.773
Ukraine	636	868	1,504	0.733
Italy	874	1,783	2,657	0.490
Taiwan	7,330	16,679	24,009	0.439
Egypt	442	1,037	1,479	0.426
India	12,581	59,570	72,151	0.211
China, PRC	9,988	47,968	57,956	0.208
World Total	233,789	266,336	500,125	0.878

Source: Open Doors 2007, "Table 2 International Students by Academic Level and Place of Origin, 2006/07."

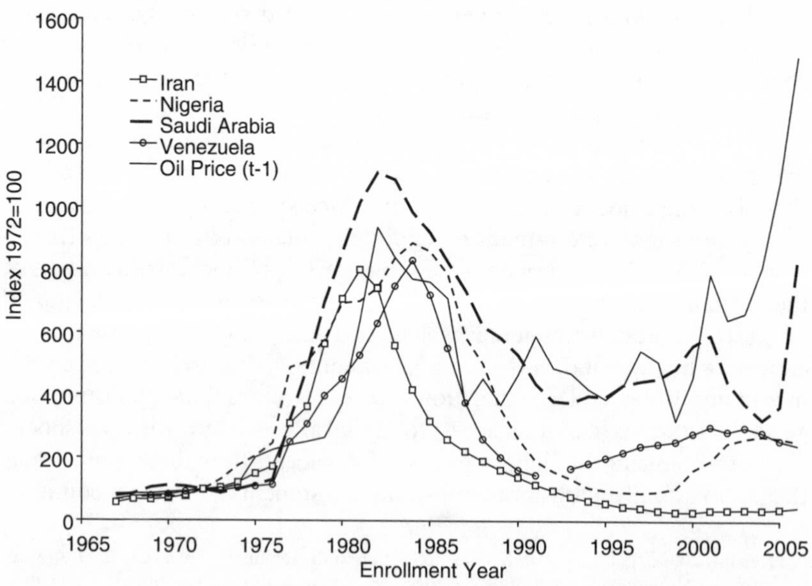

Fig. 3.5 Enrollments in the United States of students from major oil-producing countries

Sources: Enrollment data are from *Open Doors* surveys (IIE, various years); data on oil price data are from the Energy Information Administration (http://www.eia.doe.gov/aer/).

abroad who would apply to US universities if they were able to finance the tuition expenditures.[12]

One testable implication is that overall flows of graduate students should be much less sensitive to currency shocks and prices of major export goods (e.g., oil) than flows of undergraduate students. As we will pursue in more detail in subsequent sections, it is not home country financing but US university financing that is the primary source of support for foreign doctorate students; as such, we expect research funding and other determinants of university resources to be primary in determining the number of foreign doctorate students accommodated by US universities.

3.2.3 Sources of Support

It follows that we should expect to see undergraduate students heavily dependent on "own" support—paying full tuition at undergraduate institutions—while graduate students are more likely to rely on financial assistance through teaching appointments, research assistantships, and fellowships. Indeed, even as there may be many students from abroad who would like to borrow to finance investments in both undergraduate and graduate education in the United States, the absence of well-functioning international capital markets likely makes such actions impossible.

Charting the sources of support for both undergraduate and graduate students is a daunting challenge, and the following data are subject to some nontrivial problems, often recording support in broad terms like "primary," or based on imperfect institutional recording of funding sources. As international flows of students increase, better tracking of student enrollment, degree completion, and sources of support is imperative to account for the benefits and costs of globalization at US colleges and universities.

Overall, the data from Institute of International Education (IIE) show that among undergraduate students, 81.6 percent of foreign students finance their studies through "personal and family funds."[13] When we focus on doctorate students in the sciences, the distribution of funding sources is dramatically different, with only about 5 percent of foreign students relying on "own" sources as their primary support mechanism in graduate school in recent years. Indeed, foreign students are somewhat less likely to rely on own support for graduate study than their domestic peers, presumably because the latter have greater access to credit markets and family

12. To be sure, a small number of the super elite colleges and universities in the United States are able to offer need-blind admission and full financial aid to international undergraduate students; these institutions include: MIT, Harvard, Princeton, Dartmouth, Williams, and Middlebury, with most of these institutions opening aid to international students around the year 2000. See http://www.edupass.org/finaid/undergraduate.phtml for a list of universities that offer significant financial aid (both need-based and merit, but not athletic) to international students.

13. *Open Doors 2007,* "Table 15 International Students by Primary Source of Funding 2005/06 & 2006/07."

resources so they still may have an option of attending even if they are not fully funded. In turn, foreign students are somewhat more likely to have an employment source of support—either teaching assistantship or research assistantship—than their domestic US peers, while they are somewhat less likely to be supported by fellowship funding. Note that the proportion of foreign students funded through research assistantships rose markedly from the decade of the 1980s to the present, with this shift particularly prominent for students receiving their degrees from public institutions as shown in the second panel of table 3.5.

Our comparison of students from abroad at the doctorate level and undergraduate level leads to several propositions that motivate more focused consideration of the foreign students in graduate education in the next section. First, the fact that undergraduates typically pay for most—if not all—of the cost of attendance leads to quite different distributions of country of origin by level of study. In addition, the implication of the large share of students—particularly foreign students—who are funded through their doctorate studies is that their presence provides substantial benefits to the university in terms of teaching and research. In the next section, we turn to the question of how the expansion in doctorate education generated by

Table 3.5 **Sources of support for doctorate recipients in science and engineering fields by decade of PhD**

	1977–1979		1980–1989		1990–1999		2000–2005	
	US (%)	Foreign (%)	US (%)	Foreign (%)	US (%)	Foreign (%)	US (%)	Foreign (%)
				A All universities				
Teaching assistant	20.9	18.3	18.2	21.0	14.7	20.8	13.3	17.1
Research assistant	39.2	41.9	43.4	41.9	43.3	50.7	33.9	52.8
Fellowship	18.3	12.4	14.4	13.6	15.6	16.1	32.8	24.0
Loan/own/family	19.0	10.6	21.4	11.9	22.5	10.4	15.2	5.1
Others	2.6	16.7	2.6	11.6	4.0	2.1	4.8	0.9
				B Public universities				
Teaching assistant	23.8	20.3	20.5	22.6	16.4	21.9	15.4	18.2
Research assistant	39.5	43.0	43.0	41.5	42.4	52.0	36.4	56.8
Fellowship	15.0	9.3	11.6	11.9	12.8	13.6	26.7	19.2
Loan/own/family	19.9	10.6	22.8	12.2	24.8	10.7	16.6	5.0
Others	1.9	16.8	2.1	11.8	3.6	1.8	5.0	0.9
				C Private universities				
Teaching assistant	14.8	14.5	12.8	17.4	10.5	17.9	8.3	14.6
Research assistant	38.5	39.7	44.3	42.8	45.5	47.6	28.0	43.2
Fellowship	25.5	18.4	21.0	17.6	22.1	22.2	47.6	35.8
Loan/own/family	17.1	10.7	18.0	11.0	16.9	9.4	11.8	5.3
Others	4.1	16.7	4.0	11.2	4.9	2.8	4.3	1.1

Sources: Authors' tabulations. NSF, *Survey of Earned Doctorates* microdata.

foreign flows affects undergraduate degree production in both the private and public sectors of higher education.

3.3 The Effects of the Expansion of Foreign Doctorate Students on Undergraduate Education

That so many graduate students in general—and foreign doctorate students in particular—support their studies with teaching and research appointments is an implicit demonstration of the complementary role played by graduate students in the university production function. We are interested in addressing whether the complementarity is stronger in teaching or in research. Whether researchers (and the consumers of research) or undergraduate training are the most likely beneficiaries of additional graduate students represents an important dimension of university resource allocation.

While increased student demand among foreign undergraduates often comes with additional tuition dollars, foreign doctorate students often receive considerable financial support from universities. For this reason, one would expect spillovers to other dimensions of university production such as research and undergraduate education.[14] To this end, the growth of doctorate education generated by increased demand among students from abroad should make it less costly for the university to increase complementary activities like more undergraduate education or research output. Similarly, if research funding increases (e.g., positive government science shock), we would expect an increase in graduate enrollment to the extent that graduate education and research are complementary.

Our original contribution in this chapter is to explore the link between graduate flows and undergraduate flows, noting that a number of other researchers have tackled the difficult question of the link between foreign graduate flows and research output (see Black and Stephan 2007; Stuen, Mobarak, and Maskus 2007; Chellaraj, Maskus, and Mattoo 2008).

3.3.1 Undergraduate Teaching and Doctorate Education

One potential link to the expansion of doctorate training in the sciences is growth in undergraduate education. Without establishing strict causal-

14. What motivates this analysis is a model of economies of scope in the production of graduate education, undergraduate education, and research in the university. With the presence of some economies of scope in the university production function of such that the total cost (TC) of production of graduate education along with undergraduate education and research must be less than the production of these activities separately, implying the following expression is positive: $SE_G = (TC\{0, Q_G, 0\} + TC\{Q_U, 0, Q_R\} - TC\{Q_U, Q_G, Q_R\})/(TC\{Q_U, Q_G, Q_R\})$, where Q_G is the number of graduate students enrolled, Q_U is the number of undergraduates, and Q_R is the quantity of research produced. If additional doctorate students represent exogenous shifts, in the sense that at each level of financial support more students are willing to enroll, the effective price of complementary activities declines and we would expect more undergraduate output or research output in proportion to the degree of complementarity.

ity, complementarity in production between undergraduate and graduate education in the sciences would be indicated by a positive link between enrollment and degree attainment in the two areas. One mechanism is that a large influx of graduate students would make it attractive to expand undergraduate education.[15] In turn, undergraduate education in the sciences might be affected on two margins: (a) overall increases in student numbers (e.g., expansion proportionate with the university), and (b) a relative increase in undergraduate majors in fields associated with the expansion of graduate education.

To quantify the link between graduate flows and undergraduate flows, we are interested in estimating relationships of the form:

$$\ln \text{UM}_{ijt} = \alpha_i + \delta_j + \lambda_t + \beta \ln \text{PhD}_{ijt} + \varepsilon_{ijt},$$

where *i* indicates field, *j* indicates university, *t* indicates year, UM specifies undergraduate majors, and PhDs indicates the scale of the doctorate program. In turn, the estimated parameter β is the elasticity of undergraduate majors in field *i* with respect to additional PhDs in field *i*. One explanation for concurrent changes in PhDs and undergraduate majors is aggregate university expansion. Our interest is particularly focused on how changes in doctorate program scale generated by (potentially) exogenous shifts in foreign students affect undergraduate concentrations. To capture these changes we can focus on foreign PhDs as the key explanatory variable, what might be called the reduced form relationship, or present instrumental variables (IV) estimates with foreign PhDs serving as the instrument for all PhDs, as increases in participation from foreign students are plausibly (though perhaps not entirely) a result of home country changes exogenous to the US education market.

Table 3.6 presents estimates over the extended period from 1970 to the present of the effect of PhD expansion in the sciences on BA levels. Our within institution estimates tend to be precisely estimated, with effects of very modest magnitude. The IV estimates suggest elasticity estimates of 0.09 at public institutions and 0.12 at private institutions, implying that a 10 percent increase in science doctorate cohort size would be associated with an increase in undergraduate majors on the order of 0.9 percent and 1.2 percent respectively. Probing these estimates more deeply, we note that the estimate for private institutions is much smaller at the Research 1 institutions than at the other types of private doctorate institutions. We have also investigated the effects of PhD flows on relative concentrations of undergraduate majors in the sciences (share of science majors within the institution), and we find essentially no significant effects.

In discussing these results, it is worth emphasizing that while the results

15. Alternatively, increased local undergraduate demand would lower the cost of recruiting additional graduate students.

Table 3.6 Link between science PhDs and undergraduate participation in sciences

	Public (1)	Private (2)	Public (3)	Private (4)	Public (IV, foreign) (5)	Private (IV, foreign) (6)
Ln Foreign PhD	0.0432***	0.0556***				
	(0.007)	(0.012)				
Ln All PhD			0.0945***	0.0972***	0.0901***	0.1231***
			(0.007)	(0.013)	(0.014)	(0.025)
Constant	6.4705***	5.7660***	6.1781***	5.5083***	6.2442***	5.4720***
	(0.028)	(0.046)	(0.033)	(0.054)	(0.060)	(0.099)
N	5,286	2,571	5,859	2,952	5,286	2,571
R^2	0.27	0.183	0.302	0.187	n/a	n/a
Number of inst	197	99	207	116	197	99

Source: Authors' tabulations from restricted use *Survey of Earned Doctorates.*
Note: estimates in log levels with year and institution fixed effects
***Significant at the 1 percent level.

may be unsurprising to many observers, they contribute important evidence to an otherwise speculative discussion. One explanation for the very modest effects of PhD supply shocks on undergraduate education is that there may be little net change in course offerings or reductions in student faculty ratios that would make science majors more attractive to undergraduate students. New graduate students employed as teaching assistants may simply substitute for line faculty (who, in turn, may allocate more time to research), or adjunct faculty. A second, and perhaps more persuasive argument, is that additional graduate students—particularly those from abroad—adding to program size may not be deployed to teaching functions, but research functions; our pursuit of this latter hypothesis follows.

Still, there is sufficiently long history of discussion of the role of graduate students in undergraduate teaching and the expansion of university programming that we investigate the extent to which the circumstances of the 1960s were different fundamentally than those operating since the 1980s. Figure 3.6 shows the long trend in BA degrees awarded and PhD degrees awarded in the US over a century, and the broad correlation is unmistakable. However, a closer look at the data for doctorate granting institutions—that is, focusing on BA degrees awarded in the sciences by corresponding institutions—shows a much different correlation (or lack thereof) in figure 3.7. While undergraduate degree attainment continued to rise into the early 1980s, this was the period when doctorate programs were largely contracting; thereafter, contraction in undergraduate degrees corresponded with growing doctorate receipt (particularly among foreign students) in the 1980s. The most recent period shows little link between changes in undergraduate and graduate education in either the public or private sectors. Looking back

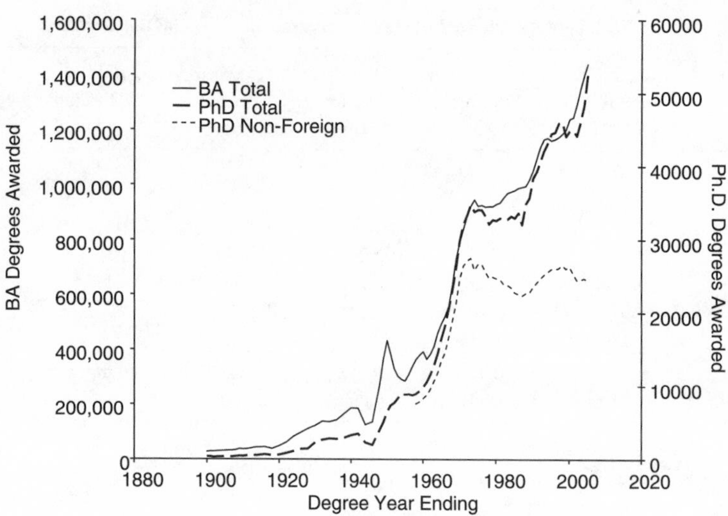

Fig. 3.6 BA degrees and PhD degrees awarded by year, 1900–2005
Source: Data assembled from government sources in Goldin (1999) with the most recent years updated from the *Digest of Education Statistics* (2007).

to the period of the 1960s, it has been argued that the dynamics generating the robust growth in doctorate attainment and dramatic decline in doctorates awarded (particularly to US residents) in the early 1970s can be attributed to a confluence of historical factors. Indeed, there is evidence that the elimination of 2-S military draft deferments for graduate study in the late 1960s, followed by erosion in the domestic academic labor market, dramatically slowed the rate of doctorate attainment among US residents (Bowen, Turner, and Witte 1992).

3.3.2 Research Funding and Doctorate Education

If additional doctorate students in the sciences—specifically, additional foreign doctorates—are not adding to the outputs in undergraduate teaching, it merits asking how the funding of these students aligns with the teaching and research functions (and outputs) of universities. As a caveat to this discussion, we note that the data available on financial support of doctorate students in the *Survey of Earned Doctorates* is far from ideal. We observe the "primary source of support" over the graduate career rather than more informative measures of the level and composition of support; in addition, the "primary source" measure is only observed from 1977 to the present. Absent other sources of information, we start with these data to fix broad trends.

Table 3.7 presents the distribution of primary source of support for for-

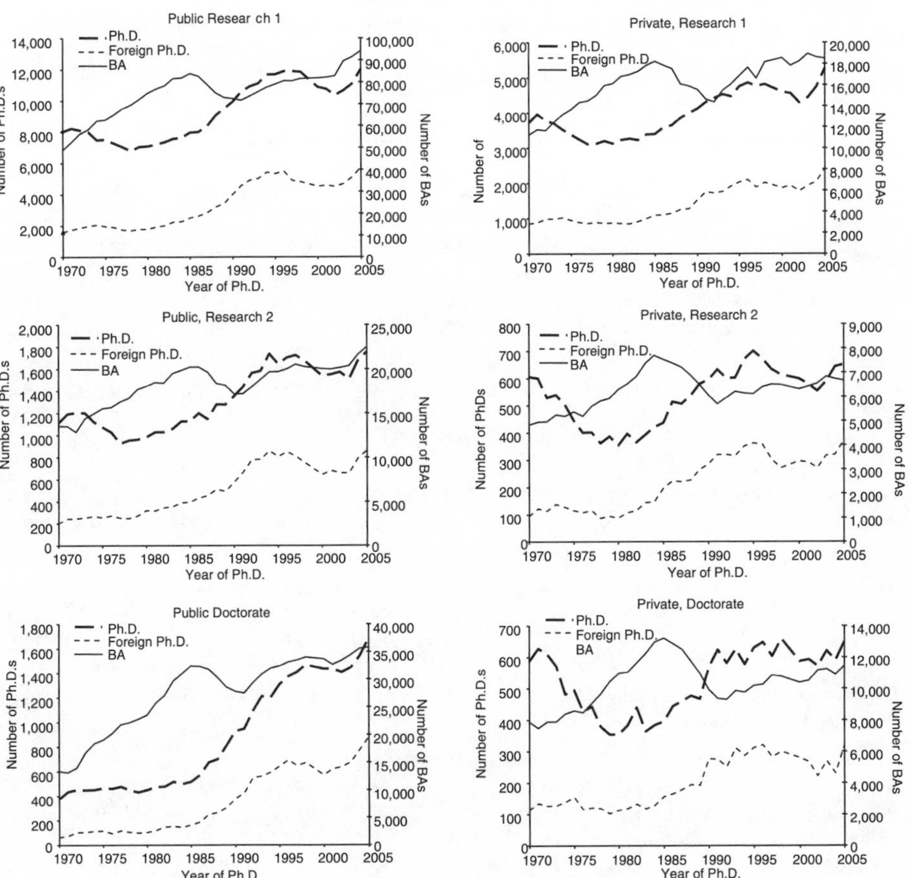

Fig. 3.7 Trends in BA and PhD degrees by type of institution

Sources: NSF, *Survey of Earned Doctorates* microdata. National origin is defined by the country in which an individual went to high school. Fields defined using NSF classification, from SED annual report.

eign and US students by field and type of institution for broad field classifications in the sciences. Outside of economics, the share of both foreign and US students reporting "teaching assistantship" (TA) as their primary source of support declines from the late 1970s to the current period, with these drops most marked in the physical sciences and engineering. As such, these data are largely consistent with the very small effects of expansion of doctorate education on undergraduate education reported in the prior section. It is worth noting that the field of economics—particularly at public universities—looks very different than the physical and life sciences in patterns of support. In economics, over 46 percent of foreign PhD recipients

Table 3.7 **Source of support by citizenship, institution type, and field (selected periods)**

	1977–1979		1980–1989		1990–1999		2000–2005	
	Foreign	US	Foreign	US	Foreign	US	Foreign	US
				Public, physical sciences				
TA	39.7	33.7	39.0	28.5	37.6	25.1	31.8	24.6
RA	36.0	38.0	39.0	45.0	46.0	43.5	50.6	43.1
Fellowship	7.7	12.2	8.4	9.5	8.1	11.0	12.8	18.7
Loan/own	6.8	14.5	7.7	15.7	7.1	18.0	4.1	10.5
Other source support	9.4	1.6	6.3	1.6	1.2	2.5	0.8	3.2
Number of observations	1,353	5,033	7,929	18,771	15,660	20,991	10,836	12,429
				Public, engineering				
TA	12.1	8.9	16.2	9.5	12.9	7.0	9.2	6.4
RA	56.7	42.0	52.0	44.0	59.0	46.4	68.4	43.8
Fellowship	6.7	18.5	9.5	16.0	10.8	16.9	14.5	25.9
Loan/own	11.4	25.3	13.4	25.4	14.6	22.4	6.3	14.4
Other source support	13.2	5.2	8.9	5.1	2.4	7.2	1.7	9.5
Number of observations	1,719	1,892	10,162	7,643	18,892	13,273	13,880	7,724
				Public, life sciences				
TA	11.8	19.1	10.7	16.9	13.1	13.0	11.7	11.9
RA	38.0	42.0	35.0	44.0	52.0	42.3	50.8	31.9
Fellowship	11.8	16.7	17.8	12.0	21.1	12.8	29.9	32.6
Loan/own	14.6	21.0	17.5	25.3	11.7	29.2	6.4	19.6
Other source support	23.9	1.1	19.1	1.6	2.2	2.7	1.2	4.2
Number of observations	1,785	7,119	8,308	29,673	16,402	29,757	11,589	21,993
				Public, economics				
TA	37.7	39.4	39.1	41.3	43.6	42.6	46.0	42.6
RA	17.0	18.0	15.0	16.0	14.7	13.0	15.0	16.7
Fellowship	12.0	13.3	11.9	9.6	18.1	8.5	26.1	14.0
Loan/own	21.8	28.2	22.1	32.3	21.4	35.0	11.5	25.0
Other source support	12.0	1.0	11.6	1.1	2.2	0.9	1.5	1.8
Number of observations	284	731	1,559	2,359	2,264	1,930	1,746	1,158
				Private, physical sciences				
TA	23.1	22.2	25.8	18.4	28.0	16.5	23.4	16.7
RA	37.0	38.0	43.0	47.0	48.7	48.7	45.1	36.8
Fellowship	19.2	24.3	14.4	20.0	15.4	19.0	26.1	35.5
Loan/own	7.8	12.6	7.6	12.0	6.0	12.1	4.2	7.8
Other source support	13.4	2.5	8.8	3.0	1.9	3.8	1.2	3.3
Number of observations	849	2,691	4,069	9,152	7,121	8,877	4,973	4,786
				Private, engineering				
TA	10.5	7.0	11.5	6.4	11.1	6.2	8.7	4.0
RA	52.0	46.0	55.0	51.0	58.7	49.9	59.8	39.7
Fellowship	11.6	18.5	12.7	18.7	16.0	22.0	23.8	39.3
Loan/own	11.6	17.7	9.7	14.6	9.9	12.2	5.8	8.5
Other source support	14.4	11.2	11.2	9.1	4.3	9.7	1.9	8.5
Number of observations	1,022	1,207	4,951	4,468	7,640	6,199	5,087	3,277

Table 3.7 (continued)

	1977–1979		1980–1989		1990–1999		2000–2005	
	Foreign	US	Foreign	US	Foreign	US	Foreign	US
			Private, life sciences					
TA	11.0	10.6	10.3	10.0	9.2	7.0	6.9	4.8
RA	29.2	42.0	28.0	45.0	39.8	45.8	29.3	21.1
Fellowship	24.8	27.5	27.5	21.3	35.4	23.6	54.5	57.9
Loan/own	14.9	17.1	20.0	21.1	13.0	20.9	7.7	13.1
Other source support	20.1	2.3	13.9	2.2	2.6	2.8	1.6	3.0
Number of observations	463	2,451	2,045	10,176	4,962	11,136	3,971	9,069
			Private, economics					
TA	10.3	14.3	20.5	17.3	25.9	21.1	21.9	16.7
RA	8.7	11.0	8.0	14.0	9.4	16.1	9.4	9.5
Fellowship	28.3	42.4	29.4	33.2	38.0	32.2	56.6	50.7
Loan/own	30.2	29.5	27.0	33.4	20.8	28.8	11.3	20.9
Other source support	22.5	2.8	15.0	2.1	6.0	1.9	0.9	2.2
Number of observations	311	495	1,291	1,686	1,863	1,399	1,587	671

Source: Authors' tabulations from restricted use *Survey of Earned Doctorates.*

Note: The first five rows of each panel show the distribution of primary support for those respondents providing usable answers to this question.

and 42.6 percent of PhD recipients from the United States at public universities relied on funding through teaching assistantships as the primary source of support in the most recent period of observation. In other scientific fields these shares are much lower and have been trending down, not up, over time, with TA positions serving as the primary source for less than 12 percent of doctorate recipients in the life sciences, and less than 10 percent in engineering.

How, then, are doctorate students financed in the most recent decades if they are decreasingly engaged in undergraduate teaching? While there are substantial differences in starting levels across fields, we see clear increases in research assistantship (RA) support for foreign graduate students. If the share of foreign PhD students funded by research positions increases while the number of foreign students is also increasing, it follows that the total number of research assistant positions held by foreign students must also be increasing. Table 3.7 shows that this shift in source of support is particularly strong at public institutions (again, excepting economics). For economics, it is likely that there are fewer scale economies in research that allow for the employment of graduate students in labs or on research grants; in turn, demand for undergraduate courses may have expanded, while demand in the sciences more generally has remained flat.

For US doctoral students, the clear shift is toward fellowship funding as a primary source of support over the last three decades.[16] If fellowship support is increasingly needed to attract US doctoral students while foreign students are willing to attend with research assistantships, the price to institutions of attracting an additional student to study in the sciences may be higher for domestic applicants than the parallel price for foreign students.

3.4 Conclusion and Next Steps

"Who pays?" and "who benefits?" are fundamental questions in higher education policy. At the undergraduate level, the answer is relatively straightforward: undergraduate students (and their parents) pay for higher education through tuition and receive largely private benefits.[17] Thus, the decisions of foreign students to pursue undergraduate education in the United States are determined largely by capacity to pay. At the graduate level, it is much more common for universities to support students through research and teaching positions, as well as fellowships. For students from abroad, these financing sources are likely to be crucial in facilitating attendance, in the absence of well-functioning capital markets.

Doctorate production in science and engineering fields plainly intersects with the research and undergraduate teaching functions of the university. Evidence presented in this chapter suggests that the expansion of foreign doctorate attainment in the sciences—particularly outside of economics—at US universities has been largely aligned with the research function at universities. The availability of research funding has been significant in supporting the increased demand among foreign doctorate students. Substantial increase in funding for science and engineering research generated by the federal stimulus (American Recovery and Reinvestment Act), and intense fiscal pressures faced by US research universities raise important questions about how US universities will incorporate the flow of talent from abroad in graduate education in the coming years.

16. Significantly, the data available to us do not distinguish between fellowship support provided by external sources (which may be restricted to domestic students) and fellowship support provided through the funds of universities. This distinction in source of fellowship funding is critical to the interpretation of the differential trends in sources of support for US and foreign students. External awards (e.g., NSF awards to individuals) are implicit subsidies to universities in the production of graduate education while university-supported fellowship awards are direct institutional costs without the direct obligation to participate in university research (as distinguished from independent research) that is implicit in research assistantship appointments.

17. To be clear, this statement is relative in the sense that tuition price is likely to be well below the actual cost of provision at many undergraduate institutions (hence many full pay students pay less than full cost); in addition, beyond the private benefits to higher education that accrue in the form of improved earnings, there may be some external benefits to consider in a full calculation.

References

Borjas, G. 2007. Do Foreign Students Crowd Out Native Students from Graduate Programs? In *Science and the University,* ed. R. Ehrenberg and P. Stephan, 134–49. Madison: University of Wisconsin Press.

Black, G., and P. Stephan. 2007. The importance of foreign PhD students to U.S. science. In *Science and the university,* ed. R. Ehrenberg and P. Stephan, 113–33. Madison: University of Wisconsin Press.

Blanchard, E., J. Bound, and S. Turner. Forthcoming. Opening (and closing) doors: Country-specific shocks in U.S. doctorate education. In *Doctoral education and the faculty of the future,* ed. R. Ehrenberg, 224–248. Ithaca, NY: Cornell University Press.

Bound, J., and S. Turner. 2006. International flows of college-educated workers: Estimates of the effect on skilled workers in the United States. University of Michigan. Working Paper.

Bound, J., S. Turner, and P. Walsh. 2009. Internationalization of U.S. doctorate education. In *Science and engineering careers in the United States: An analysis of markets and employment,* ed. R. Freeman and D. Goroff, 59–98. Chicago: University of Chicago Press.

Bowen, W., and N. Rudenstine. 1992. *In pursuit of the PhD.* Princeton, New Jersey: Princeton University Press.

Bowen, W., S. Turner, and M. Witte. 1992. The BA–PhD nexus. *The Journal of Higher Education* 63 (1): 65–86.

Chellaraj, G., C. K. E. Maskus, and A. Mattoo. 2008. The contribution of international graduate students to U.S. innovation. *Review of International Economics* 16 (3): 444–462.

Goldin, C. 1999. A brief history of education in the United States. NBER Historical Working Paper no. 119. Cambridge, MA: National Bureau of Economic Research, September.

Goldin, C., and L. F. Katz. 1999. The shaping of higher education: The formative years in the United States, 1890 to 1940. *Journal of Economic Perspectives,* American Economic Association 13 (1): 37–62.

Jan, T. 2008. Foreigners diversify face of BU; School sees record in overseas recruiting. *Boston Globe,* August 16.

Lan, X. 2008. Visa status and postdoctoral participation of non-citizen PhDs in the U.S. University of Virginia. Working Paper.

Regents, M. 2001. Research and policy issues in high-skilled international migration: A perspective with data from the United States. Institute for the Study of Labor. Discussion Paper no. 366.

Schworm, P. 2008. Foreign students flock to the US; Surge in overseas applicants driven by weak dollar. *The Boston Globe,* July 5.

Stuen, E., A. Mobarak, and K. Maskus. 2007. Foreign PhD students and innovation at U.S. universities: Evidence from enrollment fluctuations. Available at: http://www.colorado.edu/Economics/courses/mobarak/Mobarak_foreign_students.pdf.

Zhang, L. 2005. Crowd out or opt out: The changing landscape of doctorate production in American universities. Cornell University, ILR School. Cornell Higher Education Research Institute (CHERI) Working Paper no. 63. Available at: http://digitalcommons.ilr.cornell.edu/student/12/.

4

The Economics of University Science and the Role of Foreign Graduate Students and Postdoctoral Scholars

Grant C. Black and Paula E. Stephan

4.1 Introduction

Universities play an important role in the production of knowledge in the United States, authoring nearly 75 percent (fractional counts) of scientific and engineering articles written in the country.[1] Within the university, research is often performed with the assistance of graduate students, postdoctoral scholars (postdocs), and staff scientists, many of whom are foreign-born and foreign-educated. Currently, for example, over 45 percent of graduate students enrolled in science and engineering (S&E) are foreign-born and approximately 60 percent of postdocs are on temporary visas.

This chapter documents the presence and importance of graduate students and postdocs in US academic science. We are particularly interested in the role of the foreign-born and foreign-trained. We begin by examining the importance of teams in university research and then provide an overview of the way in which university research is financed and structured. Next we summarize trends in the number and proportion of foreign-born graduate

Grant C. Black is assistant professor of economics in the School of Business and Economics at Indiana University, South Bend. Paula E. Stephan is professor of economics at the Andrew Young School of Policy Studies, Georgia State University, and a research associate of the National Bureau of Economic Research.

We wish to thank Bill Kerr for graciously matching our database to his ethnic database, Kelly Wilkin for data assistance, and Mark Regets for supplying helpful information regarding postdoctoral scholars. Bill Amis, Charles Clotfelter, Harold Shapiro, and Michael Teitelbaum made useful comments on an earlier draft of this chapter as did participants at the conference "American Universities in a Global Market," held in Woodstock, Vermont, October 2008.

1. Universities also play a considerably smaller—though growing—role in invention. In 2005, universities produced 3.7 percent of all patents awarded to US owners. The underlying count of 2,725 represents a 50 percent increase over the number awarded to universities ten years earlier. (National Science Board 2008, appendix table 5-40).

students and postdocs studying in the United States. To explore the role that postdocs and graduate students play in the production of knowledge we examine articles published in *Science* during a six-month period in 2007 and 2008 that have a US academic-based scientist as the last author. Through web searches we are able to determine the status (postdoc, graduate student, staff scientist, or faculty) of virtually all US coauthors. We also examine the ethnicity of the coauthors by applying an ethnic-name database and infer nativity from ethnicity. We conclude in section 4.6, summarizing our results and discussing their implications for US universities and for the research enterprise.

4.2 The Importance of Teams

Research is rarely done in isolation, especially research of an experimental rather than a theoretical bent (Fox 1991). Scientists work in teams. One way of seeing how team size and collaboration have changed is to examine trends in co-authorship patterns among papers with one or more authors from a "top 110" US university. Adams et al. (2005) find that for this group, the mean number of authors per paper increased from 2.8 to 4.2 for the eighteen-year interval, ending in 1999.[2] The rate of growth was greatest during the period of 1991 to 1996, when use of e-mail and the Internet was rapidly accelerating.

The growth in authorship is due to a rise in the number of people working on a project within a given university as well as to an increase in the number of institutions—especially foreign institutions—collaborating on a research project. During the period 1988 to 2003, the number of addresses associated with a US-authored article grew by 37 percent and the number of foreign addresses more than tripled (National Science Board 2006, table 5-18). Despite this impressive increase, the growth in co-authorship is fueled more by an increase in the number of authors working at the same university than an increase in collaboration across universities, as evidenced by the fact that during the same period the number of names on an article grew by more than the number of addresses on an article (50 percent versus 37 percent).

Several factors contribute to the increased role that collaboration plays in research. First, the importance of interdisciplinary research and the fact that major breakthroughs often occur in emerging disciplines encourage collaboration. Systems biology, which involves the intersection of biology, engineering, and physical sciences, is a case in point.[3] By definition, no one has all the requisite skills required to work in the area; researchers must rely on working with others. Second, and related, researchers arguably are acquir-

2. The study is restricted to articles in science and engineering having one or more authors from a top 110 US university.

3. Systems biology studies the relationship between the design of biological systems and the tasks they perform.

ing narrower expertise over time in order to compensate for the educational demands associated with the increase in knowledge (Jones 2005). Narrower expertise, in turn, leads to an increased reliance on teamwork for discovery. Third, the rapid spread of connectivity, which began in the early 1980s with the adoption of BITNET by a number of universities and accelerated in the early 1990s with the diffusion of the Internet, has decreased the costs of collaboration across institutions (Agrawal and Goldfarb 2008; Winkler, Levin, and Stephan 2008). Another factor that fosters collaboration is the vast amount of data that is becoming available, such as that from the Human Genome Project (and the associated GenBank database). Although that is probably the best known, many other large databases have recently come on-line, such as PubChem, which as of this writing contained over 18,000 recorded substances, and the Worldwide Protein Data Bank (wwPDB), a worldwide depository of information regarding protein structures.[4] The practice of sharing research materials also leads to increases in the number of authors appearing on an article.

Increased complexity of equipment also fosters collaboration.[5] By way of example, in the *Science* database that we have assembled for this chapter, four co-authors are identified on web pages as electron microscopists. Barnett, Ault, and Kaserman (1988) suggest two other factors that lead persons to seek co-authors. One is the desire to minimize risk by diversifying one's research portfolio through collaboration; the other is the increased opportunity cost of time. An additional factor is quality. The literature on scientific productivity suggests that scientists who collaborate produce "better" science than do individual investigators (Wuchty, Jones, and Uzzi 2007; Andrews 1979; Lawani 1986). Some of the factors encouraging collaboration are new (such as connectivity) but growth in the number of authors on a paper is not. Wuchty, Jones, and Uzzi (2007) find that team size has grown in all but one of the 171 S&E fields studied during the past forty-five years.

Much university research occurs in a lab setting. How these labs are staffed varies across countries. For example, in Europe research labs are often staffed by permanent staff scientists, although increasingly these positions are held by temporary employees (Stephan 2008). In the United States, while positions such as staff scientists and research associates exist, the majority of scientists working in the university lab are doctoral students and postdocs. Stephan, Black, and Chang's study (2007) of 415 labs affiliated with a nanotechnology center finds that the average lab has twelve technical staff, excluding the principal investigator (PI). Of these, 50 percent are

4. The Large Hadron Collider (LHC) at CERN will create vast amounts of data. According to Kolbert (2007, 74), "If all the L.H.C. data were burned onto disks, the stack would rise at the rate of a mile a month."

5. At the very extreme are the teams assembled to work at colliders. The CERN's four colliders have combined team size of just under 6,000: 2,520 for the Compact Muon Detector (CMS.), 1,800 for the Atlas, 1,000 for ALICE, and 663 for LHCb (Overbye 2007).

graduate students, 16 percent are postdocs, and 10 percent are undergrads.[6] Some labs are quite large. A case in point is the Susan Lindquist lab at MIT, which has thirty-six members (excluding Lindquist herself)—twenty postdocs, seven graduate students, one visiting scientist, one staff scientist, three technicians, and four administrators.[7]

This way of staffing labs has been embraced in the United States for a variety of reasons. Pedagogically, it is an efficient training model. It is also an inexpensive way to staff laboratories. Moreover, and as faculty are not abashed to note, it provides a source of "new" ideas, especially given the relative young age of doctoral students and postdocs. To quote Trevor Penning, while serving as the Associate Dean for Postdoctoral Research Training at the University of Pennsylvania School of Medicine, "A faculty member is only as good as his or her best postdoc" (Penning 1998). In addition, funding is often more readily available for predoctoral and postdoctoral students than for staff scientists. The typical National Institutes of Health (NIH) grant, for example, supports both types of training, as do many other forms of grants. At least from the perspective of the National Science Foundation (NSF), it has been a conscious policy to fund students. Rita Colwell, the director of NSF from 1998 to 2004, said in an interview with *Science* that "In the 1980s, NSF asked investigators to put graduate students on their research budgets, saying it preferred to fund graduate students rather than technicians" (*Science* 1998). There is also the added advantage that postdocs and graduate students, with their short tenure, provide for more flexibility in the staffing of laboratories than do permanent technicians.

This model for staffing labs has undoubtedly contributed to the United States's eminence as a training center for both native and foreign-born students. It provides not only a hands-on learning experience but also financial support for graduate study and postdoctoral work, something that many other countries cannot provide.

4.3 The Structure and Financing of University Labs and Research Groups

Labs at US universities "belong" to the faculty PI, if not in fact, at least in name, as is readily seen by the common practice of naming the lab for the faculty member. A mere click of the mouse, for example, reveals that all of the twenty-six faculty at MIT in biochemistry and biophysics use their name in referring to their lab.[8] Sometimes, as in the case of the Nobel laure-

6. Approximately a third of the PIs were affiliated with departments of engineering, a third with departments of chemistry, and the remainder with departments of physics.

7. The Linquist lab is large compared to the labs of her colleagues at MIT in biochemistry and biophysics, which have an average of 6.3 graduate students (median of 7) and average of 5.25 postdocs (median of 5).

8. Details regarding research and staffing are available for seventeen of the twenty-six via lab web pages. Three other faculty have web pages for their labs that are not fully developed. For the other six one can find reference to the name of their lab when searching the Internet.

ate Philip Sharp, lab members and former members are referred to using a play on the PI's name—in this case "Sharpies."[9]

It is common practice for labs to maintain web pages, discussing research focus, publications, funding, and so forth. Most pages provide pictures of people who work in the lab, sometimes in a group shot; in other instances individual shots are included. While most pictures are of a traditional nature, it is not uncommon for the photos to be on the humorous side or slightly over the edge.[10]

Lab pages also traditionally provide links to "people" or "personnel," which include a list of everyone working in the lab, from undergraduate students to graduate students, postdocs, and staff scientists. Technicians and administrators are also listed. Some pages list alumni of the labs.

Research is expensive. Personnel costs alone for a small-to-medium lab, composed of three Graduate Research Assistants (GRAs), one postdoc, one technician, and the PI are approximately $210,000, including salaries and benefits but excluding the cost of buying out the PI's time for research. Each additional graduate student adds approximately $37,000; each additional postdoc adds approximately $52,000.[11] Additional expenses include the cost of supplies and equipment. For research in the life sciences, supplies can easily average $18,000 per year per lab member, or add another $108,000 to the costs for a lab of six including the PI (Pelekanos 2008). This excludes the cost of animals, which can be quite expensive. An off-the-shelf mouse costs between $17 and $60 (US) in 2009; mutant strains begin around $40 and can go to more than $500. The cost to recover a mouse from a strain that is only available from cryopreserved material starts at $1,900.[12] With the large number of mice in use (over 13,000 are already published), the cost of mouse upkeep becomes a significant factor in doing research. Universities in the United States, for example, charged from $.05 to $.10 per day per mouse (mouse per diem) in 2000 (Malakoff 2000).[13]

9. In a similar manner, graduate students and postdocs working in Alexander Pines' lab at Berkeley are referred to as "pinenuts" and alumni are referred to as "old pinenuts" (http://waugh.cchem.berkeley.edu/people/).

10. The White Lab web page (Christina White, Department of Chemistry, University of Illinois) depicts White seated on a stone throne, engulfed in flames and surrounded by twelve of her graduate students, one of whom is sporting horns. See http://www.scs.uiuc.edu/white/.

11. The graduate student amount includes stipend, fringe benefits, and tuition and is based on the amount allowed by NIH for the Ruth Kirstein National Research Service Award (NRSA) Fellowship for fiscal year (FY) 2007. Many institutions pattern their support for other students on the Kerstein Fellowship. The postdoc figure includes stipend and fringe benefits; it is the average paid under NIH guidelines for postdocs with varying experience. The fringe amount comes from Pelekanos (2008), as does the cost estimate for the technician.

12. More than 67 percent of the Jackson Labs' four thousand strains are only available from cryopreserved material (correspondence with James E. Yeadon, PhD, technical information scientist, the Jackson Laboratory, September 14, 2009).

13. This cost of mouse upkeep can rapidly add up. Irving Weissman of Stanford University reports that before Stanford changed its cage rates he was paying between $800,000 and $1 million a year to keep the 10,000 to 15,000 mice in his lab. Costs for keeping immune-deficient mice are far greater (on the order of $.65 per day), given their susceptibility to disease.

Equipping a lab adds considerably more to expenses. Pelekanos (2008) estimates that start-up equipment for a lab in the life sciences costs about $60,000. But equipment can cost much more than this. A microscope used for research in nanotechnology can cost $750,000 (http://www.unm.edu/~market/cgi-bin/archives/000132.html). A sequencer, such as Illumina's Genome Analyzer System, for example, costs $470,000. One reason research in certain fields is conducted outside the university relates to the extremely high cost of equipment and the indivisible nature of this equipment. At the extreme are costs associated with building and running an accelerator. The twenty-seven-kilometer-long Large Hadron Collider (LHC), which has recently come on-line at the European Organization for Nuclear Research (CERN), costs approximately $8 billion; the Spallation Neutron Source (SNS) at Oak Ridge National Laboratory in the United States costs $1.41 billion. (*Service* 2006).

In order to get started on an independent research career, faculty usually receive resources from the dean at the time they are hired. Included in these start-up-packages are funds for equipment and stipends to hire graduate students, staff scientists, and postdocs. Also, and of crucial importance in the lab sciences, they are assigned space. Ehrenberg, Rizzo, and Jakubson (2003) have surveyed US universities regarding start-up packages. They find that the average package for an assistant professor in chemistry is $489,000; in biology it is $403,071. At the high end it is $580,000 in chemistry; $437,000 in biology. For senior faculty they report start-up packages of $983,929 in chemistry (high-end is $1,172,222); and of $957,143 in biology (high end is $1,575,000).

Start-up packages are exactly that. After several years, the faculty member becomes responsible for procuring the resources for the lab.[14] Faculty do this primarily through the grants system, writing proposals and, if successful, receiving funds from Federal agencies and private foundations.[15] Faculty also receive support for their labs from industry. One exception to the rule is that faculty sometimes host postdocs who have received funding through a fellowship or graduate students supported on training grants (awarded to the department) who work (on a rotation basis) in a faculty lab.[16] Increasingly, faculty are expected not only to cover the research expenses of the lab through grants and contracts, but also to cover a portion of their own salary. Indeed, it is becoming increasingly common for faculty in tenured

14. Start-up packages have been known to have unintended consequences. A chair of a department recounted to one of us that new hires in the department "hoard" their start-up funds, postponing going up for NIH funding until a tenure decision has been made.

15. The primary sources of federal funds are The National Institutes of Health (NIH), the Department of Energy (DOE), the Department of Defense (DOD), and, to a lesser extent, the National Science Foundation (NSF).

16. For example, MIT distinguishes between postdoctoral associates and postdoctoral fellows. The former are supported through grants that faculty have procured at MIT; the latter have received fellowships or stipends to work with a faculty member at MIT.

positions at US medical institutions to be required to procure a portion of their salary from grants.[17]

Grant applications and administration divert scientists from spending time on research. A 2006 survey of US scientists found that scientists spend 42 percent of their research time filling out forms and in meetings; tasks split almost evenly between pre-grant (22 percent) and post-grant work (20 percent). The tasks cited as the most burdensome were filling out grant progress reports, hiring personnel, and managing laboratory finances (Kean 2006).

Organizationally, PI-labs in the United States are structured as pyramids. At the pinnacle is the faculty principal investigator. Below the PI are the postdocs; below the postdocs are graduate students and undergraduates. Some labs, as we note, also have scientists who have completed postdoctoral training in this or another lab and are hired in such non-tenure-track positions as staff scientists and research faculty. The pyramid analogy does not stop here, however. In certain ways the research enterprise itself resembles a pyramid scheme. In order to staff their labs, faculty recruit PhD students into their graduate program with funding and the promise of interesting research careers (Stephan and Levin 2002). Upon receiving their degree it is mandatory for students who aspire to a faculty position to first take an appointment as a postdoc. Postdocs then seek to move on to tenure-track positions in academe. The Sigma Xi study of postdocs, for example, found that 72.7 percent of the postdocs who were looking for a job were "very interested" in a job at a research university and 23.0 percent were "somewhat interested" (Davis 2005). In recent years, however, the transition from postdoc to tenure track has been slowed as the number of tenure-track positions has failed to keep pace with the increase in supply.

Faculty not only staff labs with graduate students and postdocs. They actively recruit and select the students who work in their lab. Unlike admission decisions to PhD programs, however, which generally occur at the department level, decisions regarding staffing are usually made by the faculty member who, in effect, is paying for the student.

Not surprisingly, given the role faculty play in staffing decisions, networks, or what may more accurately be described as "affinity effects," appear to play a role in staffing. Tanyildiz (2008) has studied paired labs in eighty-two departments of engineering, chemistry, physics, and biology. In each case she matches a lab directed by a "native" PI (as established by name and undergraduate institution) to a lab directed by a foreign PI, either of Chinese, Korean, Indian, or Turkish background. She then studies the graduate student composition of the labs, assigning nationalities to the students based on the common-name methodology used by Kerr (2008). She finds signifi-

17. A survey of medical schools found that tenure is accompanied with no financial guarantee for 35 percent of basic science faculty and 38 percent of clinical faculty (Bunton and Mallon 2007).

cant differences in the role that ethnicity plays in staffing. The mean paired difference in the percent of Chinese students in a lab directed by a Chinese PI versus a lab in the same department directed by a "native" US faculty is 37.8 percent; that for Koreans is 29.0 percent; that for Indians is 27.1 percent; that for Turkish is 36.3 percent (very small sample). When she compares labs directed by natives to nonnatives from one of these four groups the mean paired difference is 28.9 percent. Clearly, clustering by ethnicity occurs in labs. Tanyildiz also finds that affinity effects are more common in "bottom"-ranked departments; less common in "top" departments.[18]

Not all university research is organized around labs directed by faculty. In the earth sciences, for example, scientists often do not work in a lab setting. In instances of "big" science (such as experimental high energy physics, cosmology, and astrophysics), research is often organized around equipment such as a telescope or an accelerator. Often this equipment is located off-site, sometimes at national labs, such as the Stanford Linear Accelerator (SLAC), Fermi Lab, or the Lawrence Berkeley National Laboratory; sometimes it is located at international labs, as in the case of CERN.[19]

The absence of a lab on campus does not mean that graduate students and postdocs are absent nor that faculty lack a role in choosing who works with them or their group. In many instances of "big" science it is not uncommon for the group to have a web page named for its research focus—for example, the Caltech Observational Cosmology Group (with the goal of developing novel instruments)—which lists the research focus and links to faculty, postdocs, graduate students, visitors, and staff working in the group. Individual physicists in the group also maintain a web page, but physicists working in the area do not have labs with their name attached to the lab. But it is not only "big" physics that presents itself as a group. It occurs in other areas as well. For example, the Experimental Condensed Matter Research Group at Cal Tech keeps a group web page, as does the Spin Group and the Infrared Arm Group, to give but several examples. Moreover, it is not just experimentalists who speak of their group. Numerous examples can be found where theoretical physicists talk of their "group" on the web even though members of the group may be working by themselves.

18. Using NRC rankings, she finds that the mean difference is 25.9 percent in "top" departments, 35.9 percent in "middle" departments, and 53.2 percent in "bottom" departments. These calculations do not include mean differences between native students in native labs versus native students in nonnative labs.

19. By way of example, physicists at the California Institute of Technology routinely work at telescopes in New Mexico and Hawaii, and at SLAC. They also are playing key roles in developing the Compact Muon Solenoid (CMS), one of the two large general purpose particle physics detectors that will come on-line at CERN in 2008.

4.4 Trends in the Production of PhDs and Postdoctoral Students by Visa Status

4.4.1 PhD Awards

In the early 1980s, approximately 12,000 PhDs were awarded annually in the United States in science and engineering. By the late 1990s the number had grown to approximately 20,000; by the mid-2000s it had increased to over 23,000, roughly doubling over the entire period. This substantial increase, however, masks wide differences in enrollment patterns among US citizens and noncitizens shown in figure 4.1 for the period from 1980 to 2006.[20]

We see that the number of US students receiving S&E PhDs grew by only 30 percent during the period. Moreover, virtually all of the growth that occurred was among women students. The number of PhDs awarded to citizen women increased by 170 percent from 1980 to 2006, while the number of US males receiving PhDs in science and engineering changed little during the period.

In contrast, the number of temporary residents receiving PhDs grew considerably, with the increase accounting for more than 67 percent of the growth in PhD production in the United States. Permanent residents played a much smaller role, contributing only another 2.3 percent.[21] Growth of the foreign-born was especially strong during the mid-1980s to mid-1990s and again beginning in 2003. The number of foreign-born declined somewhat during the late 1990s and early 2000s.

Almost half of noncitizen PhDs come from the three countries of China, South Korea, and India (Hoffer et al. 2006, table 12). China's role has become so dominant that Tsinghua University and Peking University recently surpassed the University of California, Berkeley, as the most likely undergraduate institution for those earning a PhD at a US institution, regardless of nativity, between 2004 and 2006.[22]

The growth in the number of temporary residents receiving S&E PhDs has been dramatic across most fields, as seen from figure 4.2. The percent of PhD recipients who were temporary residents at the time the degree was

20. For these data, science and engineering excludes medical and social sciences, *citizen* means a native or naturalized citizen of the United States, *permanent resident* means a noncitizen immigrant holding a green card indicating permanent residency in the United States, and *temporary resident* means a nonimmigrant visa holder planning to remain in the United States temporarily (such as a student or temporary worker).

21. The exception was the large increase in permanent residents in the early-to-mid 1990s, which, along with the accompanying decrease of temporary-resident recipients, reflects the passage of the Chinese Student Protection Act that permitted Chinese nationals temporarily residing in the United States to switch to permanent-resident status.

22. The calculations are for degrees awarded between 2004 and 2006 (Mervis 2008). The University of California, Berkeley, is now in third place, followed by South Korea's Seoul National University, Cornell University, and the University of Michigan, Ann Arbor.

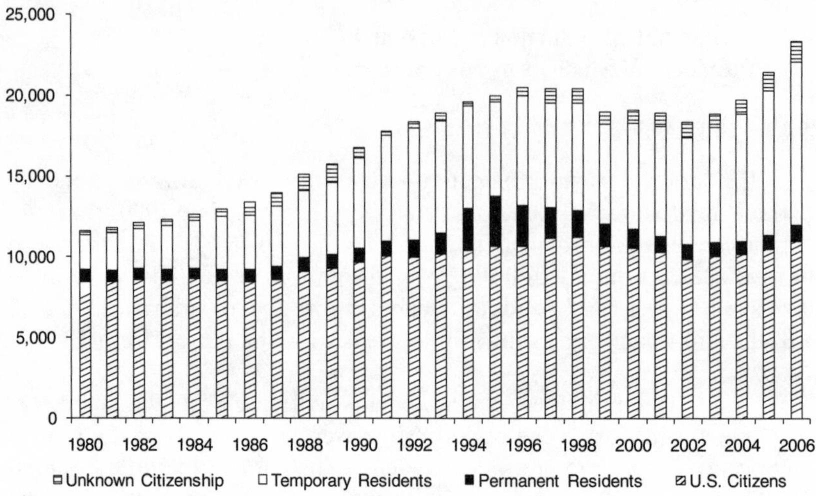

Fig. 4.1 S&E PhDs awarded by citizenship status, 1980–2006

Sources: National Science Foundation, WebCASPAR database.

Notes: Data for figures 4.1 through 4.4 come from WebCASPAR. WebCASPAR is an online integrated database of data from US academic institutions emphasizing science and engineering. WebCASPAR includes data sources from the National Science Foundation and the National Center for Education Statistics. The National Science Foundation oversees the WebCASPAR database. WebCASPAR data used in this study originally come from NSF's Survey of Earned Doctorates and Survey of Graduate students and Postdoctorates in Science and Engineering (also known as the Graduate Student Survey, or GSS). Data used in figures 4.1 through 4.4 were selected from WebCASPAR based on status as a PhD recipient, graduate student, or postdoc; citizenship status; S&E field; and year.

received more than doubled from 1980 to 2006 in the fields of math and computer sciences, the physical sciences, geosciences, and life sciences. These high growth rates dramatically increased the proportion of foreign-born receiving degrees in certain fields. For example, in math and computer sciences, the proportion rose from 19 percent to over 51 percent; in the life sciences, from approximately 12 percent to 27 percent. Growth in the number of degrees awarded to the foreign-born was lower in engineering, where temporary residents have long received a considerable share of degrees. By 2006 almost 60 percent of all PhDs in engineering were awarded to individuals on temporary visas.

The fields of the geosciences and the physical sciences owe most of their growth during the period to the large influx of foreign students. In the former, for example, temporary residents made up over 96 percent of the growth in number of degrees; in the latter, they comprised 92 percent. In terms of magnitude of change in the number of temporary residents receiving PhDs, the greatest growth took place in the fields of engineering and the life sciences. In 1980 the number of engineering PhDs awarded to temporary residents was 861; by 2006 that number had risen to almost 4,300.

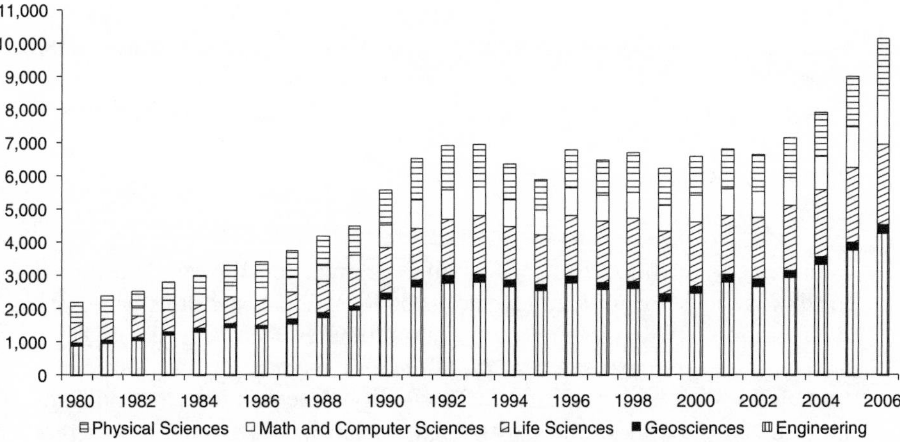

Fig. 4.2 Number of S&E PhDs awarded to temporary residents by field, 1980–2006
Source: National Science Foundation, WebCASPAR database.

In the life sciences, almost 620 temporary residents received PhDs in 1980 compared to over 2,400 in 2006. The latter was undoubtedly spurred by increased resources made available for the support of graduate students, which resulted from the doubling of the NIH budget in the late 1900s and early 2000s.

4.4.2 Recent Trends in Graduate Student Enrollments

Data concerning the number of PhDs awarded reflect conditions and decisions made six to seven years prior to the award date. Thus, the increases that we have documented were put in motion long before 9/11. Following 9/11, considerable attention was focused on the observed decline in applications and admissions of international graduate students and what this would mean for graduate education in the United States. For example, between 2003 and 2004 graduate applications across the board declined by 28 percent, admissions by 18 percent, and enrollments by 6 percent (National Academies 2005, 31).[23] These concerns have been somewhat mitigated by the modest rise in the enrollment of international graduate students experienced recently. For example, according to the Survey of Graduate Students and Postdoctorates in Science and Engineering for 2006, first-time, full-time enrollment for temporary residents in graduate science and engineering programs rose 16.4 percent between 2005 and 2006, compared to a mea-

23. Comparable figures for engineering are –36.0, –24.0, and –8.0; for the life sciences, –24.0, –19.0, and –10.0; and for the physical sciences, –26.0, –17.0, and +6.0. Data come from the Council of Graduate Schools (National Academies 2005, 31). It should be noted that application and admission data "double count" to the extent that students apply and are admitted to multiple programs.

ger 1.7 percent for US citizens and permanent residents (National Science Foundation Web Computer-Aided Science Policy Analysis and Research [CASPAR]). It remains to be seen whether this turnaround will continue. Clearly, enrollment patterns are affected not only by US visa policy but also by opportunities for study outside the United States, which in recent years have been increasing.

4.4.3 Postdocs

Estimating the population of scholars working in postdoctoral positions in the United States is complex and leads to different measures based on the methodology that is employed. Thus, estimates must be read with caution. Complications arise from several factors, including survey sampling frameworks that omit or do not easily identify some postdocs, especially in nonacademic sectors, or those with doctorates from foreign institutions; the timing of survey data collection that can miss increasingly migratory S&E PhDs; exclusions and discrepancies surrounding some S&E occupations in certain standard surveys; and institutional difficulties in identifying workers as postdocs and by visa status (National Science Board 2008; Regets 2007). By way of illustration, Regets (2007) offers the anecdotal example of officials at a major research university who expressed confidence in their ability to identify all temporary-visa postdocs at their institution on the assumption that only J-1 visas were used for postdocs. It was later discovered that Labor Condition Applications—the first step in the H1-B visa process—had been filed by the university for several hundred "postdoctoral appointments." There is also the issue of job title. It is not uncommon for individuals who are essentially postdocs to be called by another title, such as research scientist. Classification problems such as this mean that many postdocs go uncounted because of a wide range of measurement issues.[24]

Figure 4.3 shows the number of postdocs working at academic institutions in science and engineering in the United States from 1985 to 2006, based on the Survey of Graduate Students and Postdocs.[25] We see that in 1985 there were slightly more than 16,000 postdocs at academic institutions. Within a decade, that number had grown to over 25,000, and by 2006 the number of postdocs had surpassed 34,000—an increase of 110 percent from

24. The NSF is acutely aware of the many problems involved in measuring postdocs and is in the process of designing a new methodology to measure the number and characteristics of postdoctoral scholars in the United States.

25. These data are also based on science and engineering—excluding the medical and social sciences—and account only for postdocs identified by surveys of academic institutions with graduate programs in science and engineering. Although the majority of postdoctoral positions are at academic institutions, postdocs can also be found in other sectors. Using the 2006 Survey of Doctorate Recipients, Hoffer, Grigorian, and Hedbert (2008) estimate that 75 percent of postdocs in science, engineering, and health fields were at educational institutions, 12 percent were in government, 11 percent were at for-profit or nonprofit organizations, and 2 percent were at other types of institutions.

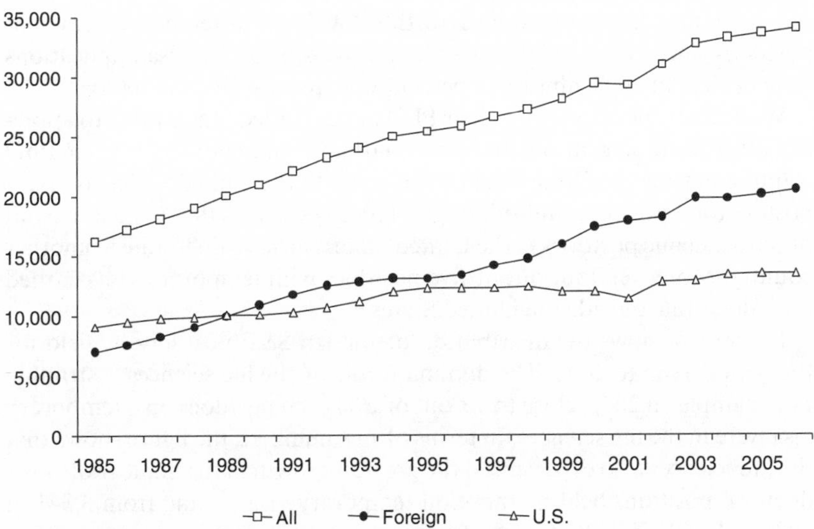

Fig. 4.3 Number of S&E postdocs working in academe, 1985–2006
Source: National Science Foundation, WebCASPAR database.

1985 to 2006. Growth was steady through the early 1990s and continued to increase in the remainder of the 1990s, but at a slower rate. The number of postdocs declined slightly in 2001 but has since increased, particularly in 2002 and 2003.[26]

Growth in the number of postdocs has been fueled largely by scholars coming from abroad. The number of postdocs with temporary-resident visas (identified as foreign postdocs in figure 4.3) almost tripled between 1985 and 2006, rising from 7,032 in 1985 to 20,521 in 2006. While in 1985 temporary residents made up just over 43 percent of all postdocs, by the 2000s they comprised approximately 60 percent of all academic postdoctoral scholars, reaching a peak of 61 percent in 2001. In contrast, the number of postdocs who are US citizens or permanent residents (identified as US postdocs in figure 4.3) grew by less than half during the same period. Indeed, the difference is so dramatic that from 1996 to 2006 alone, the number of temporary-resident postdocs grew by over 52 percent—more than the rate for U.S. citizens and permanent residents over the entire 1985 to 2006 period. The difference is so pronounced that temporary-resident postdocs grew at an annual rate of 5.2 percent, compared to only 1.9 percent for native and permanent-resident postdocs during the period. Tightened visa-security

26. The number of postdocs depends not only upon the propensity to take a postdoc but also upon the duration of the postdoc period of training. Stephan and Ma (2005) show that not only the propensity to take a postdoc but also the duration of the postdoc training period relate to the state of the academic labor market, suggesting that the postdoc position can become a "holding tank" where people wait for better market conditions.

measures may have contributed to the slowdown in temporary-resident postdocs since 2003. In 2001, less than 8 percent of J-1 visa applications were denied; in 2003, almost 16 percent were refused (Regets 2005).[27]

While many postdocs earn their PhD in the United States prior to applying for a postdoctoral position, a remarkable number receive their PhD training outside the United States and come to the United States to take a postdoctoral position. Indeed, Regets (2005) estimates that almost five out of ten academic postdocs in the United States earned a doctorate in another country. Moreover, four out of five postdocs with temporary visas earned their doctorate outside the United States.[28]

Figure 4.4 shows the distribution of foreign S&E postdocs by field for the period 1985 to 2006. The dominant role of the life sciences is striking. For example, in 2006, close to six out of every ten postdocs on a temporary visa were in the life sciences. In terms of raw numbers, the figure shows that the life sciences also experienced the greatest growth in the number of postdoctoral positions held by those on temporary visas, going from 3,341 in 1985 to 11,694 in 2006. By way of contrast, the increase in engineering was 2,193; that in the physical sciences was 1,853. The magnitude of the change in the life sciences is likely a result of the increased demand for postdocs in the field occasioned by the doubling of the NIH budget in the late 1990s and early 2000s. The fastest growth of postdocs on temporary visas occurred in the geosciences, where the number increased by a factor of more than six times. In math and computer sciences, the figure grew by over 300 percent. The number of temporary-resident postdocs grew by over 300 percent in math and computer sciences, 250 percent in the life sciences, 240 percent in engineering, and only 74 percent in the physical sciences.

4.5 Authorship Patterns in *Science*

To examine the contributions of postdocs, graduate students, and undergraduates to research in academe, we collected data on the authors of ar-

27. Foreign postdocs have traditionally been in the United States on either a J or an H visa, with some on F-1's for one year of optional practical training. The Sigma Xi survey (with a nonrepresentative sample) found that 51 percent of foreign postdocs were on J's, 41 percent on H's, and 3 percent on F-1s; the remaining 4 percent were on "other" visas (http://www.sigmaxi.org/postdoc/by_citizenship/). See also Davis (2005). Mark Regets reports (informal correspondence) that there is some evidence that the proportion on H-1B visas has been growing, based on the number of Labor Condition Applications that explicitly contain the search string "postdoc." The number on F-1 visas is expected to grow, because optional practical training time was recently increased from twelve months to twenty-nine months for most S&E advanced degrees.

28. These estimates are based on a comparison of counts from the National Science Foundation (NSF) Survey of Doctorate Recipients and the NSF Survey of Graduate Students and Postdoctorates in 2001. For example, in 2001, 17,900 academic postdocs with temporary visas were reported through the Survey of Graduate Students and Postdoctorates, while only 3,500 postdocs with temporary visas were reported in the Survey of Earned Doctorates, which only collects data on doctorates earned in the United States. Regets attributes the difference in these counts to postdocs, with PhDs earned outside the United States.

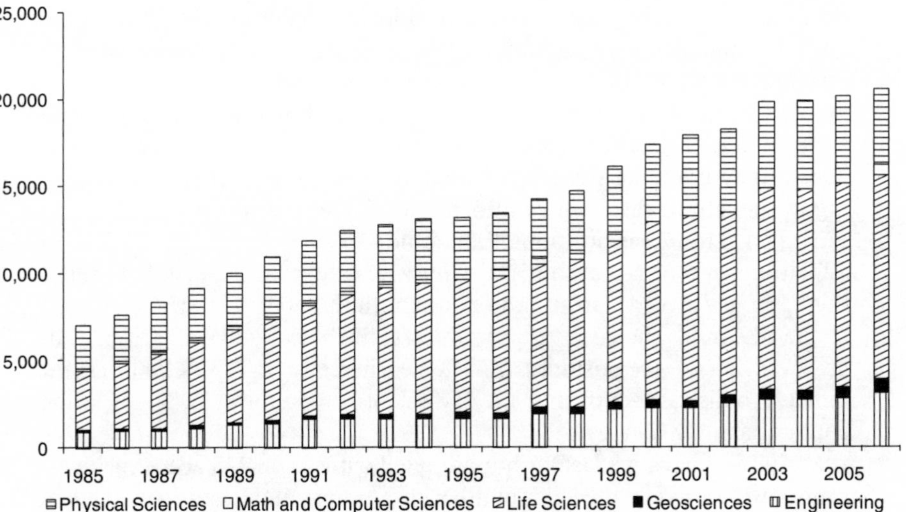

Fig. 4.4 Number of foreign S&E postdocs by field, 1985–2006
Source: National Science Foundation, WebCASPAR database.

ticles published in *Science* from November 2, 2007 to May 2, 2008.[29] We focused on papers in the Research Articles and Reports sections of the journal. In many fields of science the last author is the principal investigator; while other rules or variations exist in terms of author order, we apply this common convention to our analysis to determine if a paper has a US origin.[30] We further restrict the analysis to papers with a last author affiliated with a US academic institution, given our interest in studying science in academe.

We chose *Science* because of its multidisciplinary nature (the journal devotes 40 percent of its space to the physical sciences and 60 percent to the life sciences) and its position as a leading, if not the leading, journal in science. Moreover, and as is to be expected, the journal is highly selective. In 2007 the journal published 817 of the 12,450 articles that it received (6.6 percent; 461 of these (56.4 percent) had a first author from the United States (Franzoni, Scellato, and Stephan 2008).

For each paper we record the broad field related to the subject of the research, the number of authors, the name of each author, institutional affiliation as listed in the article, and the location (country) of the listed institutions.[31] We collect additional information from Internet searches on

29. We code twenty-two issues for the six-month period. The four issues not coded are November 23 and 30 and December 7 and 14, 2007.

30. Had we instead used the country of the first author to determine origin, the sample would have had 150 papers rather than the 159 papers we analyzed.

31. For publications with ten or more authors (twenty-six of the 159 US papers), only the first and last authors were recorded.

the authors, including the academic position of an author and whether the author is affiliated with the same lab as the last author. In some instances this information is obtained from the last author's web page but more commonly it comes from the web page for the last author's lab. Such web pages are particularly useful in identifying postdoctoral students, graduate students, undergraduate students, and staff scientists and technicians working in the lab. In cases where information could not be found (most frequently regarding the position of an author and whether the author has an affiliation with the last author's lab), missing values were coded. We believe this approach provides an accurate count of the number of students involved in the research. The count of postdocs is likely to be downward biased, however, since some postdocs, as noted earlier, have job titles that make it difficult to distinguish them from staff scientists. We thus view the postdoc count as a lower bound.

For papers having a last author affiliated with a non-US academic institution, we code only the field, number of authors, and location of the last author. Data on the fifty-one papers for which the last author is affiliated with a nonacademic institution, such as a private business, nonprofit organization, or government agency, were not collected regardless of country of last author.[32] All told, data on 267 academic papers was collected. Of these, 159 had a last author at a US academic institution and 108 at a foreign academic institution. The distribution of papers by last author affiliation is summarized in table 4.1.

The median number of authors for US academic papers is five, the minimum is one, and the maximum is seven. Web pages could be found either for the last author's lab or for the last author in all but one case.

The last authors come from sixty-nine different US academic institutions. The largest number of last authors (sixteen) come from either Harvard or Harvard Medical School; nine come from UC Berkeley, eight from Stanford, and six from the University of Michigan Ann Arbor or the University of Michigan Medical School. Five institutions have scientists publishing five articles during the six-month time period. The institutions are: California Institute of Technology, Johns Hopkins, MIT, University of Michigan-Ann Arbor, University of Washington, and Yale. Several lesser-known institutions are represented, such as Minnesota State University Mankato, Franklin and Marshall College, and Georgia Southern University.

The distribution of US academic articles by area is given in table 4.2. The distribution mirrors *Science's* overall editorial practice of having a 60/40 split between the life and physical sciences. The median number of authors is highest in genetics; it is lowest in chemistry and neurology. The most authors were on a paper in biology.

32. Of these fifty-one papers, thirty-six have a US address; four have a German address; three have a Japanese address. The remaining eight are authored by individuals in Australia (1), Canada (2), France (2), Iceland (1), the Netherlands (1), and the United Kingdom (1).

Table 4.1 **Distribution of *Science* papers by last author affiliation**

Number of issues coded	Number of articles in issues	Number for whom last author has a nonacademic affiliation	Number for whom last author has an academic affiliation	Number for whom last author has a US academic affiliation
22	318	51	267	159

Source: Authors (see chapter introduction for further information).

Table 4.2 ***Science* articles by field**

Area	Number of articles	Median number of authors	Minimum number of authors	Maximum number of authors
Biochemistry	21	5	3	15
Biology	34	6	1	71
Chemistry and related	9	4	2	9
Earth sciences	16	5	1	22
Genetics	16	7	3	42
Material science	8	5	3	10
Nano-related	6	5.5	4	15
Neurology	12	4	3	14
Physics	17	5	2	14
Other	20	5	2	11

Source: Authors.

4.5.1 Authorship Patterns

We first discuss the data for the 133 articles having nine or fewer authors; we then summarize the data for all US papers regardless of number of authors, focusing on an analysis of first and last author.

The data for articles with nine or fewer authors is summarized in table 4.3. Of the 648 authors, 585 lived in the United States.[33] We could find information on the position of 550 of these (94.0 percent). Of these, 123 were postdocs (22.4 percent); another 108 (19.6 percent) were graduate students; eight (1.5 percent) were undergraduate students; and eight (1.5 percent) were students or postdocs, specific status not known. An additional four were alumni of the program, having either been a graduate student or a postdoc.[34] The postdoc count is, as we noted before, an undercount in all likelihood given that some postdocs have titles that make it difficult to distinguish them from staff scientists. When the categories are combined, we find that almost

33. In several cases the individual is listed with two affiliations; one is in the United States; the other is outside the United States. In this case we count the individual as being in the United States.

34. This is an undercount of alums given that not all web pages list alumni of the program and in some instances faculty do not keep web pages.

Table 4.3 Descriptive data for articles with less than 10 authors (133)

Total number of authors	648
Total number of authors in United States	585
Total number of US authors for whom position is known	550
Total number postdocs	123
Total number of graduate students	108
Total number of undergraduate students	8
Total student (grad or undergrad) or postdoc; status/unknown	8
Total affiliated with lab in past	4
Number of papers with one or more author who is a postdoc, grad student, or undergraduate student	115

Source: Authors.

one out of two authors (45.6 percent) was a postdoc, a student, or a recent alum of the program.[35]

Of perhaps more interest to our study is the fact that 115 (86.5 percent) of this class of papers had either a current postdoc or student as one of the authors. Five of the eighteen papers that have neither postdocs nor students as coauthors are either singly authored or have only one US author. Two of the eighteen papers were in the field of astronomy, three in earth sciences, and two in material sciences. The field least likely to have either a postdoc or a student as a coauthor is astronomy (two for two), followed by material science (with two of the seven papers having neither a postdoc nor a graduate student author), and earth sciences (three of the thirteen had neither a postdoc nor a graduate student author). The fields most likely to have a postdoc or a graduate student as a coauthor are biochemistry, genetics, nano-related, and chemistry and chemistry-related. Indeed, all of the forty-two papers published in these four areas (with less than ten authors) had one or more graduate students or postdocs as co-authors. Fields not far behind are biology (twenty-seven of twenty-eight papers) and physics (eleven of twelve).

All but twenty-seven of the papers with less than ten authors have one or more authors working in the same lab as the senior US author.[36] These patterns differ by field. The earth science papers are the least likely to have another individual working in a lab with the senior author (six out of thirteen earth science papers have no overlap in address). By way of contrast, 90 percent or more of the articles in biochemistry, genetics, nano-related areas,

35. A third of the postdocs are the only postdoc author on the paper; another third share authorship with one other postdoc; and another third share authorship with more than one other postdoc. Two papers have five postdocs as authors; twelve papers have three postdoc authors.

36. Five of these twenty-seven papers have only one US author. In some instances the PI does not have a lab. We include these instances in this count.

Table 4.4 **First and last authorship patterns**

	All US articles	First author (restricted to counts for articles having more than one author)	Last author
Number of US papers	159	157	159
Number of authors in United States	300	141	159
Total number of US authors for whom position is known	291	136	155
Total number of postdoc authors	59	57	2
Total number of graduate student authors	45	41	4
Total number of undergraduate student authors	1	0	1
Student/postdoc; exact status unknown	4	4	0

Source: Authors.

neurology, and physics have at least one co-author working in the same lab as the senior author.

Only eleven of the 115 papers with a postdoc or graduate student as a coauthor have no authors that are in the same lab as the senior US author. But it does not follow that all of the postdoc and student authors work in the lab of the last author. In a number of instances they work outside this lab, either with someone else at the same university or with someone in another university.

First and last authorship patterns are summarized in table 4.4 for all US academic articles appearing during the six-month period. The role of postdocs and students is especially striking when one looks at first-author position, a position of particular importance since in most fields the first author does the "heavy lifting," contributing the most to the article.[37] Fully 75 percent of the 136 first authors who are from the United States and whose position is known are either a postdoc or a student. Seven of the last authors are either a postdoc or a student. Four of these papers are in the area of earth science, further confirmation that the earth sciences are organized somewhat differently than the other fields we are looking at. Two of the papers that have postdocs as last author are in biochemistry. One paper in physics has an undergraduate student, Jacob Simones from the Minnesota State University Mankato, as the last author. The article has ten other authors, including his undergraduate advisor. Simones appears to have done related work during

37. Authorship patterns vary by discipline. In the life sciences the last author is generally the PI and the one who supplied the resources. The first author is the one who contributed the greatest amount to the research. This pattern is also true in chemistry and can also be the pattern in physics. In some disciplines, such as the earth and environmental sciences, authorship order is arranged entirely in terms of contribution. Authors are rarely listed in alphabetical order on scientific papers. For example, only twenty-six of the 159 papers we identified listed authors alphabetically; nineteen of these papers had only two authors, implying that there was a 50 percent chance of their being alphabetical regardless of practice.

the summer of 2006 as a research experience for undergraduates (REU) at Minnesota State University funded by NSF.[38]

4.5.2 Ethnicity of US Authors

Ideally, we would like to know the citizenship status or birth origin of the students and postdoc co-authors. Short of fielding a survey this is not possible, because most postdocs and students do not put curriculum vitae's (CV's) on the web. Instead, we follow the approach used by Bill Kerr, drawing on the same ethnic-name database that he used to identify the ethnicity of US inventors (Kerr 2008).

Specifically, ethnicity is identified using data that Kerr obtained from the Melissa Data Corporation.[39] The Melissa data is particularly strong at identifying Asian ethnicities, especially Chinese, Indian/Hindi, Japanese, Korean, Russian, and Vietnamese names. In addition to the Asian ethnicities, we are able to distinguish four other ethnicities: Russian, English, European, and Hispanic.[40] The approach exploits the idea that authors with "the surnames Chang or Wang are likely of Chinese ethnicity, those with surnames Rodriguez or Martinez of Hispanic ethnicity and so on" (Kerr 2007).

The methodology uses both first and last names and thus minimizes ambiguity in assigning names with multiple ethnicities, such as Lee and Park. Using ethnic names to identify citizenship status of graduate students and postdocs clearly has some limitations. If Asian and Hispanic names are classified as being foreign, the technique will overcount the foreign representation, given the number of US citizens with Asian and Hispanic names. On the other hand, if English and European names are used to classify individuals as "native," the native count will be overstated, given the number of European, English, and Canadian students and postdocs working in the United States.

Some indication of the degree of bias is given by examining the ethnicity of PhD recipients in the United States and the country of origin of PhD recipients who are noncitizen (either permanent or temporary resident). For example, in 2006, 1,164 PhDs in S&E were awarded to US citizens who self-identify as being "Asian" (Falkenheim 2007, table 2). Concurrently, 7,918 PhDs were awarded to non-US citizens (permanent and temporary

38. See http://www.physics.umn.edu/outreach/reu/REU2006Proceed.pdf for papers by the REU interns.

39. We are grateful to Bill Kerr not only for providing us access to the database but also for doing the actual match.

40. In some instances, the matching procedure attributes a name to several ethnicities, providing the probability of ethnicity associated with each match. In these instances we coded the ethnicity that had a greater than 50 percent probability. By way of contrast, Kerr (2008), who has a significantly larger database and addresses different questions, summed probabilities associated with an ethnicity rather than assuming a specific ethnicity in cases that he refers to as "ties."

visas) from the Asian countries of China, India, Korea, Japan, and Thailand (Falenkeim 2007, table 4). Assuming that citizens who self-identify as "Asian" have Asian last names leads to the conclusion that 13 percent of all PhD degrees awarded in the United States to individuals with Asian names went to citizen graduate students; 87 percent went to foreign graduate students. We cannot make a similar calculation for postdocs, given that neither the ethnicity of postdocs nor the source country of postdocs is ascertained. But we have reason to believe that the 87 percent is an undercount, given that not only among US PhD recipients is the postdoc-taking rate for noncitizen Asians high (Stephan and Ma 2005) but, in addition, a large percent of postdocs receive their PhDs outside the United States. Many of these, we assume, are Asian.

We estimate that approximately 1,132 PhDs in S&E were awarded to non-US citizens from English and European countries in 2005.[41] Using "white" as synonymous with "English" and "European" and noting that the number of S&E degrees awarded to "white" citizens in 2005 was 12,514 (Hoffer et al. 2006, table 8), we "guesstimate" that 8 percent of the English and European PhD names belong to noncitizens. In a similar way we "guesstimate" that 40 percent of Hispanics receiving degrees are noncitizens.[42] In light of our counts, taken together, these "biases" come close to canceling each other out and we believe that we have fairly reasonable overall counts for noncitizen PhD students by "keying" on ethnicity of name if we classify English and European as "native" and all others as foreign. We believe this undercounts the total number of noncitizens among postdoctorates, given the large number of individuals who come with PhD in hand to take a postdoc position as well as the large number of noncitizen PhD recipients who stay in the United States for postdoctoral training.

It is more difficult to ascertain the magnitude of the bias for positions such as faculty and staff scientist. For our purposes, however, we will use the same convention as that noted previously.

The ethnicity of US authors on papers with less than ten authors is presented in table 4.5 by position. We identified no Vietnamese authors and

41. The NSF provides data on the top thirty countries of origin of non-US citizens earning doctorates regardless of field (Hoffer et al 2006, Table 12). We classify three of these countries as English: Australia, Great Britain, and Canada. The total number of PhD recipients from these countries is 800. We classify three as "European:" Germany, Italy, and France; the number of recipients from the three is 581. We estimate that 82% of all doctorate degrees awarded to non-citizens in the U.S. are in S&E (Hoffer et al 2006, Table 11). From this, we estimate that 1,132 PhDs were awarded in S&E to individuals who have European or English names and are non-US citizens.

42. We classify four countries in the "top 30 countries" list as "Hispanic," (Hoffer et al. 2006, table 12). These are Mexico, Colombia, Argentina, and Spain. Collectively, 618 PhDs were awarded to individuals from these countries. We estimate that 82 percent of these are awarded in S&E (507), using data from table 11 (Hoffer et al. 2006). There were 744 degrees awarded in S&E to citizens who self-identify as Hispanic (Hoffer et al. 2006, table 8). From these two figures we "guesstimate" that 41 percent of the degrees awarded to Hispanics are to noncitizens.

Table 4.5 **Ethnicity of authors of papers with less than ten authors**

Position	European	English	Chinese	Indian	Japanese	Hispanic	Russian	Korean	Other	Row total
Postdoc	7	42	35	6	7	10	4	3	6	120
	(5.8%)	(35.0%)	(29.2%)	(5.0%)	(5.8%)	(8.3%)	(3.3%)	(2.5%)	(5.0%)	(20.8%)
Graduate student	4	60	20	5	1	2	3	3	8	106
	(3.8%)	(5.7%)	(18.9%)	(4.7%)	(0.9%)	(1.9%)	(2.8%)	(2.8%)	(7.5%)	(18.3%)
Undergraduate student	0	5	1	1	0	0	0	0	1	8
	(0%)	(62.5%)	(12.5%)	(12.5%)	(0%)	(0%)	(0%)	(0%)	(12.5%)	(1.4%)
Student or postdoc,	0	4	1	0	0	1	0	0	0	6
status not identified	(0%)	(66.7%)	(16.7%)	(0%)	(0%)	(16.7%)	(0%)	(0%)	(0%)	(1.0%)
Faculty	19	152	19	8	2	7	1	2	6	216
	(8.8%)	(70.4%)	(8.8%)	(3.7%)	(0.9%)	(3.2%)	(0.5%)	(0.9%)	(2.8%)	(37.4%)
Staff scientist/technician	5	35	9	0	3	4	5	1	4	66
	(7.6%)	(53.0%)	(13.6%)	(0%)	(4.5%)	(6.1%)	(7.6%)	(1.5%)	(6.1%)	(11.4%)
Other	0	10	5	1	0	0	0	0	0	16
	(0%)	(62.5%)	(31.3%)	(6.3%)	(0%)	(0%)	(0%)	(0%)	(0%)	(2.8%)
Not known	2	23	6	3	1	1	2	0	2	40
	(5.0%)	(57.5%)	(15.0%)	(7.5%)	(2.5%)	(2.5%)	(5.0%)	(0%)	(5.0%)	(6.9%)
Total	37	331	96	24	14	25	15	9	27	578
	(6.4%)	(57.3%)	(16.6%)	(4.2%)	(2.4%)	(4.3%)	(2.6%)	(1.6%)	(4.7%)	(100%)

Source: Authors.

Note: Parenthetical values in ethnicity columns are percent of row total. Parenthetical values in Row total column are percent of total.

hence this category is not included in the table. "Other" refers to ethnicities not contained in the Melissa data.[43]

We find that 57.3 percent of authors with a US address (and writing with a last author at a US institution of higher education) are identified as having English names and 6.4 percent have European names. We find that 4.3 percent have Hispanic names, 16.6 percent have Chinese names, and 4.2 percent have Indian/Hindi names. Koreans, Japanese, Russians, and "other" make up the remaining 11.3 percent.

Of particular interest to our study is that seventy-one of the 120 postdoc authors are neither English nor European (59.2 percent). This is remarkably close to the 60 percent that NSF estimates for 2006.[44] We find that forty-two of the 106 graduate student co-authors have neither English nor European names (39.6 percent). This is slightly lower than the percent of US PhDs awarded in science and engineering to noncitizen PhDs in 2006 (Falkenheim 2007, table 2), but consistent with the finding of John Bound and Sarah Turner (chapter 3, this volume) that higher-ranked institutions (from which most of these authors are drawn) have a lower proportion of foreign-graduate students than do lower-ranked institutions. We note that a large percent of the faculty authors are English or European (79.2 percent); the next most likely ethnic group to be a faculty author is Chinese (8.8 percent). We also classify authors according to whether they are a staff scientist or a technician. We find that slightly more than 60 percent of authors in such positions have English or European names; 13.6 percent have Chinese names.

Focusing on articles, we find that seventy of the 133 papers (53 percent) with fewer than ten US authors have a foreign student or postdoc as a coauthor. This represents approximately 60 percent of the 115 papers that have either a student or a postdoc author. We infer that it is the norm, not the exception, to have an international student or postdoc as a coauthor in papers published in *Science.*

Table 4.6 shows position and ethnicity for US first authors from our sample of all papers. We find that 55.7 percent are either of English or European ethnicity, the remaining 44.3 percent are "foreign"—17.9 percent are Chinese, 7.9 percent are Indian/Hindi, 4.3 percent are Hispanic, and 14.3 percent are drawn from other ethnicities. The heavy representation of graduate students and postdocs in the first-author position has already been noted. But what we learn from this table is the important role of "foreign" graduate students and postdocs. To wit, using our convention, we find that almost 60 percent of the graduate student first authors are foreign—a figure significantly higher than the percent of noncitizen PhD recipients in science

43. The database used for the ethnicity match contained several edits that were not present in the database used in creating tables 4.1 through 4.4. Thus, while the counts in the ethnicity tables are very close to those in the earlier tables, they do not always correspond perfectly.

44. Note that NSF calculations classify "permanent residents" with US citizens in determining citizenship status of postdocs.

Table 4.6 **Position and ethnicity for US first authors**

Position	European	English	Chinese	Indian	Japanese	Hispanic	Russian	Korean	Other	Total
Postdoc	3	23	13	5	0	5	3	0	4	57[a]
Graduate student	2	15	8	6	1	1	1	2	5	41
Undergraduate student	0	0	0	0	0	0	0	0	0	0
Student or postdoc, status not identified	0	4	0	0	0	0	0	0	0	4
Faculty	2	12	0	0	0	0	0	0	0	14
Other (including not known)	1	16	4	0	2	0	2	0	0	25
Total	8	70	25	11	3	6	6	2	9	140/141[a]

Source: Authors.

[a]Postdoc total includes one individual whose ethnicity is not classified.

and engineering and higher than the percent of "foreign" graduate students among graduate student coauthors in general (table 4.6). Noncitizens also make up slightly more than 54 percent of the first-author postdocs. Clearly, international graduate students and postdocs are important not only in staffing labs; they play lead roles in research. It is also interesting to note that faculty play a relatively minor role as first author, while staff scientists and technicians play a relatively important role (other category).

The position and ethnicity for last authors is given in table 4.7. It is of less interest to our study, given the small role that graduate students and postdocs play as "last authors." Briefly, and using the same convention, we note that 73.6 percent of last authors are "native"; 26.4 percent are foreign. Fully one third of the "foreign" last authors are Chinese.

Our findings regarding nativity are summarized in table 4.8. Slightly more than 44 percent of first authors are foreign; almost 60 percent of postdoc authors are foreign. Last authors are very likely to be native (over 73 percent) and six out of ten graduate student authors are native.

Finally, in table 4.9, we examine "affinity effects" by comparing the ethnicity of the last author to the ethnicity of coauthors working in the United States for all papers with less than ten authors. Proceeding in such a manner, we find that 73.8 percent of the coauthors of English last authors are English. If non-last authors were distributed randomly across articles, we would expect it to be 54.5 percent, based on the distribution in our database of authors. In a similar manner, we find that 53.8 percent of the coauthors of Chinese last authors are Chinese—a figure that is strikingly higher than the 18.6 percent that we would expect. Affinity effects also appear to be present for Hispanics but the cell sizes are very small. We find no evidence of affinity effects for European last-authors.

4.6 Conclusion

4.6.1 Summary of Findings

Universities play an important role in the production of knowledge in the United States, authoring nearly 75 percent of scientific and engineering articles written within the country. Within the university, research is often performed with the assistance of graduate students, postdoctoral scholars, and staff scientists, many of whom are foreign-born and, in the case of graduate students and postdocs, are studying in the United States on temporary visas.

Here we document the important role played by students and postdocs in university research by analyzing authorship patterns for a six-month period for articles published in *Science* having a last author affiliated with a US university. We choose *Science* because of its multidisciplinary nature and its position as a leading, if not the leading, journal in science. The fast

Table 4.7 Position and ethnicity for US last authors

Position	European	English	Chinese	Indian	Japanese	Hispanic	Russian	Korean	Other	Total
Postdoc	0	2	0	0	0	0	0	0	0	2
Graduate student	0	4	0	0	0	0	0	0	0	4
Undergraduate student	0	1	0	0	0	0	0	0	0	1
Faculty	7	92	13	9	2	9	2	2	3	139
Other (including not known)	1	10	1	0	0	0	0	0	1	13
Total	8	109	14	9	2	9	2	2	4	159

Source: Authors.

Table 4.8 **Authorship patterns by nativity (percent)**

Position	Native	Foreign
First authors	55.7	44.3
Last authors	73.6	26.4
Postdoc authors	40.8	59.2
Graduate students	60.4	39.6

Source: Authors.

Table 4.9 **Affinity effects in authorship patterns**

Ethnicity of last author	Expected percent of coauthors with same ethnicity	Actual percent of coauthors with same ethnicity	Number of papers
English	54.5	73.8	88
Chinese	18.6	53.8	13
Indian	3.4	5.5	9
European	6.7	0.0	7
Hispanic	4.3	23.3	6

Source: Authors.

turnaround time (decisions are generally made in less than a month and publication rapidly follows) also means that we are able to do web research regarding the status of authors.

We analyze authorship patterns for two sets of papers: (a) papers having fewer than ten authors, in which case we determine the status of all authors residing in the United States; and (b) all papers regardless of the number of authors, in which case we determine the status of the first and the last author. The first data set contains 133 articles; the second data set contains 159 papers. We determine the status of each author with a US affiliation through web-based research, starting with the last author's web page, which often contains a link to the lab and the group working in the lab. We find the web to be a powerful tool: of the 585 US authors we can determine the status of 550. We believe we are the first to use such a methodology to investigate the role that students and postdocs play in research.[45]

Our analysis demonstrates the important role that students and postdocs play in university research. We find that 45.6 percent of all authors, or almost one out of two, is a postdoc, student, or a recent alum of the program. By category, 22.4 percent are postdocs, 19.6 percent are graduate students, 1.5 percent are undergraduate students, another 1.5 percent are student or postdoc (status not known), and a handful are alums of the program. What is even more indicative of the important role that students

45. Vogel (1999) examines authorship patterns for two issues of *Science* in 1999.

and postdocs play in university research is our finding that 86.5 percent of papers—nearly seven out of eight (133-paper sample)—have either a current postdoc or student as one of the authors.

The role of postdocs and students is especially striking when one looks at first-author position on all US papers, regardless of the number of authors. To wit, we find that 102 of the 136 first authors who are in the United States and whose position is known are either a postdoc or a student (75 percent); seven of the last authors are either a postdoc or a student.

We identify the ethnicity of authors, drawing on the ethnic-name database that Kerr (2008) used to identify ethnicity of US inventors. The methodology is particularly strong at identifying Asian ethnicities. This approach clearly has some limitations. If Asian and Hispanic names are classified as being foreign, the technique overcounts the foreign representation, given the number of US citizens with Asian and Hispanic names. On the other hand, if English and European names are used to classify individuals as "native," the native count will be overstated, given the number of European, English, and Canadian students and postdocs working in the United States. We draw upon the distribution of PhDs awarded in 2006 to investigate the degree of this bias. We conclude that approximately 87 percent of the Asians we identify are noncitizens; 8 percent of the English and Europeans we identify are noncitizens; and 40 percent of the Hispanics are noncitizens. In light of our counts, these "biases" approximately cancel each other out and we believe that we get fairly reasonable overall counts for noncitizen PhD students and postdocs by "keying" on ethnicity of name and defining "English" and "European" as native.

Using this approach, we find that 59.2 percent of postdoc authors are neither English nor European, a figure that is remarkably close to the 60 percent that NSF estimates. We find that 39.6 percent of the graduate student co-authors have neither English nor European names. This is slightly lower than the percent of PhDs awarded in science and engineering to noncitizens in 2006. At the paper level, we find that seventy of the 133 papers (53 percent) with fewer than ten US authors have a foreign student or postdoc as a co-author. This represents approximately 60 percent of the 115 papers that have either a student or a postdoc author. Clearly, it is the norm, not the exception, to have an international student or postdoc as a co-author in papers published in *Science*.

Using the same convention, we find that almost 60 percent of the graduate student first authors are foreign and that noncitizens make up slightly more than 54 percent of the postdocs who are first authors. We conclude that international graduate students and postdocs are important not only in staffing university labs; they play lead roles in university research.

4.6.2 Discussion

It has long been known that the foreign-born play an important role in US science and engineering. The basis for much of this understanding has been the role the foreign-born play as faculty or when working in industry. The results of the present study suggest that the foreign-born play an important role in doing research, much of which is of a basic nature, while they are graduate students and postdocs. The finding is not surprising, but prior to this study no one has set about to investigate the degree to which the foreign-born contribute in this way.

The contributions of the foreign-born graduate students and postdoctoral scholars to US science, of course, do not end when their training is completed. Many choose to stay in the United States. Finn, for example, finds that approximately 70 percent of PhD recipients on temporary visas in science and engineering were in the United States two years after receiving their PhD degree; the five-year stay rate was only slightly lower (Finn 2005, table 3). The rate is highest for Chinese, who have a five-year stay rate of 90 percent, followed by Indians, with a five-year stay rate of 86 percent. (Finn 2005, table 7.) No one has made comparable estimates for postdocs, but the assumption is that a number who come to train stay on after their training is completed. The ethnicity of faculty authors in this study is suggestive of this; approximately one in five had neither English nor European names. The group making up the highest percent of nonnative faculty was of Chinese ethnicity.

This is not to say that scientists and engineers contribute to US science only when they stay. Many who return end up co-authoring papers with colleagues in the United States. We see some examples of this in our data. The work of Adams et al. (2005) finds that the international co-authorship patterns of faculty at US universities are influenced by the number of foreign students trained in their department who return to their home country. Moreover, co-authorship is not the only way by which scientists in one country benefit from the work and expertise of others. Published science is a public good; regardless of whether they stay or leave, these researchers will continue to contribute to the creation of knowledge.

That foreign-born graduate students and postdoctoral fellows play an important role appears indisputable from this research. But it does not follow that their places would be left unfilled if they were not to come. Considerable debate has focused on the degree to which foreign-born students displace US students. The question is difficult to answer but there is reasonable agreement regarding several facts. First, natives, especially native males, when choosing a career are responsive to alternative opportunities. In the last twenty or so years many of these opportunities—for example, law and business—have proved relatively more attractive, requiring shorter training times and offering higher salaries. Second, if the incentive structure were to change, the number of US citizens entering S&E would arguably change as well. By way of example, Richard Freeman (2005) finds the size of the applicant pool for NSF Graduate Research Fellowships to be responsive to the relative value of the stipend and concludes "that the supply of highly skilled applicants is sufficiently responsive to the value of awards that increases in the value of stipends could attract some potentially outstanding science and engineering students who would otherwise choose other careers." Third, and by way of contrast, foreign-born have had fewer alternatives available that offer the option of support while in school and employment at a favorable relative wage. Fourth, the alternatives open to the foreign-born are changing. Programs outside the United States are becoming more and more competitive. Since the late 1980s the number of S&E PhD degrees awarded in Europe has surpassed the number in the United States. In the late 1990s, the number of degrees awarded in Asian countries surpassed the number awarded in the United States. In China alone the number accelerated from virtually zero in 1985 to approximately 13,500 by 2004 (National Science Board 2008, appendix tables 2-42 and 2-43). At the same time, programs in the United States are at risk of becoming less attractive to foreign-born students and postdoctoral scholars. This is not only because funds for graduate and postdoctoral support are diminishing as agencies such as NIH experience real decrease in funding levels, but also because of problems faced by foreign nationals in the United States since 9/11. A case in point is the special vetting required for foreign nationals to work on research supported by federal agencies and considered "sensitive but unclassified."[46]

Nor does it follow that the demand for graduate students and postdocs to work at universities will necessarily persist at its current level. The technology of discovery is changing. By way of example, in 1990 the best-equipped lab could sequence 1,000 base pairs a day. By January 2000 the twenty labs involved in mapping the human genome were collectively sequencing 1,000 base pairs a second, 24/7. The cost per finished base pair fell from $10.00 in 1990 to under $.05 in 2003 (Collins, Morgan, and Patrinos 2003) and was roughly $.01 in 2007 (http://biodesign.asu.edu/news/nih-funds-next-generation-of-dna-sequencing-projects-at-asu). As the technology of discovery changes, the need for skilled lab workers—many of whom are graduate students and postdocs—may decline. Moreover, as equipment becomes increasingly sophisticated and more expensive, research procedures may increasingly be outsourced to nonuniversity facilities. Mail-in crystallography, where crystals are sent to large nonuniversity labs for analysis, is but one example. There is also the question of whether the Federal government will continue to provide resources for graduate research assistants and postdocs at the level it has in the past.

The heavy reliance on graduate students and postdoctoral scholars in the performance of university research has contributed to the US eminence as a training center for both native and foreign-born students. It provides not only hands-on learning but also financial support for graduate study and

46. This may change in the near future. In June of 2008 DOD Under Secretary John Young wrote a directive stating that "classification is the only appropriate mechanism" for restricting participation by foreign nationals or for restricting publication (Bhattacharjee 2008, 325).

postdoctoral work, something that many other countries cannot provide. Factors that reduce either the demand for or supply of graduate students and postdocs have the potential of threatening the United States's eminence as a training center and producer of research.

References

Adams, J. D., G. C. Black, R. Clemons, and P. Stephan. 2005. Scientific teams and institutional collaborations: Evidence from US universities, 1981–1999. *Research Policy* 34 (3): 259–85.

Andrews, F. M., ed. 1979. Scientific productivity: The effectiveness of research groups in six countries. Cambridge: Cambridge University Press.

Agrawal, A., and A. Goldfarb. 2008. Restructuring research: Communication costs and the democratization of university innovation. *American Economic Review* 98 (4): 1578–90.

Barnett, A., R. W. Ault, and D. Kaserman. 1988. The rising incidence of co-authorship in economics: Further evidence. *Review of Economics and Statistics* 70 (3): 539–43.

Bhattacharjee, Y. 2008. New policy tries to ease security restrictions. *Science* 321 (5887): 325.

Bunton, S. A., and W. T. Mallon. 2007. The continued evolution of faculty appointment and tenure policies at US medical schools. *Academic Medicine* 82 (3): 281–89.

Collins, F., M. Morgan, and A. Patrinos. 2003. The human genome project: Lessons from large-scale biology. *Science* 300 (5617): 286–90.

Davis, G. 2005. Doctors without orders. *American Scientist* 93 (3, supplement). Available at: http://postdoc.sigmaxi.org/results/.

Ehrenberg, R. G., M. J. Rizzo, and G. H. Jakubson. 2003. Who bears the growing cost of science at universities? NBER Working Paper no. 9627. Cambridge, MA: National Bureau of Economic Research, April.

Falkenheim, J. 2007. *US doctoral awards in science and engineering continue upward trend in 2006.* InfoBrief, Science Resources Statistics, National Science Foundation (NSF).

Finn, M. G. 2005. *Stay rates of foreign doctorate recipients from US universities, 2003.* Oak Ridge, TN: Oak Ridge Institute for Science and Education.

Fox, M. F. 1991. Gender, environmental milieu, and productivity in science. In *The outer circle: Women in the scientific community,* ed. H. Zuckerman, J. R. Cole, and J. T. Bruer, 188–204. New York: W. W. Norton.

Franzoni, C., G. Scellato, and P. Stephan. 2008. Changing incentives to publish and the consequences for submission patterns. Paper prepared for presentation at the Dynamics of Institutions and Markets in Europe (DIME)-BRICK workshop, "The Economics and Policy of Academic Research." July, Collegio Carlo Alberto, Moncalieri (Torino), Italy.

Freeman, R. B., T. Chang, and H. Chiang. 2005. Supporting "The Best and the Brightest" in science and engineering: NSF graduate research fellowships. NBER Working Paper no. 11623. Cambridge, MA: National Bureau of Economic Research, September.

Hoffer, T., K. Grigorian, and E. Hedbert. 2008. *Postdoc participation of science, engineering, and health doctorate recipients.* InfoBrief, (NSF), March.

Hoffer, T. B., V. Welch, Jr., K. Webber, K. Williams, B. Lisek, M. Hess, D. Loew, and I. Guzman-Barron. 2006. *Doctorate recipients from United States universities: Summary report 2005.* Chicago: National Opinion Research Center.
Jones, B. 2005. The burden of knowledge and the "death of the renaissance man": Is innovation getting harder? NBER Working Paper no. 11360. Cambridge, MA: National Bureau of Economic Research, May.
Kean, S. 2006. Scientists spend nearly half their time on administrative tasks, survey finds. *Chronicle of Higher Education,* July 7.
Kerr, W. R. 2007. The ethnic composition of US inventors: Evidence building from ethnic names in US patents. Paper prepared and presented at NBER workshop on Career Patterns of Foreign-Born Scientists and Engineers Trained and/or Working in the US, November 7, New Brunswick, NJ.
———. 2008. Ethnic scientific communities and international technology diffusion. *Review of Economics and Statistics* 90 (3): 518–30.
Kolbert, E. 2007. Crash course: The world's largest particle accelerator. *The New Yorker,* May 14.
Lawani, S. M. 1986. Some bibliometric correlates of quality in scientific research. *Scientometrics* 9 (1–2): 13–25.
Malakoff, D. 2000. The rise of the mouse, biomedicine's model mammal. *Science* 288 (5464): 248–53.
Mervis, J. 1998. The biocomplex world of Rita Colwell. *Science* 281 (5385): 1944–47.
———. 2008. Top PhD feeder schools are now Chinese. *Science* 321 (5886): 185.
National Academies. 2005. *Policy implications of international graduate students postdoctoral scholars in the United States.* Committee on Policy Implications of International Graduate Students and Postdoctoral Scholars in the United States, Committee on Science, Engineering, and Public Policy. Washington, DC: The National Academies Press.
National Science Board. 2006. *Science and engineering indicators 2006.* Arlington, VA: NSB.
———. 2008. *Science and engineering indicators 2008.* Arlington, VA: NSB.
National Science Foundation. WebCASPAR, Integrated Science and Engineering Resources Data System. Available at: http:/webcaspar.nsf.gov/.
Overbye, D. 2007. A giant takes on physics' biggest questions. *New York Times,* May 15.
Pelekanos, A. 2008. Money management for scientists: Lab budgets and funding issues for young pis. Science Alliance, New York Academy of Sciences, June 16.
Penning, T. 1998. The postdoctoral experience: An associate dean's perspective. *The Scientist* 12 (19): 9.
Regets, M. 2005. Foreign students in the United States. Presentation at the Dialogue Meeting on Migration Governance: European and North American Perspectives. June 27, Brussels, Belgium.
———. 2007. An overview of foreign-born S&E workers in the United States and their measurement. Unpublished manuscript prepared for presentation at the NBER Conference on Career Patterns of Foreign-born Scientists and Engineers. November 7, New Brunswick, NJ.
Service, R. F. 2006. Tennessee scientists beaming. *Science* 312 (May): 675.
Stephan, P. E. 2008. Job market effects on scientific productivity. In *Scientific competition,* ed. M. Albert, D. Schmidtchen, and S. Voigt, 11–29. Tubingen, Germany: Conferences on New Political Economy 25, Mohr Siebeck.
Stephan, P. E., G. Black, and T. Chaing. 2007. The small size of the small-scale market: The early-stage labor market for highly skilled nanotechnology workers. *Research Policy* 36 (6): 887–92.

Stephan, P. E., and S. G. Levin. 2002. The importance of implicit contracts in collaborative research. In *The new economics of science,* ed. P. Mirowski and E.-M. Sent, 412–30. Chicago: University of Chicago Press.

Stephan, P. E., and J. Ma. 2005. The increased frequency and duration of the postdoctorate career stage. *American Economic Review Papers and Proceedings* 95 (2): 71–75.

Tanyildiz, Z. E. 2008. The effects of networks on institution selection by foreign doctoral students in the US. Unpublished dissertation, Georgia State University.

Vogel, G. 1999. Working conditions: A day in the life of a topflight lab. *Science* 285 (5433): 1531–2.

Winkler, A., S. Levin, and P. Stephan. 2008. The diffusion of IT in higher education: Publishing productivity of academic life scientists. Andrew Young School of Policy Studies Research Paper Series no. 09-01.

Wuchty, S., B. Jones, and B. Uzzi. 2007. The increasing dominance of teams in the production of knowledge. *Science* 316 (5827): 1036–39.

5

Universities as Firms
The Case of US Overseas Programs

E. Han Kim and Min Zhu

5.1 Introduction

Universities in the United States are the leading providers of higher education in the world. According to the *Newsweek* 2006 global university ranking, fifteen of the top twenty universities worldwide are American universities.[1] More than 580,000 foreign undergraduate and graduate students are currently studying in the United States. They spend around 15 billion dollars yearly, propelling the education industry into the fifth largest export service sector in the United States (Bhandari and Chow 2007). Universities in the United States are also active in a wide range of international activities, from setting up cross-country research labs to offering degree programs in foreign countries.

This chapter employs the standard economic analysis to study overseas degree programs offered by US universities. If US universities ever behave like firms, they are more likely to do so overseas, where they are not bound by the same set of obligations to domestic stakeholders as they are in the United States. We analyze how university characteristics (i.e., supply side) and host

E. Han Kim is the Fred M. Taylor Professor of Business Administration at the Stephen M. Ross School of Business, University of Michigan, where he also founded and directs the Global MBA Program. Min Zhu is a doctoral candidate at the Stephen M. Ross School of Business, University of Michigan.

We have benefited from many useful comments and suggestions from Charles Clotfelter (the editor), Peter Doeringer (the discussant), Di Li, Haizheng Li, Xiaoyang Li, Yao Lu, Scott Masten, Xinzheng Shi, Jeffery Smith, Brian Wu, Liang Zhang, two anonymous referees, and participants of NBER preconference meeting in Cambridge, finance seminar at the University of Michigan, and the NBER Conference on American Universities in a Global Market held in Vermont. We thank Joyce Buchanan for editorial assistance. We acknowledge financial support from Mitsui Life Financial Research Center at the University of Michigan.

1. Available at: http://www.msnbc.msn.com/id/14321230/, accessed August 2007.

country environment (i.e., demand side) interact to affect the likelihood of a university offering overseas programs, how universities choose location, and how they determine program pricing (tuition). We examine these issues using hand-collected data on US overseas programs from multiple sources.

Our analyses help address whether university motives for foreign direct investment (FDI) are different from those of multinational corporations (MNCs). While there are numerous studies about MNCs' FDI, to the best of our knowledge, there is no economics-based, scientific study of foreign investment by US universities. We also gather a unique data set that provides a comprehensive picture of the nature and type of overseas degree programs offered by US universities.

Although there are important differences between nonprofit universities and profit-seeking corporations, we assume universities, like firms, are subject to financial constraints and give high priority to increasing the present value of the revenue-cost difference. In such a framework, universities endued with different intellectual capital will self-select into two broad types: reputable institutions with selective admission standards and active research programs, or moderately ranked universities with relaxed admission standards and greater tuition dependency. Given these two types of universities, which type is more likely to have an overseas program? The answer is not immediately obvious. While moderately-ranked universities may be more willing suppliers, local demand would be greater for programs offered by the elite type. However, elite schools may be less willing to venture abroad because of their concerns for quality control, diluting brand names, and diverting home campus resources.

We start the chapter by comparing universities to firms. We discuss how economic motives and nonpecuniary factors affect universities' decision to offer overseas programs, providing an overview of the costs and benefits affecting the supply for and demand of US university overseas programs. This overview is based on our survey of articles published in the *Chronicle of Higher Education.* When we examine the historical archive of the *Chronicle,* we observe two major waves of US overseas programs. The first wave occurred during the late 1980s to the mid-1990s, mainly led by moderately ranked universities with less stringent admission standards. After almost a decade of relative inactivity, a new surge of overseas programs appears, with active participation by highly reputable research universities.

During the first wave, most overseas programs were apt to be supply driven and failed due to the lack of demand in the host countries. For instance, more than thirty US universities established branch campuses in Japan during its economic boom in the late 1980s. These universities had low name recognition and almost all of these overseas programs were closed by the mid-1990s due to low enrollment. In contrast, the current wave is more demand driven, and the main suppliers are large research universities with high visibility and strong reputations. It appears that the best schools are making efforts to globalize their institutions and to provide higher education opportunities overseas.

Finance plays a decisive role in offering overseas programs. Schools with greater tuition-dependency are more likely to offer overseas programs. Their location choice illustrates the important role economics plays in these programs. Real gross domestic product (GDP) per capita and tertiary school age population are two key determinants of the location choice. Universities in the United States target countries with large potential markets where the local population has the economic means to pay for their services. They also follow US multinational corporations' FDI flows and invest in business friendly countries with loose regulations. Asia and the Middle East are the most popular destinations for overseas programs, but for different reasons. Asia provides a large market with strong local demand for US-style education. Alternately, Middle Eastern countries are attractive because they grant substantial financial aid to sponsoring universities with their oil money.

Our analysis of tuition charges reveals that US universities adjust their pricing to local conditions. They discount tuition less in countries with higher real GDP per capita. Undergraduate degree programs are discounted more than master degree programs because of greater local competition in the market for undergraduate degree programs. When universities reduce costs by forging local university partnerships and/or by obtaining financial support from local governments, they do not pass on the savings to local students in the form of lower tuition.

In sum, universities behave much like multinational corporations when they make overseas investments and operate overseas programs.

5.2 Universities as Firms

5.2.1 Organizational Structure and Objective Function

Universities differ from for-profit corporations in various ways. Universities provide both private and public goods. Their two main products are knowledge creation and knowledge dissemination through research and teaching. Research results are freely available to most members of society and help stimulate economic growth. Knowledge dissemination increases human capital, and the benefits can be direct to those who receive higher education, or indirect to those who benefit from the economic growth attributable to the development and accumulation of human capital through higher education. The need for higher education has become crucial in the age of globalization, as knowledge-based workforces have become an essential ingredient to acquire and maintain a competitive edge in the marketplace.

The payoffs from knowledge creation take a long time to be realized and are highly uncertain, yet they generate positive externalities to society. In turn, society supports these activities by nonprofit universities through gifts and endowments from the private sector and subsidies from local and federal governments. The *Digest of Education Statistics* (National Center for Education Statistics 2008a) reports that during the 2004–2005 academic year, total tuition revenue represented only 16.4 percent of total revenue for all public degree-granting institutions and 29.5 percent for all private nonprofit degree-granting institutions in the United States. Society does not provide much support for for-profit universities, as it expects them to support their own profit-generating activities.[2]

Governance of universities is more complicated than governance of corporations. Unlike private enterprises with residual claim holders (stockholders), nonprofit universities have multiple stakeholders without a clearly defined pecking order, which leads to multiple objectives without well-defined priorities. Coleman (1973) compares universities to shells that encompass a variety of activities: teaching, research activities supported by government and private organizations, and external consulting. These activities often create conflicts of commitment and interest, leading to compromises in teaching and research effectiveness, although spillover effects (e.g., research and consulting experience benefiting the quality and effectiveness of teaching) may lessen the costs. Lacking well-defined priorities, faculty resource allocations are likely to be made for the benefits of individual faculty, and some universities may resemble a collection of little kingdoms built around individual faculty. Such an organizational form is not necessarily bad: it may encourage entrepreneurship on the part of individual faculty, making them more creative and productive. It also may make them more accountable for their individual actions. However, such an organizational form may make it difficult to create synergies between individual talents and for the university to act as a cohesive unit to meet various, and often conflicting, demands of the stakeholders.

Regardless of the organizational form a university takes, it must provide services to various stakeholders, who ultimately decide on the amount of its financial resources. Universities generate revenues from tuition, private gifts and endowments, state subsidies, and federal and private grants. Like firms, they strive to maximize the present value of the revenue-cost difference, not because they are profit maximizing, but because they want to maximize financial resources available for their pursuit of various goals and objectives, however ambiguous they may be.[3]

The strategies universities adopt to maximize the present value of the revenue-cost difference depends on the university type. Consider an elite university with high intellectual capital based on past research accomplish-

2. See Goldin and Katz (1999) for a review of the history of universities. Nonprofit organizations are preferred to for-profit organizations when consumers are uncertain about product quality due to asymmetric information (Easley and O'Hara 1983).

3. Winston (1999) also recognizes that nonprofit organizations' behavior may appear profit driven because of budget constraints.

ments, academic traditions, and highly selective admission standards, yielding a strong reputation and a large number of prominent and loyal alumni. Its present value of the revenue-cost difference will be higher if the school maintains its high-quality research and teaching than if it suddenly turns into a tuition-maximizing entity by compromising its standards on research and teaching.

Unlike corporations, universities have strong incentives to be selective in choosing customers because the quality of output—student academic performance, job placement, and lifetime achievement—depends on the quality of input—student quality and effort. That is, universities employ a customer-input technology (Rothschild and White 1995). Furthermore, peer effects of fellow students generate externalities to the quality of output; for example, having good students helps to improve the academic performance of fellow students (Sacerdote 2001). This is one of the reasons universities subsidize their customers (students) with financial aid and maintain certain admission standards.

Students' learning is also enhanced by the presence of research activities (Clotfelter 1999). Elite universities receive feedback effects from maintaining high-quality research and teaching because they tend to attract more high-quality faculty and students who can further improve their quality and reputation. That is, high-quality research and teaching has a "multiplier effect" (Hoxby 1997; Winston 1999).

These various attributes and effects give an elite university strong incentive to maintain its high-quality research and teaching and selective admission standards. The result is a continuation of high-quality products to serve their stakeholders, who will, in turn, provide the necessary financial resources for the university to carry on its knowledge creation and dissemination activities. At the same time, high-quality students and faculty agglomerate in elite universities with ample financial resources.

In contrast, a new university with low intellectual capital may have little chance to receive private gifts and endowments to support high-quality teaching and research. The present value of the revenue-cost difference will be higher if it forgoes costly research activities and maximizes tuition revenue by relaxing admission standards. Such universities have little chance of survival if they imitate selective admission standards and pursuit of costly research activities of elite universities, unless they can obtain unusually large public subsidies or private gifts. In other words, to universities with low intellectual capital, survival is of greater concern than taking advantage of the customer-input technology, peer effects, and the multiplier effects that are important to elite universities. Therefore, universities with low intellectual capital will be more reliant on tuition revenue and compete for customers (students) by using less selective admission standards.

Thus, we hypothesize that universities will self-select into either highly reputable institutions with high-quality teaching and research or largely tuition-dependent institutions that appear financially driven. We predict that these two types will follow different strategies in both knowledge creation and dissemination activities. Whereas the highly reputable will devote considerable resources to research and maintain highly selective admission standards, the tuition-dependent will maximize tuition revenues with relaxed admission standards.

5.2.2 Economic Motives for Overseas Ventures

Are highly reputable universities or tuition-dependent ones more likely to provide overseas degree programs? The answer is not obvious. Tuition-dependent universities will view overseas programs as opportunities to increase revenues and to distinguish themselves from rival schools in terms of international presence; thus, they will be more willing suppliers.[4] However, a successful, financially viable program requires a demand for its services in the local economy. Because education is a large, onetime investment for students, demand is determined by a trade-off between school reputation and the costs of education. The local market will be less receptive to a program offered by a US university with moderate reputation, unless it offers a deep discount in tuition. In contrast, more reputable schools will be able to charge higher tuition and/or enjoy greater demand.[5] However, an elite university may be less willing to supply overseas programs because of its concern about controlling quality from a distance. They have more to lose by putting their reputation at stake.

In this section, we provide an overview of the costs and benefits affecting the supply and demand for US overseas programs. We then explore non-pecuniary factors that may affect the programs. In the following empirical section, we analyze the interplay of these supply and demand considerations by examining the characteristics of universities offering overseas programs and of countries hosting the programs.

Supply

Financial Benefits The singular, most obvious financial benefit is tuition revenue. Successfully operating overseas programs also broaden a university's name recognition globally and attract future foreign donors. Universities with moderate reputations may have less to lose reputationally if their overseas programs lack quality. And because they are more tuition-dependent, their programs will offer more expansive admission standards.

Highly esteemed US universities, by contrast, may be less willing to pro-

4. Winston (1999) points out US universities with low financial resources tend to employ less costly teaching methods such as distance learning and also recruit more foreign and older students to generate more revenues.

5. Hoxby (1997) argues that only elite universities are able to compete for the best students at the national level. Elite universities also enjoy advantages in the global education market due to yearly publication of various worldwide university rankings readily available on the Internet.

vide overseas programs because of their concerns for quality control, possible dilution of their brand names, and diversion of faculty resources from research. However, when foreign governments seek to expand higher education opportunities for their citizens through overseas programs, they are more likely to allow/invite highly ranked universities to establish programs, and may even entice them with financial subsidies. Consequently, successful programs are more likely to be in those disciplines in which the sponsoring universities already enjoy comparative strengths.

Financial Costs Universities need physical assets (e.g., classrooms and equipment) and human capital (e.g., faculty and staff) to establish overseas programs. However, compared to manufacturing firms, universities require fewer physical assets. Although this may help keep fixed costs relatively low, variable costs tend to be higher than domestic programs because faculty often garner extra compensation for teaching in overseas programs. For example, Carnegie Mellon University gives their US-based faculty teaching on its Qatar campus a 25 percent salary increase and provides them with amenities.[6] The Global MBA Program at the University of Michigan pays its faculty an additional 18.75 percent of their base salary plus an overseas trip inconvenience fee of 2.5 percent to teach a ten-day, 2.25 credit-hour course in Asia.

To cover these higher costs, universities may pass through the additional costs as a tuition surcharge, which lowers demand and keeps class sizes small. An alternative strategy is to hire local faculty and/or offer joint programs with local universities, which tends to lower the quality and prestige of the program. Some top ranked universities also may be able to convince local governments to provide financial support to cover costs.

Demand

In developing countries, the university attendance rate of the college age population is below 15 percent, much lower than the 40 to 50 percent in developed countries.[7] To the extent that an insufficient supply of higher education opportunities contributes to the low college-attendance rate in developing countries, overseas programs provide a valuable service in satisfying the unmet demand.

Alternative Choices The extent that overseas programs resolve the unmet educational demand depends on alternative choices available to local students. The choices include attending a local university and going abroad for

6. Burton Bollag, "American's Hot New Export: Higher Education," *Chronicle of Higher Education,* February 17, 2006.

7. Beth McMurtrie, "The Global Campus, American Colleges Connect with the Broader World," *Chronicle of Higher Education,* March 2, 2007.

their degrees. Students will weigh the costs and benefits of these alternatives against attending an overseas program.

Local Colleges Students' college choices are highly sensitive to university rankings, as there is a universal belief that a degree from a higher ranked university will enable a graduate to find a better job with a higher salary (Brewer, Eide, and Ehrenberg 1999; Black and Smith 2006). Whether students perceive undergraduate overseas programs as higher-quality than programs offered by their local colleges depends upon the reputation of the provider. If the provider is a top ranked American university, students are more likely to consider the program as better than domestic programs and will be attracted to it. However, most undergraduate overseas programs are offered by moderately ranked US universities. These programs are not necessarily viewed as superior to domestic colleges and tend to be in low demand among top high school graduates. Moreover, many overseas programs hire local faculty to staff some courses, which may affect students' perceptions of program quality. The education market is considered a "trust market" where the quality of output is difficult to judge. Thus, it may take a while for overseas programs to build up their reputation, limiting the demand for the program and the price they can charge for their products.

Overseas programs usually offer courses in a limited number of disciplines, typically focusing on areas such as computer science and business, whereas local colleges offer a greater variety of courses in a wider range of disciplines. Because of their narrower offerings, students may think that overseas programs do not provide a comprehensive college experience, deterring many qualified students from enrolling. Furthermore, students may be concerned with the continuity of overseas programs. The uncertainty over the continuity may pose a risk on the value of the degree, although the adverse effects can be mitigated if the degree granting institution has a proven track record at its home campus.

Studying in the United States Local students may instead choose to attend universities in the United States. This choice gives a better opportunity to improve their English language skills, a highly valued commodity in the global market. To some students, experiencing American culture throughout their campus lives is almost as important as their college degrees. Studying in the United States also provides some students an interim step to immigrate to the United States. Those who highly value these nondegree experiences or opportunities will not be attracted to overseas programs. Furthermore, degrees earned through overseas programs may be perceived as less prestigious.

However, attending a university in the United States tends to be more costly. Students have to spend several years away from their family and friends, incurring high traveling and living expenses. They also may have to risk their career opportunities with their current employers. Overseas programs offer a less expensive alternative to studying abroad, targeting students who want foreign degrees without leaving their homeland. Individuals unwilling to incur the higher expenses, unable to obtain visas to study in the United States, and/or unwilling to leave their current jobs because of high opportunity costs (e.g., managers interested in executive MBA programs) are the primary targets of the overseas programs. Most of these overseas programs also offer the opportunity for an American campus experience before graduation.

Host Country Environment Demand also depends on the host country's institutional characteristics, which are shown to have significant impacts on how foreign ideas and systems are accepted. Djelic (1998) documents significant differences in the level of acceptance and adoption of American corporate capitalism between France, Germany, and Italy after World War II, which are attributed to the difference in local political and economic environments. Similar forces may apply to overseas programs: they are more likely to be offered and be successful in countries where government policies are friendly in terms of financial support and/or regulation.[8]

Many US universities have recently established overseas programs in the Education City of Qatar and Knowledge Valley of United Arab Emirates (UAE) because of favorable government policies and generous financial support. Some Asian countries, such as Hong Kong, Singapore, and South Korea, in their pursuit of becoming regional education hubs, actively encourage overseas programs by foreign universities.

5.2.3 Nonpecuniary Factors

Firms venture abroad mainly to generate profits, and their location choices are largely determined by economic considerations.[9] Their decisions also are influenced by nonpecuniary factors. Because universities' stakeholders are more diverse without clearly defined pecking order, nonpecuniary factors may play a more important role in setting up overseas programs.

Network Dynamics

Implementation decisions, such as location choice, are influenced by organizational and network dynamics. Setting up educational programs in foreign countries is not an easy task. It may take years to complete the whole process from selecting program location, signing a mutual agreement (if a local partner is involved), seeking government approval (if required),

8. See Green (2007) for a description of government policies regulating foreign providers of higher education.

9. For instance, firms in natural resource industries invest in countries where the resources are located. Manufacturing firms invest in less developed countries to take advantage of cheap labor. Service industries invest in countries with large customer bases. See Caves (1996) for a review on foreign direct investment of US multinational firms.

campus planning, to admitting the first class of students. To facilitate this process, some schools choose locations where they already have established connections either officially or unofficially through personal contacts. For instance, Cornell Medical School set up a branch campus in Qatar because one of their trustees encouraged them to do so and helped arrange financial support.[10] Overseas programs often have faculty directors who are born or have ethnic roots in the country of the program location.

Campus Internationalization

An important benefit of offering overseas programs is broadening international perspectives of American faculty and students. Faculty benefit from face-to-face interactions with foreign students and researchers. They gain valuable international experience from staying abroad, which helps expand the scope of teaching and research. Some overseas programs facilitate American students' study abroad, enriching their cultural experience. Courses are usually taught in English and credits can be easily transferred back to their home campuses. However, these benefits are not without costs. Faculty have to be away from home, spend less time on research, and teach in unfamiliar foreign surroundings, all of which make it difficult to secure a sufficient number of US faculty for the long term.

Status Competition

"Prestige maximization" (James 1990) and "the pursuit of excellence" (Clotfelter 1996) are often considered most important objectives for university administrators. Universities compete for high-quality faculty and students. They compete for faculty at the national level using tenure, lighter teaching loads, and plentiful research grants. This competition is especially severe among research oriented elite universities. To the extent that universities with higher status tend to receive greater endowments and gifts (e.g., Harvard), the status competition is not unrelated to economic motives.

Universities compete for students using various means, ranging from merit- and need-based financial aid to large expenditures to improve campus facilities (e.g., Clotfelter 1999). Like firms, universities advertise the beauty of their campuses and recreational facilities (Hutchins 1936). They may also collude to ease the burden of competition. In 1991, the US Justice Department charged eight Ivy League schools and MIT with violations of antitrust laws. Soon thereafter, the Ivy League universities agreed to stop comparing the aid packages of students admitted.[11] Perhaps as a consequence, the competition became stiffer, as Stanford and Harvard introduced early admission

10. This was pointed out to us by Ronald Ehrenberg during the NBER Conference on US Universities in a Global Market.

11. Scott Jaschik, "Justice Department Asks at Least 15 Colleges for Detailed Information on Admissions," *Chronicle of Higher Education,* July 24, 1991.

policies and other schools such as Yale and Princeton adopted a variety of financial aid packages (Clotfelter and Rothschild 1993; Winston 1999).

The international presence through overseas program may give a university an edge in this status competition. Setting up overseas programs signals a university's commitment to internationalization, which is given an important weight in various influential college ranking systems. For example, the *U.S. News & World Report* ranking considers campus internationalization an important aspect of college competitiveness. Higher undergraduate college rankings help recruit not only higher-quality students but also higher caliber research faculty through the halo effect (Kim, Morse, and Zingales 2009).

Altruism

It is possible that there is an altruistic motive in offering overseas programs. It is not unreasonable for American educators to believe their higher education system is the best. In their desire to help fellow mankind, they may want to set up American-style higher education institutions in countries lacking good higher education systems. What we have in mind are universities set up by missionaries in developing countries. But these are not overseas programs. They are full pledged local universities founded by missionaries.

Anecdotal evidence suggests many overseas programs set up by elite universities receive substantial financial support from foreign countries. Our empirical results indicate that universities establish programs in countries where there are sufficient student populations that can afford an American-style higher education. If altruism were an important motive for the recent surge in US overseas programs, we should have observed more media coverage of attempts to establish overseas programs in low income countries where people cannot afford higher education. However, this is not what we observe. The *Chronicle* reports very few US overseas programs in Africa, a continent desperately in need of improvement in both quantity and quality of higher education.[12]

5.3 Anecdotal Evidence

There is a dearth of empirical evidence on US universities' overseas programs. Thus, our initial step is to gather pertinent information about the overseas activities of US universities. We choose the *Chronicle of Higher Education* because it is the leading source of information on university activities. Its International Section provides numerous anecdotes on overseas activities, which vary from student exchange programs, international research collaboration, to overseas degree programs. We focus on overseas

12. It may be that there is insufficient high school graduates capable of handling course work offered by American universities overseas, discouraging even the altruistic from attempting to establish overseas programs in Africa.

degree programs. Some are financially supported by foreign governments and partners, but many programs must be financially self-sufficient to avoid draining resources from home campuses. In this regard, these programs have to be run, at least partially, like business models.

When we examine the historical archive of the *Chronicle,* an interesting pattern emerges. Most of the *Chronicle* articles on overseas programs are published in two time periods: between the late 1980s and early 1990s, and more recently, beginning in the early 2000s. The earlier articles are simple. They either announce initiation of new programs or report program failures and campus closures. The articles are short and the contents lack details. Then, after almost a decade of sporadic coverage and relative silence about overseas programs, there is a resurgence of articles beginning in 2000. They provide rather extensive coverage of overseas programs initiated mostly by top ranked US universities. These recent articles provide more details about the overseas programs, including how the deals are structured with foreign governments.

Why have elite US universities suddenly started to offer overseas programs? Is this a second wave of overseas programs with different players? Or does the new spate of articles simply reflect a resurgence of the first wave? To analyze these questions, we use the Integrated Postsecondary Education Data System (IPEDS) at the National Center for Education Statistics (NCES) and download the overseas enrollment data from IPEDS enrollment surveys conducted in 1986, 1987, 1994, 1995, 1996, and 1998. In these surveys, universities are asked to report their student enrollment numbers on branch campuses in foreign countries. In 1986, 110 schools report overseas enrollment; by 1998 the number of schools reporting overseas enrollment shrinks to sixty-one. The total overseas enrollment[13] reported on all branch campuses in 1986 is 21,090 students, peaks in 1995 at 48,043 students, and gradually decreases to 23,534 students in 1998. The majority of these overseas programs are started by lesser-known American universities and colleges without doctoral programs. Less than 5 percent of the programs during this time period are sponsored by top research universities with doctoral programs. The IPEDS dropped overseas enrollment questions from their enrollment surveys after 1998, presumably due to a significant decrease in the number of overseas programs and a concomitant decline in media interest.

The decline in the first wave of US overseas programs was preceded by a spectacular failure of American overseas programs in Japan. During the Japanese economic boom in the late 1980s, more than thirty US universities established branch campuses there, hoping their western-style education programs would attract sufficient Japanese students. However, most

13. Total enrollment includes full-time and part-time students enrolled at the undergraduate, graduate, and professional degree levels.

programs struggled with low student enrollment and were closed by the mid-1990s. Temple University Japan is one of the rare survivors after sixteen years of operation. It currently has about 3,000 students enrolled (Bhandari and Chow 2007); however, at least until 2000, the branch campus reportedly lost $50 million a year.[14]

Most US universities involved in these Japanese overseas programs had low name recognition and, as a result, they were not able to attract students who could get into the upper tier Japanese universities. Location was another contributing factor. A number of US universities, lured by financial support from local governments, set up their programs in small towns, which hoped to use the presence of US overseas programs to stem the flight of their young people to larger metropolitan areas. However, these locations only made the programs less attractive to those who preferred to attend college in large cities. Language was also a problem. Even with English preparatory courses, students struggled to achieve sufficient English proficiency to enroll in degree programs. To make matters worse, many US universities got into financial disputes with local partners, who often sacrificed academic integrity in exchange for tuition money. Some partners even committed outright financial fraud.[15] These problems contributed to eventual closure of most of the programs.

During the recent resurgence in overseas programs by US universities, the leading players are different. They tend to be well-established, highly-ranked research universities with doctoral programs. They also appear to follow the recent globalization trend, somewhat analogous to US multinationals' FDI outflows.

There is a perception that US universities are not as involved in FDI as MNCs, which derive about 30 percent of their total sales revenue from foreign affiliates. The perception could be wrong because appropriate comparisons are knowledge-based service industries such as information and banking, which have less FDI. Table 5.1 shows that contributions made by foreign affiliates to US firms' total sales revenue during 1999 through 2004 increased for most industries. More important, it shows that for information and financial services industries, foreign affiliates' contribution to total sales revenue averages only about 15 percent. Although we do not have sufficient data to make a general comparison, the case of University of Chicago Booth School of Business is illustrative. Chicago offers overseas Executive MBA programs in London and Singapore. According to its website, tuition revenue from the overseas programs represents about 14 percent of its total tuition revenue in 2006.[16] This is quite comparable to that of the

14. Beth McMurtrie, "Culture and Unrealistic Expectations Challenge American Campuses in Japan," *Chronicle of Higher Education,* June 2, 2000.

15. Ibid.

16. Our calculation is based on tuition data information obtained from the University of Chicago Booth School of Business website at http://www.chicagobooth.edu/, accessed August

Table 5.1 US foreign direct investment (selected industries)

Majority owned foreign affiliates (%)	1999	2000	2001	2002	2003	2004	Average
All industries	27.1	27.3	27.1	28.4	30.5	31.8	28.7
Mining	48.6	25.0	25.0	35.3	38.9	37.3	35.0
Utilities	12.8	14.9	15.0	15.7	11.6	10.2	13.4
Manufacturing	34.7	35.4	36.1	37.8	40.2	41.7	37.7
Wholesale trade	28.7	26.6	25.8	19.2	21.6	23.1	24.2
Information	13.1	12.4	12.3	13.8	14.8	17.2	13.9
Finance (except depository institutions) and insurance	15.3	17.8	17.3	17.4	18.5	18.8	17.5
Professional, scientific, and technical services	36.8	34.7	36.2	36.4	40.2	38.7	37.2
Other industries	13.0	14.2	15.3	15.8	16.7	15.8	15.1

Notes: This table shows the percentage of sales from majority-owned foreign affiliates, calculated as sales revenue of majority-owned foreign affiliates divided by the total sales of US parent firms and majority-owned foreign affiliates. The numbers are based on worldwide sales of US parent firms and majority-owned foreign affiliates from 1999 to 2004 obtained from Bureau of Economic Analysis website.

other knowledge-based industries, suggesting that some units of US universities are as active in generating overseas revenues as US multinational corporations.

Of late, overseas programs getting the most press coverage are those set up by upper tier US research universities in the Middle East (mainly Qatar and UAE). The Education City in Qatar, founded by the Qatar Foundation, spends $2 billion a year to host the branch campuses of Cornell University, Carnegie Mellon University, and others.[17] The Qatar Foundation pays for all the costs of these overseas programs. For example, it offered Cornell medical school $750 million to provide medical programs in the Education City.[18]

Money seems to be an important determinant in decisions to offer these overseas programs. According to one *Chronicle* article, the University of North Carolina declined to set up an overseas program in the Middle East region because the university was offered only $10 million, falling short of the $35 million the university requested.[19] Another article reports that New York University chose Dubai over Abu Dhabi because Abu Dhabi did not meet the university's demand for a $50 million upfront fee, plus payment for

2007. Because their overseas tuition includes costs of books, materials, and other fees, the 14 percent may be a slight overestimation of the actual contribution made by the school's overseas programs.

17. Zvika Krieger, "An Academic Building Boom Transforms the Persian Gulf," *Chronicle of Higher Education,* March 28, 2008.

18. Katherine S. Mangan, "Cornell's Medical School Will Open Degree Granting Branch in Qatar," *Chronicle of Higher Education,* April 20, 2001.

19. Katherine S. Mangan, "Qatar Courts American Colleges," *Chronicle of Higher Education,* September 6, 2002.

construction and expenses.[20] Michigan State University will open a branch campus in the UAE and receive a line of credit with favorable terms in several million dollars from Tecom Investments.[21]

Asia is another popular destination for overseas programs. In their efforts to become regional higher education hubs, Hong Kong, Singapore, and South Korea offer financial support and tax exemptions to attract foreign universities' overseas degree programs. Many US, UK, and Australian universities have responded by setting up degree programs there, or are currently in negotiations to do so. However, local government support does not guarantee success. The University of New South Wales set up the first comprehensive foreign university in Singapore with partial financing from Singapore's Economic Development Board. It hoped to enroll 300 students in the first semester and had a target enrollment number of 15,000 students by 2020. However, it attracted only 148 students and projected a deficit of $15 million. The branch campus was shut down in June 2007 after only three months of operation.[22] Johns Hopkins University's Biomedical Center in Singapore also closed in 2007 because of its failure to attract sufficient scientists and PhD students despite the $50 million the Singapore government spent to support the program.[23]

Other Asian countries, especially those with large college-age populations, such as China and India, also attract numerous US universities. Although we were unable to find profiles of many of these programs, one *Chronicle* article reports that at least sixty-six such programs exist in India.[24] Again, the huge potential demand in these countries does not guarantee success for overseas programs. Some business schools failed in China because they could not attract enough executives with sufficient English proficiency to enroll in their programs.[25]

Europe attracts relatively few US overseas programs, although it shares the same Western culture and is a popular destination for FDI outflow from the United States. Several factors weaken the competitive edge of US overseas programs there. First, Europe enjoys the presence of several prominent, highly-ranked universities. Second, it is easier for European students to come to the United States for higher education. Income disparities, culture,

20. Zvika Krieger, "An Academic Building Boom Transforms the Persian Gulf," *Chronicle of Higher Education,* March 28, 2008.

21. Karin Fischer, "How the Deal was Done: Michigan State in Dubai," *Chronicle of Higher Education,* March 28, 2008.

22. Pearl Forss, "University of New South Wales Singapore Campus to Shut in June," *Channel NewsAsia,* May 23, 2007.

23. Martha Ann Overland, "Singapore to Close Johns Hopkins Biomedical Center." *Chronicle of Higher Education,* August 11, 2006.

24. Shailaja Neelakantan, "In India, Limits on Foreign Universities Lead to Creative Partnerships," *Chronicle of Higher Education,* February 8, 2008.

25. Alison Damast, "China: Why Western B-Schools Are Leaving," *Business Week,* May 15, 2008.

and language present lower barriers for Europeans. It is also much easier for Europeans to obtain US visas in comparison to other nationalities, especially after 9/11. For similar reasons, Australia and New Zealand attract relatively few US overseas programs.

European and Oceania universities are also the main competitors of US universities for foreign students. According to a report by the Organization for Economic Cooperation and Development (2007), US universities enrolled about 540,000 foreign students in 2005, making it the most popular destination for international students. The United Kingdom and Australia are not far behind; their universities enrolled approximately 324,000 and 162,000 foreign students, respectively. These two countries have also been very active in setting up overseas programs.[26] The University of Nottingham was the first foreign university to set up a branch campus in China and the University of New South Wales was the first to set up a branch campus in Singapore. However, recent overseas activities of Australian universities are slowing down,[27] presumably due to low demand for their degrees.[28] Failures of UK overseas programs have also been reported in the media.[29]

For those few US universities offering overseas programs in Europe, location is important. For example, Chicago initiated a part-time executive MBA program in Barcelona in 1994, but moved to London in 2005. London is the financial center for Europe. Chicago, best known for finance, wanted to move closer to its potential clients.

There are also a number of US overseas programs in South America. The majority of these programs are established by American universities located in the southern and western regions, which are more heavily populated with Hispanics.[30] Their geographic and cultural proximity may explain why these universities are more likely to offer programs in South America.

Few US overseas programs in Africa are reported in the press.[31] Income disparities, insufficient high school graduates able to handle course work offered by American universities, government instability, and volatility in the region all may play a role in keeping US overseas programs out of a continent that desperately needs improvement in the quantity and quality of higher education.

26. New Zealand Ministry of Education (2001), available at: http://www.minedu.govt.nz/educationSectors/InternationalEducation/Initiatives/Offshore%20Education/NZsOffshorePublicTertiaryEducationProgrammes.aspx, accessed August, 2008.

27. David Cohen, "Australian Universities Cull Overseas Programs," *Chronicle of Higher Education,* July 20, 2007.

28. Luke Slattery, "'Beer and Beaches' Image Said to Hurt Australia's Higher-Education 'Brand,'" *Chronicle of Higher Education,* November 30, 2007.

29. Alison Damast, "China: Why Western B-Schools Are Leaving," *Business Week,* May 15, 2008.

30. See: http://www.censusscope.org/us/map_hispanicpop.html.

31. See Elizabeth Redden, "Cornell Degree, Offered in Africa," *Inside Higher Ed,* September 21, 2007. Redden reports that through a World Bank grant Cornell University offers a master's degree program in Agriculture and Rural Development in Ethiopia.

5.4 Empirical Analysis

To conduct an empirical investigation of the interplay of supply and demand, we collect data on overseas programs, university characteristics, and host country characteristics. We use these data to identify which universities are more likely to offer overseas programs, what characteristics of host countries are important in attracting US university programs, and how overseas programs are priced relative to their home campus tuitions.

5.4.1 Sample Construction

Data on Overseas Programs

Our data set covers US overseas programs from January 1988 through August 2008 because our online access to the *Chronicle of Higher Education* via Proquest Research Library starts in January 1988. The data is hand-collected using a three-step search process. We first search the *Chronicle of Higher Education* using the terms "overseas," "offshore," and "branch campus." We read all newspaper articles and identify universities with overseas programs in foreign countries during this period. We supplement the data with Observatory on Higher Education (OBHE) breaking news and special reports headlines,[32] American Council on Education (ACE) publications (Green 2007; Green, Luu, and Burris 2008), and Institute of International Education (IIE) *Open Doors 2007* report (Bhandari and Chow 2007). We include an overseas program in our sample whether it is failed, struggling, or forthcoming (i.e., agreement reached). An overseas program may or may not have a partner in the host country, and it may have a "brick and mortar" presence in the host country or offer degree programs only through online education. We exclude those in the discussion stage, or those awarding only certificates rather than degrees.[33] All the degree programs included in our sample require significant commitment from US universities (i.e., awarding degrees overseas) and put their reputation at stake.

For each overseas program we identify, we run additional *Chronicle of Higher Education* searches using the sponsoring university name and the location of the overseas program to obtain necessary information. When available, we record information on discipline, establishment date, curriculum, size, and financing of the programs.

For information concerning tuition and other program characteristics not covered in the articles, we search the websites of the overseas programs using

32. We read the publicly available headlines of their news articles and special reports on the OBHE website at http://www.obhe.ac.uk/news/ and http://www.obhe.ac.uk/products/reports/.

33. Medical programs are an exception. Medical programs offered by US institutions abroad usually do not award foreign students degrees or certificates qualifying them to practice medicine in the United States. However, the students are mainly trained by US institutions, and we include these medical programs in our sample.

the university's name and location of the program, and record additional information on tuition. Sometimes this additional search leads to more overseas degree programs offered by the same universities. Based on these sample selection processes and criteria, we identify 159 overseas programs offered by 86 US universities in 46 countries.[34]

Data on University Characteristics

Universities in the United States come in many different forms and shapes in both intellectual and physical contexts. To categorize university types, we rely on the Carnegie Basic Classification (2005),[35] which categorizes universities into very high research universities, high research universities, research universities, master's universities, baccalaureate colleges, associate's colleges, and other specialized institutions.

To obtain an objective measure of the ranking among research universities, we use the 2007–2008 university rankings from four sources[36]: America's best national universities from *U.S. News & World Report,*[37] the top 100 global universities from *Newsweek,*[38] THE-QS "World University Rankings" from The *Times Higher Education Supplement* (THES) and Quacquarelli Symonds (QS),[39] and "Academic Rankings of World Universities" from Shanghai Jiaotong University.[40] The last two are compiled by ranking agencies outside the United States (British and Chinese, respectively) and reflect the reputation and competitiveness of US universities outside the United States, which suits our purpose of analyzing US degree programs abroad. The *U.S. News & World Report* and *Newsweek* rankings are the most widely cited and are readily available on the Internet to all foreign

34. The Council of Graduate Schools (CGS 2007) survey of graduate schools finds that 29 percent of American graduate schools have established collaborative overseas degree programs. Our sample is smaller because their survey includes programs that award certificates. Our sample is also smaller than Green, Luu, and Burris' (2008) survey that identifies 101 US degree granting institutions. The discrepancy here seems to be mainly due to media coverage bias; namely, overseas programs offered by lower level schools and small colleges are less likely to be reported. These omissions should not affect our results because our empirical analyses focus only on overseas activities of doctoral and master degree level institutions.

35. The data is obtained from Integrated Postsecondary Education Data System (IPEDS) 2005 Institutional Characteristics Survey (NCES 2008b). Each UnitID is treated as a university. UnitID is a unique identification number assigned to postsecondary institutions surveyed by IPEDS. Institutions participating in Federal financial assistance programs are required to complete IPEDS surveys.

36. Worldwide ranking sources can be found at Wikipedia (http://en.wikipedia.org/wiki/College_and_university_rankings). When these ranking sources include foreign universities, we re-rank American universities excluding foreign universities. The *Newsweek* ranking is for year 2006.

37. Available at: http://colleges.usnews.rankingsandreviews.com/college/national-search/c_final_tier+1, accessed December 2008.

38. Available at: http://www.msnbc.msn.com/id/14321230/, accessed August 2007.

39. Available at: http://www.topuniversities.com/worlduniversityrankings/results/2007/overall_rankings/top_400_universities/, accessed December 2008.

40. Available at http://www.arwu.org/rank/2007/ARWU2007_TopAmer.htm, accessed December 2008.

Table 5.2 **Correlations among four university ranking sources and endowment per full-time equivalent enrollment (Endow_FTE)**

	USNews	Newsweek	Times	SJTU
Newsweek	0.61			
Times	0.76	0.72		
SJTU	0.54	0.90	0.70	
Endow_FTE	0.68	0.48	0.57	0.45

Notes: "USNews" refers to America's best national universities from *U.S. News and World Report,* "Newsweek" refers to top 100 global universities by *Newsweek,* "Times" refers to the THE-QS World University Rankings from the *Times Higher Education Supplement* (THES) and Quacquarelli Symonds (QS), and "SJTU" refers to Academic Rankings of World Universities from Shanghai Jiaotong University. "Endow_FTE" is the 2005 market value of endowment assets divided by full-time equivalent enrollment obtained from 2005 IPEDS College Finance Survey.

students interested in US universities. Moreover, these four rankings employ a broad range of ranking methodologies and measure different dimensions of university reputation. For example, *U.S. News & World Report* uses evaluations from peer institutions, faculty and financial resources, and student selectivity to construct the ranking. In contrast, Shanghai Jiaotong University bases its university ranking on the numbers of publications in *Science* and *Nature,* Nobel laureates, and Fields Medal winners. Relying on these four rankings takes into account both domestic and international reputation and alleviates some of the subjectivity inherent in using a single ranking methodology.

Table 5.2 shows the correlation between the four ranking sources. They are all highly correlated with each other. Yet the correlations also indicate substantial variation across the rankings. This table also contains 2005 university endowment per full-time equivalent (FTE) enrollment, *Endow_FTE,* which is obtained from 2005 IPEDS college finance survey. All four university rankings are highly correlated with the level of endowment, demonstrating the important role endowment plays in university visibility and reputation.

Sixty-seven US universities appear at least once as top fifty in at least one of the four rankings.[41] We follow Kim, Morse, and Zingales (2009) and use the Borda Count method to average the relative rankings within this group of sixty-seven universities. A university ranked first in a ranking study is given a score of 50; the second is given 49; and so on. We then take the simple average of the scores each university gets from the four ranking sources. The average Borda Count Scores (BCS) are reported in table 5.3, which shows a natural break point at the sixteenth university. We classify these

41. In *Newsweek*'s 2006 top 100 global university ranking, only forty-four are US universities.

Table 5.3 **Relative ranking of universities using average Borda Count Scores (BCS)**

Institution name	BCS	Diff	Institution name	BCS	Diff
Harvard University	50.00	—	University of Minnesota-Twin Cities	14.50	0.00
Yale University	46.75	–3.25	University of North Carolina at Chapel Hill	14.50	0.00
California Institute of Technology	46.25	–0.50	Rice University	13.25	–1.25
Stanford University	46.25	0.00	University of Rochester	13.00	–0.25
Massachusetts Institute of Technology	46.00	–0.25	Boston University	12.75	–0.25
Princeton University	44.75	–1.25	University of Virginia-Main Campus	12.50	–0.25
Columbia University in the City of New York	43.75	–1.00	Purdue University-Main Campus	10.50	–2.00
University of Chicago	42.25	–1.50	Case Western Reserve University	10.50	0.00
University of Pennsylvania	41.25	–1.00	Georgetown University	10.25	–0.25
University of California-Berkeley	40.25	–1.00	University of California-Davis	10.25	0.00
Cornell University	38.50	–1.75	North Carolina State University at Raleigh	9.25	–1.00
Duke University	38.00	–0.50	University of Notre Dame	8.25	–1.00
Johns Hopkins University	36.00	–2.00	Georgia Institute of Technology-Main Campus	7.50	–0.75
University of California-Los Angeles	35.00	–1.00	Rockefeller University	7.25	–0.25
University of Michigan-Ann Arbor	33.50	–1.50	Pennsylvania State University-Main Campus	7.25	0.00
Northwestern University	33.25	–0.25	University of California-Irvine	6.75	–0.50
University of California-San Diego	29.00	–4.25	Tufts University	5.75	–1.00
University of Wisconsin-Madison	28.00	–1.00	Wake Forest University	5.75	0.00
University of Washington-Seattle Campus	27.75	–0.25	Michigan State University	5.25	–0.50

New York University	26.00	–1.75	University of Texas Southwestern Medical Center at Dallas	5.25	0.00
Washington University in St. Louis	24.75	–1.25	Brandeis University	5.00	–0.25
Brown University	24.25	–0.50	University of Florida	5.00	0.00
Carnegie Mellon University	23.00	–1.25	College of William and Mary	4.75	–0.25
University of Illinois at Urbana-Champaign	22.50	–0.50	Texas A&M University	4.75	0.00
Vanderbilt University	22.00	–0.50	Ohio State University-Main Campus	4.50	–0.25
The University of Texas at Austin	22.00	0.00	Boston College	4.25	–0.25
University of California-San Francisco	19.75	–2.25	Rutgers University-New Brunswick/Piscataway	4.00	–0.25
University of Maryland-College Park	16.75	–3.00	Lehigh University	4.00	0.00
University of Southern California	16.75	0.00	University of Arizona	3.25	–0.75
Dartmouth College	16.50	–0.25	Rensselaer Polytechnic Institute	2.50	–0.75
Emory University	16.50	0.00	University of Massachusetts-Amherst	1.75	–0.75
University of Pittsburgh-Main Campus	16.25	–0.25	Indiana University-Bloomington	1.25	–0.50
University of California-Santa Barbara	14.75	–1.50	Yeshiva University	0.25	–1.00
University of Colorado at Boulder	14.50	–0.25			

Notes: We use the Borda Count method to average the relative rankings from four ranking sources. A university ranked first in a ranking study is given a score of 50, the second is given 49, and so on. We then take the simple average of the scores each university gets from the four ranking sources to calculate the average Borda Count Score (BCS). When the ranking sources include foreign universities, we re-rank American universities excluding foreign universities. "Diff" is the difference in BCS scores between a university and the university ranked one place above it. A natural breakpoint in BCS is at the sixteenth university. We classify the first sixteen universities as elite and the remaining forty-eight research universities (excluding specialized institutions Rockefeller University, University of California at San Francisco, and University of Texas Southwestern Medical Center at Dallas) as good.

top sixteen research universities as "elite," and the remaining forty-eight research universities (excluding specialized institutions) as "good."[42] The other research universities not included in the list of sixty-seven are defined as "moderate." We follow 2005 Carnegie Basic Classification and define all other universities that award at least fifty master's degrees and fewer than twenty doctoral degrees per year as "master." To check the sensitivity to the choice of different ranking sources, we add six more ranking sources to classify university categories. The results (unreported) are robust.[43]

We retrieve university level enrollment and financial data for these universities from the IPEDS. We use a number of IPEDS surveys, including its Institutional Characteristics Surveys, Enrollment Surveys, and Finance Surveys. From these sources we construct the following variables: full-time equivalent enrollment, *Enrol_FTE,* which is full-time enrollment plus 0.38[44] times part-time enrollment; *Part_Time,* percentage of part-time enrollment to total enrollment;[45] *Non_Resid,* percentage of nonresident alien enrollment to total enrollment; tuition revenue dependence, *Tui_Dep,* the ratio of tuition revenue to total revenue;[46] and university endowment, *Endow_FTE,* the market value of endowment assets divided by full-time equivalent enrollment.

Data on Host Country Characteristics

We obtain host countries' real gross domestic product (GDP) per capita, *GDP_PPP,*[47] and growth rate of real GDP per capita, *Growth,* in years 1999 through 2003 from Penn World Tables (Heston, Summers, and Aten 2006). The tertiary school age population, *Stu_Pop,* in years 1999 to 2003

42. We exclude from our sample highly regarded but specialized institutions such as Rockefeller University, University of California at San Francisco, and University of Texas Southwestern Medical Center at Dallas.

43. The six additional university ranking sources are: Faculty Scholarly Productivity Index from Academic Analytics, Top American Research Universities from the Center for Measuring University Performance at Arizona State University, United States National Research Council Rankings, Washington Monthly College Rankings, Avery et al. (2005), and Webometrics Ranking of World Universities by the Cybermetrics Lab. Ninety-five universities appear at least once as top fifty in at least one of the ten rankings. We use the Borda Count method to average the relative rankings within this group of ninety-five universities. We classify the top thirty-one universities as "elite," and the remaining sixty-four schools as "good." The other research universities not included in the list of ninety-five are defined as "moderate." We follow 2005 Carnegie Basic Classification and define all other universities that award at least fifty master's degrees and fewer than twenty doctoral degrees per year as "Master." All our empirical results remain qualitatively the same.

44. This number is the average full-time equivalent of part-time enrollment reported in 2005 IPEDS Enrollment Survey.

45. Total enrollment is the sum of full-time enrollment and part-time enrollment.

46. Total revenue includes tuition revenue; revenue from federal, state, and local governments; endowment income; private gifts and grants; sales and services income; auxiliary income; hospital income; independent operations income; investment income; and others.

47. It is measured in 2000 constant international dollars. An international dollar has the same purchasing power as US dollar over US GDP.

is from United Nations Educational Scientific and Cultural Organization (UNESCO) Institute for Statistics Data Center (available at: http://stats.uis.unesco.org/unesco/TableViewer/document.aspx?ReportId=143&IF_Language=eng). The US FDI outflows to other countries from 1999 to 2003 are obtained from Bureau of Economic Analysis website (BEA 2007). We also obtain measures of government stability *Gov_Stab*[48] and strength of legal system *Law_Order*[49] from the *International Country Risk Guide* in years 1999 to 2003 (Political Risk Services Group 1999–2003) and the ease of doing business index *Ease_Bus* in years 2004 to 2009 from the Doing Business website.[50]

5.4.2 Summary Statistics on Overseas Programs, Disciplines, Degrees, Finances, and Enrollments

Table 5.4 reports the number of universities with overseas programs, separately for nonprofit public, nonprofit private, and for-profit universities in each of the seven categories: elite, good, moderate, master, baccalaureate colleges, associate's colleges, and other specialized institutions. In terms of percentage, elite universities are dominant players, with 66.7 percent of public universities and 53.8 percent of private universities having overseas programs. It also shows relatively higher participation rates by public research universities than by their private counterparts. One possible explanation is that relative to private universities, public universities face greater operational constraints imposed by local governments and state legislators. For example, they are often required to charge in-state students lower tuition and give them preferential treatment in admission. These constraints no longer apply when these public universities go abroad.

Table 5.4 also shows that less than 1 percent of schools belonging to the categories of baccalaureate colleges, associate's colleges, and other specialized institutions offer overseas programs. This extremely low percentage may be due partially to the lack of press coverage on those institutions. However, the *Chronicle* usually covers newsworthy activities even by very small and little known colleges. Among for-profit universities, none belongs to the "elite" or "good" universities, and most belong to "associates" or "others." Of 2,764 for-profit universities, we are able to identify only seven that offer overseas programs, with five belonging to "masters." There are probably many more overseas programs offered by for-profit universities, which are not covered by the press and, hence, are not identified through our search

48. It ranges from 1 to 12, with 12 indicating the highest governance stability.

49. It ranges from 1 to 6, with 6 representing the strongest judicial system.

50. Available at: http://www.doingbusiness.org/CustomQuery/, accessed August 2008. The ease of doing business index ranks business regulations for 181 countries. It covers ten aspects including starting a business, dealing with construction permits, employing workers, registering property, getting credit, protecting investors, paying taxes, trading across borders, enforcing contracts, and closing business. A higher ranking means simpler regulation and stronger protection of property rights.

Table 5.4 Number of universities with overseas programs by university category and type

	Type								
	Public			Private nonprofit			Private for-profit		
	(1)	(2)	(3)	(1)	(2)	(3)	(1)	(2)	(3)
Elite	3	2	66.7%	13	7	53.8%	0	0	—
Good	27	9	33.3%	21	5	23.8%	0	0	—
Moderate	136	18	13.2%	74	10	13.5%	8	0	0.0%
Masters	270	8	3.0%	375	18	4.8%	43	5	11.6%
Baccalaureates	149	0	0.0%	511	1	0.2%	77	1	1.3%
Associates	1,073	1	0.1%	132	0	0.0%	589	0	0.0%
Others	547	0	0.0%	908	0	0.0%	2,047	1	0.0%
Total	2,205	38	1.7%	2,034	41	2.0%	2,764	7	0.3%

Notes: Column (1) shows the total number of universities in each category based on our average Borda Count Score and Carnegie 2005 basic classification. Column (2) shows the number of universities with overseas programs in each category. Column (3) shows the percentage of universities with overseas programs in each category, which is calculated as number of universities with overseas programs divided by the total number of universities in that category. Each UnitID in IPEDS is treated as a university.

process. Based on these data considerations, we focus our investigation only on nonprofit universities in the "elite," "good," "moderate," and "master" categories.

Table 5.5 shows the number of overseas degree programs offered by the four categories of universities and by nine broadly defined disciplines. "Arts and sciences" includes foreign languages, economics, physics, and others. "Engineering" includes mechanical engineering, chemical engineering, material engineering, and other traditional engineering programs. "EECS" refers to electrical engineering, computer science, and IT programs. "Business" includes finance, accounting, marketing, and management. "Public affairs" includes international relations and public policy. "Medicine" includes medical education, nursing, and health care. "Other" includes film, theater, and hotel management.

Panel A shows that among the ninety-one undergraduate overseas programs, only one is offered by elite universities. The main suppliers of the undergraduate programs are master universities, with 70 percent of market share. In contrast, panel B shows a higher participation rate by elite universities in graduate level programs, offering 9 percent of the master's degree programs. Master universities are still the biggest suppliers, offering 48 percent of the master's degree programs. This dominance by master universities simply reflects the fact that master universities outnumber elite universities by 688 to 16. Although not included in the table, when Master

Table 5.5 **Number of programs by degree level, discipline, and the sponsoring university's category**

	Arts and sciences	Education	Engineering	EECS	Business	Public affairs	Law	Medicine	Other	Total
					A Bachelor					
Elite	1	0	0	0	0	0	0	0	0	1
Good	1	1	2	2	1	1	0	0	0	8
Moderate	6	1	0	3	3	2	0	1	2	18
Master	15	1	1	13	27	5	0	1	1	64
Total	23	3	3	18	31	8	0	2	3	91
					B Master					
Elite	2	0	0	1	4	2	0	1	1	11
Good	1	0	1	8	5	2	0	1	0	18
Moderate	0	4	1	6	16	1	1	3	1	33
Master	5	5	1	3	32	6	0	3	2	57
Total	8	9	3	18	57	11	1	8	4	119
					C PhD					
Elite	0	0	0	0	0	0	0	2	0	2
Good	1	0	1	1	0	0	0	0	0	3
Moderate	0	0	1	1	1	0	1	1	0	5
Master	0	0	0	0	0	0	1	0	0	1
Total	1	0	2	2	1	0	2	3	0	11

Notes: "Arts and sciences" includes foreign languages, economics, physics, and others. "Engineering" includes mechanical engineering, material engineering, and other traditional engineering programs. "EECS" refers to electrical engineering, computer science, and IT programs. "Business" includes finance, accounting, marketing, and management. "Public affairs" include international relations and public policy. "Medicine" includes medical education, nursing, and health care. "Other" includes film, theater, and hotel management.

universities offer overseas programs, they are much more likely to offer both undergraduate and graduate programs in a variety of disciplines at the same location.

In terms of discipline, Business and EECS are by far the most popular majors offered in overseas programs. Finally, panel C shows US universities offer significantly fewer doctoral-level overseas programs, perhaps because they require substantial research expenditures without generating sufficient tuition revenue.

Table 5.6 shows the average university financial and enrollment data in years 1995 to 2005 by university category and by whether or not they have overseas programs. Higher-ranked schools are generally larger and better endowed than lower-ranked schools. Private schools are better endowed, depend more on tuition revenue, are smaller, have more nonresident alien students, and have more part-time students than public schools. This table also shows that universities with overseas programs are larger and more dependent on tuition revenue.

5.4.3 Regression Results

Likelihood of Having Overseas Programs

Our first inquiry is what university characteristics help explain the likelihood of having overseas programs. For this purpose, we use the following probit specification:

$$\begin{aligned} \Pr(\text{overseas}_i) = G(&\beta_0 + \beta_1 \times \text{Enrol\_FTE}_i + \beta_2 \times \text{Part\_Time}_i \\ &+ \beta_3 \times \text{Non\_Resid}_i + \beta_4 \times \text{Tui\_Dep}_i \\ &+ \beta_5 \times \text{Log(Endow\_FTE)}_i + \beta_6 \times \text{Reputation}_i \\ &+ \beta_7 \times \text{Public}_i + \beta_8 \times \text{interaction terms}_i + \varepsilon_i). \end{aligned}$$

The dependent variable *Pr(overseas)* is equal to 1 if a university has overseas programs and 0 otherwise. *Enrol_FTE* is full-time equivalent enrollment and measures the size of a university. *Part_Time* is the percentage of part-time student enrollment. *Non_Resid* is the percentage of nonresident alien enrollment and measures a university's openness to foreigners. *Tui_Dep* is tuition revenue as a percentage of total revenue. Log (*Endow_FTE*) is the log value of university endowment per full-time equivalent student. *Reputation* is proxied by indicator variables, *Elite, Good,* and *Moderate. Public* is an indicator variable for public university. We also include interaction terms between university ranking categories and the *Public* indicator. Subscript *i* refers to university *i*, while *G* is the probit cumulative distribution function.

Because overseas programs affect tuition revenue, expenditure, and the percentage of nonresident alien enrollment, we lag all financial and enrollment variables by using 1995 university enrollment and financial data. Of the 144 current overseas programs offered by advanced-degree awarding

Table 5.6 Summary statistics of financial and enrollment variables (1995–2005)

Category	Control	Overseas	Enrol_FTE	Part_Time (%)	Non_Resid (%)	Tui_Dep (%)	Endow_FTE
Elite	Public	Yes	33,047	8.6	9.0	15.3	65,557
		No	35,214	4.5	6.2	8.3	13,573
	Private	Yes	14,308	16.6	15.0	17.3	347,639
		No	13,729	13.9	17.9	8.4	633,932
Good	Public	Yes	29,997	16.8	8.1	19.7	8,349
		No	29,377	14.6	5.9	17.2	29,200
	Private	Yes	17,472	18.4	13.6	35.3	112,854
		No	8,800	10.8	9.7	29.6	210,896
Moderate	Public	Yes	21,338	27.6	5.8	20.9	7,846
		No	14,158	27.6	4.6	22.8	6,888
	Private	Yes	10,037	34.4	8.1	60.0	29,953
		No	5,936	32.4	6.8	60.0	29,059
Masters	Public	Yes	11,633	30.4	4.2	34.0	910
		No	6,619	31.7	2.2	26.1	2,291
	Private	Yes	3,829	42.0	4.8	69.3	10,271
		No	2,449	33.6	3.2	62.7	17,533

Notes: All variables are averaged values from 1995 to 2005. "Enrol_FTE" is full-time equivalent enrollment, which is full-time enrollment plus 0.38 times part-time enrollment. "Part_Time" is the percentage of part-time enrollment to total enrollment. "Non_Resid" is the percentage of nonresident alien enrollment to total enrollment. Tuition revenue dependence, "Tui_Dep," is the ratio of tuition revenue to total revenue. "Endow_FTE" is market value of endowment assets divided by full-time equivalent enrollment. "Endow_FTE" is adjusted by inflation and is in 2005 constant dollars. Financial variables are available in 1995, 2000, 2001, 2002, 2003, 2004, and 2005 IPEDS Finance Surveys. Enrollment variables are available in all IPEDS Enrollment Surveys from 1995 to 2005. The IPEDS surveys were not conducted in 1999. Both public and private schools follow the Old Form accounting standards until 1997, after which most of the public schools follow Governmental Accounting Standards Board (GASB) accounting rules while the others follow Financial Accounting Standards Board (FASB) accounting standards. The GASB and FASB treat revenue items differently, which render the financial data for public and private schools not directly comparable after 1997.

Table 5.7 **Summary statistics for independent variables in the likelihood regression**

Variable name	Observations	Mean	Median	Standard deviation	Min	Max	Correlation with 2005 data
Enrol_FTE	913	6,614.5	4,026.8	6,986.6	61.9	43,860.7	0.98
Part_Time	913	33.0	30.0	17.9	0.2	99.1	0.79
Non_Resid	913	3.7	2.3	4.4	0.0	35.7	0.79
Tui_Dep	913	44.7	40.6	22.7	4.9	100.0	0.89
Endow_FTE	913	17,761.4	3,352.8	73,845.3	0.0	1,703,445.0	0.88

Notes: "Enrol_FTE" is full-time equivalent enrollment, which is full-time enrollment plus 0.38 times part-time enrollment. "Part_Time" is the percentage of part-time enrollment to total enrollment. "Non_Resid" is the percentage of nonresident alien enrollment to total enrollment. Tuition revenue dependence, "Tui_Dep," is the ratio of tuition revenue to total revenue. "Endow_FTE" is market value of endowment assets divided by full-time equivalent enrollment. All variables are based on data obtained from 1995 IPEDS College Enrollment and Finance Surveys.

institutions, only four existed in 1995. At that time, both public and private schools followed the same accounting standard (the Old Form), making their financial data more directly comparable.[51] As a robustness check, we also use 2005 data as independent variables in unreported regressions. The results are quantitatively the same.

When universities have missing data in 1995, we use the average values of universities in the same category (in terms of reputation and the public/private classification) in 1995. Table 5.7 presents the summary statistics of the 1995 university enrollment and financial data.[52] The 1995 data are highly correlated with their 2005 data, indicating persistency in university characteristics.

Table 5.8 reports the estimates using probit regression.[53] University size, measured by full-time equivalent enrollment, has a positive and significant effect on the probability of having overseas programs, indicating larger universities are more likely to offer overseas programs. A 1,000 increase in full-time equivalent enrollment increases the probability of having an overseas program by 0.8 percent, holding all other variables constant at the

51. Public institutions used the Old Form until 2002, and were required to follow New Governmental Accounting Standards Board (GASB) no later than 2004. Private institutions used the Old Form until 1997, when they switched to Financial Accounting Standards Board (FASB). These accounting standards differ in their treatment of revenue and expenditure composition.

52. The average tuition dependency in table 5.7 is much higher than those reported by the *Digest of Education Statistics* (National Center for Education Statistics 2008a) for the academic year 2004 and 2005. The difference is mainly due to the difference in computing the average. The averages reported by Department of Economic Security (DES) are value-weighted—calculated as total tuition revenue of all public (or private nonprofit) institutions divided by total revenue of all public (or private nonprofit) institutions, whereas the average in table 5.7 is equal-weighted. Thus, the DES averages give greater weights to top tier, larger schools with greater endowment, which table 5.6 shows are less tuition dependent.

53. We also estimate OLS and logistic regressions. The results (unreported) are quantitatively the same.

Table 5.8 **Probit regression on the likelihood of having overseas programs**

Variable name	Coefficient	Marginal effect
Enrol_FTE	0.074***	0.008***
	(0.015)	
Part_Time	0.006	0.001
	(0.004)	
Non_Resid	0.035***	0.004***
	(0.012)	
Tui_Dep	0.011*	0.001*
	(0.006)	
Log (Endow_FTE)	–0.043	–0.005
	(0.077)	
Elite	1.640***	0.449***
	(0.505)	
Good	0.617	0.102
	(0.401)	
Moderate	0.180	0.021
	(0.234)	
Public	–0.166	–0.018
	(0.337)	
Elite*Public	–0.855	
	(0.930)	
Good*Public	–0.576	
	(0.554)	
Moderate*Public	0.020	
	(0.317)	
Constant	–2.839***	
	(0.495)	
Observations	913	
Pseudo R^2	0.22	

Notes: The dependent variable is equal to 1 if a university has overseas programs and 0 otherwise. "Enrol_FTE" is full-time enrollment plus 0.38 times part-time enrollment in thousands. "Part_Time" is the percentage of part-time student enrollment. "Non_Resid" is the percentage of nonresident alien enrollment. "Tui_Dep" is tuition revenue as a percentage of total revenue. "Log(Endow_FTE)" is the log value of university endowment per full-time equivalent student in thousands. All financial and enrollment variables are 1995 value. "Elite" is an indicator variable equal to 1 if a university's Borda Count Score is ranked in the top 16 and 0 otherwise. "Good" is equal to 1 if a university's Borda Count Score is ranked between 17 and 67 (specialized institutions excluded). "Moderate" is equal to 1 if a university is considered a research university by the Carnegie 2005 report but is ranked below 67. "Public" is an indicator variable for public university. Robust standard errors are reported in parentheses.

***Significant at the 1 percent level.

**Significant at the 5 percent level.

*Significant at the 10 percent level.

mean. This impact of size is nontrivial, considering that the likelihood of sponsoring overseas programs for an average university[54] is only 5.33 percent. Nonresident enrollment also has a positive and significant effect on the

54. An average university implies all independent variables are held at their mean values. Mean values of independent variables are reported in table 5.7.

likelihood of having overseas programs. A 1 percent increase in nonresident enrollment increases the probability of having overseas programs by 0.4 percent, holding all other variables constant at the mean. Tuition revenue dependence has a significant positive effect as well.[55] A 1 percent increase in tuition revenue dependence increases the likelihood of having overseas programs by 0.1 percent, holding all other variables constant at their mean. Elite universities are more likely to have overseas programs. Moving from master to the elite category increases the likelihood of having overseas programs by 44.9 percent for private schools, holding all other variables constant at their mean.[56]

These results suggest that the most active participants in overseas programs are large Elite research universities. Schools more open to foreign students are also more likely to have overseas programs. It appears that the best schools are making efforts to globalize their institutions and to provide higher education opportunities overseas.

The regression estimates also indicate that universities with higher tuition dependency are more likely to have overseas programs, suggesting that finance plays a role in the decision making process. How much economics matter in offering of overseas programs is the subject of investigation in the next two sections.

Location Choice

If finance plays an important role, universities' location choice may not be much different from those of multinational corporations making FDI. Thus, to examine how host country characteristics are related to the location of overseas programs, we follow the international trade literature. Specifically, we relate the number of overseas programs in a host country to measures of economic development, the recent economic growth rate, the size of the market for higher education, the US outflow of FDI, and other local environmental factors by estimating the following regression:[57]

$$\begin{aligned}\text{Density}_j = {} & \beta_0 + \beta_1 \times \text{GDP\_PPP}_j + \beta_2 \times \text{Growth}_j + \beta_3 \times \text{Stu\_Pop}_j \\ & + \beta_4 \times \text{FDI}_j + \beta_5 \times \text{Gov\_Stab}_j + \beta_6 \times \text{Law\_Order}_j \\ & + \beta_7 \times \text{Ease\_Bus}_j + \beta_8 \times \text{Continent}_j + \varepsilon_j.\end{aligned}$$

55. We also use two alternative measures of tuition dependency that account for student financial aid. The first is the ratio of tuition revenue net of financial aid to total revenue; the second ratio is based on the same numerator divided by total revenue net of financial aid. The results (unreported) are quantitatively the same.

56. We are not interpreting the marginal effects of the interaction terms, because we have three interaction terms in the probit regression. Interpreting interaction effect in nonlinear models is complicated and the widely-used Norton, Wang, and Ai (2004) interaction effect correction can only be applied to probit specification with one interaction term. Not correcting for interaction effect does not affect the marginal effects of other independent variables.

57. As a robustness check, we also estimate a conditional (fixed-effect) logit and a standard logit model with clustered standard errors (at university level) by relating a university's probability of having overseas programs in a host country (1 if having overseas programs in the

Density measures the number of overseas programs located in host country *j*. It includes all overseas degree programs offered by advanced-degree-awarding US universities in that country. As a robustness check, we include overseas programs offered by all categories of universities and colleges. The results (unreported) do not change.

All independent variables are averaged values from 1999 to 2003 except for *Ease_Bus,* which is available only from 2004 to 2009. The host country real gross domestic product (GDP) per capita is *GDP_PPP. Growth* is the growth rate of *GDP_PPP.* These two variables measure the level and the slope of economic development of host country *j*. The tertiary school age population is *Stu_Pop,* which measures the potential size of the host country's higher education market. The *FDI* is US foreign direct investment outflow to host country *j*. *Gov_Stab* is government stability of the host country, which is a proxy for political risk. *Law_Order* measures the strength of judicial system and *Ease_Bus* measures the ease of conducting business in the host country. *Continent* is a set of dummy variables that indicates whether the host country *j* is located in Africa, Asia, Europe, Middle East,[58] North America (Canada), and Oceania. We would have liked to include the likelihood of obtaining local financial support, and the quality and openness of local higher education markets; unfortunately, we can obtain such data only for a handful of countries, making it impossible to conduct meaningful tests.

Table 5.9 reports the regression estimates. We use the negative binomial model because the variance of the dependent variable (2.68) is much larger than the mean (0.77). A likelihood ratio test confirms the existence of over-dispersion.

The regression estimates in table 5.9 indicate that economics play an important role in location decisions of US universities. The two significant variables, the level of GDP per capita and student population, are both critical ingredients for financial viability. Universities in the United States target countries with large potential markets where the local population has the economic means to pay for their programs.

The regression estimates imply that a 1,000 dollar increase (in 2000 constant international dollars) in real GDP per capita increases the expected number of overseas programs in a country by 7.1 percent, holding all other variables constant. The size of the local market also has an important impact. An increase in the tertiary school age population by one million increases the expected number of overseas program in a country by 4.4 percent, holding all other variables constant. Universities in the United States also seem to follow US FDI outflow, perhaps because they regard the countries with

host country and 0 otherwise) to host country characteristics. The results (unreported) are very similar.

58. Following Bhandari and Chow (2007), the Middle East region includes Bahrain, Iran, Iraq, Israel, Jordan, Kuwait, Lebanon, Oman, Palestinian Authority, Qatar, Saudi Arabia, Syria, United Arab Emirates, and Yemen.

Table 5.9 **Negative binomial location regression**

Variable name	Negative binomial coefficient	Percentage change (%)
GDP_PPP	0.069**	7.1**
	(0.029)	
Growth	–0.006	–0.6
	(0.046)	
Stu_Pop	0.043***	4.4***
	(0.006)	
FDI	0.048**	4.9**
	(0.021)	
Gov_Stab	0.015	1.5
	(0.138)	
Law_Order	–0.379*	–31.6*
	(0.226)	
Ease_Bus	–0.016**	–1.6**
	(0.008)	
Africa	–0.183	–16.7
	(0.751)	
Asia	1.054**	186.9**
	(0.452)	
Europe	–0.350	–29.5
	(0.683)	
Middle East	1.078**	193.9**
	(0.518)	
Oceania	0.196	21.7
	(0.726)	
Constant	0.446	
	(1.655)	
Observations	117	
Log Pseudo Likelihood	–111.47	

Notes: Dependent variable is "density," which measures the number of overseas programs offered in a host country by US institutions that award advanced degrees. All our independent variables (except for "Ease_Bus," which is averaged from 2004 to 2009) are averaged values from 1999 to 2003. "GDP_PPP" is host country real gross domestic product (GDP) per capita in 2000 constant international dollars (in thousands). Growth is the growth rate of GDP_PPP. "Stu_Pop" is the tertiary school age population in millions. "FDI" is the US foreign direct investment outflows to the host country in 2000 constant US dollars (in billions). "Gov_Stab" measures government stability. "Law_Order" measures the strength of legal system. "Ease_Bus" measures the easiness of doing business. "Africa," "Asia," "Europe," "Middle East," and "Oceania" are dummy variables indicating the location of host country. The Middle East region includes Bahrain, Iran, Iraq, Israel, Jordan, Kuwait, Lebanon, Oman, Palestinian Authority, Qatar, Saudi Arabia, Syria, United Arab Emirates, and Yemen. Robust standard errors are reported in parentheses.

***Significant at the 1 percent level.

**Significant at the 5 percent level.

*Significant at the 10 percent level.

close US trade relationships as having friendlier environments for US entities to conduct business and having a higher demand for US-style higher education. An increase of one billion dollars (in 2000 constant international dollars) in US FDI outflow increases the expected number of overseas programs in a country by 4.9 percent.

Universities in the United States also are more likely to have overseas programs in countries with business-friendly environments and weaker regulations. A one point improvement in the ease of doing business index[59] increases the expected number of overseas programs by 1.6 percent, and a one point increase in the strength of judicial system[60] decreases the expected number of overseas program by 31.6 percent. We doubt that US universities purposefully target countries with weaker judicial systems; rather, the correlation seems to be due to the fact that de facto barriers against setting up overseas programs are less effective in countries with weaker judicial systems.

Table 5.9 also shows that Asian and Middle Eastern countries are more popular destinations for overseas programs. Universities in the United States offer more overseas programs in Asia because of its large market for higher education and greater local demand for US-style higher education. The main attraction to the Middle East appears to be its financial support with oil money.

To examine whether geographical and cultural proximity also matter when universities make decisions about location, we divide US universities into four regions according to US Census Bureau geographic locations: Northeast, Midwest, South, and West.[61] Table 5.10 tabulates the number of overseas programs located in the seven continents by the region. It shows that Asia and Europe have more or less equal representation from all four regions (relative to the total number of overseas programs offered by universities in each region). The Middle East has a high representation of universities from the Northeast region. Middle Eastern countries tend to target top US universities with substantial financial aid and the Northeast region has more top ranked universities. The only indication of cultural and geographic proximity affecting location decisions is the relatively higher representation of universities from the South and West regions in Latin America (relative to the total number of overseas programs offered by universities in each region). In short, although geographic and cultural distance may matter, the overriding factor in location decisions seems to be economics.

59. This variable ranges from 1 to 181, where 1 is the country where it is easiest to do business.

60. This variable ranges from 1 to 6, where 6 indicates the strongest judicial system.

61. Northeast includes ME, NH, VT, MA, CT, NY, NJ, PA, and RI. Midwest includes MI, OH, IN, IL, WI, MN, IA, MO, KS, NE, SD, and ND. South includes TX, OK, AR, LA, MS, AL, TN, KY, GA, FL, SC, NC, VA, WV, DC, MD, and DE. West includes WA, OR, CA, NV, ID, UT, AZ, NM, CO, WY, MT, AK, and HI.

Table 5.10 **Number of overseas programs offered by region and by Census Bureau geographic location of US universities**

Location of US university	Africa	Asia	Europe	Latin America	Middle East	North America	Oceania	Total
Midwest	0	29	6	1	3	0	0	39
Northeast	2	27	7	4	11	1	2	54
South	1	25	8	5	6	0	1	46
West	0	10	3	4	0	3	0	20
Total	3	91	24	14	20	4	3	159

Notes: Northeast includes ME, NH, VT, MA, CT, NY, NJ, PA, and RI. Midwest includes MI, OH, IN, IL, WI, MN, IA, MO, KS, NE, SD, and ND. South includes TX, OK, AR, LA, MS, AL, TN, KY, GA, FL, SC, NC, VA, WV, DC, MD, and DE. West includes WA, OR, CA, NV, ID, UT, AZ, NM, CO, WY, MT, AK, and HI. Middle East region includes Bahrain, Iran, Iraq, Israel, Jordan, Kuwait, Lebanon, Oman, Palestinian Authority, Qatar, Saudi Arabia, Syria, United Arab Emirates, and Yemen. This table includes all 159 overseas programs identified from the press.

Tuition Discounts

If universities behave like firms, they will adjust product pricing to suit the local environment. In this section we investigate this pricing issue by focusing on tuition discounts. We hypothesize that universities adjust their tuition based on affordability; that is, they offer higher tuition discounts in countries with lower income to attract a sufficient number of students. Other factors relevant to the local demand include the reputation of the sponsoring university, the degree level, and the discipline.

Tuition discounts may also be influenced by the cost structures of overseas programs. Costs can be lowered by inviting a local university as a partner and by employing local faculty at lower salaries than US faculty. Costs can also be lowered by obtaining financial aid from the local government and/or a third party such as the World Bank. Thus, we use the following specification to analyze overseas program tuition:

$$\begin{aligned}\text{Discount}_{ijk} = \beta_0 &+ \beta_1 \times \text{GDP\_PPP}_j + \beta_2 \times \text{Stu\_Pop}_j + \beta_3 \times \text{Gov\_Stab}_j \\ &+ \beta_4 \times \text{Reputation}_i + \beta_5 \times \text{Public}_i + \beta_6 \times \text{Prof}_k \\ &+ \beta_7 \times \text{BA}_k + \beta_8 \times \text{Joint}_k + \varepsilon_{ijk}.\end{aligned}$$

$Discount_{ijk}$ is 1 minus the ratio of overseas subprogram k's tuition in host country j to the tuition of a comparable program at the same degree level and in the same discipline on university i's US home campus. Because some universities offer several degree programs in multiple disciplines at the same location and tuition varies across degree levels and disciplines, we break down an overseas program at each location into subprograms by their degree levels and disciplines. We make tuition comparable across programs and locations by assuming that a student takes, on average, four three-credit courses per semester, or equivalently, eight three-credit courses per academic year.[62]

The average tuition discounts are 21 percent, 26 percent, 28 percent, and 8 percent for master, moderate, good, and elite universities, respectively. The discounts are significantly greater than zero at the 1 percent level for all types except elite universities.

An indicator variable for professional schools is $Prof_k$, equal to 1 if the overseas subprogram is in engineering, EECS, business, law, medicine, or other professional disciplines, and 0 otherwise. Variable BA_k is equal to 1 if the overseas subprogram is a bachelor's program and 0 otherwise. $Joint_k$ is equal to 1 if the overseas subprogram has a partner university in the host country or has received full or partial local financial support. This variable is our proxy for lower cost. Other independent variables are defined earlier.

Table 5.11 reports the ordinary least squares (OLS) regression estimates with robust and clustered (at the university level) standard errors. We exclude overseas PhD programs, because doctoral students often work as research and/or teaching assistants, receiving financial stipends and tuition waivers.

Three variables show statistical significance: real GDP per capita, "Good" university category, and bachelor's degree programs. Overseas programs offer lower tuition discounts in higher income countries. An increase in real GDP per capita by 1,000 dollars (2000 constant international dollar) leads to a 2.2 percent decrease in tuition discount, holding all other variables constant.

Tuition discounts for baccalaureate programs are 25.5 percent more than master's programs, holding all other variables constant. We attribute this greater discount to the stiffer competition undergraduate degree programs face from local universities, relative to advanced degree programs.

Indicator variable *Good* has a significant effect on tuition discounts, while *Elite* and *Moderate* do not. Moving from the master university group to the good group increases tuition discounts by 23.6 percent, holding all other variables constant. However, elites do not offer higher tuition discounts even though tuition is much higher at elite universities' home campuses than at masters. Because of their high visibility and reputation, they may not have to offer tuition discounts to attract students. Good universities, by contrast, lack the same visibility and reputation and, thus, have to offer substantial tuition discounts to fill their classrooms.[63]

62. If overseas program tuition is in foreign currency, we convert it to US dollars using foreign exchange rates as of August 29, 2008.

63. Differences in home campus tuition charged by moderate and master level universities are much smaller than those between good and master; hence, moderate schools may not need to offer significantly more tuition discounts than master schools. The average private university home campus tuitions for the 2007 and 2008 academic year are \$35,082, \$34,941, \$25,220, and \$21,084 for elite, good, moderate, and master groups, respectively. The corresponding averages for public schools are \$8,259, \$8,030, \$6,318, and \$5,374.

Table 5.11 Tuition discount regression

Variable name	OLS coefficient
GDP_PPP	–0.022***
	(0.004)
Stu_Pop	–0.000
	(0.001)
Gov_Stab	–0.050
	(0.054)
Elite	0.021
	(0.187)
Good	0.236**
	(0.114)
Moderate	0.046
	(0.113)
Public	0.006
	(0.074)
Prof	0.050
	(0.053)
BA	0.255*
	(0.131)
Joint	0.032
	(0.068)
Constant	0.913
	(0.572)
Observations	86
R^2	0.510

Notes: Discount is the ratio of overseas subprogram tuition in a host country to the tuition of a comparable program at the same degree level and in the same discipline on the sponsoring US university's home campus. We make tuition comparable across programs and locations by assuming that a student takes an average of four three-credit courses per semester, or equivalently, eight three-credit courses per academic year whenever necessary. "GDP_PPP" is host country's real per capita GDP in 2000 constant international dollars (in thousands). "Stu_Pop" is the tertiary school age population in millions. "Gov_Stab" measures government stability, which is a proxy for political risk. "Elite" is an indicator variable equal to 1 if a university's Borda Count Score is ranked in the top 16 and 0 otherwise. "Good" is equal to 1 if a university's Borda Count Score is ranked between 17 and 67 (three specialized institutions excluded). "Moderate" is equal to 1 if a university is considered a research university by the Carnegie Classification but is ranked below 67. Variable "Public" is an indicator variable for public university. "Prof" is equal to 1 if the overseas subprogram is in engineering, EECS, business, law, medicine, and other professional disciplines and 0 otherwise. "BA" is equal to 1 if the overseas subprogram is a baccalaureate program and 0 otherwise. Joint is equal to 1 if the overseas subprogram has a partner university in the host country or has received local financing support. Robust and clustered (at university level) standard errors are reported in parentheses.

***Significant at the 1 percent level.

**Significant at the 5 percent level.

*Significant at the 10 percent level.

Finally, but equally interesting, our proxy for lower costs, *Joint,* has no effect on tuition discounts, implying that US universities do not pass on any cost savings to local students in the form of lower tuition. This pricing behavior is similar to that of profit-seeking corporations.

5.5 Conclusion

This chapter examines US university overseas programs because if universities ever behave like firms, they are more likely to do so when they make investments overseas. When operating abroad, universities are not bound by the same set of implicit and explicit contracts entered over time with domestic stakeholders.

We unearth an abundance of evidence in support of our hypothesis that US universities behave like firms when they make overseas investments. Universities with higher tuition dependency are more likely to offer overseas programs. They target markets with a large pool of potential clients, in business-friendly environments, with loose regulation. Upon entering these markets, they price their products to suit local affordability and local competition. Furthermore, when they save costs by forming local partnerships or by obtaining local financial support, we find no evidence that they pass on the savings to local clients. These behaviors are exactly what one would expect from profit-seeking multinational firms in their foreign direct investments.

These findings do not necessarily imply that US universities behave like firms in their domestic operations. Because nonprofit universities face various constraints from explicit and implicit contracts entered over time with multiple stakeholders, their domestic behavior may differ substantially from their overseas behavior. Nevertheless, one can easily think of similarities in governance structures between large universities and large, diffusely held public corporations with clear separation of ownership and control: centralized administration, bureaucratic behavior, the me-first attitude often observed among those who participate in the governance process, and finally, but most important, the need to ensure sustainability by ensuring sufficient financial resources. Whether these similarities lead large modern US universities to emulate profit-seeking public corporations in operating home campuses within the US borders is an interesting subject for future research.

Finally, our results have an implication on how US universities' overseas programs affect their domestic programs. In a recent hearing by the House Committee on Science and Technology, lawmakers questioned whether university ventures abroad are undermining American economic competitiveness. Representative David Wu of Oregon says that he "wanted to be sure that colleges that established branches overseas did not price themselves too cheaply and 'start giving away the store.'"[64] Our results suggest that the public can rest assured that US universities are not diverting resources to the benefit of overseas students. Quite the contrary, US universities seem to price their products strategically, like US multinational corporations, using their competitive edge in attempts to generate more resources for the benefit of their home institutions.

References

Avery, C., M. Glickman, C. Hoxby, and A. Metrick. 2005. A revealed preference ranking of US colleges and universities. NBER Working Paper no. W10803. Cambridge, MA: National Bureau of Economic Research, October.

Bhandari, R., and P. Chow. 2007. *Open doors 2007: Report on international educational exchange.* New York: Institute of International Education.

Black, D. A., and J. A. Smith. 2006. Estimating the returns to college quality with multiple proxies for quality. *Journal of Labor Economics* 24 (3): 701–28.

Bureau of Economic Analysis (BEA). 2007. International economic account data. Available at: http://www.bea.gov/international/index.htm.

Brewer, D. J., E. R. Eide, and R. G. Ehrenberg. 1999. Does it pay to attend an elite private college? *Journal of Human Resources* 34 (1): 104–23.

Carnegie Classification of Institutions of Higher Education. 2005. The Carnegie Foundation for the Advancement of Teaching. Available at: http://www.carnegie foundation.org/classifications/.

Caves, R. E. 1996. *Multinational enterprise and economic analysis.* Cambridge: Cambridge University Press.

Clotfelter, C. T. 1996. *Buying the best: Cost escalation in elite higher education.* Princeton, NJ: Princeton University Press.

———. 1999. The familiar but curious economics of higher education: Introduction to a symposium. *Journal of Economic Perspectives* 13 (1): 3–12.

Clotfelter, C. T., and M. Rothschild. 1993. *Studies of supply and demand in higher education.* Chicago: University of Chicago Press.

Coleman, J. S. 1973. The university and society's new demand upon it. In *Content and context,* ed. C. Kaysen, 359–99. New York: McGraw-Hill.

Council of Graduate Schools (CGS). 2007. *Findings from the 2007 CGS international graduate admissions survey. Phase II: Final applicants and initial offers of admission.* Available at: http://www.cgsnet.org/portals/0/pdf/R_IntlAdm07_II.pdf.

Djelic, M.-L. 1998. *Exporting the American model: The postwar transformation of European business.* New York: Oxford University Press.

Easley, D., and M. O'Hara. 1983. The economic role of the non-profit firm. *Bell Journal of Economics* 14 (2): 531–38.

Goldin, C., and L. F. Katz. 1999. The shaping of higher education: The formative years in the United States, 1890 to 1940. *Journal of Economic Perspectives* 13 (1): 37–62.

Green, M. 2007. *Venturing abroad: Delivering US degrees through overseas branch campuses and programs.* Washington, DC: American Council on Education.

64. Goldie Blumenstyk, "House Panel Quizzes Universities on Value of Overseas Ventures," *Chronicle of Higher Education,* August 10, 2007.

Green, M., D. T. Luu, and B. Burris. 2008. *Mapping internationalization on US campuses: 2008 edition.* Washington, DC: American Council on Education.

Heston, A., R. Summers and B. Aten. 2006. Penn World Table Version 6.2. Center for International Comparisons of Production, Income and Prices at the University of Pennsylvania.

Hoxby, C. M. 1997. How the changing market structure of US higher education explains college tuition. NBER Working Paper no. W6323. Cambridge, MA: National Bureau of Economic Research, December.

Hutchins, R. M. 1936. *The higher learning in America.* New Haven, CT: Yale University Press.

James, E. 1990. Decision processes and priorities in higher education. In *The economics of American universities,* ed. S. A. Hoenack and E. L. Collins, 77–106. Buffalo, NY: State University of New York Press.

Kim, E. H., A. Morse, and L. Zingales. Forthcoming. Are elite universities losing their competitive edge? *Journal of Financial Economics.*

National Center for Education Statistics. 2008a. *Digest of education statistics 2007 (March 2008).* NCES no. 2008-022. Washington, DC: US Department of Education.

———. 2008b. [Integrated Postsecondary Education Data System] IPEDS executive peer tool and peer analysis system. Available at: http://nces.ed.gov/ipedspas/.

Norton, E. C., H. Wang, and C. Ai. 2004. Computing interaction effects and standard errors in logit and probit models. *Stata Journal* 4 (2): 154–67.

Organization for Economic Cooperation and Development (OECD). 2007. *Education at a glance, 2007.* Available at: http://www.oecd.org/dataoecd/4/55/39313286.pdf.

Political Risk Services Group (PRS). 1999–2003. *International country risk guide.* East Syracuse, NY: PRS Group.

Rothschild, M., and L. J. White. 1995. The analytics of the pricing of higher education and other services in which the customers are inputs. *Journal of Political Economy* 103 (3): 573–86.

Sacerdote, B. 2001. Peer effects with random assignment: Results for Dartmouth roommates. *Quarterly Journal of Economics* 116 (2): 681–704.

Winston, G. C. 1999. Subsidies, hierarchy and peers: The awkward economics of higher education. *Journal of Economic Perspectives* 13 (1): 13–36.

III

Emulation and Competition Abroad

6 The Structure of European Higher Education in the Wake of the Bologna Reforms

Ofer Malamud

6.1 Introduction

The United States has been the undisputed leader in higher education since World War II. According to a recent ranking of universities from around the world, seventeen of the top twenty universities are in the United States.[1] Moreover, the United States remains the predominant destination for foreign students, accounting for about 20 percent of these students in 2006 (OECD 2008). But there are growing concerns that American higher education is losing ground to other countries. Much attention is focused on the spectacular growth of higher education in India and China.[2] While these countries could be among the world's leaders in the future, at this juncture it is probably Europe that presents the main challenge to America's dominance in higher education. After trailing in college and university enrollment rates at midcentury, many countries in Europe have caught up and, in some cases, overtaken the United States.[3] Increasing numbers of foreign students are choosing to study in Europe over the United States as compared to previous

Ofer Malamud is an assistant professor in the Harris School of Public Policy at the University of Chicago, and a faculty research fellow of the National Bureau of Economic Research.

I would like to thank Charlie Clotfelter, Michael Rothschild, and other participants at the American Universities in a Global Market conference for many helpful conversations and suggestions. Cristian Pop-Eleches and Eleanor Kane also offered useful comments. Lex Borghans generously provided the CHEERS data. Alejandro Ome provided able research assistance. I am solely responsible for any errors.

1. This is according to ratings by Shanghai Jiao Tong University's Institute of Higher Education, which have been widely cited (http://ed.sjtu.edu.cn/rank/2007/ranking2007.htm).

2. See Freeman (2005) and the chapters on India and China in this volume. Fears about China and India surpassing the United States have been widespread in the popular media but there is some contention regarding the quality of these degrees.

3. The production of PhD equivalents in Germany, France, and the United Kingdom now combine to surpass the total number of PhDs granted in the United States, even though these

years. And a broader look at these same university rankings reveals that 33 of the top 100 are located in Europe while not a single university from India or China is currently listed. Thus, though the American system of higher education took the lead from Europe in the mid-twentieth century, Europe may be on the brink of a strong comeback.

Europe is also in the process of instituting some far-reaching reforms to the structure of higher education. In 1999, ministers of education from twenty-nine European countries issued the Bologna Declaration in order to modernize and harmonize the European system of higher education.[4] The ultimate aim of the Bologna process is the creation of a European Higher Education Area (EHEA) with academic degree and quality assurance standards comparable throughout Europe. However, the Bologna Declaration also makes explicit the "objective of increasing the international competitiveness of the European system of higher education" and introduces specific reforms "to ensure that the European higher education system acquires a worldwide degree of attraction." These reforms include the introduction of a standardized undergraduate and graduate degree structure and a system of transferable academic credits. With these reforms, Europe is set to adopt some of the central elements associated with the American system of higher education. That the United States drew early inspiration from the leading European models of higher education makes Europe's recent convergence to the modern American model of higher education especially striking.

How might these structural reforms affect higher education in Europe? The Bologna reforms may well serve to enhance the flexibility of student choices and improve competition among institutions of higher education, two aspects often lauded in the American system of higher education. In terms of providing enhanced flexibility, these reforms may reduce the costs associated with choosing a wrong course of study by allowing students to change fields and/or universities after completing a short (bachelor's) first degree. With the introduction of transferable credits, students may find it easier to switch fields and/or universities even in the midst of their degrees. Furthermore, the Bologna reforms might stimulate students to explore and combine a variety of different fields of study. In sum, these reforms should help induce a better allocation of students to fields and courses in university. The Bologna reforms also have the potential to encourage greater competition between universities in Europe. While not sufficient for generating competition, a more comparable degree structure will likely enable students to make meaningful comparisons across countries and encourage them to choose the best program available to them. Finally, the Bologna reforms will make the European system more compatible with other systems of higher

three countries have only two-thirds the fraction of the American population (National Science Board, National Science Foundation 2008).

4. At present, forty-six European nations (both EU and non-EU members) are signatories to the Bologna process.

education around the world, helping Europe compete on a global scale by attracting more foreign students.

The Bologna reforms in Europe may also have consequences for higher education in the United States. If the Bologna reforms do indeed attract more foreign students to Europe, this could lead to further declines in the share of foreign students in America. Moreover, the possibility of increased competition among European institutions of higher education could lead to greater demand for scarce resources such as highly talented faculty. Such increased competition among European institutions might also improve their research productivity and displace some American universities from the top of the world rankings. Whether any or all of these possibilities are actually realized, however, is likely to depend on the introduction of further reforms, such as increased autonomy and funding for European universities.

This chapter will explore the main characteristics associated with the Bologna reforms and consider the possible consequences of these reforms for higher education in the United States and Europe. Bringing data to bear on these important questions is exceedingly difficult. For one thing, the Bologna reforms are still ongoing, with many countries in the midst of restructuring their systems of higher education. Moreover, the most substantial effects of these reforms on higher education in Europe and America may take time to emerge. There is also a lack of comparable individual-level data sets on higher education that span both the United States and Europe, and cross-country comparisons are complicated by the enormous heterogeneity that still remains across different systems. However, with the adoption of a more comparable set of degree structures across Europe, future researchers will hopefully be able to make more progress in understanding the factors that help determine performance and success in higher education.

The chapter proceeds as follows: section 6.2 provides background on higher education in the United States and Europe, drawing on administrative data from the Organization of Economic Cooperation and Development (OECD) and graduate surveys in Europe and the United States. Section 6.3 briefly surveys the history of European reforms to higher education leading up to the Bologna reforms and describes the main features associated with the Bologna process. Section 6.4 considers the potential impacts of the Bologna reforms on flexibility, competition, and foreign student enrollments. Section 6.5 concludes with some final reflections.

6.2 Higher Education in Europe and the United States

6.2.1 Background

The development of higher education in the United States was greatly influenced by the rich tradition of European higher education. The University of Bologna, founded in 1088, is often regarded as the first European university. It was followed by the University of Paris (ca. 1150), the University of Oxford (1167), and the University of Cambridge (1209). The first institutions of higher learning established during America's colonial period were largely based on the English collegiate model. Harvard, Yale, and many of the other colleges founded prior to the American Revolution bore a close resemblance to Oxford and Cambridge. In the decades immediately before and after the American Revolution, France also played a role: inspiration for the University of Virginia and the University of the State of New York came largely from the contemporary French models of higher education (Paulston 1968). In the mid- to late-nineteenth century, the United States borrowed heavily from the model of the German research university. This was especially evident in the founding of Johns Hopkins University and the University of Chicago, which emphasized graduate research, introduced teaching through seminars, and began conferring doctorate degrees.[5] Thus, it is with good reason that the modern American system of higher education is often viewed as an amalgamation of the English undergraduate college and the German research university.

The American system of higher education also embodies several features that make it quite distinct from European systems of higher education. In keeping with the American tradition of limited government and freedom of expression, institutions of higher education have largely been protected from the degree of central government control present in most European nations. This tradition is reflected in a decentralized structure of higher education and a large prominent private sector. Support from federal government has generally been in the form of research grants and direct subsidies to students.[6] Indeed, a far larger proportion of funding for higher education in the United States comes from private sources as compared to Europe, where most universities are completely state-funded. Colleges and universities in the United States are also granted a great deal of autonomy in hiring, wage-setting, tuition levels, and other funding decisions. In contrast, most universities in Europe have traditionally been subject to substantial restrictions regarding faculty salaries and student tuition, as well as curriculum and enrollment decisions. However, even within Europe, there are large differences in the degree of autonomy and funding characteristics associated with institutions of higher education.[7]

5. John's Hopkins University was also the first American institution of higher education to offer an undergraduate major as opposed to a purely liberal arts curriculum. See Ulrich and Wasser (1992).

6. Prior to the mid-twentieth century, the major involvement of the federal government in higher education was through passage of the Morrill Acts, which helped establish the land-grant universities.

7. For example, Sweden and the United Kingdom have a rare degree of wage-setting autonomy, while several countries in southern Europe lack even hiring autonomy (Aghion et al. 2007).

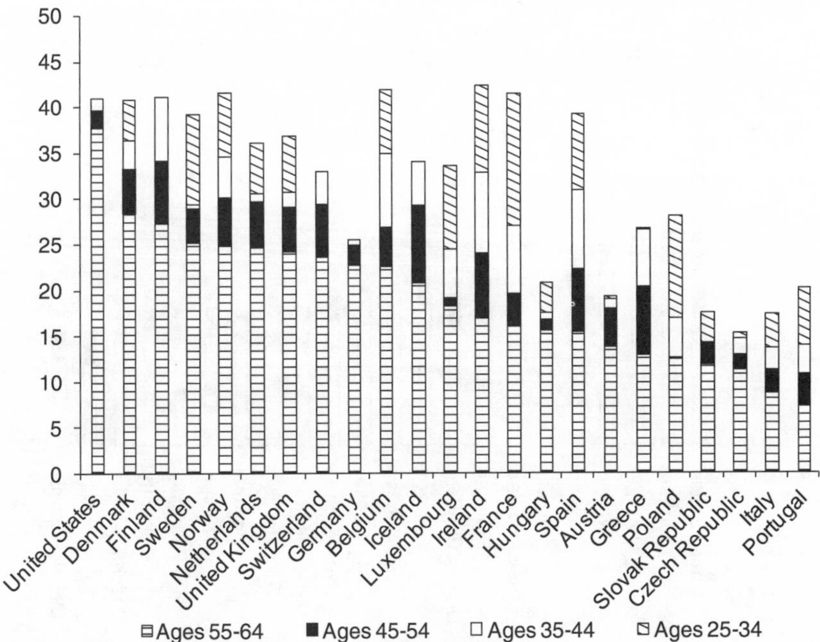

Fig. 6.1 Percent of population with tertiary education in 2006
Source: OECD (2008).

The latest statistics from the OECD help reveal some of the differences in higher education across Europe and the United States. Figure 6.1 shows the pattern of educational attainment over time by plotting the proportion of the population with tertiary education among different cohorts.[8] While the United States has the highest rates of tertiary education among individuals who were educated in the 1940s (aged fifty-five to sixty-four), most of Europe has caught up and, in some cases, surpassed the United States among those who were educated more recently (aged twenty-five to thirty-four). Figure 6.2 shows the amount of spending on tertiary education across different countries as a proportion of gross domestic product (GDP), as well as the breakdown between public and private sources. The United States spends over 3 percent of GDP on tertiary education whereas most countries in Europe spend less than 2 percent. Within Europe, the Nordic countries tend to have relatively high tertiary spending while countries in Eastern and Southern Europe tend to spend substantially less. There is also wide variation in the level of tuition: for example, Denmark, Norway, and Sweden have tended to subsidize the full cost of education for their students

8. Tertiary education consists of International Standard Classification of Education (SCED) levels 5A, 5B, 6 that include postsecondary vocational programs as well as traditional academic degrees. See Cascio, Clark, and Gordon (2008) for a discussion of these trends.

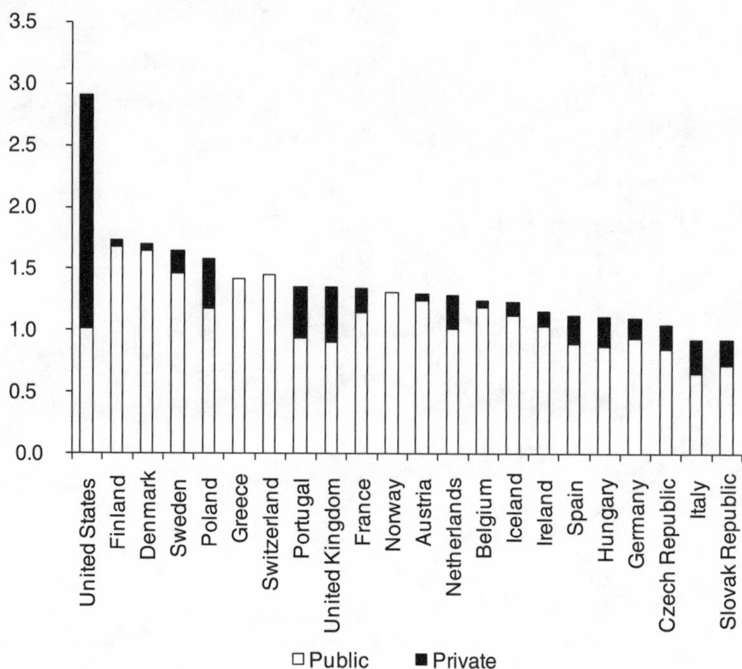

Fig. 6.2 Expenditure on tertiary education in 2005 (percent of GDP)
Source: OECD (2008).

while the United Kingdom and the Netherlands have substantially higher tuition fees (with Austria, Italy, and Spain somewhere in between). But almost all universities in Europe have low fees relative to the United States, where average tuition is much higher, especially in private institutions.

6.2.2 The Structure of Higher Education

Ahead of the reforms instituted by the Bologna process, there were also major differences in the underlying structure of higher education—that is, the manner in which courses and degrees were organized—between Europe and the United States. The United States has three main degree cycles: bachelor, master, and doctorate.[9] The bachelor's degree normally requires four years of full-time study, the master's degree one or two years of further study, and doctorates at least three years of research. This structure corresponds quite closely to the structure of higher education in the United Kingdom and other Commonwealth nations.[10] In contrast, most nations

9. Other degrees include associate's degrees, which are offered at community colleges with two years of study, and professional degrees (MD, JD, MBA, etc.), which can be earned after completing a BA.

10. Bachelor's degrees in the United Kingdom require three or four years of study. Note that, in Scotland, the first degree is sometimes referred to as an MA degree (as distinguished from MLitt or MSc, used to refer to second degrees).

in continental Europe have traditionally had a much longer first degree cycle, sometimes taking up to six or seven years to complete. The United States has also had a rather unique system for organizing courses. Since the early twentieth century, when the college credit system extended the Carnegie Unit for secondary schools, students in most American universities accumulate credits with each course taken.[11] The American credit system evolved quite naturally alongside a system of electives in which undergraduate students could choose the combination of courses that best suited their plan of study, subject to the constraints imposed by the institution.

Even within continental Europe, there has been substantial variation in the structure of higher education prior the start of the Bologna process, especially at the undergraduate level. Indeed, it was this very diversity in structures of higher education that the Bologna reforms have sought to harmonize. For example, first degree programs in Austria and Germany had a formal duration of four to five years and led to the *diplom* or *magister,* depending on the subject. First degree programs in Italy also had a formal duration of four to five years and led to a *diploma di laurea,* after which graduates could continue onto further study. France has had its own unique structure of higher education, with a broad set of degrees that span two different sectors: traditional universities and the *Grandes Écoles.* In French universities, students would first complete a two-year *diplôme* followed by a one-year *licence,* and then choose whether to complete a one-year *maîtrise.* After attaining these degrees, students could proceed to complete a *diplôme d'études approfondies* (DEA), a *diplôme d'études superieures spécialisées* (DESS), or a doctorate. The *Grandes Écoles* have had a different structure altogether, with two years of preparatory classes followed by a three year degree. In the years leading up to the Bologna reforms, some countries did introduce shorter degree cycles into their systems of higher education, often within a parallel set of institutions focusing on more applied studies. Spain has long had a dual structure where students could obtain a short three year degree (*diplomado*) or a longer five year degree (*licenciado*) depending on the subject and institution. Germany has also offered somewhat shorter degrees at Universities of Applied Sciences known as *Fachhochschulen* while Austria established their own version of the *Fachhochschulen* in 1993. The Netherlands has also offered similar degrees at *Hoger Beroeps Onderwijs* (HBOs). Of course, even this brief description is far from exhaustive and ignores many more subtleties in the systems of higher education across Europe.[12]

While differences in the formal length of degrees across Europe and the United States may not appear to be quite so stark, de facto differences have

11. See Hefferman (1973) and Shedd (2003) for a history of the credit system in American higher education.

12. This discussion has ignored intermediate postsecondary degrees corresponding to the community college level. For more details on degrees offered across Europe prior to the Bologna reforms, see EURYDICE (1999) and Murdoch (2003).

been substantially larger. Using individual-level data from the Careers after Higher Education European Research Survey (CHEERS), we can compare across European systems of higher education in more detail. This study surveyed 1994 and 1995 graduates from eleven countries in 1999, some four years after they were awarded a first degree.[13] The CHEERS study focused on first degrees, which generally required between three and six years of study at institutions of higher education as defined by national system. As a result, some countries included students enrolled in short cycle degrees (such as the German *Fachhochschulen-diploma* and Spanish *diplomado*). Although this study did not include data from the United States, the Baccalaureate and Beyond (B&B) Longitudinal Study provides somewhat comparable data on American students who received their bachelor's degree in 1992 and 1993.

Table 6.1 shows some basic descriptive statistics and detailed measures of the length of degrees for Austria, Finland, France, Germany, Italy, Netherlands, Norway, Spain, and the United Kingdom. As indicated earlier, differences in the reported formal duration of first degrees across countries do not appear to be particularly large. However, the actual length of time taken to complete the first degree, as reported by respondents, varies widely. For example, students in the United Kingdom report completing their degrees in about 3.4 years while those in France and Germany take over five years and those in Italy require almost seven years. Focusing on students enrolled in long cycle degrees reveals even larger differences. By comparison, American students who graduated in 1992 and 1993 took an average of 5.2 years from entry into postsecondary education until receipt of their bachelor degree (National Center for Education Statistics [NCES] 1996).[14] Interestingly, looking at the reported time spent on course activities reveals that students in the United Kingdom spent about four fewer hours per week on their studies as compared their counterparts in France and Germany, and almost ten hours per week less than students in Italy. Recent evidence reported by Babcock and Marks (2007) suggests that American students devote far less time to their studies than their European counterparts.[15]

The American system of using credits to measure progress through degrees has not been widely used in Europe (one notable exception is Sweden, which has had a credit system in place since the 1960s). Instead, students in

13. Sampling frames were determined by country and a weighting was undertaken so that the final sample was representative of the target population defined by type of institution, degree, field of study, and gender. For more information about the CHEERS survey and methodology, see Schomberg and Teichler (2006).

14. See Bound, Lovenheim, and Turner (2007) for a discussion of the increasing time taken for a BA degree.

15. Surveys from the Higher Education Research Institute (HERI) in 1998 and 2004 indicate that students in their fourth year of college spend approximately eleven to thirteen hours on studies and thirteen to fifteen hours of class time.

Table 6.1 Descriptive statistics and length of degrees (CHEERS data)

	Austria	Finland	France	Germany	Italy	Netherlands	Norway	Spain	United Kingdom
Descriptive statistics									
Gender	00.48	00.60	00.55	00.43	00.53	00.55	00.60	00.64	00.60
Age at graduation	32.2	33.4	27.9	31.5	31.3	29.7	32.5	28.5	30.1
Schooling prior entry	12.4	12.1	12.4	12.9	13.1	12.9	12.2	12.5	13.1
All degrees (years)									
Required length	4.65	4.51	4.03	4.27	4.43	4.03	4.29	4.19	3.51
Actual length	6.86	5.04	5.12	5.27	7.19	4.72	4.56	4.83	3.53
Calculated length	7.20	6.22	3.65	5.31	7.39	4.72	4.92	4.66	3.28
Long-cycle degrees									
Required length	4.65	4.51	4.46	4.65	4.43	4.15	5.55	4.86	—
Actual length	6.86	5.04	5.52	5.75	7.19	5.43	6.08	5.59	—
Calculated length	7.20	6.22	3.86	5.81	7.39	5.44	6.87	5.31	—
Short-cycle degrees									
Required length	—	—	2.98	3.54	—	3.95	3.24	3.18	3.51
Actual length	—	—	4.13	4.31	—	4.25	3.33	3.68	3.53
Calculated length	—	—	3.12	4.33	—	4.23	3.32	3.60	3.28
Hours spent on course activities									
Main subject: lectures	11.8	11.7	22.5	21.4	17.7	15.8	16.9	22.7	15.5
Main subject: studies	17.2	12.5	11.9	12.3	23.2	13.4	16.7	16.2	14.7
Other subjects	5.7	2.3	4.4	5.4	6.6	5.2	4.1	4.1	5.4
Extra-curriculars	1.6	5.3	0.7	1.2	0.0	3.5	0.2	2.3	1.2
Employment	7.5	5.7	3.8	5.6	4.8	6.9	4.9	4.6	6.2

Notes: Data are from the surveys "Higher Education and Graduate Employment in Europe" (CHEERS project). Austria, Finland, and Italy did not have short-cycle degrees at the time of graduation; United Kingdom did not have long-cycle degrees. Sample sizes are: Austria (2,304); Finland (2,675); France (3,050); Germany (3,442); Italy (3,120); Spain (2,495); Netherlands (2,884); Norway (3,329); United Kingdom (2,933). The dashed cells indicate that these types of degrees are not available in these countries.

Europe have traditionally applied to a specific field of study prior to entering college or university and followed a relatively rigid curriculum once admitted. Thus, European universities did not divide their curriculum into discrete units or award credits for completion of courses. A European Credit Transfer System (ECTS) was introduced in 1989 to facilitate the recognition of periods of study abroad through the European Region Action Scheme for the Mobility of University Students (ERASMUS) program. However, it was not widely used for credit accumulation in standard courses of study within Europe. Since the mid-1990s, some universities in England and elsewhere have begun offering degrees with modular courses. More recently, with the formation of the Scottish Credit and Qualifications Framework (SCQF) in 2001, Scotland has adopted a national credit transfer system. Nevertheless, prior to the introduction of the Bologna reforms, most countries in Europe had not instituted a system of credit transfer and accumulation in their institutions of higher education.

6.2.3 The Quality of Education

While differences in the structure of higher education across countries can be quantified relatively easily, differences in the *quality* of higher education are much more difficult to ascertain. In recent years, several independent sources have compiled rankings of the world's top universities. According to most such rankings, American universities dominate the top spots (with seventeen of the top twenty spots according to the Shanghai Jiao Tong University's ranking, or thirteen of the top twenty spots according to the London *Times* ranking).[16] British institutions also fare relatively well with several prominent universities in the top twenty rankings. On the other hand, the top universities in continental Europe lag behind their Anglo-Saxon counterparts. A broader look at the rankings reveals that Europe accounts for over 30 percent of the top 100 universities and over 40 percent of the top 500 universities. These rankings suggest that Europe may have a relatively more narrow distribution of university quality. Nevertheless, university rankings are heavily weighted toward research productivity, which may not reflect the benefits of education to the majority of university graduates who proceed directly to the labor market.[17]

An important aspect that may affect the quality of the first degrees is the chosen field of study. Table 6.2 documents the composition of field of study for first degrees in the CHEERS data.[18] For example, the United Kingdom

16. See http://ed.sjtu.edu.cn/rank/2007/ranking2007.htm and http://www.timeshighereducation.co.uk.

17. To assess the benefits of higher education in the labor market, one could calculate and compare the pecuniary returns to higher education across different countries. This approach is not pursued here.

18. Fields of study are aggregated to nine broad categories: education, humanities, social sciences, law, natural sciences, mathematics, engineering, and medical sciences.

Table 6.2 **Distribution of first degree by field (CHEERS data)**

	Austria	Finland	France	Germany	Italy	Netherlands	Norway	Spain	United Kingdom
Education	0.13	0.15	0.00	0.07	0.02	0.11	0.11	0.12	0.04
Humanities	0.09	0.17	0.15	0.11	0.17	0.09	0.08	0.12	0.23
Social sciences	0.26	0.23	0.38	0.31	0.27	0.41	0.26	0.35	0.30
Law	0.10	0.03	0.11	0.06	0.15	0.05	0.06	0.09	0.02
Natural sciences	0.04	0.08	0.18	0.09	0.08	0.02	0.07	0.07	0.13
Mathematics	0.05	0.05	0.08	0.05	0.03	0.04	0.03	0.05	0.07
Engineering	0.18	0.20	0.09	0.26	0.17	0.16	0.20	0.05	0.11
Medical sciences	0.14	0.10	0.00	0.05	0.11	0.11	0.21	0.15	0.10

Notes: Data are from the surveys "Higher Education and Graduate Employment in Europe" (CHEERS project). Sample sizes are: Austria (2,304); Finland (2,675); France (3,050); Germany (3,442); Italy (3,120); Spain (2,495); Netherlands (2,884); Norway (3,329); United Kingdom (2,933).

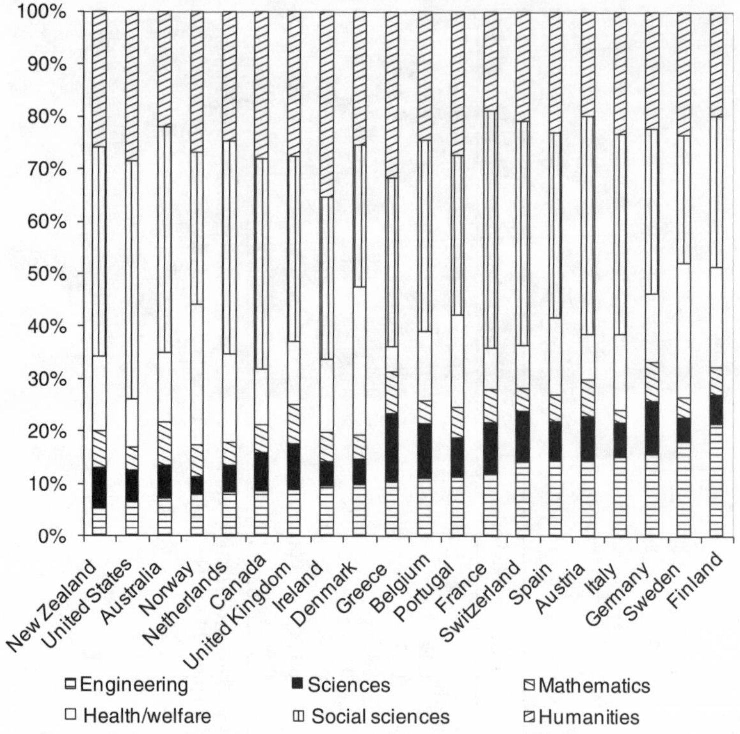

Fig. 6.3 Distribution of students across fields, 2002
Source: OECD (2005).

has a relatively high proportion of graduates in the humanities and natural sciences and Germany and the Netherlands have high fractions of engineering graduates, while Italy, Spain, and France tend to train disproportionately more lawyers. But these patterns may be affected by the differential response rates and sampling procedures, even after applying appropriate weightings. Figure 6.3 uses OECD data to provide an aggregate snapshot of the composition of fields for first and advanced degrees, including the United States. While some of the previous patterns do remain, there is substantial divergence because of different degree coverage and field categories. Most strikingly, the United States appears to have among the lowest rate of degrees awarded in engineering and the physical sciences. However, it is important to remember that the total number of slots available in each field in Europe is usually determined at the central level, not as a consequence of student demand as in the United States.

The CHEERS data also elicited retrospective views from students regarding their degrees. Specifically, students were asked how likely they were to choose certain aspects of their degree again, how they rate different aspects of their degree course, and the extent to which their studies helped them find a satisfying job, improve their long-term career prospects, and even develop their personality. In each case, table 6.3 reports the proportion of students who expressed a high likelihood or provided a high rating to each category.[19] There are no clear patterns between the likelihood of wishing to change certain aspects of their degree (panel A) or the extent to which studies were beneficial (panel B) and the structure of higher education. Focusing on nations with particularly lengthy first degrees, students in Austria and Finland are relatively more satisfied with their choice of college and course of study, while their counterparts in Italy are less satisfied. Indeed, students in Italy score comparatively lower on most measures of satisfaction. On the other hand, the broad patterns in panel C suggest that students in the United Kingdom were more satisfied with many aspects of their degree course as compared to students in other countries.

Finally, some indication of quality may be surmised from the number of foreign students choosing to study in different countries. The proportion of foreign students in the CHEERS data depends on exactly how this is determined (see alternative measures in table 6.4). Regardless of the measure, the United Kingdom has the highest rate of foreign student enrollment while Italy has extremely low rates of foreign student enrollment. However, these are undoubtedly underestimates due to reporting bias, as foreign citizens are more likely to return to their home countries after completing their studies (or may wish to avoid interacting with bureaucratic entities if they decide to stay). The OECD also collects and standardizes information on foreign student enrollments from administrative data.[20] Figure 6.4 displays the foreign student enrollments in major destination countries in 2000 and 2006. The United States remains the leading destination, but its share of foreign enrollments has declined from 25 to 20 percent. France, Germany, and the United Kingdom account for the vast majority of foreign enrollment in Europe and their combined share has remained roughly constant at 29 percent of total foreign enrollments over the same period.[21] Obviously, these countries (together with Australia, Japan, and Canada) succeed in attracting foreign students for different reasons—related to size, proximity, language,

19. Responses were elicited on a scale of 1 to 5. These are aggregated in two broad categories, with the top ratings (1 and 2) representing high likelihoods and ratings.

20. Still, there are differences in collection strategies as well as coverage of students across different sectors of higher education. In many cases, countries report the number of students with foreign citizenship rather than the number of students who moved from another country for the purpose of completing higher education. In recent years, the OECD has begun requiring countries to compile information on international students as distinct from foreign students but it is not possible to compare changes over time with this data.

21. This is mostly due to increases in foreign undergraduate enrollment in other countries. The United States has been increasing its share of foreign graduate students over recent years (OECD 2008, table C3.3).

Table 6.3 **Retrospective views on the degree (CHEERS data)**

	Austria	Finland	France	Germany	Italy	Netherlands	Norway	Spain	United Kingdom
A If you were free to choose your degree course again, how likely is that you would choose . . .									
a. the same course of study?	0.685	0.696	0.663	0.655	0.607	0.657	0.688	0.647	0.625
b. the same college/university?	0.721	0.711	0.603	0.582	0.581	0.653	0.668	0.690	0.655
c. a higher level of higher education?	0.173	0.127	0.494	0.163	0.460	0.232	0.245	0.681	0.409
d. a lower level of higher education?	0.030	0.035	0.090	0.035	0.085	0.041	0.038	0.309	0.019
e. not to study at all?	0.067	0.005	0.027	0.068	0.050	0.019	0.018	0.087	0.024
B To what extent did your studies help you . . .									
a. find a satisfying job after graduation	0.616	0.808	0.526	0.634	0.370	0.695	0.886	0.462	0.524
b. for your long-term career prospects?	0.634	0.645	0.596	0.556	0.433	0.605	0.762	0.569	0.669
c. for the development of your personality?	0.652	0.631	0.594	0.731	0.625	0.788	0.736	0.657	0.789
C How would you rate the following aspects of your degree course?									
a. Academic advice offered in general	0.208	0.364	0.283	0.245	0.104	0.133	0.305	0.141	0.522
b. Assistance with final examinations	0.228	0.447	0.191	0.359	0.390	0.369	0.464	0.101	0.521
c. Course content of main subject(s)	0.482	0.584	0.590	0.410	0.383	0.596	0.462	0.359	0.730
d. Variety of courses offered	0.547	0.465	0.609	0.462	0.420	0.677	0.424	0.380	0.593
e. Design of your degree program	0.302	0.434	0.497	0.365	0.216	0.316	0.342	0.181	0.546
f. Assessment system	0.371	0.204	0.341	0.306	0.192	0.374	0.479	0.212	0.512
g. Opportunity to choose courses/specialization	0.461	0.397	0.419	0.436	0.382	0.454	0.323	0.219	0.538
h. Practical emphasis of teaching and learning	0.155	0.271	0.259	0.193	0.084	0.413	0.337	0.172	0.449
i. Teaching quality	0.437	0.394	0.403	0.402	0.380	0.415	0.316	0.259	0.611
j. Chances to participate in research projects	0.169	0.226	0.265	0.171	0.087	0.314	0.161	0.059	0.247
k. Research emphasis of teaching and learning	0.210	0.375	0.303	0.187	0.106	0.280	0.262	0.073	0.328
p. Library resources	0.561	0.677	0.445	0.461	0.319	0.605	0.683	0.449	0.601
q. Supply of teaching materials	0.343	0.555	0.296	0.339	0.229	0.488	0.581	0.381	0.435
r. Quality of technical equipment	0.277	0.486	0.354	0.308	0.154	0.436	0.390	0.201	0.454

Notes: Data are from the surveys "Higher Education and Graduate Employment in Europe" (CHEERS project). Individuals were asked to rate each aspect on a 1 to 5 scale, where 1 was "very likely" or "very good" and 5 was "not likely at all" or "very bad." The figures present the fraction of individuals who reported a score of 1 or 2. Sample sizes are: Austria (2,304); Finland (2,675); France (3,050); Germany (3,442); Italy (3,120); Spain (2,495); Netherlands (2,884); Norway (3,329); United Kingdom (2,933).

Table 6.4 Foreign students and periods of study abroad during degrees (CHEERS data)

	Austria	Finland	France	Germany	Italy	Netherlands	Norway	Spain	United Kingdom
Study/work abroad	0.283	0.269	0.211	0.196	0.201	0.302	0.191	0.131	0.236
Study/work abroad twice	0.094	0.087	0.067	0.054	0.068	0.085	0.033	0.045	0.061
1st period abroad									
Duration (months)	6.99	7.23	8.65	6.03	3.61	4.71	8.46	4.98	6.33
For study	0.417	0.510	0.587	0.540	0.786	0.325	0.809	0.775	0.517
For work/internship	0.292	0.472	0.389	0.390	0.094	0.544	0.187	0.231	0.377
For other	0.154	0.042	0.123	0.133	0.173	0.206	0.137	0.114	0.200
2nd period abroad									
Duration (months)	5.55	4.89	6.88	5.25	2.94	4.36	6.23	5.30	6.67
For study	0.386	0.500	0.435	0.410	0.732	0.716	0.757	0.681	0.464
For work/internship	0.425	0.474	0.590	0.448	0.117	0.320	0.207	0.319	0.488
For other	0.188	0.043	0.100	0.208	0.202	0.024	0.153	0.106	0.213
Foreign students (determined according to . . .)									
Citizenship at birth	0.039	0.010	0.029	0.024	0.002	0.015	0.029	0.020	0.108
Country of secondary education	0.061	0.036	0.067	0.018	0.005	0.046	0.046	0.051	0.102

Notes: Data are from the surveys "Higher Education and Graduate Employment in Europe" (CHEERS project). Austria, Finland, and Italy did not have short-cycle degrees at the time of graduation; United Kingdom did not have long-cycle degrees. Sample sizes are: Austria (2,304); Finland (2,675); France (3,050); Germany (3,442); Italy (3,120); Spain (2,495); Netherlands (2,884); Norway (3,329); United Kingdom (2,933).

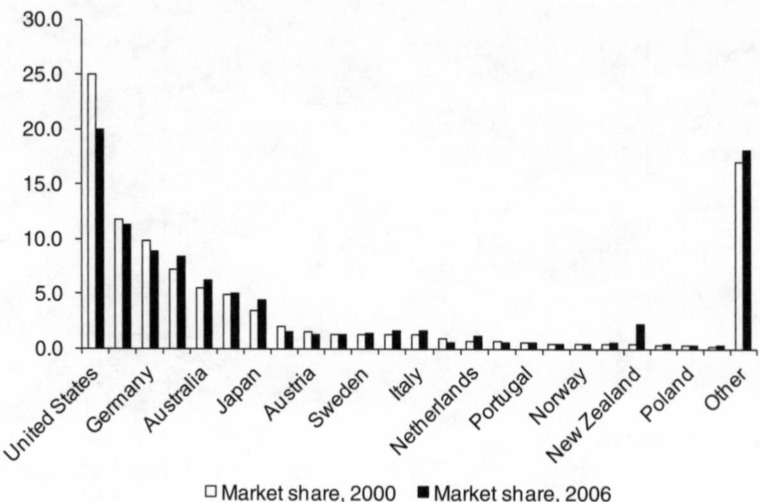

Fig. 6.4 Shares of foreign student enrollments, 2000 and 2006
Source: OECD (2008).

cost, and specific policies to encourage foreign enrollments—in addition to the quality of their higher education.

6.3 The Bologna Reforms

The Bologna reforms to European higher education came at a time of greater European integration in other social and economic spheres. The passage of the Maastricht Treaty in 1993 established the European Union (EU) and led to deeper political and economic union among many member countries. The Maastricht Treaty also dealt with education, which became an area in which the European Commission could take action, even if only as a subsidiary focus. Prior to this time, member states had limited the role of the European Community in introducing measures which could affect their own educational systems. Some successful educational initiatives were taken in the 1980s. Most notably, building on a number of earlier pilot student exchanges, the ERASMUS program was established in 1987.[22] Nevertheless, joint European action on education did not appear to be particularly high on the agenda, even after the passage of the Maastricht Treaty. Instead, the impetus for the Bologna reform came directly from the individual ministers of education acting as representatives of their national governments, outside the purview of the European Commission.

Much of the groundwork for the Bologna reforms was introduced in the

22. Participation in ERASMUS has grown from 3,244 students in 1987 to over 150,000 students in 2005. Together with other education programs, the ERASMUS program was incorporated into the SOCRATES program by the European Commission in 1994.

Sorbonne Declaration, which was signed on May 25, 1998 in Paris by ministers of education from France, Germany, Italy, and the United Kingdom.[23] The concluding document called for "the harmonization of the overall framework of degrees and cycles . . . aimed at improving external recognition and facilitating student mobility as well as employability" (http://www.bologna-berlin2003.de/pdf/Sorbonne_declaration.pdf). The need for European higher education to retain its global competitiveness was a clear motivation for the summit. According to a report of the session, "most of the major speakers referred to the fact that Europe was losing ground in the competition with the USA, and that a more 'readable' and compatible set of qualifications was needed to counteract this trend" (Knudsen, Haug, and Kirstein 1999, 29). Why did these four nations choose to introduce these reforms outside the normal channels of European action? Perhaps, as suggested by de Wit (2000), this served as a way to maintain control over the process of harmonization. The United Kingdom had already embarked on a major effort to market its higher education around the world and Germany was attempting to increase its compatibility with other systems in order to improve its attractiveness. Moreover, previous attempts in France and Italy to reform their systems of higher education had sparked major protests. A joint declaration may have enabled these countries to force some of their reluctant parties to accept reforms to higher education.

Although there was some criticism about the exclusive set of participants in the Paris summit, the general tenets of the Sorbonne Declaration were remarkably well received in other European countries. Thus, a year later, on June 19, 1999, the ministers of education from twenty-nine European countries gathered in Bologna to sign the Declaration on the European Higher Education Area. This Bologna Declaration, as it has become known, proposed a number of specific reforms to increase the "international competitiveness" and the "worldwide attraction" of the European system of higher education: (a) adoption of a system of easily readable and comparable degrees; (b) adoption of a system essentially based on two main cycles, undergraduate and graduate; (c) establishment of a system of credits; (d) promotion of mobility by overcoming obstacles for the effective exercise of free movement; (e) promotion of European cooperation in quality assurance; and (f) promotion of the European dimension of higher education. The Bologna Declaration also called for further meetings to be held every two years in order to further clarify these objectives and determine the success of individual countries in carrying out these reforms. In these subsequent meetings, several additional objectives have been proposed and a number of new signatory countries have joined the Bologna process.

Though the proposed reforms were far-reaching and multifaceted, most

23. The Sorbonne Declaration coincided with the publication of the Attali report, which offered a series of recommendations for major changes in the French system of higher education.

of the attention has focused on the changes in degree structure. The Bologna reform initially called for a two-cycle system but amendments to the original declaration added the doctoral level as a third cycle. Thus, in many ways, the proposed harmonization of the degree structure for European systems of higher education mirrors the bachelor's, master's, and doctorate degrees that underpin the structure of higher education in the United Kingdom and the United States. In particular, the Bologna reforms pushed for replacing lengthy first degrees with a three- to four-year first (bachelor's) degree followed by a one- to two-year second (master's) degree. While the Bologna Declaration did not specify the precise number of years associated with each degree cycle, most countries have adopted a model based on a three-year bachelor's degree and a two-year master's degree. As discussed earlier, a number of countries had already introduced or were in the process of introducing some type of short-cycle degree into their system of higher education. So it comes as no surprise that much progress has been made on this front. The latest 2007 Stocktaking Report, from a working group appointed by the Bologna Follow-Up Group, indicates that three-quarters of member states have a majority of students studying in a two-cycle degree system. There is some concern that these changes have been more cosmetic than substantive and that the shorter first-cycle degree is viewed by students as merely an intermediate step en route to a terminal master's degree.[24] However, it is reasonable to expect that such large structural changes require sometime before they are adopted in full.

Another important aspect of the reforms is the call to establish a system of academic credits. This feature of the Bologna reforms is similar to the modular course structure prominent in the United States where students accumulate credit for each course taken. A European Credit Transfer System (ECTS) was introduced in 1989 to facilitate the recognition of periods of study abroad through the ERASMUS program. However, with the Bologna reforms, the ECTS is set to develop into an accumulation system, which accounts for the progress that students make through their degrees. There are some important differences between the credit system proposed and elaborated by the signatories of the Bologna Declaration and the American credit system. Whereas the American credit unit is based strictly on the number of hours that faculty spent actually teaching, the European unit was intended to account for the time students spent studying, attending, and completing assignments for the course.[25] According to the 2007 Stocktaking Report, most countries are well on their way to fulfilling this aspect

24. This perception is mentioned in the European Students Union *Bologna with Student Eyes* (2007). Indeed, several countries have very high continuation rates between their newly adopted first and second degrees.

25. There was hope to include performance measures in quantifying credit units but this has generally been deemed too difficult to implement in practice. See Adelman (2008) for a detailed discussion of these issues.

of the Bologna reforms. There are twenty-seven countries in which ECTS credits are allocated in all first and second cycle programs and an additional fifteen countries in which ECTS credits are allocated in a majority of higher education programs.

In addition to these two features of the Bologna reforms that affect the structure of higher education, there are certainly other important aspects, such as the introduction of national qualification frameworks, the creation of diploma supplements to provide information to students, and the establishment and recognition of joint degrees, among others. However, in considering the consequences of the Bologna reforms, the following section will focus on the changes to the degree structure and the adoption of academic credits.

6.4 Potential Impacts of the Bologna Reforms

The changes to the structure of higher education in the wake of the Bologna reforms are likely to affect student and institutional outcomes in Europe. First, these changes in the structure of higher education may help to enhance flexibility in student choices. Second, these changes in the structure of higher education may foster increased competition among institutions of higher education. Finally, the Bologna reforms may succeed in attracting greater numbers of foreign students into Europe.

6.4.1 Flexibility

The decision to invest in higher education is usually made under considerable uncertainty. Students may be unsure about their aptitude for college or graduate school.[26] They may also be uncertain about their talents and interests in different fields of study.[27] Moreover, the labor market rewards and opportunities associated with higher levels of education and specific fields of study are never fully known. They may shift over time and differ across regions due to labor market volatility. Finally, since college or graduate school is typically a onetime investment expenditure rather than a repeated purchase, it is difficult to have complete information on the quality of the educational product being offered by institutions. Given these various sources of uncertainty, certain structures of higher education may be better suited to reveal important information and allow students the flexibility of adjusting their choices based on this information. In particular, the reforms introduced by the Bologna process—a short first-degree cycle

26. See Cunha, Heckman, and Navarro (2005) and Cunha and Heckman (2007) for attempts to separately estimate the role of this type of uncertainty (as distinguished from heterogeneity across students).

27. See Malamud (2007b) for a detailed exploration associated with this aspect of uncertainty about talents.

and a system of transferable credits—are likely to provide students with greater flexibility.

The ability to accumulate credits within an institution enables students to transfer across institutions relatively easily. Evidence from the National Longitudinal Study (NLS-72) High School and Beyond (HSB) and National Education Longitudinal Study (NELS-88) indicates that over half of American bachelor's degree recipients have attended more than one institution of higher education as undergraduates since the 1970s (Adelman 2004). Looking at bachelor's degree graduates who completed high school in 1972, over 38 percent had attended two institutions and 19 percent had attended more than two institutions. While the fraction of students attending two institutions remained roughly constant among bachelor's degree graduates who completed high school in 1982 and 1992, the fraction who attended even more than two institutions increased to almost 23 percent. In contrast, university administrative (USR) data from the United Kingdom show that the fraction of students who switched universities was less than 1 percent in both England and Wales and Scotland from 1972 to 1992.[28] Even accounting for switches across a broader set of institutions (including the former polytechnics and colleges of higher education) using the 1980 National Survey of Graduates and Diplomates, the likelihood of switching institutions is less than 5 percent. Insofar as the United Kingdom had a similar degree structure but no credit system during these years, this suggests an important role for the credit system in allowing students to switch institutions in the midst of the degree.

The ability to accumulate credits within an institution also enables students to switch their major fields of study more easily. Out of those students who completed high school in 1992 and earned a bachelor's degree, 40.5 percent changed their major during the course of their undergraduate education (Adelman 2004).[29] The likelihood that students in England switch majors during their undergraduate degree is far lower, using a very similar classification of fields of study. According to the USR undergraduate data, it appears that 7 percent of students switch their majors during university in England and Wales. The fraction of Scottish students who switch their majors during university is substantially higher at 18 percent. This corresponds to the differences in the timing of specialization between England and Scotland and indicates that it is possible to allow for flexibility within institutions without instituting a national credit system.[30] However, with a

28. The Universities Statistical Record (USR) consists of administrative data on all students in British universities undertaking courses of one academic year or longer between 1972 and 1993, amounting to almost 1.9 million undergraduates and over 1 million graduate students. Excluded are students enrolled in former polytechnics and central institutions, which only obtained university status from 1992 onwards.

29. This is based on student responses to questions asked in the 2000 survey and transcript records. Fields of study were aggregated into twelve broad categories of fields of study.

30. Malamud (2007a) explores the consequences of differences in academic specialization.

comprehensive system of credit transfer and accumulation, the degree of flexibility in higher education would probably be even greater.

A relatively short first-degree cycle should also contribute to flexibility. Students who realize that their first degrees did not provide for a good match can switch institutions and fields of study for their second and/or third degree. On the other hand, a system in which students follow a long and rigid curriculum would not provide students with the opportunity to gather information and correct their mistakes. Jacobs and van der Plaug (2006) have also argued that the Bologna reforms would encourage students to take a more demanding course of study. If the cost of switching fields or degrees is relatively high, as in traditionally long degree programs, students may avoid science and engineering degrees where the prospects of successful completion are often lower. In this case, the option value associated with a shorter degree program may lead students to experiment with more difficult majors. And starting a degree in mathematics or science may be a less daunting prospect when the expected length of study is three years rather than five or six years. On the other hand, if students tend to underestimate the difficulty of completing a degree, an inability to switch fields within a long degree program may lead to a greater rate of science and engineering degrees.

In summary, the structural reforms associated with the Bologna process are likely to enhance flexibility. A shorter first-degree cycle and a transferable credits system allows for relatively easy transfer both between institutions and within institutions across major fields of study. Students who discover that they chose the wrong institution or the wrong field of study are able to switch to a preferred alternative. Clearly, not all of these transfers and switches necessarily represent improvements ex post. Indeed, Trow (2005) discusses problems that arise when excessive flexibility leads to incoherent courses of study. But such flexibility is an important way of helping students act on new information.

6.4.2 Competition

The nature of competition in the market for higher education has been a subject of much recent research.[31] Most of this attention has focused on American higher education, with its highly decentralized institutions and large private (nonprofit) sector. Due to the hierarchical structure of institutions in the United States, not all colleges and universities necessarily compete with one another. But within certain tiers, institutions do appear to compete for students, for faculty, and for prestige. Underpinning the success of such competition is the common structure of higher education. Most American institutions award a similar set of degrees and structure their courses in a similar fashion with transferable academic credits. This

31. See Rothschild and White (1993, 1995) and Winston (1999) for insightful discussions.

no doubt helps students compare and choose among the many alternative options open to them. In other words, the market structure of higher education is likely to be influenced by the structure of degrees and courses within and across different systems of higher education.

The Bologna reforms have the potential to encourage greater competition between universities across Europe. In the absence of a comparable degree structure across countries, students may have trouble evaluating the relative benefits of different types of degrees. Employers, too, may have difficulties in assessing the value associated with a diverse set of qualifications. By introducing a more comparable degree structure, the Bologna reforms should enable students to more readily make comparisons across countries. They may also encourage institutions of higher education to improve their quality or seek certain niche markets while offering a similar set of qualifications.[32] Of course, it is also necessary to provide these institutions with autonomy and the necessary incentives to attract students (as well as faculty). In many of the state-funded and state-controlled systems of higher education in Europe today, institutional autonomy is severely lacking. Moreover, given extremely high educational subsidies, some countries may actually prefer to have their students obtain a costly education abroad (Mechtenberg and Strausz 2008). The realization of greater competition therefore depends on the introduction of further reforms, such as increased autonomy and funding for European universities.[33] Whether increased competition can result under a different institutional setting is an interesting question, but one that is beyond the scope of this chapter.

An important condition for a well-functioning market in higher education is the ability and willingness of students to relocate in order to choose among the various institutions and programs available to them. Hoxby (1997) documents the consequences of increased competition among colleges in the United States resulting from the deregulation of the airline and telecommunications industries, which lowered the cost of moving to college. The barriers to mobility for students within Europe are substantially higher due to differences in language and culture, in addition to the financial costs associated with travel and lodging.

By providing grants to subsidize travel and expenses, the ERASMUS program has led to a large increase in the number of European students studying abroad.[34] However, the length of time that students are provided with financial support has been relatively short, on the order of a six months

32. Much like Caltech and MIT have focused on particular areas of study or liberal arts colleges have focused on providing a certain type of college experience.

33. See Aghion et al. (2007) for further discussion of spending and autonomy in European higher education.

34. According to the European Commission, approximately 1.67 million students have taken part in the program since its inception in 1987.

or a year. Table 6.4 presents descriptive evidence on the pattern of student mobility prior to the Bologna reforms using the CHEERS data. A large fraction of students spend time studying or working abroad during their degrees, ranging from 13 percent in Spain to over 30 percent in the Netherlands (indeed, there are fairly large fractions of students who report spending two periods of work or study abroad). Nevertheless, the actual time spent abroad is approximately six months on average. For competition across institutions and countries to take hold, students probably need to stay abroad longer and complete their degrees there. Still, there is little doubt that a high level of student mobility is an important factor for encouraging competition in higher education.

6.5 Conclusion

The structure of higher education is an important mediating factor in determining student outcomes. Earlier empirical work on the structure of K-12 education has shown that school structure may have important consequences.[35] In higher education, structure may prove to be even more significant. A flexible course and degree structure may help allocate students more efficiently into their preferred institutions and fields of study. Moreover, having a comparable structure of higher education within and across countries may help foster competition and lead to a more efficient market in higher education. The Bologna reforms in Europe are an important development on this front. Indeed, some recent work examining the changes induced by the Bologna reforms suggest that students may respond positively to these new structures. Cappellari and Lucifora (2008) estimate a significantly higher probability of enrollment in college among high school students who graduated after the implementation of the Bologna reforms in Italy. Cardoso et al. (2008) document an increased demand for academic programs restructured under the Bologna process in Portugal. Whether these initial findings will translate into increased academic and labor market success remains to be seen.

How might these European structural reforms to higher education affect the United States? In many ways, the Bologna reforms make the European system more compatible with Anglo-Saxon systems of higher education around the world and in much of Asia and Latin America. This may help Europe to compete on the global market and attract more foreign students from around the world. Since Europe and the United States tap a common pool of foreign students, the Bologna reforms could lead to further declines

35. Bedard and Do (2005) find that shifting from a junior high school system (in which students remain in elementary school longer) to a middle school system lowers on-time high school completion.

in the share of foreign students in America. On the other hand, a common structure of higher education may facilitate the admission of European students to graduate schools in the United States. Indeed, a recent survey of US graduate admission officers indicated that most had relatively high levels of knowledge on the Bologna Process and about half reported having an official graduate admissions policy regarding first-cycle Bologna degrees.[36]

The Bologna reforms may also spur greater competition *among* European institutions of higher education, leading to increased demand for scarce resources such as highly talented faculty. Such increased competition among European institutions might serve to improve their research productivity and displace some American universities from the top of the world rankings. Whether any or all of these possibilities are actually realized, however, is likely to depend on the introduction of further reforms, such as increased autonomy and funding for European universities. And, ultimately, any benefits from the additional production of knowledge and research in Europe will be shared with the research community in the United States.

Experience with the specific reforms introduced by the Bologna process can also provide valuable lessons for higher education policy in the United States. As mentioned earlier, the new European credit unit is supposed to account for the time students actually spend studying, attending, and completing assignments for a course. This may represent an improvement over the traditional American credit unit, which simply accounts for the number of hours that faculty spend teaching a course. Other reforms such as the introduction of qualification frameworks, the creation of diploma supplements to provide information to students, and the establishment and recognition of joint degrees, may turn out to be useful innovations that make the provision of higher education more efficient.[37]

The push to harmonize the disparate European systems of higher education under the Bologna process offers another important benefit from a research perspective. As this chapter has shown, the difficulties in making cross-country comparisons in higher education are quite substantial. With a more comparable degree structure across countries, it will be possible to make even more progress in understanding the factors that help determine performance and success in higher education.

36. See IIE Briefing Paper of April 2009 (Institute of International Education 2009). Since most European nations have adopted a three-year first degree, graduate admission officers need to determine whether these are equivalent to the standard four-year BA degrees awarded in the United States. The previous survey also reveals that a third of respondents consider short Bologna degrees as equivalent and another third decide equivalency on a case-by-case basis.

37. The relevance of these reforms to the American context is explored by Adelman (2009) in greater detail. Whether American institutions will be pressured to respond to the introduction of shorter three-year European first degree remains to be seen.

References

Adelman, C. 2004. *Principal indicators of student academic histories in postsecondary education, 1972–2000.* Washington, DC: US Department of Education, Institute of Education Sciences.

———. 2008. *The Bologna club: What US higher education can learn from a decade of European reconstruction.* Washington, DC: Institute for Higher Education Policy.

———. 2009. *The Bologna process for US eyes: Re-learning higher education in the age of convergence.* Washington, DC: Institute for Higher Education Policy.

Aghion, P., M. Dewatripont, C. Hoxby, A. Mas-Colell, and A. Sapir. 2007. Why reform Europe's universities? *The Bruegel Policy Brief Series* no. 2007/04.

Attali, J. 1998. *Pour un modèle européen d'enseignement supérieur.* Paris: Stock.

Babcock, P., and M. Marks. 2007. The falling time cost of college: Evidence from half a century of time-use data. Paper presented at the All-UC Labor Workshop, International House. September 24–25, Davis, California.

Bedard, K., and C. Do. 2005. Are middle schools more effective? The impact of school structure on student outcomes. *Journal of Human Resources* 40 (3): 660–82.

Bound, J., M. Lovenheim, and S. Turner. 2007. Understanding the decrease in college completion rates and the increased time to baccalaureate degree. PSC Research Report no. 07-626.

Cappellari, L., and C. Lucifora. 2008. The "Bologna Process" and college enrollment decisions. IZA Discussion Paper no. 3444. Institute for the Study of Labor.

Cardoso, A. R., M. Portela, C. Sá, and F. Alexandre. 2008. Demand for higher education programs: The impact of the Bologna Process. *CESifo Economic Studies* 54 (2): 229–47.

Cascio, E., D. Clark, and N. Gordon. 2008. Education and the age profile of literacy into adulthood. *Journal of Economic Perspectives* 22 (3): 47–70.

Cunha, F., and J. Heckman. 2007. The evolution of inequality, heterogeneity and uncertainty in labor earnings in the US economy. NBER Working Paper no. 13526. Cambridge, MA: National Bureau of Economic Research, October.

Cunha, F., J. Heckman, and S. Navarro. 2005. Separating uncertainty from heterogeneity in life cycle earnings. *Oxford Economic Papers* 57 (2): 191–261.

de Wit, H. 2000. The Sorbonne and Bologna declarations on European higher education. *International Higher Education* 18 (5): 8–9.

EURYDICE. 1999. Organization of higher education structures in Europe (1998/99). *Eurydice Focus.* EURYDICE European Unit: Brussels.

Freeman, R. 2005. Does globalization of the scientific/engineering workforce threaten US economic leadership? NBER Working Paper no. 11457. Cambridge, MA: National Bureau of Economic Research, July.

Heffernan, J. M. 1973. The credibility of the credit hour: The history, use, and shortcomings of the credit system. *Journal of Higher Education* 44 (1): 61–72.

Hoxby, C. 1997. How the changing market structure of US higher education explains college tuition. NBER Working Paper no. 6323. Cambridge, MA: National Bureau of Economic Research, December.

Institute of International Education. 2009. Three-year Bologna-compliant degrees: Responses from US graduate schools. IIE Briefing Papers, April. Institute of International Education.

Jacobs, B., and F. van der Plaug. 2006. Guide to reform of higher education: A European perspective. *Economic Policy* 21 (47): 535–92.

Knudsen, I., G. Haug, and J. Kirstein. 1999. *Project report: Trends in learning struc-*

tures in higher education, confederation of European Union rectors. Conferences and the Association of European Universities (CRE).

Malamud, O. 2007a. Breadth vs. depth: The timing of specialization in higher education. Harris School Working Paper no. 0808. Harris School of Public Policy Studies, University of Chicago.

———. 2007b. Discovering one's talent: Learning from academic specialization. Harris School Working Paper no. 0809. Harris School of Public Policy Studies, University of Chicago.

Mechtenberg, L., and R. Strausz. 2008. The Bologna Process: How student mobility affects multi-cultural skills and educational quality. *International Tax and Public Finance* 15 (2): 109–30.

Murdoch, J. 2003. Standardisation and differentiation in the levels of diplomas in higher education systems in Europe. In *Implementing European Union education and training policy: A comparative study of issues in four member states,* ed. D. Phillips and H. Ertl, 265–76. Netherlands: Kluwer Academic Publishers.

National Center for Education Statistics (NCES). 1996. A descriptive summary of 1992–93 bachelor degree recipients: 1 year later, with an essay on time to degree. NCES 96-158 Available at: http://nces.ed.gov/pubs/96158.pdf.

National Science Board, National Science Foundation. 2008. *Science and engineering indicators 2008.* Arlington, VA: National Science Board, January. Available at: http://www.nsf.gov/statistics/seind08/.

Organization for Economic Cooperation and Development (OECD). 2008. *Education at a glance 2008.* Available at: www.oecd.org/edu/eag2008.

Paulston, R. G. 1968. French influence in American institutions of higher learning, 1784–1825. *History of Education Quarterly* 8 (2): 229–45.

Rothschild, M., and L. White. 1993. The university in the marketplace: Some insights and some puzzles. In *Studies of supply and demand in higher education,* ed. C. T. Clotfelter and M. Rothschild, 11–42. Chicago: University of Chicago Press.

———. 1995. The analytics of the pricing of higher education and other services in which the customers are inputs. *Journal of Political Economy* 103 (3): 573–86.

Schomberg, H., and U. Teichler. 2006. *Higher education and graduate employment in Europe: Results from graduate surveys from twelve countries.* Netherlands: Springer.

Shedd, J. M. 2003. The history of the student credit hour. In *How the student credit hour shapes higher education: The ties that bind. New directions for higher education,* ed. J. V. Wellman and T. Erlich, 5–12. San Francisco: Jossey-Bass.

Trow, M. 2005. Reflections on the transition from elite to mass to universal access: Forms and phases of higher education in modern societies since WWII. In *International handbook of higher education,* ed. P. G. Altbach and J. J. F. Forest, 243–80. Netherlands: Springer.

Ulrich, T., and H. Wasser. 1992. *German and American universities: Mutual influence—past and present.* Werkstattberichte 36. Kassel University, Scientific Center for Professional and University Research.

Winston, G. 1999. Subsidies, hierarchy and peers: The awkward economics of higher education. *Journal of Economic Perspectives* 13 (1): 13–36.

7

The Americanization of European Higher Education and Research

Lex Borghans and Frank Cörvers

7.1 Introduction

Over the past two decades there has been a substantial increase in the mobility of students in Europe, while also research has become much more internationally oriented. Student mobility has increased between European countries as well as between Europe, the United States, and the rest of the world. This seems to hold at bachelor, master, and PhD level. Compared to the past, European researchers publish more in foreign journals, and there is more international travel, more migration, and a strong increase in international cooperation in research. These trends have strong implications for international cooperation and competition in higher education and research.

The aim of this chapter is to document changes in the structure of research and higher education in Europe and to investigate potential explanations for the strong increase in its international orientation. The theoretical perspective we take is that the decision to study or to do research in either the home country market or the international market depends on cost and benefits, determined by the size of the market, communication costs, the transferability of knowledge between countries, and financial regulations. We argue that several dimensions of this trade-off have shifted in favor of

Lex Borghans is professor of labor economics and social policy in the department of economics and the Research Centre for Education and the Labour Market (ROA) at Maastricht University. Frank Cörvers is head of Research Dynamics of the Labour Market at the Research Centre for Education and the Labour Market (ROA) at Maastricht University.

We thank Daniëlle Claassens and Jesper van Thor for their statistical assistance. We benefited from the comments of Charles Clotfelter, Paulo Guimarães, and Hugo Sonnenschein and the participants of the NBER conferences September 2007 in Cambridge, Massachusetts, and October 2008 in Woodstock, Vermont, on earlier versions of this chapter.

international cooperation: cheaper travel possibilities, European integration, and the use of e-mail and Internet. A shift of the priorities in research from discussing and analyzing national policies toward measuring scientific output in international journals could also have stimulated this transition. An increase in the size of the home research market would have an opposite effect. The convergence of country-specific habits and institutions toward the global (US) standards has further facilitated the internationalization of research and higher education in Europe.

Using a variety of indicators we show the changes in the structure of higher education and research in Europe. While higher education started to grow substantially around 1960, only a few decades later, research and higher education transformed gradually to the American standard. Decreased communication costs are likely causes for this trend. This transformation is most clearly revealed in the change of language used in research from the national language / Latin to German / French to English. Smaller language areas made this transformation earlier while there are also clear timing differences between research fields. Sciences and medicine tend to switch to English first, followed by economics and social sciences, while for law and arts only the first signs of such a transformation are currently observed. This suggests that returns to scale and the transferability of research results are important influences in the decision to adopt the international standard.

To analyze the developments in European higher education and research, this chapter compares the developments in research in several European countries in different research areas using long time series. To illustrate some trends in more detail, particular attention will be paid to both the case of economics research and the case of the Netherlands. The developments in economics research and the Netherlands may serve as good examples of what has been or will be happening in other fields across different European countries.

Drèze and Esteban (2007) show that the United States outperforms Europe in economics research by a factor of the order three, and conclude that the Lisbon goal set by the European Union, to become the most dynamic and competitive economy in the world, is out of sight. Cardoso, Guimarães, and Zimmermann (2008) find that the quality of research by PhDs from US universities is better than the research of European PhDs.[1] The contribution of this chapter is that we take another perspective on the comparison between Europe and the United States. We document the transformation of European higher education and research not just as a change in quality, but in the first place as a change in the nature of the research performed in

1. Other papers on evaluating the performance of European and US economics research are, for example, Amir and Knauf (2008); Coupé (2003); Frey and Eichenberger (1993); Kirman and Dahl (1994); Neary, Mirrlees, and Tirole (2003); and Portes (1987). However, notice that economists typically analyze their own discipline and tend to generalize their results to draw conclusions on the overall position of Europe vis-à-vis the United States.

Europe. We include a theoretical exposition to explain the decision to adopt the American standard in research. This framework explains why the adoption of the superior American standard goes faster in some countries than in others. We argue that it is important to take account of the costs of adopting the American standard to explain how countries perform. Costs as well as benefits of the Americanization of European higher education and research seem to be to a large extent related to the acceptance of English as the lingua franca and to the specific content of what is taught and investigated. We argue that Drèze and Esteban (2007) as well as previous empirical studies in this area pay much attention to the benefits of publishing in the English language in American journals, and ignore or underestimate the productive value of publishing in the home language on European topics.

The remainder of this chapter is structured as follows. In section 7.2 we explain our theoretical framework. Section 7.3 provides data about the development of higher education in Europe and the United States. Section 7.4 describes the changes that have taken place in the Dutch higher education and research system during the last few decades, with a focus on economics. Section 7.5 deals with changes in the language used in research as an indicator of change of the structure of higher education and research in Europe. Section 7.6 concludes.

7.2 Theory of Internationalization

Higher education and research is not a homogeneous good. Different countries teach other things in science, economics, or law, and the aims and focus of research can be rather different across countries. One important dimension of the differences is whether a country's higher education and research system builds on national structures and traditions, or adopts and perhaps interferes with international standards. This implies that universities/researchers/students can decide to join the national research discussion or to join the international discussion. The value of each choice depends on the quality of the research, its relevance to the country concerned, and the costs of research. For nationally-oriented research this value equals:

$$V_{\text{nat}} = v_q Q(n) + v_r R - k,$$

in which $Q(n)$ is the quality of the research and n the size of the research community. The quality depends on the size of the community. Variable R represents the relevance of research and k the costs. Variables v_q and v_r are the weights attached to quality and relevance. For internationally-oriented research the value equals:

$$V_{\text{int}} = v_q Q(N) + v_r \tau R - K.$$

Variable N is the size of the international research community. If the benefits from research are subject to returns to scale, a researcher who joins the international debate profits from a larger peer group. These benefits are counterbalanced, however, by a reduced benefit of the research findings for the situation in the home country and higher communication costs. Variable τ represents the degree of transferability of research findings to the national situation ($0 \leq \tau \leq 1$). The transferability might depend on the research area. In some fields the relevance of research will not depend on the country that is investigated, while for other fields of research this might be very country specific. Furthermore, internationally-oriented research might incur higher costs, due to higher travel and communication costs. These costs are indicated by K ($K > k$).

The trade-off between national or international research might also be influenced by the value attached to quality versus relevance. A researcher will choose to join the international research community when $V_{\text{int}} > V_{\text{nat}}$. Given the difference in quality of research but also the costs in the international versus the national context, the threshold level of transferability can be calculated for which researchers are indifferent between joining the national or the international debate:

$$\bar{\tau} = 1 - \frac{v_q}{v_r}\frac{Q(N) - Q(n)}{R} + \frac{K - k}{v_r R}.$$

If the actual transferability exceeds this threshold, the international debate will be chosen. So if the transferability of research findings increases, the costs of international research decrease or the scale effects increase, researchers participating in the national debate will switch to the international debate when this threshold is reached. Also, a change in the valuation of quality versus relevance might lead to this change. At the point of transition, the value of research will change only gradually. The move from the national to the international debate will affect quality and relevance substantially, however. In figure 7.1 we show for certain parameters of this model what would happen to the quality and relevance of research per unit of costs when transferability increases (panel A) and the costs of international research decrease (panel B). Panel A shows that the transition from the national to the international debate is associated with a decrease in relevance and an increase in quality. Once the transition is made, a further increase in transferability will not affect the research quality but will increase relevance. When costs of international research are reduced (panel B), a similar shift toward higher quality and lower relevance is observed. A further reduction of the costs of international research will benefit both quality and relevance per unit costs.

If the size of the market, communication costs, transferability, and incentives determine the choice for either nationally- or internationally-oriented research, the following predictions can be made.

Size of the market: The growth of higher education in Europe and the process of European integration will shift the attention of researchers toward

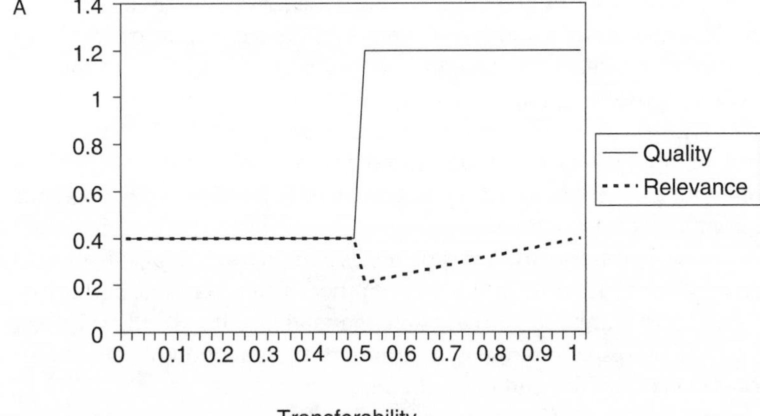

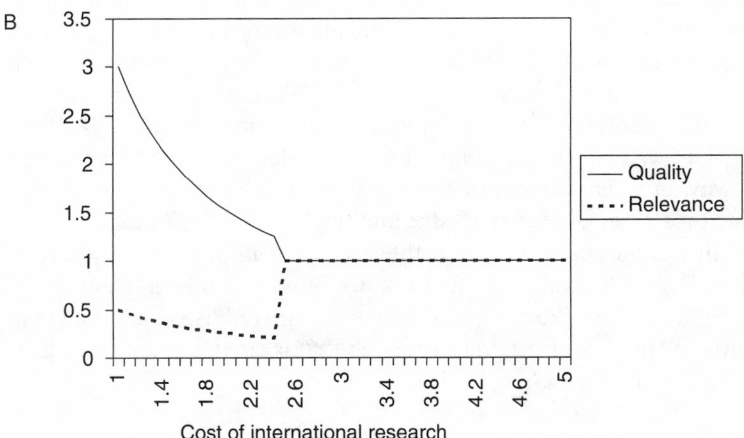

Fig. 7.1 Quality and relevance of research per unit costs as a function of transferability (panel A) and costs of international research (panel B)

Note: The figure is based on the following parameters: $v_q = v_r = 1$, $Q(n) = 1$, $Q(N) = 3$, $k = 1$, and $K = 3$ in panel A and $\tau = 0.5$ in panel B.

the European market. This will imply a decrease of the importance of research aimed at specific European countries, but would also reduce the focus on international research.

Communication cost: There are many reasons to assume that communication costs are decreasing. Travel is cheaper, and Internet and e-mail provide important tools for long distance communication between researchers, while European integration (the use of English and the introduction of the bachelor's-master's degree (BA-MA) system) has improved comparability and therefore facilitates communication.

Transferability: Differences in transferability of research in the first place might predict differences between research fields. For sciences it will be relatively easily to join one international research discussion, while, for example, for literature and law national differences might be too large to allow for international cooperation, because of the importance of distinctive national institutions, cultural traditions, and history. Economics and social sciences will be an intermediate case. Although these disciplines apply general theories, specific circumstances and institutions within countries might affect the relevance of certain research questions and limit international comparability.

Finance: In many European countries there is a trend toward subsidies based on research output; for example, the number of publications, number of diplomas, and number of PhDs. Such financial incentives will also affect decisions with respect to research, although the direction of these influences is sometimes difficult to predict.

To facilitate cooperation between researchers in either the national or the international research discussion, it is likely that conventions will be adjusted toward a common standard. The most obvious case of this is the language, but one could also think about a standardization of other aspects to facilitate comparability. Standardization of diplomas, both in terms of names and content, is such an example. The adoption of the BA-MA structure in place of historically unique European degrees can be interpreted in this way, but also the use of terminology such as assistant professor, associate professor, and full professor and the role of a PhD thesis could be affected by changes in the values of the research community.

In this chapter we will therefore look not only at trends in the language used in research, the nationality of researchers who publish in national journals, and the country of origin of research that is cited, but also the age at which the PhD thesis is typically finished.

7.3 Developments in Higher Education

Like in the United States, many of the richer European countries faced a rapid increase of participation in higher education in the 1960s.[2] Universities were transformed from small elite schools to mass universities.[3] Figure 7.2 shows the increase in participation in higher education in Western

2. See Eurydice (2000) for the developments in higher education since the 1960s in eighteen Western European countries. For the development of the highest level of educational attainment in the United States from 1940 to 2007, see figures 3 and 4 in the *Digest of Education Statistics: 2007* of the National Center for Education Statistics (2008).

3. Windolf (1997) discusses the educational expansion in Germany, the United States, Japan, and some other European countries between 1870 and 1990. To explain the expansion of higher education he refers to human capital theory and the needs of society, and theories from educational sociology that are based on competition for status between individuals or between social groups. He also discusses the relevance of the increasing enrollment of women for educational expansion.

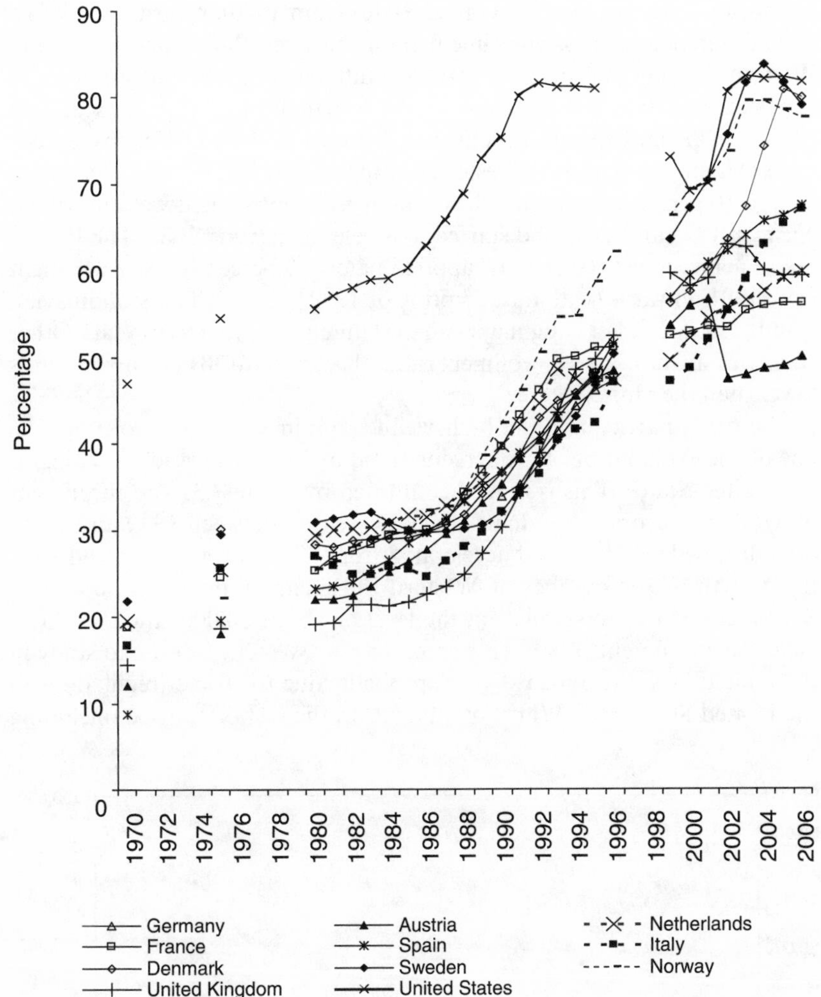

Fig. 7.2 Gross enrollment ratios in Western European countries and the United States, 1970–2006

Source: Unesco Institute for Statistics.

Notes: The gross enrollment ratio is defined as the number of students enrolled in tertiary education expressed as a percentage of the population in the theoretical age group for tertiary education. There may be changes in the measurement of the gross enrollment ratio between 1996 and 1999 for some countries, like the United States. There also seems to be a break in the series for the United States and Austria between 2001 and 2002. For Germany, data is only available from 1990 to 1996.

European countries and the United States from 1970 onwards. There is a huge difference in gross enrollment ratios between the United States and Western Europe. This does partly reflect differences in the educational system, such as a strong emphasis on a solid system of intermediate vocational education in many European countries. Between 1970 and 1975 gross enrollment in higher education in Western Europe and the United States increased by 5 to 10 percentage points. The trend in gross enrollment was almost flat between 1975 and 1985 and started to accelerate around 1985. The United States achieved a maximum of approximately 80 percent gross enrollment from 1991 onwards (with the exception of 1999 to 2001). The Scandinavian countries more or less caught up with the United States in recent years. Other countries still have gross enrollment ratios that are 15 to 30 percentage points lower than the United States.

The rising participation in higher education in Western Europe may be one of the explanations for the rising trend of European students going to the United States. This is indeed confirmed by figure 7.3. The enrollment of Western European students slowly increased between 1949 and 1970, then dropped till 1975, and accelerated from 1975 onwards. Around 1993 the growth of the number of Western European students in the United States leveled off, to stabilize at the level of about 50,000 students. After 2000 the enrollment of students coming from Western Europe to study in the United States dropped slightly, probably due to stricter regulations in the United States after 9/11. For students in the rest of Europe (including

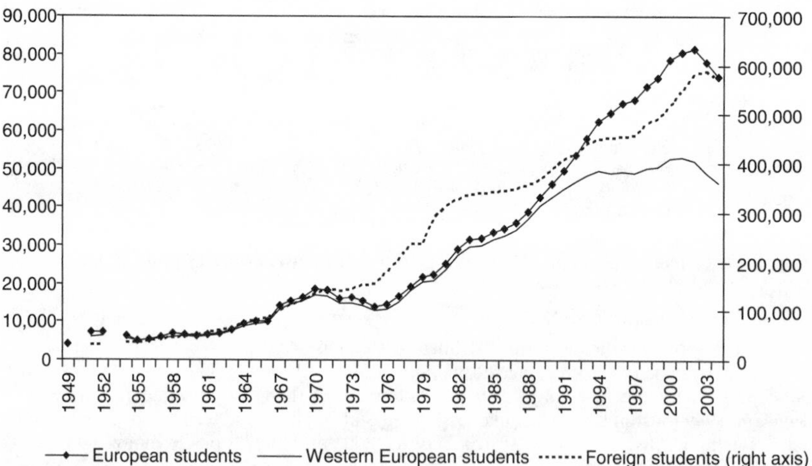

Fig. 7.3 Total number of European and foreign (non-US) students in the United States, 1949–2004

Source: Institute of International Education.

Notes: The data has been drawn from the *Open Doors* database of the Institute of International Education. For international students in the United States, *Open Doors* surveys count both enrolled degree students as well as students who are taking shorter, nondegree courses.

Central and Eastern Europe) figure 7.3 shows that outbound mobility in absolute numbers was rather low until the second half of the 1980s. After that time outbound mobility sharply increased, to reach a maximum of more than 30,000 students in 2002. During the last two years of the time series the outbound mobility from Europe as a whole to the United States decreased. For the total number of foreign students going to the United States the decrease started in 2004.

One could suppose that the rising number of European students going to the United States can be explained by rising "globalization." Figure 7.4 shows that this can only be partly true. The figure shows outbound mobility

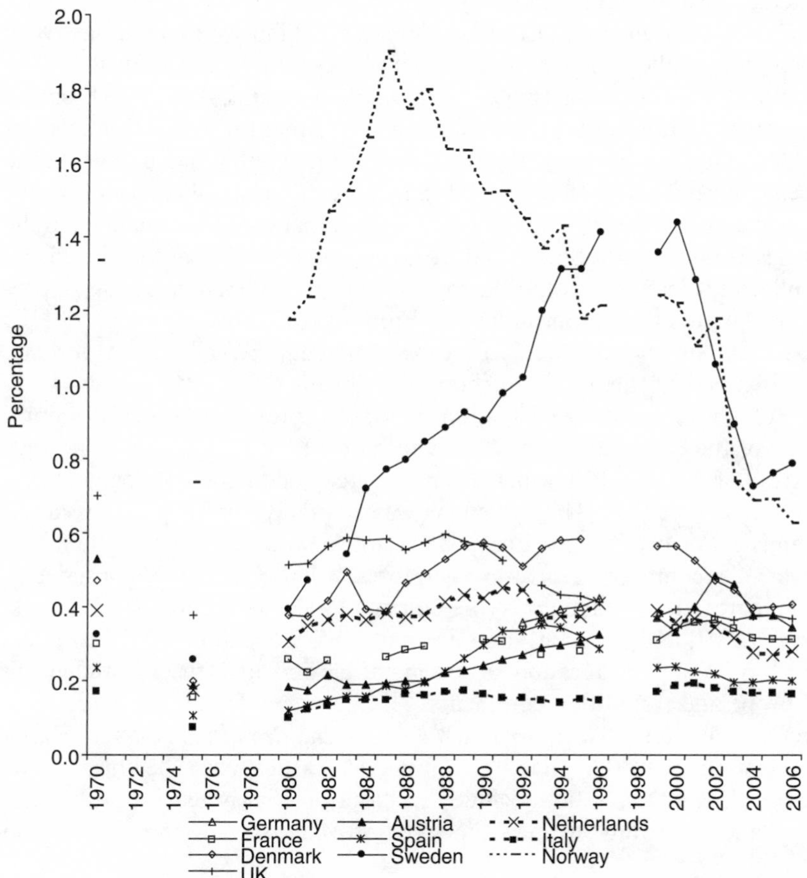

Fig. 7.4 Students of Western European countries in the United States as percentage of enrollment in home country, 1970–2006

Source: Institute of International Education and the Unesco Institute for Statistics.

Note: The percentages have been calculated by dividing the number of students of a particular country in the United States (*Open Doors* surveys, see figure 7.2) by the number of enrolled degree students in the respective home country (Unesco).

of Western European students to the United States as a percentage of the number of students enrolled in higher education in ten different Western European countries. For most countries the percentage of outbound mobility is relatively high in 1970, even higher than in 2006, the last year of the time series. With 1975 as the reference year, all countries show an upturn, but sooner or later outbound mobility starts to fall again for each country. Thus, there is no clear upward trend of outbound mobility since 1970. Almost all countries show a downward trend during the last five to ten years. For the United Kingdom the share started to fall in 1988, for Norway even in 1985. The percentages remain relatively high for the Scandinavian countries till the end of the time series. Italy, and to a lesser extent Spain, typically have low shares of outbound mobility to the United States.

It may be argued that European Union (EU) inner mobility flows compensated for the decline in outbound mobility from Western Europe to the United States. On the one hand, the inner EU programs, such as the Erasmus program, indeed seem to be expanding over time (European Commission 2008).[4] On the other hand, figure 7.5 suggests that outbound mobility as the percentage of home enrollment declined after 2002 in all countries of our sample. An explanation for this difference is that enrollment data from the Unesco Institute for Statistics does not include mobility flows of students collecting credits in another European country, nor student exchange programs within the European Union. From figure 7.5, we can conclude that Norway, Austria, and Sweden have the highest numbers of students enrolled in foreign countries relative to home enrollment.

A higher students' participation in inner EU programs fits into the ambition of the European Union of establishing a European Higher Education Area (EHEA) by 2010, which has been agreed upon in the Bologna Declaration of June 1999. This agreement was originally signed by the education ministers of twenty-nine European countries and developed into a major reform encompassing forty-five countries. It has put in motion a series of new agreements and reforms (the Bologna Process, see European Commission [2007] and Association of International Educators [2007]) to make European higher education more compatible and attractive for students in Europe and from other continents. The European Union considers these reforms as a requirement to match the performance of the best performing systems in the world, notably the United States and Asia. The objectives of the Bologna Declaration include the adoption of a system of easily readable and comparable degrees, the adoption of a system essentially based on

4. One has to notice that mobility in the European Union is typically so called "horizontal mobility." In programs like the Erasmus program, students spend a substantial time (from three to twelve months) at another European institution of higher education, having all the academic credits recognized by and transferred to the home institution. As is remarked by Spinelli (2005), students in the US practice "vertical mobility"; that is, they mainly pursue a graduate degree at a different institution from where they have received their undergraduate degree.

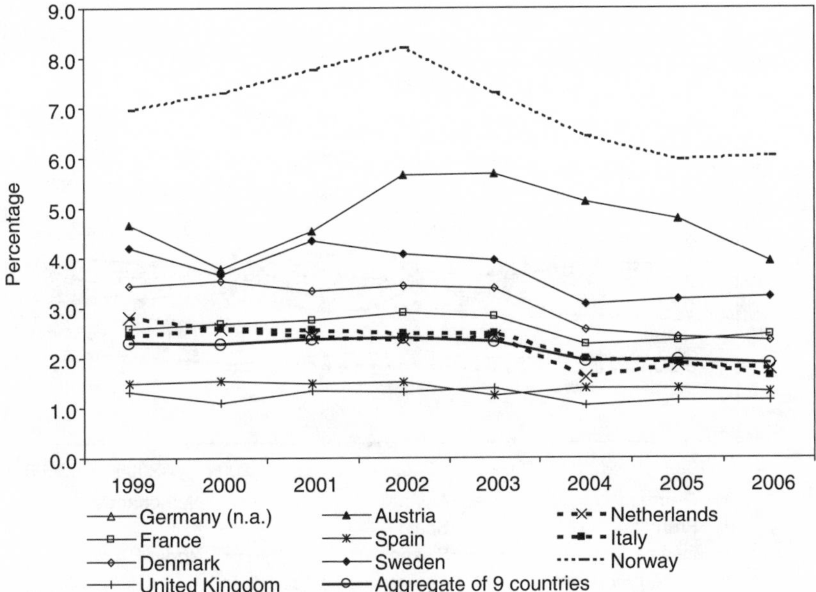

Fig. 7.5 Outbound mobile Western European students as percentage of enrollment in home country, 1999–2006

Source: Unesco Institute for Statistics.

Notes: Unesco counts the number of degree students enrolled in the home country and in foreign countries. Home enrollment data is not available for Germany.

two main cycles, the establishment of a system of credits, the promotion of mobility, the promotion of European cooperation in quality assurance, and the promotion of the European dimension in higher education.

For stimulating transatlantic mobility in particular the adoption of a system based on two main cycles, undergraduate and graduate, is important,[5] as well as the establishment of a system of credits (such as the European credit transfer system [ECTS]). Before the Bologna Process, the higher education system of continental European countries generally had one integrated tier only, leading to the title necessary for entering PhD courses. In the Bologna Declaration it has been agreed that the bachelor's degree awarded after the first cycle, lasting a minimum of three years, shall become relevant on the European labor market as an appropriate level of qualification. Access to the second cycle requires successful completion of first cycle studies. The second cycle leads to the master's degree. Initially only two cycles were men-

5. For example, Spinelli (2005) refers to difficulties for US administrators to understand the level of European students who had not completely finished their European degree in the one tier system. There were problems even for students who graduated from a five-year integrated course (i.e., master's level), to whom US administrators generally offered admission to master instead of PhD courses since they were holding one degree only.

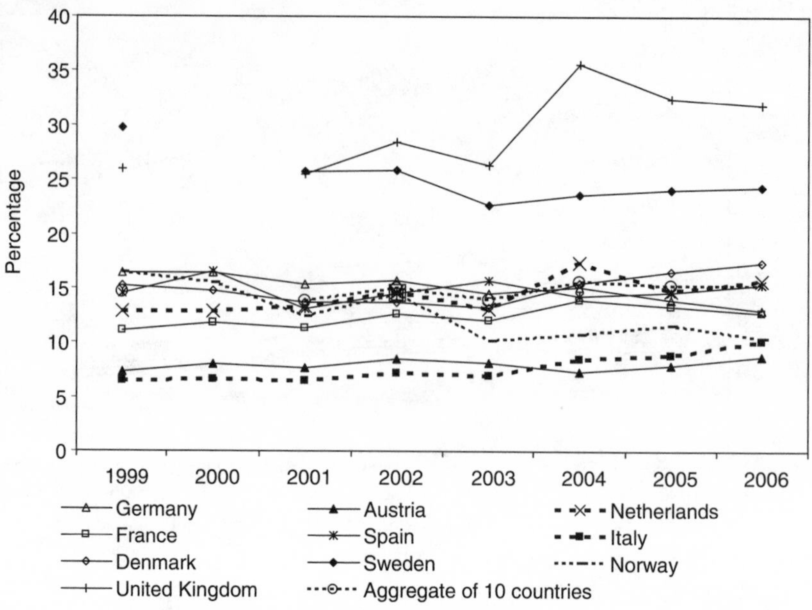

Fig. 7.6 Outbound mobile students that study in the United States as percentage of total outbound mobility per country, 1999–2006

Source: Unesco Institute for Statistics.

Note: Unesco counts the number of degree students enrolled in the home country and in foreign countries.

tioned, equivalent to undergraduate and graduate. Later the doctoral (or doctorate) degree was introduced as the third cycle.[6] Although European countries are committed to convert their existing higher education programs to a three-year bachelor's and two-year master's, in reality there is a large variation between countries in the length of the cycles and in the intermediate credentials traditionally offered (Adelman 2009).

Figure 7.6 shows the percentage of outbound students per country who are going to the United States for the period 1999 to 2006. The percentages are relatively high for the United Kingdom and Sweden, with about one-quarter to one-third of their outbound students enrolling in the United States. Italy and Austria have low shares of students enrolling in the United States. The shares dropped relatively much for students from Norway and Germany between 1999 and 2006. On average the market share of the United States in total outbound mobility of the ten Western European countries in our sample was approximately 15 percent in this period. We can conclude that the United States has not become less attractive for European students that want to study abroad, either within or outside Europe. However, since

6. See Witte (2006) for a detailed account and analysis of the evolution of the three cycles.

enrollment of Western European students outside their own country seems to have decreased during the last years or more for many countries, this also holds for the number of Western European students studying in the United States. This development may be caused by the increasing popularity of mobility programs like the Erasmus program, which stimulates European students to study in another European country, which is not counted as enrollment in the Unesco figures.

Figure 7.7 depicts the number of US students abroad between 1955 and 2003. Total study abroad of Americans increased between 1955 and 1990, then dropped slightly and started to accelerate after 1992. The share of Europe in study abroad decreased due to the rise of Asian countries. The US students hardly go to European countries outside Western Europe. Whereas the number of Western European students in the United States accelerated from 1975 onwards, the number of US students in Western Europe only started to grow strongly after 1992, thus much later.

Table 7.1 shows the number of US students relative to the number of students enrolled in the country they go to. The table does not reveal a clear

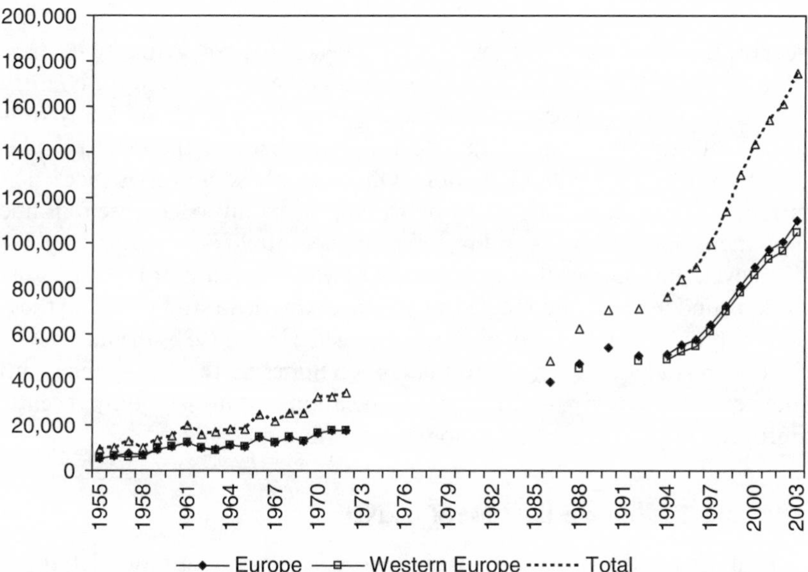

Fig. 7.7 Total number of US students abroad, 1955–2003

Source: Institute of International Education.

Notes: The data has been drawn from the *Open Doors* database of the Institute of International Education. For Americans overseas, *Open Doors* surveys count the number of students that study abroad. This consists of short-term programs of one year or less that are held in another country, but which the American student receives credit for toward their US degree. There are far more Americans participating in these types of study abroad programs than are enrolled in degree courses overseas. The Unesco measures this enrollment, which equals about 48,000 students in 2006.

Table 7.1 **US students as percentage of enrollment in Western European countries, 1970–2003**

	1970	1986	1992	1996	2003
Germany	—	—	0.16	0.17	—
Austria	0.42	0.95	0.69	0.51	1.22
Netherlands	0.06	0.05	0.12	0.15	0.34
France	0.94	0.51	0.53	0.38	0.62
Spain	0.64	0.44	0.52	0.48	1.02
Italy	0.24	0.33	0.33	0.42	0.99
Denmark	0.12	0.41	0.36	0.27	0.56
Sweden	0.27	—	0.14	0.13	0.20
Norway	0.31	—	0.06	0.05	0.13
United Kingdom	0.35	1.33	1.52	1.06	1.39

Sources: Institute of International Education and the Unesco Institute for Statistics.
Notes: The percentages have been calculated by dividing the number of US students that study in a particular country (*Open Doors,* see figure 7.7) by the number of enrolled degree students in that country (Unesco). The percentages in the 1992 column refer to 1990 for France and the United Kingdom. The percentages in the 1996 column refer to 1995 for France and Denmark.

general trend for all countries between 1970 and 1996. After 1996 there is an upward trend. The United Kingdom is the most attractive country for American students because of the English language. Remarkably, during recent years Austria, Spain, and Italy have become the most popular countries after the United Kingdom. Obviously these countries succeed in attracting American students by reforming their university system in line with the Bologna Process and by offering good quality courses in English. Moreover, the relatively large communities with a Spanish or Italian family background in the United States may induce American students from these communities to study in Spain or Italy. So while in the 1980s the number of European students that went to the United States increased—in line with the increased participation in higher education in Europe—only recently European universities became more open to foreign students.

7.4 Americanization: The Case of the Netherlands

To illustrate the outcomes of the theoretical model in more detail, we discuss the developments in higher education and research for the case of the Netherlands, and where useful refer to other European countries or the United States. Figures 7.8 and 7.9 summarize some basic facts about the size and growth of higher education in the Netherlands. Figure 7.8 depicts the growth in the country's two major higher education sectors, distinguishing the number of students in universities from students in professional higher education (*Hoger Beroeps Onderwijs,* or HBO). Dutch universities are always research universities, and incorporate business schools, law schools, and medical schools. The HBO institutions are typically not engaged in

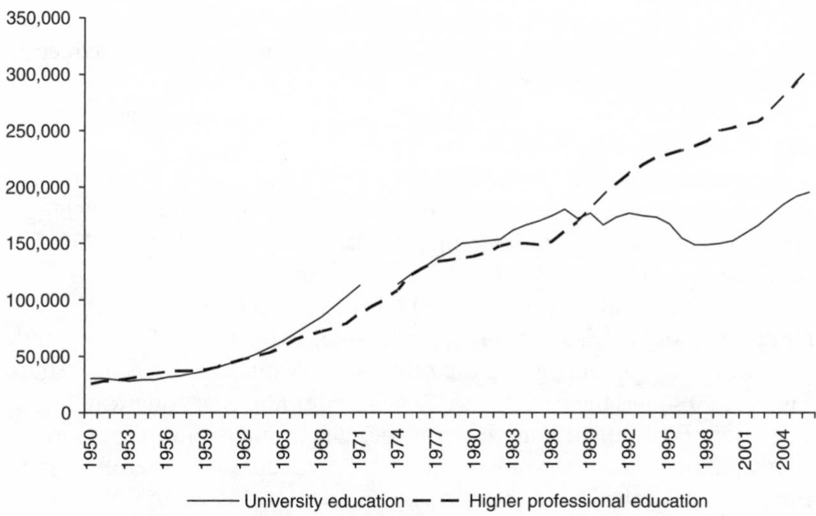

Fig. 7.8 Growth of higher education in the Netherlands, 1950–2006
Source: Statistics Netherlands.
Note: The data concerns students in full-time education.

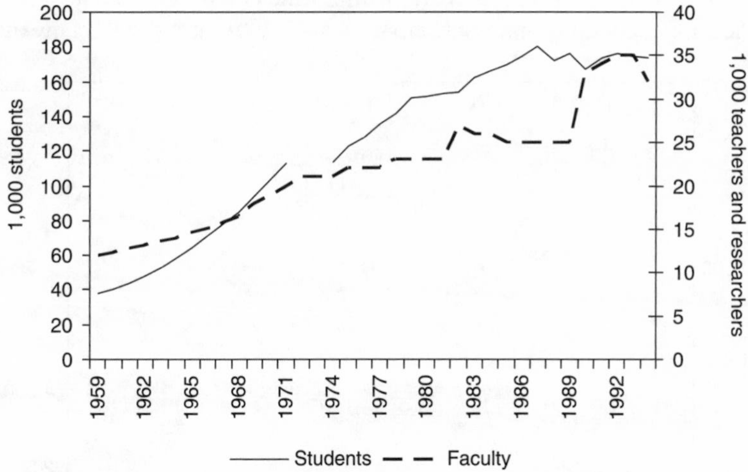

Fig. 7.9 Students versus faculty at universities in the Netherlands, 1959–1994
Source: Statistics Netherlands.
Note: See figure 7.8.

research, and teach professional skills; for example, for nurses, teachers, therapists, accountants, and practically-oriented engineers. The strongest increase in the number of students is during the 1960s, but the number keeps increasing until the early 1980s. From the 1980s on the growth in participation at the universities stagnates, while participation at the professional colleges continues to grow. Fluctuations in participation rates for universities from the 1980s onward mainly reflect new regulations that aim at a reduction of the years spent at university.

Figure 7.9 focuses on universities and compares the enrollments with the size of the faculty. In line with the growth of the number of students, the number of teachers and researchers also grows. The growth rate of faculty is about 50 percent of the growth rate in student population, implying an increase in the student-faculty ratio from 3 to 7 between 1960 and 1990. The break between 1990 and 1991 is due to a change in definition.

The internationalization of Dutch higher education is evident in the growing numbers of Dutch university students going to the United States to study and American students going the other way, to study in the Netherlands. Figure 7.10 shows the participation of Dutch students in American higher education. For comparison, the corresponding trend is shown for German participation, which, as shown in figure 7.3, is representative of Western Europe as a whole. For both countries the start of this growth in the early 1960s coincided with the growth of higher education in Europe. Around 1975 there was a sharp decline in the participation of Dutch and German students at US universities, but after 1975 this trend recovered. From 1975 until 1992 the participation of Dutch students in the United States grew faster than the German participation, after which Dutch enrollment fell. The same happened to German participation after 2001, as it did in many other

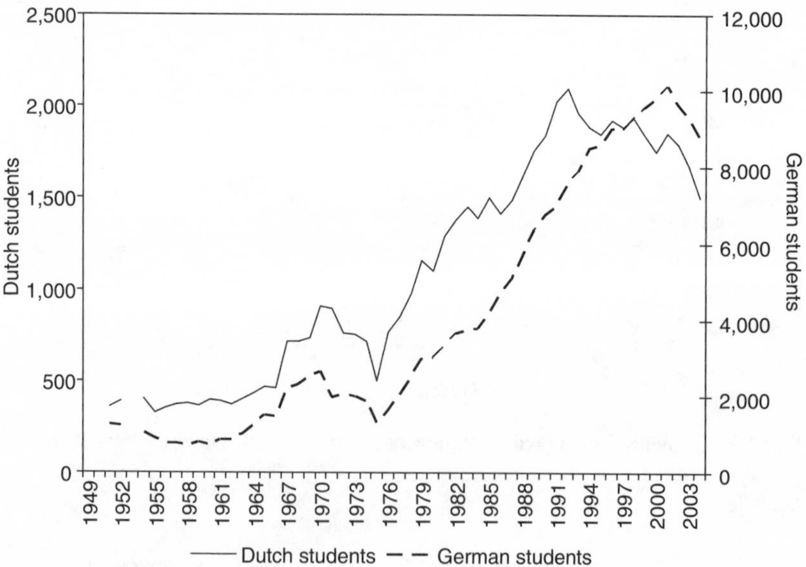

Fig. 7.10 Dutch and German students in the United States, 1949–2004

Source: Institute of International Education.

Notes: See figure 7.3.

Western European countries during the last decade, as has been revealed in the discussion of figures 7.3 and 7.4.

Initially only a very small fraction of foreign students in the Netherlands came from the United States, but this changed in the 1990s when some universities started to provide courses in English in some fields. Figure 7.11 shows the increase of US students in the Netherlands in those years. Between 1995 and 1998 the participation of US students more than doubled and has continued to increase since then. Participation of Dutch students in the United States increased much earlier, and was related to the rise of higher education in the Netherlands. Similar trends can be seen for other Western European countries (compare figure 7.4 and table 7.1 of the previous section). Significantly, the magnitudes of these mobility flows differ by discipline, with disciplines such as law being more nationally-oriented than others. This fact is clearly demonstrated in figure 7.12, which shows that the percentages of foreign students are lowest in fields like health care, law, education, and language and culture. The more science-oriented studies and economics display a much higher influx of foreign students. Finally, note that the total number of foreign students enrolled in Dutch higher education has been increasing since 2004, as has the percentage of US students (see table 7.1).

"Americanization" of Dutch higher education is more starkly evident in the transformation that has taken place in the very degrees, titles, and objectives that define academic institutions. Table 7.2 describes several key characteristics of Dutch universities in 1980 and 2008. The focus is on eco-

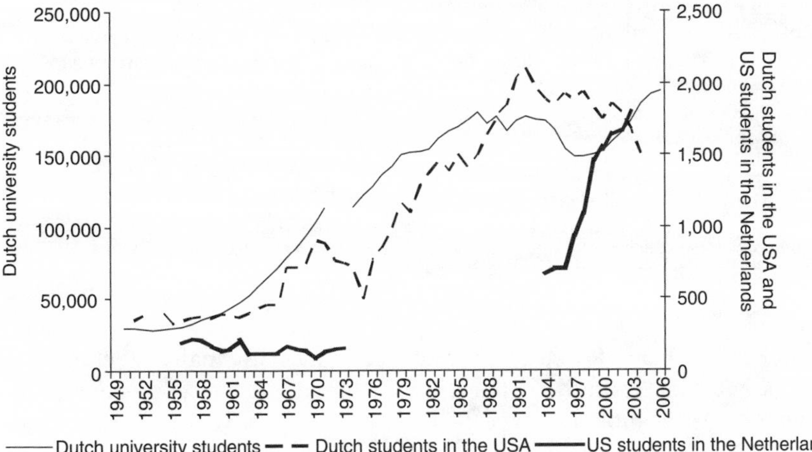

Fig. 7.11 Dutch university students and mobility flows between the Netherlands and the United States, 1949–2006

Sources: Statistics Netherlands and Institute of International Education.

Notes: See figures 7.3, 7.7, and 7.8.

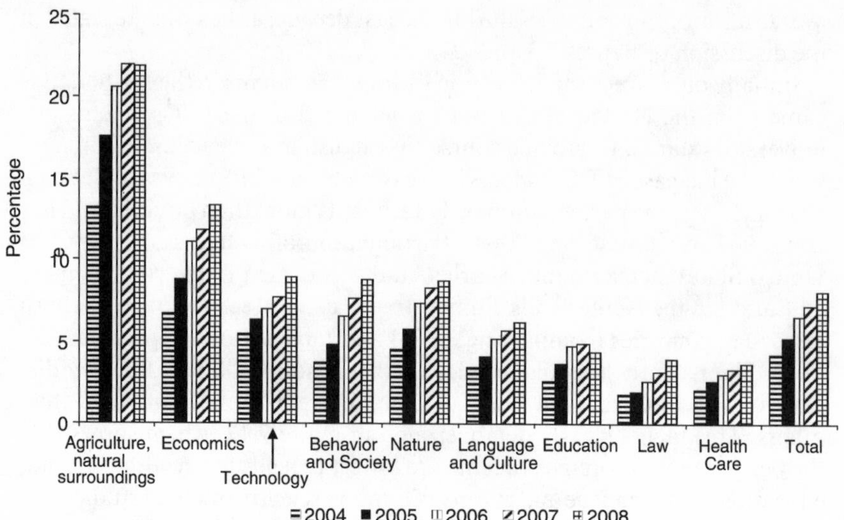

Fig. 7.12 Foreign students as percentage of Dutch enrollment per discipline, 2004–2008

Source: Nuffic (2008).

Note: Data concerns foreign students enrolled at publicly-funded Dutch universities.

Table 7.2 Characteristics of education and research in economics at Dutch universities in 1980 and 2008

1980	2008
Drs-diploma, 5–8 years of study	BA and MA, 3 + 1 years of study
A drs could become member of the faculty	Then "AIO" = employee who writes a thesis
Some wrote a thesis	Gradual shift:
Often as a magnus opus	From employee to student
	Introduction of course work
	Use of term PhD rather than AIO
Aim: Participation in national discussion	Aim: Publish in international (American) journals
Some researchers have an international focus	Most researchers have an international focus

nomics. In 1980 a degree program in economics nominally required five years, but in fact most students spent as much as six to ten years to complete their study. The diploma was called "drs." and was regarded as equivalent to a MA diploma. In 1982 the nominal duration was reduced to four years, although the diploma remained officially unchanged. Furthermore, measures were taken to reduce the time spent at university to a maximum of six years. Later, further measures were taken to reduce the length of the stay. In 2002—following the Bologna Declaration of 1999—the structure was changed into a BA-MA-structure, with three years of bachelor's and one (sometimes two) years of master's.

In the 1980s it was very common for members of the faculty not to have a PhD. Some wrote a "proefschrift" (PhD thesis) as a member of the faculty. Some of them used this thesis as an opportunity to bring together all their research at the end of their career as a magnus opus. Others never wrote a PhD thesis, but could nevertheless become full professor. Famous professors in economics at that time were often involved in the national political discussion about economics. Many were affiliated with a political party and joined national committees advising the Dutch government about economic policy. Gradually this situation shifted. Obtaining a PhD became a prerequisite to become assistant professor, and an official PhD program was implemented (*Assistant in Opleiding,* or AIO). Initially, AIOs just had to write their thesis, but gradually course work was introduced in these programs. Joining the national debate and publishing in national journals became less important while success in international publications gradually became the measure of success.

Initially there was not one European system for higher education. Like the Netherlands, most countries in Europe had their own specific characteristics. Germany had and still has a "habilitation", a kind of second thesis after PhD, which is required to become full professor. France distinguishes many different diplomas for different levels obtained in higher education, and has a distinction between universities that focus mainly on teaching, and *écoles superieure.* In international comparisons such differences are not always acknowledged, for several reasons. First, international communication about higher education is clearly affected by selection bias: those who go to international conferences prefer the international system and therefore behave most of the time in accordance with the American standard and tend to describe their home situation by using the American terminology. Second, for international statistics, degrees are translated to facilitate comparison, hiding the obvious differences between degrees in different countries. Third, when norms change about what constitutes good research, there is a tendency to judge research in the past using these new norms. Consequently, researchers who do not publish in international journals are easily considered to be lazy; differences in the system are therefore regarded as a lack of appropriate incentives.

To show how the PhD has changed in the Netherlands, we constructed a time series on doctoral dissertations defended at Dutch universities before 1995 using information from the library of Maastricht University that holds all these titles. Figure 7.13 compares the number of PhDs awarded with total university enrollment. The figure makes clear that these two indicators follow very different patterns. Initially, writing a PhD thesis was not a requisite for faculty, as shown in table 7.2. There were many full professors who did not obtain a PhD and some wrote their PhD later in their career

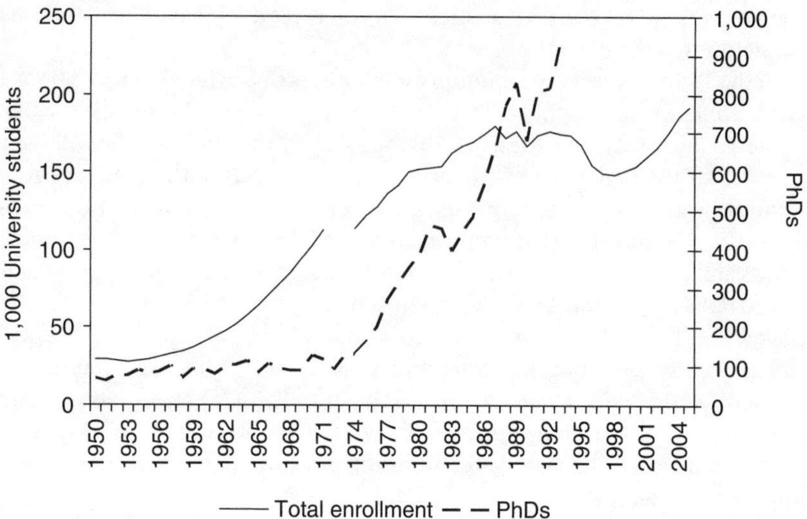

Fig. 7.13 Number of PhDs and total enrollment at universities in the Netherlands, 1950–2005

Sources: Statistics Netherlands and Library of Maastricht University.

as a summary of all their main research. Only in the mid-seventies did this start to change and nowadays a PhD is required for most positions as an assistant professor.

Figure 7.14 shows the average age of PhDs by discipline for the doctoral dissertations in our library sample from 1970 till 1995. As has been argued before, we expected that the age at which candidates received their PhDs would fall over time due to the transition of the Dutch to the Anglo-American system. After 1980 the average age did indeed fall for all disciplines except arts. The decrease was most prominent for science and economics. In these disciplines the transition to the Anglo-American system may have been most prominent.

7.5 Importance of Language for Research

One way to illustrate the increasing dominance of Anglo-American academic research is to look at the language in which Continental European researchers are publishing. Nowadays it is common in many research fields and countries to publish in English. However, for some fields, like law and national history, this seems to be less relevant due to a lack of international academic audience that is interested in country-oriented research. In contrast, for areas like physics, chemistry, and medicine the international academic community is more or less dealing with the same questions everywhere. Therefore, in these areas the interest to understand each other and

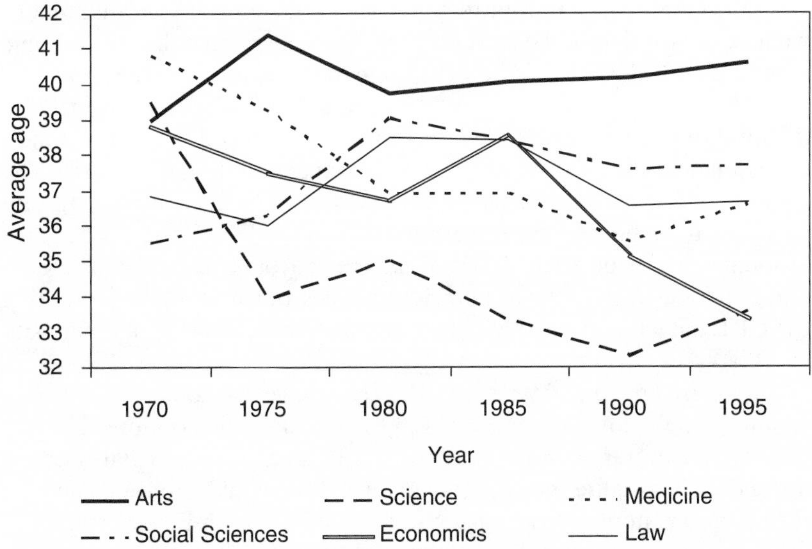

Fig. 7.14 Average age of graduating PhDs by discipline in the Netherlands, 1970–1995

Source: Library of Maastricht University.

to communicate in the same language is much bigger. Moreover, due to globalization and converging institutions—think of financial markets, international law, the end of communism in many countries, but also the higher education system—societies may have become more similar over time. Therefore the interest in sharing the knowledge that emerges from research is probably increasing. Communicating in one instead of different languages makes it easier to ensure that research output gets feedback from others all over the world, and that new knowledge will be generalized and used for practice.

7.5.1 Doctoral Dissertations

International

To illustrate the growing dominance of the English language in academic research on the European continent we use data of the foreign doctoral dissertation database of the Center for Research Libraries (CRL) in Chicago.[7]

7. The Center for Research Libraries (CRL) is a consortium of North American universities, colleges, and independent research libraries. The consortium acquires and preserves newspapers, journals, documents, archives, and other traditional and digital resources for research and teaching. These resources are then made available to member institutions cooperatively, through interlibrary loan and electronic delivery. The CRL website for foreign dissertations is: http://catalog.crl.edu.

For nine Continental European countries in the database we analyzed to what extent the doctoral dissertations have been written either in the home language or in English, and how the share of dissertations in the home language has evolved over the last hundred years. The CRL collection includes doctoral dissertations submitted to institutions outside the United States and Canada. A list of these institutions is available at the CRL website. The subjects of the dissertations are very mixed, but the database contains no variables to categorize the dissertations by discipline. We did some provisional analyses on recent years of databases from French, Danish, German, and Austrian national libraries to check our results. We found that the CRL data are reasonably well in line with those in other national data sources.

Figure 7.15 presents by country the percentages of home language dissertations in the total of home and English language dissertations. The percentages are averages for ten-year periods between 1908 and 2007 (see the appendix). The figure shows that in many Continental European countries the development of increasingly writing dissertations in English started as far back as the beginning of the previous century. This holds in particular for the Scandinavian countries. The Netherlands had a somewhat slower start, but caught up with these countries. Italy seems to follow the Netherlands till the 1960s, but then remained more or less constant. During the last ten

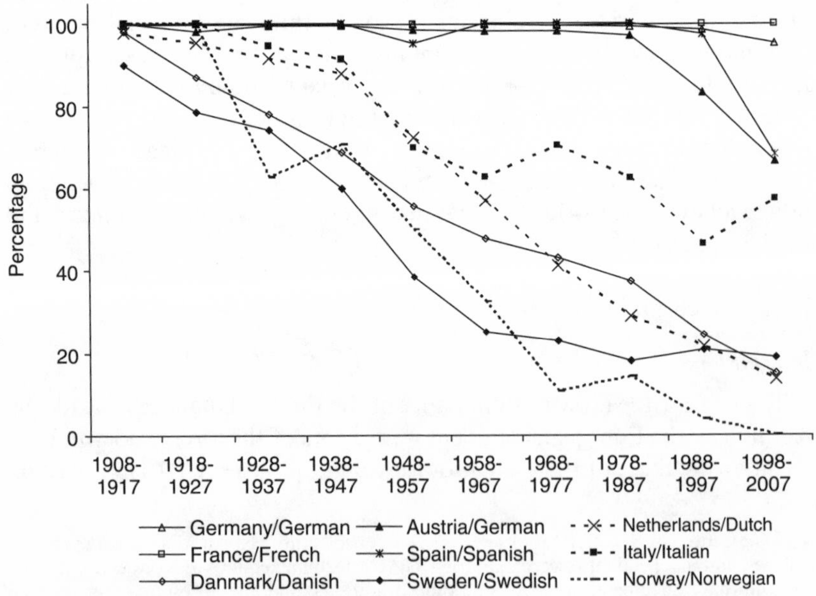

Fig. 7.15 Percentage of doctoral dissertations in the home language, 1908–2007
Source: Center for Research Libraries.

to twenty years, PhDs in Spain and Austria increasingly wrote their thesis in English. In Germany this process seems to have started up only recently. Based upon the CRL database, 5 percent of the doctoral dissertations in Germany were written in English by 1998 to 2007.

In France there is only the barest indication of movement toward English.[8] It seems that countries that are part of big language areas (i.e., French, German, and Spanish) have small incentives to switch to publishing in English. Moreover, France is known for its language policies in many different areas of life.[9] As has been argued in section 7.2 of this chapter, the costs of switching to publishing in English are the largest for countries that are part of big language areas due to economies of scale. However, Drèze and Estevan (2007) conclude that the big four Continental countries (France, Germany, Italy, and Spain) should accept English as the lingua franca to catch up in performance in economics research with the United Kingdom and the small countries in Western Europe. Although their paper is measuring the performance in economics research only, their conclusion may hold for other fields as well.

The Netherlands

Figure 7.16 shows the language that was used in the doctoral dissertations in our sample of dissertations in the Maastricht University library system. We distinguished among the five languages that appear to have a substantial frequency: Latin, Dutch, German, French, and English. The figure shows the cumulative shares of these languages. Until about the 1850s Latin was the main language in doctoral dissertations at Dutch universities. After the 1850s this changed very rapidly, and Dutch became the main language. Also the importance of German and (later on) French increased. The share of English dissertations began to increase only after World War I. This share started to increase very rapidly in the 1960s. Latin was still used in a number of Dutch doctoral dissertations till the 1960s.

The use of English in doctoral dissertations differs very much between disciplines, as figure 7.17 reveals. Science and medicine have the largest share of doctoral dissertations in English, followed by economics and social sciences. In law, the use of English is even smaller than in arts. The figure also reveals that the share of dissertations in English increased very much in medicine. Substantial increases are also evident for science, economics, and social sciences. The increase for arts and law was only moderate.

8. From the extensive "'Système universitaire de documentation'" of French academic libraries, we found that until 1997 almost all doctoral dissertations in France had been written in French. In 2002, 1 percent of the dissertations were written in French, and in 2007 this percentage increased to 3 percent.

9. For example, the use of French is required by law in commercial and workplace communications (Toubon Law). However, we do not know exactly how French governmental language policies can affect the use of language in academic publications.

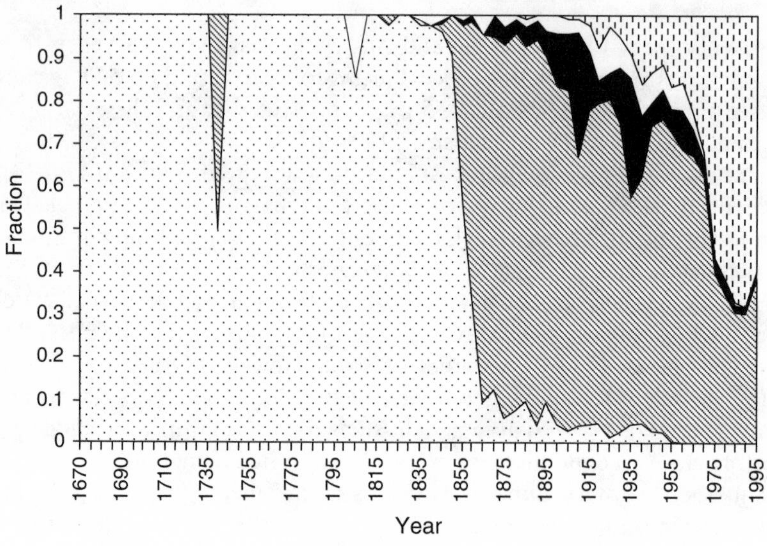

Fig. 7.16 Shares of languages of doctoral dissertations in the Netherlands, 1674–1995

Source: Library of Maastricht University.

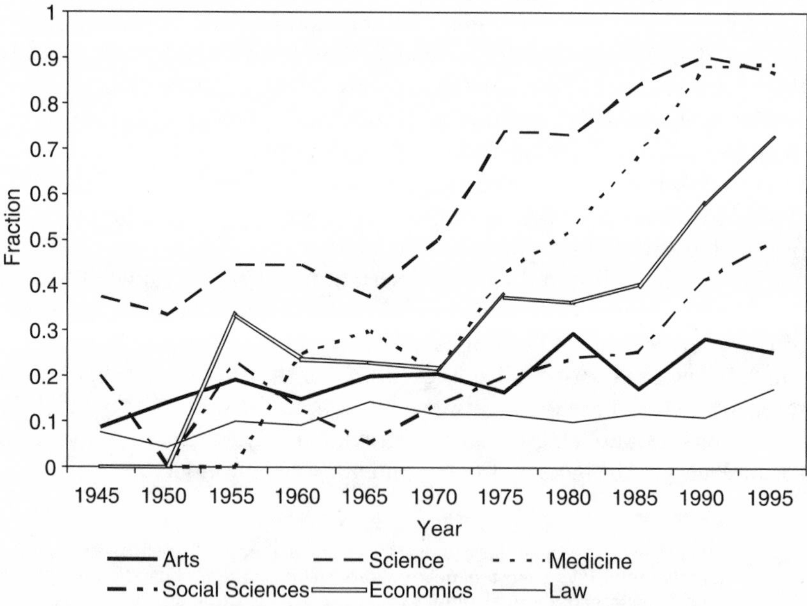

Fig. 7.17 The fraction of doctoral dissertations published in English by discipline in the Netherlands, 1945–1995

Source: Library of Maastricht University.

7.5.2 Economics Journals

International

The switch to the use of the English language can also be analyzed for academic journals. We looked at the publishing language of many Continental European and Anglo-American economics journals since the emergence of the first academic journals in economics around 1850. We follow these journals from the year of foundation, and noted when they switched from their home language to English. The selection of economics journals in different Continental European and Anglo-American countries is based on the overview by Gonçalo L. Fonseca. The list of selected journals has been published on the website "Economics Journals: A Chronological Account."[10] Only journals founded before 1990 were included on this website. We checked the year of foundation and the year when the journal stopped publishing with other data sources.

For none of the twelve Continental European countries in our data set is English a native language. Countries can have more than one national language (like German and French in Switzerland), and obviously the same language can be spoken in different countries. Journals may start in English from the foundation year (like an Italian and two Soviet journals), or switch to English at a later stage (see the appendix for detailed data). Information on the year of switching to English was drawn from data sources such as home pages of journals, national libraries, and EconLit. Journals need to publish all regular articles (i.e., excluding book reviews, etc.) in English to be considered as an English language journal. The first year in which this happens is noted as the transition year (this can also be after 1990).

In figure 7.18 the emergence of Continental European economics journals and their language use is presented. The total number of journals has gradually increased since 1844. Only after World War II did the number of journals suddenly increase, and the first English language journal on the continent was published (the Italian *Banca nazionale del lavoro quarterly review*). This journal was a new journal, as were also two Soviet journals founded in 1958 and 1964. The first old economics journal that switched to English was the Swedish *Ekonomisk Tidskrift* in 1964. In the same year it also changed its name to *Scandinavian Journal of Economics.* Starting from the first half of the 1990s the use of German (in journals from Germany, Austria, and Switzerland) and other languages (Italian, Spanish) seriously declined. By 2001 only four German and two other language journals were left. Many economics journals in these languages switched to English or disappeared. On the contrary, all French language journals from France,

10. See http://www.newschool.edu/nssr/het/essays/journal.htm. We selected the period from 1850 onwards, when the first academic economics journals emerged. We excluded the light and news-oriented journals, or journals not principally dedicated to economics, which are all marked as such on the website.

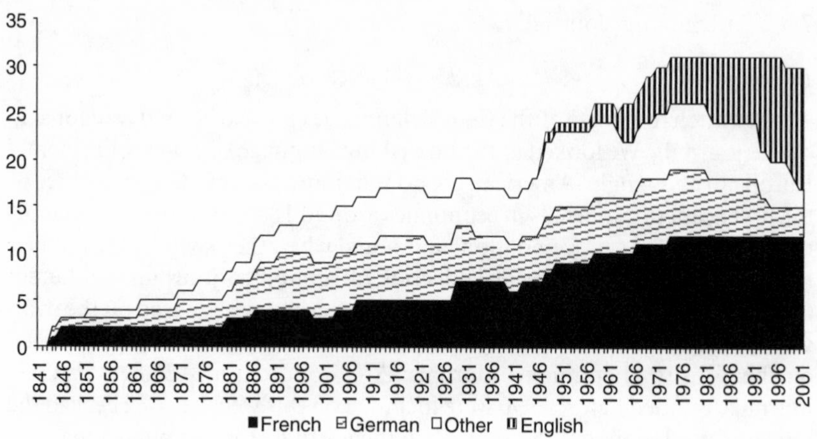

Fig. 7.18 Language of Continental European journals in economics, 1844–2001
Sources: Fonseca; Periodicals Service Company & Schmidt Periodicals GmbH, and some additional sources (see table 7A.2 in appendix).

as well as from Belgium and Switzerland, kept publishing in French. It has to be noticed that some French journals are bilingual, publishing French as well as English articles. These journals are not counted as English language journals in our data set. Even taking this strict definition, the English language journals on the European continent outnumber the French language journals during the last few years (thirteen versus twelve in the year 2001).

Figure 7.19 shows the development of the number of English language economics journals in Anglo-American countries from 1859 until 1990. For some years there was only one serious academic economics journal, according to our source (the British *Macmillan's Magazine,* 1859 to 1907; see the appendix). In 1886 the first US journal was founded (*Quarterly Journal of Economics*), and in 1891 the first well-known British economics journal emerged (*Economic Journal*). Only after World War II did the US journals begin to outnumber the journals in the United Kingdom and other English-speaking countries (Australia, Canada, South Africa). The first international journal (i.e., without a real home country) was published in 1921. Around 1970 the number of international journals suddenly increased. In 1990 there were twenty-six international journals, twenty-eight US journals, and fourteen English journals in the United Kingdom and other English-speaking countries.

The Netherlands, Austria, and Italy

To show the development in international orientation of economics journals in more detail, we analyzed three general interest journals. These journals are *De Economist,* founded in 1852 in the Netherlands; the *Journal of Economics,* founded in 1892 in Austria as the *Zeitschrift für Nationalökonomie;* and *Research in Economics,* founded in 1947 in Italy as *Ricerche*

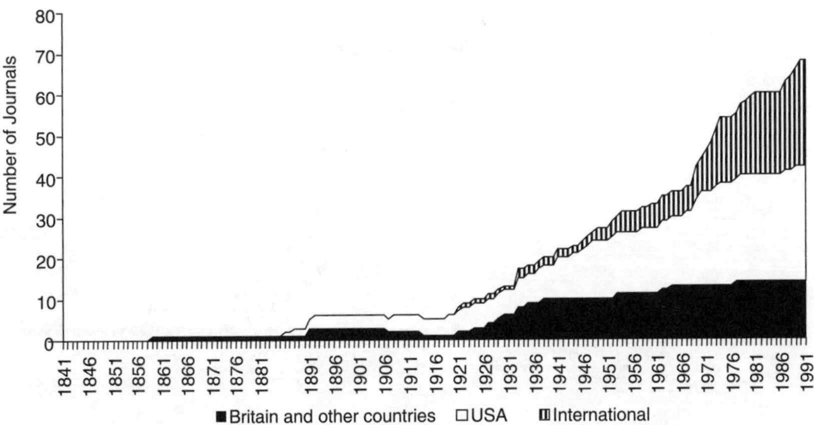

Fig. 7.19 Country of origin of English language economics journals in Anglo-American countries, 1859–1990

Sources: Fonseca; Periodicals Service Company & Schmidt Periodicals GmbH, and some additional sources (see table 7A.3 in appendix).

Economiche. For these journals we drew information from databases on the Internet with respect to the language of articles, the nationality of the authors, and the language of the references to other publications.[11]

Figure 7.20 shows the decline of the use of the home language in the Netherlands, Austria, and Italy. For the Netherlands the decline went rather fast after the beginning of the 1970s. Within less than a decade the language switched from Dutch to English. From 1983 onwards no regular articles have been published in Dutch anymore. For Austria, figure 7.20 shows that the switch from German to English in the Austrian *Journal of Economics* started about a decade earlier compared to *De Economist.* However, it took about two decades to transform the journal from German to English. From 1982 onwards no regular articles have been published in German. In Italy, as in the Netherlands, the switch from Italian to English was accomplished in about a decade. Figure 7.20 shows that the switch for Research in Economics took place later than for *De Economist* in the Netherlands and the *Journal of Economics* in Austria. From 1993 onwards no regular articles in this journal have been published in Italian anymore.

The language change in *De Economist* certainly coincided with the nationality of the authors. The decline of the fraction of Dutch authors, however, developed more gradually than the decline of the fraction of articles in Dutch, as is shown in figure 7.21. Moreover, the fraction of articles by German or Austrian authors in the *Journal of Economics* declined rapidly after

11. For *De Economist* and the *Journal of Economics,* we used the website http://springer.com; for *Research in Economics* we used http://www.Elsevier.com for the years after 1996; and the following website for the period from 1960 to 1996: http://www.biblio.liuc.it/essper/schedper/p78.htm.

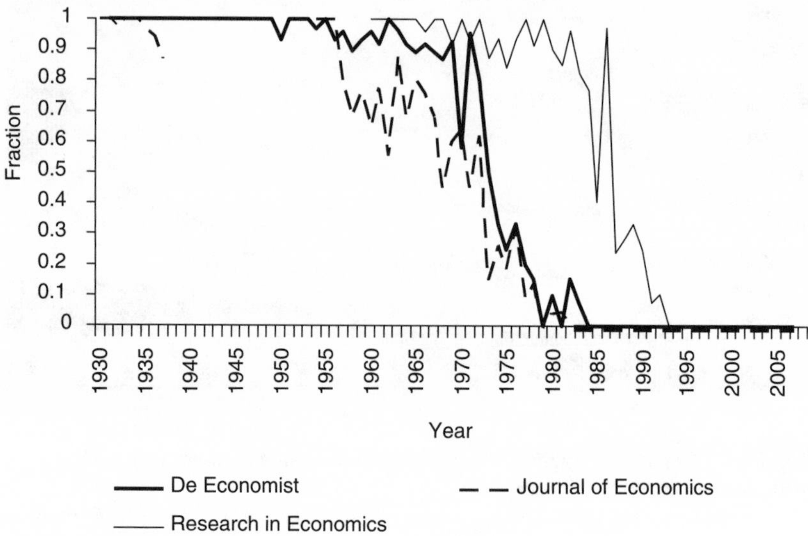

Fig. 7.20 The fraction of articles written in home language in *De Economist* (Netherlands), *Journal of Economics* (Austria/Germany), and *Research in Economics* (Italy), 1930–2007

Sources: Springer, Elsevier, and website of *Research in Economics* for 1960–1996 (http://www.biblio.liuc.it/essper/schedper/p78.htm).

World War II. The fraction reaches a level below 20 percent in the late 1980s and the early 1990s. In recent years, however, the fraction of German and Austrian authors increased again. Figure 7.21 also provides information about the nationality of the authors in *Research in Economics.* Since the 1980s the fraction of Italian authors gradually decreased, reaching a level of about 20 percent in recent years.

Figure 7.22 shows the developments in the language of the references in English-written papers published in *De Economist* and the *Journal of Economics.* The change in international orientation of *De Economist* had a clear impact on the language of the publications, which was referred to in the articles. In the 1960s, between 40 and 50 percent of the references were in the Dutch language. During the last decades this share was less than 10 percent for most years. Also, for the *Journal of Economics* the change in international orientation had a clear impact on the fraction of references to publications in the home language. The fraction decreased over years. In particular after 2000 this fraction is very low.

7.6 Conclusions

In this chapter we document the shift of the European research and higher education system from a national to an international—and American—orientation. This gradual process did not start immediately after the expan-

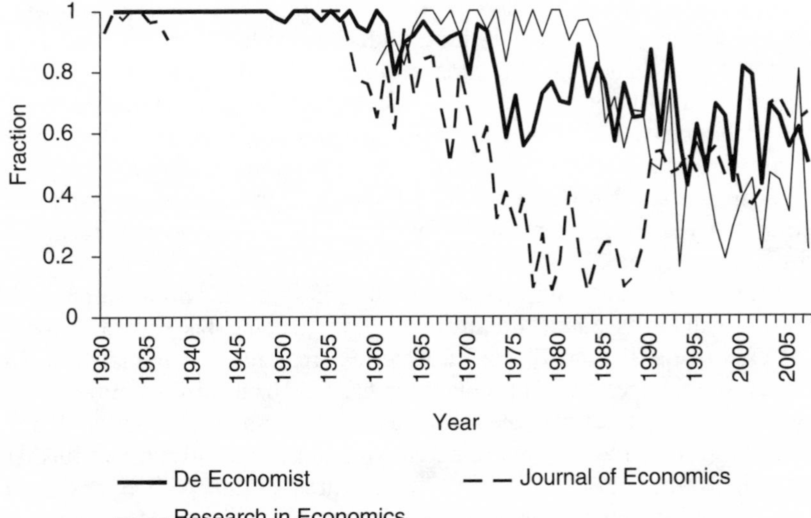

Fig. 7.21 The fraction of articles written by native authors in *De Economist* (Netherlands), *Journal of Economics* (Austria/Germany), and *Research in Economics* (Italy), 1930–2007

Sources: Springer, Elsevier and website of *Research in Economics* for 1960–1996 (http://www.biblio.liuc.it/essper/schedper/p78.htm).

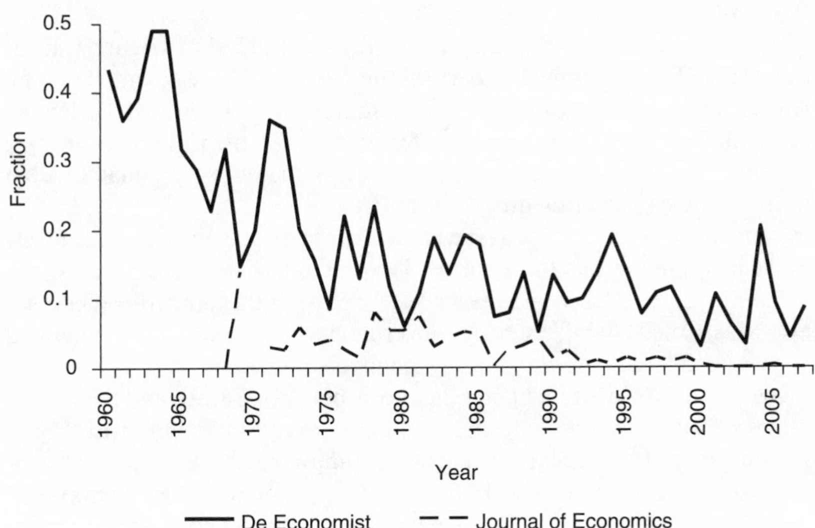

Fig. 7.22 The fraction of references in English articles to publications in home language for *De Economist* (Netherlands) and *Journal of Economics* (Germany), 1960–2007

Source: Springer.

sion of higher education, but developed over time. Smaller countries with smaller language areas were the first to adopt English as a research language and to adjust their system to American standards, suggesting that returns to scale are an important factor in the decision to join the international research society. Comparing between fields of study, sciences and medicine turn out to make this change earlier than economics and social sciences, while in arts and law the majority of the work still is focused on the home country. Differences in the transferability of research outcomes may account for these differences.

These trends might imply that mobility of students and researchers in Europe will increase substantially in the years to come. The standards used, the use of English, and a focus on American research go hand in hand. So once these changes start, it becomes increasingly beneficial to continue this process. At the same time, when more researchers join the international society, the scale of the national research communities shrinks, which further stimulates internationalization. When research in Europe becomes more harmonized and more focused on American research, the need for European students to study in the United States might be reduced, while at the same time the system will become more attractive for students and researchers from outside Europe. Until now the inflow of students from outside Europe is still relatively small, so we can only speculate about the potential size of these developments. Another remaining question is whether law and arts will follow other disciplines in their shift toward the American/international standard.

Further progress in the establishment of a European Higher Education Area (EHEA), which is part of the Bologna Process, can create an American-like competitive European standard for higher education, in particular when the European Union succeeds in the full adoption of a system based on two main cycles for undergraduates and graduates with a transparent system of credits. As is noticed by Drèze and Estevan (2007), the introduction of English as the lingua franca of universities, particularly in the big four continental countries, is a prerequisite to increase European competitiveness. Other conditions for increasing its competitiveness (see also Mas-Colell [2003]) are better governance at European universities and concentrating PhD programs at fewer universities.

In our analysis of student mobility flows between Europe and the United States we found the first indications of a declining enrollment of European students in the United States, whereas studying abroad in Europe by US students seems to be on the rise. In the long term, similar developments could occur for the number of PhD students and researchers going to the United States. Only if international/American standards are adopted in European higher education and research can Europe as a whole become more attractive for students and researchers all over the world, and challenge the United States as the number one.

Appendix

Table 7A.1 **Numbers of dissertations by country and language, ten-year periods 1908–2007**

	Year									
	1908–1917	1918–1927	1928–1937	1938–1947	1948–1957	1958–1967	1968–1977	1978–1987	1988–1997	1998–2007
Austria										
German	86	112	245	191	375	302	336	205	79	22
English	0	2	1	1	6	6	6	6	16	11
% German	100	98	100	99	98	98	98	97	83	67
Germany, West										
German	35,326	34,764	60,550	11,833	11,020	42,177	63,229	63,253	70,751	24,594
English	56	10	23	13	21	80	269	514	1,042	1,222
% German	100	100	100	100	100	100	100	99	99	95
Netherlands										
Dutch	622	1,207	1,978	1,448	1,643	1,648	1,796	1,360	1,169	435
English	13	57	183	201	630	1,243	2,551	3,342	4,287	2,771
% Dutch	98	95	92	88	72	57	41	29	21	14
France										
French	7,148	10,187	8,733	6,808	4,861	10,331	18,213	6,993	18,120	7,591
English	6	5	17	9	4	22	87	17	24	21
% French	100	100	100	100	100	100	100	100	100	100
Spain										
Spanish	4	28	41	11	20	188	436	59	234	32
English	0	0	0	0	1	0	0	0	6	15
% Spanish	100	100	100	100	95	100	100	100	98	68

(*continued*)

Table 7A.1 (continued)

	Year									
	1908–1917	1918–1927	1928–1937	1938–1947	1948–1957	1958–1967	1968–1977	1978–1987	1988–1997	1998–2007
Italy										
Italian	8	5	18	21	23	49	31	60	56	8
English	0	0	1	2	10	29	13	36	65	6
% Italian	100	100	95	91	70	63	70	63	46	57
Denmark										
Danish	112	133	213	247	249	256	260	260	222	66
English	2	20	60	113	198	280	342	438	696	377
% Danish	98	87	78	69	56	48	43	37	24	15
Sweden										
Swedish	240	249	243	267	294	288	622	842	1,411	1,084
English	27	68	84	177	469	864	2,102	3,854	5,440	4,695
% Swedish	90	79	74	60	39	25	23	18	21	19
Norway										
Norwegian	5	7	22	12	9	13	15	34	6	0
English	0	0	13	5	9	27	127	206	153	51
% Norwegian	100	100	63	71	50	33	11	14	4	0

Source: Center for Research Libraries (CRL).

Table 7A.2 **Language of Continental European academic journals in economics**

Country	Original language	National journal name	English journal name	Publishing years	Year of publishing solely English articles
Austria	German	Zeitschrift für Nationalökonomie	Journal of Economics	1892–	1982
Belgium	French	Revue Économique Internationale	n.a.	1904–1940	n.a.
Belgium	French	Recherches Economiques de Louvain	Louvain Economic Review	1929–	Still partly in French
Belgium	French	Cahiers Économiques de Bruxelles	Brussels Economic Review	1958–	Still mix of French and English language
Europe	English	European Economic Review	n.a.	1969–	1969
France	French	Annuaire de l'Économie Politique et de la Statistique	n.a.	1844–1899	n.a.
France	French	Annales d'Économie Politique	n.a.	1846–	Still in French
France	French	Revue d'Économie Politique	n.a.	1887–	Still mainly in French
France	French	Les Etudes Social	n.a.	1881–	Still in French
France	French	Histoire, Économie et Société	n.a.	1908–	Still in French
France	French	Annales d'Histoire Économique et Sociale	n.a.	1929–	Still in French
France	French	Économie Appliquée	n.a.	1948–	Still mainly in French
France	French	Revue Économique	n.a.	1950–	Still mainly in French
France	French	Economies et Sociétés	n.a.	1967–	Still in French
France	French	Cahiers d'Économie Politique	n.a.	1974–	Still mix of French and English language
Germany	German	Zeitschrift für die gesamte Staatswissenschaft	Journal of Institutional and Theoretical Economics JITE	1844–	1993
Germany	German	Jahrbücher für Nationalökonomie und Statistik	n.a.	1863–	Still in German
Germany	German	Schmollers Jahrbuch	Journal of Applied Social Science Studies	1871	Still partly in German
Germany	German	Die Neue Zeit: Revue des geistigen und öffentlichen Lebens	n.a.	1883–1923	n.a.
Germany	German	Archiv fur Sozialwissenschaft und Sozialpolitik	n.a.	1888–1933	n.a.
Germany	German	Weltwirtschaftliches Archiv	Review of World Economics	1913–	1995
Germany	German	Kredit und Kapital	n.a.	1968–	Still in German

(*continued*)

Table 7A.2 (continued)

Country	Original language	National journal name	English journal name	Publishing years	Year of publishing solely English articles
Italy	Italian	Giornale degli Economisti e Annali di Economia	n.a.	1875	2000
Italy	English	Banca nazionale del lavoro quarterly review	Previously: Quarterly review. Banca nazionale del lavoro; Nowadays: BNL Quarterly Review	1947–	1947
Italy	Italian	Ricerche Economiche	Research in Economics	1947–	1993
Italy	Italian	Economia internazionale	n.a.	1948–	2001
Netherlands	Dutch	De Economist	De Economist Netherlands Economic Review	1852–	1983
Norway	Norwegian	Norsk Økonomisk Tidsskrift	n.a.	1887–	Still in Norwegian
Soviet Union	English translations	Problems of Economic Transition	n.a.	1958–	1958
Soviet Union	English translations	Matekon	n.a.	1964–1998	1964
Spain	Spanish	Revista Española de Economia	Spanish Economic Review	1971–	1999
Spain	Spanish	Revista de Historia Económica	Journal of Iberian and Latin American Economic History	1945–	Submissions in English, Spanish, or Portuguese
Sweden	Swedish	Statsvetenskaplig tidskrift för politik-statistik-ekonomi	n.a.	1897–1963	n.a.
Sweden	Swedish	Ekonomisk Tidskrift	Scandinavian Journal of Economics	1899–	1964
Switzerland	German	Kyklos	Kyklos International Review for Social Sciences	1947–	1993
Switzerland	French	Revue Économique et Sociale	n.a.	1943–	Still in French

Sources: Fonseca; Periodicals Service Company & Schmidt Periodicals GmbH, home pages of journals, national libraries, EconLit, and so forth.

Notes: Continental European Journals selected from 1850 onwards (emergence of academic economics journals, excl. light and news-oriented journals, or journals not principally dedicated to economics). Only journals that were founded until 1990 have been included.

n.a. = not applicable.

Table 7A.3 **English language journals (only English-speaking countries)**

Country	National journal name	Publishing years
Australia	Economic Record	1924–
Australia	Australian Economic Papers	1962–
Britain	Macmillan's Magazine	1859–1907
Britain	Economic Journal	1891
Britain	Economic Review	1891–1914
Britain	Economica	1921–
Britain	Economic History Review	1927–
Britain	The Manchester School of Economic and Social Studies	1929–
Britain	Lloyds Bank Review	1930–
Britain	Review of Economic Studies	1933–
Britain	Oxford Economic Papers	1938–
Britain	Scottish Journal of Political Economy	1953–
Britain	Journal of Development Studies	1964–
Britain	Cambridge Journal of Economics	1977–
Canada	Canadian Journal of Economics[a]	1935–
International	International Labour Review	1921–
International	Econometrica	1933–
International	Metroeconomica	1949–
International	Journal of Industrial Economics	1952–
International	IMF Staff Papers	1954–
International	International Economic Review	1960–
International	Journal of Economic Theory	1969–
International	History of Political Economy	1969–
International	Journal of International Economics	1971–
International	International Journal of Game Theory	1971–
International	Journal of Public Economics	1972–
International	Journal of Monetary Economics	1972–
International	Journal of Econometrics	1973–
International	Atlantic Economic Journal	1973–
International	Journal of Mathematical Economics	1974–
International	Journal of Development Economics	1974–
International	Economics Letters	1978–
International	Journal of Economic Dynamics and Control	1979–
International	Journal of Economic Behavior and Organization	1980–
International	Mathematical Social Sciences	1981–
International	The New Palgrave: A dictionary of economics	1987–
International	Review of Austrian Economics	1987–
International	Economic Systems Research	1988–
International	Games and Economic Behavior	1989–
International	Structural Change and Economic Dynamics	1990–
International	Journal of Evolutionary Economics	1990–
South Africa	South African Journal of Economics	1933–
US	Quarterly Journal of Economics	1886–
US	Journal of American Statistical Association	1888–
US	Journal of Political Economy	1892–
US	Bulletin of the American Economic Association[b]	1908–1910
US	American Economic Review	1911–
US	Review of Economics and Statistics	1919–

(*continued*)

Table 7A.3 (continued)

Country	National journal name	Publishing years
US	Journal of Business	1922–
US	Southern Economic Journal	1933–
US	Encyclopedia of the Social Sciences	1937–
US	Journal of Economic History	1941–
US	American Journal of Economics and Sociology	1941–
US	Review of Social Economy	1944–
US	Journal of Finance	1946–
US	International Organization	1947–
US	Monthly Review	1948–
US	Economic Development and Cultural Change	1952–
US	Journal of Law and Economics	1958–
US	Western Economic Journal	1962–
US	Journal of Economic Issues	1967–
US	Journal of Economic Literature	1969–
US	Review of Radical Political Economy	1969–
US	Journal of Money, Credit and Banking	1969–
US	Brookings Papers on Economic Activity	1970–
US	Bell Journal of Economics[c]	1970–1973
US	Carnegie-Rochester Conference Series on Public Policy	1973–
US	RAND Journal of Economics	1974–
US	Eastern Economic Journal	1974–
US	Journal of Post Keynesian Economics	1978–
US	Journal of Economic Perspectives	1987–
US	Review of Political Economy	1989–

Sources: Fonseca; Periodicals Service Company & Schmidt Periodicals GmbH, home pages of journals, national libraries, EconLit, and so forth.

Notes: Continental European Journals selected from 1850 onwards (emergence of academic economics journals, excl. light and news-oriented journals, or journals not principally dedicated to economics). Only journals that were founded until 1990 have been included.

[a]Formerly published as *Canadian Journal of Economics and Political Science.*

[b]Predecessor of *American Economic Review.*

[c]Predecessor of *RAND Journal of Economics.*

References

Adelman, C. 2009. *The Bologna Process for US eyes: Re-learning higher education in the age of convergence.* Washington, DC: Institute for Higher Education Policy.

Association of International Educators. 2007. The Bologna Process. International Educator Bologna 2007. Supplement. http://www.nafsa.org./_/Document/_/bolognaprocess_ie_supp.pdf.

Amir, R., and M. Knauff. 2008. Ranking economics departments worldwide on the basis of PhD placement. *Review of Economics and Statistics* 90 (1): 185–90.

Cardoso, A. R., P. Guimarães, and K. F. Zimmermann. 2008. Comparing the early research performance of PhD graduates in labor economics in Europe and the

USA. Institute for the Study of Labor, Bonn., Germany. IZA Discussion Paper no. 3898.

Center for Research Libraries. *Catalog of foreign doctoral dissertations database.* Available at: http://catalog.crl.edu.

Coupé, T. 2003. Revealed performances: Worldwide rankings of economists and economics departments, 1990–2000. *Journal of the European Economic Association* 1 (6): 1309–45.

Drèze, J. H., and F. Estevan. 2007. Research and higher education in economics: Can we deliver the Lisbon Objectives? *Journal of the European Economic Association* 5 (2–3): 271–304.

European Commission. 2007. *The Bologna Process: Towards the European Higher Education Area.* Available at: http://ec.europa.eu/education/policies/educ/bologna/bologna_en.html.

———. 2008. *Erasmus—statistics, Erasmus student and teacher mobility.* Available at: http://ec.europa.eu/education/programmes/llp/erasmus/statisti/table1.pdf.

Eurydice. 2000. Two decades of reform in higher education in Europe: 1980 onwards. Education and Culture Directorate General, European Commission. Brussels, Belgium.

Fonseca, G. L. *Economics journals: A chronological account.* Available at: http://newschool.edu/nssr/het/essays/journal.htm (accessed October 23, 2009).

Frey, B., and R. Eichenberger. 1993. American and European economics and economists. *Journal of Economic Perspectives* 7 (4): 185–93.

Institute of International Education. *Open Doors 1948–2004: Report on international educational exchange.* CD-ROM. Sewickley, PA.

Kirman, A., and M. Dahl. 1994. Economic research in Europe. *European Economic Review.* 38 (34): 505–22.

Mas-Colell, A. 2003. The European space of higher education: Incentive and governance issues. *Rivista di Politica Economica* 93 (11–12): 9–27.

National Center for Education Statistics. 2008. *Digest of education statistics: 2007,* March. Washington, DC. Available at: http://nces.ed.gov/programs/digest/d07/index.asp (accessed October 23, 2009).

Netherlands organization for international cooperation in higher education (nuffic). 2008. *Internationalization in education in the Netherlands 2007.* The Hague.

Neary, P. J., J. A. Mirrlees, and J. Tirole. 2003. Evaluating economics research in Europe: An introduction. *Journal of the European Economic Association* 1 (6): 1239–49.

Periodicals Service Company & Schmidt Periodicals GmbH. Available at: http://www.periodicals.com/download.html.

Portes, R. 1987. Economics in Europe. *European Economic Review* 31 (6): 1329–40.

Spinelli, G. 2005. Mobility and admission of graduate students across the Atlantic: New challenges with the Bologna Process. *IIENetworker Magazine* (Spring). Available at: http://www.iienetwork.org/?p=Spinelli (accessed October 23, 2009).

Unesco Institute for Statistics. Data for 1970–1996. Available at: http://www.uis.unesco.org/pagesen/ed.htm.

———. Data for 1999–2006. Available at: http://stats.uis.unesco.org/unesco/tableviewer/document.aspx?ReportId=143.

Windolf, P. 1997. *Expansion and structural change: Higher education in Germany, United States, and Japan, 1870–1990*. Boulder: Westview Press.

Witte, J. K. 2006. Change of degrees and degrees of change: Comparing adaptations of European higher education systems in the context of the Bologna Process. PhD diss., University of Twente, Netherlands.

8

Higher Education in China
Complement or Competition to US Universities?

Haizheng Li

8.1 Introduction

In 2006, a total of 134,000 Chinese students went abroad to further their education, a number almost as large as the total number of new international students (142,923) coming to the United States from all countries.[1] Chinese students accounted for 11.6 percent of the total number of international students in the United States in that year. In recent years, China has ranked first, or second to India, in numbers of students studying in the United States. Since 1978, when China began to open to the outside world, the United States has been receiving an increasing number of Chinese students. In 2005, 23 percent of all overseas Chinese students were in the United States (Fazackerley and Worthington 2007).

Chinese students mostly enroll in graduate programs in the United States, and they are in all major universities, especially Research I universities. Chinese graduate students traditionally mostly studied in the fields of science, such as physics and mathematics, but now they are in many other fields, including business, economics, law, and medicine. Moreover, the reliance of Chinese students on financial aid from the hosting institutions that was characteristic of earlier cohorts has declined significantly in recent years

Haizheng Li is associate professor of economics at the Georgia Institute of Technology.

I am grateful to Sumei Guo, Fei He, Chongyu Lu, Yang Peng, Hua Wang, Ying Wang, Yanni Xu, Luping Yang, Xiaobei Zhang, and Xiaojun Zhang for data collection, and especially to Lan Ding for excellent assistance. I would like to thank Hongbin Cai, Yongjun Chen, Li Gan, Yongmiao Hong, Yifu Lin, Baoyun Qiao, Xiangdong Qin, Guoqiang Tian, Wei Xiong, and Gene Zhang for helping with the survey, and participants at the National Bureau of Economic Research (NBER) preconference and conference, especially Charles Clotfelter, Debra Stewart, and Hugo Sonnenschein, for insightful comments and suggestions.

1. See the Institute of International Education (IIE) Network, http://opendoors.iienetwork.org/page/92270/.

because more Chinese students are coming to the United States with funding from their families.

At the same time, China is increasingly becoming an important destination for international students. According to the Institute of International Education (2007a), China now ranks fifth as a destination country for international students, behind the United States, the United Kingdom, France, and Germany. The number of Americans studying abroad in China increased fivefold in the past ten years, making China one of the top ten study abroad destination countries for U.S. students, and U.S. students now account for 7 percent of all international students in China.

As the Chinese economy and family incomes grow and college tuition in China increases, studying abroad will become more affordable, and, thus, more Chinese students are likely to come to the United States to study. But the rapid expansion of higher education in China will also offer more educational opportunities and, thus, encourage many Chinese students to stay home for higher education. Meanwhile, the increasing job and career opportunities in China will attract an increasing number of overseas trained scholars and students to return to work in China, helping to build world-class education and research programs.

Therefore, the dynamics in the higher education system, both within China and in its interactions with the United States and other countries, raise many interesting questions. How will higher education in China affect universities in the United States? Will those American-trained Chinese students help American universities become more competitive in the global market? Or will they help China build world-class universities? Will Chinese universities eventually compete with American universities, or will they continue to serve as complements, preparing high-quality students for universities in the United States? Those questions have important implications for both American and Chinese universities. This chapter addresses questions regarding the prospects for higher education in China, focusing on its influences on American universities. In addition to the use of publicly available data, we also collected our own data for the analysis and conducted a small survey about the recruitment of faculty members by Chinese universities in the U.S. academic job market.

There are a few studies of China's higher education system and its impact on universities in other countries. An Agora report edited by Fazackerley and Worthington (2007), "British Universities in China: The Reality Beyond the Rhetoric," presents a comprehensive review of the relationship between British universities and Chinese universities. The article by Xin and Normile (2008) published in the Newsfocus section in *Science* discusses issues related to Chinese universities in their efforts to become world-class institutions. Ma (2007) reviews top universities in China and their role in economic transition. Liu (2007) provides an overview of research universities in China. In this study, we discuss China's higher education system from a different angle, that is, its relationship with the outside world, especially the United States.

The remainder of the chapter is organized as follows. In the next section, we briefly describe the history of higher education in China. Section 8.3 discusses the rapid growth of higher education since economic reform began in 1978. In section 8.4, we present major policies adopted by the Chinese government for fostering world-class universities. The trends and patterns of Chinese students studying abroad are discussed in section 8.5. In section 8.6, we discuss the situation of Chinese students and scholars in the United States. Section 8.7 analyzes the trends and policies related to overseas Chinese students returning to work in China. Section 8.8 discusses the challenges in the higher education in China and concludes.

8.2 A Brief History of Higher Education in China

In the imperial era before the twentieth century, Chinese education focused on the Confucius doctrines. There was no institution that could be called a university. One element of Chinese ancient higher education was in the form of Taixue and Guozijian (imperial college), which taught mostly Confucianism and Chinese literature for high-level civil services. The imperial examination system (*Keju*) was the major mechanism by which the central government identified and recruited elites all over the country.

Following the defeat of the Chinese Empire in the Opium Wars in 1840, modern Western education was introduced to China. Western style professional schools began to be established, and some of these later became the earliest universities in China. In 1912, China had one university and ninety-four professional training colleges. By 1923, there were thirty-five university-level institutions of higher education and sixty-eight provincial training colleges (Yang [2005] and references therein). Chinese students had been going abroad to study as early as the late nineteenth century. Starting in 1872, the government of the Qing Dynasty selected 120 children aged twelve to fourteen years old and sent them to study in the United States, thirty students per year for four years.

From the very beginning, the modern Chinese higher education system was greatly influenced by foreign countries. The country's higher education first followed the Japanese system and then the American model. Western missionaries and Chinese scholars returning from Japan and Western countries played significant roles in the development of the modern institutions of China's higher education (Yang 2005). The war with Japan and the following civil wars hindered the growth and development of higher education. By 1949, when the new People's Republic of China was established, there were only 205 colleges and universities, with a total enrollment of 116,504 students (table 8.1). Beginning in 1949, the higher education system in China completely switched to the Soviet model and for the next sixteen years grew

Table 8.1 **Higher education institutions in operation and students in China, 1949–1977 (no. of persons)**

Year	No. of institutions of higher education (1)	New enrollment: undergraduate students (2)	Total enrollment: undergraduate students (3)	New enrollment: graduate students (4)	Total enrollment: graduate students (5)
1949	205	30,573	116,504	242	629
1950	193	58,330	137,470	874	1,261
1951	206	51,689	153,402	1,273	2,168
1952	201	78,865	191,147	1,785	2,763
1953	181	81,544	212,181	2,887	4,249
1954	188	92,280	252,978	1,155	4,753
1955	194	97,797	287,653	1,751	4,822
1956	227	184,632	403,176	2,235	4,841
1957	229	105,581	441,181	334	3,178
1958	791	265,553	659,627	275	1,635
1959	841	274,143	811,947	1,345	2,171
1960	1,289	323,161	961,623	2,275	3,635
1961	845	169,047	947,166	2,198	6,009
1962	610	106,777	829,699	1,287	6,130
1963	407	132,820	750,118	781	4,938
1964	419	147,037	685,314	1,240	4,881
1965	434	164,212	674,436	1,456	4,546
1966	n.a.	0	533,766	0	3,409
1967	n.a.	0	408,930	0	2,557
1968	n.a.	0	258,736	0	1,317
1969	n.a.	0	108,617	0	n.a.
1970	n.a.	41,870	47,815	0	n.a.
1971	328	42,420	83,400	0	n.a.
1972	331	133,553	193,719	0	n.a.
1973	345	149,960	313,645	0	n.a.
1974	378	165,084	429,981	0	n.a.
1975	387	190,779	500,993	0	n.a.
1976	392	217,048	564,715	0	n.a.
1977	404	272,971	625,319	0	226

Source: Ministry of Education of the People's Republic of China (various years), *China Education Statistical Yearbook* (1949–1981).

Notes: In column (1), the numbers of schools for the period of 1957–1963 fluctuated dramatically. For example, it increased from 229 in 1957 to 791 in 1958 and then dropped from 1,289 in 1960 to 845 in 1961. This is related to the government "Great Leap Forward" policy in 1958, which was aimed at catching up developed countries in a few years, and the resulting dramatic readjustments in the years followed. During the Cultural Revolution starting in 1966, most universities were closed, and statistical work was interrupted, and, thus, some data are missing. In column (2), there was no new undergraduate enrollment during 1966–1969 and no national college entrance examinations for 1966–1976. In column (4), there was no new graduate enrollment during 1966–1977 due to the Cultural Revolution. For graduate students, data for 1961 and before only include graduate students at universities; for 1962 and after, data also include graduates from the Chinese Academy of Science and research institutes. In column (5), when new enrollment goes to zero due to the political movement to close universities, there were still formerly enrolled students. They needed to finish or took time to leave school. That is why the total enrollments for those years were declining but still nonzero. n.a. = not available.

rapidly. Total enrollment grew almost sixfold between 1949 and 1965, peaking at almost one million in 1960.

The Cultural Revolution of 1966 to 1976 had a devastating impact on China's higher education. Colleges and universities were closed or stopped functioning. National entrance examinations for higher education were abandoned. From 1966 to 1969, no new students were admitted to colleges or universities. Graduate student admission was suspended even longer, for the twelve years from 1966 to 1977. Although official statistics show new enrollment starting in 1970, those students were mostly admitted into college based on their family background and political considerations. Such admissions were only allowed for a few universities. There were no academic standards for either admission or for graduation. During this period, the curricula, classes, and grading system were all distorted, not following the academic standards of higher education.

The year 1977 brought the end of the Cultural Revolution and a new beginning for higher education in China. In that year, China held its first national college entrance examinations for higher education since the beginning of the Cultural Revolution in 1966. Some 5.7 million aspiring students took part in the exams, but only 273,000 were admitted to colleges and universities, yielding a miniscule admission rate of only 4.8 percent.[2] As a result, the Class of 1977 was both extraordinary and renowned because it was selected from the accumulation of ten years' worth of potential students.

8.3 Growth after the Cultural Revolution

With the beginning of the economic reforms of 1978, Chinese higher education began expanding rapidly. As can be seen in table 8.2, from 1978 to 2006, the number of institutions of higher education more than tripled, and total enrollment exploded, increasing by a factor of 20. The acceleration in enrollments began around 1999, coinciding with government policies for expanding higher education. From 1999 to 2006, new enrollments grew at the astonishing average rate of 23 percent a year. As a result, the number of graduates also increased accordingly.

The expansion also increased the probability of getting into college for those taking the national college entrance examinations. Whereas the rate of admission before 1981 was below 10 percent, it increased to 48 percent in 1999 and to 62 percent in 2004. Since 1999, more than half of those who participated in the entrance exams have been admitted into college.[3]

Table 8.3 provides information about the distribution of undergraduate students by field of study. Engineering had the largest number of students,

2. Those admitted to universities in 1977 started their higher education in spring 1978. From 1978 on, the national higher education entrance exams have been held in summer time, and the students who received admission began school in fall of that year.

3. Admission rates are from http://www.neea.edu.cn/.

Table 8.2 Higher education institutions and students in China, 1978–2006

Year	No. of institutions of higher education (units)	No. of faculty members (thousands)	No. of graduate students (persons)			No. of undergraduates (thousands)		
			Total enrollment	New enrollment	Graduated	Total enrollment	New enrollment	Graduated
1978	598	206	10,934	10,708	9	856	402	165
1979	633	237	18,830	8,110	140	1,020	275	85
1980	675	247	21,604	3,616	476	1,144	281	147
1981	704	250	18,848	9,363	11,669	1,279	279	140
1982	715	287	25,847	11,080	4,058	1,154	315	457
1983	805	303	37,166	15,642	4,497	1,207	391	335
1984	902	315	57,566	23,181	2,756	1,396	475	287
1985	1,016	344	87,331	46,871	17,004	1,703	619	316
1986	1,054	372	110,371	41,310	16,950	1,880	572	393
1987	1,063	385	120,191	39,017	27,603	1,959	617	532
1988	1,075	393	112,776	35,645	40,838	2,066	670	553
1989	1,075	397	101,339	28,569	37,232	2,082	597	576
1990	1,075	395	93,018	29,649	35,440	2,063	609	614
1991	1,075	391	88,128	29,679	32,537	2,044	620	614
1992	1,053	388	94,164	33,439	25,692	2,184	754	604
1993	1,065	388	106,771	42,145	28,214	2,536	924	571
1994	1,080	396	127,935	50,864	28,047	2,799	900	637

1995	1,054	401	145,443	51,053	31,877	2,906	926	805
1996	1,032	403	163,322	59,398	39,652	3,021	966	839
1997	1,020	405	176,353	63,749	46,539	3,174	1,000	829
1998	1,022	407	198,885	72,508	47,077	3,409	1,084	830
1999	1,071	426	233,513	92,225	54,670	4,134	1,597	848
2000	1,041	463	301,239	128,484	58,767	5,561	2,206	950
2001	1,225	532	393,256	165,197	67,809	7,191	2,683	1,036
2002	1,396	618	500,980	202,611	80,841	9,034	3,205	1,337
2003	1,552	725	651,260	268,925	111,091	11,086	3,822	1,877
2004	1,731	858	819,896	326,286	150,777	13,335	4,473	2,391
2005	1,792	966	978,610	364,831	189,728	15,618	5,045	3,068
2006	1,867	1,076	1,104,700	397,900	255,900	17,388	5,465	3,775

Sources: National Bureau of Statistics of P.R. China (2005), "Comprehensive Statistical Data and Materials on 55 Years of New China"; National Bureau of Statistics of P.R. China (various years); *China Statistical Yearbook* (2003–2006); Ministry of Education of the People's Republic of China, "The Statistic Communiqué of Education Development in 2006."

Notes: In 1978, a total of 10,708 new graduate students were admitted. Although universities were mostly closed for the 1966–1976 period, there were still many people with university degrees who were eligible to apply for graduate schools at that time. Some of newly admitted graduate students may be left over from the early period when the universities closed.

Table 8.3 **New enrollment by field of study at each degree level for 2001 and 2007 (%)**

	Undergraduate		Master's		Doctoral	
Field	2001	2007	2001	2007	2001	2007
Philosophy	0.07	0.04	1.1	1.3	1.6	1.6
Economics	5.2	5.2	5.0	4.9	5.9	4.9
Law	5.5	3.4	7.4	8.0	4.0	5.5
Education	5.9	4.7	3.1	4.0	1.5	1.9
Literature	15.6	15.5	7.1	9.4	4.0	4.8
History	0.6	0.3	1.4	1.3	1.9	1.7
Science	9.6	5.3	11.8	10.5	17.7	15.4
Engineering	33.3	36.9	37.9	34.4	39.2	37.9
Agriculture	2.4	1.8	3.4	3.7	3.7	4.2
Medicine	6.5	6.5	9.7	10.4	12.4	13.4
Military Science	n.a.	n.a.	0.04	0.06	0.05	0.06
Management	15.5	20.6	12.3	12.2	8.1	8.6
Total	100.00	100.00	100.00	100.00	100.00	100.00

Sources: Ministry of Education of the People's Republic of China (various years), *China Education Statistical Yearbook* (1994–2007); National Bureau of Statistics of P.R. China (various years), *China Statistical Yearbook* (2005–2008)

Note: The year 2001 is chosen as the starting year because the field classification was changed in 2000. n.a. = not available.

accounting for approximately 37 percent of all undergraduate students in 2007. Management ranked second, with 21 percent of all students. The third largest field was literature with 16 percent of students, followed by medicine, science, and economics (accounting for 5 percent). Growth rates by field differed, with the fastest growth in economics, literature, engineering, medicine, and management.

Graduate enrollments expanded even faster, given the increasing focus on research in China's universities. In 1978, there were only 10,934 graduate students in total. However, by 2006, the number had grown to 1.1 million, as shown in table 8.2, a breathtaking hundredfold increase from 1978. Growth was sporadic until 1992, but new admissions grew in every year after that. In 2006, the number of graduate students who completed their degree was 255,900, which was equivalent to the entire fifteen-year total of graduates between 1978 and 1992. Corresponding to the national entrance examinations for college, there is also a national entrance examination for graduate study although the admission rate for master's students is much lower than that for undergraduate students. As it is with undergraduate enrollment, engineering is also the largest field for master's students, accounting for more than one-third of the total in 2007. It is followed by management, science, and medicine. Unlike the undergraduate level, enrollment in master's programs increased rapidly between 2001 and 2007 for almost all fields.

Doctoral programs in China restarted in 1982, when there were only a few hundred doctoral students in the country. By 1988, the number of doctoral students enrolled had reached 10,000 (see table 8.8 later in this chapter). It took fourteen years for the total enrollment to reach 100,000 (in 2002), but only another four years after that for total enrollment to increase by another 100,000 doctoral students. In 2006, there were 55,955 new doctoral students admitted to institutions in China, and the total enrollment of doctoral students reached 208,038. In that year, 36,247 students were awarded a doctoral degree. In comparison, there were 45,596 doctoral degrees awarded that same year in the United States. China's growing doctoral production is illustrated by this fact: whereas China's output of doctoral students in 1996 had been only 13 percent of the number awarded by U.S. universities, by 2006, China's production had reached 79 percent of the U.S. level. A very large proportion of Chinese doctoral students are in engineering. In 2007, the share was 38 percent (table 8.3). In contrast to the distributions for undergraduate and master's programs, science is the second largest field for doctoral study, accounting for 15 percent of all students.

Faculty size has not increased as fast as enrollments. In 1999, when undergraduate admission rose by approximately 50 percent and graduate admission rose by about 30 percent, the total number of faculty members increased by merely 5 percent. Although the faculty size grew at a faster pace after 1999, it is still far below the speed of enrollment. In particular, the average annual increase of faculty size from 1999 to 2003 was 12 percent, far below the growth of admission. The implication is that, since 1999, China has educated more college students with relatively fewer faculty members. Thus, the student-faculty ratio rose from 8.8 in 1998, before the expansion, to 10.3 in 1999. The ratio continued to rise to 16.2 in 2003 and 17.2 in 2006, which almost doubled the ratio since the start of recent expansion. This ratio is considerably higher than that in the United States. In particular, in the United States, the average ratio of students to faculty for four-year private schools is 12.2, and for four-year public schools it is 14.8.[4] Given the huge economic gap between the two countries, it is unclear whether the ratio in China is too high.

In China, graduate students can be advised only by professors who hold either the title full professor or associate professor. High student-faculty ratios at the graduate level are probably a bigger threat to quality at the graduate level than at the undergraduate level. The ratio of graduate students to the sum of full and associate professors was relatively low, mostly below 2 or even 1 before 2002. Yet the ratio increased quite quickly. For example, in a ten-year period from 1992 to 2001, the ratio more than doubled, from 0.90 to 1.85. Unfortunately, the data on professors at the full and associate levels are not available after 2001, and we cannot get the ratios for recent years.

4. See the National Center for Education Statistics, http://nces.ed.gov/programs/digest/d07/tables/dt07_237.asp.

However, anecdotal evidence suggests that a typical professor advises an increasingly large number of graduate students, especially master's students. It has become very common for a graduate student to have only very limited interaction with his or her advisor during the entire period of graduate study. Such a situation would likely lower the quality of graduate education.

8.4 Major Reforms and Government Policies to Foster "World-Class Universities"

Since the economic reforms started in 1978, the Chinese government has implemented a number of major market oriented reforms in higher education. First, the government abandoned the traditional command system on admission and placement so as to give schools some flexibility in enrollment. More important, it also abandoned the job assigning system and let graduates find jobs in the labor market. Second, it transformed the traditional free higher education to a tuition-based system. Third, it opened higher education institutes to the outside world and encouraged collaborations and exchanges with universities worldwide.

In addition to changes in the institution and system, the Chinese government also launched a number of specific programs with special funding in order to help some universities become world-class schools. The major initiatives include the "211 Project," the "985 Project," and some related projects like the "863 Project" and the "973 Project."

The 211 Project was designed to provide special support to the top 100 universities to help improve their teaching, research, and infrastructure. It includes improvements in faculty, labs, and infrastructure for those universities, support for some selected programs to help them become leading programs in the fields, and improvements in information technology, including the Internet and libraries. The total funding for the 211 Project for the five-year period from 1995 to 2000 was RMB 18.37 billion Yuan ($2.3 billion). In this project, the amount of RMB 6.4 billion Yuan ($0.8 billion) was for supporting the selected priority programs.[5] The fund supported a total of 107 universities and 602 priority programs. Among the programs supported, 42 percent were in engineering and new technology, 20 percent in social science and humanity, 15 percent in basic research, 11 percent in medical and health, and the remaining 12 percent in environmental and agriculture.[6]

The 985 Project is aimed at helping the top forty universities to become world-class universities. Its provisions include (a) reforming and improving university administrative and operational mechanisms; (b) recruiting lead-

5. In this period, the exchange rate was approximately $1 = RMB 8.0.

6. The figures are from the official Web site of Ministry of Education, China, http://www.moe.edu.cn/edoas/website18/level3.jsp?tablename=724&infoid=5607; and http://www.moe.edu.cn/edoas/website18/level3.jsp?tablename=724&infoid=3568.

ing scholars inside or outside China to establish strong research teams; (c) establishing the Science and Technology Innovation Platform and the Social Science Research Base in those selected universities; and (d) improving university infrastructure and supporting international collaborations.[7] The 985 Project provides special financial support to those universities, ranging from RMB 300 million to RMB 1.8 billion per school.[8] The funding comes from the Ministry of Education and local provincial governments. Compared to the 211 Project, the 985 Project is weighted more heavily on research. Table 8.4 lists all universities supported by the 985 Fund and some basic information about those schools, including the size of faculty, students, graduate students, location, and date of founding. This list includes the top research universities in China.

The 863 Project focuses on research and development of high-level technology, while the 973 Project supports basic research. Both projects represent a large investment in science and technology by the Chinese government. Universities in China have received a considerable share of the funding from these two projects for their research. For example, by 2002, there were forty-nine universities that each received funding in the amount of 10 million Yuan or more from the 863 Project for specific research projects.[9] In addition, every year, the National Natural Science Foundation and Social Science Foundation in China provide a large amount of financial support to faculty members in universities for their research.

It is difficult to evaluate the direct effects of those policies. Yet it is clear that Chinese universities have made significant progress since the beginning of economic reforms in 1978. The relative importance of Chinese universities in the world can be inferred from rankings of world universities, as shown in table 8.5. This table lists three rankings by three different agencies for two years each. As of 2008, according to the Shanghai Jiaotong University (SJTU) Ranking, no Chinese university was among top 200 in the world. However, the progress has been impressive. In 2004, only two Chinese universities were among the top 300, but the number increased to five in 2008. The Times ranking put five Chinese universities in the top 200 in 2004 and six universities in this rank range in 2008, and most of those schools had a big jump in the ranking within this time period. The Webometrics ranking is based on different criteria, but the trend is similar; that is, as time goes on, more Chinese universities join the ranks of the elite universities of the world.

7. See the official Web site of Ministry of Education, China. http://www.moe.edu.cn/edoas/website18/level3.jsp?tablename=684&infoid=5120.

8. The exchange rate varied from $1 = RMB 6.8 - 8.3 in this period.

9. See China Education Online, October 28, 2005, http://www.51paihang.cn/html/edu/716.html.

Table 8.4 **Top universities in China supported by the government 985 Project (no. of persons)**

School name	Enrollment	Faculty	Graduate students	Date of founding	Location
Beihang University	22,768	1,851	9,695	1952	Beijing
Beijing Institute of Technology	21,914	1,927	7,666	1939	Beijing
Beijing Normal University	19,500	2,198	8,999	1902	Beijing
Central South University	50,004	2,732	15,796	1953	Changsha
China Agricultural University	22,414	1,490	7,821	1905	Beijing
China University of Mining and Technology	44,900	1,500	4,900	1909	Beijing
Chongqing University	52,000	3,010	16,063	1929	Chongqing
Dalian University of Technology	30,780	2,025	11,392	1949	Dalian
East China Normal University	25,640	1,660	7,730	1951	Shanghai
Fudan University	29,359	2,250	11,542	1905	Shanghai
Harbin Institute of Technology	46,701	3,027	20,474	1920	Harbin
Huazhong University of Science and Tech.	56,307	2,290	18,005	1953	Wuhan
Hunan University	30,000	1,970	10,600	A.D. 976	Changsha
Jilin University	60,067	6,428	19,614	1946	Jilin
Lanzhou University	27,397	1,758	9,190	1909	Lanzhou
Nanjing University	27,600	1,990	11,316	1902	Nanjing
Nankai University	21,942	1,773	9,522	1919	Tianjin
National University of Defense Technology				1953	Changsha
Northeastern University	30,010	2,003	9,271	1923	Shenyang
Northwest A&F Technology	26,885	1,490	5,942	1934	Yangling
Northwestern Polytechnical University	25,100	1,300	9,200	1938	Xi'an
Ocean University of China	19,681	1,298	5,573	1924	Qingdao
Peking University	29,854	1,597	15,119	1898	Beijing
Renmin University of China	22,329	1,700	9,378	1937	Beijing
Shandong University		4,000		1901	Ji'nan
Shanghai Jiaotong University	50,225	2,930	9,649	1896	Shanghai
Sichuan University	60,000	3,946	21,000	1896	Chengdu
South China University of Technology	38,253	2,213	12,859	1952	Guangzhou
Southeast University	26,303	2,185	11,436	1902	Nanjing
Sun Yat-Sen University	53,356	5,097	19,908	1924	Guangzhou
The Central University for Nationalities	14,296	1,040	2,691	1941	Beijing
Tianjin University	24,875	2,000	8,800	1895	Tianjin
Tongji University	42,205	2,851	18,663	1907	Shanghai
Tsinghua University	31,395	2,789	17,495	1911	Beijing
University of Electronic S&T of China	25,000	1,900	9,000	1956	Chengdu
University of S&T of China	26,601	1,098	12,087	1958	Anhui
Wuhan University	50,235	3,500	17,467	1893	Wuhan
Xiamen University	33,979	2,391	11,513	1921	Xiamen
Xi'an Jiaotong University	31,441	2,438	12,690	1896	Xi'an
Zhejiang University	40,910	3,539	16,214	1897	Hangzhou

Sources: The list of universities in the 985 Project: http://bmxxfb.cic.tsinghua.edu.cn/docinfo/board/boarddetail.jsp?columnId=0090401&parentColumnId=00904&itemSeq=2131. The data are from the official Web sites of the universities (collected in December 2008).

Notes: China University of Mining and Technology and East China Normal University were added to the project in 2007. The location and date of founding is based on the main campus. Blank cells indicate "not available."

Table 8.5 **The ranks of universities in China among universities in the world**

	SJTU ranking		Times ranking (top 200)		Webometrics ranking	
School name	2008	2004	2008	2004	2008	2007
Peking University	201–302	202–301	50	17	112	120
Fudan University			113	195		
Nanjing University	201–302		143	192		
Shanghai Jiaotong University	201–302		144		285	
Tsinghua University	201–302	202–301	56	61	238	270
University of S&T of China	201–302		141	154		

Notes: The SJTU Rankings are published in "Academic Ranking of World Universities" by the Institute of Higher Education at the Shanghai Jiaotong University (SJTU). The key ranking criteria are quality of education, quality of faculty, research output, and size of institution. The SJTU Ranking does not distinguish ranks for universities ranked after 200. Instead, it groups every 100 universities into one group such as group 200-300 (the number 201 or 302 in the table is caused by the same rank of some schools above or below; available at http://www.arwu.org/. The Times Higher Education-Quacquarelli Symonds World University Rankings are a composite measure based on four key criteria: research quality, teaching quality, graduate employability, and international outlook. It only ranks top 200 universities and is available at http://www.timeshighereducation.co.uk/hybrid.asp?typeCode=142&pubCode=1&navcode=105. The Webometrics Ranking measures volume, visibility, and impact of the Web pages published by universities, with special emphasis in the scientific output (referred papers, conference contributions, preprints, monographs, theses, reports) but also taking into account other materials (courseware, seminars or workshops documentation, digital libraries, databases, multimedia, personal pages) and the general information on the institution, their departments, research groups, or supporting services and people working or attending courses (available at http://www.webometrics.info/premierleague.asp).

8.5 Chinese Students Studying Abroad

It has been a long tradition for Chinese students to go abroad to study, beginning as early as 1872, as discussed in the preceding. From the founding of the People's Republic of China until the Cultural Revolution, most students going abroad were sponsored by the government. From 1950 to 1966, the Chinese government sent a total of 10,678 students to study in approximately twenty-five countries, mostly in the Soviet Union, Eastern Europe, and other socialist countries. The policy of studying abroad was largely abandoned during the Cultural Revolution, along with other programs involving international exchanges in education. For the ten-year period from 1966 to 1976, only 1,629 students were sent to other countries, mostly to study foreign languages.[10]

Following the start of economic reform in 1978, the government resumed the policy of sending students and scholars to study abroad. In 1979, a total of 1,750 people were dispatched to other countries to study. Most of them (74 percent) were visiting scholars. Among those, 82.6 percent studied

10. Data are from *China Education Statistical Yearbook 1949–1981.*

natural science, 16.1 percent language, and only 1.3 percent social science.[11] This natural science-oriented pattern continued for a number of years.

Individuals going abroad to study can be classified as visiting scholars and students, who generally will not get a foreign educational degree, or as formal students, who are to pursue degrees in foreign countries. Most visiting scholars and students from China were sponsored by the government or their employers, while most degree students going abroad were sponsored by the hosting schools in the form of fellowships or assistantships. In 1981, the Educational Testing Service (ETS) from the United States entered China to offer the Test of English as a Foreign Language (TOEFL), Graduate Record Examination (GRE), and Graduate Management Admission Test (GMAT) for Chinese students. Those tests make it possible for Chinese students to apply for formal graduate degree programs and financial aid from the schools to which they applied. Before 2000, due to the relatively low level of family income, financial aid was almost the only financial resource for Chinese students to study abroad for a graduate degree.

Since 1978, the number of Chinese students going abroad has increased continually except for the period of 1988 to 1991, due to the Tiananmen Square demonstration.[12] Figure 8.1 shows the total number of Chinese students and scholars studying abroad. The number increased from 860 in 1978 to 134,000 in 2006. In this period, there were more than 900,000 Chinese students and scholars who studied abroad. Based on the Institute of International Education (2007a), China has been the overall largest supplier of international students to countries around the world over the past decade. Since 1992, especially after 1998, the growth in the total number of Chinese students going abroad to study has accelerated. The total number of students going abroad increased from 2,900 in 1991 to 6,540 in 1992, an increase of 126 percent. The second fastest increase occurred in 2001, growing that year by 115 percent.

As can be seen in figure 8.1, almost all students and scholars studying abroad before 1992 were funded by the Chinese government. The number of students without government funding increased rapidly after that. Before 2000, it was almost impossible for Chinese students to get a U.S. entry visa if he or she did not get some sort of scholarship from the hosting institute. Thus, most of the nongovernment sponsored students were funded by financial aid from the hosting institutes in the foreign country. Since 2000, due to the rapid increase in family income in China, it has been much easier for a Chinese student to get a U.S. entry visa with self-funding.

For the ten-year period from 1996 to 2006, the average annual growth rate of students studying abroad was 25.7 percent.[13] The largest increase

11. The numbers are from *China Education Statistical Yearbook 1949–1981.*

12. In 1989 and 1990, the number of students going abroad funded by the government dropped 21 percent and 25 percent, respectively, compared to the previous year.

13. Data before 1996 were either missing or noncomparable. For example, the official statistics before 1991 does not include self-funded students.

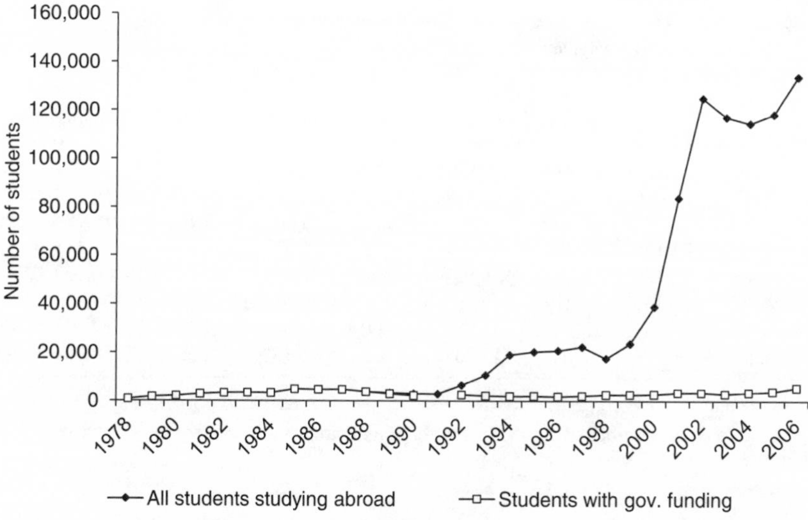

Fig. 8.1 Chinese students studying abroad (1978–2006)

Sources: National Bureau of Statistics of P.R. China (various years), *China Statistical Yearbook* (2006); Ministry of Education of the People's Republic of China (various years), *China Education Statistical Yearbook* (various years).

Note: Year 1991 is excluded for lack of data.

is in the group of self-funded students, with an annual growth rate of 31.7 percent, although annual changes fluctuated from year to year. Obviously, the increase has been driven mostly by these self-funded students, given the lower annual average growth rates of 12.3 percent and 5.3 percent for government-funded and employer-funded students, respectively. The proportion of self-funded students was about 65 percent in 1996, but it increased to 90 percent or above after 2001.[14] As the income level continues to grow, we can expect that more Chinese students can afford to study abroad with their own financial resources.

The distribution of Chinese students in selected countries is listed in table 8.6. Since 1999, the United States has received the largest number of students from China, followed by Japan. Since 2001, the United Kingdom has surpassed Germany to become the largest hosting country for Chinese students after the United States and Japan. In fact, in the United Kingdom from 2000 to 2006, the number of Chinese students increased more than sevenfold. No wonder the Agora report (Fazackerley and Worthington 2007) admits "that the UK is financially dependent on a tide of Chinese students flooding into this country . . ." (1, introduction). Similar or even larger increases in the number of Chinese students for the same period can be found for Australia, New Zealand, South Korea, and France. In contrast, the increase in

14. Self-funded students include those who received financial aid from hosting schools in a foreign country.

Table 8.6 **The flows of new students from China to selected countries at the tertiary level (no. of persons)**

Year	Australia	Japan	New Zealand	Republic of Korea	Canada	France	Germany	United Kingdom	United States
1999	4,578	25,655	247	902	n.a.	1,934	5,355	4,250	46,949
2000	5,008	28,076	1,133	1,182	n.a.	2,111	6,526	6,158	50,281
2001	n.a.	31,955	3,338	1,645	n.a.	3,068	9,109	10,388	51,986
2002	17,343	41,180	8,481	2,407	n.a.	5,477	14,070	17,483	63,211
2003	23,448	51,656	16,479	4,025	n.a.	10,665	20,141	30,690	92,774
2004	28,309	76,130	24,215	6,462	n.a.	11,514	25,284	47,738	87,943
2005	40,316	83,264	23,260	10,093	17,913	14,316	27,129	52,677	92,370
2006	n.a.	86,378	n.a.	15,288	n.a.	17,132	n.a.	50,753	93,672

Source: http://stats.uis.unesco.org/unesco/TableViewer/tableView.aspx?ReportId=171.
Notes: The data is the number of new Chinese students going to the country for that year. n.a. = not available.

the United States is slower but steadier. In 2005, Australia, Germany, and New Zealand ranked four, five, and six, respectively, in receiving Chinese students.

The rapid increase of Chinese students in Europe, Australia, and other non-U.S. countries has undoubtedly been spurred by the efforts of those countries to actively recruit students in China and in teaming up with Chinese universities. Some universities in those countries have even set up offices in China to market their programs and to recruit students. Europe is reforming its higher education and research, trying to become more competitive. Australia would like to see itself as the graduate education and research anchor for all of Asia. Therefore, high quality Chinese students would contribute to both graduate programs and research there, and the revenue derived from Chinese students would also be important to those education systems.

The significance of study abroad for higher education in China, especially in graduate education, can be seen in figure 8.2. It shows the ratio of students studying abroad to undergraduates who completed their degrees in that year. We can see that, since 1978, those going abroad to study have accounted for an increasing proportion of graduated college students, assuming that most students studying abroad pursue graduate degrees. The percentage reached more than 9 percent in 2002. In other words, about 10 percent of graduating Chinese college students in that year went to other countries to further their study. The ratio declined to around 3.5 percent in 2006, though. One reason for the declining proportion is the enrollment hike in China because students affected by the 1999 expansion in enrollment reached graduation time in 2002 to 2003.

On the other hand, the ratio of students studying abroad to domestic new graduate admissions is much higher, and it shows a stronger rising trend.

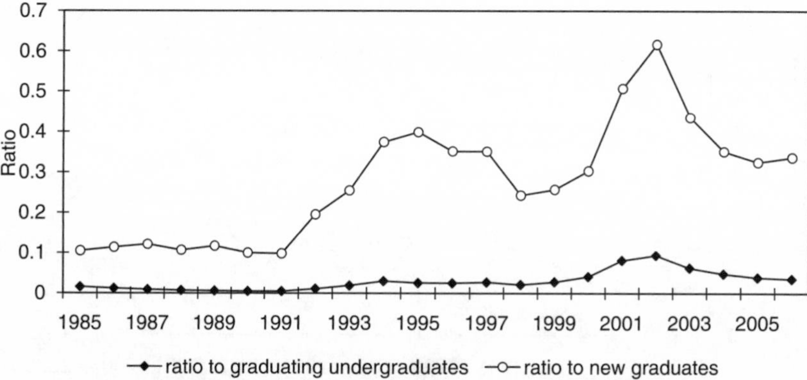

Fig. 8.2 The significance of studying abroad in China's higher education

Sources: National Bureau of Statistics of P.R. China (various years), *China Statistical Yearbook* (2006); Ministry of Education of the People's Republic of China (various years), *China Education Statistical Yearbook* (various years).

Note: The lower line is the ratio of the number of new students studying abroad to total undergraduate students graduated in China for that year. The upper line is ratio of the number of new students studying abroad to total new graduate students admitted in China for that year.

In particular, in 1995, the ratio was 40 percent, meaning that those going abroad for graduate education were almost 40 percent of those who stay home for graduate education. For most of the years since 1994, the number of Chinese students going abroad for graduate study is approximately one-third of those joining domestic graduate programs. Therefore, studying abroad is an important component for Chinese students after finishing an undergraduate degree.

However, the enrollment boom that started in 1999 does not seem to have significantly increased the flow of Chinese students studying abroad. The first wave of the enrollment boom started in 1999, and those students began to graduate in 2003. From 2003 to 2006, the average annual growth rate of graduation for undergraduate students and graduate students was 30 percent and 33 percent, respectively. Yet the annual average growth for studying abroad for the same period was merely 2 percent. The growth of studying abroad showed a different pattern, decreasing in both 2003 and 2004 and increasing only slightly in 2005. Therefore, the proportion of students studying abroad among those who newly completed their undergraduate and graduate degrees declined in this period.

It is unclear though whether the decline is caused by diminishing propensity to study abroad or by other social and economic factors. In general, the candidate pool for studying abroad is mostly recently graduated undergraduate students plus current graduate students. We calculate a proxy for study abroad propensity by dividing the number of students studying abroad by

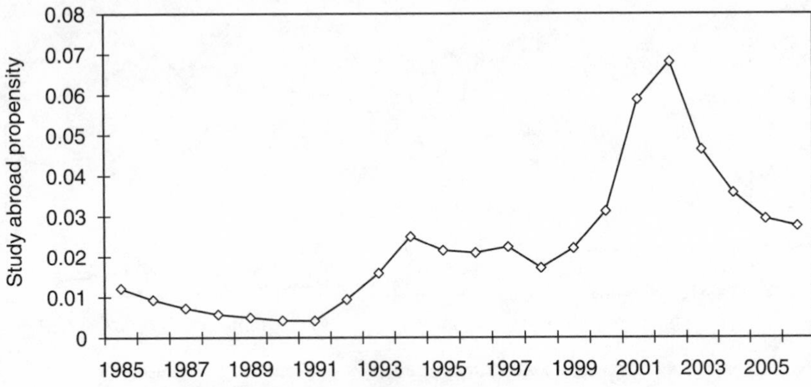

Fig. 8.3 Study abroad propensity (1985–2006)

Sources: National Bureau of Statistics of P.R. China (various years), *China Statistical Yearbook* (2006); Ministry of Education of the People's Republic of China (various years), *China Education Statistical Yearbook* (various years).

Note: Study abroad propensity year t = (students studying abroad in year t)/(total undergraduates completed the degree in year t + total graduate students enrollment in year t).

the candidate pool. Figure 8.3 shows the trend of the studying abroad propensity. The trend is generally upward until 2002 when it was 7 percent, and then the proxy declined continuously to around 3 percent in 2006. It appears that a smaller proportion of the students who benefited from expanded college admission studied abroad.

On the other hand, the Chinese government expanded the scope and scale in sponsoring graduate students to study in developed countries. In 2007, the Chinese government launched a new program called the Graduate Students Joint Training program (GSJT). This program sponsors first or second year doctoral students currently studying in universities in China to do dissertation work in a number of designated universities in developed countries for a period of one to two years, as well as provides partial financial support to the students who have been admitted into a formal graduate program to study for a graduate degree, mostly for doctoral degrees, for up to four years.[15] The funding comes from the China Scholarship Council (CSC), with a monthly stipend of approximately $1,000, plus a round-trip international airline ticket.[16] Based on the current government plan, from 2007 to 2011, China will support 5,000 GSTJ graduate students each year. To get an

15. In order to get the GSTJ's support for degree study in other countries, the student must obtain admission and tuition waiver from the overseas university. Because it is generally more competitive to get a tuition waiver, students supported by this program have been mostly nondegree students.

16. The China Scholarship Council (CSC) is a nonprofit institution affiliated with the Ministry of Education. The objective of the CSC is to provide financial assistance to Chinese citizens wishing to study abroad and to the foreign citizens wishing to study in China. The CSC is financed mainly by the state's special appropriations for scholarship programs.

idea of the magnitude of this program, in 2006, the total new enrollment of doctoral students was about 56,000. Thus, the scale of the GSJT program is almost one-tenth of all new doctoral students admitted into domestic programs.

The new GSJT program reflects a much more open view of the Chinese government on studying abroad. Traditionally, students studying abroad were viewed somewhat as "dissidents" and faced various restrictions from the government. Now, the Chinese government is starting to view higher education systems in developed countries as a part of the domestic higher education system and is interested in partnering with U.S. and other research universities around the world in an effort to train its own research talent who will return to China. Such a cooperative view on higher education is certainly a welcome development in China although it may take a while for universities in other countries to see the benefits of this program.

8.6 Chinese Students and Scholars in the United States

The number of Chinese students in the United States has risen in almost every year since 1979, reaching 81,127 in 2007. As shown in figure 8.4, the majority of Chinese students are in the United States for graduate studies. In general, undergraduate students, both international and domestic, are self-funded in the United States. It is likely that the number of Chinese undergraduate students will increase in the future, as tuition in U.S. universities becomes more affordable for Chinese families. A similar trend is possible for graduate students, especially for the professional master's programs (like

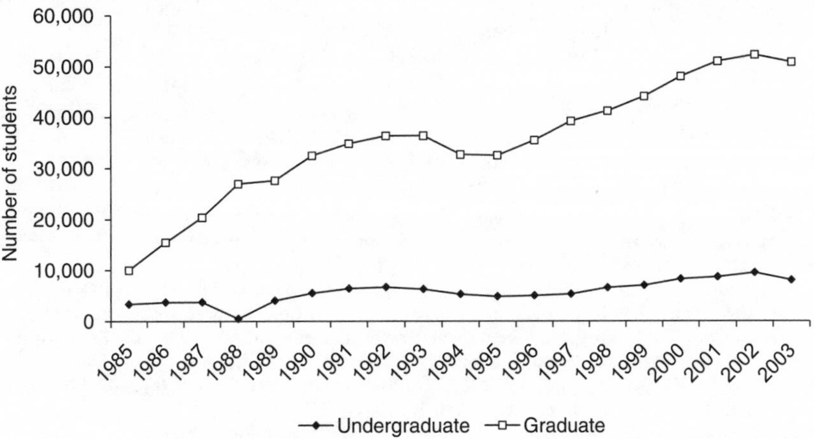

Fig. 8.4 Chinese graduate students and undergraduate students in the United States

Sources: Institute of International Education. 2007b. *Open Doors: Report on International Exchange (1948–2006),* CD version, New York. Data collected from tables for various years.

MBA) and PhD programs in non-STEM (Science, Technology, Engineering, and Mathematics) fields.

Table 8.7 lists the number of new Chinese students coming to the United States, as well as student flows from Taiwan, India, South Korea, and Japan. The flow of Chinese students to the United States with an F-visa increased steadily from 1997 to 2001 and then dropped for 2002 and 2003. A similar decline from 2002 to 2003 can be found for India. The September 11 attacks in 2001 and the related change in U.S. policy for foreign students might have contributed to the decline. However, the flow of students picked up speed between 2004 and 2005 and then accelerated. For the years 2006, 2007, and 2008, the annual growth of Chinese students coming to the United States with an F-visa was 27 percent, 35 percent, and 40 percent, respectively. The increase with J-visa students followed a similar pattern with a somewhat slower pace. It appears that, after slowing down in 2001 to 2003, the flow of Chinese students going abroad accelerated beginning in 2006, when the number of students grew 13 percent compared to 2005.

The trend in the flow of Chinese students to the United States and other

Table 8.7 **Foreign students in the United States, by type of visa, 1997–2007 (no. of persons)**

	China-Mainland		China-Taiwan		India		South Korea		Japan	
Year	F	J	F	J	F	J	F	J	F	J
1997	11,909	5,206	14,794	967	10,532	2,874	36,188	3,886	35,157	7,344
1998	13,958	6,462	13,867	995	12,154	2,855	21,271	3,087	34,063	7,605
1999	16,303	6,470	14,709	1,111	15,286	3,288	20,883	4,022	33,762	8,041
2000	21,586	7,708	16,084	1,274	20,469	3,740	27,520	5,525	32,661	8,304
2001	25,218	7,579	15,821	1,403	24,106	4,073	28,977	6,391	32,237	8,300
2002	21,784	6,790	13,952	1,629	20,771	3,626	26,670	7,399	25,036	7,638
2003	19,251	8,020	12,071	2,151	20,320	5,311	34,697	14,218	25,962	11,377
2004	21,227	9,459	14,880	2,472	19,567	4,838	35,365	15,169	25,581	10,810
2005	24,653	12,341	16,137	2,850	21,312	5,231	40,721	15,891	25,567	10,343
2006	31,199	15,098	17,398	3,508	27,555	5,932	49,414	16,706	24,435	9,922
2007	42,248	20,024	15,545	4,500	35,959	7,678	53,169	17,452	22,831	9,915
2008	58,942	25,792	15,165	5,498	37,890	8,815	56,309	17,157	20,714	9,382

Sources: Visa statistics report by U.S. Department of State, http://www.travel.state.gov/visa/frvi/statistics/statistics_4396.html; 2008: http://www.travel.state.gov/pdf/FY08-AR-TableXVII.pdf; 2007: http://www.travel.state.gov/pdf/FY07AnnualReportTableXVII.pdf; 2006: http://www.travel.state.gov/pdf/FY06NIVDetailTable.pdf; 2005: http://www.travel.state.gov/pdf/FY2005_NIV_Detail_Table.pdf; 2004: http://www.travel.state.gov/pdf/FY2004_NIV_Detail_Table.pdf; 2003: http://www.travel.state.gov/pdf/FY2003_NIV_Detail_Table.pdf; 2002: http://www.travel.state.gov/pdf/FY2002_NIV%20Detail_Table.pdf; 2001: http://www.travel.state.gov/pdf/FY2001_NIV%20Detail_Table.pdf; 1999: http://www.travel.state.gov/pdf/FY1999_NIV_Detail_Table.pdf; 1998: http://www.travel.state.gov/pdf/FY1998_NIV_Detail_Table.pdf; 1997: http://www.travel.state.gov/pdf/FY1997_NIV_Detail_Table.pdf.

Notes: F and J are two types of visas issued by the U.S. Department of State to foreign students and scholars coming to the United States for a short period of study or scholarly visit. Visa issuance includes the Border Crossing Cards. Also, we do not exclude possibilities that students who obtained an F or J visa and came to the United States for immigration purposes.

countries raises some interesting questions. What determines the flow of Chinese students studying abroad? How will the flow change over time as the higher education system in China expands and as the Chinese economy continues to grow?

It is possible that only the top students in China go abroad to study. If so, the expanded enrollment in China's higher education will not have much impact on this group. Also, the rapid expansion of graduate programs in China offers Chinese students more chances to do graduate study home, thus reducing the demand to further their studies in a foreign country. Additionally, it is also possible that, with growing career opportunities in China, students are becoming less interested in going abroad. Other factors hindering Chinese students' going abroad include restrictions placed by foreign universities and the economic condition in destination countries. For the United States, because some other countries, such as the United Kingdom, France, Australia, and New Zealand, are actively attracting Chinese students to their universities, such competition may take students away from the United States.

On the other hand, with the rapid increase in family income in China (magnified by the appreciation of the Chinese currency), the greater openness of the country, the higher degree of connections with universities around the world, and the relaxation of visa restrictions on Chinese students by foreign countries, more Chinese students may well decide to study abroad.

Among those Chinese students coming to study in the United States, many of them come for a doctoral degree. In 2006, the number of doctoral degrees awarded to Chinese students in the United States was 4,774 (table 8.8). This represents 30 percent of all doctoral degrees awarded to all foreign students and 10 percent of all doctoral degrees awarded in the United States for that year. In 2006, the number of doctoral degrees awarded in China was 36,247. Thus, the number of doctoral degrees awarded to Chinese students in the United States was 13 percent of the number of doctoral degrees awarded in China. In other words, U.S. universities have played a significant role in training Chinese doctorates. As a result, the total number of Chinese students who received a doctoral degree in both countries in 2006, 41,021, was more than the total of doctoral degrees awarded to all non-Chinese students in the United States.

Table 8.9 shows the number of U.S. doctoral degrees in science and engineering (S&E) earned by students from China, India, and Korea, the top countries for foreign-born PhDs in the United States. In every year from 1996 to 2006, the number of doctorates earned by Chinese students in S&E was larger than the combined number of doctorates in S&E earned by students from India and South Korea. Since 2004, for both Chinese and Indian students, the number of doctorates has increased at a very fast pace, much faster than that for Korean students, a fact probably related to the economic boom in those two countries.

Table 8.8 **Doctoral degrees awarded in China and in the United States (no. of persons)**

	Doctoral students in China			Doctoral degrees awarded in the United States			
Year	Total enrollment	New enrollment	Awarded	To Chinese students	To all foreign students	To U.S. citizens	Total awarded
1983	737	172	4			24,393	31,280
1984	1,243	492	39			24,045	31,334
1985	3,639	2,633	287			23,388	31,295
1986	5,654	2,248	284			23,097	31,897
1987	8,969	3,615	464			22,984	32,365
1988	10,525	3,262	1,583			23,290	33,497
1989	10,998	2,776	2,046			23,402	34,325
1990	11,345	3,337	2,457			24,913	36,065
1991	12,331	4,172	2,610			25,583	37,530
1992	14,558	5,036	2,528			26,009	38,886
1993	17,570	6,150	2,940			26,449	39,800
1994	22,660	9,038	3,723			27,150	41,033
1995	28,752	11,056	4,641			27,740	41,747
1996	35,203	12,562	5,430			27,777	42,437
1997	39,927	12,917		2,408	11,390	28,160	42,539
1998	45,246	14,962	8,957	2,571	42,683	28,456	42,637
1999	54,038	19,915	10,320	2,400	11,368	27,986	41,097
2000	67,293	25,142	11,004	2,594	11,597	27,986	41,365
2001	85,885	32,093	12,867	2,670	11,602	26,907	40,737
2002	108,737	38,342	14,638	2,644	11,353	25,936	40,025
2003	137,000	48,740	18,806	2,784	12,063	26,413	40,757
2004	165,610	53,284	23,446	3,209	13,000	26,431	42,123
2005	191,317	54,794	27,677	3,827	14,225	26,312	43,385
2006	208,038	55,955	36,247	4,774	15,916	26,917	45,596

Sources: National Bureau of Statistics of P.R. China (2005), "Comprehensive Statistical Data and Materials on 55 Years of New China"; National Bureau of Statistics of P.R. China (various years), *China Statistical Yearbook* (2003–2006); Ministry of Education of the People's Republic of China (2007), "The Statistic Communiqué of Education Development in 2006; NSF/NIH/USED/NEH/USDA/NASA, Survey of Earned Doctorates; the Doctorate Recipients from United States Universities Summary Reports, http://www.norc.org/projects/Survey+of+Earned+Doctorates.htm (various years).

Notes: The total awarded does not equal the sum of all foreign students and U.S. citizens because of the group of unknown citizenship. Blank cells indicate "not available."

Table 8.10 provides some information on specific fields in S&E. The table shows that from 1985 to 2000, there were a total of 28,698 Chinese students who earned doctoral degrees in the United States, and 92.5 percent of them were in S&E. Among different fields, engineering has the most recipients, accounting for more than 25 percent, followed by biological sciences, accounting for 24 percent. The physical sciences have the third most recipients, accounting for 22 percent. Although the number of Chinese doctorates from the mainland is much larger than that from Taiwan, India, and South Korea, the number in non-S&E is much smaller. Clearly, students from mainland China have been mostly focused on S&E when pursuing the

Table 8.9 **Non-U.S. citizens earning science/engineering (S&E) doctorates at U.S. institutions by country, 1996–2006 (no. of persons)**

Year	China	India	South Korea
1996	3,033	1,287	991
1997	2,395	1,281	901
1998	2,502	1,134	822
1999	2,233	915	760
2000	2,378	834	753
2001	2,404	817	865
2002	2,401	681	856
2003	2,495	769	956
2004	2,877	863	1,056
2005	3,448	1,103	1,170
2006	4,323	1,524	1,219

Source: NSF Division of Science Resources Statistics, *Survey of Earned Doctorates.*

Table 8.10 **Asian recipients of U.S. science/engineering (S&E) doctorates by field and country/economy of origin, 1985–2000 (no. of persons)**

Field	China	Taiwan	India	South Korea	Total of these four countries/economies
Physical sciences	6,356	1,923	1,856	1,852	11,987
Earth, atmospheric, and ocean sciences	972	327	180	252	1,731
Mathematics	1,954	614	438	579	3,585
Computer/information sciences	673	839	1,178	531	3,221
Engineering	7,207	7,518	6,146	5,052	25,923
Biological sciences	6,790	2,175	1,766	1,520	12,251
Agricultural sciences	901	601	316	515	2,333
Psychology/social sciences	1,681	1,490	1,394	2,954	7,519
Non-S&E	2,164	3,021	2,755	3,820	11,760
S&E	26,534	15,487	13,274	13,255	68,550
All fields	28,698	18,508	16,029	17,075	80,310

Source: NSF Division of Science Resources Statistics, *Survey of Earned Doctorates,* special tabulations (2003)

Note: Foreign doctorate recipients include permanent and temporary residents.

highest degree in the United States. Comparing table 8.8 and table 8.9, we can see that, even in recent years, most doctoral degrees awarded to Chinese students are in S&E, approximately 90 percent. One important reason for such a field distribution is the funding opportunities.

Given the large number of Chinese students studying in the United States, it is clear that American universities play a significant role in providing higher education to Chinese students, especially in graduate education. On the other hand, foreign recipients of U.S. doctoral degrees are an important part of the internationally mobile, high-skilled labor force. When they return to their home countries after completing their degrees, they add to the stock of potential leaders in research and education, making those countries more competitive in related fields. Those who remain in the United States enhance the competitiveness of U.S. enterprises and universities. Many Chinese students stay in the United States to work after graduation and, thus, make contributions to the U.S. economy. Given the competitive labor market in the United States, Chinese students who get a job in the United States after graduation must be at least as productive as any others in the same job.

Ultimately, the supply of highly educated Chinese students to the U.S. labor market is determined by their intention to stay in the United States. Table 8.11 provides information on intentions to stay in the United States for U.S. doctorates in S&E. It shows that the intent to stay is the highest for students from mainland China, much higher than for students from Japan, South Korea, and Taiwan. In 1998 to 2001, more than 96 percent of Chinese students who earned doctorates in the period planned to stay in the United States. These high stay rates are perhaps largely attributable to the higher income, better environment, and higher level of social stability available in the United States. Interestingly, when it comes to firm plans to stay (those reporting accepting firm offers), the percentage of Chinese doctorates is smaller than that for Indian doctorates, suggesting that Chinese doctorate recipients may be less likely to find jobs than those from India. One likely reason is differences in English language proficiency.

Research by Finn (2007) confirms the high stay rates of foreign-born doctoral recipients in general and for those from China in particular. Of foreign citizens who received S&E doctorates from U.S. universities in 2003, two-thirds still lived in the United States in 2005. As can be seen from table 8.12, among those who came to the United States on temporary visas and got their doctoral degrees during the years 1990 to 1991, 79 percent from

Table 8.11 **Plans of foreign recipients of U.S. science/engineering (S&E) doctorates to remain in the United States, by place of origin, 1990–2001 (%)**

	Plans to remain			Firm plans to remain		
Place of origin	1990–1993	1994–1997	1998–2001	1990–1993	1994–1997	1998–2001
All non-U.S. citizens	63.4	69.3	76.3	40.9	43.3	54.1
East/South Asia	68.6	75.4	83.2	44.1	46.2	58.5
China	93.5	96.6	96.2	58.0	57.3	67.5
Taiwan	56.0	54.3	68.8	33.8	28.9	42.2
Japan	42.7	44.0	54.9	29.6	31.6	36.8
South Korea	38.7	42.3	65.7	24.4	25.8	45.1
India	85.6	90.1	94.0	62.6	61.8	73.2

Source: NSF Division of Science Resources Studies, *Survey of Earned Doctorates,* http://www.nsf.gov/statistics/seind04/append/c2/at02-31.xls.

Note: Firm plans include plans for future education and employment.

Table 8.12 Percentage of foreign students on temporary visas receiving science/engineering doctorates who remain in the United States (%)

Country of origin	1987–1988 doctorate recipients in 1992	1990–1991 doctorate recipients in 1995	1992–1993 doctorate recipients in 1997	1994–1995 doctorate recipients in 1999	1996 doctorate recipients in 2001	1998 doctorate recipients in 2003	2000 doctorate recipients in 2005
China	65	88	92	91	96	90	92
India	72	79	83	87	86	86	85
United Kingdom	n/a	59	56	60	53	60	58
Canada	32	46	48	55	62	58	56
Greece	44	41	46	49	53	60	54
Germany	n.a.	35	38	53	48	51	49
Taiwan	47	42	36	42	40	47	50
Japan	17	13	21	27	24	37	39
Brazil	13	25	15	21	25	25	30
Korea	17	11	9	15	21	34	42
All average	41	47	53	51	56	61	65

Source: This table is taken from Finn (2007), table 8; Oak Ridge Associated Universities, http://orise.orau.gov/sep/files/stayrate07.pdf.

India and 88 percent from China were still working in the United States in 1995. In contrast, only 11 percent of the corresponding group from South Korea were still in the United States in 1995. Since 1990, the stay rate of Chinese doctorates has been the highest among the countries shown, averaging 90 percent. Countries whose doctoral recipients have the lowest stay rates include Korea and Japan. The high stay rate of Chinese doctorates in the United States has made them become an important component in the U.S. academic labor force.

To learn where Chinese scholars are in American universities, we collected data for a sample of ninety-five universities.[17] Most of them are among the top 100 colleges and universities as ranked by *U.S. News & World Report.* Those ninety-five institutions had 6,230 Chinese faculty members, accounting for 3 percent of total faculty size. Table 8.13 lists the institutions with the largest number and share of Chinese faculty. The University of Michigan and the University of Pittsburgh had the largest number of Chinese faculty; Stevens Institute of Technology and the Georgia Institute of Technology had the largest shares.

Although data are lacking on both the rate of growth in Chinese faculty and its size relative to faculty from other nations, it is reasonable to expect that the absolute and relative size will continue to grow, given the large number of Chinese students now in the United States. The career paths of American-trained Chinese students, most of whom are top students from China, reveal an interesting dynamic in what is effectively the integration of higher education among these two countries. In this sense, higher education in China and the United States is complementary and mutually beneficial.

8.7 Enticing Foreign-Trained Chinese Scholars to Return Home

Before 1992, very few Chinese students who received graduate degrees in the United States and other countries returned to China. In the United States, Chinese doctorates worked in academia, industry, and even government. Together with other highly educated Chinese students, they quickly entered the American middle class after graduation. In order to attract such well-established scholars to return to work in China, the Chinese government has adopted a number of preferential policies specifically aimed at them. Those policies provide attractive packages, including relatively high compensation, generous research support, and prestigious awards.

For example, in 1998, The Ministry of Education and the Li Ka Shing Foundation in Hong Kong jointly established the Changjiang Scholar Fellowship program. This program sets up the "Changjiang Professorship,"

17. Those schools are chosen because they hosted more than five Chinese graduate students sponsored by the GSJT program in 2007. Details about the sample can be found in Ding and Li (2009).

Table 8.13 **U.S. universities with the largest number and the highest percentage of Chinese faculty, 2007**

Institute	Chinese faculty (no. of persons)	Chinese faculty to total faculty ratio (%)
By number of Chinese faculty		
University of Michigan, Ann Arbor	139	2.6
University of Pittsburgh, Pittsburgh	133	3.1
University of Missouri, Kansas City	131	7.0
University of California, Los Angeles	129	3.6
Cornell University	127	6.2
Purdue University, West Lafayette	124	4.5
Ohio State University, Columbus	122	2.9
Vanderbilt University	120	3.8
Yale University	119	3.6
University of Florida	111	2.3
By percentage of Chinese faculty		
Stevens Institute of Technology	56	11.6
Georgia Institute of Technology	69	7.6
University of Missouri, Kansas City	131	7.0
University of Missouri, Rolla	32	6.8
Case Western Reserve University	87	5.5
Baylor College of Medicine	105	5.5
Rensselaer Polytechnic Institute	27	5.5
University of California, Riverside	43	5.2
The University of Texas, Arlington	57	5.1

Source: Ding and Li (2009).

the "Changjiang Lecture Professorship," and the "Changjiang Scholar Achievement Award" in Chinese universities and research institutes. A Changjiang Professor is expected to work in the awarding institute at least nine months, and a Changjiang Lecture Professor at least two months. Changjiang Scholars are expected to play a leading role in research, in building research and graduate programs, in teaching core courses, and in advising young scholars and graduate students. From 1998 to 2006, there were 803 Changjiang Professors, 304 Changjiang Lecture Professors, and 14 Changjiang Scholar Achievement Awards bestowed in ninety-seven Chinese universities.[18] Among those Changjiang scholars, 94 percent had studied or worked overseas, a figure showing that a majority of China's leading scholars have some training in other countries. Of those named Changjiang Professors, 231 (or 29 percent of the total) were overseas scholars, whereas all 304 Chang-jiang Lecture Professorships were awarded to overseas scholars, including some prominent non-Chinese scholars.

Following the Changjiang scholarship program of the central govern-

18. See http://www.cksp.edu.cn/news/16/16-20070319-136.htm.

ment, provincial governments and universities established similar fellowship programs to attract well-established scholars, such as the "Furong Scholar Fellowship" program in Hunan Province and the "Zhujiang Scholar Fellowship" in Guangdong province. Although such local fellowships are not as prestigious as the Changjiang fellowship, their funding amounts are comparable. Such funding has become one of the important channels to attract established overseas scholars into the higher education sector in China.

In addition, the Natural National Science Foundation of China (NSFC) also sets up specific funds to support overseas scholars to do research in China. For example, it established the "Distinguished Young Scholar" fund for overseas scholars in 2005. Recipients of this fund must work full time in China to do research. The program granted RMB 9.4 million in 2005, increasing to RMB 24 million and 20 million in 2006 and 2007, respectively.[19] In order to encourage joint research, the NSFC has also established the Joint Research Fund for Overseas Chinese Young Scholars to do joint research with a Chinese institute. All of those research resources provide incentives for overseas Chinese scholars to collaborate with researchers in China or to return to work in China permanently.

With more internationally established scholars working in Chinese universities, young Chinese scholars and especially fresh PhDs in other countries have begun to consider universities in China in their job search. Taking a faculty position in a university in China is becoming much more acceptable than in the past and is sometimes a better option for many fresh Chinese PhDs or even senior scholars in foreign countries, including some in the United States.

In the meantime, universities in China have started to actively recruit faculty overseas. Although detailed data on the recruiting efforts of universities in China are still not available, we are able to collect data for the economics field via *Job Openings for Economists* (*JOE*), published by the American Economic Association (AEA). Every year in early January, the AEA, in conjunction with approximately fifty associations in related disciplines, holds a large scale annual meeting in the United States, as part of the Allied Social Science Association (ASSA) annual convention. In this convention, the AEA provides a job placement service to which universities and some nonacademic employers submit their job opening advertisements for economists (mostly with PhDs in economics). In addition, the *JOE* publishes job openings on a regular basis.

The archives of *JOE* reveal a marked increase in recruiting by Chinese universities and research institutes. The first year that Chinese universities listed job openings was 1995. Two units listed job openings for this year, Peking University's China Center for Economic Research and Nanjing Uni-

19. See http://www.nsfc.gov.cn/nsfc2008/index.htm. In this period, the exchange rate was approximately $1 = RMB 7.0 to 8.0.

versity's Hopkins-Nanjing Center. After that, from 1996 to 1999, Hopkins-Nanjing Center was the only employer listed. In 2000 and 2001, Peking University was the sole employer, and in 2002 and 2003, Tshinghua University began recruiting at the AEA meetings. In 2004, another university, Shanghai University of Finance and Economics started to recruit faculty in the ASSA placement market, and it listed ten openings for that year. Since then, the number of schools and institutes recruiting in the ASSA market increased very quickly, reaching eight and seven in 2005 and 2006. The number doubled to fourteen in 2007 (plus three other research institutes). As the number of Chinese universities recruiting in the American academic job market increased, so did the total number of positions. Whereas the total number of economics faculty positions from China in the ASSA job market was below ten until 2003, the number increased to 108 in 2005 and 2006 and was eighty in 2007.[20]

Given the large gaps in salary between universities in China and in the United States, the biggest concern for job candidates considering a job in China is likely to be the level of compensation. In 2002, Tsinghua University was the first to publish a salary range in its *JOE* advertisement: $25,000 to $75,000 plus housing subsidies and research support. Although that salary was not high by U.S. standards, it was five to ten times the salary earned by faculty members with the same rank in that university, and it was in the very highest percentile of all salaries in China. Since then, it has become common for Chinese universities to put a salary range in their *JOE* job advertisements. In 2007, the highest advertised salary was from Shanghai University of Finance and Economics, in the range of $43,000 to $214,000. Given the relatively low cost of living in China, such a pay scale is becoming increasingly attractive, especially with the additional housing subsidy and research support.

In order to find more detailed information about faculty hiring packages from universities in China and to assess their competitiveness, we conducted a survey of Chinese universities. The survey covers seven of the fourteen universities recruiting economics faculty in the ASSA job market in 2007. All seven are major Chinese universities and have been listed in the *JOE* for three or more years. The survey questionnaire was completed by the chairs or deans to provide information for their departments or colleges. Because some universities have multiple departments engaged in hiring, our sample includes a total of ten departments from those seven universities.

Based on the survey, the faculty size varies dramatically in those departments, from 3 to 140. This is because some departments are newly established. So far, there are two hiring models for adding faculty members with

20. The number for 2005 and 2006 should be interpreted with caution because one school, Southwestern University of Finance and Economics, advertised fifty and forty positions in the *JOE* for those two years, respectively.

overseas doctoral degrees. One is to add new faculty members to the existing faculty in a department but with different pay schemes and evaluation standards. The other one is to set up an entirely new department for overseas faculty. The latter model is easier to implement, as it can reduce potential conflicts between faculty groups caused by the huge differences in pay scale and promotion standards. A direct consequence of these policies is that the ratio of U.S. trained faculty is very high, 45 percent on average for full-time faculty and as high as 97 percent in the sample.

Because tenured, senior faculty members in the United States are generally difficult to recruit, due to the uncertainty associated with positions in China, most Chinese with doctorates in economics who return to China are fresh PhDs. But senior faculty members from overseas are generally in very high demand, owing to the need to build programs, to mentor young faculty and to advise graduate students. In order to find a practical way to recruit senior faculty from the United States, many universities in China have established some type of special-term professorship, which is a part-time position specifically designed for overseas senior faculty members. Such professors can go to teach at the Chinese university during summer break or during sabbatical leave. To accommodate such short-term appointments, many universities in China have set up specially condensed courses or even condensed semesters. These short-term professors serve to bolster Chinese programs by teaching courses and advising graduate students. In our survey, the average number of special-term professors was about four, and the ratio of special-term professors with U.S. academic appointments to full-time faculty with U.S. PhD degrees averaged 0.65. These findings suggest that the flexible special-term professorship plays an important role in overseas faculty recruiting.

Learning from the policy of establishing special economic zones in China, Chinese universities established new departments, institutes, and centers subject to special policies on recruiting, promotion, and compensation. In such "Special Platforms," teaching is mostly in English, special-term faculty members are mostly from the United States and Europe, full-time faculty are mostly those with PhD degrees from the United States and Europe, and the system is similar to the American academic system. Moreover, in order to start at a higher level in education and research, most newly established departments and programs have hired as director (or chair or dean), on a part-time basis, a senior overseas faculty member. This overseas director normally resides in China during summer and winter breaks and works on program building (not teaching). In our survey, 70 percent of departments or academic units have an overseas head. The obvious advantage of having a director and special-term professors from overseas is that they can help to quickly build the program to international standards and to attract more faculty members from overseas. This reflects the combination of competition and cooperation, noted in the preceding, between universities in China and in the United States and around the world.

Table 8.14 **Information on recruiting packages for U.S.-trained faculty in economics**

Survey indicator	Average From	Average To	Min.	Max.	No. of observations
Junior starting salary	36,143	43,429	28,571	57,143	10
Senior starting salary	47,143	67,143	42,857	78,571	5
Junior annual housing subsidy	6,589	7,244	3,429	9,571	8
Junior housing subsidy (in years)	4		3	6	8
Junior annual research support	5,486	6,771	2,857	14,286	10
Senior annual housing subsidy	8,524	11,952	6,857	26,190	5
Senior housing subsidy (in years)	5.6		3	10	5
Senior annual research support	5,095	6,048	2,857	11,429	6

Source: The survey of overseas faculty recruiting in economics from universities in China, 2008.

Note: Numbers are U.S. dollars unless otherwise indicated.

The survey revealed ambitious plans for expansion. On average, the surveyed departments planned to hire over the following three years more than thirteen new faculty members from overseas, or about four a year. This number of planned overseas hires would far exceed the existing number of U.S. trained faculty and would, if acted on, lead to more than doubling of overseas faculty in three years.

Table 8.14 provides information on the compensation packages that are being used to recruit overseas faculty. The average starting salary offered for a fresh PhD in economics in 2008 was approximately $36,000 to $43,000 and could go as high as $57,000. Housing subsidies offered for a limited number of years were in the range of $6,600 to $7,200 per year, and annual research support for junior faculty was in the range of $5,500 to $6,800. Compensation packages for senior faculty were generally higher, with a base salary ranging from $47,000 to $67,000, on average. This compares to an average in the United States of $118,000 for full professors in 2007.[21] Although the typical salary plus housing subsidy offered by Chinese universities is still low by U.S. standards, it is at least close to the U.S. range. Moreover, the cost of living is much lower in China, the teaching loads in China (two to three semester courses per year) tend to be lower than in most economics departments in the United States, and the annual research support is comparable to that in the United States.

On the strength of hiring packages such as these, universities in China have become more competitive in recruiting Chinese faculty in the U.S. academic market. As evidence, consider the responses given to the survey question asking the name of two top universities in the United States from

21. This is based on American Association of University Professors (AAUP); in 2007, for doctoral institutes, the average salary for an assistant professor is $68,112, and for an associate professor and a full professor is $80,043 and $118,044, respectively. See "The Annual Report on the Economic Status of the Profession, 2007–08," http://www.aaup.org/.

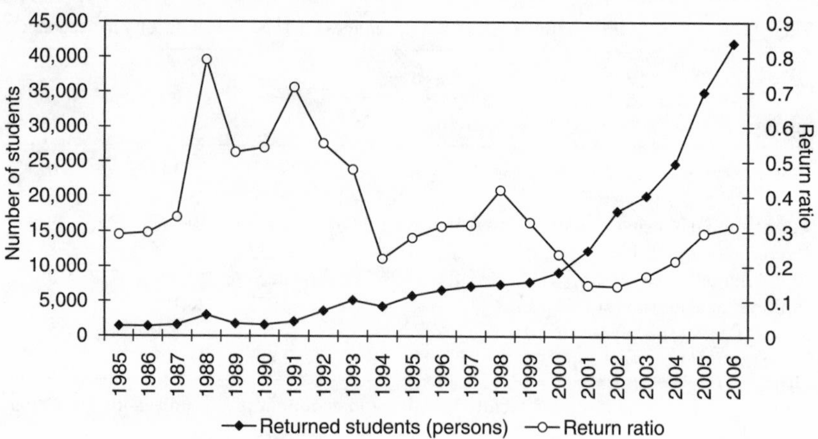

Fig. 8.5 Chinese students returned to China

Sources: National Bureau of Statistics of P.R. China (various years), *China Statistical Yearbook* (2006); Ministry of Education of the People's Republic of China (various years), *China Education Statistical Yearbook* (various years).

Note: Return ratio = the ratio of returned Chinese students to those going abroad to study for that year.

which their U.S.-trained full-time faculty members received their degrees. The answers included top-ranked institutions like Harvard, Princeton, Stanford, and Berkeley.

As a result of all these efforts, in aggregate, the number of Chinese students with overseas degrees who returned to work in China began to grow at an accelerated pace after 2000, reaching 42,000 in 2006, as shown in figure 8.5. Between 2002 and 2006, the average annual growth in returned students and scholars was 29 percent, which is higher than the growth rate of those going abroad to study.[22] Although there are still many more students going abroad than returning home (in 2006, the number who returned was 31 percent of those who left China), the ratio of those who returned to those going abroad has shown a steady increase. It will be interesting to see whether this trend continues.

8.8 Challenges and Conclusions

This chapter discusses the higher education system in China and the study-abroad behavior of Chinese students, focusing on those in the United

22. For recent anecdotal evidence on the return of Chinese scholars in other fields, see, for example, "Back-to-China Syndrome," *Business Week,* September 15, 2008, 53, and "China Entices Its Scholars to Come Home," *The Chronicle of Higher Education,* December 19, 2008.

States. In the era of globalization, higher education in most countries is not isolated. This is especially the case for China as it becomes more integrated into the world. Additionally, because of the large number of Chinese students and scholars studying abroad, the development of higher education in China will also inevitably affect universities in other countries.

We show that China's higher education has been growing rapidly since the beginning of economic reforms, made possible with the resources generated by rapid economic growth. However, there are still many challenges facing China's higher education. First, rising college tuition makes higher education an increasing financial burden for Chinese families (see Wang et al. 2009). Since 1989, China's higher education began to transform from tuition-free (with some living allowances to students) to tuition-based. By 1997, tuition became mandatory in all colleges in China. By 2002, the average tuition per student had reached 46 percent of per capita gross domestic product (GDP), roughly the same ratio for private colleges and universities in the United States.[23] Second, the rapid expansion of college enrollments has probably had a negative impact on job placement. In 2003, the job placement rate for college graduates was only about 70 percent. The slower growth in college admissions in 2005 and 2006 may improve the job prospects for college graduates if economic growth remains steady.[24]

A third problem lies in the objectives and quality of graduate programs. The objective of master's programs is not well defined in China. It is unclear whether such programs are for training researchers or just for a professional degree. Moreover, doctoral programs in China generally need dramatic improvement in quality, design, and curriculum in order to train the best researchers. Unfortunately, such an effort has been hindered by the fact that a large number of government officials and business executives are getting their doctoral degrees, mostly in economics and business-related disciplines, on a part-time basis. Such desire for "window dressing" from those in control of administrative and financial resources compromises efforts to improve doctoral education in China and makes doctoral education, especially in social science and humanity fields, to some extent, effectively an Executive Master of Business Administration (EMBA) type program. A final challenge is still the central planning administrative system for higher education. Unlike much of the economy, which is in transition toward a market system,

23. The tuition and enrollment data include only regular institutes of higher education. The ratio for the United States is based on a per capita GDP of $37,626 for 2003 and an average tuition for private four-year institutions of $16,826, yielding a ratio of 0.45. U.S. Council of Economic Advisers, *Economic Report of the President,* 2008, table B-31, http://www.gpoaccess.gov/eop/tables08.html, 2/5/09; U.S. Department of Education, *Digest of Education Statistics,* 2007, table 320, http://nces.ed.gov/programs/digest/d07/tables/dt07_320.asp, 2/5/09.

24. The placement rate is based on the September number of that year, *China Education Statistical Yearbook* (various years), and http://edu.people.com.cn/GB/8216/52456/52459/106207/index.html.

the higher education system in China is still largely centrally planned. Government intervention is observed in almost every aspect of teaching and research in universities.

In the face of so many challenges, an effective strategy to improve Chinese universities is to continue to engage with universities in developed countries. From its earliest days, China's modern higher education system has been influenced by foreign countries. Many Chinese students have gone abroad to receive the best education in world-class universities, making foreign universities a significant part of the education of Chinese students, especially at the graduate level. Chinese scholars and faculty who return to China help improve the quality of higher education in China. At the same time, many overseas Chinese students contribute to the economies in the hosting countries through their employment after graduation. Moreover, Chinese faculty in increasing numbers contributes to higher education in those countries as well. Such dynamics between universities in China and in other countries help to reinforce the mutual positive impact on higher education on both sides.

The large number of Chinese students in the United States makes it impossible to ignore the impact of the development of China's higher education system on American universities. First, high quality Chinese students and Chinese faculty should help make American universities more competitive. Second, the increasing number of Chinese students with self-funding may also contribute to the financial resources of American universities. Moreover, the collaboration between Chinese and American universities will help to expand education and research experiences for American students and faculty.

Therefore, although higher education in China will continue to expand, for the foreseeable future, a large portion of best students from Chinese universities will still come to the United States to further their education. Given the big economic and political gap between China and the United States, many of the best trained Chinese students in the United States will be likely to stay to work in the United States after graduation, especially in American universities. In this sense, Chinese universities are a complement to American universities.

On the other hand, the accelerating return of established Chinese scholars from overseas—spurred by the aggressive recruiting policies of Chinese universities—may help to speed up the process of building world-class programs in China. As a result, some Chinese students may choose to stay home for further education instead of going abroad, and more international students may come to China to study. Universities in China are starting to compete with American universities in faculty recruiting and in attracting students. Thus, there are some signs that Chinese universities compete with American universities.

Given the significant differences between the Chinese and the United

States' higher education systems as well as in their economic and political systems, it seems likely that the relative standing of Chinese and American universities will not change significantly in the foreseeable future. In recent years, the Chinese government and universities have shown greater openness in higher education, and they are willing to partner with world-class universities around the world in order to promote their own schools to the elite status among world universities. The combination of competition and cooperation between universities in China and in other countries is most likely the model for the future, and such a model should have a positive impact on higher education in the world.

References

Ding, Lan, and Haizheng Li. 2009. Social network and study abroad: The case of Chinese students in the US. Georgia Institute of Technology, School of Economics, Working Paper.

Fazackerley, Anna, and Philip Worthington. 2007. British universities in China: The reality beyond the rhetoric. Agora Discussion Paper. http://www.agora-education.org.

Finn, Michael G. 2007. Stay rates of foreign doctorate recipients from U.S. universities, 2005. Oak Ridge Institute for Science and Education. http://orise.orau.gov/sep/files/stayrate07.pdf.

Institute of International Education. 2007a. Educational exchange between the United States and China. IIE Briefing Paper. New York: IIE, July.

———. 2007b. *Open doors: Report on international exchange (1948–2004).* New York: IIE.

Liu, Nian Cai. 2007. Research universities in China: Differentiation, classification, and future world-class status. In *World-class worldwide—Transforming research universities in Asia and Latin America,* ed. Philip G. Altbach and Jorge Balan, 54–69. Baltimore: Johns Hopkins University Press.

Ma, Wanhua. 2007. The flagship university and China's economic reform. In *World-class worldwide—Transforming research universities in Asia and Latin America,* ed. Philip G. Altbach and Jorge Balan, 31–53. Baltimore: Johns Hopkins University Press.

Ministry of Education of the People's Republic of China. 2007. The statistic communiqué of education development in 2006. Beijing: May. Available at: http://www.stats.edu.cn/tjdt/tjdt20070608.htm.

———. Various years. *China education statistical yearbook.* Beijing: People's Education Press.

National Bureau of Statistics of P.R. China. 2005. Comprehensive statistical data and materials on 55 years of new China. Beijing: China Statistics Press.

———. Various years. *China statistical yearbook.* Beijing: China Statistics Press.

National Science Foundation (NSF). 2006. *Survey of earned doctorates.* http://www.norc.org/projects/Survey+of+Earned+Doctorates.htm.

State Statistical Bureau. Various years. *China statistical yearbook.* Beijing: China Statistical Publishing House, China Statistical Information and Consultancy Center.

UNESCO Institutes of Statistics. http://stats.uis.unesco.org/unesco/TableViewer/tableView.aspx.

Wang, Xiaojun, Belton Fleisher, Haizheng Li, and Shi Li. 2009. Access to higher education and inequality: The Chinese experiment. Ohio State University, Department of Economics. Working Paper.

Xin, Hao, and Dennis Normile. 2008. Gunning for the ivy league. *Science* 319 (January): 148–51.

Yang, Rui. 2005. Higher education in the People's Republic of China: Historical traditions, recent developments and major issues. Paper presented at 5th national and the 4th international conference, Challenges and Expectations of the University: Experiences and Dilemmas of the Reformation, Tamaulipas, Mexico.

9

Indian Higher Education

Devesh Kapur

9.1 Introduction

If physical capital—its growth and distribution—was central to debates on economic development in the twentieth century, human capital increasingly occupies center stage (Kapur and Crowley 2008). While much of the attention has been on primary education, tertiary education is increasingly receiving greater attention. However, the very promise of higher education for developing countries is also making this a politically contentious issue. Because universities influence the minds of young adults, they have always been sites of politics. Increasingly, however, a growing awareness of the distributional implications of higher education has led to issues of access and financing becoming more salient (often at the expense of quality). Many of the underlying handicaps faced by students from lower socioeconomic groups appear to occur much earlier in the life cycle—at the primary and secondary school level—but policies to overcome these handicaps seem to be more politically expeditious in higher education. Unsurprisingly, the attention to higher education in developing countries has focused mainly on its economic effects, especially its links with labor markets. However, there is little understanding about the how the impact of higher education is mediated by the type of education and its beneficiaries.

The paper first outlines the principal characteristics of Indian higher education and its recent rapid growth, especially the number of students and

Devesh Kapur is director of the Center for Advanced Study of India and Madan Lal Sobti Associate Professor for the Study of Contemporary India at the University of Pennsylvania.

I am grateful to Arvind Pangariya and other discussants at the conference for their comments and suggestions. I am especially grateful to Charles Clotfelter for his detailed comments. Ritu Kamal and Arjun Raychaudhuri provided excellent research assistance.

institutions, the fields of study, and the sources of supply. The next section focuses on the key challenges facing Indian higher education resulting from a massive increase in the demand for higher education. What are the specific fields of higher education for this growing demand, and how is it being met? It then analyzes two key questions: why, despite India's robust growth and a legacy of one of the better higher education systems in developing countries, has quality deteriorated so markedly? And, second, if quality is indeed poor, then why is this not manifestly handicapping India's rapid growth? It concludes with some questions on possible nonlabor market effects of the current structure of Indian higher education.

9.2 Growth

The past quarter century has seen a massive expansion in higher education worldwide and especially in developing countries, reflecting shifting demographics, changing economic structures, and significant improvements in access to primary and secondary education. Tertiary education is a rapidly growing service sector, enrolling more than 80 million students worldwide and employing about 3.5 million people. Demand pressures have been acute, the result of a population bulge in the relevant age group, increasing enrollment in secondary education, increasing incomes (and with it the capacity to pay), and rising wage premiums accruing from higher education. Meeting this escalating demand has placed public systems and resources under severe strain. And because this demand group is more urban and vocal, it also poses major political challenges.

As countries and university systems strain under the pressure of increasing demand, new supply responses are rapidly changing the higher education landscape in most countries. The financing, provision, and regulation of higher education are witnessing two major shifts. The first is from pure public to private and mixed systems; the second is a shift from provision and regulation that has traditionally been purely domestic to greater international influence. These trends broadly mimic what has been occurring in almost all aspects of the economy. This is true in India as well—but, if anything, the trend toward the private provision of higher education is even greater.

9.2.1 Indian Higher Education: Basic Facts and Trends

In 1950 to 1951 India had twenty-seven universities, which included 370 colleges for general education and 208 colleges for professional education (engineering, medicine, education). The system has grown rapidly, especially since the mid-1980s, with student enrollment growing at about 5 percent annually over the past two decades. This growth is about two-and-half times the population growth rate and results from both a population bulge in lower age cohorts as well as increased demand for higher education. The gross enrollment ratio in higher education is approximately 11 percent of the age cohort with women constituting about 40 percent of enrollments.

By end 2008, India had 449 universities—265 state universities, 25 central universities, 121 deemed-to-be universities (also known as "deemed universities"), 33 institutes of national importance established under Central Legislation and 5 institutions established under legislations by various state legislations.[1] In addition, there were 22,064 colleges. At the beginning of the academic year 2008 to 2009, the total number of students enrolled in universities and colleges was about 12.4 million. Of this 1.6 million (13 percent) were enrolled in university departments and 10.8 million (87 percent) in affiliated colleges. Women comprised 40.5 percent of total enrolment.

The number of doctoral degrees awarded by various universities in 2006 was 20,131. Out of the total number of doctoral degrees awarded, faculties of arts had the highest proportion followed by the faculties of science. These two faculties together accounted for over 70 percent of the total number of doctoral degree awarded. In contrast, the number of engineering PhDs is about a thousand—less than one per engineering college. The number of faculty was about half million, of which 16 percent was in universities and the rest in the affiliated teaching colleges.

The bulk of students (nearly two-thirds) are enrolled in arts and science, with another one-sixth in commerce/management. Recent growth has been much greater in technical education (engineering, management, pharmacy) and professional education (medicine, teacher training, and law), as well as in private vocational courses catering especially to the information technology (IT) sector (table 9.1). The private sector has accounted for the bulk of recent supply as cash-strapped state governments have virtually ceased to expand the list of government aided institutions, thereby increasing the percentage of "self-financed" or "private unaided institutions," most noticeably in professional and technical education (Agarwal 2006; Kapur and Mehta 2007). The vast majority of these, however, are affiliated to public universities whose role is increasingly an affiliation and degree granting one rather than teaching or research. Consequently, enrollment at public universities is still almost a hundred fold that of private universities, principally because of onerous entry regulations on the latter.

These private institutions are helping to meet the growing demand that the public sector cannot. Private institutions are less subject to political instabilities and day-to-day political pressures that often bedevil public institutions in developing countries. They are also more nimble and able to respond to changes in demands from employers and labor markets. Yet despite these positives, these institutions are of highly variable—and

1. Deemed-to-be-universities are an institutional innovation that may be *sui generis* to India. These institutions have narrow domains but can grant degrees. The original criterion was that they should be engaged in research and teaching in chosen fields of specialization that were innovative and of very high standards.

Table 9.1 Higher education in India: technical education intake capacity

	No. of students	No. of Institutions
Engineering (degree)	627,082	1,617
Engineering (diploma)	333,296	1,403
Business Management	104,084	1,150
Master's in Computer Applications	56,004	999
Hotel Management and Catering Technology	5,229	80
Pharmacy	44,476	736
Architecture	4,707	116
Fine Arts	650	9

Source: Government of India, Ministry of Human Resource Development. Data are from July 31, 2007.

often dubious—quality. They are mostly teaching shops, and very rarely knowledge-producing institutions. Although most private provision occurs domestically, there is a small but growing trend toward international private provision.

The public-sector supply, which has been stagnant since the early 1980s, is, however, poised for significant expansion if the targets announced for the XI plan (2007–2008 to 2011–2012) come to pass. It has targeted a gross enrollment ratio (GER) of 15 percent (21 million students), implying an annual growth rate of nearly 9 percent or an additional enrolment of 870,000 students in universities and about 6 million in colleges in the next five years. To this end, the central government intends setting up and funding thirty new central universities across the country, has ambitious plans in "technical education," and intends supporting state governments to set up colleges in the 340 districts that have extremely low college enrolments.[2] In December 2008, the Indian parliament passed a bill establishing a science and engineering research board (SERB) to serve as the apex research agency for planning and supporting research. Ideally, such a body would identify research priorities and then fund researchers (and their institutions) through a competitive grant process. A host of funding initiatives has also been announced that follow the student instead of the institution.[3] By providing merit scholarships to 2 percent of total students in higher education, the government hopes that universities will have an incentive to compete and attract students

2. This includes setting up eight (new) India institutes of technology (IITs), seven India institutes of management (IIMs), five India institutes of science and engineering research (IISERs), two schools of planning and architecture (SPAs), ten national institutes of technology (NITs), twenty India institutes of information technology (IIITs), and fifty centers for training and research in frontier areas.

3. Schemes under the Innovation in Science Pursuit for Inspired Research (INSPIRE) launched in XI Plan include (a) Scheme for Early Attraction of Talents for Science (SEATS), (b) Scholarships for Higher Education (SHE), (c) Assured Opportunity for Research Careers (AORC).

rather than have all their costs covered. And in order to increase the pool from which universities will be able to draw students, in late 2008, the Indian government announced a new $5 billion program to boost secondary school enrolment from just above half to 75 percent within five years.[4]

9.3 Quality

The prevailing view regarding higher education in India is discouraging: by most quality indicators, Indian bachelor's, master's, and PhD programs are lagging behind domestic demand in terms of required quality of graduates. There are numerous studies that detail both the need for better higher education in the country and the challenges in recruiting a scientifically competent workforce. According to the prime minister, the Indian university system "is, in many parts, in a state of disrepair . . . In almost half the districts [340] in the country, higher education enrolments are abysmally low, almost two-third of our universities and 90 per cent of our colleges are rated as below average on quality parameters . . . Its erstwhile Human Resources Development (HRD) Minister (who is responsible for higher education), called higher education the 'sick child of education.'[5]

Various indicators employed to study the quality of higher education in India, such as research output, infrastructure, and placement of graduates, point to the need for reform in the higher education public and private sector. In the Times Higher Education World University Rankings 2008, of the top 200 universities, two were Indian: the Indian Institute of Technology, Delhi, and the Indian Institute of Technology, Bombay.[6] And the Academic Rankings of World Universities by Shanghai Jiao Tong University ranked only two Indian universities in the top 500 (Indian Institute of Technology, Kharagpur and the Indian Institute of Science, Bangalore, both between 303 and 401).[7] Note that even the handful included in these rankings is dominated by engineering- and technology-specific institutions, a sorry testament to the extreme weakness of broad-based universities in the country.

In science and engineering, the part of Indian higher education that has grown most rapidly in recent years, India produced three times more graduates than the United States in 2006 (table 9.2). Various industry surveys

4. The program called the *Rashtriya Madhyamik Shiksha Abhiyan* aims at providing additional enrollment of 3.2 million through strengthening of about 44,000 secondary schools and opening 11,188 new secondary schools and appointment of 179,000 additional teachers and construction of 88,500 classrooms.

5. Prime Minister Manmohan Singh's address at the 150th Anniversary Function of University of Mumbai, June 22, 2007, http://pmindia.nic.in/lspeech.asp?id=555; Arjun Singh, cited in http://inhome.rediff.com/news/2007/oct/10arjun.htm.

6. Data available at http://www.timeshighereducation.co.uk/hybrid.asp?typeCode=243&pubCode=1.

7. Data available at http://www.arwu.org/rank2008/EN2008.htm.

Table 9.2 **Science and engineering higher education in China, India, and the United States**

	India (2006)	China (2003)	United States (2006)
Bachelors	237,000	351,500	74,200
Masters	20,000	35,000	39,000
Doctorates			
Science	5,500	32,000	14,200
Engineering	1,000	4,300	8,400
Total	6,500	36,300	22,600
Masters/Bachelors (%)	8.4	10	52.6
Doctorates/Bachelors (%)	0.4	1.2	11.3
Bachelors per million population	214	272	246
No. of institutions	1,511	n.a.	4,314[a]
Faculty	67,000	n.a.	26,700
Publications in science and engineering (2003)	12,774	60,067	211,233

Sources: Banerjee and Muley (2007). For China, data taken from Vivek Wadhwa, Duke Outsourcing Study: Empirical Comparison of Engineering Graduates in the U.S., China, and India, 2005.

Notes: Data are from most recent year available.

[a]Taken from http://nces.ed.gov/programs/coe/2008/analysis/sa_table.asp?tableID=1053.

indicate that about a fifth of these are of comparable standards to their U.S. counterparts. The contrast is most stark in the number of PhDs. Between 1985 and 2002, the ratio of the number of PhDs to bachelors degrees in India dropped from 2.2 percent to just 0.66 percent, while it doubled in the United States from 4.1 percent to 8.4 percent (table 9.3). The annual number of PhD engineers produced in India around 2005 was about half per engineering school per year.

The contrast with China is stark. In the last two decades, the number of PhDs in science and engineering (S&E) in India increased by around 50 percent (from 4,007 in 1985 to 6,318 in 2003), whereas in China, the numbers increased from a tiny 125 in 1985 to 12,238 in 2003 and 14,858 in 2004 (see figure 9.1). According to one analysis, in 1990, publications from India were about 50 percent more than China. Over the next fifteen years, publications from India increased 40 percent. The increase from China was nearly sixfold, a number more than double compared to India (see figure 9.2).

The problems are even more acute in the social sciences. The number of PhDs produced by India's premier economics faculty—Delhi School of Economics—has dropped from about 4.5 a year in the 1970s and 1990s to barely 1.5 a year in this decade. This is despite the fact that the number of economics departments in Indian universities grew from 72 in 1971 to 119 in 2001. As a recent official review of Indian social sciences put it, "an even more serious problem [than funding] is the severe, and increasing, shortage, of qualified researchers. Even research institutes and universities that have

Table 9.3 **Ratio of engineering PhDs to bachelors engineering degrees**

	1985	1987	1989	1991	1993	1995	1997	1999	2000	2001	2002
India	2.21	2.13	2.03	n.a.	n.a.	0.58	0.4	0.93	0.87	0.83	0.66
China	0.09	0.15	0.65	0.67	0.88	1.11	1.51	1.67	2.11	1.98	n.a.
United States	4.08	4.99	6.79	8.38	9.09	9.48	9.81	n.a.	8.94	9.28	8.36

Source: Banerjee and Muley (2007), "Engineering Education in India," Observer Research Foundation Report. Data from tables 1.10, 1.11 and 1.12.

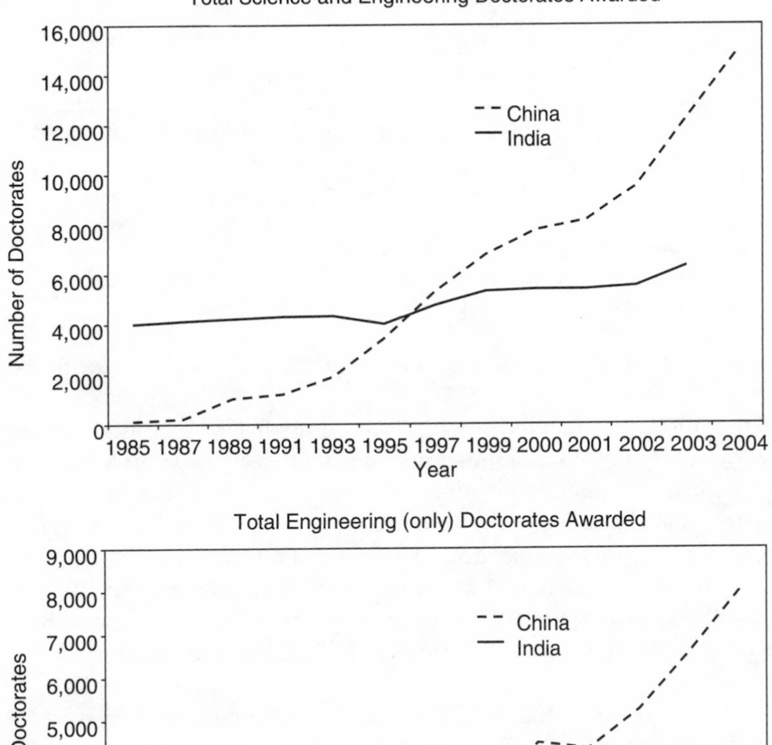

Fig. 9.1 Science and engineering doctoral degrees: Selected years, 1985–2005
Source: NSF, *Science and engineering indicators, 2008,* appendix table 2-43.

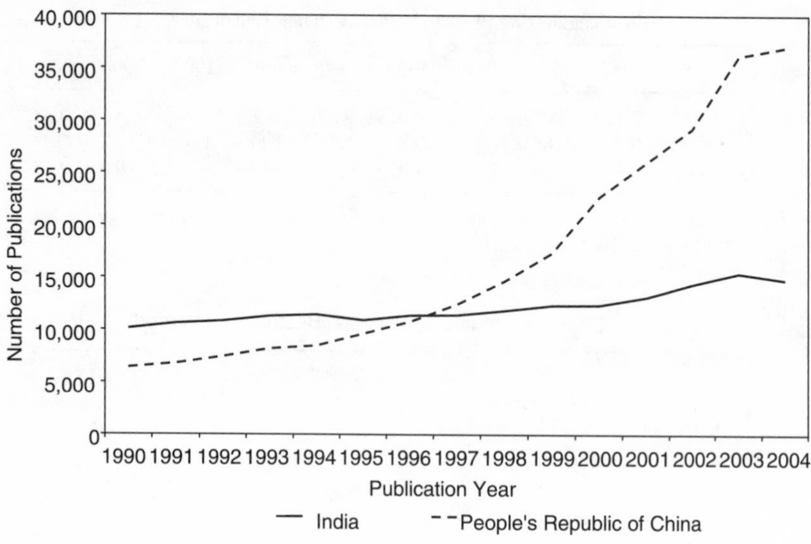

Fig. 9.2 Publication productivity of India and China
Source: Kademani, Sagar, and Kumar (2006).

a good reputation for quality are faced with a decline in both the number and quality of Ph.D. students."[8]

The shortage of faculty is ubiquitous across fields. According to a survey by the Pay Review Commission of the University Grants Commission, 44.6 percent of sanction positions of lecturers at the university level and 41 percent at the college level were vacant.[9] In December 2008, the Indian government approved a pay hike of 70 percent for the nearly half a million faculty in universities and colleges across India. However, while this measure will help, it does not address the core questions of governance, which is the central reason for the weaknesses of Indian higher education and even more of a deterrent to attracting talent.

The poor quality of Indian higher education is evident in the results of the Indian administrative service exams. The applicants to posts ratio (APR), an index of the number of candidates aspiring for civil service posts through various examinations is an astounding *755* candidates for every post filled (for 2005). Even then, suitable candidates are not found, and positions are left unfilled (table 9.4). More than 5,000 candidates applied for just thirty positions for the Indian Economic Service/Indian Statistical Service through civil services examinations. Even then, barely twenty-three made the grade.

8. The Indian Council of Social Science Research, "Restructuring the Indian Council of Social Science Research," Report of the Fourth Review Committee, March 2007, 22.

9. University Grants Commission, *Report of the Committee to Review the Pay Scales and Service Conditions of University and College Teachers,* 2008.

Table 9.4 **Indian civil service exams**

Name of examination	No. of posts	No. of applicants	No. of recommended candidates	APR	RPR
Civil Services	457	345,106	425	755	0.93
Engineering Services	262	74,363	229	284	0.87
Combined Medical Services	624	28,878	562	46	0.90
Central Police Forces	256	92,568	224	362	0.88
Indian Economic Service/ Indian Statistical Service	30	5,017	23	167	0.77
Geologists	95	3,433	95	36	1.00
Total	1,724	549,365	1,558	319	0.90

Source: Union Public Service Commission 57th Annual Report, 2006–07, table 5.
Note: APR = applicants to posts ratio; RPR = recommended to post ratio.

It should be noted that this is a different problem from the disincentives to join the public sector because of (relatively) poor pay or working conditions, which might result in fewer applications and lead the best to leave after a few years. There are clearly a very large number of students with degrees in economics and statistics who want to apply—it is just that less than half of 1 percent conform to certain standards. The result is that the Indian Statistical Service, a cadre of the federal government that over the decades has produced one of the best government statistics among developing countries, is being starved of talent with adverse consequences for the quality of government statistics. Indian newspaper editors, when queried about the main constraint facing them, say it is the lack of availability of young people who can write even two pages of correct English prose.

9.4 The Political Economy of Indian Higher Education: Why Is Quality Poor?

There are several reasons why Indian higher education, and the bulk of its universities in particular, is in a poor state. A structural reason stems from a decision made in the 1950s to create separate research institutions outside the university system. Over time, as universities became politicized, researchers fled the university system and migrated to public institutions under the umbrella of the Council of Scientific and Industrial Research (CSIR), the Department of Atomic Energy, the Indian Space Research Organization, and the Indian Council of Social Science Research (ICSSR). The bifurcation of research from teaching and the in-breeding of faculty, gradually led to an entrenchment of mediocrity. The most acute weakness plaguing India's higher education system is a crisis of governance. Indeed the Indian Prime Minister, a former professor at Delhi University, himself has commented,

"I am concerned that in many states university appointments, including that of vice-chancellors, have been politicised and have become subject to caste and communal considerations, there are complaints of favouritism and corruption." The core of the governance problem lies in the nature of highly centralized state regulation of higher education that seeks to micro-manage who can teach what to whom at what cost. Table 9.5 gives an overview of the regulatory structure of Indian higher education. Its effects on Indian higher education can be gauged by the bleak assessment of a former science and technology (S&T) minster, "There is not such a thing as UGC [University Grants Commission] there is not such a thing as AICTE [All India Council for Technical Education], there is not such a thing as MCI (in the western world). They [have] destroyed our entire efforts to take education forward."[10]

One might presume that an independent regulatory framework for any sector would shield it from the political interference. In the Indian case, they are simply another mechanism for political influence and rent-seeking. And when they do exercise regulatory independence, they are quickly overridden by the ministries even flouting the courts. To take one example: in 2003, the Supreme Court of India ruled that the Medical Council of India (MCI) was the only authority that could recommend an increase of student strength or renewal of permission for medical colleges. That order had directed the central government "not to grant any further permission without following the procedure prescribed under the Indian Medical Council Act." In 2008, the MCI denied permission to two medical colleges to take new students based on a report by a government appointed lawyer that their facilities were "inadequate."[11] The very same day the Health Ministry permitted the very two private medical colleges to take in more students!

There is sufficient awareness of the problems afflicting Indian higher education at the highest levels of the Indian government as evident by the quotes cited in the preceding by a range of key cabinet members. Why then has the Indian state not acted and addressed them? One reason may be that higher education is arguably one of the most difficult sectors to reform—and not just in India. In the case of public universities, employees (both faculty and administration) and students are among the most vocal and well-organized political groups in any country. Even as unions have weakened in virtually all aspects of economic activity, education remains a rare exception. Direct exit options—such as closing down poor performing departments or

10. Kapil Sibal, quoted in *Business Standard* July 9, 2008, http://www.business-standard.com/india/storypage.php?autono=328167. In April 2009, Kapil Sibal became the new minister for Human Resource Development, which included higher education.

11. Amitav Ranjan, "Denied SC nod for admissions, 2 medical colleges get Health Ministry OK same day," *Indian Express,* September 29, 2008, http://www.indianexpress.com/news/denied-sc-nod-for-admissions-2-medical-colleges-get-health-ministry-ok-same-day/367138/0.

Table 9.5 **Structure of higher education regulation**

Function	Institution	Purpose
Higher education policy	Central Advisory Board of Education (CABE)	Apex body that advises the central and state governments in the field of education.
Universities	University Grants Commission (UGC)	Regulates all aspects of universities and also provides funds.
All aspects of "technical education," including engineering/technology, architecture, management, hotel management & catering technology, pharmacy, and applied arts & crafts	All India Council for Technical Education (AICTE)	Maintenance of norms and standards and quality assurance through accreditation, and funding in priority areas. Except with the approval of the Council, no new technical institution or university technical department shall be started; or no course or program shall be introduced by any technical institution, university, or university department or college; or no technical institution, university or deemed university, or university department or college shall continue to admit students for degree or diploma courses or program; no approved intake capacity of seats shall be increased or varied. Approval is based on the fulfilment of certain preconditions.
Medical education	Medical Council of India (MCI), Pharmacy Council of India (PCI), Indian Nursing Council (INC), Dentist Council of India (DCI), Central Council of Homeopathy (CCH), Central Council of Indian Medicine (CCIM), Rehabilitation Council of India (RCI)	Accreditation and standards.
Legal education	Bar Council of India (BCI)	Accreditation and standards.
Teaching	National Council for Teacher Education (NCTE), Distance Education Council (DEC)	Accreditation and standards.
Agriculture	Indian Council for Agriculture Research (ICAR)	
	National Assessment and Accreditation Council (NAAC)	Assess and accredit institutions under the purview of the UGC that volunteer for the process, based on prescribed criteria.
	National Board of Accreditation (NBA)	Assess the qualitative competence of institutions in technical education approved by AICTE.

colleges—sharply increases the risks of an immediate political reaction. Visible strategies such as increasing fees are also fiercely resisted even when they could raise quality or lead to a less regressive income transfer to elites.

Public universities (and their affiliated colleges) are plagued by misguided attempts at equity, poor administration, and bureaucratization. The lack of institutional autonomy and poor academic governance has made it increasingly difficult for higher education to attract talent, especially because (unlike the past) that talent has alternatives. In many cases, talent out has been driven out, and as individuals at the upper end of human capital distribution leave, the remaining pool is of poorer quality. This not only prompts the more talented to also consider leaving, but also discourages those who left earlier from returning, ensuring that mediocrity becomes entrenched in these institutions. While low salaries are an issue, in many cases, a poor overall academic environment is perhaps more important. In most government institutions, the focus is on process rather than performance, appointments are politicized, and autonomy in administration, financial, and academic content is minimal. Resources are an undoubted constraint, but more flexible rules, access to modest research resources, and a work environment that encourages innovative practices and research can achieve much.

Consequently, changes have occurred largely because the majority of public institutions focus on liberal arts programs, which have deteriorated to such an extent as to force students to seek private-sector alternatives. In other cases, fiscal constraints have limited public-sector led supply increases, resulting in increasing rationing as demand escalates, thereby forcing excess demand to spill over to a burgeoning private sector. The latter largely focus on technical and professional education and, as I note later, are also plagued by poor quality and corrupt practices. In both cases, the result is the same—a massive increase in the share of the private sector in higher education.

A second reason for the problems afflicting the Indian university system is the rent-seeking behavior that is the inevitable consequence of detailed administrative regulation. The sector is the last refuge of the "license raj" with severe political, administrative, and regulatory interference on virtually every aspect of higher education, be it admissions policies, internal organization, fees and salaries, and the structure of courses and funding.[12] While the private sector has ramped up supply, the quality of most of the new private-sector colleges (many linked to politicians) leaves much to be desired. Their governance problems may be different from public institutions, but are no less acute. As a recent report by a commission appointed by

12. Prior to the onset of economic liberalization in India in 1991, firms were required to seek government approval for what they produced, how much they produced, what technologies they could use, and the sources of financing. Tight quantitative restrictions on imports were enforced through import licenses. The system, whose original logic lay in a planned economy, degenerated into a labyrinth of red tape and rent seeking by state functionaries and businesses, and came to be known as the "license raj."

the Indian government put it, "mushrooming engineering and management colleges, with some notable exceptions, have largely become, mere business entities dispensing very poor quality education."[13]

Ironically, at the same time, the Indian state has made it very difficult for *quality* private universities to come up, jeopardizing the supply of faculty—and the training of future generations.[14] First, the process of regulatory approvals diminishes the capacity of private investment to respond to market needs. Second, the regulatory process produces an adverse selection in the kind of entrepreneurs that invest because the success of a project depends less upon the pedagogic design of the project than the ability to manipulate the regulatory system. Consequently, private investment in higher education is driven principally by profit making goals and not education as a public trust. Consequently, private-sector investment has been confined to professional streams, bypassing the majority of students, and also suffers severe governance weaknesses, raising doubts as to its ability to addresses the huge latent demand for quality higher education in the country. Third, there are significant market failures in acquiring physical assets that are necessary for institutions, especially land. Fourth, regulatory approvals are extremely rigid with regard to infrastructure requirements (irrespective of costs or location) and an insistence on academic conformity to centrally mandated course outlines, degree structures, and admissions policies. Fifth, a key element of a well functioning market—competition—is distorted by not allowing foreign universities to set up campuses in India, limiting benchmarking to global standards. Sixth, the central element of a well-functioning market, informational transparency, is woefully inadequate.

A third reason—and the most important—lies in the key cleavages and drivers of India politics. The contention of a former cabinet minister responsible for higher education, that "inclusion and access with equity are the core issues that confront us today [in higher education]," is noteworthy in that the absence of excellence or the abysmal quality of governance that has made the pursuit of excellence so difficult are simply not deemed as core issues.[15] While higher education is a prime casualty of the populism and fragmentation of the Indian polity, the underlying reason is that it has become a key battleground of distributional conflicts (and not just in India). The main reason is rising skill premia. While this is a global phenomenon—the last two decades have seen a significant increase in the skill premium in both industrialized and developing countries—it is more puzzling in developing countries. Despite numerous problems that afflict the measurement of skill premia, Goldberg and Pavcnik (2007) argue that because virtually all country studies show large skill premium increases, "it is unlikely that they

13. Report of *The Committee to Advise on Renovation and Rejuvenation of Higher Education,* June 2009.

14. The discussion in this paragraph draws from Kapur and Mehta (2008).

15. http://inhome.rediff.com/news/2007/oct/10arjun.htm.

are all a figment of the measurement problems," although the exact magnitudes may be affected by these measurement problems.[16] In India, the skill premium (as measured by the return to a university degree) has increased by 13 percent (relative to primary education) between 1987 and 1999 (Kijima 2006) and 25 percent between 1998 and 2004 (Dutta 2006; OECD 2007).

With identity politics emerging as the principal fulcrum of political competition in India, debates on affirmative action (or "reservations" as it is known in India) as *the* means to increase the representation of socially marginalized groups have been so contentious as to overwhelm virtually every other issue in Indian higher education. While the framers of India's constitution were deeply concerned with the ideals of social justice and equality, these progressive ideas ran contrary to the pervasive and deep-rooted social hierarchy and severe discrimination deeply imbedded in India's caste system. In order to redress centuries of discrimination against India's lowest castes (so-called untouchables, or *Dalits* as they are now known) and indigenous peoples, the Indian constitution enshrined the most comprehensive system of compensatory discrimination for these groups known as "reservations." Seats in federal and state legislatures and jobs in civil services and state-owned enterprises were reserved in proportion to their share in the population. The same was the case in public higher education institutions (except in those run by minorities).[17]

But like the infant-industry argument, affirmative action programs tend to take on a life of their own, as more and more groups press their claims to avail of its benefits. The Indian constitution contains a clause allowing the federal and state governments to make "any special provision for the advancement of any socially and educationally backward classes of citizens or for the Scheduled Castes and Scheduled Tribes" (Constitution of India, Article 15, clause 4). Over time, the expansiveness and ambiguity of the clause "any socially and educationally backward classes of citizens" opened up a Pandora's Box and became a favorite hunting ground for political populism. While affirmative action has had some success (albeit modest) in reducing intergroup inequality, it has tended to amplify intragroup inequalities. Broad social categories like "Scheduled Castes," "Scheduled Tribes," and "Other Backward Castes" tend to gloss over the fact that these are themselves extremely heterogenous categories with hierarchies within them. Consequently, the benefits of reservations are disproportionately garnered by some subgroups—those who were better off to begin with. Moreover,

16. The skill premium increases have been largest in Mexico, where the return to university education (relative to primary education) increased by 68 percent between 1987 and 1993 (Cragg and Epelbaum 1996). In Latin America, a worker with six years of education earns on average 50 percent more than someone who has not attended school, a high school graduate earns 120 percent more, and someone with a university diploma earns on average 200 percent more (World Bank and UNESCO 2000).

17. Article 15 of the Indian Constitution prohibits discrimination, based on religion, race, caste, sex, and place of birth.

while the creation of educated elites from these social groups is indicative of some success, their children benefit much more than the vast majority in the group who, given the limited number of seats, are crowded out. This points to one chronic weakness in these programs—the absence of nondiscretionary sunset clauses that allows the benefits of these policies to spread to other households *within* the group. Finally, perhaps the most inimical impact is that these policies have resulted in a political economy akin to that of rent-seeking. Enormous political energy and effort is spent by politicians promising ever more benefits to more and more social groups rather than improving and expanding the quality of supply by focusing on primary and secondary education. The Indian supreme court has ruled that reservations cannot exceed 50 percent (that would violate equality guaranteed by the constitution), but this has been flouted by several states setting the stage for a possible future constitutional crisis.

Debates on affirmative action are, of course, by no means unique to India. There continues to be widely divergent views on the role of higher education in society. Governments increasingly want universities to be "engines of social justice" on the one hand as well as "handmaidens of industry" or "implementers of the skills agenda" on the other. Alison Richard, Cambridge University's vice-chancellor, has argued that while institutions such as hers "try to reach out to the best students, whatever their background," and "one outcome of that is that we can help to promote social mobility. But promoting social mobility is not our core mission. Our core mission is to provide an outstanding education within a research setting."[18] And even if social mobility is an important goal, how should group rights be balanced against individual rights? Advocates highlight the important "role-model" effect of such programs for disadvantaged groups and the many positive pay offs of diversity, while critics argue that these programs perpetuate racial stereotypes. How valuable is diversity in an educational environment? And what exactly is "diversity"? What criteria (or sunset clauses) should be used to phase out these programs? There is little agreement on even the most basic question. Under what conditions do such programs entrench identity politics or instead gradually erode them? Then there are practical questions of how to implement these programs. To what extent should governments use control or incentive mechanisms to oversee such programs? What should be the policy at private institutions given their growing importance? And how should design of such programs reflect not just the normative aspects but the reality of how political considerations will impact implementation?

In 2006, in an attempt to bolster its electoral base among India's largest social group, the Congress-led United Progressive Alliance (UPA) gov-

18. Jessica Shepard, "Cambridge Mission 'Not Social Mobility,'" *The Guardian,* September 10, 2008, http://www.guardian.co.uk/education/2008/sep/10/accesstouniversity.higher education/print.

ernment extended reservation benefits to the "Other Backward Castes" (OBCs) in educational institutions run by the federal government. There are ongoing disputes about statistical data used by the government of India and Indian states for offering reservation benefits to these groups, especially because the possibility of entitlements has led to more and more social groups to claim they are more backward than the others.[19] Sundaram (2007) argues that representation of a social group can only be judged by a comparison of its share in enrollments in a given level of education with its share in the population eligible for entry into that level of education rather than the population as a whole. By this criterion, India's OBCs (and, especially, for over 70 percent of them who are above the poverty line), the extent of underrepresentation of the OBCs in enrollments in Indian universities is less than 5 percent. Affirmative action programs that are based on identity rather than income or poverty, for a social group such as India's OBCs whose social and economic conditions reflect the average in the country, risk the better off within the group monopolizing all the privileges, with little benefit to the vast majority in that group.

Another analysis (Basant and Sen 2009) also confirms that the underrepresentation of socially marginalized groups in higher education is much less once the likelihood of completion of high school is taken into account. The likelihood of undertaking higher education increases dramatically for the marginalized groups after they cross the threshold of school education. This increase is particularly the case for women and in rural areas. Table 9.6 lays out the degree of under- or overrepresentation across socioreligious groups. All socioreligious groups except upper caste Hindus and "other minorities" are underrepresented. However, this declines once flow (rather than stock) measures are considered (suggesting improvements over time) and decline significantly when we compare across only the eligible population, that is, those who have completed high school. Take, for example, the OBC group that will now benefit from reservation in higher education. Of the total population in the age group seventeen to twenty-nine, this group has a share of about 34.5 percent; the group's share in the eligible population in this age group is 30.1 percent, while their share in the currently studying population is 28.2 percent.

19. As India's Supreme Court has observed, "The paradox of the system of reservation is that it has engendered a spirit of self-denigration among the people. Nowhere else in the world do castes, classes or communities queue up for the sake of gaining the backward status. Nowhere else in the world is there competition to assert backwardness and to claim 'we are more backward than you.' This is an unhappy and disquieting situation, but it is stark reality. Whatever gloss one may like to put upon it, it is clear from the rival claims in these appeals and writ petitions that the real contest here is between certain members of two premier (population-wise) caste community classes . . . each claiming that the other is not a socially and educationally backward class and each keen to be included in the list of socially and educationally backward classes." Justice O. Chinnappa Reddy in *K.C. Vasanth Kumar v. State of Karnataka* (1985) [Supp. SCC 714, para. 23].

Table 9.6 **Participation in higher education by socioreligious category, 2004–2005**

	Share in 20+ age group			Share in 22–35 age group			Share in 17–29 age group		
Socioreligious group	Total population	Graduates	Eligible population	Total population	Graduates	Eligible population	Total population	Currently studying	Eligible population
H-SC	17.3	6.3	7.9	17.8	7.5	8.9	18.0	10.4	9.9
H-ST	6.9	1.7	2.2	7.2	1.9	2.5	7.1	4.0	2.9
H-OBC	34.9	23.0	27.0	34.8	25.6	29.3	34.5	28.2	30.1
H-UC	23.9	55.4	48.1	22.9	51.7	44.9	22.1	41.8	41.6
M-OBC	4.4	1.7	2.2	4.6	1.7	2.1	5.0	3.2	2.8
M-G	6.8	4.1	4.2	7.2	4.1	4.1	7.8	5.2	4.6
OM	5.8	7.8	8.4	5.5	7.5	8.2	5.5	7.2	8.0
Total	100	100	100	100	100	100	100	100	100

Source: Basant and Sen (2009).

Note: H-SC = Hindu, scheduled caste; H-ST = Hindu, scheduled tribe; H-OBC = Hindu, other backward caste; H-UC = Hindu, upper caste; M-OBC = Muslim, other backward caste; M-G = Muslim, general; OM = other minorities.

If the problem of access is less acute than warranted by recent populist measures, the performance of "reserved" candidates compared to the rest raises further questions on the limits of this strategy. It is not just that reservations at elite educational institutions benefit at best a tiny minority of candidates from socially marginalized groups. The evidence is also strongly suggestive that admission alone will be insufficient to equalize career outcomes even for this tiny minority in the absence of better school-level opportunities. Chakravarty and Somanathan (2008) use data from one of India's most elite institutions (Indian Institute of Management [IIM]-Ahmedabad) and find that that graduates who came through affirmative action (Scheduled Caste [SC] or Scheduled Tribe [ST] or SC/ST) get significantly lower wages (between a fifth and a third) than those admitted in the general category. However, this difference disappears once they account for lower grade point averages of SC/ST candidates, suggesting that the wage differences could be due to the weaker (on average) academic performance of SC/ST candidates.[20] This appears to be the result of poor quality of schooling prior to entering higher education rather than discrimination per se in access to higher education (which in any case in India is almost entirely based on standardized exam scores, such as state wide high school exam results or nationwide standardized entrance tests). Nonetheless, all major actors, be they politicians, courts, media, and even many academics, have focused on access issues in higher education.

9.5 The Evolution of a Surrogate Higher Education System

There is little doubt that the Indian university system is in deep crisis. Given its well documented travails, its limited impact on India's growth needs some explanation. If the traditional university system is doing such a poor job, how have Indian firms addressed their human capital needs in recent years? Sectors such as IT have been growing at a scorching pace. From a few million dollars in the mid-1980s, its revenues crossed 70 billion dollars for FY2008 to 2009. More recently, the life-sciences sector (biotech and pharmaceutical) industry has also been growing rapidly, with revenues of nearly $25 billion in 2007.

Of course it could be argued that a better higher education system would have resulted in even higher growth rates or that the poor quality has imposed economic costs. Large increases in wage premia at the top end of India's talent pool imply that supply of quality talent simply has not kept up with the demand. Other costs may not be visible as yet—they may be more long term or their negative effects may be more social and political rather

20. They also find that (at least in this case) controlling for work experience and grades, there is no wage penalty to being female, and unlike studies from U.S. and British labor markets, there is only weak evidence of any wage premium to being more attractive.

than economic. While I will return to this issue in the conclusion, here it is sufficient to discuss why the travails of Indian universities have not had a more inimical impact on Indian firms. I argue that just as Indian firms have been forced to adapt to chronic weaknesses in infrastructure, labor laws, and so on, they have also adapted to the weaknesses of the Indian university system. A surrogate higher education system has evolved and, in particular, workforce skill development is occurring outside the traditional domestic university model—within firms, by commercial providers, overseas, through open-source or virtual learning, and in narrow specialized institutions, the so-called deemed-to-be universities.

9.5.1 Skill Development by Firms

The private sector has long contributed to higher education through four key mechanisms: directly funding research (indeed, in Japan, doctorates called *ronbun hakase,* were awarded by universities to dissertations that were written by researchers working solely in firms, with appropriate company personnel serving as advisers instead of university professors); private philanthropy supporting gifts and endowments; working with weak public institutions to improve the quality of instructional material and infrastructure; and, most important, through so-called corporate universities—in-house company training and development initiatives. These have been around since the nineteenth century, when large companies such as DuPont and General Electric introduced "corporate classrooms" to provide additional training for employees.

In most market economies, the direct and indirect training costs incurred by the private sector make it the largest provider of professional training. Corporations often have greater access to resources than do public universities and offer training in functional skills and new technologies that may not be otherwise available. Although most of these institutions serve only company employees, some corporate universities are opening their programs to fee-paying students or launching subsidiary for-profit universities.

Recently the new multinational corporations (MNCs) from emerging markets have become innovators in this area, having to compensate for the weakness of the higher education systems in their countries by developing ambitious in-house programs. In principle, there are many benefits when firms organize and pay for the labor market skills they need. Indeed all firms do that to some extent—in most cases relying on some variant of an apprenticeship system. However, developing countries have few large firms that can internalize the costs of these training universities. Moreover, as labor markets become more flexible, the greater turnover of employees reduces the incentives for in-house universities because the benefits of such training are not fully internalized.

Nonetheless, as Wadhwa, Kim De Vitton, and Gereffi (2008) argue, with firms forced to recruit from a subpar pool to fill their skilled labor needs,

Indian industry has addressed this handicap by investing heaving in providing the necessary workplace training and development of their employees. An array of workforce skill development practices including new employee training, continual training, hiring managers from within the company, advanced performance appraisal systems, and investing in education by partnering with universities have all gone a long way in improving the skills of their workforce.

The private sector has also become involved in creating "corporate universities" to try and fill the gap between the skills required for employment and those produced by traditional universities. The most organized effort in this regard has been by the IT industry, whose rapid expansion has led to growing skill shortages.[21] Industry leaders, Infosys, Tata Consultancy Services (TCS), and Wipro, have all set up large campuses and training programs and are also working collectively through the industry body, NASSCOM, to improve pedagogy and training in Indian engineering schools. Infosys has set up a $450 million facility capable of training 18,000 fresh graduates annually at a cost of about $5,000 per student. Each of the candidates recruited by the software company has to spend eight hours a day at a residential company campus studying software programming and attending team-building workshops. In order to graduate, every trainee has to pass two three-hour-long comprehensive exams.[22] Similarly, the Wipro Academy of Software Engineering recruits and trains about 14,000 annually. It screens science graduates and trains them in a four-year program with a well-known private engineering school (Birla Institute of Technology and Science [BITS]-Pilani), at the end of which they graduate with a master's in software engineering and are employed by Wipro. Under a program called TCS Ignite, TCS hires science graduates from over 200 colleges in nine states and then puts them through an intensive seven-month customized curriculum before they are inducted as full-time employees. The condition is that these candidates must agree to stay on with the company for two years.

Collectively, efforts of companies like Infosys's Campus Connect Program and Wipro's Academy of Software Excellence aim to improve the quality of engineers through curriculum development and training in colleges. NASSCOM, the apex body representing the IT industry, has been directing its efforts at standardized skills assessment and verification program and improve the skills of 10,000 faculty members in 1,500 engineering colleges over the next three years.

The surrogate education system is extending well beyond software companies. In finance and banking, accounting firm Ernst & Young, faced with

21. See, "India's Corporations Race to Train Workers and Avoid Being Left in the Dust," India Knowledge@Wharton, September 18, 2008.

22. Infosys's Global Education Centre (GEC) is spread over 335-acres. It has over 500 faculty rooms and 10,300 residential rooms in a built-up space of 6 million square feet and is capable of training 13,000 students in a single sitting.

a severe shortage of freshly qualified chartered accountants for its tax audit business, has opened a tax academy, which trains recruits as tax associates. While India's largest public-sector bank, State Bank of India, annually recruits about 20,000 new employees (from 2.4 million applicants) and has a long-established training program, new private-sector banks are following suit. ICICI Bank recruits undergo a one-year residential classroom training at the ICICI Manipal Academy of Banking and Insurance, a joint venture between the bank and the private Manipal University. The bank and university have jointly designed the course content with courses in treasury, international banking, and microfinance. The costs are paid by ICICI Indian Institute of Banking and Finance (IIBF).

Recently, even a seemingly lower skill sector, the rapidly expanding organized retail sector, has followed suit. Pantaloon (a large retail firm) has started a three-year bachelor of business administration (BBA) program with a focus on retail in association with the Madurai Kamraj University. The Bharti Group has started the Bharti Academy of Retail Academy for Insurance and is also setting up sixty learning centers across the country to offer courses in insurance, telecom, and retail. Other training initiatives in this regard include Reliance Retail, the Future Group and Retailers Association of India.

Industry has also become involved in redesigning curricula. For instance, the Confederation of Indian Industry (CII) has been putting together courses to improve soft skills, training the trainers for this course and to integrate related courses into the university curriculum. This initiative has been launched in the state of Tamil Nadu and will be extended to universities across other states. Firms and industry bodies, with the efforts of state governments are all working at enhancing skill development. The CII is also working closely with the government and large companies in a public-private partnership model to upgrade the government-owned industrial training institutes (ITIs) and align them more closely with the needs of industry.[23] To address the shortage of civil engineers, Volvo Construction Equipment has joined hands with Visveswaraya Technological University (VTU) for offering hands-on industry education to postgraduate students of the university. Under this partnership, the university has recognized Volvo's Resource Centre for Asphalt and Soil Testing Academy as an extension center to offer postgraduate courses in road technology.

Even public-sector organizations such as the Department of Space, the Council for Scientific and Industrial Research (CSIR), and the Defense Research and Development Organization (DRDO) are seeking to address their difficulties in recruiting qualified research and development (R&D) personnel by setting up captive "deemed universities." For instance, the

23. Companies that have adopted ITIs include Bosch; Hero Honda; Ashok Leyland; Larsen & Toubro; and Bharat Heavy Electricals, Ltd.

Department of Space has set up the Indian Institute of Space Science and Technology, and the Department of Atomic Energy the National Institute of Science, Education, and Research. The Bhabha Atomic Energy Research Center (BARC) training schools (established by the founder fathers of India's atomic energy program in 1957), provided the scientific personnel for the Department of Atomic Energy for nearly a half-century. The programs were modeled on the Argonne International School of Nuclear Science and Engineering (1955) and Oak Ridge School of Reactor Technology (1950) in the United States where many of the BARC pioneers had been trained. This is now being transformed into a deemed-to-be university—the Homi Bhabha National Institute (HBNI). Faced with a shortage of trained personnel, the CSIR, a network of thirty-eight government laboratories in applied research, is planning to set up a research university. This would allow the CSIR to impart a quality education and award degrees and thereby create the human capital it desperately needs.

9.5.2 Buying Higher Education Abroad

Higher education and learning has always had a strong international flavor. Where political constraints make any change unfeasible and the supply of higher education institutions with any signaling effect is severely limited, there is an increasing tendency to purchase higher education overseas. Since the late 1990s, the number of students crossing borders to receive education has increased by more than 50 percent. It is estimated that the number of students from developing countries studying abroad is likely to double before 2015 and double again by 2025. While China has emerged as the largest country of origin for international students, there has been a surge of students from India as well.

International student outflows from India have been growing rapidly. In contrast to past decades when these outflows were more the result of low pay offs to skill rather than underinvestment in higher education capacity, with the rapid rise in skill premiums and the difficulties of access to quality institutions within the country, the latter has become more important. Data from the Indian government indicate that more than a quarter million Indian students were studying abroad in 2008 to 2009.[24] In 1993, there were barely 300 Indian students in Australia. In 2008 to 2009, the figure crossed 97,000. However, most of this increase has been either at the undergraduate level and (especially) master's level, not at the doctoral level.[25] Indeed, the number of S&E doctorates received by Indians in the United States peaked

24. Of these, 104,522 were in the United States; 97,035 were in Australia; 25,905 were in the United Kingdom; and 6,040 were in New Zealand. Figures are from a report of the Ministry of Overseas Indian Affairs cited in "Desi Students Are Latest Globe Trotters," *Sunday Times of India*, Bangalore, July 26, 2009, p 7.

25. More than 70 percent of Indian students in the United States were in graduate programs, IIE *Open Doors 2007*.

in the late 1990s (around 1,300 annually) and subsequently declined to about 800 annually between 2001 to 2003.

Until about the mid-1960s, Indians who went abroad for higher education tended to return. And when they did, the reentry vehicle was generally the public sector. From the mid-1960s to the end of the millennium, return rates fell sharply, especially for those with advanced degrees. The pendulum has again begun to swing back, but with one key difference: the reentry of Indians with advanced degrees is now almost entirely to the private sector (especially the growing number of MNC R&D labs), with few joining public-sector research institutions. In the latter case, many researchers have postdoctoral experience abroad, rather than doctoral degrees (this is especially true of the biological sciences).

While there are many gains from these outflows, there are two significant costs. One, a large number of students, especially those engaged in research, do not return. Despite the increasing attractiveness of India, the percentage of Indians obtaining PhDs in S&E who had "definite plans to stay" in the United States increased from 56.3 percent in 1994 to 1997 to 62.7 percent in 2002 to 2005, even as the number of Indians obtaining PhDs in S&E declined by 30 percent (from 5,014 to 3,587). And two, students (and parents) incur very large expenditures, which are almost the same as the total higher education expenditures in the country—for a tiny fraction of the number of students in the country. While public higher education spending in India was about $4.5 billion in 2006 to 2007, Indians were spending nearly $3.5 billion buying higher education overseas (Kapur and Mehta 2008).

Although the number of students from developing countries seeking education abroad has sharply increased in recent years, the phenomenon itself is not new. What is newer, however, is the reverse: foreign higher education institutions, establishing programs in developing countries under a variety of arrangements ranging from cross-border franchised agreements, twinning agreements, joint programs, validation programs, subcontracting, and distance learning activities.[26] For example, the growing demand for nurses in India (and abroad) has led to a burgeoning number of private nursing schools. Although these are accredited by the Indian Council of Nursing, this carries little signaling value. Recently, a group of private nursing schools in India approached the Commission on Graduates of Foreign Nursing Schools (CGFNS), a statutory U.S. body, to create a set of standards that could become an imprimatur and have a distinct signaling value.[27] The importance of external validation mechanisms is likely to increase.

26. Under twinning arrangements, after initial training in their home country, students relocate overseas to receive their final training and degree from the foreign university. Under franchising programs, the entire program takes place in the home country, with the foreign institution providing curricula and assessment and certifying the program with the university crest on the degree.

27. Interview with Barbara Nichols, CEO, CGFNS, Cambridge, September 27, 2008.

The other alternative, attracting foreign higher education providers to India, has faced strong resistance. There is no dearth of critics who fear the entry effects of foreign providers of higher education. Some fear that foreign providers—by importing curricula with little consideration of local traditions and culture—might prove to be Trojan horses of cultural imperialism. Others argue that foreign providers arguably undermine the sovereignty of the state, especially in its capacity to regulate education and its nation-building functions. A third concern is that because transnational education is aimed primarily at upper socioeconomic groups, foreign providers may simply engage in "cream-skimming," exacerbating inequities in access to tertiary education. A fourth concern is of an internal "brain-drain"—wage differentials between faculty at public and private (foreign) institutions would result in public universities stripped of their most talented teachers.

These concerns must be juxtaposed against a reasonable counterfactual. It is not as if the current "closed" system higher education system has either sharply reduced social inequality or brought about exemplary "nation-building." If the choice is between students going overseas and spending money there or spending it mainly at home, the latter is surely a less-worse option. Indeed, a policy of allowing any university ranked in the world's top 1,000 could only improve Indian higher education given the handful of Indian universities that make the grade, as noted earlier.

But India's political economy has made liberalization in this sector exceedingly difficult. However, the return of the Congress party led government in 2009 with a stronger mandate, and the weakening of the left parties led to renewed hopes that a policy change would occur. Such a change would require the government to pass a bill in parliament that could only occur if it ensured a level playing field between foreign and domestic suppliers with regard to the sensitive issue of social obligations, namely affirmative action. This would make it very unlikely that reputed foreign universities would enter India, at least at the undergraduate level. The few that might will confine their activities to graduate, specialized degrees.

9.5.3 Virtual Education

Technology is driving another mechanism of availing of higher education—virtual education. Distance learning is not a new phenomenon in developing countries—students have enrolled in correspondence courses for decades, especially in teacher training programs.[28] But these classes had little interaction between faculty and students and were plagued by high dropout rates. However, significant improvements in technology in the past

28. In 1996, all of the five largest distance-learning programs were based in lower- or middle-income countries (World Bank and UNESCO 2000). These include Anadolu University in Turkey, founded in 1982; China TV University, founded in 1979; Universitas Terbuka, Indonesia, founded in 1984; Indira Gandhi National Open University (IGNOU), India, founded in 1985; Sukhothai Thammathirat Open University, Thailand, founded in 1978.

decade have transformed these programs, drastically increasing their size and scope. Despite skepticism on numerous fronts, especially perceived weaknesses on key components of quality education—discussion, collaboration, and reasoning skills—virtual education has been increasing rapidly. There has been a dramatic expansion of resources available online, specifically through the use of "open courseware," in which high quality "open knowledge" materials, including course content, library collections, and research data is being made available online. In 2006, more than 100 higher education institutions and associated organizations from around the world launched the Open Courseware Consortium, each pledging to place course materials for at least ten courses online for free.[29] By reducing constraints on access to quality content and instruction at low cost, virtual education has much promise. Nonetheless, making these resources available online does not solve the problem of access for the less privileged without addressing the availability of affordable Internet access, which continues to be a critical impediment.

The principal driver of virtual education in India has been the Indira Gandhi National Open University (with more than 1.8 million students). Despite the brouhaha about India's IT prowess, until recently there were only limited attempts at leveraging its potential for virtual education. However, a recent joint venture funded by the Indian government that includes all Indian institutes of technology (IITs) and the Indian Institute of Science (IISc), called the National Programme on Technology Enhanced Learning (NPTEL), aims to enhance the quality of engineering education in the country by developing curriculum-based video and Web courses. Dissemination is through an agreement with Google and YouTube. The NPTEL YouTube channel covering the courses hosts about seventy-four courses currently and has had more than 1.3 million visitors. However, the didactic importance of this mechanism is unclear as yet.

A major handicap is that 80 percent of India's Internet connections are in the country's twelve largest cities (which account for about one-tenth of the population). To address this issue, the Indian government launched a new $1 billion initiative in 2009—National Mission in Education through Information and Communication Technology—to provide content generation, connectivity, and computing infrastructure to all higher educational institutions across the country.

9.6 Conclusion

The paper has argued that while there has been a substantial growth in higher education in India, whether measured by the number of students or

29. Other examples include Connexions, the Open University in the United Kingdom, and CMU's Open Learning Initiative. They offer some advantages in that they are specifically designed for online distance learning.

expenditures (especially private), serious governance issues have hobbled the Indian university system. To the extent the Indian system has succeeded, it is largely the result of Darwinian selection mechanisms. The formal labor market invariably selects from such an enormous pool, with selection ratios often less than 1 percent, with the assumption that those selected may have limited skills but have the attributes to be trainable. A parallel surrogate higher education system has, however, evolved to impart job-related skills that are more akin to vocational education rather than a conventional university system.

In June 2009, a committee set up by the Indian government a year earlier submitted its report.[30] The report was a severe indictment of the Indian higher education system and largely corroborates many of the weaknesses emphasized in this paper. It called for sweeping changes to the regulatory system, abolishing the plethora of regulatory bodies and replacing them by a single body: a Commission for Higher Education and Research (CHER). In order to shield the new regulator against political pressures, the report emphasized that this commission be established through a constitutional amendment and have a constitutional status. It also highlighted the dangers of the growth of specialized institutions of higher education in the country at the cost of broad-based universities, short-changing the possibilities of a broad-based undergraduate education and cross-fertilization of ideas across disciplines. At the time of writing this paper, however, it was unclear if the Indian government would adopt the roadmap for reforms suggested by this commission or put into place some other ideas.

In addition, this paper also raises fundamental questions about just what we mean about higher education and the purposes it serves. Beyond selection, it is unclear what is the value added by higher education in India. It is entirely possible that the limited numbers of good higher education institutions benefit the few who have access to them and crowd out from labor markets others with similar ability but who lack access. Furthermore, with formal educational qualifications becoming more prevalent, the pressures to get credentialed are mounting, without the corresponding skills and training. However, just as an arms race does not lead to greater security despite much greater spending, the upward spiral in education credentialing in India, as elsewhere, may not yield social benefits commensurate to the expenditure (e.g., Wolf 2004; Murray 2008).

The success of the evolving surrogate education system has (at least now) depended mainly on drastic selection mechanisms and the ability to pay private providers. But for the vast majority of graduates with worthless degrees, who are not selected into these training programs and left to the

30. Government of India, *Report of the Committee to Advise on Renovation and Rejuvenation of Higher Education,* June 2009. The report is also known as the Yash Pal Committee report after the Chairman of the Committee that drafted the report.

vagaries of the informal sector, the risk of being locked into low productivity occupations is very real. The rapid increase in the number of credentialed but poorly educated young people posed significant political challenges for India in the 1970s at a time of economic stagnation. In an era of rapid growth these dangers are less apparent—but the sharp increase in their numbers and expectations, coupled with weak formal job market prospects for the majority of India's graduates, may well come back to haunt the country if its growth falters.

Even otherwise success in labor markets does not imply success in knowledge creation. India's knowledge needs in areas with large public goods pay offs, in social sciences and a host of basic sciences, be it climate change, health economics, infectious diseases, or agricultural technologies, have been woefully neglected. The Achilles heel of the system is that higher education in India has become so completely focused on professional education that the less instrumental aspects of higher education—research and training in the "liberal arts" and "pure" sciences—have atrophied significantly.[31] It is hard to gauge the long-term effects of this decline because there is little agreement on even the most fundamental question about higher education: what is the purpose of higher education? To train people for a labor force or train a labor force that is, in turn, trainable by employers? To create a middle class? Be an engine of innovation? Provide a ladder for social mobility or create national elites? To influence and mold the minds of young people? If the answer is "all of the above" (however weakly), the prognosis may be less bright than currently thought.

Given the enormous pool of young people in India, the future of India's higher education system will have considerable effects on the U.S. higher education system given that students from India constitute the largest number of foreign students in the United States. In the foreseeable future, at least that demand will remain, given the growing cohort of India students and the weaknesses of the Indian higher education system. However, the more noticeable change is likely to come when India modifies its policies to attract foreign universities and a new generation of Indian higher education institutions gets established. During the 1950s and 1960s, the collaboration between U.S. and Indian institutions established some of India's leading higher education institutions (see box 9.1). While those arrangements will not be precisely replicated, there are likely to be growing linkages between the large number of new central government as well as private institutions that are being set up and U.S.-based institutions on faculty training and exchanges, pedagogy, collaborative research programs, and student

31. For a view on India's attempts at improving science education, see Shobo Bhattacharya, "India's Education Experiment in Basic Sciences: The IISER Solution," *India in Transition,* January 7, 2009, http://casi.ssc.upenn.edu/iit/Bhattacharya.

Box 9.1 Examples of successful United States-India collaborations in higher education

Successful collaborations between the United States and India have a left a strong legacy, not just for India but for the United States as well. The Indian Institute of Technology, Kanpur, established in 1959, benefited in its first decade from the Kanpur Indo-American Programme, where a consortium of nine U.S. universities (Massachusetts Institute of Technology [MIT]; University of California, Berkeley; California Institute of Technology; Princeton University; Carnegie Institute of Technology; University of Michigan; Ohio State University; Case Institute of Technology; and Purdue University) helped set up the research laboratories and academic programs. The Indian Institute of Management, Ahmedabad established in 1961, collaborated with Kellogg School, Wharton School, and Harvard Business School in its initial years, while Indian Institute of Management, Calcutta, was developed in collaboration with MIT's Sloan School of Management and the Ford Foundation. Faculty training and program design were the key elements in these collaborations.

A less heralded, but equally successful collaboration, was the U.S. role in developing Indian agriculture higher education institutions. During the 1960s and 1970s, the Ford Foundation financed a large-scale extension build up, the Rockefeller Foundation helped strengthen agricultural research, and the United States Agency for International Development (USAID) helped conceptualize and finance a new institutional innovation—state agricultural universities. Because of the lack of knowledge about U.S. institutions, the Rockefeller Foundation awarded ninety short-term travel grants to Indian scientists and teachers to visit agricultural colleges and experiment stations in the United States between 1959 and the early 1970s, while resisting pressures to invest in university buildings and equipment.

In the 1950s, an Indian delegation visited the United States. Impressed by the contribution of the land grant universities, it recommended the establishment of at least one state agricultural university (SAU) per state. In 1960, India decided to create SAUs that were directly responsible to the states and outside the control of the Ministry of Education. The USAID provided funding for five American universities to enter into partnerships with nine of the newly established SAUs. The five American universities supplied 300 professors on assignments of two or more years to these nine Indian universities. An Agricultural Universities Commission was established in 1960. The Indian government invited the Rockefeller Foundation to help to help to craft a system of core institutions to support the development and spread of the Green Revolution and the Ford Foundation to help the Indian Council of Agricultural Research build centers of excellence to serve all of India at some of the state universities during the 1960s.

Today, the Gates Foundation is poised to play a similar role by assisting in the establishment of new public health schools in India to address India's poor record in this area. These collaborations have not only served India well through a cadre of excellent engineering and managerial human capital, and the technological basis for India's agricultural growth, but also helped supply the United States with excellent talent who over time created strong bridges between the two countries.

exchanges. In addition, programmatic research in global goods, such as sustainable agriculture, climate change, energy, transport, tropical diseases, and water, are likely to grow as well. India will represent one of the biggest overseas opportunities for U.S. higher education well into the future.

References

Agarwal, Pawan. 2006. Higher education in India: The need for change. ICRIER Working Paper no. 180. New Delhi, India: Indian Council for Research on International Economic Relations.

Basant, Rakesh, and Sen, Gitanjali. 2009. Who participates in higher education in India? Rethinking the role of affirmative action. Ahmedabad: Indian Institute of Management Working Paper no. 2009-11-01.

Chakravarty, Sujoy, and Eswaran Somanathan. 2008. Discrimination in an elite labour market? Job placements at the Indian Institute of Management—Ahmedabad. Indian Statistical Institute Discussion Paper no. 08-01. Delhi, India: Indian Statistical Institute.

Dutta, Puja Vasudeva. 2006. Returns to education: New evidence for India, 1983–1999. *Education Economics* 14 (4): 431–51.

Goldberg, Pinelopi Koujianou, and Nina Pavcnik. 2007. Distributional effects of globalization in developing countries. *Journal of Economic Literature* 45 (1): 39–82.

Kademani, B. S., Anil Sagar, and Vijai Kumar. 2006. Indian science & technology research: A scientometric mapping based on Science Citation Index. http://www.scientificcommons.org/17474092.

Kapur, Devesh, and Megan Crowley. 2008. Beyond the ABCs: Higher education and developing countries. Center for Global Development Working Paper no. 139. Washington, DC: Center for Global Development.

Kapur, Devesh, and Pratap Mehta. 2008. Mortgaging the future? Indian higher education. Brookings-NCAER India Policy Forum 2007.

Kijimi, Yoko. 2006. Why did wage inequality increase? Evidence from urban India 1983–99. *Journal of Development Economics* 81 (1): 97–117.
Murray, Charles. 2008. Are too many people going to college? *The American,* September 8.
Organization for Economic Cooperation and Development. 2007. *Economic survey of India, 2007.* Paris: OECD.
Wadhwa, Vivek, Una Kim De Vitton, and Gary Gereffi. 2008. How the disciple became the guru. http://ssrn.com/abstract=1170049Duke/Harvard.
Wolf, Alison. 2004. Education and economic performance: Simplistic theories and their policy consequences. *Oxford Review of Economic Policy* 20 (2): 315–33.
World Bank and UNESCO. 2000. Higher education in developing countries: Peril and promise. Washington, DC: World Bank.

10

From Brain Drain to Brain Competition

Changing Opportunities and the Career Patterns of US-Trained Korean Academics

Sunwoong Kim

10.1 Introduction

As other chapters in this volume have shown, many students around the world are coming to the U.S. universities to study, and some of them return to their native countries, while others stay in the United States. More and more PhDs, particularly in science and engineering (S&E), are awarded to foreign nationals, particularly from the students from China, India, and Korea, and they are becoming a major component of the research activities of the U.S. universities. Currently, the majority of Chinese and Indian PhDs intend to stay in the United States after their graduation.[1] However, based on the experience of Korean PhDs trained in the United States, it is not clear this pattern will continue into the future, raising the question whether and how the U.S. research universities will continually maintain their preeminence. The Korean experience shows that the situation in the home country plays a decisive role in determining the career choice of those foreign-born talents.

Clearly, PhDs are the core resource in research and development activities, and where and how they work will determine the effectiveness of not

Sunwoong Kim is professor of economics at the University of Wisconsin, Milwaukee.

I would like to thank the participants of the conference and, in particular, the organizer and the editor of this volume, Charles T. Clotfelter, for comments and suggestions.

1. According to the 2006 Survey of Earned Doctorates, among 45,596 doctorates awarded in the United States, about one-third (15,916) were awarded to foreign nationals. In engineering, the share of foreign nationals was 63 percent, and in physical science 53 percent. Chinese are the largest group with 4,774 degrees, followed by Indians with 1,742, then followed by Koreans with 1,648. 89.8 percent of Chinese, 88.1 percent of Indian, and 60.9 percent of Korean said they intended to stay in the United States (Hoffer et al. 2007). The share of the people who intended to stay has increased over time recently, but the trend reflects the increasing number of students from China and India.

only the higher education sector but also the national innovation system as a whole. The decision of those people to stay or return to their native country will depend on several professional and personal considerations. In this paper, we examine employment opportunities and career patterns of the U.S.-trained Korean PhDs in academia over the past several decades. Korea is an interesting country to study the employment and residence choice of the U.S.-trained highly skilled knowledge workers. Over the last fifty years, Korea has transformed itself from a low-income agrarian country to a fledgling advanced economy. Consequently, the Korean labor market situation for academics has changed significantly. In fact, the desirability of staying in the United States after gradation has changed significantly due to the Korean government's policy as well as the forces of internationalization in higher education and the globalization of the professorial market. The purpose of this paper is to highlight the changes in government policies, institutional arrangements, and market forces in Korean higher education system, and relate them to the employment choices and career patterns of the U.S.-trained Korean academics.

If one examines the post-Korean War period from the perspective of employment choice of the U.S.-trained Korean academics, three different periods can be identified: brain drain (1953–1970), brain gain (1970–1997), and brain competition (since 1979). The first period is typical of low-income countries: talented Korean students left for the United States to study abroad and stayed there after their education and training by being de facto immigrants. In the second period, a large number of Korean graduate students came to the United States for advanced degrees and returned to seek lucrative employment opportunities in the burgeoning Korean economy. During this period, Korea effectively outsourced its graduate education to the United States. In the third period, more U.S.-trained Korean PhDs sought employment opportunities outside of Korea. The professorial market became more globalized, and their midcareer movements were more diverse and complex. The Korean academic labor market became more competitive as a result of the greater supply of PhDs and the adaptation of merit-based personnel policies. Also, the competition among elite universities to seek world-class status became more evident, and they actively recruited midcareer researchers working in the United States. At the same time, there has been an increase of migration of Korean-educated postdocs to the United States. More professional cooperation and competition for and among talents across borders are emerging.

The paper is organized as follows. In the next section, we describe the large presence of Koreans in U.S. higher education and the large influence of U.S.-trained academics in Korean higher education. In section 10.3, historical context before the Korean War (1950–1953) explaining the close relationship between Korean and U.S. higher education is provided. In section 10.4, the first period of brain drain (1953–1970) is discussed. In section 10.5, we discuss how Korea used the brain gain (1970–1997) of the Korean expatriate for economic development and increasing the capacity of the Korean higher education sector. At the same time, we highlight the structural characteristics of the academic job market and explain why the Korean model of brain gain worked but could not be sustained. In section 10.7, we discuss the emerging trend of increased competition and mass internationalization of higher education since the Asian economic crisis (1997). We highlight the private and public responses to the changing market environment resulting in global brain competition. Finally, in the conclusion, we discuss the implications of this new trend of global brain competition to American universities.

10.2 The Importance of Korea and the United States in Each Others' Higher Education Sector

According to the data provided by the U.S. Institute of International Education, there were 564,766 foreign students enrolled in higher education institutions in the United States in the academic year of 2005 to 2006 (Institute of International Education [IIE] various years). There were 58,847 Korean students in the same year, representing 10.5 percent of all foreign students. Korea ranks third in terms of the number of students in U.S. higher education, following India with 76,503 students and China with 62,582 students. Considering the fact that both China and India have much bigger populations, Korea sends the most students per capita to the United States in the world. Among them, 46 percent are registered in undergraduate programs, 41 percent in graduate programs, and the rest in special programs. In addition to the students enrolled in the regular academic programs, there are about 10,000 Korean students studying in intensive English programs in the United States. Currently, Korea sends the largest number of students to the United States for English language training in the world, followed by Japan, which used to occupy the top position until recently.

Korean presence in U.S. higher education is prominent at the doctorate level as well. According to the 2006 Survey of Earned Doctorates, the number of PhDs awarded to Korean nationals was 1,648, only outranked by China (4,774) and India (1,742; Hoffer et al. 2007). Despite the large supply of PhDs, the number of Korean faculty members in American Universities is relatively small. The 2008 Directory of the Korean American University Professors Association (KAUPA) lists about 2,500 faculty members working in North America, and the majority of them are in the United States. While this number is relatively small, it has been growing rapidly for the last ten years due to the changes in the Korean and world academic labor markets. In addition, there are about 8,000 Korean visiting scholars and substantial number of Korean postdocs in U.S. universities.

On the other side of the ledger, the presence of U.S. universities in the

Korean higher education sector is also quite remarkable. Among Korean academics working in Korea who received their PhDs abroad, the United States is the biggest contributor. According to the data provided by the Korean Research Foundation, 52.8 percent Korean researchers with foreign PhDs who registered their degree during the period between January 2000 and August 2007 at the Foundation received their degrees in the United States. Following the United States, the proportion of Japanese PhDs accounts for 17.7 percent, followed by Germany (7.1 percent), the United Kingdom (5.5 percent), and China (4.6 percent). (*Dong-A Daily,* October 24, 2007). Because these data are based on self-reporting and ignore the fact that many U.S. PhDs don't tend to return to Korea immediately after their degree (compared to the degree recipients from other countries), the U.S. proportion is likely to be higher.

Currently, U.S. PhDs dominate the professorial positions in Korean universities. The pattern is most striking in top-rank universities. In Seoul National University, 886 out of 1,683 professors with PhDs (52.6 percent) received their PhDs in the United States. Some disciplines have much higher proportions than others. In general, management, social sciences, natural sciences, and engineering have higher proportions of U.S. PhDs than humanities, law, medicine, and nursing. Almost 90 percent of business school faculty members have U.S. PhDs. In social sciences, the proportion is 78.8 percent, in natural sciences 77.6 percent, in engineering 76.8 percent, and in biological and life sciences 76.8 percent. (*Chosun Daily,* October 18, 2007). The other two premier science and engineering universities in Korea, Korea Advanced Institute of Science and Technology (KAIST) and Pohang School of Technology (POSTECH), also have a very high proportion of U.S. PhDs. At KAIST, 84 out of 101 (83.2 percent) science professors and 170 out of 239 (71.1 percent) engineering professors received their PhDs in the United States. At POSTECH, 73 out of 81 (90.1 percent) science professors and 99 out of 120 (82.5 percent) engineering professors received their PhDs in the United States (data from KCUE *Faculty Directory of Universities in Korea, 2004*). Beyond their sheer number, the U.S.-trained academics form the basic tenets and methodology of many academic disciplines (e.g., see Choi [1997] on the influence of U.S.-trained academics on economic science in Korea).

In the second-tier universities, the proportion of U.S.-trained PhDs is smaller. For example, at Hanyang University, a private university whose overall ranking in Korea is around five or seven among all Korean universities, 41.1 percent of professors in sciences and 40.3 percent in engineering are U.S. PhDs. At Kyunghee University, another private university whose overall ranking is around ten, 43.4 percent of science professors and 33.3 percent of engineering professors are from the United States. At Kyungbook University, a national university in Daegu (a major provincial city), 51.5

percent of science professors and 27.9 percent of engineering professors received their PhDs from major U.S. universities.

10.3 Historical Legacy (from Late Nineteenth Century to the Korean War, 1950–1953)

It is natural to wonder why Korea, a relatively small country located far away from the U.S. mainland, has such a strong relationship with the U.S. higher education system. In order to answer this question, one needs to start with longer and broader historical backgrounds since the beginning of modern education in Korea. The American influence started in the nineteenth century when several U.S. missionaries established several modern higher education institutions in Korea. During the Japanese colonial period (1910–1945), the United States provided a safe haven for overseas Korean expatriates working for Korean independence. More direct and stronger influence started in the aftermath of World War II and the Korean War, when the United States took a great part in Korean politics and national security. Since then, the Korean higher education system has been heavily influenced by U.S.-trained academics (Lee 1989).

During the period between 1880 and 1910, when the Chosun Dynasty struggled to cope with the encroachment of the powerful imperialistic nations of the period, the student flow to the United States was minimal because of the obvious difficulty of traveling the long distance between the nations at that time. Most foreign cultural and intellectual influence from advanced nations was through the students who studied in neighboring Japan and China. However, American missionaries during the time period actively participated in the beginning of modern education in Korea by establishing higher education institutions. Many such institutions, such as Yonsei University, Soongsil University, and Ewha Womans University, are still in existence today and constitute top-rung private universities in Korea.

During Japan's forced annexation of Korea between 1910 and 1945, the development of modern education in Korea was severely suppressed by the colonial government. For the first twenty-five years of the colonial rule, no universities were allowed in the Korean peninsula, and all institutions of higher learning were converted to technical colleges in order to provide technical manpower necessary in governing the colony. Most top Korean students who wanted to further their study went to Japan for several reasons. First, Japan was the colonial power, and the elites who were attached to the colonial government were favored in Japan, and their children were welcome in Japanese higher education institutions. Second, as the economic and social ties between Japan and its Korean territory increased, more information regarding study in Japan was available to the potential students.

However, there were only a few dozen Koreans in the U.S. universities at any given time until 1940s.[2] However, the United States provided an alternative to Japan to those who overtly or covertly worked for Korean independence. For those students, Japan was a dangerous place, and the United States provided a safe haven for their independence activities. In contrast to the education in Japan, which stressed the importance of the national power and the collective ethos, American social philosophy was based on individual freedom and democracy. Therefore, the philosophy and attitude of the Korean students in the United States were very different from those in Japan regarding Japanese colonialism and Korean nationalism.

The victory of the United States over Japan in World War II gave the scholars and leaders who were trained in the United States a great deal of leverage, and they often served as the conduit of the American policy toward the occupied land. In fact, many of those who studied in the United States felt quite strongly about such social responsibility. The list of the Who's Who in the independence movement and early Korean government, business, and social leaders were dominated by those who studied in the United States during the colonial period (e.g., Ahn Chang-Ho, Rhee Syngman, Ahn Ick-Tae, Yeom Sang-Seop, Cheon Young-Taek, Paik Nack-Jun, Helen Kim, Yun Chi-Young, Hong Nan-Pa, and so on). In particular, Rhee Syungman, who studied at Harvard and Princeton, mobilized Koreans in Hawaii for the nation's independence movement during the Japanese colonial period and became the first president of the newly independent South Korea in 1948. Despite the large influence of the U.S.-educated Korean leaders, the number of Koreans who were exposed to U.S. universities was very small. However, the outbreak of the Korean War (1950–1953) and the U.S. military involvement in the war changed the picture dramatically.

10.4 Brain Drain: The First Wave of Study Abroad (1953–1970)

Figure 10.1 depicts the changes in the number of Korean students in U.S. higher education institutions since 1954, the first year that the Institute of International Education (IIE) started to keep track of the statistics. According to the figure, there were two major waves of study abroad in the United States by Koreans. The first wave, a relatively small one, started immediately after the Korean War. The second wave, a major wave that started around 1980, does not show any sign of slow down despite a temporary setback during the Asian Financial Crisis of 1997 to 1999. However, the nature of the study in the United States and the behavior of the students in the two waves are quite different from one another. The first wave was a typical brain drain in which talented students went to the United States and

2. Around 1930, it was reported that there were about 300 Korean students in the U.S. higher education institutions, while there were more than 3,000 in Japan (Chang 2005).

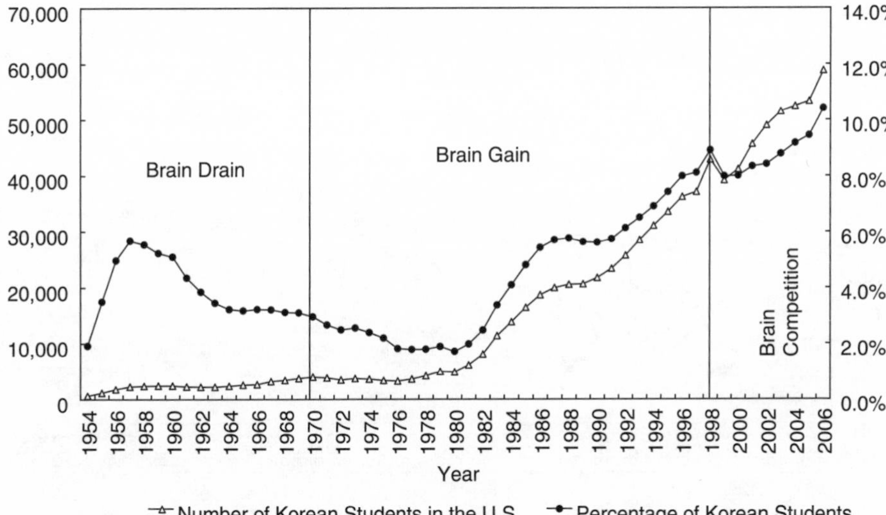

Fig. 10.1 Korean students in U.S. higher education
Source: IIE *Open Doors* (various years).

stayed there after their education and training by being de facto immigrants. The second wave is a large-scale internationalization of higher education between Korea and the United States.

During the first wave, increasing numbers of Koreans started to come to the United States for study abroad. Motivations and financial support for those students were quite diverse. Some students were sent by the Rhee government. Any students who planned to go overseas to study were exempted from the mandatory military service. The Rhee government wanted to use them as a vehicle for technology transfer in order to reconstruct and develop the war-torn nation. Most of these students concentrated in graduate studies in S&E. Some students were supported by the U.S. government, including Fulbright Scholarships and East-West Center Fellowships. Some students were adopted or sponsored by American soldiers and missionaries, whose number increased dramatically since the Korean War. Some were financed by their own families.

In any case, many bright Korean students who finished their advanced degree in the United States ended up settling down in the United States. This phenomenon was particularly keen in the science and engineering fields, where scholarships for graduate students and employment opportunities in the United States after graduation were much more abundant. Korea lost these talented people for two major reasons.

First, there was a large difference in living standards between the United States and Korea. Figure 10.2 shows the relative income between Korea and

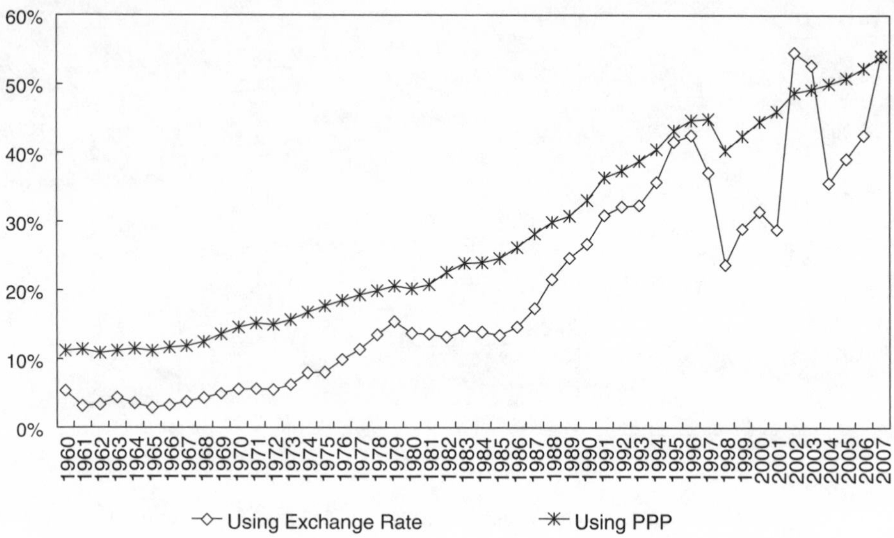

Fig. 10.2 The ratio of per capita GDP between Korea and the United States
Sources: http://www.NationMaster.com and U.S. Bureau of Labor Statistics.

the United States between 1960 and 2007. The ratio of the Korean gross domestic product (GDP) per capita to the U.S. GDP per capita was calculated using the official exchange rate and purchasing power parity (PPP). The graph using the exchange rate is more volatile of the two because of the exchange rate fluctuation as Korea has maintained the managed flexible exchange rate regime since the late 1960s. The figure shows that the relative income between the two countries remained pretty stable up until 1967 (3–5 percent using the exchange rate and 11 percent using PPP). Since the late 1960s, the relative income has steadily increased to around 45 percent until the Asian Financial Crisis in 1997 to 1998. After this significant negative shock, the Korean economy recovered fairly quickly, and the relative income reached about 54 percent in 2007. Rapidly rising income in Korea certainly had an important influence on the return decisions of the students in the later period, which will be discussed later.

The second reason for the drain was the lack of professional opportunity, due to the underdevelopment of research infrastructure in Korea. When the student returned to Korea after the successful study, he or she would find that the working conditions in Korea were much inferior to the ones in the United States. Even if the student were financed by the government and were obligated to return home, the government found it difficult to place the returnee. Consequently, the returnee was often forced to work in a field different from his or her specialization or went back to the United States.

It is difficult to obtain quantitative measures of the extent of the brain drain in this period. However, the pattern is not very different from the current brain drain of highly educated and trained professionals from low-income countries to high-income countries, widely observed in many countries (Beine, Docquier, and Rapport 2001; Kao and Lee 1973; Kwok and Leland 1982; Wong and Yip 1999; Katz and Stark 1984).[3] In the case of Korea, however, its brain drain was not a total waste. Rather, it can be regarded as a "brain saving" because some of the expatriate Korean talents were effectively mobilized during the subsequent push for rapid economic growth and the expansion of the higher education sector.

10.5 Brain Gain (1970–1997)

10.5.1 Human Capital and Economic Growth in Korea

In explaining the Korea's successful economic development experience since early 1960s, economists usually point out several reasons. Rapid expansion of production capacity through heavy investment in capital goods and infrastructure, stable governments, high domestic savings rates, disciplined Confucian work ethic, and well-timed government-led economic policies have been often cited as the major determinants of Korea's high growth rates (e.g., Amsden 1989; Song 1997). However, the accumulation of Korea's human capital has been relatively ignored in the discussion of Korea's successful economic development process.

Domestically, when the Park Chung-Hee Administration (1961–1979) started to implement the government-led economic development plan, Korea was already prepared with quite substantial human resources as a result of more than a decade of intensive human capital investment by the previous administration. Immediately after independence, the previous Rhee Syngman Administration (1948–1960) pushed for universal primary school education under the guidance of American education planners (McGinn 1980). Although the effort had been seriously jeopardized by the outbreak of the Korean War, the successful postwar implementation of universal primary schooling increased the primary school enrollment from 1.37 million students in 1945 to 2.27 million in 1947 to 4.94 million in 1965. Despite the substantial foreign aid provided by the United States, Rhee's government failed to establish a peaceful and prosperous economy, due to widespread corruption among its political elite and political instability. But its legacy of expanding universal primary education paid off handsomely several years later. The number of teachers increased from 20,000 in 1945 to 79,000 in 1965. By 1965, the goal of universal primary school education

3. 63 percent of foreign-born students who earned science and engineering doctorates from U.S. institutions between 1988 and 1996 said they planned to locate in the United States. Two-thirds of those who planned to stay had firm plans for further study or employment (Johnson 1998).

had been more or less achieved, and the human resources for Park's export promotion policies by specializing labor intensive manufacturing industries were already in place (Korean Ministry of Education and Human Resources 1998).

The second important aspect of human capital resources in that era was the availability of highly educated people that assumed leadership roles in Korean economy. Many of these people received advanced degrees in the United States. The Korean government did not pursue a systematic policy of "learning from the West" that the Meiji government of Japan adopted in the middle of nineteenth century. However, many Korean talents went to the United States for advanced study through personal and religious affiliations because the United States was heavily involved in the Korean War and the reconstruction efforts afterward. As early as 1953, the number of Korean students enrolled in U.S. higher education jumped to around 2,000 to 3,000 (IIE various year). During the 1950s, there were about 50,000 to 60,000 foreign students in the United States, and Korean students accounted about 5 to 6 percent of them. Surprisingly, Korea ranked between fifth and tenth in terms of the number of students enrolled in U.S. higher education in the late 1950s despite the lower income and relatively small population. When the Park Administration set the goal of economic development by recruiting U.S.-trained engineers and economists, there were already substantial numbers of Korean expatriate professionals in the United States.[4]

10.5.2 Push for Brain Gain

As a part of economic development strategy, the Park Administration actively recruited and utilized the U.S.-trained knowledge workers. For example, in 1966, the Korea Institute of Science and Technology (KIST) was established, and wholesale recruitment of Korean scientists and engineers from abroad, particularly from the United States, began.[5] The Korea Development Institute (KDI) was established in 1971 in order to advise the government for the active economic planning exercise. To launch these institutions, which were created outside of the existing universities and other government agencies, their presidents began by recruiting qualified scientists, engineers, and economists who could lead their research groups. Salaries were set much higher than the local pay level. Generous allowances for research equipment and assistants were provided. In addition, modern housing and educational allowance for their children were provided (Yoon 1992; Song 1997).

From the perspective of Korean PhDs in the United States, such job offers presented opportunities as well as substantial risks. On the one hand, they

4. See Kapur (2001) and Vasegh-Daneshvary, Schlottmann, and Herzog (1987) for international migration of professionals and technology transfer.

5. Major funding for the establishment of KIST was provided by the Johnson Administration as a quid pro quo to Park's decision to send fighting forces to Vietnam War.

presented a great opportunity to go back home and contribute to the development of the homeland. Although the working conditions and the material reward were comparable to the existing jobs in the United States, the positions offered more professional freedom because they were given wider and greater responsibility. There was a certain personal satisfaction about being able use their knowledge and skills in promoting the welfare of the people in the homeland. Also, being able to be close to relatives (particularly aging parents) and friends was a plus. On the other hand, there were certain personal and professional risks. Other family members, particularly young children, might not adjust well to Korean society and be unhappy about the move back. Professionally, the move could lead to a dead-end career prospect and loss of valuable professional connections in the United States. Based on this obvious trade-off, not all expatriates welcomed such offers. But some were willing to take the risk and come back to Korea in such an environment.

Overall, the government-sponsored institutions were a great success. The institutions were able to recruit enough expatriates to Korea, and the returnees were able to contribute greatly to the scientific, engineering, and economic progress (Song 1997; Yoon 1992). Observing the success of government-sponsored research institutes, universities and private firms also participated in the recruitment of the U.S.-trained talents. Because the supply of talents was rather limited, their labor market return was quite high. Such a positive market signal for the U.S.-educated professionals and rising income in Korea created a bonanza of going to the United States for the purpose of studying. Having seen the successful career developments of the U.S.-trained professionals, large-scale study abroad started.

With the strong market signal, many bright young people leave Korea to study in the United States. Some of them may end up staying in the United States because of its superior working conditions and quality of life. However, if the Korean economy provided high enough incentives, a majority of these talents would come back to Korea. The high incentives of the returnee created strong incentives for more young people to go to the United States. In effect, Korea virtually outsourced its graduate education to the United States. As long as the incentive existed, the process of brain gain continued. In Korean universities, the U.S.-educated PhDs started to fill many professorial positions in Korea. Following their favorite professors' advice, the brightest students who aspire to obtain advanced degrees go abroad, and the United States has been the most popular destination for those expecting to obtain a professorial position in Korea (Mountford 1997). In 1999, about 80 percent of 40,000 full-time faculty members in Korean universities have doctoral degrees, and about 50 percent of them earned PhDs from abroad, with 67.2 percent of the foreign doctorates being from the United States (Korean Council for University Education 2000). This ratio is undoubtedly higher among younger faculty members.

There are several reasons that the Korean government's initiative to invite back the high-skilled expatriates was successful. First, the timing of the recruitment strategy worked out well. There was enough supply of highly educated and skilled Korean knowledge workers in the United States already so that there were enough people who would be willing to return despite the risks mentioned in the preceding. Second, the success of the subsequent economic growth for an extended period gave enough confidence to the potential returnees. Third, the size of the recruitment was substantial enough so that the potential recruit felt that he or she was not alone, and the community of returnees can form a community to support one another in Korea. Fourth, the stronger political and military ties between Korea and the United States due to Korea's participation in the Vietnam War gave confidence to the Korean government officials as well as to the returnees. Fifth, the government was able to provide special privileges and much higher compensation to the returnees than existing domestic workers as they were absorbed to the newly created institutions rather than the existing ones.

10.5.3 Professorial Market in Korea and Brain Gain

During the Park Administration (1961–1979), the expansion of higher education in Korea was heavily suppressed. During the administration, the enrollment in secondary schools increased more than five times; the graduates are encouraged to follow technical careers after their graduation rather than advancing to universities. In the previous Rhee Administration, the higher education sector was left to the market. With little government support and supervision, the sector was expanded mainly by profit-seeking academic entrepreneurs. Consequently, a substantial part of the private higher education sector was plagued with low quality and corruption. Although all the private universities in Korea are de jure nonprofit institutions, many behave like de facto for-profit institutions on behalf of the founder's family.

The Park government that obtained the power through a military coup was trying to gain legitimacy by cleaning up the corruption. Heavy regulation toward the higher education sector was adopted as an anticorruption measure. For example, individual institutions are required to obtain specific permission by the government in order to increase the size of the department within the institution. Moreover, the economic development plan during the Park Administration called for the rapid increase in the supply of semiskilled production workers. Meanwhile, professors and students in universities were regarded as trouble makers to the government because of their incessant criticism and protests against the dictatorial government.

The natural consequence of the enrollment quota in higher education and restricted supply of university-educated workers was a large wage premium for university graduates. As the government's support for higher education was relatively small, tuition revenue was the major source of income for

Korean universities. Naturally, households are required to bear the bulk of the higher education expenditure, and student tuition and fees were set relatively high. At the same time, Korean universities have enjoyed the freedom to choose students albeit the government's heavy regulations on the methods of student selection. As a result of the freedom and the competition among students, universities have a well-known pecking order.[6] As the perceived monetary and social gain for the elite universities was high, the competition to enter universities in Korea was extremely fierce even with high tuition payment.

The phenomenon of brain gain made the pursuit of graduate education, in particular PhD programs in top American universities, even more desirable. An advanced degree was regarded as an important credential for professorial positions, and this credential was more important than teaching and research performance. As we shall discuss in the following, professors in Korean universities are granted de facto tenure when they are hired, and salaries and promotions are mostly determined by years on the job. Their salaries were quite high, and the job security was extremely high. Consequently, professorial positions were very desirable. The mandatory retirement age for professors was sixty-five, which was five to ten years later than most private-sector jobs. While their teaching load was typically higher than U.S. norms (typically nine credit hours per semester in research universities and twelve credit hours in teaching schools), compared with private-sector employees in Korea, their working lives were much more pleasant.[7]

Until 1975, Korean professorial positions were well protected. The Korean Constitution and higher education related laws guarantee the independence of higher education institutions, and academic staffs in those institutions enjoyed de facto tenure when they were appointed as a full-time lecturer, both in public and private universities.[8] They move up to the rank of assistant professor, associate professor, and professor over time. There were part-time lecturers as well, but they were subject to one- or two-year limited time appointments.

In 1975, the dictatorial government introduced a reappointment system for university personnel. Professors and associate professors were supposed to be reappointed every six to ten years, and assistant professors and full-

6. Lee and Brinton (1996) examined how university prestige generates advantage for entry into the labor market. Social background of the new job seeker does not directly influence the job search outcome, but institutional social capital (the help of the placement office, professors, or friends and alum) play an important role.

7. Korea has by far the longest working hours among OECD countries.

8. The Korean university system has public universities and private universities. Most of the public universities are national universities that are run by the Ministry of Education. Other public universities are run by local governments and other government agencies. Private universities (some with religious affiliations and others independent) are governed by the board of trustees. The Korean higher education system is dominated by private universities, and about three-quarters of university students are enrolled in private universities. See S. Kim (2008) for more detail on Korean higher education system.

time lecturers every two to three years. Although the stated objective of the new system was to sanction academic staff who were not doing their jobs properly, the real motivation was to control one of the most vocal and influential social groups opposing the dictatorship, professors. While some politically active professors failed to be reappointed, the number of them not reappointed was in fact extremely small. Between 1975 and 1999, only 226 professors failed to be reappointed, and 115 universities did not have a single case of no reappointment (Lee and Im 2000; Ham and Hong 2007; Seo, Jeong, and Kwak 2000).

In 1987, the dictatorial government backed by the military gave away to a democratically elected government. As part of the regime change, students and faculty members had struggled for a more democratic internal and external governance of the universities. The new government changed the appointment of presidents in national universities to direct election by the full-time regular faculty members. In private universities, while the boards of trustees still appointed the president, the faculty council gained a stronger voice against the administration.

Korean professors have been relatively well-paid as well. In 1990, the average salary of full professors was 27 million Korean won (about 5.5 times the GDP per capita), and that of full-time lecturers was 16.7 million won (about 3.5 times the GDP per capita). Professors in private universities were paid, on average, about 10 percent more than those in public universities. Most universities have a seniority-based salary system, that is, salary is mostly determined by the years on the job. While there is a component based on the performance and the area of specialty, the difference is marginal. For example, in 1995, the average salary of professors in humanities and social science was 42 million won, science and engineering 39 million, and medical science 44 million based on the salary survey done by Kim (1996). In 2000, the average salary at the rank of full professor was $40,422; associate professor, $33,231; assistant professor, $28,948; and instructor, $24,305 (Lee 2003).

Performance played very little role in determining the salary. The total compensation includes a substantial amount of various nontaxable components, including a research fund, which ranges from 10 to 30 percent of the total compensation, children's educational expenses, and so on. The nonsalary components account for 40 to 60 percent of the total compensation depending on institution. There are other perks associated with being professors in Korea. Korean universities have a very liberal leave policy. Professors have been allowed to take a leave of absence for a variety of reasons without much penalty. For example, they commonly run for public offices, such as members of the National Assembly or mayors. When they fail or decide to come back to the old position, they have been routinely taken back to the previous positions. Second, professors have been able to actively participate in social and public activities. Some are paid activities such as consulting for the government or private firms or voluntary civic actions such as in nongovernmental organizations.

Because the professorial positions have been coveted by most PhDs, exit from the professorial positions to other types of jobs are extremely rare. According to Lee et al. (2007), out of 372 job transfers who moved out of industry during the period between 1994 and 2006, 47 percent moved to higher education institutions and 8.3 percent to research institutions, and the remainder to other private firms. Among 400 transfers out of higher education institutions, 81 percent moved to other higher education institutions, 12 percent to research institutes, and only 7 percent to private firms. Among 233 transfers out of research institutes, 73 percent moved to higher education institutions, 16.7 percent to research institutions, and only 9.4 percent to private firms. According to the same survey, of PhDs working in science and engineering fields, 68.3 percent received their degrees outside of Korea. Among the foreign PhDs, 64 percent are from the United States.

10.5.4 Brain Gain Was Not Sustainable: PhD Glut

Up until the mid-1990s, Korea did relatively well in minimizing brain drain. Compared to other Asian countries such as China and India, the percentage of Korean PhD recipients who intended to stay in the United States was substantially lower. In this regard, the large influx of Korean students into the United States during this period can be regarded effectively as a mechanism for training high-level human resources without much domestic investment. In particular, the Korean higher education sector had been able to allocate substantial human resources to professorial positions in a relative short time period. However, despite its strong growth, this Korean model of brain gain could not be sustained for an extended period. Rigid personnel policies in universities characterized by very low turnover rates of faculty members, lack of performance-based personnel policy, and the politicized governance structure generated a stale system that is not flexible enough to absorb the rapidly rising supply of PhDs efficiently.

Figure 10.3 shows the dramatic increase in the number of Korean PhDs received during the 1980s both in Korea and in the United States. In 1980, only 249 PhDs in the fields of humanities, social sciences, natural sciences, and engineering (150 of them were in natural sciences and engineering) were awarded in Korea. In 1990, the number reached 1,916 (1,137 in S&E). In the United States, the number of PhD degrees awarded to Koreans increased from 116 (87 in S&E) to 1,275 (767 in S&E) during the same period. This Korean bonanza of U.S. PhDs culminated in 1993 to 1994. In those years, more than 6 percent of total PhDs granted in U.S. institutions were awarded to Koreans. Much of this study abroad phenomenon was driven by individual students and occurred outside of formal government programs.

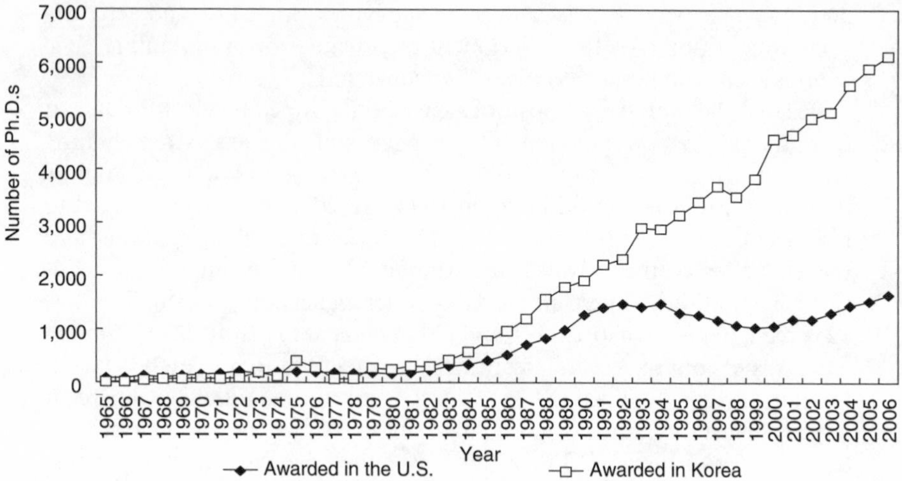

Fig. 10.3 Number of doctorates awarded to Koreans in the United States and in Korea

Sources: Survey of Earned Doctorate (United States) and author's tabulation based on the *Korean Education Statistics Yearbook.*

Note: Korean statistics do not include professional doctorate degrees such as law and medicine.

Most of the students came to the United States with temporary visas, and more and more students are supported by personal means since 1985 (see table 10.1).[9]

The sharp increase in the number of Korean PhDs during the period was due to several factors. First, the number of undergraduate students in Korea increased very rapidly after the late 1970s. Because of the burgeoning number of high school graduates and increasing advancement rate to universities, the government was forced to increase the quota of college enrollments. In 1978, the enrollment in the Korean university system was about 278,000. In the education reform pushed by the Chun Doo-Hwan Administration in 1980, the quota for university students increased substantially. Due to the relaxation of the quota, the enrollment figure increased to 932,000 in 1985. The sharp increase in the number of undergraduate degrees created higher demand for graduate degrees, including the PhD.[10]

Second, the economic rate of return to PhD was quite high. As the number of PhDs was very small, and the higher education sector was expanding quite rapidly, the domestic demand for professors was quite high. Until the early 1990s, despite a substantial gap in earning potential between the

9. These figures include any partial supports by the university or the government.
10. See S. Kim (2008) for more on the rapid expansion of higher education in Korea.

Table 10.1 **Statistical profiles of Korean doctorates received in the United States**

	1975	1980	1985	1990	1995	2000
Total number of PhDs earned	190	158	392	1,259	1,306	1,048
Natural Science and Engineering (%)	59.5	55.0	64.2	60.9	52.4	53.2
Social Science including Psychology (%)	21.6	28.5	18.7	16.9	24.6	18.0
Humanities, Education, and Professional (%)	18.9	16.5	17.1	22.2	23.0	28.8
Some personal financial support (%)	44.2	53.8	79.7	72.4	74.1	96.5
With permanent visa (%)	36.3	21.5	12.0	5.6	10.0	9.7
Intend to stay in the United States[a] (%)	46.8	48.5	33.5	31.5	38.7	64.1
Firm plans to stay in the United States[a] (%)	37.7	40.9	25.8	23.0	20.9	42.9
No. with firm plan to stay[a]	58	54	84	225	210	320
No. with firm employment[a]	35	21	31	68	35	115
Postdoc[a]	23	33	53	157	175	205
Educational institution[a]	13	6	12	30	18	29
Industry/business[a]	20	12	16	31	15	82

Source: Johnson (1998).
[a]Only for science and engineering (including social sciences).

United States and Korea, many U.S.-educated talents gladly chose a career in Korea because the jobs in Korea tended to be higher in status and responsibility. Korean jobs tended to have more stress and longer hours, but they could be more fulfilling, as they carry more responsibility. Between 1965 and 1995, the Korean economy was growing rapidly, and there was a strong demand for such talents as firms and society needed highly educated manpower for its leadership positions. Most of the U.S.-educated PhDs were able to take up such positions.

Third, as the process of brain gain continued, the number and the capacity of graduate faculty increased within Korean universities. Most of the faculty members in top Korean universities have PhDs from elite universities around the world, particularly from the United States. Consequently, more graduate programs were established domestically, and the number of PhDs awarded by those institutions started to increase rapidly.

Given the low turnover among professors due to de facto tenure at hire, the supply of PhDs quickly outnumbered the domestic demand. During the late 1980s and early 1990s, it became evident that the job prospects for new PhDs dimmed as the number of U.S.-educated PhDs grew rapidly. More graduate students then wanted to stay in Korea for their PhD in order not to lose contact with the professors who could help in securing teaching positions. Also, the quality of faculty and graduate education in Korea improved substantially, thanks to the quality of the new faculty and the establishment of graduate and research-oriented universities. Consequently, the relative attractiveness of pursuing a PhD in Korea (vis-à-vis in the United States) increased substantially. At the same time, the Korean government provided military service exemptions to those who pursue graduate education in

Table 10.2 Earned doctoral degrees awarded in Korea

Year	Total	Humanities	Social sciences	Natural science & engineering	Professional
Pre-1965	563	15	3	40	505
1965	117	2	0	8	107
1970	407	7	6	62	329
1975	994	26	17	69	220
1980	528	54	50	168	300
1985	1,400	157	105	528	610
1990	2,747	439	340	1,137	831
1995	4,429	617	447	1,820	1,243
2000	6,555	746	679	3,148	1,982
2003	7,623	779	675	3,622	2,547
2006	9,314	952	858	4,320	3,184

Source: KMOE (various years), *Education Statistics Yearbook.*
Note: Humanities include literature, philosophy, and theology; social sciences include economics, political science, business administration, and public administration; natural science and engineering also includes agriculture and fishery; professional includes law, medicine, pharmacy, dentistry, oriental medicine, public health, nursing, home economics, and education.

Korea.[11] Because of all these factors, the number of graduate students and PhDs awarded in Korea has risen rapidly since 1985. As shown in table 10.2, the number of doctoral-level degrees (PhDs and professional doctorate degrees including law, medicine, and so on) awarded in Korea increased from only about 400 in 1970 to 9,314 in 2006.

As the supply of qualified PhDs increased, many of them with degrees from top-notch universities around the world, Korean universities could afford to be choosier over time. Universities tended to look for PhDs from higher ranking universities over time. As the supply of PhDs from top universities became more plentiful, universities could consider not only the university from which the candidate received the degree, but also her or his research output (particularly in the form of publications) after graduation. Naturally, younger faculty members tended to have better credentials and have stronger research capability.

Many of the new PhDs have been hired by universities, and the proportion of PhDs in academic staff has increased very rapidly (see table 10.3). However, the glut of PhDs made the job market prospects of the recent PhDs rather dismal. A peculiar trap resulting from this excess supply PhDs is the underemployed "part-time instructor." Most Korean universities, particu-

11. Korea maintains a compulsory military service for all men. Because of the post-War baby boom, the military was not able to take all draftees. One principle that was accepted as the reason for the exemption of the service was the contribution to the nation in alternative way. Apparently, graduate-level education in S&E was regarded to meet the criterion to policymakers.

Table 10.3 **Doctoral degree holders in four-year colleges and universities in Korea**

Year	Full-time teaching staff (A)	Doctorate holders (B)	B/A (%)
1970	7,944	1,440	18.1
1975	10,242	2,807	27.4
1980	14,696	4,835	32.9
1985	26,459	9,090	34.3
1990	33,340	16,055	48.5
1995	45,087	26,771	5934
2000	41,943	34,666	82.7
2005	49,300	41,397	84.1
2006	51,859	43,362	83.6

Note: Full-time teaching staff before 1997 includes teaching assistants.

larly private universities under strong incentives to reduce expenditure on teaching personnel, have relied heavily on cheap part-time instructors.[12] In 2007, the number of full-time academic staff in four-year universities was 52,592, whereas the number of part-time lectures in those institutions was 59,848 (KEDI and MOE database). There has been a steady increase of part-time lecturers: in 2001, there were 38,050 part-time lecturers and 46,283 full-time academic staff in four-year universities (Kang and Paik 2005). In two-year junior colleges, the situation is worse: that same year there were 11,543 full-time staff and 22,180 part-time lectures. This heavy reliance on part-time lecturers became a serious structural problem in Korean higher education. Private universities used them to reduce the instruction costs, and even with a PhD, they cannot make a decent living. After investing so many years in schooling and for PhDs, part-time instructors struggle with low earnings for many years, hoping eventually to secure full-time teaching positions (W.-Y. Kim 2008).[13] Because of the slow turnover of the regular professorial positions and the sluggish expansion of new positions, the wait becomes longer every year.

The situation is worse for domestic PhDs because foreign PhDs typically have better reputations. In the academic year 2007, 4,749 new faculty members were hired in four-year universities, and 1,595 of them (42.5 percent) received their final (mostly PhD) degrees abroad. In fact, the proportion of foreign PhDs has been increasing, not decreasing, steadily over the last few years. In 2002, it was only 34.6 percent. A similar pattern is found in two-year junior colleges: the proportion of new hires in the colleges with foreign degrees increased from 19.2 percent in 2002 to 28.7 percent in 2007.

12. Most part-time instructors do not have other meaningful occupations, but teach several courses, sometimes in several schools simultaneously.

13. The issue of part-time instructors has been surfaced to a social problem by the suicide of a long-time, part-time instructor at Seoul National University in June 2003. There has been an effort to organize a labor union for part-time instructors recently. For more information, visit http://www.kangno.com.

In 2002, full-time, nontenure-track instructors were introduced, and by 2005, fifty-three universities had adopted this type of position. Although there are only 557 of them, the system became more popular, and in some universities, they account for more than 30 percent of the instruction staff. Their working conditions are substantially worse than full-time, tenure-track positions. They have lower salaries (50–80 percent of the tenure-track counterpart) and heavier teaching loads (the majority of them have more than twelve credit hours per semester).

10.6 Drivers for Global Brain Competition (since 1997)

For the last two decades, the Korean higher education system became more deregulated and internationalized. Consequently, universities became more responsive to the changing market environment. *Joong-Ang Daily*, one of the leading daily newspapers, now regularly publishes a Korean university ranking similar to that produced by *U.S. News and World Report*. As the tuition fees of Korean universities, even the public universities, are quite substantial, students and parents are quite sensitive to the education value of the universities. The recent sharp decline of the age cohort of college going age despite of large expansion of higher education system has also encouraged many universities to actively recruit students. Attractive academic programs and star faculty members in addition to better student services became major tools for student recruitment.

As the Korean economy continued to grow, study abroad became more affordable and popular. In addition to traditional graduate students, a growing number of Korean students go abroad for their undergraduate degrees or intensive language courses (particularly English). According to a recent study done by the Korea Trade Association, the number of Korean students seeking degrees or language training abroad in 2003 was about 350,000. The amount they spent in one year was estimated at about 4.6 billion U.S. dollars, which is about a quarter of the budget of the Korea Ministry of Education and Human Resources.[14] There has been a steep increase in these numbers.

The excess supply of PhDs, increased competition among universities, and the mass internationalization of higher education generated a changing environment in the higher education sector, and major stakeholders actively sought better market opportunities. Individual PhDs need to adjust to the professorial labor market with increasingly greater supply. At the same time, they want to look for a better professional and personal environment when they decide where to live, as Korea's income increases and the country becomes more integrated with the global economy. Universities want to improve their reputations in order to attract better students and academic

14. *Hankyoreh Daily Newspaper*, http://www.hani.co.kr, February 19, 2003.

staff. The government and businesses seek ways to move the economy to an increasingly more knowledge-based economy. Since the early 1990s, they recognized the importance of research and development in S&E as the new engine of economic growth. The IMD's ranking of national competitiveness has been adopted as the new objective of the government interventions in the economy. Additional resources to and institutional reform in higher education became important priorities in the national agenda. We shall discuss these various aspects in more detail in what follows.

10.6.1 Mass Internationalization of Higher Education

Internationalization of higher education promotes the competition in the Korean higher education system. While there are as yet no credible foreign institutions that effectively compete with top Korean universities in Korea, many top high school students opt to study at elite U.S. universities. Currently, there are about 150,000 Korean students enrolled in higher learning institutions abroad. Out of these students, about 60,000 (40 percent) are in the United States. Other popular destinations are English speaking countries, such as Canada and Australia, which take an additional 30,000 students. Moreover, increasing numbers of primary and secondary school students are seeking study abroad.

The trend of early study abroad is motivated by the dissatisfaction over the current secondary education system. Korea regularly attains one of the highest ranks in standardized international tests of academic achievements such as the Trends in International Math and Science Study (TIMSS) and Programme for International Student Assessment (PISA).[15] However, many parents and educational specialists are concerned about the level of education spending. In 2003, the government spent 3.5 percent of GDP on primary and secondary education, a relative size of public expenditure that is in line with other Organization for Economic Cooperation and Development (OECD) countries. At the same time, the household sector spends an additional 3.2 percent of GDP (2.3 percent in private tutoring and 0.9 percent for high school tuition payments, textbooks, and other teaching material) in primary and secondary education (Kim and Lee 2010). In addition

15. The International Associations for the Evaluation of Educational Achievement (IEA) conducts standardized achievement tests in about fifty countries and reports the results as TIMSS since 1995. Korea's scores have been consistently at the top. According to the latest reported tests conducted in 2003, Korea ranked the second in math and the third in science among forty-four countries that participated in the tests. Another well-known international test is PISA, conducted by the OECD. While TIMSS tries to measure scholarly achievements based on the standard curricular material, PISA tries to measure more applied ability such as problem-solving skills. Korea ranks very highly in PISA as well. In 2003 tests, fifteen-year old Korean students ranked number one in problem solving, ranked second in reading, third in math, and fourth in science among forty countries where the tests were conducted. The dispersion of the test scores of Korean students is known relatively small, and this finding was considered as that Korean education system not only produces high average academic achievements but more equalized outcomes than most OECD countries.

to the resulting financial burden, Korean secondary students spend an inordinate amount of time in private tutoring in addition to regular schooling. The heavy financial and emotional costs of education translate into genuine dislike for schools. Another major dissatisfaction over the secondary educational system is that it emphasizes rote memorization over creativity and critical thinking. Consequently, many upper-middle-class households are willing to take their children out of the Korean system and send them to foreign countries to study. While the effectiveness of this growing early study abroad is not certain, its socioeconomic costs are not trivial.

In an attempt to reduce the education deficit, estimated to be between US $3 to 10 billion a year, the Korean government has been trying to attract foreign universities and research institutions into the 52,000 acre Incheon Free Trade Zone by giving generous incentives such as rent-free buildings and tax-free land. The State University of New York (SUNY), Stony Brook and North Carolina State University have signed agreements to operate degree programs and research projects, and the University of Southern California (USC), George Mason, and George Washington University are reportedly in the process of negotiation (*Chronicle of Higher Education,* March 21, 2008, vol. 54, no. 28).

At the same time, more English-only institutions are starting to operate. Underwood College of Yonsei University started its operation by attracting Korean and foreign students. Virtually all major universities offer some classes exclusively taught in English, and some programs or schools are planning to offer all classes in English. Most major Korean universities have exchange programs that send students abroad regularly.

However, the Korean push for internationalization of its higher education institutions has not produced any noticeable changes in inbound internationalization. In the 2007 Ministry of Education Survey, twenty-three public universities employed a total of only twenty-two full-time foreign professors. Private universities have hundreds of foreign professors, but most of them are English instructors. Korean universities have tried to attract foreign students, but the result is rather dismal. There are only 22,000 foreign students in Korea, compared to about 100,000 in Japan. Kim (2005) observed that despite the official goal of "30% of academic staff by 2005," the bureaucratic rules have not been updated. For example, a rule that only Korean scholars are allowed to receive research grants from Korea Research Foundation was on the books until 2008. Cultural and bureaucratic exclusion of the small number of foreign faculty members were common.

10.6.2 Reform Initiatives by Universities

The massive outbound internationalization of students and increased competition among institutions encouraged some innovative academic administrators to implement a variety of reform measures, including more rigorous tenure evaluations, merit pay schemes, and large prizes for high visibility publications. In 2000, Seoul National University (SNU) asked a blue ribbon commission, composed of internationally known scholars and academic administrators, to review the university and to provide recommendations to make SNU a world-class university. The commission's recommendations (Seoul National University 2001) were quite relevant in pointing out the malaise of SNU and other Korean universities in general. The first set of recommendations concerned the governance structure of SNU. Instead of having the university president elected through direct vote among faculty, it recommended the establishment of an independent board of directors, which would appoint the president for a longer (or indeterminate) term of office. Also, it recommended more rigorous review of the program and faculty. Up until then, the rate of granting tenure in SNU was 100 percent, and there was no effective program review. Without such reviews, it was natural to expect the quality of research and teaching at SNU to be mediocre. Third, it recommended that resources should be allocated based on merit and scholarly excellence.

By and large, many top-rung universities recognize their weakness and have tried to improve their competitiveness in a more globalized higher education market. Since the late 1990s, several private universities started to introduce performance-based pay for faculty, a marked change from previous practice in which salaries were rarely based on market rates across disciplines or individual performance within the department. The faculty reaction to this new pay system was decidedly mixed. Predictably, the faculty in humanities and social sciences objected, while those in medical schools, business schools, and other popular disciplines usually welcomed the new scheme, as did younger faculty (Na 2000).

The Asian Financial Crisis of 1997 to 1998 sounded a wake-up call to the Korean economy. In order to increase profitability, many private-sector firms abandoned the lifetime employment policy. After observing massive restructuring and wholesale lay offs during the crisis, many Korean professionals no longer viewed the jobs in Korea as a lifetime commitment. Realizing that they could lose their jobs at a whim unless they upgraded themselves continuously, workers started to view individual performance as more important than organizational harmony and company loyalty.

The changes in personnel policies in the private sector started to influence higher education institutions. Until the early 1990s, faculty positions had been rationed by the availability of the PhDs and the ranking of the university where the candidate received his or her PhD. Beginning in 2002, regulations regarding the personnel policy of professors shifted, allowing universities to have explicit contracts with individual professors similar to those in the United States. Since then, some professors were given tenure, some were given probationary contracts with tenure evaluation (tenure track), and other others were given temporary contracts (adjunct or part-time lecturers). In most universities, the tenure evaluation occurs some years after the faculty member is appointed as full professor. The new personnel policy change has been gradually taken seriously, particularly by top research universities. For example, in the 2007 tenure evaluation, KAIST dropped fifteen out of thirty-five applicants (43 percent). Such a low success rate had been unheard of in Korea. However, the strict tenure evaluation policy pushed by the KAIST President Dr. Suh Nam-Pyo, a long-time MIT professor in mechanical engineering, has been reluctantly accepted by the faculty. However, his predecessor, a physics Nobel Laureate from Stanford, failed to be reappointed, owing to the opposition of the faculty when he tried to impose more selective faculty research support. Although the ultimate success of KAIST's stricter tenure policy remains to be seen, many top universities, including SNU, seem to have adopted substantially tighter tenure requirements recently.

Faculty mobility among universities in Korea is increasing, as universities are more willing to outbid others in order to attract better faculty members. According to Son (2007), among the 1,135 hires in the 182 universities in the fall 2005 semester, 213 (18.9 percent) were transfers from one university to the other. This type of lateral move had been very rare in the previous environment in which seniority and loyalty were regarded a more important consideration than the individual record of performance in the hiring process.

While the incentive pay scheme and more rigorous tenure evaluations have been accepted gradually, the governance structure turned out to be much more difficult to implement. The governance structure of national universities is still highly bureaucratic. The faculty and administrative staffs are civil servants, and their personnel matters (appointment, promotion, salary, and so on) are managed by the government, not by the president of the university. In most cases, the president is elected by a popular vote by the faculty. Consequently, their tenure is relatively short (typically four years), and they are not able to formulate or implement any measures of substance. The level of autonomy by individual university is rather limited. In this environment, it is difficult to expect universities to adopt innovative measures to make their institutions more efficient.

The difficulty of institutional reform in university governance can be seen at KAIST as well. Korea Advanced Institute of Science and Technology is a public university founded by the Ministry of Science and Technology in 1971, not by the Ministry of Education that supervises most of the national universities and provides funding. In this regard, KAIST is different from a typical national university. Its aim, from the beginning, was to be a world-class research university that specializes in science and technology. The basic rationales for establishing the institution were first, science and technology would be one of the most important determinants of economic growth in the future; and second, the Ministry of Science and Technology would be the better agency to supervise the new institution because it would be free of heavy regulation imposed by the Ministry of Education on other national universities. Its basic model of operation is heavy government subsidy of elite students with an emphasis on graduate education, particularly PhDs. In order to attract the best students, KAIST charged no tuition. At the same time, KAIST hired top-notch faculty, many of whom had advanced degrees from top research universities in the United States, with the expectation of high research productivity and minimal teaching loads. In 2004, KAIST hired a Nobel Laureate in physics, Dr. Robert B. Laughlin from Stanford University, as the president. The goal of hiring Dr. Laughlin, who had no prior administrative experience, was to provide credibility to the in-stitution as a world-class research university.

This hiring of a non-Korean reflected the national sentiment that foreign experts would be better able to adopt revolutionary reform to improve the efficiency of the organization because they have no existing ties to domestic stakeholders whose interests might be jeopardized by reform. The success of Mr. Gus Hiddink, who led the Korean soccer team to the quarterfinals of the 2002 World Cup, was an inspiration for such bold recruiting efforts at the executive level.

However, the rosy expectations of Hiddink-like institutional reform at KAIST were not realized. On the contrary, there was a tremendous backlash against the Laughlin strategy. President Laughlin suggested that in order to become an elite university (such as MIT or Stanford), KAIST should be privatized. For a physicist, his analysis was surprisingly economic. The original KAIST model, he suggested, would not be sustainable, as the government budget allocation would never be enough for KAIST to compete effectively among the major research universities in the world. The emphasis on graduate education at KAIST, which is expensive to maintain, would not be sustainable without the cross-subsidy from the tuition revenues generated by undergraduate students attracted by the prominent faculty members and the reputation of the institution. Also, he wanted to have more diverse undergraduate programs (with substantial tuition fees), which are attractive to a wide variety of talented undergraduate students, not just techies and nerds. In order to attract such tuition-paying students, KAIST's undergraduate programs would need to be responsive to the market demand. These are the reasons why he wanted to privatize KAIST.

The proposal was not well received at all, as there were no key stakeholders who were willing to support such drastic change. Faculty did not like the more market-oriented structure and the subsequent unequal distribution of resources within the institution. Students fear a big hike in tuition and fees. The government does not want to lose the control of the institution. The widespread dissatisfaction with Laughlin's leadership featured an open letter from twenty department heads threatening to resign if Laughlin remained. In 2007, the KAIST board did not renew Laughlin's contract.

A related issue of institutional reform is the privatization of public universities proposed by the Ministry of Education in 2007. The basic idea of this reform is to create an independent board for each national university along the lines of a Japanese law passed in 2003 that created an individual board of trustees responsible for the operation of each university. The law also establishes endowments from the government in the form of land, building, and other assets. The Korean Ministry of Education has been holding various focus group meetings, but the general reaction has been quite negative.

10.6.3 Government Programs: Limited Success but with Steep Learning Curve

The Korean government's investment in higher education has been very minimal due to the historical legacy of ambitious plan for the programs of universal primary education and secondary school equalization. These two previous initiatives, in effect, precommitted the government's educational resources. Given the large number of primary and secondary students in the school system, the government simply did not have enough resources available for the higher education sector. However, as the number of recent students in primary and secondary schools decreased, the government increasingly had more resources available for higher education. In addition, the need for a competitive higher education sector has become apparent for this country that does not have many natural resources. Thus, the government has undertaken for the last two decades policy initiatives for upgrading the competitiveness of Korea's higher education sector. However, because Korean law bans successive five-year terms for the president, the government's policy often serves short-term visibility at the expense of long-term capacity building, and even those attempts have been manipulated by powerful stakeholders to protect and further their interests.

Korea has a long tradition of government control over the economy, including the higher education sector. Although government regulations have been relaxed over time, it still maintains great control over the higher education sector by operating public universities, distributing resources, and enforcing regulations. The professors and administrative staffs in national universities are appointed by the government and regarded as civil servants. Therefore, the president of the university lacks the power to hire and fire workers in the university, making the personnel policy one of the most rigid aspects of the Korean public university system. Because the government provides substantial resources to public universities (about 30 percent of the total expenditure), its annual budget allocation substantially influences the fiscal capability of public universities. At the same time, the government successfully fended off the request of private universities to support their operational budget, and the government does not have any direct fiscal responsibility to support private universities. The only government funding to private universities is in the form of research support or special programs designed with specific policy objectives. Over the years, the government has instituted many higher education policies. The following are the most noteworthy.

Brain Pool Program (1994–Present)

Initiated in 1994 during the Kim Young-Sam (1992–1997) Administration, the Brain Pool program allows Korean researchers to invite foreign talents (mostly Korean expatriates) for short stays, rather than the longer visits supported by previous brain gain programs. Another characteristic of the program is its emphasis on established researchers, on the principle that brand-new PhDs, albeit their excellent training, are not particularly productive, owing to their relative inexperience in setting up independent cutting-edge research programs and their lack of familiarity with local research environments. Through the program, researchers at universities and research institutes invite foreign researchers (with at least five years of experience) for a fixed-time (three months to two years) to carry out joint research. The program supports the invitee's salary, living, and travel expanses. While the program aims for already established researchers, however, the level of support is small (e.g., up to $2,000 per month salary), and host institutions have been reluctant to put in substantial cost-sharing to invite established researchers. At the same time, an established researcher in the United States would be reluctant leave for Korea while sacrificing the progress of his or her ongoing research activities. Consequently, the program has not been able to attract active researchers who are in the middle of active research activities as intended. Instead, most of the invitees have been either young postdocs who would like to go back to Korea, but do not have firm employment prospects, or retirees who would like to spend some time in Korea. However, many Korean professors used this program for expanding their publication effort in international journals. Although the program has changed somewhat and the level of funding has declined over the years, it is still being maintained.

Brain Korea 21 (1999–2012)

During the next Kim Dae-Jung Administration (1998–2002), an ambitious government initiative to promote research universities and graduate education was launched. The motivation of this program was the realization that the top Korean universities were losing their top students to top U.S. universities. Recognizing the prospect that obtaining a PhD at a top Korean university will not generate a promising career, many talented Korean students either pursue lucrative nonacademic careers (such as business management, medical, and legal professions) or go to the United States for further study. By the early 1990s, the faculties in top Korean universities were filled with PhDs from top U.S. research universities.

The Brain Korea 21 (BK21) Program's major objective was to upgrade

Korean graduate education. The basic design of the program was to select a handful of research groups (three to six, depending on subjects) and support their graduate programs. During Phase I (1999–2005), BK21 allocated about US $1.4 billion, and in Phase II (2006–2012), an additional US $2.1 billion was allocated. The bulk of the funding went to graduate student tuition, stipends, travel, and research allowances, although the program also allows some limited funding for faculty. While the program's explicit objective was for education (i.e., graduate education), the selection criteria heavily rely on the participating faculty group's aggregated research output. The basic rationale for selecting research groups rather than individuals was to "concentrate" resources on "substantial size" programs.

Despite the opposition by many active research professors who work outside of the top research universities, the plan was implemented. Predictably, the main beneficiary of the program was the small group of large top research universities such as Seoul National University, KAIST, POSTECH, Yonsei University, and Korea University. Approximately 500 programs, covering 25 percent of all graduate students in science and technology and 5 percent of those in humanities and social sciences, were supported by the program. Seoul National University was awarded about 20 percent of the total allocation.

Dr. Zhang-Hee Cho, Professor of Radiological Science at the University of California, Irvine, and a member of the U.S. National Academy of Sciences, heavily criticized the design of the program. While he had been involved substantially in the public policy formulation of the science and engineering policies in the previous administration, he argued that the government's initiative lacked the main ingredient of the research university: hiring talented researchers. In evaluating the BK21 program, Seong et al. (2008) suggested that although supporting the department as a unit may have some merits, individual graduate students should be the main beneficiaries so that they can take the fellowship and choose the university to attend rather than channel the resource to the university in order to attract students.

New University for Regional Innovation (NURI) Program (2004–Present)

In 2004, during the next Roh Moo-Hyun Administration (2003–2007), the NURI Program was launched. The Roh Administration's top policy agenda was balanced regional development. With about a quarter of Korea's population and more than a half of its GDP, the Seoul Metropolitan area dominates the country's economy. Because the administration regarded the heavy concentration of higher education in the area as an impediment to the nation's healthy economic growth, the NURI Program was designed to strengthen the capability of universities located outside of this populous region so that they could be the pillar of regional innovation. The program supports graduate students, faculty appointment, and cooperation with local government and industry. The NURI Program was operated jointly with BK21 so that all universities compete in BK21, and only the ones outside of the Seoul region compete in NURI.

World Class University

The new Lee Myung-Bak Administration (2008–2013) is starting the World-Class University (WCU) Program with a budget of $850 million between 2008 and 2012. The objective of this program is to recruit top-notch faculty members (Koreans as well as non-Koreans) permanently into Korean universities in the fields of emerging technologies and interdisciplinary programs. The program subsidizes the salary of the recruit up to US $200,000 per year for five years, after which the host university is expected to cover the full expense. The program also allows these faculty members to be part time or full time. Because the Program has not yet started as of 2008, its effects remain to be seen.

Besides the concern for the effectiveness of the top Korean universities in the national economy, the most recent government program was heavily motivated by the recent hoopla of the world rankings on universities, such as *Academic Rankings of World Universities* by Shanhai Jiatong University started in 2003 and *Times Higher Education-Quacqarelli Symonds* (*THE-QS*) *World University Rankings* published in *Times Higher Education* supplements started in 2004. Other rankings of world universities proliferated by trying to address several criticisms of those rankings.[16] The Korean government took those world rankings seriously as it tried to move up the ladder of advanced countries. By focusing on the indicators used in those well-known rankings, the current administration wanted to improve domestic and international public relations. Other nations such as China and Singapore have already adopted a national objective to improve top domestic universities at the level of world-renowned major research universities. The Korean government does not want to be left behind in this international competition of global prominence in top universities. The worldwide reputation of their top universities can satisfy the collective ethos of their citizens who want to be recognized as one of the leading nations in the world as such desire cannot be satisfied only through the success in major sporting events such as the Olympics or the World Cup soccer tournament.

Overall, the effects of these government initiatives have been mixed. On one hand, they provide a strong medium for reform because they are considered major discretionary resources that universities can utilize. The incentives and evaluations that they provide gave institutions strong signals of the government's objectives. On the other hand, government programs

16. Shanghai Jiatong rankings are mainly based on research outputs such as publications in peer review articles and research, Nobel prizes, and so on, which favor institutions in English-speaking countries, particularly the United States. The *THE-QS* relies heavily on reputation of the peer and internationalization.

have been driven by short-term political objectives that are prone to change from administration to administration. Another major problem is that the government-led initiatives have been ill-targeted because they are designed and managed by bureaucrats who do not know exactly how research universities operate.

As the experience of the successive rounds of government programs accumulates, the program design becomes more compatible with incentive structures of the major stakeholders. While most of the government programs in general favor the insiders of the system (i.e., government bureaucracies and major universities), the evaluation process in which the beneficiaries are determined becomes more transparent. Also, the amount of resources set aside for the programs becomes large enough to attract international talents who may be able to make a difference in shaping the culture of the Korean academic community.

10.6.4 Aspiration for Global Prominence and Globalized Professorial Market

During the past ten years, Korea's research output and capability have increased substantially. The number of published articles in Science Citation Index (SCI)-indexed journals has jumped from 9,444 in 1998 to 23,515 in 2005. In terms of world ranking based on number of publications, Korea's rank has risen from eighteenth in 1998 to twelfth in 2005. Kim (2007) reports that the research output of SNU, Korea's flagship research institution among comprehensive universities, has grown to become quite substantial and comparable to major U.S. public universities. According to him, the number of articles indexed in the SCI by SNU professors ranked seventy-fifth in the world in 1999, and jumped to thirty-first in 2004 with 3,116 articles. In the same year, Harvard ranked number 1 with 9,421 articles, followed by Tokyo University with 6,631, and the University of California Los Angeles (UCLA) with 5,232. Seoul National University's total research funding in the same year reached US $270 million, which is quite comparable to Harvard's $648 million, Tokyo University's $426 million, and UCLA's $611 million. While the quality of its articles was not comparable to those universities, SNU's overall quality of publications has improved a great deal. Measured by the number of citations in SCI, SNU's quality was 35 percent of the "top three" universities in the United States and 53 percent of the "high-ranking (top 20 to 30)" U.S. universities in 1999. The measure in 2004 has also jumped to 74 percent of the "top three" and 137 percent of "high-ranking" universities.

While these measures of research quantity and quality are not perfect, they show a pattern of great progress for Korea's top universities. Although there exists a great deal of institutional rigidity and the fundamental governance structure is unlikely to change in the near future, the changed incentive system of faculty hiring, promotion, and salary setting have already generated a substantial shift toward more research orientation. While the bulk of those research products may not be creative and high impact at the world's highest level, Korea's research capability has been improving greatly during the last ten years or so. Some authors like Leydesdorff and Zhou (2005) have predicted that China and Korea will become the new science and engineering research powerhouses in the near future.

Certainly, the competition for top researchers has increased recently. Korean universities and research institutes are now willing (and able) to pay comparable (and higher) wages compared with top research universities in the United States, thus intensifying the global competition for talents. However, as the domestic professorial market deteriorates over time, along with more stringent career prospects and tougher tenure evaluations and promotion, more and more U.S.-trained Korean PhDs are opting to stay away from Korea, at least immediately after receiving the degree. Market salaries for fresh PhDs have plummeted, but those of the world-class researchers have gone up. Therefore, young PhDs are likely to start out their professional careers in the United States or any other place in the world that can sustain their research activities (Kim 2004; Jin et al. 2006). The percentage of Korean doctorates who intend to stay in the United States after the completion of their degree increased from 58.4 percent in 2000 to 63.0 percent in 2006 (Hoffer et al. 2007). Among the Korean S&E PhDs (including social sciences), the "intend to stay rate" has gradually increased from 32.7 percent in 1992 to 68.8 percent in 2005 (data provided by Michael Finn [2007]). The percentage of Korean S&E PhDs who have definite plans for U.S. employment has increased from 3.0 percent in 1993 to 12.1 percent in 2005. The stay rate in the United States of Korean S&E PhDs five years after graduation for 1992 to 1993 doctorate recipients was only 9 percent, and the proportion has increased to 42 percent for 2000 doctorate recipients.

Also, employment prospects of American-trained PhDs in third countries such as Singapore, Australia, Hong Kong, the United Kingdom, the Netherlands, and other European countries are increasing. More and more universities in those countries are willing to hire professors without the local language expertise because English is or becomes the main medium in teaching. It is not totally clear who stays in the United States, who goes to the third country, and who decides to go back. However, such decision will surely be dependent on personal as well as professional considerations.[17] Regarding the former, the United States and Korea generally offer better environments than a third country. For most young doctorate recipients, Korea offers familiarity and opportunities to be close to relatives and friends, and the United States offers a better environment in which to educate their chil-

17. Unlike their older colleagues who had grown up in tougher economic situations, the new generation enjoyed more comfortable material lives and tended to be more individualistic and to value quality of family life over a more fulfilling career. Many of these people viewed the high-pressure working conditions in Korea less favorably than the U.S. situations.

dren. In terms of professional opportunities, it may be difficult to generalize because it is not only the job itself, but the connectivity to the wider research community that is important. For some, Korea may offer better opportunities because of the future prospects. For others, the United States may offer better working environments by being able to be connect to the larger professional community (Miyagiwa 1991).

10.7 Conclusions: What Does It Mean for American Universities?

Despite its relatively small population size and substantial geographical distance to the United States, Korea has been sending a large number of students to U.S. universities over the last few decades. How many and what kind of these students come to the United States and go back to Korea after their education and training? As many of the graduates, particularly PhDs, engage in research and teaching, these questions are very important in gauging the potential for the competitiveness of U.S. universities as well as of Korean universities.

Over the last decades, the number and the quality of these students changed quite dramatically. At the same time, the relationship between the graduates and U.S. universities has changed substantially depending on what is happening in Korea. When Korea was a low-income country and the potential for a successful professional career within Korea was bleak, most of the talents from Korea stayed in the United States after their higher education and training in the United States. This pattern of brain drain is similar to the current situation of the students from China and India. However, when Korea began to actively recruit the talented expatriates to promote economic growth and the development of higher education sector and the career prospects of the returnees improved, the majority of the Korean expatriates started to return home. A pattern of active brain gain by virtually outsourcing graduate education was established. Many talented and promising students came to the United States for graduate studies and returned home to work in Korea. Based on this experience, many Chinese and Indian talents educated and trained in the United States may start to go back to their home countries on a large scale when the economic conditions of their homelands are more amenable to these U.S.-trained professionals.

While the full-scale outsourcing of graduate education will fade away as the quality of teaching and the research capacity of Korean universities improve, large-scale study abroad of Korean students to the American universities is likely to continue in the near future. As long as the top American universities maintain their worldwide reputations, they will continuously attract top Korean graduate students. In addition to the attraction represented by the great global reputation of the top American research universities, a large number of Korean undergraduate and high school students will continue to come to the United States because of the continuing internationalization of higher education and the dissatisfaction with the Korean education system.

Recent changes are likely to encourage more Korean talents to seek employment opportunities in the United States after their education and training. Rapid increases in the supply of PhDs, particularly within Korea, have made job prospects in Korea less promising. As the seniority-based personnel policy gave away to a more merit-based system, Korean universities started to demand research output in the form of publications and patents rather than just the degrees from prestigious universities. In this environment, promising young Korean scholars and researchers favor more productive research environments, at least at the beginning of their careers. As long as the research environment of the American universities is more favorable than those of other nations, they will continuously attract top Korean researchers. Recently, with the government initiatives and increasing market pressure, Korean top universities have improved their research output and working environments tremendously. While the quality and the impact of their research output may not yet reach the level of the top research universities in the United States, the gap has narrowed quickly during the last decade.

As Korean professors become more active in the international scholarly community, the interaction between Korean and American universities will become more complex and frequent. In the earlier brain drain phase, Korea simply provided talented students to the U.S. universities. In the brain gain phase, Korean students earned graduate degrees and returned home to work and teach there. In the new phase of brain competition, Korean academics will have more cooperation and competition with their U.S. colleagues in joint research projects. To American universities, Korea will provide not only graduate students but undergraduate students and post-docs. Also, there will be more lateral moves among Korean expatriates across the national border temporarily or permanently. More Korean professors will be incorporated into the wider U.S. and international community of scholars who compete and cooperate with one another at the same time.

References

Amsden, Alice H. 1989. *Asia's next giant: South Korea and late industrialization.* New York: Oxford University Press.

Beine, Michel, Frederic Docquier, and Hillel Rapoport. 2001. Brain drain and economic growth: Theory and evidence. *Journal of Development Economics* 64:275–89.

Center for Research on Innovation and Society. 2001. *German scientists in the United States: Challenges for higher education and science policies.* Bonn, Germany: German Federal Ministry of Education and Research.

Cho, Zang-Hee. 1999. Brain (dead) Korea 21? Letter to the editor. *Korean American Science Technology Newsletter (KASTN),* August 4.

Choi, Kang-Shik. 1996. The impact of shifts in supply of college graduates: Repercussion of educational reform in Korea. *Economics of Education Review* 15:1–9.

Choi, Young Back. 1997. The Americanization of economics in Korea. In *The post-1945 internationalization of economics,* ed. William Coates, 97–122. Durham, NC: Duke University Press.

Finn, Michael. 2007. Stay rates of foreign doctorate recipients from U.S. universities, 2005. Oakridge Associated Universities. Unpublished Manuscript.

Ham, Seok-Dong, and Mi-Jeong Hong. 2007. An examination of university professors reappointment appeal (in Korean). *Kyoyuk Haengjung Yeonku* 25 (4): 341–68.

Hill, Susan T. 2001. *Science and engineering doctorate awards: 2000.* NSF 01-314. Arlington, VA: National Science Foundation.

Hoffer, Thomas, Mary Hess, Vincent Welch, Jr., and Kimberly Williams. 2007. *Doctorate recipients from United States universities: Summary report 2006.* Chicago: University of Chicago, National Opinion Research Center.

Institute of International Education (IIE). Various years. *Open doors: Report on international educational exchange.* New York: IIE.

IMD. Various years. *World competitiveness yearbook.* Lausanne, Switzerland: IMD.

Jin, Mi-seok et al. 2006. *Kwahak kisool boonya haeeoi baksaei jinrowa kokeub inlyeokjawon jeongchaek* (Career paths of science and engineering Ph.D.s who received their degrees abroad and human resource policies for highly skilled workers). KRIVET Research Report no. 2006-3. Seoul, Korea: Korea Research Institute of Vocational Education and Training.

Johnson, Jean M. 1998. *Statistical profiles of foreign doctoral recipients in science and engineering: Plans to stay in the United States.* NSF-99304. Arlington, VA: National Science Foundation.

———. 2001. The reverse brain drain and the global diffusion of knowledge. *Science and Technology* 125–131.

Kang, Byung-Yoon, and Jung-Ha Paik. 2005. University personnel policy after the contract system (in Korean). *Kyoyuk Haengjeong Yeonku* 23 (2): 375–98.

Kao, Charles H. C., and Jae Won Lee. 1973. An empirical analysis of China's brain drain into the United States. *Economic Development and Cultural Change* 21 (3): 500–513.

Kapur, Devesh. 2001. Diasporas and technology transfer. *Journal of Human Development* 2 (2): 265–85.

Katz, Eliakim, and Oded Stark. 1984. Migration and asymmetric information: Comment. *American Economic Review* 74 (3): 533–34.

Kim, Byung-Joo. 1992. An analysis of university professors' pay system (in Korean). *Kodeung Kyeoyuk Yeonku* 4 (1): 153–87.

Kim, Ki-Seok. 2007. A great leap forward to excellence in research at Seoul National University, 1994–2006. *Asia Pacific Education Review* 8 (1): 1–11.

Kim, Kwang-Yoon. 1996. A study on the pay system of the academic staffs in private universities (in Korean). *Kyeongyeonghak Yeonku* 25 (4): 73–111.

Kim, Sunwoong. 2004. Brain drain, brain gain, and brain drain again? Changing market for Korean science and engineering Ph.D.s. *KSEA Letters* 32 (3): 19–27.

———. 2008. Rapid expansion of higher education in Korea: Political economy of education fever. In *The worldwide transformation of higher education,* ed. David P. Baker and Alexander W. Wiseman. International Perspectives on Education and Society Series, vol. 9. Oxford, UK: Emerald Publishing.

Kim, Sunwoong, and Ju-Ho Lee. 2110. Private tutoring and demand for education in South Korea. *Economic Development and Cultural Change,* forthcoming.

Kim, Terri. 2005. Internationalisation of higher education in South Korea: Reality, rhetoric, and disparity in academic culture and identities. *Australian Journal of Education* 49 (1): 89–103.
Kim, Won-Yeol. 2008. The problem of part-time lecturers: Diagnosis and alternatives. *Sidae Wa Cheolhak* 19 (1): 77–102.
Korean Council for University Education. 2000. *University education* (in Korean).
Korean Ministry of Education (KMOE). Various years. *Education Statistics Yearbook.* Seoul, Korea: KMOE.
Korean Ministry of Education and Human Resources. 1998. *50 years of education history* (in Korean). Seoul, Korea: Korean Ministry of Education and Human Resources.
Kwok, Viem, and Hayne Leland. 1982. An economic model of brain drain. *American Economic Review* 72 (1): 91–100.
Lee, Jeong-Jae et al. 2007. *The survey on the current status of science and engineering manpower.* Seoul, Korea: Korea Ministry of Science and Technology.
Lee, Sungho. 1989. The emergence of modern university in Korea. *Higher Education* 18:87–116.
———. 2003. The changing academic workplace in Korea. In *The decline of the guru: The academic profession in developing and middle-income countries,* ed. Philip G. Altback. New York: Macmillan.
Lee, Sunhwa, and Mary C. Brinton. 1996. Elite education and social capital: The case of South Korea. *Sociology of Education* 69 (3): 177–92.
Leydesdorff, Loet, and Phing Zhou. 2005. Are the contributions of China and Korea upsetting the world system of science? *Sociometrics* 63 (3): 617–30.
Miyagiwa, Kaz. 1991. Scale economies in education and the brain drain problem. *International Economic Review* 32 (3): 743–59.
Mountford, Andrew. 1997. Can a brain drain be good for growth in the source economy? *Journal of Development Economics* 53:287–303.
Na, Min-Joo. 2000. A direction on the design of pay system in national universities. *Kodeung Kyoyuk Yeonku* 11 (1): 129–62.
OECD. 1998. *Knowledge-based economy.* Paris: OECD.
Seo, Jung-Hwa, Ki-O Jeong, and Chang-Shin Kwak. 2000. A study on the university personnel system (in Korean). *Kyoyuk Haengjeong Yeonku* 18 (3): 173–207.
Seong, Somi et al. 2008. *Brain Korea 21 phase II: A new evaluation model.* Santa Monica, CA: Rand Corporation.
Seoul National University. 2001. *Elevating Seoul National University to a world class: Findings and recommendations from the Panel on Educational Excellence.* Seoul, Korea: SNU.
Son, Jun-Jong. 2007. A study on the intention of turnover of the university professors. *Kyoyuk Moonjae Yeonku* 29:45–71.
Song, Byung-Nak. 1997. *The rise of the Korean economy.* New York: Oxford University Press.
Song, Hahzoong. 1997. From brain drain to reverse brain drain. *Science, Technology and Society* 2 (2): 317–45.
Vasegh-Daneshvary, Nassar, Alan M. Schlottmann, and Henry W. Herzog, Jr. 1987. Immigration of engineers, scientists, and physicians and the U.S. high technology renaissance. *Social Science Quarterly* 68 (2): 311–25.
Wong, Kar-yiu, and Chong Kee Yip. 1999. Education, economic growth, and brain drain. *Journal of Economic Dynamics and Control* 23:699–726.
Yoon, Bong-Soon. 1992. Reverse brain drain in South Korea: State-led model. *Studies in Comparative International Development* 27 (1): 4–26.

IV

Looking Ahead

11

What Does Global Expansion of Higher Education Mean for the United States?

Richard B. Freeman

University education, once the privilege of a modest number of well-to-do persons in high-income countries, spread massively throughout the world in the latter part of the twentieth century and beginning of the twenty-first century (Shofer and Meyer 2005). Between 1970 and 2006, the number of students enrolled in institutions of higher education increased from 29 million to over 141 million. The numbers studying science and engineering, where the content of courses is relatively similar around the world, increased commensurately. The global expansion of higher education eroded the U.S. position as the country with the most highly educated workforce and potentially endangers the U.S. lead in science and technology. In the 2000s, diverse business and academic groups issued reports that warned that the faster growth of the supply of science and engineering students overseas than in the United States risked national competitiveness and national security (National Academy of Sciences 2005; Council of Competitiveness 2005).

In which countries has university education spread rapidly? Why have so many more students gone on to higher education outside the United States, and why have so many countries expanded their higher education system in the past thirty or so years? What are the implications for the United States? How might the country best respond to the rest of the world closing the higher education gap with the United States?

This study examines these questions in two stages.

Part I documents the global expansion in university training in terms of the increased *proportion* of young persons enrolled in university in advanced

Richard B. Freeman holds the Herbert Ascherman Chair in Economics at Harvard University, is the faculty director of the Labor and Worklife Program at Harvard Law School, and is a research associate of the National Bureau of Economic Research.

countries; the increased *absolute number* of young persons obtaining university training in developing countries; the influx of women into higher education, which has brought the female share above 50 percent of university students in many advanced countries; and the growing number of international students from developing countries. The bottom line of part I is that the United States will continue to lose its quantitative edge in higher education, including science and engineering, in the foreseeable future.

Part II examines the implications of this development for the U.S. labor market, university system, and economy writ large. With respect to the labor market, the expansion of higher education overseas and the influx of international students in the United States have contributed to the growing supply of highly educated immigrants to the country. Because the U.S. higher educational system is the world leader, in the short and medium run, it benefits from the increased supply of students worldwide, as many of the world's best and brightest seek a U.S. education and later seek jobs at U.S. universities. But as the quality of higher education improves in other countries, their universities will invariably become more competitive with the American institutions in attracting students and faculty. The globalization of higher education should benefit the United States and the world economy by accelerating the rate of technological advance associated with science and engineering and speeding the adoption of best-practices around the world, which will lower the costs of production and prices of goods. But the increased number of graduates in other countries threatens U.S. comparative advantage in graduate-intensive sectors of production, particularly if the graduates cost much less than comparable U.S. workers. The United States has responded to the great increase of university graduates overseas by "importing" highly educated workers through immigration. U.S. firms have also off shored work to highly educated workers overseas. I conclude this essay by examining the benefits and costs of these two alternatives and considering government and university policies that might enhance the net benefits to the United States from the global expansion of higher education.

11.1 Part I: Expansion of Higher Education

Table 11.1 presents estimates of the number of persons enrolled in higher education worldwide and the U.S. proportion of world enrollees in selected years from 1970 to 2006. The data are from the UNESCO Institute for Statistics, which reports enrollments in "tertiary" education for most countries over this period.[1] The figures are best viewed as giving orders of magnitudes

1. UNESCO Institute for Statistics (UIS) Data Centre, based on data provided by UNESCO Member States through the UIS annual data collection with most recent data from http://stats.uis.unesco.org/unesco/TableViewer/tableView.aspx?ReportId=175, table 3B, enrollment by

Table 11.1 **Millions of enrollments and shares of world enrollments in higher education, including enrollments for less than four years, by country, 1970–2006**

	1970	1980	1990	2006
	Millions of enrollments			
World	29.4	55.3	67.6	141.5
United States	8.5	12.1	13.7	17.5
Other advanced	4.9	8.2	12.9	29.5
Developing[a]	16	35	41	102.5
China	<0.1	1.7	1.8	23.4
India	2.5	3.5	5	12.9
	Shares of world enrollments (%)			
United States	29.00	22.00	20.00	12.00
Other advanced	16.70	14.8	20.3	17.7
Developing[a]	54.4	63.3	60.7	72.4
China	0	3.1	2.7	16.5
India	8.5	6.3	7.4	9.1

Source: UNESCO, online files: http://stats.uis.unesco.org/TableViewer/tableView.aspx?ReportId=47; http://www.uis.unesco.org/en/stats/centre.htm; http://www.uis.unesco.org/pagesen/DBGTerIsced.asp.

Note: The UNESCO Web site also reports table II.S.3 enrollment by level of education for major areas and groups of countries. The UNESCO division of countries between advanced and developing shows an even greater increase from 1970 in the developing country share. My division places the ex-Soviet countries in the group outside the United States and other advanced countries.

[a]Developing indicates developing and other countries beyond the United States and advanced.

rather than precise statistics. One reason is that definitions of tertiary education and counts of students vary across countries. Another reason is that UNESCO does not report data annually for every country so that to get numbers for some countries in a given year, I used data from the nearest surrounding year. Even with a large window to find a near year with data (going back to 2000 in a few cases to obtain estimates for 2006), data for some countries was still missing (such as Sri Lanka, Syria, and Serbia, among others). Finally, the UNESCO database lacks information for the ex-Soviet Union, ex-Yugoslavia, and the two Germanys from 1970 to 1997.[2] To deal with this problem, I used enrollment figures from the Banks Cross National Time Series Archives.[3] While it is likely that data from national sources are

International Standard Classification of Education (ISCED) level enrollment in total tertiary. See also http://stats.uis.unesco.org/unesco/TableViewer/tableView.aspx?ReportId=167, table 14, tertiary indicators.

2. http://www.uis.unesco.org/en/stats/centre.htm; http://www.uis.unesco.org/pagesen/DBGTerIsced.asp.

3. Cross National Time Series Data Archive, 2004 Arthur S. Banks, http://www.databanksinternational.com.

more accurate than UNESCO figures, for consistency, I use the UNESCO data for all countries, including the United States.

The table shows that in 1970, approximately 29 percent of the world's college students were in the United States, although the country had approximately 6 percent of the world's population.[4] Thereafter, the U.S. share of world college enrollments dropped rapidly so that by 2005 to 2006, the United States had 12 percent of enrollments—about two-fifths of its 1970 share. During this period, tertiary enrollments in other advanced countries went from barely half of U.S. enrollments to 23 percent greater than U.S. enrollments; while enrollment in developing countries, most spectacularly China, increased by such large numbers that in 2006 nearly three-quarters of the world's tertiary-level enrollments were in those countries. Chinese government statistics (Ministry of Education of the People's Republic of China 2007), which differ somewhat from the UNESCO data, show an increase in full time enrollment from 924,000 in 1993 to 5.4 million students in 2006 and an increase in total enrollment from 5 million to 25 million, or from 5 percent to 22 percent of the age cohort over the same period.[5]

Table 11.2 turns to the number of first university degrees and the number relative to the number of twenty-four-year-olds in the United States compared to the rest of the world in 2004. It gives the number of bachelors' degrees in total, the number in the natural sciences and engineering, the number of twenty-four-year-olds, and the numbers of degrees relative to the number of twenty-four-year-olds for the United States and the world, respectively. Column (1) records these figures for the United States. Column (2) records these statistics for the world. Column (3) shows the ratio of the U.S. numbers to the world numbers. The United States had 14 percent of all bachelor's degrees and 9 percent of science and engineering degrees, compared to about 5 percent of the world's twenty-four-year-olds. The proportion of twenty-four-year-olds earning first degrees and earning first degrees in natural science and engineering was larger in the United States than in the world.

Table 11.3 examines the changing position of the United States in the world's production of first degrees overall and in natural science and engineering from 1995 to 2004. Because the National Science Foundation (NSF) reports degrees only for three regions for 1995—Europe, Asia, and North America—the trend data compare the United States to those regions. The 1995 to 2004 trend shows that the U.S. share of bachelor's degrees fell by 8 points, while the U.S. share of natural science and engineering degrees

4. The United States had such a large proportion because it developed the first mass higher education system in the world. Land grant colleges gave opportunities for university education throughout the country. The GI Bill spurred enrollments in colleges and universities. Refugees from Europe contributed to building first-rate science and engineering research programs. Sputnik led to large investments in R&D and university education.

5. www.albertachina.com/upload/IB_BEIJING-_123071-v1-China_Higher_education.

Table 11.2 **Numbers of degrees and 24-year-olds in the United States compared to world, and ratios of degrees to 24-year-olds, 2004**

	United States (1)	World (2)	Ratio, United States/World (3)
First degrees, total (in thousands)	1,407	10,926	0.14
First natural science/engineering degrees (in thousands)	236	2,772	0.09
24-year-olds	3,850	79,360	0.05
Proportion of 24-year-olds with first degrees	0.37	0.14	2.64
Proportion of 24-year-olds with natural science/engineering first degrees	0.06	0.035	1.71

Source: National Science Board (2008), *Science and engineering indicators, 2008,* appendix table 2-37, where the number of degrees is for 2004 or the most recent year. Number of 24-year-olds from National Science Board (2006), *Science and engineering indicators, 2006,* appendix table 2-37, where the number of 24-year-olds refers to 2002 or the most recent year.

Table 11.3 **Ratios and changes in numbers of degrees and 24-year-olds in the United States relative to comparable numbers for Three Regions (Asia, Europe, North America), 1995–2004**

	Ratio, United States/ Three Regions		Change in ratios, 1992–2004
	1992	2004	
First degrees, total (in thousands)	0.23	0.15	–0.08
First natural science/engineering degrees (in thousands)	0.13	0.10	–0.02
24-year-olds	0.06	0.06	0.0
Proportion of 24-year-olds with first degrees	4.10	2.50	–1.60
Proportion of 24-year-olds with natural science/engineering first degrees	2.35	1.61	–0.74

Sources: 1995, calculated from National Science Board (1998), *Science and engineering indicators, 1998,* appendix table 2-1, where the number of degrees and 24 year olds is for 1995 or the most recent year. 2004, calculated from National Science Board (2004), *Science and engineering indicators, 2008,* appendix table 2-37, and National Science Board (2006), *Science and engineering indicators, 2006,* appendix table 2-37, for Asia, Europe, and North America.

Note: The ratios measure the relevant statistic for the United States divided by the statistic for Asia, Europe, and North America because those are the only areas for which the National Science Board provides data.

declined by 2 points, and that the U.S. edge in first degrees and in first degrees in natural science and engineering per twenty-four-year-old fell commensurately. Data on degrees for the entire world would presumably show the U.S. share of degrees declining by larger amounts than in table 11.3 because enrollments grew rapidly in areas with missing degree data—South America, Africa, and Oceana.

Given that the United States has about 5 percent of world population and that most of the rest of the world is in catch-up mode in mass higher education, the decline in the U.S. advantage in the proportion of the population with university training is likely to continue for some time.

11.1.1 PhD Graduates in Science and Engineering

The PhD is the critical degree for advanced research and, thus, for increasing the stock of knowledge on which economic growth ultimately depends. Table 11.4 records the ratios of PhDs earned in science and engineering in major PhD producing countries relative to the numbers in the United States from 1975 to 2004. PhDs in science and engineering outside the United States increased sharply, while the number granted in the United States stabilized at about 26,000 per year before increasing modestly to 29,000 by 2006. In 2004, the European Union (EU) granted 78 percent more science and engineering (S&E) PhDs than the United States.

The greatest growth in PhDs granted is in China. In 1975, China produced almost no science and engineering doctorates. In 2004, NSF figures show that the country graduated 23,000 PhDs, approximately 63 percent in science and engineering. Between 1995 and 2003, first-year entrants in PhD programs in China increased sixfold, from 8,139 to 48,740. At this rate, China will produce more science and engineering doctorates than the United States by 2010. The quality of doctorate education surely suffers from such rapid expansion, so the numbers should be discounted, but as the new Chinese doctorate programs develop, quality will undoubtedly improve.

Within the United States, moreover, international students have come to earn an increasing proportion of S&E PhDs. In 1966, universities awarded

Table 11.4 Ratio of science/engineering (S&E) PhDs from foreign universities to U.S. universities and U.S. share of world S&E PhDs, 1975–2010

	1975	1989	2001	2004	2010
Asia major nations[a]	0.22	0.48	0.96	1.23	n.a.
China	n.a.	0.05	0.32	0.57	1.26
Japan	0.11	0.16	0.29	0.29	n.a.
European Union major (France, Germany, United Kingdom)	0.64	0.84	1.07	1.02	n.a.
All advanced European Union[b]	0.93	1.22	1.54	1.78	1.92
Chinese "diaspora"/United States[c]	n.a.	n.a.	0.72	n.a.	n.a.
U.S. share of world science/engineering PhDs	n.a.	n.a.	22.3%	17.6%	n.a.

Sources: National Science Board (2008), *Science and engineering indicators, 2008:* table 2-40; 2002: table 2-36; Weigo and Zhaohui National Research Center for S&T Development (China), private communication; NSF (1993, 1996).

[a]China, Japan, India, Korea.

[b]Includes Norway, Switzerland, excludes new European Union entrants, extrapolation to 2010.

[c]"Diaspora" includes estimates of Chinese doctoral graduates from the United Kingdom, Japan, and the United States (with temporary visas). U.S. natives = citizens and permanent residents.

23 percent of science and engineering PhDs to the foreign-born; 71 percent to U.S.-born males and 6 percent to U.S.-born females. In 2006, universities awarded 48.2 percent of science and engineering PhDs to the foreign-born; 26.3 percent to U.S.-born males and 25.5 percent to U.S.-born females.[6] Looking among fields, the foreign-born received 23.2 percent of all doctorates awarded in the social and behavioral sciences, 32.3 percent in the life sciences, 50.6 percent in the physical sciences, and 63.6 percent in engineering. Because few U.S. students earn S&E PhDs overseas, the ratio of S&E PhDs earned by U.S. citizens or residents to those earned by citizens of other countries fell more rapidly than the ratio of degrees granted by U.S. universities to degrees granted by foreign universities. If we add the number of S&E PhDs granted to Chinese students in the United States and other countries to the numbers granted in China, the ratio of Chinese degrees to U.S. PhDs granted less those given to the Chinese rose to 0.71 in 2001. But because many Chinese who gain PhDs in the United States remain in the United States, it is more appropriate to count them as part of the U.S. supply than of the supply of S&E PhDs in China.

11.1.2 Propensity to Enroll and Graduate: Advanced Countries

The Organization for Economic Cooperation and Development (OECD) and NSF provide data on the proportions of young persons enrolling and graduating university. Table 11.5 displays the rank of the United States in "entry rates" into tertiary education and in first-time graduation relative to the relevant age group in 1992 and 2005 from the OECD data.[7] In 1992, the United States was second (to Canada) in entry rates and third in graduation rates among the twenty or so OECD countries that reported data. In 2004, the United States was seventh and thirteenth, respectively. The lower ranking of the United States in graduation rates than in entry rates reflects what the OECD calls the low "survival rate" of students in the United States, where a smaller proportion of entrants to higher education graduate with four-year degrees than in other advanced countries. The United States was tied for seventeenth position of the eighteen countries in the OECD survival rate data. The table also displays the rank of the United States in bachelor's graduates overall and in the natural sciences and engineering relative to the age group in 1992 and 2004 (based on NSF data). The United States has a lower rank in natural science and engineering degrees per twenty-four-year-old than in all bachelor's degrees per twenty-four-year-old because Americans are less likely to major in science and engineering than students in other countries.

Comparing the proportion of workers with college degrees across

6. The 1966 figures are from Freeman, Jin, and Shen (2007); the 2006 from NSB (2008).

7. These are cumulated entry rates for countries so that if 20 percent of twenty-year-olds enter tertiary education and 21 percent of twenty-one-years-olds enter, the rate is 41 percent.

Table 11.5 **U.S. rank in propensity for university training, 1992–2005**

Graduation data from OECD/NSF		
	1992	2005
"Tertiary A" graduation rates (OECD)	2 of 15	13 of 20
Bachelor's degrees/24-year-olds (NSF)	2 of 21	14 of 23
Natural science & engineering/24-year-olds (NSF)	3 of 21	19 of 23
PhD or equivalent graduation rates (OECD)	n.a.	9 of 20
All science graduates/25–34-year-olds (OECD)	n.a.	12 of 20
Enrollment data from OECD		
	1995	2005
First time entry as percentage of age group	2 of 15	7 of 20
Enrollment percentage of 20–29-year-olds	9 of 20	12 of 20
Survival rates for advanced countries from OECD		
Graduation/new entrants for type A	2004, 17 tie out of 18[a]	

Sources: OECD, *Education at a Glance, 2005;* NSB, *Science and Engineering Indicators* (various years).

Notes: OECD = Organization for Economic Cooperation and Development; NSF = National Science Foundation. n.a. = not available.

[a]17th out of 18 tie means that the United States is tied for 17th out of 18 countries in the comparison.

cohorts/age groups provides another way to document the declining relative position of the United States in higher education. Because most graduates obtain their degree in their twenties, the share of persons with degrees in different age groups reflects the share of young persons earning degrees when the age group was in their twenties at different time periods. The OECD data on higher educational attainment by age group show that in all of the advanced countries save the United States, the proportion with university education is much higher in younger than older age groups. In the United States, there is little difference in the graduate shares by age. The implication is that the college share of young persons stabilized in the United States while growing among other advanced countries over this period.[8]

It is natural, at least for labor economists, to wonder if the differences in the shares or changes in the shares of young persons investing in higher education across countries are related to cross-country differences in the economic payoff to higher education. Within countries, college-going appears

8. See OECD (2005), *Education at a Glance 2005: OECD indicators,* table A1.3a. Regressions of the ln of the college share of each age group and a trend indicator for when the group was in the age group of the youngest cohort, twenty-five to thirty-four years old (four for age twenty-five to thirty-four; three for age thirty-five to forty-four; two for age forty-five to fifty-four; and one for age fifty-five to sixty-four) give a 0.028 coefficient on time in the United States with a standard error nearly as large. By contrast, the coefficient on the time indicator for the other countries was 0.19 with a standard error one-fourth the size.

to respond to differences in returns, measured in various ways (Freeman 1975, 1976; Edin and Topel 1997). To see if there is a similar relation between returns and college-going across countries, I display the proportions of young persons graduating university and OECD estimates of the ln wage differential between university graduates and secondary school graduates in figure 11.1, and the proportion of young persons graduating and estimated internal rates of return to investing in higher education that take account of costs of tuition, among other factors, in figure 11.2 (Baorini and Strauss 2007). Because recent graduates make up only a small proportion of the overall college graduate population, the relative earnings or rates of return

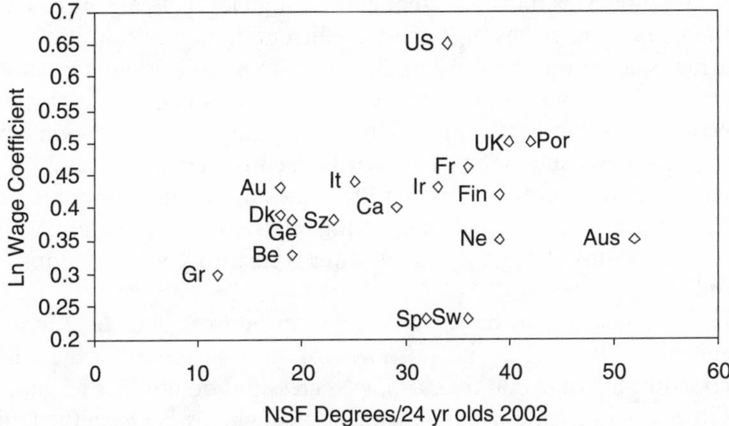

Fig. 11.1 OECD estimated Ln wage coefficient and proportion of twenty-four-year-olds getting bachelor's degree ($r = 0.19$)

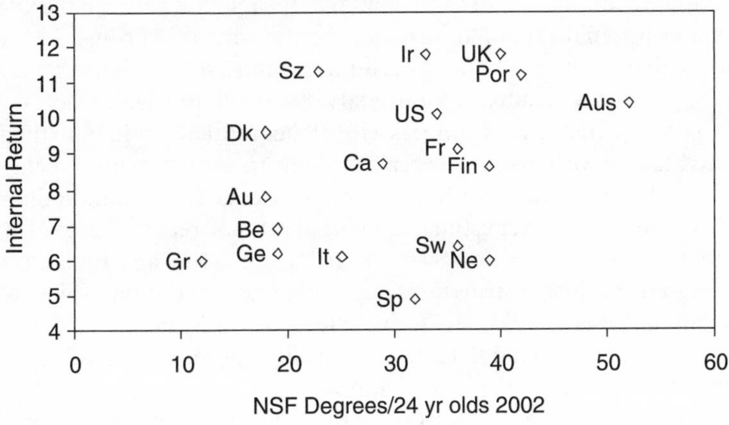

Fig. 11.2 OECD estimated internal rate of return to college degree and proportion of twenty-four-year-olds getting bachelor's degree ($r = 0.39$)

for all university graduates should be largely exogenous to the supply of the youngest group. Put differently, the earnings differentials for the stock of graduates would be determined by the interaction of current demand conditions with the supply of all graduates set years or decades earlier per the "cobweb type" models of the market for graduates (Freeman 1971). Thus, the relation between the flow of new graduates and earnings differentials or rates of return should largely reflect supply behavior and, thus, be positively related.

Figure 11.1 shows that, indeed, there is a modest positive correlation ($r = 0.19$) between the earnings differentials and the influx of young graduates relative to the population among the OECD countries. One reason the correlation is modest is that consistent with its high level of earnings inequality, the United States has the largest coefficient on higher education in the ln earnings equation, but only a moderate rate of college-going. Another reason the correlation is modest is that at the other end of the spectrum, countries with narrow distributions of earnings and low college/high school wage differentials, such as Sweden, have high enrollment ratios despite their low earnings differentials. Sweden graduates approximately three times as many PhDs in science and engineering relative to the age group as does the United States, despite having a lower return to post-bachelor's education!

What might explain the weak correlation between the coefficients on college education and the proportions going to university in these data? One possible factor is that the earnings regressions do not take account for the direct costs of college-going, which differs greatly between the United States, with its high tuition, and European countries. To deal with this and differential taxes and other factors that may influence the return, the OECD calculated internal rates of return using comparable cross-country earnings data for individuals. Figure 11.2 shows that the relation between the OECD estimated internal rate of return and the proportions earning degrees is stronger than is the relation between the earnings differentials themselves and the proportion graduating university ($r = 0.39$). But again, there is a lot of variation. Three of the countries with higher rates of graduation than the United States have higher internal rates of return per labor supply behavior, but four of the countries with higher rates of college graduation than the United States have lower estimated internal rates of return. Three of those low rate of return countries, Sweden, the Netherlands, and Finland, have compressed earnings distributions in general and low tuition, which would make investments in university training less risky than in the United States and might make smaller differentials in earnings more meaningful as signals of opportunity than in the United States.

In any case, these calculations show that while high returns to university training have driven some of the growth of investing in higher education in advanced countries, there is sufficient country variation for other factors, including educational and earnings policies that do not directly affect private monetary returns, to also affect enrollment and graduation rates.

11.1.3 China and India

The huge and increased numbers of university graduates in China and India have attracted attention as part of the discussion of the offshoring of computer programming and multinational corporate investments in research in those countries. In 2005, top executives from high-tech firms reported that China graduated as many as ten times the number of engineers as the United States and that India also graduated more engineers than the United States to call for policies to increase the supply of science and engineering graduates in the United States. More detailed investigation, however, found that part of the reported China/India to U.S. gap in engineering degrees reflected comparisons of numbers with different definitions of degrees (Duke University 2005; Wadwha et al. 2008). Chinese and Indian data included graduates from short courses comparable to U.S. two-year degree programs, while the U.S. data excluded computer science degrees that the other countries counted with engineering. Adjusting the numbers for comparability brings the United States, China, and India numbers closer but does not overturn the trend growth of degrees in China and India compared to the United States. It simply displaces the increase in four-year comparable degree production two to three years behind the publicized figures.

The massive growth of university graduates in China in the 2000s created a major problem in the Chinese job market even before the world economy fell into the most devastating recession since the 1930s. The Chinese government estimated that approximately 1.5 million graduates of the graduating class of 2008 were unemployed over a year later—for an unemployment rate of over 20 percent.[9] With 6.1 million graduates coming onto the labor market, in 2009, Chinese Premier Wen Jiabao declared that employment of higher education graduates was a priority for the government. The state encouraged graduates to find jobs at the urban and rural grassroots in poorer western regions and in small- and medium-sized businesses rather than sitting jobless in big coastal cities.[10]

The extent to which the huge supplies and joblessness of graduates in China and other developing countries will create problems for university graduates in the United States depends in part on the quality of the education received in those countries. In an effort to determine the qualifications of new graduates in developing countries, the McKinsey Global Institute (2005) asked recruiters for multinational firms to estimate the proportion

9. Jamil Anderlini, "China Battles Unemployment to Deter Unrest," *Financial Times,* December 21, 2008, http://www.ft.com/cms/s/0/fa2ecbc2-cf76-11dd-abf9-000077b07658.html?nclick_check=1.

10. Reuters, "China Pushes to Ease Grim Graduate Unemployment," January 7, 2009, http://www.reuters.com/article/worldNews/idUSTRE5062AD20090107.

of graduates from different countries that might be suitable candidates for their firm in terms of skills and *language and potential mobility*. The recruiters estimated that in engineering, 10 percent of graduates from China and 25 percent of graduates from India were so qualified (McKinsey Global Institute 2005, exhibit 2, 8) and gave figures for graduates from most other developing countries in the same range. But it is difficult to know how to assess these estimates. The McKinsey survey did not ask whether graduates could perform successfully for subcontractor firms in their local area in their own language. It did not explore whether the lower pay of graduates in developing countries would compensate for the lower qualifications so that, while multinational firms might not hire them directly, those firms would subcontract work to firms with the less-qualified but cheaper graduate in the developing countries. Finally, the study never asked for the proportion of graduates from U.S. engineering schools that recruiters viewed as qualified.

11.1.4 Surge of Women into Higher Education

Underlying the increase in university enrollments and degrees has been a huge movement of women into higher education.

Table 11.6 shows the ratio of the proportion of females of college age attending university to the proportion of males of college age attending university in advanced countries, as reported by the OECD and by the United Nations (UN) for 2004. When the ratio of female to male enrollment rates is 1.0, the same proportion of the relevant age group is in university. When the ratio is below 1.0, there are more men than women enrolled relative to the age group and, conversely, when the ratio is above 1.0. For most of the post-World War II period and in earlier decades, university students consisted disproportionately of men. Beginning roughly in the 1970s, enrollments of women began to increase more rapidly than enrollments of men in virtually all advanced countries so that by 2004, women made up a majority of university students in twenty-one of the twenty-five advanced countries in the table. The surge of women into higher education in the United States increased the ratio of female to male enrollments to above 1.0 at the bachelor's and master's level (which includes many school teachers) and just a bit below 1.0 for law, PhD, and MD enrollments as of 2006 (U.S. Census Bureau 2007). Among doctorates granted to the U.S.-born, the ratio of female to male PhDs rose to 1.03. In 2004, 22 percent more women than men were granted graduate research fellowships by the National Science Foundation, implying that the female to male ratio among PhDs in science and engineering will continue to rise.

Table 11.7 turns from female to male enrollments in the advanced countries to the female to male enrollments in the entire world. It shows the ratio of female to male enrollments in the world, for advanced and developing

Table 11.6 **Enrollment ratios of women and men in higher education, by age group, advanced countries, 2004**

Country	Organization for Economic Cooperation and Development	United Nations
Norway	1.54	1.38
Iceland	1.78	1.82
Australia	1.23	1.14
Ireland	1.28	1.28
Sweden	1.55	1.47
Canada	1.36	n.a.
United States	1.39	1.27
The Netherlands	1.08	1.17
Finland	1.20	1.26
Luxembourg	1.18	n.a.
Portugal	1.32	n.a.
Germany	n.a.	0.97
Japan	0.89	0.73
Switzerland	0.80	0.97
Korea	0.61	0.87
Belgium	1.21	1.06
Austria	1.19	1.24
Denmark	1.42	1.58
France	1.28	1.47
Italy	1.34	1.27
United Kingdom	1.37	1.17
Spain	1.22	1.41
New Zealand	1.41	1.41
Israel	1.33	n.a.
Greece	1.17	1.23

Sources: OECD, *Education Statistics at a Glance;* United Nations.
Note: n.a. = not available.

countries as a group, and in selected countries from 1988 to 2005. Worldwide, the number of female to male enrollees increased by over 40 points in the period, putting the ratio above 1.0 in 2005. The developing countries had lower ratios of female to male enrollments than the advanced countries but also had greater increases in the ratios. In China, female to male enrollments jumped from 0.55 to 0.95. In Brazil, 32 percent more women than men were university students in 2005. While in many countries in Africa, Latin America, and in the Arab world, the ratios are still noticeably below 1, the direction of change is clear: feminization of higher education is proceeding rapidly around the world. As women contribute to an increasingly large supply of new university students, companies and countries whose institutions and policies (family friendly policies, most likely) allow them to attract and use female graduates efficiently are likely to have an edge in the marketplace.

Table 11.7 Ratio of female to male tertiary enrollment rates

Group/Country	1988	2005
World	64	105
Advanced	106	121
United States	116	140
The Netherlands	81	108
All developing countries	54	91
Chile	82	96
Malaysia	87	131
Most populous developing countries		
India	47	70
China	55	95
Indonesia		79
Brazil	106	132
Pakistan	46	88
Bangladesh	25	53
Nigeria		55
Mexico	66	99
The Philippines		123
Vietnam		71

Source: UNESCO.

11.1.5 International Students

The proportion of students who study in countries other than their own has also been increasing rapidly since at least the mid-1970s. The first column of table 11.8 shows that from 1975 to 2005, the number of international students increased from 0.6 million to 2.7 million—nearly fivefold. The second column shows that the number of international students to the United States increased somewhat more slowly over the whole period, from 0.15 million to 0.58 million—a bit less than fourfold. The third column shows the U.S. share of international students rising in the 1970s and then dropping in the late 1990s to 2000s. Although the U.S. share of international students fell in the latter period, the growth rate of international students in the United States was still sufficient to increase the international student share of U.S. enrollments.

Countries differ in the extent to which they recruit or attract international students at the undergraduate or graduate level. Some countries like Australia and, to a lesser extent, the United Kingdom specialize in undergraduate education for international students, whose tuition payments help fund higher education institutions that receive relatively modest government support and lack the endowments of U.S. private universities. By contrast, table 11.9 shows that the U.S. intake of international students consists disproportionately of graduate students, many in PhD programs. In addition, the United States attracts many international postdoctorate students/workers. Most U.S. international students are from Asia, with India and China

Table 11.8 **Millions of international students worldwide and in the United States, and U.S. share, 1975–2007**

Academic year	Millions of international students in: World	United States	U.S. share of international students (%)
1974–1975	0.6	0.15	25.00
1979–1980	0.8	0.29	36.25
1984–1985	0.9	0.34	37.80
1989–1990	1.2	0.39	32.50
1994–1995	1.3	0.45	34.60
1999–2000	1.9	0.51	26.80
2006–2007	2.9	0.58	20.00

Sources: For millions of international students worldwide, OECD (2008), *Education at a glance: OECD indicators,* box C31; for international students in the United States, Institute of International Education, figure 1B International Students and US. Higher Educational Enrollment Trends, http://opendoors.iienetwork.org/?p=131533.

Notes: Project Atlas reports somewhat smaller numbers: "In 2006, UNESCO estimated that over 2.5 million students were being educated at the tertiary level in countries other than their homes, up from an estimated 1.7 million in 2000" (http://www.atlas.iienetwork.org/?p=46572).

Table 11.9 **Proportion of international students by academic level and major source country, 2006–2007**

% by academic level:
- Graduate, 45.4
- Bachelor's, 29.2
- Associates, 11.6
- Other, 13.8

% by top ten source countries:
- India, 14.4
- China, 11.6
- Korea, 10.7
- Japan, 6.1
- Taiwan, 5.0
- Canada, 4.9
- Mexico, 2.4
- Turkey, 2.0
- Thailand, 1.5
- Germany, 1.5

Sources: International Educational Exchange, Open Doors 2007; table 3 International Students by academic level, 2005 to 2006 and 2006 to 2007; figure 2A Top 20 leading places of origin of international students 2005 to 2006 and 2006 to 2007; http://opendoors.iienetwork.org/?p=113136 and http://opendoors.iienetwork.org/?p=113121.

Note: Total international student to the United States was 582,984 (over two-thirds were from Asia with nearly 85% from developing countries).

Table 11.10 **Share of U.S. degrees to non "citizens/permanent" residents, 1985–2005**

	All		Natural science/ engineering		Engineering	
Degree	1985	2005	1985	2005	1985	2005
Bachelor's	3.0	3.1	5.4	5.2	7.2	8.0
Master's	9.4	12.8	27.2	38.6	26.2	39.7
Doctorate	25.3	39.3	33.1	50.9	59.6	68.8

Sources: Degrees, NSF, National Science Board (2008), *Science and Engineering Indicators, 2008,* chapter 2, tables 2-28, 2-30, and 2-31; Postdocs, enrollments, grad. table 2-22.

being the largest source countries. The foreign-born share of enrollments and degrees is particularly high in graduate science and engineering and increased greatly in those areas from 1985 to 2005 (table 11.10).

Although the foreign-born make up a much smaller share of undergraduate than of graduate students, they are an important source of immigrant scientists and engineers. There are three reasons. First, because the undergraduate student population is much larger than the graduate student population, the absolute number of foreign-born undergraduates is of similar magnitude to the absolute number of foreign-born graduate students. Second, foreign-born undergraduates are far more likely to do graduate work in the United States than foreign-born undergraduates educated outside the country. In 1993, 36.6 percent of foreign-born residents who obtained a master's degree in science and engineering had a U.S. bachelor's degree (over half of them also had a U.S. secondary school degree). Multiplying this by the 24.7 percent of S&E master's degrees going to the foreign-born in that year, approximately 9.7 percent of all S&E master's degrees were awarded to foreign-born persons with U.S. bachelor's degrees. This is 2.5 times the foreign-born share of U.S. bachelor's degrees in science and engineering. At the doctorate level, 19.1 percent of foreign-born residents with a science and engineering PhD had a U.S. bachelor's degree (with nearly half also having graduated from a U.S. secondary school). Given that the foreign-born had 40.6 percent of S&E PhDs in that year, about 10 percent of all S&E PhDs were awarded to foreign-born persons with U.S. bachelor's degrees. This is 2.8 times the foreign-born share of U.S. bachelor's degrees in science and engineering.[11]

What these statistics suggest is that attracting international students at the bachelor's level (and the high school level) raises the probability that those students continue their studies at U.S. institutions and eventually remain in the country to work. But the statistics do not establish that the relation is causal. It could be that the foreign-born undergraduates are selectively

11. The 1993 estimates are from Mark Regets, "Foreign Students in the U.S." PowerPoint presentation, June 27, 2005, Brussels Dialogue Meeting on Migration Governance, OECD.

drawn from a population of persons who would end up working in the United States regardless of where they were educated. To determine whether studying in the United States or any other country leads to further study and immigration to the country of study requires some independent variation in opportunities to study in a foreign country, of the type that I discuss in section 11.2. To presage that discussion, there does indeed appear to be a causal link: attracting students to study in a country induces them to study and work later on.

In the aftermath of 9/11, the academic and research communities feared that tightened visa requirements would reduce the number of international students in the United States. The State Department rejected more students applying for visas than in the past, particularly from China, and made it more difficult for international students to travel outside the United States. The number of international students applying to and enrolling in U.S. universities fell from 2002–2003 through 2005–2006, breaking an upward trend that stretched back at least from 1959–1960. But the State Department responded to complaints about the difficulties faced by international students and remedied many of the problems (National Academy of Sciences 2005). Even with the post 9/11 drop, the United States attracted 560,000 or so international students in 2003 to 2005, and the number increased from 2005–2006 to 2006–2007.

What factors lie behind the huge increase in international students and their choice of countries in which to study? Using a cross-section regression design, Rosenzweig (2006) found that the number of U.S. students obtaining visas in the early 2000s from different countries was larger the larger the population in the country of origin and the closer the distance to the United States, and was also larger the greater the number of universities in the students' home country and level of gross domestic product (GDP) per capita. He also reported that the number of visas was *inversely* related to the return to skills in the home country: the higher the skills in the home country, the less likely were students to come to the United States. The implication is that many come to the United States with the intention of remaining to work in the United States. This fits well with the fact that a large proportion of international students in science and engineering do eventually end up working in the country. But Hwang (2008) finds that analyses that look at changes in student visas by country are positively related with earnings differentials in the student's country, which implies that many may have chosen to study in the United States because returns to higher education are high in their home country (though they may later decide to remain in the United States).

11.1.6 The University Sector

The supply of university students and graduates is only part of the story of the growth of higher education around the world. The other part relates to the increased number or scale of the institutions of higher education that employ faculty and other staff to "produce" graduates. In many countries, the central government determines the number of places in departments to which students apply so that the distribution of graduates among fields depends on government policies. In the United States, state governments have been the major force in expanding the number of institutions of higher education, though student choices determine the distribution of graduates. In yet other countries—Korea, the Philippines—much of the expansion of higher education has come through the private sector. Australian universities actively recruit for international students, largely because the national government has reduced public funding (Marginson 2001; Welch 2002).

Expansion of higher education in the United States between 1960 and 2005 first took the form of large increases of enrollments in existing institutions and then of large increases in the number of institutions. Between 1960 and 1980, enrollments in institutions of higher education in the United States nearly tripled, from 3.3 million students to 12.1 million students. The number of institutions increased more modestly, from 2,008 to 3,231 (including two-year institutions) so that approximately two-thirds of the 1960 to 1980 expansion took the form of increased enrollments at existing institutions.[12] Between 1980 and 2005, enrollments increased from 12.1 to 17.5 million—a 45 percent increase, while the number of institutions increased from 3,231 to 4,276, by 32 percent. In this period, 86 percent of the expansion took the form of increased numbers of institutions[13]—a lagged response to the huge growth of enrollments in the 1960s and 1970s.

What about the expansion of higher education worldwide? The International Association of Universities (IAU) provides information on over 16,000 institutions of higher education around the world (IAU 2008, 2009). In addition, several Internet sites provide data on universities outside the United States during the 1990s period of rapid enrollment growth (http://univ.cc/; www.braintrack.com/about.htm). These data provide potentially detailed information on the development of mass higher education around the world that goes beyond this study but that gives some insight into the incredible expansion of the university sector worldwide.[14] Table 11.11 records the names and years of founding (or of changes in the nature of an institution into a university) in two developing countries: Bangladesh and Chile. Many of the institutions in both countries were developed in the 1990s. In Bangladesh, the new institutions were public sector, but in Chile, there was an expansion of private-sector colleges and universities. Bangladesh has

12. Calculated using ln metric, the growth of enrollments was 1.30 ln points, while the growth of the number of institutions was 0.48 ln points.

13. Calculated using ln metric, the growth of enrollments was 0.37 ln points, while the growth of the number of institutions was 0.32 ln points.

14. The IAU data are in computer form but not publicly available as of 2008, but earlier data may exist only in paper form. I am currently trying to get all of these data organized in research-friendly forms.

Table 11.11 **Universities in Bangladesh and Chile, 2004, by year founded (with multiple years reported due to changes in status comparable to founding)**

Name	Year founded
Bangladesh universities	
Bangabandhu Medical	1965 (1998)
Bangabandhu Medical Agric	1983 (1998)
Bangladesh Agricultural Univ	1961 (1972)
Bangladesh Open Univ	1992
BUET	1947 (1992)
Chittagong	1964 (1966)
Dhaka	1921
HMDSTU	1976 (2002)
Islamic	1979 (2000)
Jahangirnagar	1970 (1972)
Khulna	1991
National University	1992
Rajshahi	1953
Shahjalal	1987
American International	1994
Ahsanullah	1995
AUB	1996
DIU	1989
Dhaka	1995 (2000)
EWU	1996
Gono Bishwabidyalay	1998
IUB	1993
IUBAT	1992
Islamic University of Techl	1981
North South Univ	1992
People's University	1996
Queens	1997
Asia Pacific	1996
Univ Sci & Tech. Chittagnong	1992
Chilean universities	
arturo prat	1984
metropolitan of education	1986
metropolitan of tech antofagasta	1981
atacama	1857
bio bio	1988
chile	1738
magallanes	1961 (1981)
santiago chile	1849 (1981)
talca	1981
tarapaca	1982
valparaiso	1911 (1981)
Adolfo Ibanez	1953 (1989)
Alberto Hurtado	1997
Andres Bello	1988
Autonomous Univ Christian	1975 (1988)

(*continued*)

Table 11.11 (continued)

Name	Year founded
Autonomous Univ of South	1989
Bernardo O'Higgins	1990
Bolivariana	1988
Catholic-Cardinal Henriquez	1990 (1993)
Catholic	1888 (1930)
Catholic Univ of Holy Concept	1991
Catholic Univ of Maule	1991
Catholic Univ of North	1956 (1969)
Catholic Univ of Temuco	1991
Catholic Univ of Valparaiso	1928 (1961)
Central	1982 (1993)
Chile Adventist	1965 (1990)
Diego Portales	1982 (1993)
Federico Santa Maria Tech	1932 (1935)
Finis Terrae	1981 (1996)
Francisco De Aguirre	1990 (2001)
Gabriela Mistral	1981 (1992)
Ibero_American Tech	1989
International	1892 (1988)
Jose Santos Ossa	1992
Las Condes	1987
Mariano Egana	1988
Maritime	1990
Miguel de Cervantes	1998
Panamerican	1989
El Libertador	1990
San Andres	1994
San Sebastian	1989 (2001)
Santo Tomas	1988
Southern	1955
Aconcagua	1978 (1989)
Americas	1988 (1997)
Andes	1989 (2001)
Arts, Science and Comm	1981 (1999)
Arts and Social Sciences	1982
Computer Science	1989
Concepcion	1919 (1980)
for Development	1990
Mayor	1988 (1996)
of the Pacific	1990
of the Republic	1988
of the Sea	1989
VP Rosales Tech	1982 (1992)
Vina del Mar	1984 (1990)

an Open University. The universities in both countries report connections with universities in advanced countries.

11.2 Part II: Implications

The globalization of higher education has implications for supply and demand in the labor market, for the U.S. university system, and for the economy writ large.

11.2.1 Immigration and the Labor Force

Increased numbers of foreign-born university graduates trained outside the United States and increased numbers obtaining degrees as international students in the United States provide new growing sources of highly educated workers for U.S. firms. By coming to the United States, these immigrants strengthen the country's comparative advantage in high-tech and university workforce-intensive sectors. At the same time, however, by augmenting the supply of highly educated workers in the United States and worldwide, the greater number of highly educated foreign-born persons reduce the payoff to investing in higher education in the United States. The supply of highly able programmers from India and other developing countries willing to work at lower pay than Americans has dampened the growth of the supply of programmers in the United States. Looking at PhDs, Borjas (2006) finds the increased number of foreign-born S&E graduates in the United States reduces the employment opportunities and earnings of U.S.-born S&E graduates (Borjas 2006), which presumably lowers U.S. supply.

The 1990s economic boom provides striking evidence of the extent to which immigrant scientists and engineers can increase the total labor supply of graduates in the United States in times of great demand. Census data show that from 1990 to 2000, the foreign-born share of bachelor's science and engineering graduates increased from 11 percent to 17 percent, that the foreign-born share of master's degree science and engineering graduates increased from 19 percent to 29 percent, and that the foreign-born share of doctorate science and engineering graduates increased from 24 percent to 38 percent, while the foreign-born share of those aged less than forty-five nearly doubled from 27 percent to 52 percent. Nearly 60 percent of the *growth* in the number of PhD scientists and engineers in the country in the 1990s came from the foreign born. Data from the Current Population Survey for the 2000s show that the foreign-born share remained in ensuing years as well. In 2005, the foreign born made up 18 percent of bachelor's S&E workers, 32 percent of master's S&E workers, and 40 percent of the PhD S&E workforce, and continued to supply over half of doctorate scientists and engineers under the age of forty-five. Looking at all college graduates, in 2007, the foreign born were 18 percent of the U.S. college graduate workforce and 28 percent of the growth of college graduates from 2000 to 2007.[15]

As intimated in the earlier discussion of international students, a huge proportion of immigrant scientists and engineers come to the United States first as students.[16] Table 11.12 shows that nearly 60 percent of all foreign-born scientists and engineers working in the United States obtained their degrees in the United States. The proportion of U.S. degree recipients among the foreign-born was larger at the PhD and master's level than at the bachelor's level, though even among bachelor's graduates, half of foreign-born S&E workers in the United States were U.S. university-educated. The proportions obtaining degrees in the United States versus in their home or in other countries does, however, differ markedly by country. Many S&E workers from India, the Philippines, the former Soviet Union, and the United Kingdom were educated outside the United States, whereas the majority of foreign-born S&E workers from China, Taiwan, South Korea, Mexico, and Germany were educated in the United States. Because the United States accounts for about 10 percent of all S&E degrees granted in the world (about 8.5 percent of bachelor's degrees compared to 17.6 percent of PhDs), if the country of degree was unrelated to the likelihood of working in the United States, 10 percent of the foreign-born scientists and engineers in the United States would have been U.S.-educated compared to the 60 percent who in fact were U.S.-educated.

What is the actual probability that U.S.-educated foreign-born scientists and engineers end up working in the United States? To estimate this statistic, I compare NSF estimates of the stock of foreign-born S&E workers with highest degrees in the United States in the country to the cumulated number of the foreign-born who obtained a U.S. degree in the preceding thirty or so years at the doctorate, master's, and bachelor's levels. The NSF (NSB 2008, appendix table 3-8) reports that in 2003, the United States had 1.34 million foreign-born S&E workers with a highest degree in the United States, of whom 176,000 had a PhD from the United States, 438,000 had a U.S. master's as their highest degree, and 723,000 had a U.S. bachelor's degree as their highest degree. These statistics are the numerator for my estimates.

15. The 2007 data are from the Bureau of Labor Statistics, Foreign Born Workers: Labor Force Characteristics in 2007 (http://www.bls.gov/news.release/pdf/forbrn.pdf). The 2000 data are from the Migration Policy Institute (2005), migration information source, table 1: Demographic, Social, and Labor Market Characteristics by Nativity: College-Educated Workers, Ages 25 to 64, Census 2000. (http://www.migrationinformation.org/Feature/feb05_spotlight_table1.cfm.)

16. Neither the Current Population Survey nor the Census ask where someone earned their degree, so they do not distinguish between international students who stay in the United States and immigrants who come with foreign degrees. The 2000 Census reported a much higher number of foreign-born S&E workers than did the NSF's SESTAT data system because the latter counts foreign-born recipients of U.S. degrees but not immigrants with overseas degrees between Census years. The New American Community Survey asks an open-ended question about the specific major of bachelor's degree recipients.

Table 11.12 **Proportions of U.S. science and engineering workers that are foreign-born and the proportion of the foreign-born that have highest degree in the United States, 2005 (%)**

Degree	Foreign-born share of workers	Share of foreign-born with highest degree
Bachelor's	15.2	54.3
Master's	27.2	68.5
Doctorates	34.6	64.00

Source: National Science Board (2008, table 3-8).

To estimate the number of foreign-born persons who obtained PhDs in science and engineering doctorates from whom the 176,000 foreign-born but U.S.-trained doctorates came, I use the number of PhDs granted to persons who were not U.S.-born nor permanent residents from the Survey of Earned Doctorates between 1970 and 2003.[17] There were about 250,000 such persons. Dividing the 176,000 estimated stock in 2003 by 250,000 suggests that about 70 percent of the PhDs in the thirty-three year period were in the United States in 2003. This statistic is of the same order of magnitude as Survey of Earned Doctorates data that show that 70 percent to 75 percent of foreign doctoral recipients plan to stay in the United States after they graduate (NSB 2008, indicators, table 2-33) and with Michael Finn's (2007) estimates that in the 2001 PhD graduates cohort, 66 percent of foreign-born doctorates were working in the United States for at least two years and that 62 percent of the 1995 graduates were still working in the United States ten years later.

For masters' graduates, I estimate that about 600,000 noncitizen, non-permanent residents obtained a degree between 1965 and 2003, a slightly longer period due to their being younger than doctorate graduates. Dividing the 438,000 estimated stock in 2003 by this number suggests that around two-thirds stayed to work in the country. For bachelor's graduates, I estimate that on the order of 550,000 noncitizens and nonpermanent residents obtained S&E degrees in the United States from 1960 to 2003 (again a bit longer to allow for the younger age of these graduates). In this case, the 2003 stock of 723,000 exceeds the estimated number of foreign born persons with a U.S. S&E bachelor's highest degree. While this comparison suggests that there are some serious problems with the bachelor's graduate statistics, it does not gainsay the conclusion that a huge proportion of international students who obtain U.S. degrees end up working in the country years later.

Turning to foreign-born S&E graduates who obtain degrees overseas, the

17. There is a problem with using temporary residents because the United States gave permanent resident status to Chinese students following Tiananmen Square incident, and those students would be counted with U.S. citizens/permanent residents.

NSF estimates that in 2003, there were 0.9 million foreign born S&E workers with their highest degree outside the country. On the basis of estimates of the number of bachelor's and higher graduates outside the United States and the proportion of those who studied science or engineering, there were about 31 million university-educated S&E workers outside the country.[18] Dividing the 0.9 million foreign-educated S&E workers in the United States by the 31 million degree recipients, I estimate that approximately 3 percent of foreign-born S&E workers with highest degrees outside the country immigrated to the country.

To what extent might the huge difference between the likelihood that foreign-born S&E graduates with U.S. highest degrees end up working in the United States and the likelihood that a foreign-born graduate earning an S&E degree outside the country migrates to the United States reflect the causal impact of being an international student on immigration behavior, as opposed to selectivity of persons with greater desire to move to the United States? Lacking experimental or pseudo-experimental variation in studying in the United States to answer this question, I seek an answer in estimates of the *causal* impact of international study on a graduate's future location of work from analyses of the European Union's ERASMUS program (http://en.wikipedia.org/wiki/ERASMUS_programme). This program provides financial incentives to students to study outside their country for one or two terms. Comparing cohorts of students before and after introduction of the program and groups eligible and ineligible due to the timing of their university's involvement with the program, Parey and Waldinger (2008) estimated causal impacts on location decisions on the order of 20 percentage points—far below the huge difference in the proportion of international students who immigrate to the United States and the proportion of non-U.S.-trained graduates who migrate to the United States given in the above. Other studies of student migration and employment in the EU (Oosterbeek and Dinand 2009; de Grip, Fourage, and Sauerman 2008; Dreher and Poutvaara 2005) find similar orders of magnitude for the impact of being an international student and future work in a foreign country. As to the mechanism by which study abroad causally affects working abroad, Parey and Waldinger (2008, table 11) find that social factors in the form of a partner are important in leading former international students to work outside their home country and that assessments of career prospects also

18. My estimate is based on NSF estimates that 26 percent of the stock of university graduates in the world was in the United States in 2000 "or most recent year" (NSB, *Science and Engineering Indicators 2008,* figure 3-52). In 2003, 50 million persons aged twenty-five and over had four or more years of higher education in the United States (U.S. Census Bureau 2004, table 214). The supply of university graduates outside the United States was, thus, on the order of 150 million persons. From the statistics in table 11.2 of this study, I estimate that 27 percent of bachelor's graduates outside the United States are in science and engineering. This gives an estimate of 31 million science and engineering graduates outside the United States.

influence the decision to work overseas, presumably by linking the students to potential future employers.

The estimated causal impact of foreign study on immigration decisions from the ERASMUS program is likely to understate the causal impact of being an international student in the United States on migration behavior. The reason is that the ERASMUS program is a smaller treatment than four to six or so years of study for a degree in the United States, during which time the student could very well build up job and social connections that could make returning home feel more like immigration than remaining in the United States. In addition, whereas students in the ERASMUS program move between countries with roughly similar standards of living, most U.S. international students are from developing countries such as China and India rather than from comparable advanced countries. The rates of staying for PhD graduates are much higher for persons from lower-income countries than for those from higher-income countries.

The increased number of university graduates overseas and of international students who return to their homeland will also create competition for highly educated U.S. workers. Increasing their stock of university graduates improves the ability of other countries to compete with the United States in high-tech and other sectors that use highly educated workers. With large numbers of graduates outside the U.S., multinationals are more likely to locate overseas research and development work and other activities that require university education. Consistent with this, between 1994 and 2004, research and development (R&D) employment increased by 94 percent in the majority-owned foreign affiliates of U.S. multinationals, while employment in the parent firm increased by 39 percent.[19]

11.2.2 The Impact of Globalization of Higher Education on the U.S. University System

The growing number of students and universities in other countries impacts the U.S. university system in several ways. Increased numbers of bachelor's graduates from other countries raises demand for places in U.S. graduate and professional schools. If U.S. universities treat foreign and domestic applications equally, the increased share of bachelor's degrees outside the United States will reduce the proportion of U.S. graduates admitted to particular programs. In 2008, the bright U.S. graduate from, say, Haverford, must compete for admission to Berkeley, Harvard, Michigan, or Massachusetts Institute of Technology (MIT) with students from China, Brazil, India, France, Germany, and so on as well as with top graduates from Texas, Syracuse, Dartmouth, and so on. In July 2008, the *Chronicle of Higher Edu-*

19. In 1994, R&D employment was 92,400 in majority-owned foreign affiliates of U.S. multinational corporations (MNCs) and 591,200 in U.S. parent firm (http://www.bea.gov/scb/account_articles/international/1296iid/table17.htm). In 2004, it was 179,300 in majority-owned foreign affiliates and 818,7000 in parent firm (Yorgason 2007, tables 1 and 3).

cation reported that the three leading major undergraduate institutions for U.S. PhD programs were Tsinghua, Beijing, and Seoul National University.[20] Given that the top U.S. graduate and professional schools have not increased the number of graduate slots much (Freeman, Jin, and Shen 2007), the chances of graduates of U.S. institutions gaining admission to these programs has been and is likely to continue to fall.

But this does not mean that overseas applicants push students from U.S. bachelor's programs out of postgraduate education. The United States has a large number of universities that have expanded graduate enrollments. The expansion of U.S.-born women into graduate programs occurred more or less simultaneously with increased foreign student enrollments. Many foreign-born graduate students enrolled at less-prestigious universities, which enabled those institutions to improve their graduate programs (Freeman, Jin, and Shen 2007). To the extent that the supply of U.S. students to graduate programs diminishes due to the increased attraction of masters of business administration (MBA) or law programs, bachelor's graduates from overseas will keep some graduate programs in business.

International ratings of universities place U.S. institutions at the top of the world tables. The Institute of Higher Education, Shanghai Jiao Tong University, rates eight of the top ten universities as American, nine of the next ten, and thirty-seven of the top fifty. (http://ed.sjtu.edu.cn/rank/2005/ARWU2005_Top100.htm). In its league tables, the *Times of London* places more UK universities among the top, but the UK numbers still fall far short of those for the United States (http://www.timesonline.co.uk/tol/life_and_style/education/article502890.ece). Associated with the dominance of the U.S. university system is its ability to attract outstanding foreign-born scientists and engineers, many of whom first came to the country as international students, as noted. In 2003, a large proportion of full-time doctoral instructional faculty in research institutions in the physical sciences/math/computer sciences/engineering were foreign born—47 percent compared to 38 percent in 1992 (NSB, 2008, appendix table 5-21).

Over time, foreign universities will improve their quality so that the expansion of higher education outside the United States will create greater competition for American universities in attracting international students. For American students and faculty, the benefit will be a greater number of quality universities at which to obtain an education or a job. The challenge to U.S. universities will be to remain world centers of excellence in spite of increased overseas competition. This presumably requires that they innovate in various ways, taking advantage of their "brand names," culture of openness, ties with business, and so on. Some U.S. institutions have developed

20. Jeffrey Brainard, "Graduates of Chinese Universities Take the Lead in Earning American PhDs," *Chronicle of Higher Education,* July 14, 2008, http://chronicle.com/article/Graduates-of-Chinese/41297.

overseas branch campuses to increase enrollments in particular countries (for instance, Carnegie Mellon in the Qatar). This may work in some countries but not in others. In the early 1990s, about forty U.S. universities had branches in Japan, but the Japanese educational authorities did not accredit them and all but three have shut down.

Foreign universities, particularly from Australia and the United Kingdom, have been more active than U.S. universities in seeking international students as undergraduates. Some Australian universities award degrees to students who do part of their education at lower-cost universities in their home country. The Australian government gives preference in immigration to graduates from Australian institutions. British universities have more branches overseas than American universities, particularly in Commonwealth countries. In non-English-speaking countries, many universities have switched their education into English, which increases their attractiveness for international students. Among the developing countries, China's Project 985 policy for creating a number of first-rate universities of international advanced standing represents perhaps an extraordinarily bold effort to leapfrog a low-income country to the forefront of higher education. It involved providing sizable financial grants to nine universities—Beijing Fudan, and Nanjing among traditional universities and to Tsinghua and five other institutions oriented primarily to science and technology. In 2004, the government expanded financial support to an additional thirty institutions. While it will take time, and perhaps increased democratization of China for these universities to challenge the very best American universities, the Chinese university system has greatly improved its attractiveness to faculty and students worldwide. In fall 2008, the *Chronicle of Higher Education* reported that China had become the fifth top college destination for international students, particularly attracting those from Asia (Hvistendahl 2008).

In the face of global competition, it is difficult to imagine the United States maintaining the dominance it has had in the latter part of the twentieth century (just as it is difficult to imagine the United States maintaining its dominance of the global economy). But barring some horrific policies or events, I would expect U.S. universities to continue to rank among the world's leaders in higher education into the foreseeable future and, thus, to keep attracting high-skill immigrants to the country.

11.2.3 Impacts on the Economy

The increased number of science and engineering and highly educated workers around the world has two major positive impacts on the economy. First, it should accelerate the growth of scientific and technological knowledge and the economic progress that flows from this knowledge. One does not have to be a devotee of "the singularity" view of technological progress to believe that having three or so times as many university graduates, particularly in science and engineering, than a quarter century ago, the Internet to spread knowledge, and computers to perform calculations unimaginable two or so decades ago could produce a golden age for humanity.[21] We benefit from advances in our understanding in biology or nano-technology or robotics or economics for that matter, regardless of whether the increased knowledge comes from the United States or other places or from U.S.-born persons or foreign-born persons. To the extent that taxpayers in some other country fund research and education, we win without paying for it. Second, the increased number of highly educated workers overseas should raise productivity in foreign countries, which, in turn, should reduce the cost of their exports to the United States. This will benefit all Americans who do not compete in producing those goods. If Romanian scientists and engineers figure out ways to improve the production of shoes, the price of shoes on the global market will fall, and the United States as a major importer of shoes will benefit.

But there is a negative side. The increased supply of university graduates in other countries will enhance their ability in the high-tech sectors that employ relatively many college graduates, where the United States has comparative advantage. In the context of the North-South model of trade in which the advanced North does the R&D that produces innovative products and the developing South produces products based on low-wage labor, this competition will squeeze U.S. earnings and job opportunities. With more highly educated workers, developing countries should be able to increase their rate of innovation and their rate of imitation. The prices of U.S. exports in high-tech and other university-graduate-intensive sectors should decline, with adverse consequences for the workers in those sectors and for workers with similar skills elsewhere.

In some cases, given the lower cost of labor, the United States may lose its position as the major producer of high-tech goods or of the research and development on which they are based. The NSF (NSB 2008) data show that China has, in fact, increased its share of export markets in high-tech goods. The Georgia Tech index of the technical prowess of countries based on a variety of statistics shows a huge rise in the position of China's prowess. The index will surely show increases in the position of other developing countries in the next decade or two.

In response to the growth of highly educated workers worldwide, the United States can seek to attract international students on the notion that many will stay in the country as immigrants and can encourage high-skilled immigrants to come to the country. Given that the multinational firms in the forefront of technology can locate activities in the United States or offshore activities overseas, the policy issue for the United States would seem to be whether it is better to attract immigrant specialists or to have the multinationals offshore an increasing proportion of their work overseas. Which

21. http://en.wikipedia.org/wiki/Technological_singularity.

is better for the United States—offshoring or immigration? Grossman and Rossi-Hansberg (2008) make a case for offshoring. Assuming that wages in the developing countries are lower for similar work than wages in the United States, offshoring costs less than the same work done by immigrants in the United States. Offshoring is equivalent to an improved technology that allows U.S. workers to do their tasks better. Foreign-born workers compete on the offshorable tasks but not on other activities with Americans for whom they are substitutes. By contrast, immigrants compete with Americans in all sorts of jobs, including those in nontraded sectors. Taking a broadly similar approach, Ruffin and Jones (2007) argue that under some conditions, it is even desirable to give our best technology to the low-wage foreign countries because we will then get the products back at the lowest cost. In the case of science or engineering, better to have an inventor doing their work overseas at lower cost than than doing it in the United States at higher cost.

But can the same person do as good work in a developing country as in the United States? There is diverse evidence that the huge pay and productivity difference between workers in the United States and in developing countries cannot be explained by human capital-labor or capital-labor ratios or any other observable measure, for that matter. Analyzing research papers, MacGarvie and Khan (2009) show that the number of papers written is higher for nominally similar international students in the United States than for those whose fellowships make them return to their native countries. The implication of these findings is that the same person working with the same capital produces more in the United States than in most other countries. Why? One possible reason is the United States's business and work culture, which is difficult to replicate. But whatever the reason, the greater productivity in the United States implies that immigration raises output more than offshoring and, thus, is to be preferred on that criterion.

Does the productivity of U.S. workers benefit more from immigration or offshoring? Working in direct contact with someone would appear to raise productivity more than buying their goods because of the greater likelihood of learning about work activity from them. Kremer and Maskin's (2006) model of the mixing of low- and high-skilled workers does not deal with immigration and offshoring, per se, but it gives conditions for the sorting of workers between advanced and developing countries that shows that the answer to the productivity question will depend on relative numbers and productivities of skilled and less-skilled workers outside and within the United States as well as on the strength of complementarity reflected in the production function.

11.3 Conclusion

This paper has documented the spread of higher education around the world. It has shown that the rising proportion of young persons going to college in advanced countries, which has risen above those in the United States in some countries, and in the huge populous developing countries has greatly diminished the United States's share of the world's university students and graduates. Because international students make up roughly half of university graduate immigrants, the ability of U.S. universities to attract the world's best and brightest international students has important consequences for its success in attracting immigrant talent.

The growing number of foreign-born persons getting PhDs outside the United States as well as in U.S. universities will undoubtedly diminish the gap between U.S. universities and those in other countries. The world ranking of top universities in 2020 is likely to include many more from other countries. Increasingly, new knowledge will come from workers outside the country, but there is much the United States can gain from this. We do not know whether the United States will do better through immigration or through offshoring of some university graduate-level work. My guess is that by educating some of the best students in the world, attracting some to stay in the country, and positioning the United States as an open hub of ideas and connections for university graduates worldwide, the country will be able to maintain excellence and leadership in the "empire of the mind" and in the economic world more so than if it views the rapid increase in graduates overseas as a competitive threat.

References

Boarini, Romina, and Hubert Strauss. 2007. The private internal rates of return to tertiary education: New estimates for 21 OECD countries. OECD Working paper no. 591. Paris: Organization for Economic Cooperation and Development.

Borjas, George. 2006. Immigration in high-skill labor markets: The impact of foreign students on the earnings of doctorates. NBER Working Paper no. 12085. Cambridge, MA: National Bureau of Economic Research.

Council on Competitiveness. 2005. *National summit on competitiveness: Investing in innovation.* Washington, DC: National Association of Manufacturers.

Dreher, Axel, and Panu Poutvaara. 2005. Student flows and migration: An empirical analysis. IZA Discussion Paper no. 1612. Bonn, Germany: Institute for the Study of Labor.

Duke University, Master of Engineering Management Program. 2005. *Framing the engineering outsourcing debate: Placing the United States on a level playing field with China and India.* Durham, NC: Duke University.

Edin, Per Anders, and Robert Topel. 1997. Wage policy and restructuring: The Swedish labor market since 1960. In *The welfare state in transition: Reforming the Swedish model,* ed. Richard Freeman, Robert Topel, and Birgitta Swedenborg, 155–201. Chicago: University of Chicago Press.

Finn, Michael. 2007. Stay rates of foreign doctorate recipients from U.S. universities 2005. Oak Ridge Institute for Science and Education.

Freeman, Richard B. 1971. *The market for college-trained manpower.* Cambridge, MA: Harvard University Press.

———. 1975. Overinvestment in *college* training? *Journal of Human Resources* 10 (3): 287–311.

———. 1976. *The over-educated American.* New York: Academic Press.

Freeman, Richard B., Emily Jin, and Chia-Yu Shen. 2007. Where do new US-trained science-engineering PhDs come from? In *Science and the university,* ed. Ronald G. Ehrenberg and Paula E. Stephan, 197–220. Madison, WI: University of Wisconsin Press.

Gomory, Ralph, and William Baumol. 2007. *Global trade and conflicting national interests.* Cambridge, MA: MIT Press.

Grip, Andries de, Didier Fouarge, and Jan Sauermann. 2008. What affects international migration of European science and engineering graduates? Research Memoranda no. 006. Maastricht, The Netherlands: ROA, Research Centre for Education and the Labour Market.

Grossman, Gene M., and Esteban Rossi-Hansberg. 2008. Trading tasks: A simple theory of offshoring. *American Economic Review* 98 (5): 1978–97.

Hvistendahl, Mara. 2008. China moves up to fifth as importer of students. *Chronicle of Higher Education,* September 19.

Hwang, Jung Eun. 2008. MIT or Tsinghua? A panel data analysis of the determinants of domestic higher education and international student mobility. Bachelor's thesis, Harvard College.

International Association of Universities. 2008. *The international handbook of universities.* 20th ed. Hampshire, UK: Palgrave Macmillan.

———. 2009. *World higher education database.* New York: Palgrave MacMillan.

Kremer, Michael, and Eric Maskin. 2006. Globalization and inequality. http://www.economics.harvard.edu/faculty/kremer/files/GlobalizationInequality_Oct06.pdf.

MacGarvie, Megan, and Shulamit Khan. 2009. How important is U.S. location for research in science? Boston University Working Paper.

Marginson, Simon. 2001. The global market in foreign higher education: The case of Australia. Paper presented at Association for Studies in Higher Education (ASHE) 26th annual conference, Richmond, Virginia.

McKinsey Global Institute. 2005. The emerging global labor market: Part I. White Paper no. 2005-06-01. New York: McKinsey Global Institute.

Ministry of Education of the People's Republic of China. 2007. Gross enrollment rate of schools by level. Beijing. Ministry of Education of the People's Republic of China. http://www.moe.edu.cn/edoas/website18/level3.jsp?tablename=2233&infoid=33487

National Academy of Sciences (NAS). 2005. *Policy implications of international graduate students and postdoctoral scholars in the US.* Washington, DC: NAS Press.

National Science Board (NSB). 1998. *Science and engineering indicators 1998.* Arlington, VA: National Science Foundation.

———. 2004. *Science and Engineering Indicators 2006.* Arlington, VA: National Science Foundation.

———. 2006. *Science and Engineering Indicators 2006.* Arlington, VA: National Science Foundation.

———. 2008. *Science and Engineering Indicators 2008.* Arlington, VA: National Science Foundation.

National Science Foundation (NSF). 1993. *Human resources for science & technology: The Asian region.* NSF no. 93-303. Arlington, VA: NSF.

———. 1996. *Human resources for science & technology: The European region.* NSF Special Report no. 96-316. Arlington, VA: NSF.

Organization for Economic Cooperation and Development (OECD). 2004. *Internationalisation and trade in higher education: Opportunities and challenges.* Paris: OECD.

———. 2005. *Education at a glance 2005: OECD indicators.* Paris: OECD.

———. 2007a. *International migration outlook 2007.* SOPEMI 2007 ed. Paris: OECD.

———. 2007b. *Science, technology and industry scoreboard 2007.* Paris: OECD.

———. 2008a. *Education at a glance: OECD indicators.* Paris: OECD.

———. 2008b. *Main science and technology indicators (MSTI) 2008-2 edition.* Paris: OECD.

Oosterbeek, Hessel, and Webbink Dinand. 2009. Does studying abroad induce a brain drain? *Economica,* forthcoming.

Parey, Matthias, and Fabian Waldinger. 2008. Studying abroad and the effect of international labor market mobility: Evidence from the introduction of ERASMUS. IZA discussion paper no. 3430. Bonn, Germany: Institute for the Study of Labor.

Rosenzweig, Mark. 2006. *Global wage differences and international student flows.* Washington, DC: Brookings Institution.

Ruffin, Roy J., and Ronald W. Jones. 2007. International technology transfer: Who gains and who loses? *Review of International Economic* 15 (2): 209–22.

Schofer, Evan, and John W. Meyer. 2005. Worldwide expansion of higher education. Center on Democracy, Development, and the Rule of Law, Stanford Institute on International Studies Working Paper no. 32.

U.S. Census Bureau. 2004. *Statistical abstract of the United States: 2004–2005.* 124th ed. Washington, DC: U.S. GPO, December.

———. 2007. *Statistical abstract of the United States: 2008.* 127th ed. Washington, DC: U.S. GPO.

Wadwha, Vivek, Gary Gereffi, Ben Rissing, and Ryan Ong. 2008. Getting the numbers right: International engineering education in the United States, China, and India. *Journal of Engineering Education* 97 (1): 13–25.

Welch, Anthony. 2002. Going global? Internationalizing Australian universities in a time of global crisis. *Comparative Education Review* 46 (2): 433–71.

Yorgason, Daniel. 2007. Research and development activities of U.S. multinational companies. *Survey of Current Business* (March):22–39.

Contributors

James D. Adams
Department of Economics
Rensselaer Polytechnic Institute
3406 Russell Sage Laboratory
Troy, NY 12180-3590

Eric Bettinger
Stanford University School of Education
CERAS 522, 520 Galvez Mall
Stanford, CA 94305

Grant C. Black
School of Business and Economics
Indiana University, South Bend
1700 Mishawaka Avenue
South Bend, IN 46634

Lex Borghans
Department of Economics and Research Centre for Education and the Labour Market (ROA)
Maastricht University
P.O. Box 616
6200 MD Maastricht, The Netherlands

John Bound
Department of Economics
University of Michigan
Ann Arbor, MI 48109-1220

Charles T. Clotfelter
Sanford School of Public Policy
Box 90245
Duke University
Durham, NC 27708

Frank Cörvers
Research Centre for Education and the Labour Market (ROA)
Maastricht University
P.O. Box 616
6200 MD Maastricht, The Netherlands

Richard B. Freeman
National Bureau of Economic Research
1050 Massachusetts Avenue
Cambridge, MA 02138

Devesh Kapur
University of Pennsylvania
Centre for Advanced Study of India
3600 Market Street, Suite 560
Philadelphia, PA 19104-2653

E. Han Kim
Stephen M. Ross School of Business
University of Michigan
701 Tappan Street
Ann Arbor, MI 48109-1234

Sunwoong Kim
Department of Economics
College of Letters and Science
University of Wisconsin, Milwaukee
P.O. Box 413
Milwaukee, WI 53201-0413

Haizheng Li
School of Economics
Georgia Institute of Technology
Atlanta, GA 30332-0615

Ofer Malamud
Harris School of Public Policy Studies
University of Chicago
1155 E. 60th Street, Suite 172
Chicago, IL 60637

Paula E. Stephan
Department of Economics
Andrew Young School of Policy Studies
Georgia State University
Box 3992
Atlanta, GA 30302-3992

Sarah Turner
Department of Economics
University of Virginia
2015 Ivy Road, Room 312
P.O. Box 400182
Charlottesville, VA 22904-4182

Min Zhu
Stephen M. Ross School of Business
University of Michigan
701 Tappan Street
Ann Arbor, MI 48109

Author Index

Subject Index

The letters f *and* t *following page numbers refer to figures and tables, respectively.*